FUNDAMENTA~
OF
FINANCIAL
MANAGING

3rd Edition

FRANK M. WERNER
Fordham University
Associate Professor of Finance

JAMES A.F. STONER
Fordham University
Professor of Management Systems

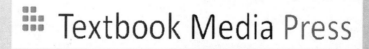

Acquisitions Editor: Edgar Laube
Text Design and Editing: Philip Schrömbgens
File Management, Editing, and Production: Kyle Houghton, Phungporn Jaroonjetjamnong,
John Fernandez, Elizabeth Tam, Shui Hwang
Cover Design: Frank Werner

For permission to use copyrighted material, grateful acknowledgement is made to the copyright holders on page xxiv which are hereby made part of this copyright page.

Fundamentals of Financial Managing, 3rd Edition

Library of Congress Cataloging-in-Publication Data

Werner, Frank M., 1944-
  Fundamentals of Financial Managing, 3rd Edition / Frank M. Werner,
James A.F. Stoner.

      p. cm.
Includes bibliographical references and index.
  ISBN 1-930789-43-2

To my parents, Anne and Jules Werner,
who opened my eyes to the joys of learning.

FMW

To Barbara, Alexandra, and Carolyn, who continue
to do a wonderful job of "saving Jim from himself."

JAFS

BRIEF CONTENTS

DETAILED CONTENTS

PART V   RETURNING VALUE TO SHAREHOLDERS

PART VI   LOOKING AHEAD

Where to find it: Web-based appendixes and cases can be found at the *Fundamentals of Financial Managing* section of the Textbook Media website: www.textbookmedia.com

TO THE INSTRUCTOR

Thank you and congratulations for adopting this book. We and the many leading finance professionals throughout North America who encouraged us to write it and who reviewed our work think you have made an important decision for your students and for global competitiveness. Change is never easy, as we ourselves found out when we began asking the questions that led to this textbook.

Fundamentals of Financial Managing is a different kind of undergraduate finance text. Although all financial management texts cover finance, we know of no other undergraduate "financial management" textbook that has anything to do with management. We're excited about the book since we believe this is the way we will all be seeing finance in the coming years. We hope we've communicated our excitement to you and your students

1. Our Goals for the Book

In writing *Fundamentals of Financial Managing,* we set seven goals for ourselves:

To present finance in a clear and consistent manner The book is designed—through its choice of language, illustrations, and design—to be easy to read and use. The approach for analysis and problem-solving is straightforward and is applied consistently. The book is approachable and user-friendly, thanks to features such as its realistic cases and problem scenarios, cartoons, hypertext cross-references, and dual glossary.

To organize the book based on the way financial managers conceive their work The flow of the book is consistent with the financial managing job: raising money, using money to add value to the firm, and returning value to shareholders. This makes it easier for students to understand the "big picture."

To make the book consistent with the direction of business education The book includes extensive material in response to four concerns of contemporary business education: (1) globalization, (2) ethics, (3) cross-disciplinary activities, and (4) small business. International content is integrated throughout the book. Ethics appears naturally in the context of the worldwide quality-management and sustainability revolutions. Cross-disciplinary activity, a requirement in modern business practice, is explicitly addressed wherever financial decision making is discussed. The special needs and limitations of small business appear throughout the book, making it applicable to organizations of all sizes.

To capture the implications of the quality and sustainability revolutions for financial practice The book uses the experiences of leading companies to report the progress finance organizations are making in identifying and serving finance's customers, in improving finance's processes, and in contributing to global sustainability. A consistent theme throughout the book is bridging

the gap between traditional and new management practices, a current fact of life for finance professionals we refer to as "living in both worlds."

To equal or surpass the best features of other textbooks We benchmarked over 50 features of both finance and nonfinance texts, looking for the best example(s) of each, and set out to do as well or better on every one.

To provide instructors flexibility in using the book The book contains full coverage for an introductory course of either one or two semesters. It can be used in a traditional financial management course, or in a survey of finance course since its broad coverage introduces many areas of finance, not just large corporation financial management. We have put more-advanced subjects, more-detailed explanations, and derivations on the web in "Web Appendixes" to provide greater flexibility in selecting and assigning materials. Cross-reference footnotes connect material that appears in multiple chapters, helping instructors and students alike to tie pieces of the finance subject together.

To keep the size of the book reasonable Even with all its new coverage, the book has only 18 chapters.

2. Advantages for Students, Instructors, and Society

We think there are important advantages to a finance book that is consistent with the best management practice.

For students The approach of *Fundamentals of Financial Managing* makes students more attractive to employers, not only by teaching them the core competencies of finance but also by showing them how to use those skills effectively within a modern, world-class organization.

For instructors *Fundamentals of Financial Managing* permits instructors to teach best practice—financial managing as it is done in companies recognized as business leaders. It supports teaching, as students find the book intuitively clear and easy to read and understand. By integrating international and ethical issues throughout the book, it builds those subjects naturally into students' analyses and removes the need to treat them as separate topics.

For society *Fundamentals of Financial Managing* joins the increasing supply of educational materials attempting to change the way business schools prepare their students. Business is changing so fast today that schools often have understandable difficulty keeping up. The observation of Walt Kelly's lovable cartoon possum, Pogo, that "We have met the enemy, and it is us!" has been applied with some wisdom to business education. *Fundamentals of Financial Managing* is our contribution to moving business schools from being "part of the problem" to a "part of the solution" of educating students to compete successfully in today's global markets and to contribute to global sustainability.

3. Who Should Use the Book

Because of its tone and approach, *Fundamentals of Financial Managing* has been appreciated by instructors, students, and employers alike. We think the book is especially appropriate for nontechnical students, since it minimizes the use of derivations and formulas, and for students who are employed full- or part-time and who will immediately see the validity of the book's approach and its relevance to their work. Its graduate-level sibling, *Modern Financial Managing—Continuity and Change*, has been successfully used at the M.B.A., and executive M.B.A. levels and was reviewed during its development both by professors and senior financial executives from some of North America's leading companies.

4. Pedagogical Aids

We have included many pedagogical aids to make your job of teaching easier and your students' job of learning more rewarding and more fun. Among the features to look for and take advantage of are:

Tightly integrated chapter structure Each chapter begins with a set of learning objectives entitled "Key Points You Should Learn from This Chapter." These points correspond precisely to the A-heads, or major sections of the chapter. At the end of each chapter is a "Summary of Key Points" that repeats and reviews the learning objectives.

Chapter opening and closing vignettes Each opening vignette describes a scenario faced by a finance professional and is designed to involve your students in the material by putting them "on the job." Each closing vignette shows how the concepts of the chapter can be used to address the opening issue. Since the closing vignettes do not give a single definitive answer (there rarely is one), the opening story can be used as a case for class discussion, homework, or examinations.

Presentation of current finance practices of world-class companies (and some not quite so accomplished)   Four types of boxes are scattered throughout the book. "Finance in Practice" boxes describe recent activities of companies and business leaders as well as modern applications of finance theory. "Serving Finance's Customers" boxes illustrate how a finance organization can add value by meeting the needs of its internal and external customers. "Improving Finance's Processes" boxes describe examples of adding value to a corporation by doing finance's job more efficiently and effectively. "Contributing to Global Sustainability" boxes illustrate how financial activities can enhance the environment and society.

Frequent, clearly labeled, fully worked-out examples   Students learn from examples, and we have tried to err on the side of too many rather than too few. Where the examples are closely linked to finance theory, we often have presented the example first followed by the theory, rather than the other way around, so that the theoretical concepts may be related immediately to a shared and understood example. Examples are in a standard format: a problem scenario paragraph followed by a "Question," "Solution steps," and "Answer." Often the "Answer" contains further commentary to enhance students' understanding of the example.

Appeal to intuition rather than to formula   While some students are very comfortable with mathematical presentations, all too many are not and never learn finance because of their "math anxiety." This is a shame because the majority of finance can be a very intuitive subject. We have avoided formulas wherever possible or placed them in Web Appendixes where they are available for those who find them helpful. We have standardized the notation in the algebra that is included: in all cases, capital letters stand for a money amount (e.g., PV for present value) while lower case letters stand for a rate (e.g., t for the marginal tax rate).

Use of the financial calculator and spreadsheet for time-value analyses   We have purposely minimized the use of time-value tables with this text. Although some instructors find the tables useful for illustrating the basic time-value relationships, financial calculators and spreadsheet programs are universal tools in business today. It is the rare finance professional who does not use them; it is the rarer finance professional who still uses time-value tables. Also, it is often cheaper for a student to purchase a calculator than to buy the textbook itself. All problems involving time value are fully worked out, showing the correct keystrokes and spreadsheet functions. At the end of the book you will find a calculator appendix "Using Your Financial Calculator" illustrating the location of each time-value key on the most widely used financial calculators and a "Spreadsheet Functions" appendix listing financial functions in Microsoft Excel and Corel Quattro Pro. By illustrating how each time-value example may be solved with calculators and spreadsheets, the book provides students with extensive hands-on experience. Another advantage of this approach is that our examples can be much more realistic and not confined to a narrow set of interest rates or time periods.

Use of visual aids   Charts and tables are used throughout the book to support learning. Each discussion of financial market instruments features a copy of the relevant quote(s) from a recent edition of *The Wall Street Journal* or the Bloomberg.com website as seen "Through the Looking Glass" in which we magnify a section of the newspaper to study the numbers in more detail.

Complete glossary, both in the margin, and at the end of the book
The marginal glossary defines terms as they are encountered in the text, so students have the definitions when they need them. The end-of-text glossary is a reference students can go back to when they review and study. Also, the end-of-text glossary serves as a second index since each definition contains the number of the page on which the parallel marginal definition appears.

Questions that follow each chapter   We have tried to make the chapter-ending questions both thought-provoking and useful for reviewing the chapter concepts. They may be used for homework, class discussion, or examinations.

Extensive set of homework problems   The problems that follow each chapter are presented in the same order as the chapter material and are clearly labeled to identify the topic(s) they refer to. Problems come in pairs: problems 1 and 2 cover the same material; so do problems 3 and 4, problems 5 and 6, etc. You can assign one problem of each pair for homework and keep the other in reserve for classroom work, examinations, or for the student who asks for additional examples. The problems range from the simple to the complex—the first problems are narrowly targeted at specific concepts and relationships, while the later problems tend to be broader and integrate the chapter materials. Most problems have multiple parts in which the value of one variable is systematically changed. Students may do all the parts at one sitting or may save one or two parts for later review. When all parts of a problem have been completed, they illustrate the sensitivity of the result to the variable that was changed, providing another learning opportunity.

Accompanying web-based cases   These cases provide additional opportunities to explore the chapter concepts and may also be used for assignments and examinations.

End-of-book summary of mathematical relationships and summary of financial ratios   These handy summaries can be used as study aids by students. They are also useful as reference materials for examinations if you permit students to bring in a list of formulas.

"NET Present Value"—references to interesting and useful websites
These references, which appear throughout the book in the margin, direct students to interesting sites on the "net" where they can learn more about a topic and see practical, real-time applications of finance.

5. Supplements

We are creating a full set of supplements to accompany the book. For this edition there are:

- **A solutions manual** with answers to all questions and detailed, step-by-step solutions to all problems.

- **An instructors manual** containing several suggested syllabi for both a one semester and full-year course, and teaching notes for each chapter and case.

- **A test bank** with short-answer questions and problems available both in hard copy and on diskette for Macintosh and PC-compatible computers.

- **PowerPoint™ slides** for each chapter to support and supplement classroom presentations containing the chapter content plus formulas, figures and tables from the text.

Additional supplements planned for the future include:

- **A study guide** containing an outline of each chapter, worked out sample problems, and self tests.

- **A CD-ROM** containing computerized versions of various end-of-chapter problems which may be used with many popular spreadsheet programs.

- **A CD-ROM** containing "listen to the Authors" audio files in which we discuss and elaborate concepts presented in the book.

For both instructors and students there are five books summarizing our research findings:

- *Joining Forces—Integrating Shareholder Value and Quality Management*, published by Fordham University Graduate School of Business. This monograph reports on a 1996 seminar at Fordham in which senior finance and other executives presented their progress in adopting shareholder value management and measurement systems, such as Stern Stewart's Economic/Market Value Added and the Boston Consulting Group's Total Shareholder Return/Cash Flow Return on Investment.

- *Internal Audit and Innovation,* published by the Financial Executives Research Foundation (FERF) in 1995. Written for executives and practitioners, this book reports on how the internal audit groups of five companies—American Standard, Baxter International, Gulf Canada Resources, Motorola, and Raychem—have changed their auditing philosophies and practices to be more consistent with their evolving management systems. FERF, the research arm of the Financial Executives Institute, was the generous sponsor of this research.

- *Managing Finance for Quality—Bottom-Line Results from Top-Level Commitment,* published by ASQ Quality Press and the Financial Executives Research Foundation in 1994. Also written for executives and practitioners, this book reports how the quality management revolution is changing financial management practice. The book includes case studies of five quality-leading companies—Corning Incorporated, Federal Express, Motorola, Solectron, and Southern Pacific. FERF was also the generous sponsor of this research.

- *Finance in the Quality Revolution—Adding Value by Integrating Financial and Total Quality Management,* published by the Financial Executives Research Foundation in 1993. This shorter version of *Managing Finance for Quality* contains an executive summary, the five case studies, and a chapter on "Lessons Learned." It was published for and distributed to the 11,000 senior financial executives and academics who are members of the Financial Executives Institute.

● *Remaking Corporate Finance—The New Corporate Finance Emerging in Quality-Leading Companies,* published by McGraw-Hill Primis in 1992. A monograph describing transformations in finance work as seen through the observations of senior executives from leading corporations, venture capitalists, consulting organizations, and universities.

6. Moving Forward Together

We have worked very hard to make *Fundamentals of Financial Managing* an exciting and superior textbook. However, we believe that everything is subject to continuous improvement, and we know that you all have wonderful ideas that could enhance the book and its supplements. We would love to hear from you. Tell us how we can (further) assist your teaching in any way; help us make the book better. Feel free to contact us any time at:

Fordham University
Graduate School of Business Administration
113 West 60th Street
New York, NY 10023

Frank: (212) 636-6213, fwerner@fordham.edu
Jim: (212) 636-6178, stoner@fordham.edu

You are our customers, and delighting you and exceeding your expectations is and will always be our primary goal.

◼ Acknowledgments

Writing a textbook takes the efforts of many people over many years. We extend our hearty thanks to all of them. Although we will never be able to thank each person adequately, we wish to identify those who played a particularly important role in the book's development.

1. Genesis

The beginnings of this textbook were the teaching materials Frank Werner developed for use in his finance classes at Fordham University and in the *Management Training Program—Finance* at Manufacturers Hanover Trust Company, now part of JPMorganChase. Thanks go to Corporate Professional Development staff at Manufacturers Hanover—especially Mort Glantz, Carol Johnson, Tom Kennedy, Tom McCaskill, Charlie Stipp, and Barbara Taylor—who helped Frank to identify the best content and sequencing of the materials, and to Dale Broderick, who, more than any other teacher, taught Frank how to write for the classroom.

In 1989, Frank and Jim began their work on the interrelationships between financial managing, globalization, and quality management by conducting the first of a series of graduate seminars with that theme. The seminars led to our stimulating and fruitful relationship with the Financial Executives Institute's research arm, the Financial Executives Research Foundation (FERF). FERF's research grants, and the strong support of Roland Laing and Bill Sinnett, gave us exceptional opportunities to learn from many CFOs and other financial executives of companies that are leaders in changing financial management practice. These financial executives are showing how finance can add increasing value to their companies by recognizing and taking advantage of the opportunities arising from the integration of globalization, technology, quality management, sustainability and financial practice. Many of the examples in this book are drawn from their successes.

We owe a great intellectual debt to the finance and quality professionals throughout the United States who taught us quality management and how it must be an integral part of the job of financial managing. In particular, we wish to single out:

Fred Allerdyce, CFO, American Standard

David Baldwin, former CFO, Florida Power and Light

Len Bardsley, former Manager, Continuous Improvement, Du Pont

Richard Buetow, VP and Director of Quality, Motorola

Chauncey Burton, Senior Quality Administrator, Finance, Federal Express

Jim Chambers, Assistant Treasurer, Corning Incorporated

Winston Chen, former Chairman, Solectron

W. Edwards Deming, consultant

Joe Doherty, Assistant VP—Finance, Southern Pacific

Keith Elliott, CFO, Hercules Corporation

Bill Fitton, Senior Manager, Corporate Financial Audit, Motorola

Justin Fox, Director—Quality, Southern Pacific

Blan Godfrey, Chairman and CEO, The Juran Institute

Larry Grow, VP and Director of Corporate Financial Planning, Motorola

Sandy Helton, VP and Treasurer, Corning Incorporated

David Hickie, former Executive VP and Vice-CFO, Motorola

Alan Hunter, CFO, Stanley Works

Ken Johnson, VP, Corporate Controller, and Director of Internal Audit, Motorola

Joseph M. Juran, Chairman Emeritus, The Juran Institute

Ralph Karthein, Controller, IBM Canada

Bob Lambrix, former CFO, Baxter International

Bill Latzko, President, Latzko Associates

Ken Leach, VP Administration, Globe Metallurgical

Karen May, VP, Corporate Audit, Baxter International

Paul Makosz, General Auditor, Gulf Canada Resources

Ko Nishimura, President and CEO, Solectron

Gabriel Pall, Vice President, The Juran Institute

James F. Riley, Vice President, The Juran Institute

Pete Sale, Team Member—Finance Reengineering, Baxter International

Paul Schnitz, Director, Corporate Operations Review Group, Raychem

Bob Siminoni, Director of Strategic Planning, Treasury, Westinghouse

Ben Stein, VP and General Auditor, American Standard

Kent Sterett, Executive VP, Quality, Southern Pacific

Kent Stemper, Director, Corporate Audit, Baxter International

Bob Talbot, VP, Management Services, IBM Credit Corporation

Susan Wang, CFO, Solectron

Len Wood, Corporate Operations Review Group, Raychem

Larry Yarberry, CFO Southern Pacific

At Fordham, Frank and Jim have had the good fortune to work with excellent colleagues in an environment where good teaching is encouraged and supported. Our faculty colleagues, particularly Victor Marek Borun, Sris Chatterjee, John Finnerty, Gautam Goswami, Steven Raymar, Allen Schiff, Robert Wharton, and Milan Zeleny continue to provide much of that environment. Our deans past and present of the Fordham Schools of Business—Susan Atherton, Arlene Eager, David Gautschi, Robert Himmelberg, Janet Marks, Lauren Mounty, Donna Rapaccioli, Ernest Scalberg, William Small, Sharon Smith, Arthur Taylor, Maureen Tierney, and Howard Tuckman—have consistently supported us emotionally and financially. Bobby Wen repeatedly played key roles in the early seminars and courses we conducted.

2. Modern Financial Managing—Continuity and Change

In December 1991 we were introduced to Kirsten Sandberg, finance acquisition editor at HarperCollins College Publishers. Kirsten was quick to see the potential of our approach and immediately understood our desire to produce a family of textbooks using quality management techniques. In a large sense, our first textbook, *Modern Financial Managing—Continuity and Change*, would not have existed if it were not for her unfailing energy, good humor, and consistent faith in us and the project. Ed Yarnell worked closely, patiently, and creatively with us in the final crunch, and arranged for our work to be read by the following academic and professional reviewers who responded to the manuscript in its various stages of completion and who gave us many good ideas for improvement:

Peter Bacon, Wright State University

Omar M. Benkato, Ball State University

T. K. Bhattacharya, Cameron University

James Booth, Arizona State University

Kuang C. Chen, California State University-Fresno

Michael C. Ehrhardt, University of Tennessee

Janet Hamilton, Portland State University

David W. Hickie, Motorola Corporation

Sherry L. Jarrell, Indiana University

H. Thomas Johnson, Portland State University

John M. Joseph, Jr., Thomas College

John Kensinger, University of North Texas

Russell L. Kent, Georgia State University

Nancy E. Kin, Lake Forest Graduate School of Management

Rose Knotts, University of North Texas

John H. Lea, Arizona State University

Bryan Malcolm, University of Wisconsin-Stout

Steven Mann, University of South Carolina

Kyle Mattson, Rochester Institute of Technology

Thomas H. McInish, Memphis State University

Vivian Nazar, Ferris State University

Chec K. Ng, Jackson State University

M. Megan Partch, University of Oregon

Shafiqur Rahman, Portland State University

Robert G. Schwebach, University of Wyoming

Hugh D. Sherman, York College of Pennsylvania

David Y. Suk, Rider University

Kenneth R. Tillery, Middle Tennessee State

Philip M. Van Auken, Baylor University

Charles H. Wellens, Fitchburg State University

Len Wood, Raychem Corporation

Thomas V. Wright, St. Louis University

Robert M. Zahrowski, Portland State University

As we began to create *Modern Financial Managing*, we class-tested each chapter extensively in the introductory courses at Fordham University. Hundreds of stu-

dents provided written feedback as they read each chapter. While it is impossible to single out each by name, they are responsible for many of the book's examples and innovations. Particular thanks go to Fordham professors Christopher Blake, Sris Chatterjee, Iftekhar Hasan, and Rohinton Karanjia who used draft sections of the book in their classes and provided valuable feedback.

3. Fundamentals of Financial Managing

With the successful publication of *Modern Financial Managing—Continuity and Change*, we turned to writing *Fundamentals of Financial Managing*, the second book in the family. We were fortunate to have the support of Trond Randøy, Cynthia Leonard, and the excellent staff at Authors Academic Publishing as we prepared the first edition of this book.

When Authors Academic Publishing closed its doors, we discovered the new, exciting, and innovative textbook distribution concept developed by Textbook Media. Like the people at Textbook Media, we believe that the price of traditional textbooks has become far too high. Our thanks go to Ed Laube and Tom Doran of Textbook Media who made the second and third editions possible and who pioneered the process to bring it to students at a price they can afford.

Particularly special thank yous go to Philip Schrömbgens, Kyle Houghton, Phungporn (Bee) Jaroonjetjamnong, John Fernandez, Elizabeth Tam, and Shui Hwang, Frank's graduate assistants at Fordham, who worked closely with Frank and Jim to prepare the manuscript. Philip managed the computer files, designed page layouts and edited text and artwork to produce the first edition. Kyle, Bee, and John picked up where Philip left off and produced the second edition. Elizabeth and Shui produced this third edition. Their skill and creativity improved immeasurably the quality of this book, and we are most grateful for all their efforts.

A special thank you goes to Eric Werner whose brilliant sense of humor and artistic skill are responsible for most of the cartoons of this edition.

4. And, of Course . . .

Finally, we both feel a debt of love and gratitude to our families—Marie, Allison, and Eric; and Barbara, Alexandra, and Carolyn—who accepted our many late nights at the office and frequent trips to visit finance and quality professionals with very few complaints and many warm welcomes upon our return. For both of us they formed our ultimate support system.

TO THE STUDENT

Welcome to *Fundamentals of Financial Managing*. We have tried to make the book easy to read and learn from and a lot of fun as well. Unlike many introductory finance books, this one talks about two facets of finance: analytical finance, the theory that guides financial analysis and decision making (which is in all finance texts), and operational finance, the way finance is practiced in world-class companies (which is in no other undergraduate finance text we know of). You are fortunate to have a professor who is forward-looking and in touch with the enormous changes taking place in business practice.

As you begin to study finance you are embarking on an exciting adventure, and we hope this book will be a good companion and guide. To help your learning further, we offer these suggestions:

Skim the entire book in advance   Take an hour or so to look over the table of contents and to skim the glossary and index. Then read the "part openers," the short sections that begin each of the six parts of the book, and read the section "Key Points You Should Learn from This Chapter" at the beginning of each chapter. By taking the time to do this at the beginning of the term, you will get a good overview of the subject and will be able to set each topic in the appropriate context when you get to it.

Read the section entitled "To the Instructor"   It is always useful to know as much as possible of what is on your professor's mind. In our comments to your instructor, we have written about what is new and special about this book. We have described some of the major features of the book—most of which were designed to make your work as a student easier.

Put yourself in the chapter opening vignettes   Each chapter opens with a scenario you might find yourself in (or may already have been in) at some point in your business career. Before you read the chapter, think of how you might try to deal with the situation our characters are facing. As you read the chapter, relate the concepts to the vignette, and see how much more you could add. When you reach the end of the chapter, and read the closing vignette, match up your observations with those of the protagonist. While there is rarely a single "right answer," finance provides helpful ways of approaching each problem. You will be delighted as you observe your thinking and analytical processes sharpen throughout the course.

Work each example problem you encounter while you are reading a chapter   Take out your financial calculator or boot up your computer and go through the problem step by step. Doing each problem will reinforce your reading and help you to become proficient at using the financial calculator and/or

Jim discovers the true value of his textbooks

spreadsheet which have become universal tools of financial professionals. You will learn more, and the new knowledge will stay with you longer.

Relate the examples about company practices to your experiences
If you have worked for a while, you may have been involved in or seen similar examples of financial practice. However, even if you have little or no work experience, you have been a customer of business for years. In many ways, all the examples talk about universal phenomena: serving customers, increasing quality, improving work, discovering when benefits exceed costs, finding the best way to do something. In what ways are these examples different or the same as those you have experienced? What could you have done differently if you had this knowledge back then? What about these examples makes them illustrations of "world-class" performance?

Use the footnotes labeled "Cross-reference" as a hypertext device
Whenever a reference is made to something that appears in another chapter, there is a footnote identifying that other location. Jump back and forth as needed to pick up and review supporting concepts.

Look carefully at the total results of each homework problem   Where a problem has multiple parts, you may find yourself doing the same analysis several times. Feel free to do only one or two parts at first and come back to the rest later to reinforce your learning. However, when you have completed all parts of a repeating problem, look at the range of results. Observe how the results changed in response to the one variable that changed, an important insight beyond what is asked in the problem.

Take advantage of the end-of-book "Summary of Mathematical Relationships" and "Summary of Financial Ratios"   These handy pages include every formula in the book and serve as useful references when doing homework problems or preparing for examinations.

Use the end-of-book "Glossary" as a second index When you wish to review a concept, you can look up the definition of a related term in the glossary. At the end of the definition you will find the number of the chapter and page on which the term was first defined. Turn to that page, and you are at the beginning of the section to review.

Help us make the book better As we teach financial managing to our students at Fordham, we ask each student to write a weekly memo to us telling us how well we did each week as teachers and authors. Was the class clear and useful? Did this week's chapter read well or make no sense? What didn't you understand, and which parts of the chapter worked well for you? What could we do to make the book better? Hundreds of our students have written those memos. They have taught us a huge amount, and helped us to improve the book significantly. We invite all of you to join our Fordham students as we continue to improve the book. Please address any comments, criticisms, and suggestions to either of us at:

> Fordham University
> Graduate School of Business Administration
> 113 West 60th Street
> New York, NY 10023

We promise to read your letters and consider them seriously for the next edition. You are the ultimate customers of our work, and as we have learned from our studies of world-class companies, delighting you and exceeding your expectations must always be our primary goal.

Enjoy! Most important, as you study finance, HAVE FUN!! We know that there will be times during the course where many of you will be convinced that finance is anything else *but* fun, but this doesn't have to be so. We believe that one of the most important goals for every worker—whether a student, professor, finance professional, or anyone else—is to find what the renowned management thinker W. Edwards Deming called "joy in work." If you put in the effort to read carefully, to do the assigned problems, to go over the sticky points, to review your work, and to discuss the material with your friends who are also taking the course, you will be rewarded handsomely with useful and important learning that will last a lifetime. And as it has for your professor and us, finance will become a true labor of love.

ABOUT THE AUTHORS

Frank M. Werner is Associate Professor of Finance at the Schools of Business Administration of Fordham University. He received his Ph.D. in Finance from Columbia University in 1978. He also received an M.Phil. in Finance from Columbia in 1975 and an M.B.A. from Harvard in 1968. His undergraduate degree, also from Harvard, was in Engineering and Applied Physics in 1966. Dr. Werner is the author of a variety of journal articles, a computer-based simulation of corporate finance decision making, and numerous monographs and cases for instructional use. He is a member of the American Finance Association, the American Society for Quality, Financial Executives International, the Financial Management Association, and the Academy of Business Education. In addition to his responsibilities at Fordham, Dr. Werner advises companies in the areas of corporate finance and quality management. He has given seminars on various quality and finance topics, in both English and Spanish, throughout North, Central, and South America; Europe; Asia; Africa; and the Middle East. His novel, *The Amazing Journey of Adam Smith* (CreateSpace, 2010), explores the connection between financial self-interest and the evolving needs of society, often referred to as 'global substainability.'

James A.F. Stoner is Professor of Management Systems at the Schools of Business Administration of Fordham University. He received his Ph.D. from the MIT School of Industrial Management (now the Sloan School) in 1967. He also earned an S.M. in Management from MIT in 1961 and a B.S. in Engineering Science from Antioch College in 1959. Dr. Stoner is author and co-author of a number of books and journal articles. These include *Management,* sixth edition, Prentice Hall; *Introduction to Business,* Scott Foresman; and *World-class Managing—Two Pages at a Time,* Fordham University. He is a member of the Academy of Management and past chair of the Management Education and Development Division; the American Society for Quality; the Academy of Business Education, and the Organizational Behavior Teaching Society, of which he is a former board member. In addition to his responsibilities at Fordham, Dr. Stoner advises several major companies on the movement toward quality management and teaches in executive seminars on quality and management. He has taught in executive programs in North and South America, Europe, Africa, and Asia. In 1992, Fordham University established the James A.F. Stoner Chair in Global Sustainability.

Drs. Werner and Stoner are the authors of five books studying changes in finance in companies that are leaders in quality management: *Remaking Corporate Finance—The New Corporate Finance Emerging in High-Quality Companies* (McGraw-Hill Primis, 1992), *Finance in the Quality Revolution—Adding Value by Integrating Financial and Total Quality Management,* (Financial Executives Research Foundation, 1993), *Managing Finance for Quality—Bottom-Line Results from Top-Level Commitment* (ASQ Quality Press and the Financial Executives Research Foundation, 1994), *Internal Audit and Innovation* (Financial Executives Research Foundation, 1995), and *Joining Forces* (Fordham Graduate School of Business monograph, 1998). They are also the authors of the textbook *Modern Financial Managing—Continuity and Change.*

CREDITS

PART I

ABOUT

FINANCE

AND MONEY

In Part I we introduce key concepts of finance.

Chapter 1 introduces finance and the task we call financial managing. We define finance, relate it to economics, and look at two ways to organize the subject. We trace its historical development and discuss its continuing evolution in response to the dramatic changes in today's business environment. We then examine the modern finance goal—maximization of shareholder wealth—look at how companies that have moved toward new management systems are following a "sequenced goal approach," and speculate about the future.

Chapter 2 identifies the data used in financial analysis and decision making. The chapter also discusses how the use of all data derives from theory and suggests some difficulties in making accurate use of data.

Chapter 3 introduces time value of money, the fundamental concept that the value of money depends on both its amount and when it is received or paid. We develop the basic time value relationship and then systematically extend it to describe more complex patterns of cash flows.

Chapter 4 looks at interest rates and foreign exchange rates. We introduce a model of interest rates that points to why interest rates differ. We then describe exchange rate systems and business exposure to changing rates.

CHAPTER 1
WHAT IS
FINANCIAL
MANAGING?

*L*iz Horne and Mike Cantrell shut the door to the conference room and sat down around the circular table. Liz spoke first, "This should be an interesting assignment. I really think the boss is right. The company could do a much better job of providing education for members of the finance organization."

Liz and Mike are on the staff of the chief financial officer (CFO) of their company. Earlier today, the CFO asked them to study the knowledge and skills within the finance department and to recommend what kind of education the company should provide to its finance employees.

Mike walked over to a flip-chart in the corner of the room and started making notes. He spoke as he wrote. "We could start by interviewing our colleagues. After all, they're the ones who know the most about what education they don't have."

"I'm not so sure," Liz replied. "How can they know what they don't know? Maybe we should talk to some experts in finance, like the professors at the university. They can tell us what our people should know. Then we can go around the department and see how everybody measures up."

"Do we want to ask only finance professors?" Mike countered. "When I was in school, I remember my teachers emphasizing how the various parts of any organization are interconnected. It seems to me that we have to look at the big picture and see how the finance department fits into the entire company. Why don't we try to list the various functions that the finance organization plays in the company and see where that takes us?"

Two hours later, the walls of the conference room were covered with Liz and Mike's notes. Liz sat back and looked around the room. "One thing is clear," she commented. "Finance certainly is a large and fascinating field. Our company's education program will have to cover a lot of ground."

Liz and Mike have a challenging task in front of them. As their brainstorming revealed, well-educated finance professionals are comfortable with two bodies of knowledge. First, they must understand finance theory, a particularly useful way to view how the worlds of money and business work. Over the years, students of finance have developed many useful techniques for the analysis and solution of business problems. Second, finance professionals must understand how finance relates to the rest of the organization and the external environment. The finance function serves as a support system—obtaining money resources and providing technical expertise. A seemingly brilliant solution to a financial problem that is not compatible with the way the rest of the organization or the external world functions is not really useful at all!

financial managing—the art of integrating financial theory and practice with the rest of an organization's management systems to support the delivery of low-cost, high-quality goods and services to customers and to maximize the value of the organization to its stockholders and other stakeholders

A successful business operates efficiently and effectively and maintains cooperative and productive relationships with people and other organizations. It delivers value to its customers—competitively priced, high-quality products and services that not only satisfy those customers but make them want to return to purchase more. An effective finance organization supports the company's relationships and operations. It helps the business deliver value to its customers and, as a result, deliver increased value to employees, suppliers, neighbors, and ultimately to investors. We call this task **financial managing.** In this book we discuss what financial managing is and how skillful financial managing can add value to any business organization.

Key Points You Should Learn from This Chapter

After reading this chapter you should be able to:

- Identify what the subject of finance deals with and how it differs from traditional economics, and organize finance along two useful dimensions.

- Recount how the finance discipline evolved and is continuing to evolve in response to changes in the business environment.

- Explain why it is important for a business to have goals, why profit maximization was the original goal recommended by the early microeconomists, and why shareholder wealth maximization replaced profit maximization as the firm's financial goal.

- Identify longstanding concerns about the undesirable side effects of shareholder wealth maximization being the goal of business firms.

- Explain how emerging approaches may reduce some of the concerns about shareholder wealth maximization as a goal.

Introductory Concepts—What Is Finance?

finance—the study and practice of how money is raised and used by organizations

Finance is a broad subject. In simplest terms, it covers anything to do with the use and management of money. Since money is a required ingredient in the recipe for all businesses, finance plays an important role in any business organization. Since businesses that run out of money cease to exist, skillful financial managing can easily be the difference between a successful and an unsuccessful company.

Of course, money is also a topic within the subject of economics, the discipline that has made the greatest contribution to financial theory and practice. The supply of and demand for money are very important issues in understanding how economies function. One group of economic theorists, the "monetarists," represented most notably by Nobel Prize winner Milton Friedman, argues that the money supply-demand relationship is practically the sole determinant of how well an economy performs. This book will touch on the **macroeconomic** implications of money where appropriate, but this is not our focus.

macroeconomics—the study of the functioning of economies taken as a whole

microeconomics—the study of individual units within an economy, specifically consumers and producing firms

Neither will we dwell on the micro side of economics, even though finance is an outgrowth of **microeconomics.** The branch of microeconomics commonly known as "the theory of the firm" has long dealt with the economics of a business organization but from a very narrow point of view. The organization is typically assumed to produce a product, as opposed to a service. It is studied in terms of the physical transformation of inputs into outputs: what is the optimal mix of land, labor, and capital to produce the firm's products at the lowest cost? What is the

FIGURE 1.1

Money flows of a business. The firm
(1) raises money,
(2) purchases inputs and
(3) sells outputs,
(4) shares its profits with governments and society,
(5) pays its debts, and
(6) provides returns to its investors.

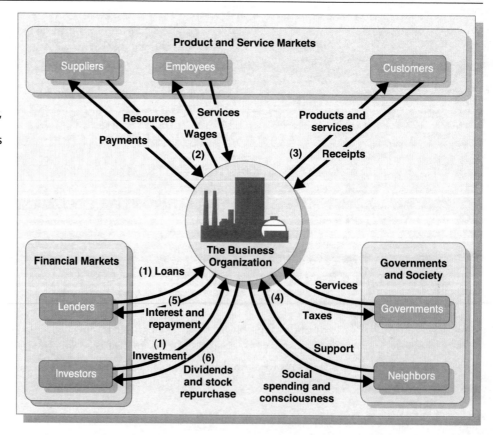

optimal mix of products to generate the highest revenue? It is also studied in terms of market structure: how should the firm price its product, and how much should the firm produce if it is a perfect competitor? an oligopolist? a monopolistic competitor? a monopolist?

The characteristics that distinguish finance from traditional economics are a focus on the business firm and the individual (hence finance is not quite macroeconomics) and a focus on financial flows rather than production transformations (hence it is not quite microeconomics either). Finance looks at how money enters the firm, is used within the firm, and exits the firm. It studies who gives the firm money and why, how to raise and use money, and how the firm distributes money. Figure 1.1 diagrams the flow of money into and out from a typical firm and identifies the firm's **stakeholders,** all those affected by the actions of the business.

stakeholders—persons and organizations affected by the actions of a business firm

Like many broad subjects, it is helpful to divide finance into component parts for ease of understanding. Two useful divisions are: (1) by academic studies and career paths and (2) by areas of concern to financial managers.

1. Organizing Finance by Academic Studies and Career Paths

One useful way to categorize the subject of finance is by the academic studies and career paths you might follow should you choose to take additional finance courses or work in a finance job. Most universities organize their finance curriculum into three broad tracks which correspond to the way many finance professionals organize job opportunities: (1) financial managing within an organization that produces and sells products and/or services, (2) analysis and management of investments, and (3) work within financial markets and institutions. Figure 1.2 shows these three paths and identifies some of the common course titles and job activities on each. Figure 1.2 also identifies an important insight: although this book concentrates primarily on the financial managing path, the key finance concepts you will encounter in the book underlie and are fully applicable to all three paths.

FIGURE 1.2

Three branches of finance. The core concepts of this book support further study and employment in (1) financial managing, (2) investment analysis and management, and (3) financial markets and institutions.

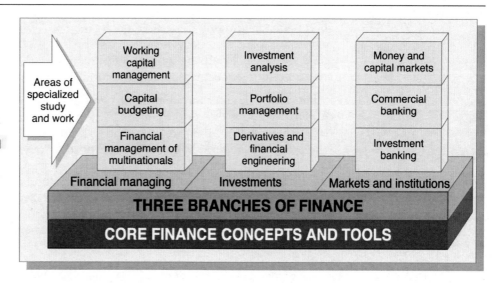

2. Organizing Finance Around the Concerns of Financial Managers

Another useful way to categorize the subject of finance is to divide it into three broad areas as seen by someone managing finance within an organization: (1) the financial environment, (2) financial instruments, and (3) management of the finances of the business firm.

financial environment—the business and social forces which impact the financial operations of an organization

financial instrument—a document giving the holder a claim to present or future cash flows

security—a financial instrument such as a bond or share of stock

stock—a type of financial instrument that gives the holder ownership of a portion of a corporation

bond—a type of financial instrument that is a long-term loan, giving the holder the right to receive interest payments and repayment of the loan principal

investment banker—an individual or organization that specializes in helping firms issue new securities and in trading existing securities

commercial banker—an individual or organization that specializes in taking deposits from investors and in making loans to individuals and organizations

financial manager—a person responsible for analyzing and improving the money flows of an organization

chief financial officer (CFO)—the senior finance professional responsible for all of a company's financial activities

The financial environment   The **financial environment** includes all the economic, political, legal, ethical, social, and other issues that define the surroundings within which finance people operate. It includes the financial markets where lenders and investors provide money to business firms, and the product and service markets where firms purchase resources and sell their products and services. It includes the tax environment within which income is shared with various governmental agencies. It also includes the political/social environment in which society makes demands and places limits on the firm.

Financial instruments   **Financial instruments** are legal agreements giving investors ownership of the results of a business's operations. They include notes, such as bank loan agreements, and **securities,** such as **stocks** and **bonds.** Finance professionals active in the creation of financial instruments include **investment bankers,** who help the business firm to structure and issue securities; **commercial bankers,** who make loans to the firm; and professional investors and fund managers, who trade in the firm's securities to earn money for their clients. Financial managers study financial instruments to understand how and why (or why not) they can add value for these stakeholders and the firm.

Financial managing   The **financial manager** is responsible for an organization's money. Accordingly, financial managers must understand in detail the company's money flows and must ensure that money is consistently used in the best ways possible to further the company's objectives.

This book deals primarily with managing the finances of the business firm. It also includes information about the financial environment and financial instruments because good financial managers base financial management decisions upon a solid understanding of all parts of the finance discipline. This book is also about managing financial processes and operations. Good financial managers understand and use not only the tools and techniques of finance but also the tools and techniques of management. One without the other is incomplete.

If you choose to enter the finance area of a business, your first job typically will call for the use of technical finance skills; little management knowledge will be required. As you grow in responsibility within the firm, however, the nature of your job will change. While you will still need to be well versed in financial theory and practice, you will be managing tasks and people and dealing more frequently with senior managers. At this level, an understanding of management will be of significant help in your work. Eventually, you might reach the post of **chief financial officer (CFO)** or perhaps president of your company. Success at this level requires a thorough understanding of management.

◼ The Development of the Finance Discipline

Finance as a discipline did not exist prior to the beginning of the twentieth century. Small businesses were the norm. Because they were small, they needed few financial resources and were believed to be efficient and self-regulating. The few large businesses were, for the most part, financed by a wealthy owner and a few equally wealthy banker friends. Although the concept of financial accounting had been around for centuries, there was no set of standards to make financial statements available or meaningful. The financial markets were the province of a few insiders. Little information about the firm was publicly available, and few outside the business and its associates were interested in the firm's finances.

1. The History of Finance

NET Present Value
The American Finance Association is recording interviews and lectures by many of the giants in the field which may be found at: www.afajof.org/association/historyfinance.asp

Finance as we know it today evolved since the turn of the twentieth century, as summarized in Figure 1.3. The first tentative analyses of the firm from a financial point of view were largely descriptive and followed the trends of the day. Between 1900 and 1910 the focus was on the building of the great trusts: merger, consolidation, and economies of scale. From 1910–1920, the focus shifted to include divestiture in response to early antitrust legislation. Also during this period, the Federal Reserve system was created and the banking system was studied intently. The boom of the 1920s encouraged firms to raise funds for expansion and redirected the descriptive focus of finance toward securities and the stock market. By 1930, the boom was over and finance followed soberly, turning its attention to describing reduction in scale and bankruptcy.

It was not until the mid-1930s that finance began to grow into its own as a discipline. John Burr Williams's development of the theory of time value marked a turning point in the history of finance.[1] Finance was no longer solely descriptive.

FIGURE 1.3
A timetable of financial thought. The finance discipline continues to evolve in response to changes in the business environment.

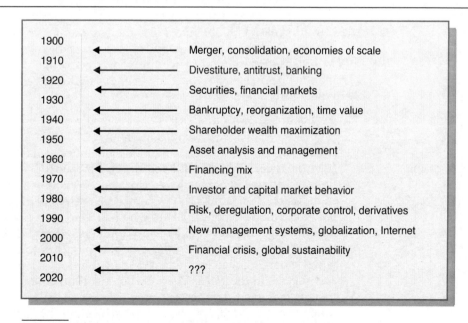

1900	Merger, consolidation, economies of scale
1910	Divestiture, antitrust, banking
1920	Securities, financial markets
1930	Bankruptcy, reorganization, time value
1940	Shareholder wealth maximization
1950	Asset analysis and management
1960	Financing mix
1970	Investor and capital market behavior
1980	Risk, deregulation, corporate control, derivatives
1990	New management systems, globalization, Internet
2000	Financial crisis, global sustainability
2010	???
2020	

---

[1] **Reference:**   John Burr Williams published his insights in *The Theory of Investment Value* (Cambridge, Mass.: Harvard Univ. Press, 1938).

For the first time, there was a theory that could instruct financial managers in what they *should* do to add value to the firm. After that, with a bit of a pause during World War II, finance spurted ahead in leaps and bounds. A goal of maximizing shareholder wealth was formulated (more about this later in this chapter), and techniques and theories were developed to achieve this goal. Mathematics and statistics were married to finance, and the power of computers was harnessed to permit complex modeling.

During the 1950s the focus of these efforts centered on the analysis and management of assets as time value theory was applied to the flows of money from asset purchases. By 1960, theories of liability/equity mix had begun to emerge, and the methods by which the firm raises money—for many years a subject only of description—got a thorough analytical treatment. The 1970s saw the development of theories of the behavior of investors and of capital markets. Theories of risk were developed, permitting financial managers to quantify risk for the first time and relate it to return. As a result, the actions of firms were linked with the behavior of investors and capital markets, and financial managers could begin to quantify how shareholders might react to corporate financial decisions.

The "oil shock" of the early 1980s as the OPEC cartel sharply raised petroleum prices, the "currency shock" as world currencies floated free of gold and the dollar, and the "inflation shock" as prices rose at double-digit rates, all created a financial environment much more volatile than experienced at any time in recent history. New financial instruments were developed to assist financial managers in coping with the increased risk. The decade of the 1980s was also a period of wrenching change for many companies. In the early 1980s, a number of U.S. industries—the financial industry included—were partially or totally deregulated in response to competition from countries with less regulation and to the political success of "free-market" advocates. (Airlines, railroads, banks, and telecommunication companies are examples of industries that experienced significant deregulation.) Although finance theory provided much advice on managing in an increasingly deregulated world, not all newly deregulated industries made the transition easily. By the mid 1980s the "market for corporate control" was flourishing: U.S. business was engulfed in a wave of mergers and takeovers as "financial raiders" sought to acquire poorly performing companies and sell off the worst-performing units. *Junk bonds, greenmail,* and *leveraged buyout* became household words.

Events in the 1980s and early 1990s forced many observers to rethink the basic premises of how organizations are managed and how the finance function contributes to that process. Existing management systems, consistent with traditional financial theory, were considered the best means for achieving a vibrant, innovative, and competitive business sector; yet we experienced competitive difficulties in industry after industry. U.S. companies responded by paying much more attention to management thinkers who had long been proposing new methods for running organizations. And finance thinkers began to reformulate theories of finance to be consistent with these new approaches to management. Beyond the newly emerging management systems, other forces emerged to change business and finance in the 1990s. As political, institutional and geographic barriers fell, nations realigned. Former enemies became allies, free-trade zones were established and expanded, and the European Community adopted a common currency. Improvements in information and communication systems permitted companies to operate as truly transnational enterprises. The Internet, previously a backwater communication channel for government and academic research, expanded into an information resource available to every computer user and became an important new distribution channel for many retail and financial businesses.

As the new millennium dawned, the dot.com boom of the late 1990s came to a screeching halt, and many businesses had to cope with the financial impacts of downsizing and restructuring. The emergence of global terrorism curtailed and refocused much business activity. Serious flaws in executive compensation, financial reporting, and corporate governance became very visible at Enron, WorldCom, Tyco International, and the New York Stock Exchange.

securitization—issuing securities backed by the cash flows of a group of financial assets

By the mid-2000s, the confluence of deregulation, technology, and creativity led to a dramatic expansion of **securitization**. Almost any cash flow stream—mortgage payments, legal settlements, recording contract receipts—could be packaged together and resold in the financial markets. However, these new securities were created faster than investors' ability to understand them, and when many companies found themselves holding investments that were far riskier than they had anticipated the investments plunged in value and financial markets shut down. The ensuing "financial crisis" pushed the world into a recession that has been characterized by many as the worst since the Great Depression of the 1930s.[2] The decade of the 2000s was also marked by an increased understanding of climate change and the need for concerted global action to reverse decades of environmental and social damage. Financial theorists began to rethink finance goals to be more consistent with the growing demands of society for a cleaner and more just world, a broader goal often referred to as **global sustainability**.[3] This is an exciting time to be studying business and finance.

global sustainability—the long term maintenance and improvement of human well-being through the combination of economic success, a cleaner and healthier environment, and increased social justice

2. The Continuing Evolution of Financial Managing

We are living in a time of dramatic and accelerating change. Every day some new technology, social development, political movement, or other event appears and alters the way we live and work. A few years ago, individuals who predicted such things as the rise of global terrorism, the extent of the AIDS epidemic, the emergence of China as a global economic power, and the Internet were considered to be engaging in wild speculation. Today, events such as these are shaping our environment, and we must learn to respond to them as individuals and as members of business organizations if we are to survive, much less prosper.

Change and the need to respond to it have always been characteristics of our environment. What is striking about change today, however, is its rapid pace and its dramatic consequences for many companies and industries.

● The U.S. banking industry hardly changed during the first three quarters of the twentieth century. Local personal relationships, unchanging products and services, and "bankers' hours" were the norm. Today, the industry has been

---

[2] **Cross reference:** See Web Appendix 1B for a detailed discussion of the Global Financial Crisis.

[3] **Elaboration:** The most widely quoted definition of sustainability is that of the United Nations World Commission on Environment and Development, often called the Brundtland Commission after its Chair, Dr. Gro Harlem Brundtland: "Sustainable development is development that meets the needs of the present without compromising the ability of future generations to meet their own needs." The social justice aspect is "a world that works for everyone with no one left out."

deregulated, is rapidly consolidating and competing globally, and is struggling to use new technologies effectively.

- The U.S. automobile industry "owned" the domestic market until the 1970s. General Motors was the country's largest company and virtually defined the industry's products and practices. Today, foreign-owned manufacturers have captured a large portion of the market, and GM is recovering from bankruptcy.

- The U.S. computer industry was dominated since its inception in the late 1940s by IBM, whose increasingly powerful mainframes and marketing sophistication were so effective that the U.S. government spent the entire decade of the 1970s attempting to break up the company's "monopoly." But where legal challenges failed, the changing environment succeeded. Today, the microprocessor, the Internet, social networking, and consumer-focused design rule the industry; the most influential players are Intel, Google, Facebook, and Apple; and IBM has had to rethink its business.

The rapid pace of change is making effective response more necessary at the same time that it is making it more difficult. In general, business organizations have not been very good at dealing with change. It is fascinating to study the lists of the 500 largest U.S. corporations published each year by *Fortune* and *Forbes* magazines. Far more interesting than which companies are on the lists is to discover which have dropped off. We might expect considerable stability from year to year; these are, after all, some of the biggest, wealthiest, most powerful organizations on the planet. The startling fact, however, is that some 40% of the companies on the list at the beginning of each decade are no longer on the list at decade's end. They have not kept up with change. They have lost out to their competitors, or they have merged with or been acquired by another company.

Of course, not everything is changing. Some time-tested theories, methods, and behaviors continue to work as well as ever; others are becoming less successful. Rapid change increases the need to identify and hold on to what works while simultaneously adapting to the ever new environment.

NET Present Value Summaries of current key ideas in business and management can be found (for a small fee) at www.leadershipandchange books.com

Major forces for change   The first step in dealing with change is understanding what is causing it to occur. We can identify nine major forces for change in today's environment that, acting alone and interacting among themselves, are dramatically modifying business practice.

- *Increased international cooperation, communication, and competition*   As late as the 1970s, most business was domestic; companies primarily served their national markets. Although the European Community was conceived in the late 1950s to reduce barriers to trade, it was still years away from having any real economic meaning. In the last 40 years, however, the economies of most of the world's nations have become significantly intertwined. The success of Japanese companies in penetrating foreign markets—notably in automobiles and electronics, the emergence of free trade areas,[4] and the information and telecommunications technologies which supported these developments have created the "global village." Today, any company's partners and competitors can just as easily be half a world away as around the corner.

---

[4] **Observation:** Although the European Community took more than 40 years to go from concept to today's relationships, the nations that have formed free trading areas more recently, including the signatories of NAFTA and Mercosur, expect to cut that time at least in half, another example of the increasing pace of change.

- *Revolutionary rates of improvement in the quality of goods and services*   New technologies for error detection, analysis, and prevention have permitted many companies to produce low-cost products at levels of quality unheard of only a decade ago. Whereas automobile warranties once rarely extended past one year, on some automobiles they now cover 100,000 miles of driving. We routinely expect electronic equipment to work for years without failure—so much so that the retail electronics repair business is now nearly defunct. Today, in an increasing number of industries, it is impossible to compete without proficiency in these quality technologies.

- *Global sustainability*   There is nearly universal consensus in the scientific community that the temperature of the earth is rising and that human activity is the primary cause. Awareness of the damage we have caused to the natural environment and the harm this will cause future generations is growing rapidly. We are also becoming more aware of opportunities previously ignored to serve the roughly one-half of the world's population that lives in poverty. Today, developments in areas such as clean energy, biotechnology, eco-friendly design, carbon markets, and microfinance promise to change the way much business is done.

- *Increased diversity in organizations' work forces, customers, and suppliers*   Changes in social norms and inexpensive worldwide transportation and communications have increased the probability that a company's next encounter will be with a person or organization from a different cultural background. We are in the midst of a major transformation as a society in our attitudes toward people different from ourselves. Rather than talking about how to "deal with" different people, companies are learning to embrace diversity and make it a positive and constructive force. Today, understanding different backgrounds and cultures is becoming a requisite of doing business.

- *Rapid changes in available information technologies*   In only 30 years, computers moved from large, centralized, frigidly air-conditioned, tightly controlled rooms to everyone's work station, desk, lap, and palm. Wireless networks connect company members to each other, to their customers and suppliers, and to databases holding vast amounts of information. E-business is growing at an explosive rate. E-mail is now as common as voice mail. Search-engine advertising and social networking sites have changed the way companies reach their customers. Today, individual employees and consumers have immense and growing analytical power at their fingertips.

- *A shift from physical capital to human capital*   Fifty years ago, the most important resource for most firms was the money used to construct the plant and equipment that produced its products. But for many firms in today's increasingly information-based service economy, the most important resource is now intellectual capital—the intelligence and creativity of its people. Today, these firms are seeking new ways to attract, measure, utilize, and reward intellectual capital, and the financial markets are struggling to place a value on it.

- *Changes in ethical standards and expectations*   Social norms are changing, and so is business conduct. Members of all racial, ethnic, and social groups increasingly expect nondiscriminatory behavior in the workplace. Businesswomen have made the problems of sexual harassment and the "glass ceiling" more visible. We are struggling to balance the requirement of any democracy for open discourse with our concerns for treating everyone fairly and equally, a conflict that often surfaces in discussions of "political correctness." We are looking more carefully at business leaders, due in part to the notoriety of illegal business activities such as the

use of multiple partnerships to hide Enron's deteriorating financial condition while enriching senior managers, fraudulent accounting at WorldCom and HealthSouth, the theft of company resources by executives at Adelphia Communications and Tyco International, and the actions of many in the finance and real-estate industries that precipitated the recent economic "crisis." In the public arena, there has been a notable trend in many countries to hold politicians to ever higher moral standards. Today's rules of behavior are markedly different from those of even a few years ago.

● *Changes in the ways organizations are managed* Over the past three decades in the United States, management methods underwent the greatest change since scientific management and the assembly line revolutionized production early in the twentieth century. Many companies discovered they could operate more effectively by moving decision making "lower" in the organization, eliminating layers of management, and breaking down the "functional silos" that separated specialist units of the organization. Today, many companies are rethinking almost every facet of the way they operate.

● *Changes in governmental policies and actions* In the United States, the 1980s was a decade of deregulation of industry. With technologies changing, the government concluded that natural monopolies were dissolving so that previously regulated companies would now respond to the discipline of the markets. Outside the United States, many countries began the shift toward market economies. Other countries moved to transfer state-owned companies to private owners. At the same time, many governments became much more active in working with domestic industries to increase their global competitive positions. Today, the interaction of business and government continues to evolve.

Implications of these forces for financial managing There are many implications for finance professionals in each of the nine change forces we have identified. For the most part, we discuss these implications throughout the book wherever we cover a topic that is changing. However, three implications transcend all finance activities: the need for intensified education and training, the importance of viewing an organization as a system, and the imperative of responding to society's increasing demand for global sustainability.

- Education has moved from being preparation for the workplace to being a life-long requirement. It is too easy for any of us to become obsolete given the rapid pace of change. Avid reading, seminars, business training programs, refresher courses, and further degree studies must be on the agenda of anyone who does not want to fall behind.

- As companies adopt modern quality-focused management practices and adapt them to their own circumstances, they quickly discover that one core concept involves viewing the organization as a system tied together by processes that cross conventional functional boundaries. Every traditional department—including finance—must be involved in the company's quality-focused efforts for the company to obtain the full benefits of this powerful way of managing. The finance functions of many companies are learning that they can add considerable value to their firms by being full partners and participants in their company's quality management efforts.

- As companies become aware of the demands of consumers and governments for sustainable products, services, and activities, they quickly realize that their ways of doing business will have to change. The products and production technologies of the future must have little or no negative effect on the environment. A huge market awaits for companies that can develop clean products or can devise ways to market to the poor. Companies that take the lead in becoming sustainable will be the ones that position themselves for future success; those that do not will risk the viability of their businesses. Evaluating and supporting these new business approaches will become a critical contribution of every company's finance function.

The Purpose of the Firm

goal—the objective of (a business's) actions

Before we can consider *what* the financial manager should do, we must first ask *why*. All decisions, financial or otherwise, can be judged only if they are measured against some **goal** or goals. A good decision is one that helps the company achieve its goals; a bad decision is one that moves the firm further away from its goals.

1. The Need for Goals

The need for goals applies to all forms of endeavor, not just the actions of a business firm. Consider personal decisions, for example. Why are you studying finance? There are many possible reasons. Is it to get a job? to get a better job? to make more money? to satisfy a demanding boss or parent? to meet an academic requirement? to broaden yourself as a person? to contribute to the well-being of society? to have fun? If you are studying finance for the right reasons, your efforts will prove rewarding. If you are studying finance for the wrong reasons, this could well be a frustrating and empty experience.

Or consider the decision to accept a new job. Is the new job right for you? The best way to approach the decision is first to be honest with yourself: what are your goals here? money? status? autonomy? personal growth? ability to contribute? intellectual challenge? If you clearly define your goals and ask how the new job measures up against those goals, you are far more likely to make a good decision than if you choose blindly.

Prior to the 1930s, before the finance discipline had developed any significant theory, the goal of finance was the microeconomic rule of maximizing profits. Since then, however, profits have been replaced by shareholder wealth as the number to maximize. Today, shareholder wealth maximization is itself being challenged by a much broader definition of the firm's goals.

2. The Role of Business in Society

NET Present Value
The International Association for Business and Society, at www.iabs.net, brings together scholars who study these issues

Business plays a vital role in our society. It is the primary means by which the necessities of life—food, clothing and shelter—are manufactured and made available to the public. It provides jobs, which define much of our lives and give us much of our sense of self-worth. But business does much more. It provides pharmaceuticals and medical care. It provides banking, insurance, and pensions. It provides education at all levels. It engages in research and development activities, which bring us new products and services enhancing our lives. By freeing us from economic want, business allows us to pursue leisure activities. All societies require a healthy business sector, and a healthy business sector is required for a healthy society.

capitalist economic system—an economy marked by private ownership of businesses and the resources necessary for producing goods and services

Yet, in a **capitalist economic system** such as ours, society and business are quite distinct from each other. And while business firms can indeed benefit society, they are usually owned and operated by people for other reasons entirely. The entrepreneur who devotes time, energy, and money to creating and nurturing a business rarely makes benefit to society the primary goal of the firm. Rather, individuals create business firms for personal reasons, usually to make money. Since the Industrial Revolution, when the earliest businesses were formed, economists and philosophers have been examining whether, given the personal motivations of those who form and manage businesses, the actions of privately owned firms really do lead to a high degree of social welfare.[5]

3. The Microeconomic Goal: Profit Maximization

It was Adam Smith who first put forward the idea that individual business firms, each acting for its own benefit could, in the aggregate, benefit society. More than 200 years ago he wrote:

> (The businessman) by directing . . . industry in such a manner as its produce may be of greatest value . . . intends only his own gain, and he is in this, as in many other cases, led by an invisible hand to promote an end which was not

---

[5] **Observation:** This question, of the consistency between personal and societal goals, is particularly relevant in a capitalist economy, in which the means of production (businesses) are privately owned and separate from society as a whole. An alternate approach is that of Karl Marx, who, concerned about just this potential conflict of interest, proposed an economic system in which society owned all businesses. In this socialist economy, Marx argued, business and society would join together, and government would insure that business success equalled societal success. However, as events in socialist economies throughout the world (most notably in Eastern Europe and the former Soviet Union) have demonstrated, the side effects of socialism—centralization of political power, misallocation of resources due to the lack of market pricing signals, alienation of people—have repeatedly prevented the system from achieving either a well-functioning economy or a high degree of social welfare.

economic profits—the money returns to the investors in a firm

a part of his intention. . . . pursuing his own interest he frequently promotes that of society more effectually than when he really intends to promote it.[6]

This most famous of passages offered the managers of the Industrial Revolution a simple primary goal. The object was for each firm to maximize **economic profits;** in practical terms this translated to efficiency of production. Since it was observed that efficient firms survived and prospered, **profit maximization** attracted many adherents. As elaborated by subsequent economists, in highly **competitive markets,** with well-informed participants and prices accurately reflecting values, profit maximization by all businesses leads to the **efficient allocation of resources** and produces the greatest amount of those goods and services demanded by society at the lowest cost given the resources available.

profit maximization—the act of managing a firm so as to increase its economic profits to the maximum possible level

competitive market—a market in which no participant has enough economic power to influence prices

efficient allocation of resources—directing the resources of an economy (money, labor, machinery, land, etc.) to those businesses where they can produce goods and services of the greatest value

However, when the early economists described the role of profits, they had no way of anticipating the complexity of modern business practice and the multiplicity of ways present-day accountants record and interpret financial numbers. One firm can have many possible numbers for its **accounting profits,** depending on the choices made by its managers and accountants. It is increasingly difficult to measure profits and to know whether they are being maximized.

accounting profits—the bottom number on an income statement using rules of measurement determined by accounting authorities

There are other difficulties as well with profit maximization as a goal—difficulties also not foreseen by Adam Smith and his followers. For one thing, profits do not come at once but over time, as firms invest their resources in long-term investment projects. As a result, investments with the same total profits might not have the same value.

Example

| **Different Timing for Two Profit Streams** |

Investments A and B each have a three-year life and total profits of $6,000. However, Investment B returns its profits earlier than Investment A.

	Profits from	
Year	Investment A	Investment B
1	$ 1,000	$ 3,000
2	2,000	2,000
3	3,000	1,000
Total	$ 6,000	$ 6,000

Question: Which investment will be preferred by the company's owners?

Answer: Although both investments have the same $6,000 *total* profits, there is considerable difference as to *when* the profits come. The firm's owners would probably prefer Investment B, which earns the greater amount sooner. However, if the two investments have impacts beyond year 3, the answer could be different. For example, if Investment B's declining performance is the result of customer dissatisfaction and Investment A's performance resulted from a gain in market share that will continue in years 4, 5, and beyond, the firm's owners would probably prefer Investment A.

risk—the possibility that the result of some activity will not be exactly as (and particularly, will be worse than) forecast

Another difficulty is that of **risk,** the lack of certainty in the profits from an investment. Profits do not consider risk, but investors do.

---

[6] **Reference:**   Adam Smith, *The Wealth of Nations,* 1776, bk. 1, chap. 2.

Example

Different Risk Levels

Investments C and D each have a one-year life. However, each investment's profitability depends on the state of the economy.

Event	Profits from Investment C	Profits from Investment D
Good economy	$ 50,000	$ 90,000
Poor economy	50,000	10,000
Average profits	50,000	50,000
Variability of profits	0	80,000

Question: Which investment will be preferred by the company's owners?

Answer: Although both investments have average (expected) profits of $50,000 (assuming good and bad economies are equally likely), there is considerable difference as to the *certainty* with which the profits will be received. The profits from Investment C will be $50,000 regardless of the state of the economy; however, Investment D could earn $90,000 or $10,000. The firm's owners would probably prefer <u>Investment C</u> which exposes them to much less risk than Investment D.

There is still one more problem with profits. In Adam Smith's day, the manager of a business was normally its owner and thus directly received its profits. Profits equaled return to the investor. Over time, however, as firms required additional equity capital to finance growth, shares of stock were sold to outside investors. Today, in most large companies, outside shareholders make up the majority of owners; the companies typically are run by **professional managers,** who own relatively little of the firm. In these firms the owners receive dividends and stock-price appreciation, which are rarely equal to the firm's profits. Profits no longer equal return to the investor.

professional managers—individuals employed by a firm to direct its activities because of their expertise. They are distinguished from owner-managers, individuals who find themselves managing a firm because they own it

Profits, then, do not convey enough information in a complex world. They are hard to measure, and they ignore the timing and riskiness of benefits. In addition, profits are something which happen within the firm, yet the firm's owners are often outside shareholders who do not receive the firm's profits as they are earned. For these reasons, finance turned away from maximizing *profits* as the goal of the firm and toward maximizing the *wealth* of the firm's owners.

4. The Traditional Finance Goal: Maximization of Shareholder Wealth

For many years it has been accepted in finance that the proper goal of every business is to maximize the wealth of its owners. For a corporation, owned by shareholders, this is referred to as **shareholder wealth.** In this perspective, shareholders provide the investment needed to start and expand the firm, and most companies exist because of shareholders' desire to increase the value of their investment. Shareholders hire management, whose primary responsibility is to increase the wealth of their employers.

shareholder wealth—the total value of an investment in the common stock of a company, measured by the price at which the stock could be sold

Shareholders obtain wealth from the firm in two ways: (1) dividends and other direct cash payments, and (2) appreciation in stock price. In general these two methods of adding to shareholder wealth do not conflict; that is, actions that lead to the ability to pay a high dividend stream are the same actions that increase the firm's stock price. It is therefore customary to equate the maximization of shareholder wealth with the maximization of stock price.

efficient capital market—a financial market in which security prices fully contain the meaning of all known information

By looking at stock price we avoid the problems of profit maximization. A well-functioning or **efficient capital market** should look beyond accounting choices and evaluate the timing and risk of promised benefits to determine their true worth.[7] Even though the price of a share of stock may be affected on a day-to-day basis by many factors having no relation to the performance of the firm, in the long-run the stock market will recognize all the components of value and reward stockholders whose managers act to increase their wealth.

In addition to rewarding shareholders for the use of their funds and for the risks they bear, it has further been accepted that the goal of maximizing shareholder wealth leads to two additional contributions to the economic welfare of society:

- *The effective allocation of new investment funds.* Companies often need infusions of additional money from outside investors to finance their operations. The firms most deserving of these funds are those that use the money best in satisfying their customers. But firms that do an excellent job of satisfying their customers should be highly profitable and should have a high stock price. Therefore, firms that act to maximize their share price will be the ones that deserve to attract new investment capital. This is particularly important to financial managers, since a key part of their job is to raise money. Companies must always be positioned to obtain funds as needed.

- *The evaluation of investment risks.* As they consider giving their money to a business firm, investors evaluate the risks they would face. What is the likelihood that the firm will do well? be average? do poorly? fail? Investors in general are averse to taking risks and will do so only if properly compensated. They will demand a higher return from a risky investment than from one with less risk and will reduce the price they are willing to pay for the firm's stock if they see the company taking excessive risks. Management will be able to maximize the value of the firm's stock only if it can provide returns commensurate with the risks it takes.

signaling—the process of conveying economic information

Notice how investors provide a powerful signal to a company's management through the price they are willing to pay for the firm's stock. This **signaling** aspect of the stock market, providing feedback about risk and return levels, is considered one of its most important properties.

Figure 1.4 presents the logic of share-price maximization as the traditional financial goal of the firm. The ultimate objective is to achieve the greatest level of economic efficiency. An important requirement for economic efficiency is a vibrant, well-functioning business sector. This can only be achieved by private enterprise—entrepreneurial businesses willing to compete and take risks. If successful, many

---

[7] **Elaboration:**   In financial terms, an efficient capital market is one in which security prices are always "correct" in that they reflect investors' best judgment about the future. All available information has been properly evaluated, and new information is rapidly analyzed and incorporated into security prices. Studies of the efficiency of the stock market (in particular of the New York Stock Exchange) have suggested a very high level of efficiency.

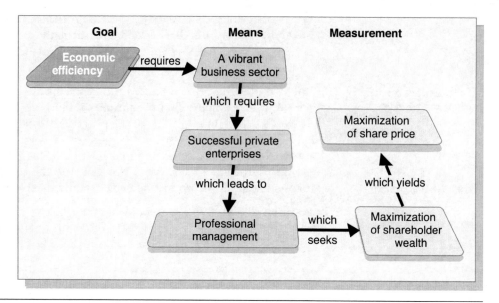

FIGURE 1.4
The logic of share-price maximization. Private enterprise, professionally managed to maximize share price, should lead to the highest degree of economic efficiency.

of these businesses will become large enough to require professional management, and ownership and management will become separated. Managers will be asked to act in the best interest of the owners, who will measure them by how much they have increased the firm's share price, hence their wealth. In summary, then, we ask managers to work in the best interests of society, and we measure their success by how much they increase the firm's share price.

Concerns About Shareholder Wealth Maximization

Earlier in this chapter we pointed out the separation between business and society characteristic of capitalist economies. Important concerns persist about whether an economy of corporations, each maximizing the wealth of its shareholders, produces undesirable side effects. We summarize these concerns under two questions: (1) Does accepting this goal yield a desirable mix of outcomes for society? (2) Does accepting it lead to desirable actions within corporations?

1. Outcomes for Society

Even when pursuit of shareholder wealth maximization yields the full advantages of economic efficiency its advocates claim for it, it may still not lead to the best mix of outcomes for society. A well-performing economy is only one facet—although a very important one—of social welfare. Other aspects of social welfare must be successfully addressed for nations and the world to survive and prosper. In particular, is shareholder wealth maximization always consistent with a clean and healthy environment or with society's notions of economic and social justice? Major concerns about this issue have persisted for years. In many countries it is the defining issue that separates social groups and political parties.[8]

---

[8] **Elaboration:**   In the United States, for example, this division is the primary distinction between many of the positions of the Republican and Democratic parties. Although it is dangerous to summarize any one of a political party's positions in a few words, for the most part, the Republicans see the benefits from a well-functioning economy as a paramount goal and the precursor to most social possibilities, while the Democrats believe that more far-reaching social goals must be pursued in parallel to economic goals, even if that results in somewhat less economic efficiency.

Three topics regularly discussed as part of this debate are: (1) income inequality, (2) the failure of corporations to take socially responsible actions, and (3) poorly directed business activities.

Income inequality   In most societies there is a widely held belief that there is a tradeoff between economic efficiency and equality of incomes. If the tradeoff does exist, companies acting to maximize shareholder wealth may be hurting society at the same time as they contribute to it. And even if these beliefs are not accurate, the debate could persist indefinitely because the relationship is so hard to test empirically.

Failure to take socially responsible actions   Companies pursuing shareholder wealth maximization may perceive little or no incentive to use their resources to provide for the social welfare either of their employees or of nonemployees. For example, until mandated by legislation, many companies spent very little on workplace safety, employee health care, or employee pensions. And even though, when viewed in hindsight, the benefits companies derived from being more socially responsive might well have been greater than the costs in many cases (thus actually increasing the companies' success in pursuing shareholder wealth), this does not mitigate the social losses arising from the companies' earlier lack of social responsibility.

Poorly directed business activities   The pursuit of shareholder wealth maximization leads to a mixture of products and services that is not always consistent with the needs or desires of the overall population. Rather it reflects the demands of those at the high end of the income distribution. To some, it seems inconsistent with social welfare that there are over 50 brands of sugared cereals on supermarket shelves at the same time that many people cannot find adequate shelter or health care. Similarly, profit maximization by itself does not discourage producing and marketing products and services harmful to society.[9] In fact, the more profitable an activity, the more it is encouraged by a goal that looks only at the benefits accruing to shareholders and ignores the costs borne by society.

2. Actions Within the Firm

At least four concerns exist about the internal operations of companies using shareholder wealth maximization as their goal. These concerns can be expressed in terms of four questions many managers have had trouble answering to their own satisfaction: (1) Is the shareholder wealth maximization goal a useful measuring stick? (2) Does it create the right image for the company? (3) Does it inspire employee commitment? (4) Does it encourage ethical behavior?

A useful measuring stick?   To be useful in guiding day-to-day action, shareholder wealth maximization needs to provide clear and valid guidance to managers. Some financial managers are convinced it does exactly that. However, other finance professionals see limitations to share price maximization as a useful managerial guideline. Perhaps the greatest concern is about the temptation to take actions that increase short-run share price at the expense of long-run share price. Many financial managers believe it is possible to fool the market—at least in the

---

[9] **Observation:**   Illicit drugs, tobacco, and handguns are examples of highly profitable products that cause significant damage to many people as are activities that pollute or otherwise degrade the environment.

very short run—to look good this week or month at the expense of things not going as well at some time in the future. They are very uncomfortable with measurement systems that encourage them to sacrifice the future strength of their company for current appearances of high performance.

Creating the right image?   One major disadvantage of shareholder wealth maximization as the goal of a company is the message it sends to those outside the firm. The consistency between maximizing shareholder wealth and serving customers with excellence, treating suppliers with integrity as partners, and contributing to society has not been easy to communicate. The public is aware of so many examples of companies that in their single-minded search for profits have not achieved desirable social outcomes, that any company touting such a goal faces the task of explaining how its pursuit of only a high share price will lead to behavior different from that of other companies with apparently the same goal.

Inspiring commitment?   Many managers are also concerned about the image this goal would project within their company. Think back to the most recent time you made a personal sacrifice in contributing to a company you were working for—when you inconvenienced yourself to go well beyond the minimum required of you and when you knew there was almost no likelihood you would be rewarded or even recognized for your extra effort. Did you put the company's interest ahead of your own in the hope that you would add 0.00000001 dollars to the value of each share in your company? We suspect not.[10]

Much more likely, you did what you did for a very different reason. Perhaps you did not want to let down an internal or external customer or a member of your work group. Maybe you cared about how the company would look if you did not put forth the extra effort, or perhaps the reason was simply that the personal pain of doing less than your best was greater than the sacrifice required to do what you knew was right. The trouble with telling people that the entire purpose of their work is to enrich someone else is that it sends the wrong message—that we are being used for a purpose that sounds less than noble to most of us and seems to demean our commitment and our sacrifices.

Encouraging ethics?   Many managers believe that high corporate ethics are not just morally correct but also good business. However, the call for maximizing share price may not always carry with it an equally loud insistence on maintaining high ethical standards while doing so. Where the only goal is share price, ethics has sometimes taken a back seat to making more money.

Emerging New Approaches That Begin Re-Integrating Societal and Shareholder Interests

We have seen that relying on shareholder wealth maximization to provide the best mix of benefits for the community raises problems that are real and may never be solved fully. However, the seriousness of these concerns and frustrations in deal-

---

[10] **An invitation:**   If that *was the reason,* please write or call us and tell us about it (our addresses and phone numbers are in the "To the Instructor" and "To the Student" sections at the beginning of the book). We are delighted to learn when our predictions are inaccurate. However, we don't anticipate getting many calls.

ing with them, both within and outside corporations, continue to encourage new solutions. Two emerging approaches may offer new alternatives for reducing such concerns: (1) efforts to align goals throughout the organization, and (2) a recognition of the value of a sequence of goals.

1. Aligning Goals Throughout the Organization

The requirements of global competitiveness and modern quality-focused management systems stress the pursuit of harmony and alignment of interests of all parties within a company and between the firm and its environment. Unless all parts of a business work together, it is impossible to produce low-cost products and services of competitive quality. And without competitive products and services, the firm cannot survive, much less maximize shareholder wealth. Fortunately, modern management approaches offer new solutions to integrating the interests of shareholders and society.

Using process-focused goals   Modern quality-focused management approaches seek to concentrate every employee's and manager's attention on the connection between the needs of customers and the internal productive processes that meet those needs. Efforts are directed toward improving the way the firm designs, produces, markets, delivers, finances, etc. its products and services. By doing so the firm lowers its costs while creating more value for its customers, often permitting it to charge premium prices. The result is increased profitability and share price, but this comes from a focus on processes not on financial numbers.

Building on people's integrity   Many organizations have extensive controls within their management systems that focus on the dark side of our nature, our selfishness and lack of integrity, and ignore our good side, our trustworthiness and selflessness. Implicitly they say that organizations must be designed to protect themselves from those of us who cannot be trusted. In doing so, they invite all of us to respond in kind—to earn that distrust.

A major aspect of modern management approaches is the pursuit of organizational designs based on the "98% of us who can be trusted to work collaboratively with others in pursuit of valued organizational goals" rather than on the "2% who cannot be trusted to do so." One approach involves asking all organizational members to identify their customers and suppliers, inside or outside the firm, and to create **customer–supplier alignments.** These alignments permit both parties to gain a fuller understanding of the other's needs, permitting suppliers to meet and exceed their customers' expectations.

Another approach is to support individuals and work units in designing, installing, and operating their own control methods—a system of self-control. Early experiences with such systems have been very encouraging, even at a stage when our knowledge and skills for developing them are quite modest.

Focusing on cross-functional relationships   Modern quality-focused management approaches recognize that the formal organization chart is often an impediment to cooperation. As a result they place great emphasis on breaking down those barriers and work hard to forge the cross-functional relationships necessary to make their processes work smoothly and accurately.

customer-supplier alignment—a close working relationship between two parties, one of whom supplies the other, to ensure that the needs of each are being met

FIGURE 1.5
The Johnson & Johnson Company credo. Notice their use of the sequenced goal approach: first customers, then employees, then communities, and finally stockholders.

Our Credo

We believe our first responsibility is to the doctors, nurses and patients,
to mothers and fathers and all others who use our products and services.
In meeting their needs everything we do must be of high quality.
We must constantly strive to reduce our costs
in order to maintain reasonable prices.
Customers' orders must be serviced promptly and accurately.
Our suppliers and distributors must have an opportunity
to make a fair profit.

We are responsible to our employees,
the men and women who work with us throughout the world.
Everyone must be considered as an individual.
We must respect their dignity and recognize their merit.
They must have a sense of security in their jobs.
Compensation must be fair and adequate,
and working conditions clean, orderly and safe.
We must be mindful of ways to help our employees fulfill
their family responsibilities.
Employees must feel free to make suggestions and complaints.
There must be equal opportunity for employment, development
and advancement for those qualified.
We must provide competent management,
and their actions must be just and ethical.

We are responsible to the communities in which we live and work
and to the world community as well.
We must be good citizens — support good works and charities
and bear our fair share of taxes.
We must encourage civic improvements and better health and education.
We must maintain in good order
the property we are privileged to use,
protecting the environment and natural resources.

Our final responsibility is to our stockholders.
Business must make a sound profit.
We must experiment with new ideas.
Research must be carried on, innovative programs developed
and mistakes paid for.
New equipment must be purchased, new facilities provided
and new products launched.
Reserves must be created to provide for adverse times.
When we operate according to these principles,
the stockholders should realize a fair return.

Johnson & Johnson

2. A Sequence of Goals

NET Present Value
You can learn more about
Fedex Corporation at
www.fedex.com and
about Johnson & Johnson
Corporation at
www.jnj.com

To maximize stock price, management must integrate its goals into a sequence that builds from one goal to the next. FedEx Corporation captures this concept in its motto "People, Service, Profits," which identifies the order in which value is created. Federal Express managers think first about their employees (the people in the motto): how to empower them and provide the resources they need to excel at their jobs, to act boldly on their own initiatives when unforeseen customer needs arise, and to improve every part of the company. Success with employees is the critical prerequisite for high-quality service. And sustained profitability is only possible after people and service have been taken care of. This is not to say that profits are a lower priority than people or service—rather, to achieve profits it is first necessary to have well-treated employees and well-served customers.

The Johnson & Johnson Company has described the sequenced goal approach as well as any company. The statement they call "Our Credo," is reprinted as Figure 1.5. The sequenced goal approach translates in practice to continually striving to exceed the expectations of *all* stakeholders. In doing so firms will:

On a Day-to-Day Basis

1. Treat customers like royalty, providing the best possible products and services at attractive prices at all times.
2. Treat employees fairly, paying a fair wage and providing employee benefits, excellent working conditions, and opportunities for personal and professional growth.
3. Treat suppliers and creditors with respect and courtesy, negotiating firmly yet also seeking win/win agreements and scrupulously honoring contracts.
4. Treat neighbors as they would wish to be treated.
5. Constantly strive to reduce costs, increase quality, and add to market share in all aspects of the business.

On a Long-term Basis

6. Treat shareholders to the high returns that will come from properly implementing the day-to-day actions.

The sequenced goal approach provides a practical method of achieving the finance goal of shareholder wealth maximization by putting customers and other stakeholders first. Yet there is an irony here: as recounted in this chapter, firms that directly pursue a high stock price may, in that pursuit, do many things that eventually drive their stock prices to progressively lower levels. In the sequenced goal approach, share price maximization still plays a role. But it is restored to its rightful original place—as the result of doing other things well and not as the first place for management to direct its attention. Only by first satisfying the firm's other stakeholders can management produce a successful and valuable firm.

Seemingly the reverse of the traditional approach, this far-from-new approach begins with customers and employees and ends with shareholders. By beginning with share price, management often can get derailed before reaching its other stakeholders. By beginning with customers and employees, the firm rarely gets derailed on the way to a high stock price.

3.   Global Sustainability

The goal of shareholder wealth maximization is intended to achieve the highest level of economic efficiency in a society. However, the goals of many societies are not solely financial but include social and environmental objectives as well. Businesses are expected to pursue these additional goals as they seek to maximize their economic value.

One widely accepted set of additional goals for business is the principles of the UN Global Compact, an initiative of the United Nations. Participating businesses voluntarily commit to uphold ten social and environmental principles with respect to the protection of fundamental human rights, the elimination of discriminatory and abusive labor practices, the protection of the environment, and the abolition of corruption as they pursue their financial goals. Figure 1.6 lists these ten principles.[11]

Another way to capture the increasing desire of societies to integrate financial goals with environmental and social objectives is captured in the term "global sustainability," the simultaneous pursuit of financial/economic success, environmental preservation, and social inclusion as suggested by Figure 1.7. Unlike the small businesses that Adam Smith studied at the time of the Industrial Revolution—firms that had little or no impact on the environment or society—today's large corporations can significantly damage or contribute to the world's ecological and social well-being by the way they operate and through the products and services they produce.[12] Society is increasingly demanding that companies consider all three objectives as they set their business goals. And, as recent experience has demonstrated, firms that pursue shareholder wealth maximization at the expense of social and environmental goals run the risk of serving neither society nor their shareholders.[13]

*T*hree days after Liz Horne and Mike Cantrell put their initial ideas for a financial training program on flip-chart pages, they returned to the same conference room with their laptops to hammer out a short report to the CFO.

"Wow," said Liz, "you can learn a lot—and get pretty confused—in three days when you ask a question that a lot of people are interested in, can't you?"

"Yep," Mike replied. "The treasurer points out how different the finance course he took three decades ago was from the current business school syllabus we showed him. And then, in the same breath, he points out a bunch of concepts in that same syllabus that he learned 30 years ago and still uses today. It looks as if there's lots of change and lots of stability at the same time."

---

[11] **Reference:**   United Nations, *Corporate Citizenship and the World Economy*, 2008.

[12] **Reference:**   The relationship between the increased power of business to impact the environment and society and the goal of the firm is the subject of Frank Werner's recent novel, *"The Amazing Journey of Adam Smith,"* CreateSpace, 2010.

[13] **Example:**   The Deepwater Horizon oil spill by British Petroleum in 2010 was due in part to decisions about how much to spend on ensuring the integrity of the well. Although the company avoided some spending in the short term, the ensuing spill severely damaged the ecology and economy of the Gulf of Mexico while costing the company, hence its shareholders, tens of millions of dollars in fines, cleanup costs, and lost revenues.

Human rights

Principal 1:   Businesses should support and respect the protection of internationally proclaimed human rights; and

Principal 2:   make sure that they are not complicit in human rights abuses.

Labour

Principal 3:   Businesses should uphold the freedom of association and the effective recognition of the right to collective bargaining;

Principal 4:   the elimination of all forms of forced and compulsory labour;

Principal 5:   the effective abolition of child labour; and

Principal 6:   the elimination of discrimination in respect of employment and occupation.

Environment

Principal 7:   Businesses are asked to support a precautionary approach to environmental challenges;

Principal 8:   undertake initiatives to promote greater environmental responsibility; and

Principal 9:   encourage the development and diffusion of environmentally friendly technologies.

Anti-corruption

Principal 10: Businesses should work against corruption in all its forms, including extortion and bribery.

FIGURE 1.6

The ten principles of the United Nations Global Compact. The principles deal with human rights, fair labor practices, environmental protection, and anti-corruption efforts.

"Okay," said Liz, "here's my memory of what we agreed upon late yesterday: (1) there are some key concepts and tools to be learned; (2) finance has specialized skills and a unique role in the company. In that sense finance people are different—and at the same time, finance people are members of the whole organization; in that sense they are the same as everyone else. And (3) some of what finance does today will change and some will not . . . and nobody knows for sure which part is which.

"Let's summarize what the program might look like. We start with an introduction to finance where we cover data, time value of money, and money rates. Next we look at how the company raises its money. Then we cover risk and return. From there we study the financial decisions that add value to the firm. We finish up with a look at how the company provides returns to its investors. How does it sound?"

"It sounds like a new kind of textbook!," Mike replied laughing. "Let's see what the CFO says."

FIGURE 1.7

Global Sustainability. The simultaneous achievement of economic, social, and environmental success is the emerging goal of many societies.

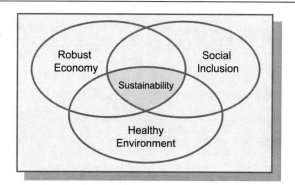

Summary of Key Points

■ **Identify what the subject of finance deals with and how it differs from traditional economics, and organize finance along two useful dimensions.** Finance is about money: how a firm gets it, uses it, and distributes it. Finance draws heavily from economic thinking but is distinct from economics. Unlike macroeconomics, which looks at economies taken as a whole, finance studies individuals and business firms. Unlike microeconomics, which looks at physical transformations within a business, finance studies money flows. Finance may be divided into three areas of academic study and career paths: financial managing, investment analysis and management, and financial markets and institutions. The concerns of financial managers may also be divided into three areas: the financial environment, financial instruments, and financial managing. Financial managers must also know how to manage well to be successful.

■ **Recount how the finance discipline evolved and is continuing to evolve in response to changes in the business environment.** Finance evolved over the twentieth century from a descriptive subject to an analytic discipline. Theory, mathematics, statistics, and computing power have been joined to create a rich body of knowledge which can guide the financial manager in making good decisions. Of late, theorists have been recasting financial concepts in a broader framework in response to new developments in the business environment and in management systems

■ **Explain why it is important for a business to have goals, why profit maximization was the original goal recommended by the early microeconomists, and why shareholder wealth maximization replaced profit maximization as the firm's financial goal.** Goals are necessary to judge the value of any action. Since business has such an enormous effect on most aspects of society, it is important that the goal(s) of business be chosen wisely to provide maximum benefit. Early economists demonstrated that profit maximization leads to an efficient use of resources and a high degree of economic efficiency under conditions of perfect competition. As the world grew more complex in the post-World War II era, the difficulty of measuring profits, as well as the new dimensions of the timing and risk of benefits, convinced economists that a more comprehensive goal than profit maximization was needed. They concluded that an economy composed of firms acting to maximize their stock prices would achieve the classical benefits of economic efficiency. In addition it would provide for the effective allocation of investable funds and the proper evaluation of business-related risks.

■ **Identify longstanding concerns about the undesirable side effects of shareholder wealth maximization being the goal of business firms.** Even strong advocates of shareholder wealth maximization have long recognized important social trade-offs inherent in this goal. Although an economy of firms acting to maximize shareholder wealth can achieve significant economic benefits, the accompanying social costs such as income inequalities, failure to take socially responsible actions, and poorly directed business activities are unattractive to most of us. Concerns about what may happen when shareholder wealth is used to guide a company include difficulties in applying the concept in practice, problems communicating to society the advantages of this goal, its weakness as a theme for inspiring commitment, and its potential for encouraging selfish and unethical behavior.

■ **Explain how emerging approaches may reduce some of the concerns about shareholder wealth maximization as a goal.** Aligning goals throughout the organization, the sequenced goal approach, and global sustainability all emphasize the consistency of interests among parties. They provide more effective ways to manage, and they suggest that maximizing shareholder wealth can only be accomplished on a sustained basis by serving the needs of customers, employees, and other stakeholders on both a day-to-day and long-term basis. These new approaches hold the promise of reducing or removing many of the concerns about undesirable societal consequences of shareholder wealth maximization.

Questions

1. How is the discipline of finance (a) similar to and (b) different from the discipline of economics?

2. Give an example of how each piece of the financial environment listed below affects the business firm:

   a. the economy
   b. the political scene
   c. the law
   d. ethical standards
   e. social norms

3. What does a financial manager do for a living?

4. What is a stakeholder? For each stakeholder listed below, identify its relationship to the business firm:

   a. customers
   b. employees
   c. suppliers
   d. governments
   e. neighbors
   f. lenders
   g. investors

5. Identify an industry affected significantly by recent environmental changes. List some of the ways the industry has been altered.

6. Identify nine forces for change in today's environment. Give an example of how each has affected business in general or a specific company.

7. If you were to start a business, what would you set as its goal? Suppose your business grew to employ 50 people. Would this change your answer? What if you had 1,000 employees?

8. What are the problems with the economic rule of maximizing profits? In what ways does the use of shareholder wealth as the firm's goal solve these problems?

9. Why is an efficient capital market necessary for the shareholder wealth maximization goal to be effective?

10. Identify an instance from your experience or readings in which a firm, aiming to maximize shareholder wealth, has caused damage to society.

11. What is the sequenced goal approach? Why is it important for managers to sequence their goals?

12. What is the UN Global Compact? Identify the Global Compact's ten principles.

13. What is meant by Global Sustainability? Why are some companies looking beyond shareholder wealth as they set their goals?

14. Why do you think finance is the most popular area of concentration at many schools of business?

CHAPTER 2
DATA FOR
FINANCIAL DECISION
MAKING

*S*teven Barbara was worried. His company was profitable, yet there never seemed to be enough cash to meet all the firm's obligations. Just today he had received a telephone call from his banker threatening not to renew the company's line of credit unless the company improved its financial condition. He had assured the banker he would get to work to solve the problem immediately, but where to start?

And now, when he needed to lock himself in the office, Steven had a doctor's appointment to go to. He had made the appointment two months ago. Given his time pressure at work he wished he could cancel it, but his wife would not hear of it. "Damn," he thought as he entered the doctor's office, "It's only a general physical examination. Why do I have to waste time on this now?"

Steven's doctor carefully measured and recorded data on his physical condition. Then he compared Steven's measurements to past data from his records and to standards for individuals of Steven's age, height, and weight as published by the medical profession. He found that Steven was essentially in good condition but could afford to lose 20 pounds. He told Steven, "Take off the weight, and you'll feel a whole lot better. Your heart won't have to work as hard, you'll have much more energy, and you'll be able to get a lot more done. You'd be surprised how one improvement like that has so many ripple effects throughout your system."

On the way back to his office, Steven thought about what his doctor had said. He wondered if the process by which the doctor had reached his diagnosis and prescription was in any way applicable to his problem at work.

Like a doctor who takes responsibility for the physical health of a patient, the financial manager is responsible for the financial health of a business. A healthy business, just as a healthy person, lives longer and is capable of pursuing many more interesting and rewarding activities. It has less stress and can more easily handle shocks to its system. It invests fewer resources to produce a profitable result, raising the return to all stakeholders.

In this chapter we look at the data required to make good financial decisions. We look at data provided by the accounting system: the financial accounting data reported to the public and the managerial accounting data used for internal decision making. We also look at data that do not come from the accounting system: information about the economy and industry; data to help us understand the needs of the people with whom the company works—its employees, customers, and suppliers; data that can tell us how well financial processes are functioning and point toward opportunities for improvement; and data capturing the firm's contributions to global sustainability.

Key Points You Should Learn from This Chapter

After reading this chapter you should be able to:

- Identify the meaning of *financial analysis* and the data used for financial decision making.

- Realize that financial accounting data are an important but imperfect source of information, and understand why it is necessary to compare numbers when doing financial analysis.

- Recognize financial ratios that measure profitability, use of working capital, use of fixed and total assets, and the choice and management of funding.

- Prepare a cash flow spreadsheet and recognize different types of costs.

- Understand the importance of economic data; of collecting information about customer and employee satisfaction; of measuring the performance of financial processes; and of environmental, social, and governance (ESG) data.

Introductory Concepts—The Need for Good Data

financial analysis—the use of financial and other data to understand the financial health of an organization

Financial analysis is using financial and other data to reach judgments about the financial health of an organization.[1] It is done within a company by financial managers as they work to keep the business healthy. It is also done outside the company by its stakeholders—investors, creditors, customers, suppliers, governments, unions—as they decide how they want to interact with the firm.

The medical analogy is quite appropriate since, in performing financial analysis, we do virtually the same things as a doctor who analyzes and cares for a patient. First, we collect and organize data about the firm to describe its present condition in useful financial terms. Second, we use this information to diagnose the firm's strengths and weaknesses and identify issues that require our immediate attention. Third, we use our knowledge of the firm, plus other data about similar firms and the environment, to predict where financial problems are likely to arise in the future. Finally, we prescribe financial medicine if required to nurture the company back to full financial health, recommend a changed financial routine if required to improve its health, or simply advise the firm to continue doing what is working well to insure that a healthy firm stays that way.

While we identify data collection as the first step in financial analysis, there is actually a *prior* step: before we collect data, we must have theory. Without a theory we cannot know what information is relevant to study and hence to collect. Steven Barbara's doctor used his knowledge of medical theory to select information that he knew would provide insight into Steven's health.

The primary information set used by financial executives today is based on the traditional economic-financial theory of the firm, in which the fundamental objective of a business is to maximize owners' wealth. Thus financial managers collect measures of cash flow, profitability, liquidity, leverage, and resource use, because finance theory has discovered relationships between these numbers and value for the owners. *Health* is defined in financial terms. In many ways this traditional financial analysis has been quite successful in identifying problems and pointing toward better financial condition.

 However, many firms are in the midst of supplementing financial data with nonfinancial data. Financial managers are often major players in identifying meaningful nonfinancial data to collect, in collecting it, and in reporting it to the rest of the organization. For example, companies that place a particularly high priority on customer satisfaction and continuous improvement of production and service processes measure the business to assess these components of its health. To improve customer satisfaction they collect data about customer dissatisfaction; to improve processes they measure them in ways that disclose their limitations. Today many companies are using customer and process data along with traditional financial measures to give a fuller picture of the firm.

Financial Accounting Data

Financial accounting data are information collected by the firm's accounting system that are used to produce the financial statements presented to the public: the

---

[1] **Observation:**   While we look at a business in this chapter, the same concepts, with relatively minor modifications, can be used to analyze other types of organizations, both public and private.

income statement, balance sheet, and statement of cash flows. They are constrained by the pronouncements of the Financial Accounting Standards Board and the Securities and Exchange Commission, the organizations that establish the rules for public reporting.

1. The Limitations of GAAP

NET Present Value
GAAP rules are promulgated by the Financial Accounting Standards Board (FASB) at www.fasb.org

Although public financial statements are required to conform to Generally Accepted Accounting Principles (GAAP),[2] GAAP rules are not always designed with the financial analyst in mind. In fact some of the rules make it quite difficult to reach meaningful conclusions from the financial statements.

Two different valuation methods mixed together   A first concern is that two different and somewhat incompatible methods are used to value the firm's assets and liabilities. Monetary items, those that can be measured directly in money terms (cash, marketable securities, receivables, payables), are recorded at their cash value. However, nonmonetary items, those whose worth depends on future economic events (inventories, plant and equipment, receipts-in-advance) are valued at "historical cost"—for assets, the amount originally paid for them less depreciation; for liabilities, the amount received.

To accountants this makes sense. The alternative to historical cost is to estimate the money benefits the company will obtain from its nonmonetary assets and the costs of satisfying its nonmonetary liabilities, and any estimates of future benefits and costs clearly would be subjective and easy to misstate. To an analyst, however, historical cost can be just as arbitrary, since the depreciation formulas used may not relate at all to market conditions.

The use of two valuation methods complicates comparisons. Two firms with the same numbers might be worth very different amounts.

Example

Different Valuation Methods
The Monetary Company and the Nonmonetary Company both report $10 million of assets on their most recent balance sheets. Monetary Company's assets are U.S. Treasury bills and are carried at market value. Nonmonetary Company's assets are land and buildings purchased ten years ago.
Question: Are the assets of both firms worth the same amount?
Answer: Most probably no! It is likely that Monetary Company's assets are worth close to the $10 million reported since they are carried at market value and probably could be sold for that amount. The value of Nonmonetary Company's assets, however, cannot be determined from the balance sheet. If their real estate is run down and in a poor location, it might be worth considerably less than $10 million. On the other hand, if it is well maintained and well located, its value could be far above $10 million.

Alternative numbers for the same event   A second problem with GAAP is the flexibility allowed accountants in describing an event since one method might not fit all economic circumstances. Unfortunately, when management has

---

[2] **Recommendation:**   We encourage you to refer to your textbook in financial accounting if you need to refresh your knowledge of accounting principles.

a choice of accounting methods, it does not always choose the one that best describes the economics in question. Rather, managers often choose to put their best face forward—highest income, lowest costs, highest asset values—or to minimize taxes—lowest income, highest costs, lowest asset values.

Alternative accounting treatments show up throughout the financial statements. Some common examples[3] are: (1) Revenues—differences in the point in a firm's economic process (production, sale, delivery, collection) when revenue is recognized (appears) on the income statement. (2) Expenses—differences in measuring the use of nonmonetary assets such as inventory (alternatives include LIFO, FIFO, and average cost) and capital equipment (depreciation may be calculated using the straight-line method or an accelerated method). (3) Assets—differences in the treatment of inventory and capital equipment, as above, plus differences in how leases are recorded (as capital or operating leases). (4) Liabilities—differences arising from the choice to include certain obligations or to treat them as "off-balance sheet" financing (e.g., contingent claims, nonconsolidated subsidiaries).

The variety of accounting treatments for a given event often makes it difficult to compare numbers. Two firms, identical except for accounting, might look very different to an analyst not aware of the accounting differences.

Example

Alternate Accounting Treatments

Two companies are identical in every respect except that FIFO Company uses the first-in, first-out method to value its inventories while LIFO Company uses the last-in, first-out method. The sum of beginning-of-year inventory value plus purchases of inventory this year is $800 for both companies; this amount will be allocated between ending inventory and cost of goods sold. However, prices have risen over the years. FIFO Company, applying the lower, earlier prices to the product it sold this year, reported cost of goods sold of $500. Its inventory balance of $300 reflects the most recent price level. LIFO Company, on the other hand, reported cost of goods sold of $700 based on the higher, more recent prices, and applied earlier prices to value its inventory at $100. Both firms report $1,000 of assets other than inventory.

	FIFO Company	LIFO Company
Inventory value	$ 300	$ 100
Other assets	1,000	1,000
Total assets	1,300	1,100
Cost of goods sold	500	700

Question: Do the two companies look the same to financial analysts?

Answer: <u>No!</u> FIFO Company appears to be more *profitable* since it reports that it produces at a lower cost (cost of goods sold of $500 versus $700) and owns more valuable assets ($1,300 versus $1,100) than LIFO Company. On the other hand, LIFO Company seems to be more *efficient*, reporting that it generates the same sales with less need for inventory ($100 versus $300) and total assets ($1,100 versus $1,300). In fact, <u>there is no real difference</u> between the companies. The "difference" is only within the accounting records.

---

[3] **Observation:**   You will recognize some or all of these differences depending on how much accounting you have studied.

Important information omitted   With its focus on money transactions between the firm and outside parties, GAAP ignores data that might be of critical interest to some financial analysts. Some examples: Financial accounting does not measure the quality of a company's products and processes, increasingly important determinants of future success. Financial accounting places no value on human resources, yet in an increasingly knowledge-based world, the attitudes and skills of its employees are often a company's most valuable assets. Financial accounting does not report on backlog of orders, a critical variable for firms with a long production cycle. Financial accounting does not value intangible assets that were not purchased—a company that has developed valuable patents, copyrights, or brand names finds little of that value reflected in its financial data.

Nevertheless, with all its imperfections, the financial information produced by a company is normally an excellent source of information for describing its financial health. While good analysts are appropriately skeptical and constantly searching for additional data to strengthen their conclusions, most analyses still begin with a thorough going over of the firm's financial statements.

2. The Need to Compare Numbers

A common error in working with data is to use a number out of context. It does a doctor little good to know a person's weight, for example 150 pounds, and nothing else about the person. A weight of 150 pounds could be too low, too high, or quite good, but to determine this the doctor must have some other information about the person (for example, height). In the same way, we must always make comparisons to make sense out of financial data. It is impossible to make a judgment about a business using one number alone.

Example

Attempting a Judgment with Only One Number

A company has a cash balance of $1 million.

Question: Is this cash balance sufficient? too high? too low?

Answer: <u>There is no way to know</u> without at least one other piece of data to compare to the $1 million so we can set the cash balance in context. One alternative is to compare the cash balance to the firm's size. Is it a small proprietorship?—if so, $1 million is likely much too large a cash balance. Is the company a giant corporation?—if so, $1 million is likely much too small. Another alternative is to look at the level and predictability of cash inflows and outflows. How much does the firm need to cover its day-to-day needs? Each comparison provides some insight; without comparison, the cash number is interesting perhaps, but not very informative.

There is a series of natural relationships between the financial numbers of any company, just as there are inherent relationships between a person's height and weight, or arm length and leg length, etc. A doctor uses an understanding of these relationships to spot those that seem to be abnormal. In a similar manner, as you learn more about which numbers to compare, you will develop the background and skill to locate financial abnormalities within a business.

Three types of comparisons are generally used to test the meaning of financial and other data: (1) benchmark comparisons, (2) time-series comparisons, and (3) cross-section comparisons.

benchmark comparison—
comparison to a norm
which is valid across many
companies and/or industries

Benchmark comparisons   Whenever we compare a number to some standard value we are making a **benchmark comparison.** A benchmark is a norm that is valid across many companies and industries. For example, the number 2.0 has been a benchmark for the current ratio for many years. Financial analysts seek benchmark comparisons when they believe there is a universal relationship governing the numbers in question. However, because of differences between companies and industries, there have been few useful financial benchmarks with which many analysts have felt comfortable.

Recently a new kind of benchmarking technique has been used by many companies to improve the quality of their products and services. In **competitive benchmarking,** we look for the *best* example of what we are trying to accomplish and set our goal to match or (preferably) exceed that standard. To illustrate, the manager of a real estate management company responsible for cleaning office buildings must set a standard for the level of cleanliness to strive for. Traditional benchmarking would have the manager compare the company's cleaning operation to those of similar real estate companies. Competitive benchmarking, on the other hand, would have the manager search for the best cleaning operation in any industry—perhaps in a hospital or in the "clean room" of a highly dirt-sensitive manufacturing facility. Some companies are now beginning to use competitive benchmarking to set financial standards and refusing to let traditional comparisons be their guide.

competitive
benchmarking—using the
best example available,
regardless of source, as the
firm's target

time-series comparison—a
tracking of some number
across time to see if it is
changing, and if so, the
direction and amount of
change

Time-series comparisons   Whenever we can calculate measures for more than one year, we can study their trends across time. This is a **time-series comparison.** We can see which measures are deteriorating and which are improving. Often a time-series comparison gives us warning of a developing problem so we can take action before the problem becomes serious.

cross-section comparison—
comparison of some
number to equivalent data
from other companies or
from the industry over a
common period of time

Cross-section comparisons   Whenever we have the same measure over a common period of time from more than one company we can make a **cross-section comparison.** We use a common time period to hold the environment constant. Then we can conclude that differences between measures must reflect differences between the firms and not just different points in the business cycle. We must also take care to be sure that other differences between the firms—size, product mix, markets, manufacturing technology, accounting policy, etc.—are not so great as to make comparisons meaningless. In part to overcome this problem, it is common to compare a company's ratios to **industry-average ratios.** This generally improves the analysis as it forces the comparison to reflect the overall economics of the industry in question.

industry-average ratio—a
ratio calculated by
averaging the ratios of
firms within an industry

It is important to note, however, that industry ratios often are not useful guides for financial managers. In some industries, even the "best" firms might be doing poorly, or business practice might not be up to date. And even if the industry is well managed, comparing a firm to the industry averages simply tests to see if the firm is average. Good financial managers do not use averages as their guide, for this leads to an average (mediocre) firm. This is another reason why the use of competitive benchmarking is becoming more and more widespread. By comparing themselves to the best, regardless of industry, businesses can break away from traditional thinking and identify possibilities for improvement.

IMPROVING FINANCE'S PROCESSES

Financial Benchmarking at Southern Pacific

The Southern Pacific Transportation Company, a unit of the Union Pacific Railroad, uses railroad industry data published by the United States Interstate Commerce Commission (ICC) in a very creative way. Each year, the ICC publishes its R1 report, a summary of financial and operating data from major U.S. railroads. Included in the report are detailed expense numbers for each company, that permit Southern Pacific to compare itself to its competitors. Southern Pacific uses the numbers to locate and prioritize opportunities for improvement and to support the company's shared belief that improvement is possible. Over the next decade, Southern Pacific is aiming to match or beat the best competitor in each cost category, which would make it the lowest-cost major western railroad in the United States.

Analysts normally calculate a company's ratios directly from its financial statements. To make a comparison with other companies and with industry groups, however, additional data are needed. Several information services collect financial data and report common ratios of companies and industries. Among the most popular sources are Standard & Poor's, Moody's Investors Service, Robert Morris Associates, and Dun & Bradstreet.

Financial Ratios

NET Present Value
A good source of financial ratios including comparisons with industry and overall market rations is msn money:
moneycentral.msn.com/investor/invsub/results/compare.asp?symbol=msft

The most common form of financial comparison is financial ratios. Like all other mathematical ratios, they are fractions: a numerator over a denominator. They guarantee a comparison since at least two numbers are needed to construct them.[4]

It is common to organize ratios into groups. While there are several ways to do this, we favor a scheme that emphasizes the role of ratios in financial analysis. Thus each group below contains ratios that pertain to a specific question an analyst might have about the business. Although there are other ratios we could describe, those that follow are the most basic and most commonly used.

1. Ratios That Measure Profitability

An important measure of the health of a business is its ability to produce profits. Each ratio in this group measures the firm's profit level in some way. They differ in which income statement item is chosen to represent the firm's profit and in which measure profit is compared to. Often, ratios of this type are referred to as "measuring a rate of return."

Profitability compared to sales   There are several ratios that compare profits to sales:

$$\textbf{Gross profit margin} = \text{gross profit}/\text{sales}$$

---

[4] **Observation and cross-reference:**   The ratios are introduced in this chapter without numerical examples. The same ratios are presented over again in Web Appendix 2A where they are applied to the financial statements of a sample company providing numerical examples for each.

Gross profit is sales less cost of goods sold. Cost of goods sold summarizes the costs of producing the firm's products. Sales is the sum of cost of goods sold and the firm's profit margin. As a result, this ratio measures the firm's pricing policy relative to its production costs.

$$\text{Operating profit margin} = \text{EBIT}/\text{sales}$$

Earnings before interest and taxes (EBIT) summarizes sales revenue less all operating expenses. Not included are financing costs and taxes. This ratio measures the firm's economic earnings, the earnings from delivering its products and services to customers. It is useful for comparing the economic performance of firms.

$$\text{Pre-tax profit margin} = \text{earnings before taxes}/\text{sales}$$

This ratio measures the firm's profit after satisfying its creditors but before taxes and shareholders.

$$\text{Net profit margin} = \text{earnings after taxes}/\text{sales}$$

This ratio measures the profitability seen by shareholders as it takes all expenses into account.

The GAAP format for the income statement groups expenses according to those related to the product (cost of goods sold) and those related to the passage of time (expenses such as rent or interest). However, a different expense classification, dividing costs according to those that are variable and those that are fixed, often makes good analytical sense.[5] When using this alternate scheme for cost classification, we can calculate:

Johnson solves the income statement problem.

---

[5] **Cross-reference:** Fixed and variable costs are discussed later in this chapter on pages 46-47.

$$\text{Contribution margin} = \text{contribution/sales}$$

Contribution is the subtotal of sales less variable costs. Thus, this ratio gives us the increase to the firm's profits from an additional dollar of sales.

Profitability compared to assets   We are often interested in the firm's ability to generate sales from its investment in assets. Two ratios that look at this are:

$$\text{Basic earning power} = \text{EBIT/average total assets}$$

This ratio shows the firm's economic earnings relative to its investment in assets.

$$\text{Return on assets (ROA)} = \text{earnings after taxes/average total assets}$$

This ratio shows the firm's total earnings in relation to its investment in assets.

Note the use of *average* total assets in these ratios. Earnings come from the income statement and measure activity throughout the entire year. Total assets is a balance sheet figure which represents only one point in time, the balance sheet date. A fair comparison requires us to match profitability throughout the year with the (average) balance of assets also throughout the year. Whenever we calculate a ratio which compares an income statement or cash flow statement figure with the balance sheet, we can improve the calculation by using an average for the balance sheet number. A simple way to obtain the average is to use the beginning-of-year and end-of-year figures: add them and divide by 2. The beginning-of-year figure, of course, is the prior year's balance sheet number. For more accuracy, we could average quarterly or even monthly numbers. However, sometimes only the end-of-year balance sheet is available or the analyst feels that the balance sheet data has not changed significantly during the year. In these cases it is common to simply use the end-of-year balance sheet numbers without taking an average.

Profitability compared to equity   Another way that we can examine profitability is to compare it to the level of shareholders' investment to see if the company is providing shareholders a sufficient rate of return on their invested money.

$$\text{Return on equity (ROE)} = \text{earnings after taxes/average total equity}$$

When used with return on assets, this ratio shows how the firm uses leverage to raise its return on assets to a higher return for its shareholders.

2. Ratios That Measure Effective Use of Working Capital

working capital—a firm's current assets minus its current liabilities

The term **working capital** refers to a firm's current assets and current liabilities.[6] Besides involving a large amount of money, these accounts require a great deal of day-to-day attention; current assets arrive daily and current liabilities must be paid when due. The first two of these ratios measure the firm's overall working capital position. The others measure how well the firm is managing one component of its working capital.

---

[6] **Elaboration and cross-reference:**   Mathematically, *working capital* is normally used to mean current assets minus current liabilities. In day-to-day usage, however, the term is often used to refer to all current accounts taken together, regardless of any particular mathematical combination. See Chapter 12 for further elaboration.

Measures of overall liquidity   **Liquidity** refers to a company's ability to have cash as needed. If a firm has enough cash, it is liquid by definition. If its resources are not in the form of cash it is not liquid and it could have problems paying its current liabilities. The broadest measure of liquidity is the current ratio:

$$\text{Current ratio} = \text{current assets}/\text{current liabilities}$$

Current assets (such as cash and accounts receivable) are assets that are now cash or will turn into cash within the accounting period, typically the next year. Current liabilities (mostly payables) are obligations that must be paid within the accounting period. The current ratio, therefore, measures a firm's ability to generate cash to meet its upcoming obligations. A good current ratio is at least equal to 1.0, since, at that level, current assets equal current liabilities and are (barely) enough to cover the firm's current debts. If cash flows are variable, with inflows not matching outflows, the average value of the current ratio should be above 1.0 so the firm can meet its obligations when cash inflows drop off.

A current ratio that is too high can be almost as bad as a very low current ratio. A very high current ratio could indicate an excess of current assets, a wasteful use of resources. It could also indicate inadequate use of current liabilities. A traditional rule-of-thumb used by many analysts is that a current ratio near 2.0 indicates that the current accounts are somewhat in balance.

Some companies are **seasonal,** their level of business changing throughout the year. In these firms there is a normal build-up of working capital, especially inventories and accounts receivable, as the busy season approaches, followed by a reduction of working capital after the seasonal peak as inventories are sold and receivables are collected. The current ratio of a seasonal firm will fluctuate with the seasons as well, and the good analyst will calculate it at various points during the seasonal cycle to test the firm's liquidity throughout the year.

A stricter test of liquidity is the quick ratio:

$$\text{Quick ratio} = \text{quick assets}/\text{current liabilities}$$

Quick assets are those current assets that can be converted quickly to cash. Typically included as quick assets are cash (it's already cash), marketable securities (it only requires a phone call to the firm's securities broker to produce cash), and accounts receivable (which usually can be sold to a financial institution for cash). Typically omitted from quick assets is inventory that could be out of date or out of fashion. Inventory could also be work in process which might never be completed and would be of no use to anyone else. Also typically omitted are prepaid expenses, unless the money could be retrieved in an emergency. This ratio is a much narrower measure of liquidity than the current ratio. Analysts who forecast a crisis[7] in which the company has to raise cash immediately use this ratio to test the firm's ability to cover its obligations under that scenario.

Measures of the effective use of accounts receivable   Companies extend credit to their customers to facilitate their customers' purchases and, hence, to increase sales. A well-managed receivables balance is then collected in a reasonable time so the money can be reused (turned over) to produce more prod-

---

[7] **Elaboration:**   Because this ratio is particularly applicable in times of difficulty when the firm is being pushed to its financial limits, it is also called the *acid-test* ratio.

ucts for additional customers. These ratios measure the speed with which the firm collects its accounts receivable. They are especially important for a company in which credit is an important competitive tool.

Accounts receivable turnover = credit sales/average accounts receivable

Collection period = (average accounts receivable/credit sales) × 360

Accounts receivable turnover is the number of times the firm sells and then collects each year. This equals the number of times each year the firm reuses the money invested in accounts receivable. Collection period expresses the same concept in days. It measures the time it takes (number of days after sale) to collect the typical receivable. Since firms normally instruct their customers how long they may take before payment is due, a company's collection period may be compared to its invoice terms to test whether its customers are, on average, complying with its billing instructions.

Credit sales is used in these ratios because only credit sales produce accounts receivable. When credit sales is not known, it is common to use total sales although this will overstate the turnover ratio and understate the collection period should there be any significant amount of cash sales.

Note the use of 360 to measure the number of days in the year. While some analysts insist on the precision of 365 or even 366 every fourth year, ambiguities within the accounting numbers are typically great enough so that 360 works very well. Using 360 days for the year is also quite convenient, since it is easily divisible into halves, quarters, twelfths (it makes each month exactly 30 days), etc.

Measures of the effective use of inventories Traditionally, firms have invested in inventories for several reasons. Raw material and finished goods were used to separate the production process from purchasing and sales in the belief that this would permit each to operate in the most efficient manner. Work-in-process inventories were used to "smooth" production. Finished goods and merchandise inventories were kept to provide immediate delivery and a choice of products to customers. The belief was that the costs associated with inventory were worth paying since they lowered production costs and increased sales.

just-in-time inventory system—a system in which inventory is received and produced only as needed keeping the balance of inventory-on-hand as close as possible to zero

Recently, an inventory management system known as **just-in-time** has been adopted by many companies. Under this system, the ideal inventory balance is zero! Raw material is scheduled to arrive as it enters production; finished goods are produced as demanded by the customer. Work-in-process is kept to an absolute minimum. Just-in-time comes from the experiences of these companies that the benefits of holding inventories seem not to be worthwhile. Production can be smoothed in less costly ways than by holding inventory; in fact inventory is often found not to smooth production but to simply hide inefficiencies—production time too long, scrap and rework levels too high. Today there is a drive by companies in a wide variety of industries to use their inventories more effectively, and inventory balances are trending down.

A well managed inventory balance, therefore, ties up as little (ideally none) of the firm's funds as possible. It permits the money invested to be turned over quickly to purchase the next round of inventory. These ratios measure the speed with which the firm moves its inventory. They are especially important for a firm in which inventory is perishable and must be turned over quickly to avoid spoilage or other damage.

$$\text{Inventory turnover} = \text{cost of goods sold/average inventory}$$

$$\text{Inventory days} = (\text{average inventory/cost of goods sold}) \times 360$$

Inventory turnover is the number of times each year the firm reuses the money invested in inventories. Inventory days expresses the same concept in days. It measures the length of time the average item remains in inventory.

Some analysts compute inventory ratios using sales in place of cost of goods sold, in part because of the practice of Dun & Bradstreet (D&B), a company that produces ratio and other credit-related information. D&B uses sales in these ratios as it cannot always get good data for cost of goods sold. However, this practice can lead to erroneous conclusions because it distorts the inventory ratios. Since sales contains profits as well as the cost of inventories, the inventory ratios now change with changing profit margins. A firm with a high gross profit margin would show a much higher inventory turnover than a firm which moves its inventory just as often but has a low gross profit margin. To measure inventory use accurately, the inventory balance should be compared to cost of goods sold.

The inventory ratios are also affected by the accounting method—LIFO, FIFO or average cost—the firm uses. Analysts must be especially careful when comparing firms to be sure they use the same inventory method, as an earlier example in this chapter pointed out.

Measures of the effective use of accounts payable   A well-managed firm pays its bills when due. Yet trade credit can be an important source of funds, especially for the smaller firm. These ratios measure the firm's ability, and perhaps willingness, to pay its obligations to suppliers.

$$\text{Accounts payable turnover} = \text{purchases/average accounts payable}$$

$$\text{Payables period} = (\text{average accounts payable/purchases}) \times 360$$

Accounts payable turnover measures the number of times each year a company pays its accounts payable. More useful is the payables period ratio, which tells us how long it takes the firm to pay its bills. When compared with the terms of sale offered to the firm, we can determine whether the company is responsible and able to pay its obligations when due.

The cash conversion cycle   The ratios that describe accounts receivable, inventories, and accounts payable in days can be combined to measure the firm's total commitment to working capital in support of its operations. This produces the **cash conversion cycle,** the time it takes to recover the funds invested in inventory and accounts receivable.

cash conversion cycle—the length of time from the outflow of cash to purchase inventory until the inflow of cash from the collection of accounts receivable

The cash conversion cycle is diagrammed in Figure 2.1. Working capital activity begins when inventory is ordered, yet it is typical not to pay for inventory immediately (payables period). After some time has passed (inventory days), the firm sells its product. Still later (collection period), the customer pays and the firm retrieves its cash (plus profits). Cash flows out when accounts payable are paid and does not flow back in until the corresponding account receivable is collected.

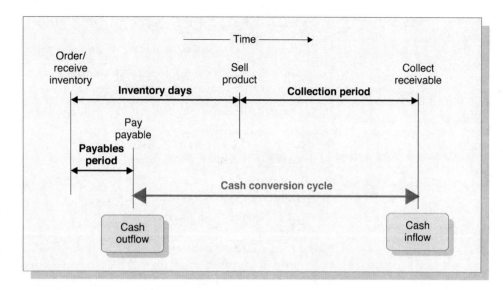

FIGURE 2.1
The cash conversion cycle. The firm's cash is tied up in current assets from the time it pays its accounts payable to its suppliers until it collects its accounts receivable from its customers.

Algebraically:

Cash conversion cycle = inventory days + collection period − payables period

While the length of the cash conversion cycle varies from industry to industry (the inventory days ratio is influenced by the nature of the production and selling process, and trade credit is often a function of industry practice), the shorter the cash conversion cycle the better. A short cash conversion cycle means that money invested in current assets comes back to the firm and can be reused quickly. A company can rapidly redirect its funds in response to changes in its environment. It also has a low reliance on outside funding to finance its investment in working capital.

3. Ratios That Measure the Use of Fixed and Total Assets

While the turnover concept is particularly applicable to current assets and liabilities since they flow into and out of the firm several times per year, it is also applied to a company's fixed assets and to its total assets.

A measure of the productivity of fixed assets

Fixed asset turnover = sales/average fixed assets

This ratio captures the effectiveness of fixed assets in generating sales. It is meaningful for firms in which fixed assets are an important resource. Correspondingly, it has little meaning for firms whose sales do not depend on fixed assets, for example, many service companies.

Recall that fixed assets are recorded at historical cost. A firm with old assets that have been depreciated to a low book value would show a higher turnover than a competitor with newer, less depreciated assets. Yet the second firm is probably in a better position, especially if its assets reflect more modern technologies.

A measure of the productivity of total assets

$$\text{Total asset turnover} = \text{sales/average total assets}$$

This ratio summarizes the relationship of all the firm's assets to its sales. It is effectively a weighted average of the accounts receivable turnover, inventory turnover, and fixed asset turnover ratios.

4. Ratios That Measure the Choice and Management of Funding

How a firm chooses to finance itself is an important indicator of its risk as well as its ability to generate returns for its stakeholders. Each of these ratios looks at one part of the firm's financing choice.

Measures of the financing mix   These ratios examine the mixture of debt and equity funds on the balance sheet. Creditors worry about too much debt since their interest and principal payments might be threatened. Shareholders, on the other hand, enjoy the magnification of their earnings, or **financial leverage**,[8] which the judicious use of debt can provide. These ratios provide broad statements about the firm's financing mix.

financial leverage—the use of debt to magnify the returns to equity investors

$$\textbf{The debt ratio} = \text{total liabilities/total assets}$$

This ratio measures the fraction of the firm's assets financed with debt. Correspondingly, the remainder must be financed with equity.

$$\textbf{The funded debt ratio} = \text{funded debt/total assets}$$

Funded debt is debt on which interest must be paid. It does not include the various payables which carry no interest charge. This ratio gives a first, if general, picture of a company's interest obligations.

$$\textbf{The debt/equity ratio} = \text{total liabilities/total equity}$$

This is a popular variation on the debt ratio, indicating the amount of debt relative to equity financing.

$$\textbf{The assets/equity ratio} = \text{total assets/total equity}$$

This is another variation on the debt ratio, highlighting the amount of assets supported by each dollar of equity financing.

Measures of the ability to service debt   The above ratios tell us the amount of debt a company has incurred. We need additional tests to determine whether the firm can make the payments its debt requires. The following ratios compare a firm's earnings to the amount it must pay to service its debt.

$$\textbf{Times interest earned} = \text{EBIT/interest}$$

This ratio compares operating earnings to interest. If its value exceeds 1.0, then earnings are sufficient to pay the year's interest obligation. Analysts look for a

---

[8] **Cross-reference:**   We will study financial leverage and the best mix of debt and equity financing in Chapter 14.

value in excess of 1.0, since earnings may well fluctuate in the future; 1.0 should be the absolute worst case for this ratio under any foreseeable economic scenario.

The times interest earned ratio ignores the repayment of principal. In effect it assumes that principal will not be repaid from earnings but will be "rolled over" by extending the maturity of the existing debt or by taking a new borrowing to repay the loan falling due. If earnings must be sufficient to pay both interest and principal, it is better to use:

$$\text{Fixed charge coverage} = \frac{\text{EBIT}}{\text{interest} + \text{principal}\left(\dfrac{1}{1-t}\right)}$$

Note the term $\dfrac{1}{(1-t)}$ multiplying the principal amount in the denominator (where t is the firm's marginal income tax rate). This adjustment is required because it takes more than \$1 of EBIT to repay \$1 of debt principal. Debt principal is repaid with after-tax dollars. To repay \$1 of principal, the firm must earn enough so that after taxes, there is \$1 remaining. By contrast, interest is paid on a pre-tax basis, and \$1 of EBIT will fully cover \$1 of interest.

This ratio compares operating earnings to both interest and principal obligations. A value of 1.0 means earnings are just sufficient to cover both.

Measures of payments against equity   Some investors buy a company's shares in order to receive regular dividends. Others prefer that the firm not pay dividends but rather retain and reinvest its earnings. As we will see in Chapter 16 there is a variety of reasons why a particular dividend payout is appropriate for a given firm. These ratios measure the choice made by management.

Dividend payout ratio = dividends/earnings after taxes

Retention ratio = earnings retained/earnings after taxes

Since earnings after taxes must be either paid out as dividends or retained, the sum of these two ratios must be 1.0.

■ Managerial Accounting Data

NET Present Value
More information on management accounting topics can be found at the Institute of Management Accountants website, www.imanet.org

Managerial accounting information is data collected by the firm's accounting system for use in internal planning, analysis, and decision making. While generally coming from the same database as the information used to produce the company's public financial statements, it is not constrained by the pronouncements of the Financial Accounting Standards Board (FASB) or the Securities and Exchange Commission (SEC), the organizations that establish the rules for public reporting. Rather, the information can take any form management finds useful in its work.

Three particular aspects of managerial accounting data are useful to keep in mind as you study finance: (1) the difference between cash flows and accrual accounting data, (2) different types of costs, and (3) alternate methods of cost allocation. All three imply that the numbers available in the accounting system must be looked at carefully to see if they are appropriate for any specific analysis.

1. Cash Flows vs. Accrual Accounting Data

cash flow—money received
or paid by an organization

Most financial analysis and decision making is based on cash flows. A **cash flow,** the receiving or paying of cash, is a real, tangible event and is clearly identifiable. Cash has clear and immediate value. A firm that has cash can use it to acquire resources or invest it to earn interest. A firm that must make a cash payment loses the opportunity to put that money to another use. If it is short of cash, the firm must raise the money, for example, by borrowing it and incurring interest charges.

accrual accounting—a
system of recording
accounting numbers when
economic events have been
achieved

By contrast, the data appearing in accounting records often are not based on cash. Most companies use the **accrual accounting** system, in which revenues and expenses enter the accounting records when products or services are sold (for example, the accounts "sales revenue," or "cost of goods sold"), or as time passes (the account "interest expense" is an example). The amount of sales revenue will not equal the amount of cash brought in if there are accounts receivable. Similarly, the firm's expenses will differ from cash paid out if there are any payables. Throughout this book we will be careful to extract cash flow data from accounting records for use in financial analysis and decision making.

Whenever we need to summarize cash flows, we will use a "cash flow spreadsheet" in which each row represents an event producing a cash flow and each column stands for a point in time. Columns are identified with the date and/or a time-point number beginning with 0 to represent "now." Each cash flow is inserted in the appropriate cell. For clarity, it is common to use the accountant's convention of parentheses to indicate negative numbers since negative signs can easily be overlooked. After all cash flows have been entered into the table, we total the amounts in each column to produce the net cash flow at each point in time.

Example

Cash Flow Spreadsheet

A company is trying to organize the following cash flows:

● Buy a machine for $25,000 in 2012.
● Increase cash inflows by $15,000 in 2013, 2014, and 2015.
● Pay additional taxes of $8,000 in 2014.
● Sell the machine for $10,000 in 2015.

Question: Prepare a cash flow spreadsheet to summarize this information.

Solution:

Event	Year 0 2012	Year 1 2013	Year 2 2014	Year 3 2015
Buy machine	(25,000)			
Additional cash inflows		15,000	15,000	15,000
Additional taxes			(8,000)	
Sell machine				10,000
Net cash flows	(25,000)	15,000	7,000	25,000

2. Types of Costs

Because the word *cost* is used in so many ways, it is important to distinguish among several types of costs that are particularly useful for the financial manager to understand.

Total, average, and marginal costs   When a company manufactures many units of a product or provides many instances of its service, it is unlikely that every unit costs the same amount to create. It is normal for the first units of anything to be expensive to produce due to start-up costs and the unfamiliarity of employees with how to make them. As more is produced, efficiencies and learning set in, and costs decline. Eventually, resources become strained, and costs tend to rise again. Economists capture this pattern with the concept of the "U–shaped cost curve" illustrated in Figure 2.2. Note that each unit has a different cost, making it difficult to specify "the cost of one unit of product." The concepts of total, average, and marginal cost provide ways to describe this operating environment. As the words suggest, **total cost** is the sum of all costs, **average cost** is the cost per unit, and **marginal cost** is the cost of producing the next unit of output.

Total and average cost numbers are particularly useful for analyzing long-term, optimization decisions. Marginal numbers, on the other hand, are used in analyzing short-run, incremental decisions.[9]

total cost—the sum of the costs of making each unit

average cost—total cost divided by the number of units made

marginal cost—the cost of making one additional unit

Example

Total, Average, and Marginal Cost

A company estimates the following costs to produce each of the first 11 units of its product:

Unit:	1	2	3	4	5	6	7	8	9	10	11
Cost:	$25	$21	$18	$16	$15	$15	$16	$18	$21	$25	$30

FIGURE 2.2

A U-shaped cost curve. Per-unit costs are normally high at first, then decline, and finally increase again.

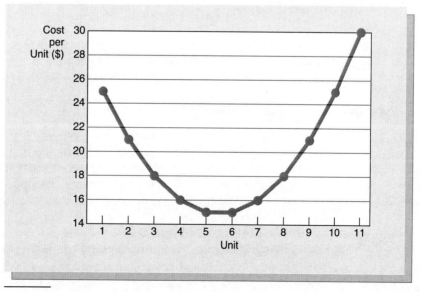

[9] **Cross-reference:**   Examples of optimization decisions are the best mix of financing which we study in Chapter 14 and the best dividend policy discussed in Chapter 16. Incremental decisions, such as acquiring assets, are examined in Chapters 11 and 12.

Question: What are the total and average costs to produce the first 10 units?

Solution steps:

Total cost $= 25 + 21 + 18 + 16 + 15 + 15 + 16 + 18 + 21 + 25$ $= \underline{\$190}$

Average cost $= \$190 / 10 = \underline{\$19}$

Question: What is the marginal cost to produce the eleventh unit?

Answer: $\underline{\$30.}$ The marginal cost is simply the cost of producing that unit.

Incremental cost   The marginal cost concept is commonly extended to other actions beyond producing more of the firm's products or services. Whenever the company considers taking any action that will change its costs, the amount of the change is the **incremental cost.** Equally, we must consider any incremental revenues that will come from the change.

incremental cost—the additional cost from taking a particular action

Example

Incremental Cost (and Revenue)
A company is considering the purchase of a new machine which is expected to increase revenues by $10,000 and increase costs by $6,000 per year. Because these numbers capture the <u>changes</u> from purchasing the new machine, they are incremental and must enter the analysis.

sunk cost—money previously spent

Sunk cost   A **sunk cost** is money spent in the past. The cost is unrecoverable—the fact that the money was spent is history and can never be changed. Sunk costs are always ignored in financial decision making.

Example

Sunk Cost
A company purchased a machine three years ago for $100,000. Today it is evaluating whether to sell it. Because the $100,000 was spent in the past, it is a sunk cost and should play <u>no role</u> in the analysis of whether to sell the machine.

opportunity cost—a benefit forgone by the making of a financial decision

Opportunity cost   Often, a financial decision prevents a firm from obtaining some other benefit. Whenever this happens, the lost benefit, or **opportunity cost,** must be taken into account in analyzing the decision.

Example

Opportunity Cost
A company owns a building which is currently leased for $1,000 per month. It is considering whether to expand one of its product lines which would require the use of the building, resulting in the termination of the lease. The analysis of the expansion must take into account the opportunity cost of $1,000 per month, the income that would be lost if the building were taken off lease.

variable cost—a cost that changes with changes in sales

fixed cost—a cost that remains constant when sales changes

Variable and fixed costs   Costs that vary as sales (and hence production volume) changes are called **variable costs.** By contrast, costs that do not vary as sales changes are called **fixed costs.** For any analysis in which sales and production volume are expected to change, it is important to identify which costs are variable and which are fixed, since only the variable costs will be affected.[10]

---

[10] **Cross-reference:**   One particular use of variable and fixed costs is break-even analysis, described in Web Appendix 2C.

Example

Variable and Fixed Costs
A company is evaluating the costs of increasing production of one of its products. Raw materials and direct production labor costs are variable, since they will increase as production levels increase, and must be included in the analysis. On the other hand, the costs of operating the company's administrative offices are fixed with respect to sales and production levels and will not enter the decision.

3. Tax Rates

A consistent theme throughout this book is that financial value comes from cash flows. A company that can produce high cash flows for its stakeholders is a valuable firm. Since taxes typically represent a large cash flow that goes to one stakeholder at the expense of the others, it is important for financial managers to understand the basics of the income tax system. In particular:

● Virtually every financial decision changes the amount of taxes the firm or its stakeholders will pay. It is thus impossible to evaluate a decision in financial terms without including the impact of taxes.

● If there are more ways than one to accomplish a goal, and if they differ in their tax impact, the value of the tax differential must enter the decision-making process for the comparison to be complete.[11]

● The government as a stakeholder requires only what is specified by the law, and a business fully satisfies its tax obligation by paying that amount. A firm that overpays its taxes is taking value away from the firm's other stakeholders. By not paying unnecessary taxes, the firm avoids lowering the value of the firm to its other stakeholders.

NET Present Value
Go to the Internal Revenue Service website, www.irs.gov, for detailed tax information

Because of the complexity of the U.S. tax system, it can be quite time-consuming to calculate the correct amount of tax that results from a given transaction. To avoid unnecessary (but unfortunately very real) complications in the illustrations and problems of this book, we have chosen to treat all businesses as corporations subject to a flat tax rate of 34% or 35%, rates in the U.S. tax code that apply to many corporations.[12]

Other Data

While the accounting system provides important data for financial managing, other data sources are also important. In this section we look briefly at four other data sets: (1) economic data, (2) data about people, (3) data about processes, and (4) environmental, social, and governance (ESG) data.

---

[11] **Elaboration:**   The government recognizes this and often uses the tax code to motivate firms to act in ways judged beneficial to the public welfare. Two examples: A business that locates in an area deemed to be in need of economic revitalization can receive a reduction in its taxes. A business that employs minorities or the underprivileged can also receive a tax reduction. In both cases, it is the hope of the government that these tax savings will offset any other costs involved and make the socially responsible decision the economically more valuable decision as well

[12] **To delve further:**   More detail about how income taxes are calculated in the United States is provided in Web Appendix 2D, "The U.S. Personal Income Tax System," and Web Appendix 2E, "The U.S. Corporate Income Tax System."

1. Economic Data

Almost all companies are affected by the state of the economy. If the economy is doing well, people will have money to spend and businesses will be expanding their operations. For most firms, this translates to increased demand for their products. Conversely, in an economic downturn, most companies find their business slowing down with the economy. To anticipate and respond to economic events, companies collect economic data that relate to their success, data such as GNP growth, inflation rates, interest rates, foreign exchange rates, etc. Companies also carefully monitor their industries to gauge competitive actions and pressures.

2. People Data

Since satisfied people play an important role in the financial health of a business, it is important to collect and analyze data about their needs and about how pleased they are with the firm. Satisfied employees are the most important asset of many companies. They delight the customers they serve and contribute to process improvements leading to higher-quality products and services and to cost reduction. Satisfied customers raise the firm's revenues by buying its products and services again and again and by recommending the firm to others. Often they are willing to pay a premium price for what they perceive as superior quality.

Finance has customers both inside and outside the firm. Everyone who gets financial output—for example, the external customer who receives a bill, the supplier who receives a payment, the employee who receives a paycheck, the lender who receives an interest payment—is a customer of the finance function. It is important to understand the needs of each of these customers and to measure how well they are being fulfilled. Many companies talk of customer/supplier alliances, close relationships between each customer and supplier, to emphasize the importance of working actively to improve these relationships by seeing them in cooperative terms. (At the same time, finance is a customer of other parts of the company, such as purchasing, which supplies data on material costs. It is equally important for finance people, acting as the customer, to form customer/supplier alliances with its suppliers to ensure that finance gets the inputs it needs on time, without error, and in the most useful form.)

Most data about customer satisfaction come from direct contact or from systematic surveys. Surveys may be taken of external customers and also of customers internal to the firm. Many firms also survey employees to discover their concerns so these concerns may be promptly addressed. Some firms include questions about leadership, asking employees to rate their direct supervisor and the company's management in general. To ensure that management takes this information seriously, a company may incorporate it into its compensation policy. At FedEx, for example, senior management can earn a full year-end bonus only if their leadership score on the employee survey has increased over the previous year's score.

3. Process Data

Every activity of finance professionals is part of a process, whether it be raising money, performing financial analysis, or producing internal reports. In a well functioning company, these processes are understood, under control, and repeatable.

They are also being studied to locate additional opportunities for improvement—either to continue reducing errors, waste, and rework or to shorten the time it takes to complete them.

Three ways that companies measure the performance of their processes are by calculating: (1) the absolute number of failures, (2) the relative number of failures—the number of failures as a fraction of the number of opportunities to fail, and (3) process cycle time.

Absolute number of failures   Individual processes can be measured by counting the number of times they fail to deliver the desired output. Simple tally sheets and graphs are often used to record the number of failures. A summary number, which captures the objective and indicates the functioning of the process, is identified and tracked. At Corning, Incorporated, these numbers are called "Key Results Indicators (KRIs)." For example, Corning's treasury is responsible for delivering cash throughout the company where and when needed. One of its goals is to have no missed deliveries, and it counts and plots—as one of its KRIs—the number of times per month it fails to deliver, thereby failing to meet the needs of its internal customers. The graph of this KRI is prominently posted on the wall outside the corporate treasurer's office along with similar graphs of the treasury group's other KRIs.

six sigma—a statistical measure of process accuracy, only 3.4 errors per million opportunities

NET Present Value
The company best known for its use of six sigma is General Electric. To learn more go to:
www.ge.com/sixsigma/makingcustomers.html

Relative number of failures   Where processes have many steps, or repeat many times, statistical techniques often are employed to measure process accuracy. One system, based on the number of failures per opportunity to fail, is known as **six sigma,** after the goal for process accuracy set by its creators. Developed at Motorola, Inc., six sigma is based on the normal (bell curve) probability distribution and represents the tiny area under one tail of the distribution further than six standard deviations from the mean. Motorola's studies have shown that, without the application of systematic quality management, the norm for many human processes is to perform with approximately four sigma accuracy. This translates to 6,210 errors per million opportunities, a success rate of 99.38%. When a process is operating at six sigma accuracy, however, there are only 3.4 defects per million opportunities, a 99.9997% success rate. At that level of precision, someone typing 20 pages of single-spaced text every working day would hit the wrong key roughly once a week.[13]

cycle time—the time from the beginning to the end of any process or process step

Cycle time   If a process can be completed quickly, unnecessary costs are avoided, there is less chance for errors to creep in, and customers receive the output of the process in a more timely fashion. Many companies have begun to measure **cycle time**—the time it takes to complete each process, either in absolute hours or in person-hours—and to set goals for cycle time reduction. For example, after achieving six sigma accuracy in many of its processes, Motorola set a new corporate goal of ten-times cycle time reduction in every process over the next five years. A process that once took ten hours should now take only one hour to complete. Cycle time reduction comes from process redesign to eliminate complexity and waste. Unnecessary steps are eliminated and the steps that remain are simplified. In doing so, errors are also reduced.

---

[13] **Observation and cross-reference:**   From this example it should be clear that systematic quality management is necessary for processes to reach six sigma accuracy. We look further at financial processes, their measurement and improvement in Chapter 13.

4. Environmental, Social, and Governance (ESG) Data

NET Present Value
A good summary of ESG data and its use is "Translating Environmental, Social and Governance Factors into Sustainable Business Value: Key Insights for Companies and Investors," a joint report of the World Business Council for Sustainable Development and the United Nations Environment Program Finance Initative which may be accessed at www.unepfi.org/work_streams/investment/index.html

The growing demand of society for business to contribute to global sustainability has led companies to collect and act on data about their impact on the environment and social justice, and about how they are governed to achieve these as well as their traditional financial goals. Many companies now publish annual sustainability reports that compliment their annual financial reports and detail their ESG progress.

Environmental data includes a company's energy use and efficiency, greenhouse gas emissions, water use, and eco-friendly product innovation. Social data includes information on employee health and safety training and development and diversity as well as the company's record on human rights, community support, and product safety. Governance data includes information on the independence of the company's board of directors, the transparency of its public reporting, and how the company implements its code of conduct.

Recently, Bloomberg began incorporating publicly-available ESG data on more than 3,000 companies in its database so that its subscribers could use the information in their analyses and planning. Thompson Reuters provides ESG data— 250 Key Performance Indicators (KPIs) plus 750 individual data points—on 3,200 companies through its ASSET4 unit. The KLDGlobalSocrates database of KLD Research & Analytics includes more than 200 ESG indicators and over 2,000 data points on more than 4,000 companies. And, in 2008, fourteen of the largest US institutional investors requested that the Securities and Exchange Commission require public companies to disclose and discuss ESG risks, including risks from climate change, in their annual reporting cycle.

*S*teven Barbara sat down at his desk, pulled out a pad of paper, and started to summarize his thoughts. On the way back from the doctor's office, he had contemplated the doctor's advice, and the connection between his personal health and the company's health was becoming clearer.

Diagnosing a company's problems was very similar to diagnosing a person's health problems. To understand his business and locate its problems it was necessary to have accurate data about the overall financial performance of the firm, the cash flows and costs of running the business, conditions in the economy and industry, the attitudes of key stakeholders, the functioning of key processes, and the firm's ESG performance. Steven wrote down each item on a separate sheet of paper and listed underneath the information his company was currently collecting and using. It was clear there were significant gaps.

Just then the phone rang. It was the firm's banker calling back to ask whether Steven had made any progress toward resolving the bank's cash flow concerns. "I sure have," Steven replied with a smile. "It will be a couple of days before I can tell you how we'll lose the weight, but now I know where to look to find those extra 20 pounds!"

Summary of Key Points

▪ **Identify the meaning of** *financial analysis* **and the data used for financial decision making.**   Financial analysis is the use of financial and other data to study the financial health of an organization. It is of interest to all stakeholders since they all benefit if the firm remains vibrant and healthy. It is of particular use to management as it can help uncover problems that deserve management's attention within the firm's finances. It makes use of data that conform both to the traditional economic-financial theory of the firm and to recent insights into the contributions of people and processes to financial health.

▪ **Realize that financial accounting data are an important but imperfect source of information, and understand why it is necessary to compare numbers when doing financial analysis.**   GAAP rules permit choices in the preparation of financial accounting numbers. Analysts must understand how the statements were prepared and must be careful in comparing financial data among firms. Particular concerns include the use of both monetary and historical cost valuation, LIFO vs. FIFO inventory treatment, differing depreciation formulas, etc. Financial analysis typically involves comparisons since one number out of context is usually meaningless. We compare numbers to benchmarks, across time, and to other comparable companies.

▪ **Recognize financial ratios that measure profitability, use of working capital, use of fixed and total assets, and the choice and management of funding.**   We create comparisons of financial data by using financial ratios, fractions which compare a numerator to a denominator. The ratios listed in this chapter are among the most common used in financial analysis.

▪ **Prepare a cash flow spreadsheet and recognize different types of costs.**   A cash flow spreadsheet organizes cash flows by their cause and when they take place. The managerial accounting system is used to obtain the data for internal decision making. It is important to isolate cash flows and to understand types of costs to insure that the correct data are used for each type of analysis.

▪ **Understand the importance of economic data; of collecting information about customer and employee satisfaction; of measuring the performance of financial processes; and of environmental, social, and governance (ESG) data.**   Economic data allow the firm to anticipate and respond to market and competitive conditions. Customer satisfaction is an important determinant of a company's revenues. Employees' satisfaction affects their ability and willingness to use resources wisely and to improve the firm's processes to serve customers, improve quality, and reduce costs. Companies and their finance functions collect information on processes to locate opportunities for improvement. ESG data capture a company's contributions to global sustainability.

Questions

1. Why is it critical to have theory prior to collecting data about a company?

2. Why is it often difficult to compare the financial statements of similar companies?

3. You have just learned that a company has 10,000 employees and have been asked to determine if this is good or bad. What would you like to learn to make that judgment?

4. Why is competitive benchmarking superseding traditional benchmarking?

5. Why is it possible to talk of a "rule-of-thumb" number, such as 2.0, for the current ratio, but not have a comparable rule-of-thumb number for the times interest earned ratio?

6. If the value of one of a firm's ratios is cut in half, can we be sure that the firm's condition has improved?

7. Which ratios would be of most interest to:
   a. Managers?   e. Employees?
   b. Customers?   f. Governments?
   c. Shareholders?   g. Neighbors?
   d. Creditors?

8. Why do industries that have low total asset turnover ratios tend to have high net profit margins and vice versa?

9. What would be the effect of inflation on ratios? How would an analyst take inflation into account in interpreting ratios?

10. Why might an analyst pay more attention to average balance sheet values in looking at a seasonal or growing firm than when studying a firm that remains constant throughout the year?

11. Is the fixed asset turnover ratio more relevant in the analysis of McDonald's Corporation or General Motors Corporation? Why?

12. Distinguish between cash flows and accrual accounting data. When would you use each?

13. Give an example of each of the following costs:
    a. Total cost   e. Sunk cost
    b. Average cost   f. Opportunity cost
    c. Marginal cost   g. Variable cost
    d. Incremental cost   h. Fixed cost

14. In what ways do the attitudes of customers and employees affect the financial worth of a business?

15. Identify a financial process. What data would you like to have in order to learn if it is functioning properly?

16. What is the meaning of "six sigma"? How does it differ from the normal success rate of human activity?

17. Why are many companies collecting and reporting ESG data? How might this change a company's behavior and performance?

Problems

1. **(Profitability ratios)** A firm had the following income statement for last year:

Sales	$ 37,611
Less: Cost of goods sold	20,889
Gross profit	16,722
Less: Operating expenses	11,483
Less: Depreciation	1,575
Operating profit (EBIT)	3,664
Less: Interest expense	1,400
Earnings before taxes (EBT)	2,264
Less: Tax expense	792
Earnings after taxes (EAT)	$ 1,472

Calculate the firm's:

a. Gross profit margin ratio
b. Operating profit margin ratio
c. Pre-tax profit margin ratio
d. Net profit margin ratio

2. **(Profitability ratios)** A financial analyst calculated the following ratios from a firm's income statement:

Gross profit margin = 60%
Operating profit margin = 27%
Pre-tax profit margin = 14%

The firm had sales of $500,000 and paid federal income taxes at a 35% rate.

a. Reproduce the firm's income statement.
b. Calculate the firm's net profit margin ratio.

3. **(Rates of return)** The firm of Problem 1 finances itself with equal amounts of liabilities and owners' equity. Calculate the firm's basic earning power, return on assets, and return on equity if its average total assets last year were equal to:

a. $ 5,000   c. $25,000
b. $15,000   d. $35,000

4. **(Rates of return)** A financial analyst calculated the following ratios from a firm's financial statements:

Operating profit margin = 22%
Net profit margin = 6.5%
Return on assets = 9%
Return on equity = 14%

The firm had sales of $2,500,000. Calculate the firm's:

a. Earnings before interest and taxes (EBIT)
b. Earnings after taxes (EAT)
c. Average total assets
d. Average total equity

5. **(Liquidity ratios)** A firm has current assets at year-end consisting of:

Cash	$12,000
Marketable securities	5,000
Accounts receivable	22,000
Inventory (work-in-process)	8,000
Total current assets	$47,000

Calculate the firm's year-end current ratio and quick ratio if its current liabilities equal:

a. $10,000   c. $40,000
b. $25,000   d. $60,000

6. **(Liquidity ratios)** A firm has a year-end current ratio of 1.85 and a quick ratio of 1.18. Total current assets equal $125,000. Calculate the firm's balance of:

a. Total current liabilities
b. Quick assets
c. Inventory

7. **(Seasonality)** A firm has the following partial quarterly balance sheets:

	Quarter 1	Quarter 2
Cash	$ 3,000	$ 1,000
Marketable securities	3,000	500
Accounts receivable	6,000	2,000
Inventory (work-in-process)	4,000	10,000
Total current assets	$16,000	$13,500
Total current liabilities	$10,000	$15,000

	Quarter 3	Quarter 4
Cash	$ 1,500	$ 2,000
Marketable securities	500	5,000
Accounts receivable	11,500	4,000
Inventory (work-in-process)	6,000	2,000
Total current assets	$19,500	$13,000
Total current liabilities	$12,000	$ 6,000

a. For each quarter, calculate the firm's current ratio and quick ratio.
b. In which quarter are the firm's ratios the strongest? why?
c. In which quarter are the firm's ratios the weakest? why?
d. Where is the firm's asset risk exposure in quarters 2 and 3?

8. **(Seasonality)** At the end of the first quarter, a firm has $50,000 of inventory. In the second quarter, all of the inventory is sold for $70,000 on 90-day credit terms. In the third quarter, the full $70,000 is collected as cash. The firm has no other inventory and has other current assets equal to $15,000. Total current liabilities remain constant at $40,000 throughout the period. Calculate the firm's current ratio and quick ratio:

a. At the end of the first quarter
b. At the end of the second quarter
c. At the end of the third quarter
d. How much of the change to the ratios is due to the firm's seasonality and how much is due to the recording of the $20,000 profit?

9. **(Accounts receivable ratios)** A firm has annual sales of $5 million, of which 20% is for cash and the remainder is credit sales. What is the firm's accounts receivable turnover and average collection period if its average balance of accounts receivable is:

a. $250,000?   c. $ 750,000?
b. $500,000?   d. $1,000,000?

10. **(Accounts receivable ratios)** A firm has annual sales of $9,000,000 and an average balance of accounts receivable of $500,000. What is the firm's accounts receivable turnover and average collection period if the percentage of its sales that is made on credit is:

a. 50%?   c. 90%?
b. 75%?   d. 100%?

11. **(Inventory ratios)** A firm reported cost of goods sold of $100,000 last year. Determine the firm's inventory turnover and inventory days ratios if the firm maintained an average balance in inventory of:

a. $100,000   c. $10,000
b. $ 50,000   d. $ 1,000

12. **(Inventory ratios)** A firm reported cost of goods sold of $2,500,000 last year. Determine the firm's average inventory balance if its:

a. Inventory turnover is 5 times
b. Inventory remains on hand for an average of 60 days
c. Inventory turnover is 15 times
d. Inventory remains on hand for an average of 5 days

13. **(Accounts payable ratios)** A firm purchased $60,000 of merchandise inventory. Determine the firm's accounts payable turnover and payables period ratios if the firm maintained an average balance in the account "accounts payable—merchandise inventory" of:

a. $3,000   c. $10,000
b. $6,000   d. $20,000

14. **(Accounts payable ratios)** A firm purchased $400,000 of merchandise inventory last year. Determine the average balance in the firm's account "accounts payable—merchandise inventory" if:

a. Accounts payable turnover is 10 times
b. It takes an average of 45 days to pay accounts payable
c. Accounts payable turnover is 20 times
d. It takes an average of 10 days to pay accounts payable

15. **(Cash conversion cycle)** Last year a firm had an inventory days ratio equal to 15 days and a payables period ratio equal to 30 days. Calculate the firm's cash conversion cycle if its collection period was:

a. zero (all sales on a cash basis)
b. 18 days
c. 30 days
d. 60 days

16. **(Cash conversion cycle)** Last year a firm had an inventory turnover ratio of 8 times and an accounts payable turnover ratio of 12 times. Calculate the firm's cash conversion cycle if its accounts receivable turnover was:

a. 3 times,   c. 12 times
b. 8 times   d. 30 times

17. **(Fixed and total asset ratios)** A firm had an average balance of total assets equal to $100,000 last year of which 40%, on average, were current assets. Calculate its fixed asset turnover ratio and total asset turnover ratio if the firm's sales was:

a. $100,000   c. $ 500,000
b. $250,000   d. $1,000,000

18. **(Fixed and total asset ratios)** Last year a firm had a fixed asset turnover ratio of 6.5 times and a total asset turnover ratio of 4.2 times. Calculate the average balance of total assets, fixed assets, and current assets if sales was:

a. $1,000,000   c. $ 5,000,000
b. $2,000,000   d. $25,000,000

19. **(Financing mix ratios)** A firm's year-end balance sheet reported total liabilities of $250,000 of which noninterest-bearing liabilities (accounts payable, wages payable, etc.) made up $75,000. Calculate the firm's debt ratio, funded-debt ratio, and debt/equity ratio if the firm's total assets equal:

a. $1,000,000   c. $450,000
b. $ 750,000   d. $300,000

20. **(Financing mix ratios)** A financial analyst calculated the following ratios from a firm's balance sheet

Debt ratio = 45%
Funded debt ratio = 35%

The firm's total assets were $900,000. Calculate:

a. Total liabilities
b. Interest-bearing liabilities
c. Noninterest-bearing liabilities
d. Debt/equity ratio

21. **(Debt service ratios)** A firm reported EBIT of $85,000 last year. The firm paid interest of $25,000 and repaid $15,000 of debt principal. The firm is in the 35% federal income tax bracket. Calculate the following ratios for this firm:

a. Times interest earned
b. Fixed charge coverage

22. **(Debt service ratios)** A financial analyst calculated the following ratios from a firm's financial statements:

    Times interest earned = 6 times
    Fixed charge coverage = 3 times

    The firm had an EBIT of $500,000 and is in the 35% federal income tax bracket. Determine the firm's:

    a. Interest expense
    b. Principal repayments

23. **(Dividend ratios)** Last year a firm earned $65,000 after taxes. Calculate its dividend payout ratio and retention ratio if its dividend payment was:

    a. nothing   c. $30,000
    b. $10,000   d. $50,000

24. **(Dividend ratios)** A firm is considering the cash-flow implications of its dividend policy. Last year's earnings were $140,000. Calculate the amount of its dividend and the amount of earnings retained, if it sets its dividend payout ratio at:

    a. zero   c. 65%
    b. 30%   d. 100%

25. **(Cash flow spreadsheet)** A company is investigating an activity that would generate the following incremental cash flows over the next five years:

Purchase machinery immediately	$100,000
Increase revenues in years 1–2	30,000 per year
Increase revenues in years 3–5	50,000 per year
Reduce costs in years 1–5	20,000 per year
Pay additional taxes in years 2–4	10,000 per year

    Prepare a cash flow spreadsheet to summarize this information.

26 **(Cash flow spreadsheet)** A company is investigating an activity that would generate the following incremental cash flows over the next four years:

Purchase an office building immediately	$250,000
Increase revenues in years 1–4	85,000 per year
Reduce costs in years 1–4	30,000 per year
Pay additional taxes in years 2–4	20,000 per year
Sell building in year 4	400,000
Pay tax when building is sold	50,000

    Prepare a cash flow spreadsheet to summarize this information.

27. **(Total, average, and marginal costs)** A company estimates the following costs to produce the first five units of its only product:

Unit number:	1	2	3	4	5
Cost in $:	100	90	83	79	76

    a. What is the total cost to produce the five units?
    b. What is the average cost per unit for the first five units?
    c. What is the marginal cost to produce the second unit?
    d. What is the marginal cost to produce the fifth unit?

28. **(Total, average, and marginal costs)** A company estimates the following costs to produce the first seven units of its only product:

Unit number:	1	2	3	4	5	6	7
Cost in $:	60	51	44	39	36	35	35

    a. What is the total cost to produce the seven units?
    b. What is the average cost per unit for the first seven units?
    c. What is the marginal cost to produce the sixth unit?
    d. What is the marginal cost to produce the seventh unit?

CHAPTER 3

THE TIME VALUE

OF MONEY

*J*ay Herman boarded his morning train, settled in to a seat, and opened his attaché case. He took out the box containing his new financial calculator and the instruction manual that came with it. Jay smiled as he thought of how his wife had teased him about "one more high-tech toy," but even he was impressed by the number of buttons on the calculator and the size of the manual. This was one heck of a sophisticated "toy!"

Jay had recently joined the finance group of a medium-sized consumer products company. Because of his experience in manufacturing, his first assignment was to participate on a team studying improvements in an important production process. As preparation for that assignment, the company had provided him with the calculator.

Jay thought back to the group's last meeting, where group members had had a good discussion of process measurements, identified problems, and brainstormed solutions. The team had agreed that one solution looked particularly promising and should be studied further. Jay's role, as the finance person on the team, was to analyze the cash flow benefits and costs of implementing that solution and report back at the team's next meeting.

The cry of the conductor announcing the next station interrupted Jay's recollections. As he watched the throng on the platform squeezing toward the narrow train doors, Jay looked again at his new calculator. He remembered the awkwardness of the old time-value tables he had used in school, and realized how much he looked forward to learning how to use the calculator to help him make a positive contribution to the team's efforts.

As he gets more deeply into his analysis, Jay is going to find that the proposed process improvement will change his company's cash flows. There will be new costs and benefits while other costs and benefits will disappear. In addition to identifying the amounts of these changed cash flows, the team will have to estimate *when* they will occur so Jay can establish their "time value." Jay will indeed put his new financial calculator to very good use.

time value of money—the concept that the value of money depends on the date of its receipt or payment

Every organization is regularly receiving and paying money. Regardless of the size of the enterprise, time value underlies all financial decision making. A knowledge of the concepts of the **time value of money** is crucial for good financial managing.

Key Points You Should Learn from This Chapter

After reading this chapter you should be able to:

■ Understand why the value of money depends on the time of its receipt or payment and, therefore, why money amounts can only be compared after they have been adjusted for time.

■ Calculate the present value and future value of cash flows, the interest rate that describes any pair of cash flows, and the length of time it takes to reach a financial goal.

■ Analyze a set of uneven cash flows.

■ Recognize when time value analysis can be simplified because the cash flows form a standard pattern.

Introductory Concepts—The Money Rules

If your rich uncle offered you a gift of either $100 or $150, which would you choose? Assuming there were no strings attached, most of us would choose the $150. We all know that it is better to have more money than less, other things being equal. The same concept works in the other direction as well. Suppose your uncle brought a car to your home and told you that you could own it by paying him either $3,000 or $4,000. What would you do? It is clearly better to pay only $3,000. In fact, if the car were really worth $4,000, buying it for $3,000 would add $1,000 to your wealth.[1] We summarize these ideas as Money Rule #1:

> MONEY RULE #1:   Value depends on the AMOUNT of money involved.
> Choose to receive MORE.
> Choose to pay LESS.

Suppose now that your uncle offered you a slightly different choice. You could have $100 today or the same $100 next year. Now which would you choose? Again, in the absence of "strings," most of us would choose to get the $100 today. Getting money sooner is better than getting it later. Turn the problem around. Which would you rather pay: $100 now or $100 a year from now? The better choice is to pay the $100 next year. These insights lead us to Money Rule #2:

> MONEY RULE #2:   Value depends on the TIMING of money flows.
> Choose to receive money SOONER.
> Choose to pay money LATER.

Of the several reasons why money depends on time, by far the most important is that money can be invested to earn positive interest rates. $100 received today can be invested to earn interest and to grow to be more than $100.[2]

Example

Earning Interest
If you deposited the $100 in a bank account that paid 6% interest, your $100 would grow to $106 (the $100 deposit or "principal" plus 6% of the $100 or $6 interest). You would have $6 more than if you simply got the $100 next year.

Virtually all business deals involve trades of money. We invest some money today with the expectation of receiving a greater amount in the future. We insist that we get back more than we invest in order to create a gain (that is, we follow the advice of Money Rule #1), but the very fact that we pay money now and receive money later creates an offsetting loss (we violate Money Rule #2). Every

---

[1] **Observation:** This is the basic idea underlying most financial transactions: buy something for less than it is worth to you. In particular, you could sell the car for its $4,000 value and turn the $1,000 gain into cash.

[2] **Elaboration:** Other reasons why time affects the value of money include the ability to take advantage of a special opportunity to purchase something, the loss of purchasing power due to inflation, and the risk associated with having to wait for a cash flow. However, if interest rates correctly contain compensation for postponing consumption, for inflation, and for risk, these concerns are all "priced" in today's rates and are included in the analysis of this chapter. We will explore the makeup of interest rates in more detail in the next chapter.

business deal, therefore, requires a comparison: we must determine if the gain from receiving more money than we invest outweighs the loss from investing today but not receiving the return on our investment until some later date. This is Money Rule #3:

> MONEY RULE #3:   The value of a business deal involves a TRADEOFF between the amount of the money flows and the time of their receipt or payment

To make this test, we must first do a time value of money calculation since it is impossible to combine or compare cash flows and values that occur at different times. This is Money Rule #4:

> MONEY RULE #4:   Money flows can only be compared after they have been adjusted for their time value

Sometimes the appropriate time value calculation is simple enough so that you can do it without any computational help.

Example

Calculating a Rate of Return: A Simple Case

Imagine you can invest $100 today in order to receive $125 in one year. What is the rate of return on this investment? The answer is 25%, and most people can easily do this calculation in their heads. If you were able to do this, your brain is functioning at least as well as a low-level financial calculator.

Most of the time, however, time value calculations are too complex for even the geniuses among us, and we must rely on a calculator, computer, or computer-generated table of numbers to give us the solution.[3]

Example

Calculating a Rate of Return: A More Difficult Case

Now imagine you invest $100 today in order to receive $40 in one year plus $60 one year after that plus $50 after three years. What is the rate of return on this investment? Most people cannot do this calculation without some computational help. The answer is 22.40%, a result that required an advanced financial calculator to compute. Don't be too upset if you couldn't solve this problem in your head!

The concept of time value of money is perhaps the single most important concept in finance. It underlies the analysis of all investments and all forms of financing. In this chapter we will develop the basics of time value analysis. These techniques will then be applied over and over in many of the subsequent chapters.

---

[3] **Elaboration:**   This book is written with the assumption that students will have financial calculators or spreadsheet programs available for their use. Financial calculators and spreadsheets are far more efficient and capable than the limited time-value tables they replaced. In addition, they have become standard equipment in most modern businesses. Calculators can be purchased for as little as $25, making them cheaper than many school supplies, including textbooks. (Time-value tables are on pages T–1 through T–4 at the back of this book and instructions for their use appear in this chapter for those students and instructors who might wish to explore their use.)

FINANCE IN PRACTICE

A Classic Tale: The U.S. Government Learns About Time Value of Money

It took a three-year $500,000 study for the federal government to finally discover the time value of money. New practices are being introduced throughout the Treasury Department in an attempt to significantly improve the government's cash management systems.

The Office of Management and Budget (OMB) is already reporting success. According to the OMB, efforts to accelerate the collection of tax and other revenues, stop paying bills early, and ensure that idle cash balances are deposited into interest-bearing accounts are already generating interest savings and earnings of some $450 million a year.

In 1980, federal interest costs are expected to be $64.3 billion.

Reference: "Get Receipts Sooner and Pay Bills Later Is New Federal Rule," The Wall Street Journal, Aug. 18, 1980, page 3.

The Fundamental Relationship

The amount of interest money can earn depends on the following three factors:

- Its amount (the principal)
- The interest rate it can earn (rate)
- How long it is invested (time)

You most likely saw this idea for the first time in elementary school, where you were taught the relationship for **simple interest:**

simple interest—interest paid only on the initial principal and not on previously paid interest

$$\text{Interest} = \text{Principal} \times \text{Rate} \times \text{Time}$$

This formula is true as long as the interest earned is removed (withdrawn) from the investment as it is paid. In business, however, it is much more usual for interest earnings <u>not</u> to be withdrawn from an investment. When interest earnings remain in an investment, they become part of the principal and earn interest in subsequent periods of time. This phenomenon, interest paid on previous interest, is called **compound interest.**

compound interest—interest paid on both the initial principal and previously paid interest

The fundamental time value relationship is the compound interest formula:

$$Future\ value = present\ value\ (1 + interest\ rate)^{number\ of\ time\ periods}$$

You will see where this relationship comes from as we solve the first set of examples that follow.

The compound interest formula contains four variables. We will use the following notation to refer to them (we will add additional notation later as needed):

FV = **Future Value:** a single cash flow or value at the end of a time frame.

TABLE 1   Future Value Factors $= (1 + r)^n$
         (**FV** of $1 after **n** periods at interest rate **r**)

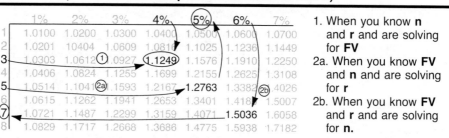

	1%	2%	3%	4%	5%	6%	7%
1	1.0100	1.0200	1.0300	1.0400	1.0500	1.0600	1.0700
2	1.0201	10404	1.0609	1.0816	1.1025	1.1236	1.1449
3	1.0303	1.0612 ① .0927	1.1249	1.1576	1.1910	1.2250
4	1.0406	1.0824	1.1255	1.1699	1.2155	1.2625	1.3108
5	1.0514	1.1041 ②ₐ .1593	1.2167	1.2763	1.3382 ②ᵦ	.4026
6	1.0615	1.1262	1.1941	1.2653	1.3401	1.418	1.5007
⑦	1.0721	1.1487	1.2299	1.3159	1.4071	1.5036	1.6058
8	1.0829	1.1717	1.2668	1.3686	1.4775	1.5938	1.7182

1. When you know **n** and **r** and are solving for **FV**
2a. When you know **FV** and **n** and are solving for **r**
2b. When you know **FV** and **r** and are solving for **n.**

FIGURE 3.1
Using a time value table. The tables can be used to obtain the value of $(1 + r)^n$ or to solve for **n** or **r**.

PV = **Present Value:** a single cash flow or value at the beginning of a time frame.[4]

n = **number of time periods** between present and future value.

r = **rate of interest** per time period. Also represented by the letter **i** when the financial calculator is to be used.

Using this notation, we can rewrite the compound interest formula as:

$$FV = PV(1 + r)^n$$

The potentially difficult part of this equation is the term $(1 + r)^n$. As a result, tables of values of $(1 + r)^n$ have been used for many years to simplify the calculation effort.[5] Figure 3.1 is an excerpt from Table 1, the table to use when calculating the future value of a present amount. Each row represents a value of **n**, each column a value of **r**. To use the table, follow one of two strategies, depending on which variable is the unknown:

1. If **FV** is the unknown, look up the value of $(1 + r)^n$ at the intersection of row **n** and column **r**. Then multiply that number by **PV** to obtain **FV**.

2. If **n** or **r** is the unknown, rearrange the future value equation to obtain the value of $(1 + r)^n$:

$$(1 + r)^n = FV/PV$$

Then (a) if you are solving for **r,** scan across the row for **n** until you find the number closest to your value of $(1 + r)^n$ and look at the top of that column to find **r.** (b) If you are solving for **n,** scan down the column for **r** until you find the number closest to your value of $(1 + r)^n$ and look at the left of that row to find **n.** (Note: it is also possible that the unknown is **PV,** but Table 2 is typically used for that problem.)

NET Present Value
A fun website with lots of financial calculators is
www.moneyadvisor.com/calc

Time value problems may also be solved with a financial calculator or spreadsheet program by entering the data of the problem and letting the machine handle the arithmetic. The first three variables, **FV, PV,** and **n,** correspond precisely

---

[4] **Elaboration:**   Since most business problems begin today (the present) and extend into the future, the terms *present value* and *future value* have become the standard usage for *beginning value* and *ending value.*

[5] **Cross-reference:**   We have included such a table at the end of this book—it's identified as "Table 1—Future Value Factors"—as well as three additional tables for other time value problems.

to the labels on the keys of your financial calculator. However, it is usual for calculators to use some variation of the letter "i" (such as **i, I/Y, I/YR,** or **I%YR**) rather than "r" to represent the interest rate.[6]

In solving time value problems we start with the values of three of the variables and then solve for the fourth. It does not matter which three we know and which is the unknown variable. In the examples that follow, we will illustrate all four possibilities, solving for: (1) future value, (2) present value, (3) the time period between two cash flows, and (4) the interest rate that joins two cash flows.

future value—a single cash flow or value at the end of a time frame

compounding—adding compound interest to a present value to produce a future value

1. Finding Future Value

If we wish to determine the amount to which an investment will grow if our money earns interest for some period of time, we are looking for a **future value.** Solving for a future value is often referred to as **compounding** a present value.

Example

Compounding for One Year

Imagine you plan to deposit $1,000 into a bank account that pays 10% interest.

Question: How much will you have in your account after one year?

Solution steps:

1. Identify the data you have to work with. The $1,000 is a **present value,** a single beginning cash flow. You are also given the 10% **rate** and that the **number of time periods** (years) is one.

2. Identify what you are calculating. The answer will be a **future value,** a single value at the end of the one-year time frame.

3. Plug in the data and calculate the result. You can do this in several ways:

   a. By formula:

   $$FV = \text{Principal} + \text{interest}$$
   $$= PV + r \cdot PV$$
   $$= 1{,}000 + .10\,(1{,}000) = 1{,}000 + 100 = \underline{1{,}100}$$

   Or, using the compound interest relationship:

   $$FV = PV\,(1 + r)^n$$
   $$= 1{,}000\,(1.10)^1 = 1{,}000\,(1.10) = \underline{1{,}100}$$

   b. Using the time-value tables:

   (1) Write the time value formula:

   $$FV = PV\,(1 + r)^n$$

---

[6] **Elaboration:**   In formulas, the rate of interest is always expressed in decimal form, thus 10% is represented as .10. In financial calculators, however, the rate of interest is always entered in percentage form. You would enter 10% into the calculator by keying in 10, not .10. Our choice of the letter **r** for formulas and **i** for calculators is intended to make this distinction. However, since time value tables are used with formulas, we will use **r** to denote the interest rate, even though most tables (ours included) show rates in percentage form.

(2) Since **r** and **n** are known, look up the time value factor. Factors for the future value of a single present value are found in Table 1.

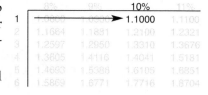

(3) Substitute into the formula and solve:

$$FV = 1,000 \ (1.1000) = \underline{1,100}$$

c. By financial calculator or spreadsheet program:[7]

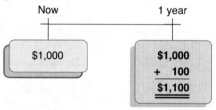

Answer: $\underline{\$1,100}$. You will still have your principal of \$1,000 plus you will have earned interest equal to 10% of \$1,000 or \$100.

Now	1 year
\$1,000	\$1,000 + 100 \$1,100

Example

Compounding for Two Years

Suppose you leave your \$1,000 deposit in the bank for a second year.

Question: How much will you have in your account after two years if you can continue to earn 10% interest?

Solution steps:

1. By formula (looking at the second year):

$$FV = Principal + interest$$
$$= PV + r \bullet PV$$
$$= 1,100 + .10 \ (1,100) = 1,100 + 110 = \underline{1,210}$$

Or, using the compound interest relationship (looking at both years together):

---

[7] **Elaboration:**   A minus sign attached to a cash flow identifies it as an outflow while a positive cash flow is an inflow. In this problem we are telling the calculator we will *invest* 1,000 (hence the minus sign). The calculator responds with an answer of positive 1,100 indicating that in return for *giving* 1,000, we will *get* 1,100.

$$FV = PV (1 + r)^n$$
$$= 1,000 (1.10)^2 = 1,000 (1.21) = \underline{1,210}$$

2. Using the time-value tables:

   a. Write the time value formula:

      $$FV = PV(1 + r)^n$$

   b. Since **r** and **n** are known, look up the time value factor. Factors for the future value of a single present value are found in Table 1.

   c. Substitute into the formula and solve:

      $$FV = 1,000 (1.2100) = \underline{1,210}$$

	8%	9%	10%	11%
1	1.0800	1.0900	1.1000	1.1100
2	1.1664	1.1881	1.2100	1.2321
3	1.2597	1.2950	1.3310	1.3676
4	1.3605	1.4116	1.4641	1.5181
5	1.4693	1.5386	1.6105	1.6851
6	1.5869	1.6771	1.7716	1.8704
7	1.7138	1.8280	1.9487	2.0762
8	1.8509	1.9926	2.1436	2.3045
9	1.9990	2.1719	2.5379	2.5580
10	2.1589	2.3674	2.5937	2.8394
11	2.3316	2.5804	2.8531	2.1518
12	2.5182	2.8127	3.1384	3.4985

3. By financial calculator or spreadsheet program:

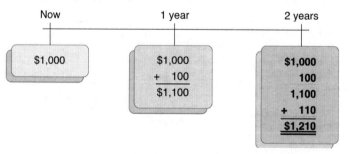

	1,210
Clear TVM	
Enter	
−1000 as	PV
10 as	i
2 as	n
Compute	FV

B5	▼	f_x =FV(+B2,+B3,0,+B1)	
	A	B	C	D
1	PV	-1000		
2	r	0.10		
3	N	2		
4				
5	FV	1,210		
6				

Answer: $\underline{\$1,210}$. By the end of the first year your account will have grown to $1,100. In the second year you will earn 10% interest on $1,100, or $110.

Now	1 year	2 years
$1,000	$1,000 + 100 $1,100	$1,000 100 1,100 + 110 $1,210

Example   **Compounding for Three Years**

Finally, suppose your $1,000 deposit remains in the bank and continues to earn 10% interest for a third year.

Question: How much will you have in your account after three years?

Solution steps:

1. By formula (looking at the third year):

   $$FV = Principal + interest$$
   $$= PV + r \bullet PV$$
   $$= 1,210 + .10 (1210) = 1,210 + 121 = \underline{1,331}$$

Or, using the compound interest relationship (looking at the three years together):

$$FV = PV\,(1 + r)^n$$
$$= 1,000\,(1.10)^3 = 1,000\,(1.331) = \underline{1,331}$$

2. Using the time-value tables:

   a. Write the time value formula:

   $$FV = PV(1 + r)^n$$

   b. Since **r** and **n** are known, look up the time value factor. Factors for the future value of a single present value are found in Table 1.

	8%	9%	10%	11%
1	1.0800	1.0900	1.1000	1.1100
2	1.1664	1.1881	1.2100	1.2321
3	1.2597	1.2950	1.3310	1.3676
4	1.3605	1.4116	1.4641	1.5181
5	1.4693	1.5386	1.6105	1.6851
6	1.5869	1.6771	1.7716	1.8704
7	1.7138	1.8280	1.9487	2.0762
8	1.8509	1.9926	2.1436	2.3045
9	1.9990	2.1719	2.5379	2.5580
10	2.1589	2.3674	2.5937	2.8394

   c. Substitute into the formula and solve:

   $$FV = 1,000\,(1.3310) = \underline{1,331}$$

3. By financial calculator or spreadsheet program:

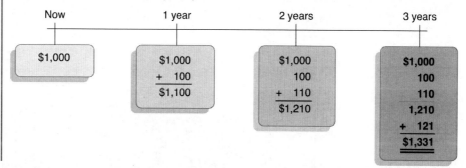

Answer: $\underline{\$1,331}$. By the end of the second year your account will have grown to $1,210. In the third year you will earn 10% interest on $1,210, or $121.

Do you see a pattern here? In each year, you get back the beginning principal and earn interest on that amount. Another way to say this is that each year's beginning principal is multiplied by $(1 + r)$, where the "1" represents the return of principal and the "r" adds on the interest:

After 1 year: $FV = PV\,(1 + r)$

In the second year, the principal is $[PV(1 + r)]$, and

After 2 years: $FV = [PV(1 + r)] \bullet (1 + r) = PV\,(1 + r)^2$

In the third year, the principal is [PV(1 + r)(1 + r)], and

> After 3 years: FV = [PV(1 + r)(1 + r)]•(1 + r) = PV (1 + r)^3

Continuing the pattern:

> After n years: $FV = PV (1 + r)^n$

and this is the compound interest relationship!

2. Finding Present Value

present value—a single cash flow or value at the beginning of a time frame

discounting—removing compound interest from a future value to produce a present value

If we wish to determine how much we must invest today to produce a given future value, we are looking for a **present value.** An important use of this calculation is to establish a price for benefits we expect to receive in the future. Solving for a present value is often referred to as **discounting** a future cash flow.

The present value of a future amount is found by rearranging the compound interest formula to solve for **PV**:

$$PV = \frac{FV}{(1 + r)^n} = FV \frac{1}{(1 + r)^n}$$

Just like solving for future value, we can solve this equation in one of three ways: (1) directly, by plugging in values of **FV, r,** and **n;** (2) with the aid of a time value table, in this case "Table 2—Present Value Factors," to obtain a value for $1/(1 + r)^n$; or (3) with a financial calculator or spreadsheet program.

For a brief period of time, until scientists corrected the equation, Tim was money.

Example

Finding a Present Value (Discounting)

You can purchase an investment that will return $50,000 in five years, and you wish to earn an annual rate of return of 15%.

Question: How much should you pay for this investment?

Solution steps:[8]

1. Using TVM tables:

   a. Write the relevant time value formula:
   $$PV = FV \frac{1}{(1 + r)^n}$$

   b. Since **r** and **n** are known, look up the time value factor. Factors for the present value of a single future value are found in Table 2.

   c. Substitute into the formula and solve:
   $$PV = 50{,}000 \, (.4972) = 24{,}860$$

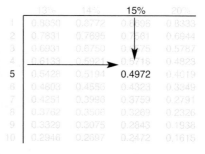

2. Using a financial calculator[9] or spreadsheet program:

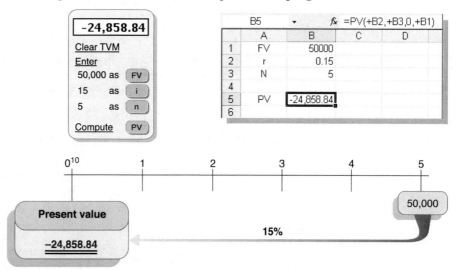

Answer: If you pay (notice that the present value calculates as a negative number—thus "pay") $24,858.84, you will earn exactly 15% per year over the five-year period.

---

[8] **Observation:**   Note the (small) difference between the calculator/spreadsheet solution and the answer found with the table. The calculator/spreadsheet result is the more precise one. There is round-off error when using time value tables since the time-value factors are rounded to four decimal places. For small dollar amounts this error is not meaningful.

[9] **Tip:**   Don't forget to clear the part of your calculator that stores time value information before each calculation to prevent numbers left over from prior problems from accidently entering your current analysis. On most calculators, this is *not* done by pressing the **C** or **CLR** key (which simply clears the display), but rather by pressing a key or key sequence labelled **CLEAR TVM, CLEAR FIN, CLEAR DATA, CLEAR ALL,** or the like.

[10] **Observation:**   We often will use a time line such as this one to diagram time value problems. Each number marks the end of a year, hence the label "1" means the end of the first year, etc. "0" (literally the end of the 0th year) stands for the *beginning* of the first year (or "now"), the point at which present values are normally located.

3. Finding a Time Period

We may wish to determine how long it would take, given a rate of interest, for a present value to grow to a particular future amount.

Example

Finding a Time Period

You have $10,000 today and wish to see it grow to $37,000. You can earn interest at an annual rate of 8%.

Question: How long will this take?

Solution steps:

1. Using TVM tables:

   a. Write the relevant time value formula:

   $$FV = PV\,(1 + r)^n$$

   b. Since **n** is the unknown, rearrange the equation to solve for the time value factor:

   $$(1 + r)^n = FV/PV$$
   $$= 37,000/10,000 = 3.7000$$

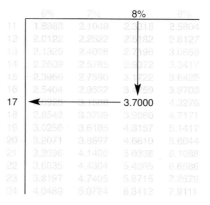

   c. Factors for the future value of a single present value are found in Table 1. Scan down the 8% column until you reach the number closest to 3.7000. Then look left to find the number of years for that factor:

   $$n = 17 \text{ years}$$

2. Using a financial calculator or spreadsheet program:

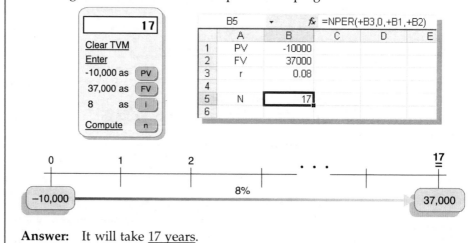

Answer: It will take <u>17 years</u>.

4. Finding an Interest Rate

We often wish to learn what interest rate, compounded over a specified number of time periods, would make a present value grow to a given future amount.

Example

Finding an Interest Rate

You have $10,000 today and wish to see it grow to $170,000 in 25 years.

Question: What interest rate will accomplish this?

Solution steps:

1. Using TVM tables:

   a. Write the relevant time value formula:

   $$FV = PV (1 + r)^n$$

   b. Since **r** is the unknown, rearrange the equation to solve for the time value factor:

   $$(1 + r)^n = FV/PV$$
   $$= 170{,}000/10{,}000 = 17.000$$

	11%	12%	13%	14%
18	6.5436	7.6900	9.0243	10.575
19	7.2633	8.6128	10.197	12.056
20	8.0623	9.6463	11.523	13.743
21	8.9492	10.804	13.021	15.668
22	9.9336	12.100	14.714	17.861
23	11.026	13.552	16.627	20.362
24	12.239	15.179	18.788	23.212
25		→17.000	21.231	26.462
26	15.080	19.040	23.991	30.167
27	16.739	21.325	27.109	34.390
28	18.580	23.884	30.633	39.204
29	20.624	26.750	34.616	44.693
30	22.892	29.960	39.116	50.950
31	25.410	33.555	44.201	58.083

   c. Factors for the future value of a single present value are found in Table 1. Scan across the 25 year row until you reach the number closest to 17.000. Then look up to the top of that column to find the interest rate for that factor:

   $$i = 12\%$$

2. Using a financial calculator or spreadsheet program:

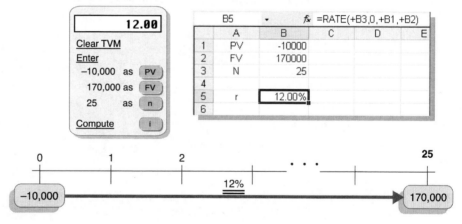

Answer: You will reach your goal if you can earn <u>12.00%</u>.

Multiple Cash Flows—Uneven Flows

So far we have looked at calculations involving two cash flows only: one present value and one future value. However, often we must analyze more than two cash flows. When finding a present or future value (as opposed to finding an interest rate, which requires that all cash flows be considered together), one strategy is to analyze each cash flow individually and then combine the results.[11]

---

[11] **Cross-reference and observation:**   See Web Appendix 3B for a time-saving method of solving these problems using the cash flow list feature of financial calculators. Since that method begins with inputting all the cash flows of the problem, it can also be used to solve for a rate of interest.

Example

Present Value of Uneven Cash Flows

The state lottery promises a grand prize of $1,000,000. The winner will be paid $100,000 per year for the first three years, $200,000 per year for the two years after that, and $300,000 in the sixth year. If 8% is the appropriate rate of interest, what is the lottery really worth today? (Note that even though the winner receives the advertised $1,000,000 in cash, the lottery must be worth less than that since the winner does not receive all of the money at once!)

Question interpreted: Find the present value of this package of cash flows.

Solution steps: Calculate each present value individually and then add them together:

1. Using TVM tables:

   a. Write the relevant time value formula:

   $$PV = FV/(1 + r)^n$$

   b. Since **r** and **n** are known, look up the time value factors for each number of years. Factors for the present value of a single future value are found in Table 2.

   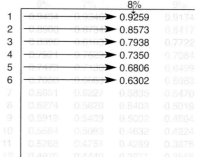

   c. Substitute each cash flow and time value factor into the formula in turn and solve:

$$PV = 100,000\ (.9259) = \$\ 92,590$$
$$PV = 100,000\ (.8573) = \ \ \ 85,730$$
$$PV = 100,000\ (.7938) = \ \ \ 79,380$$
$$PV = 200,000\ (.7350) = \ \ 147,000$$
$$PV = 200,000\ (.6806) = \ \ 136,120$$
$$PV = 300,000\ (.6302) = \ \ 189,060$$

   Total $\underline{\$729,880}$

2. Using the financial calculator:

   $\boxed{\text{CLEAR}}$ the time value part of your calculator, then:

Year	As $\boxed{\text{FV}}$	As $\boxed{\text{n}}$	As $\boxed{\text{i}}$	Compute $\boxed{\text{PV}}$
1	100000	1	8	$ −92,592.59
2	100000	2	8	−85,733.88
3	100000	3	8	−79,383.22
4	200000	4	8	−147,005.97
5	200000	5	8	−136,116.64
6	300000	6	8	−189,050.89
			Total	$−729,883.19[12]

[12] **Elaboration and observation:**   The negative sign attached to the answer can be interpreted as follows: If a person *invested* (an outflow, hence negative) $729,883.19 today at 8% interest, the investment would grow exactly to provide the six cash flows of this problem. Thus $729,883.19 is the "correct price" to *pay* (−) for this investment in order to earn 8%. Of course, if you could buy these cash flows for the price of a lottery ticket, you would be way ahead!

3. Using a spreadsheet program:

	A	B	C	D
		B9	▾	*fx* =NPV(+B7,B1:B6)
1	Year 1	100000		
2	Year 2	100000		
3	Year 3	100000		
4	Year 4	200000		
5	Year 5	200000		
6	Year 6	300000		
7	r	0.08		
8				
9	PV	729,883.20		
10				

0	1	2	3	4	5	6
	100,000	100,000	100,000	200,000	200,000	300,000

Present value
- −92,592.59
- −85,733.88
- −79,383.22
- −147,005.97
- −136,116.64
- −189,050.89
- **−729,883.19**

Answer: Winning this lottery is worth only $729,883.19 and not $1 million if 8% measures the value of time.

Multiple Cash Flows—Cash Flows That Form a Pattern

Sometimes the cash flows of a problem form a pattern for which a quick solution already exists. If we recognize these patterns when they occur, we can save ourselves much time (and increase the odds that we get the correct answer as well!).

Consider, for example, the problems facing John Platini, a lending officer at the Local National Bank. Yesterday, a customer purchasing a house asked John to calculate how much she could borrow if she could repay $1,000 per month. Since the bank makes home mortgage loans for a 30-year period (360 months), John had to calculate 360 present values and add them together. Today, another customer inquired about borrowing $20,000 and offered to repay the loan in ten annual installments. John was asked to calculate the amount of each payment, ten equal future values whose combined present value is $20,000. John will be doing a lot of calculations, many by trial-and-error, unless we can give him some help.

Fortunately the mathematics has been worked out for these and similar problems and is included in our financial calculator. We will look at three patterns of cash flows: (1) the annuity, (2) the growing cash stream, and (3) the perpetual annuity or "perpetuity."

1. The Annuity

annuity—a series of cash flows that are equal in amount, direction of flow, and time distance apart

Both problems facing John Platini involve annuities. An **annuity** is defined as a set of cash flows that are identical in amount, direction of flow, and spacing. The following examples of cash flow patterns should help you identify annuities:

Examples

Recognizing Annuities

These cash flow patterns _are_ annuities:

1	2	3	4	5	6	7	time ⟶
5	5	5	5	5	5		
	5	5	5	5	5	5	(The starting date does not matter)
−5	−5	−5	−5	−5	−5	−5	(The direction of flow does not matter as long as it is consistent)
5		5		5		5	(The time distance between flows does not matter as long as it is uniform)

These cash flow patterns _are not_ annuities:

1	2	3	4	5	6	7	time ⟶
5	4	5	5	5	5	5	(The second flow is different)
5	5	−5	5	5	5	5	(The third flow is in the opposite direction)
5	5	5		5	5	5	(The fourth flow is missing so that the time distance between flows is not uniform)

Annuity calculations   Like the problems we have already examined, we can solve annuity problems using time value tables, a financial calculator, or a spreadsheet program.[13] The variable we use for each cash flow in an annuity is **PMT** which stands for the word **PayMenT.** You may have noticed there is a fifth time value key on your calculator labeled **PMT.** This is the key we use for an annuity.

payment—one of the cash flows in an annuity

There are five types of annuity calculations. We can compute (1) the present value of an annuity, (2) the amount of each annuity payment, (3) the future value of an annuity, (4) the length of an annuity, or (5) the interest rate in an annuity. With the help of John Platini, the banker, we will look at each calculation:

Example

Present Value of an Annuity

John's first problem involved finding the present value of an annuity, in this case the amount of a loan. His customer was willing to pay $1,000 per month for 360 months. Suppose John's bank charges 1% interest per month on this loan. How much can John lend?

Question: What is the present value of this annuity?

---

[13] **Looking ahead:** From this point on, all solutions will be illustrated as they are done on the financial calculator and spreadsheet. For interested students Web Appendix 3A illustrates how to solve annuity problems using the time value tables.

Solution steps:[14]

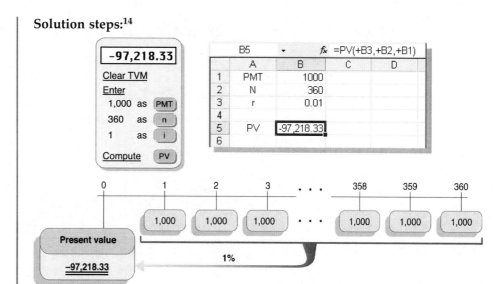

Answer: If the loan is for $97,218.33, John's customer's payments of $1,000 per month will repay the loan plus interest at the rate of 1% per month in 360 months or 30 years.

Example

Amount of an Annuity

John's second problem involved finding the amount of an annuity. His customer wished to borrow $20,000 to be repaid in ten equal annual installments. John's bank charges 14% annual interest on this loan.

Question: How much will each annuity payment be?

Solution steps:

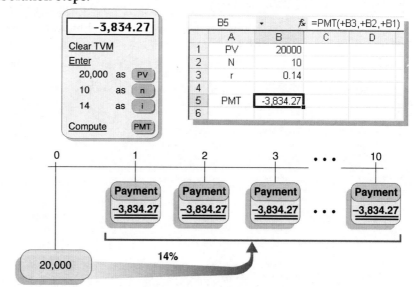

Answer: Payments of $3,834.27 at the end of each of the next ten years will exactly repay the $20,000 loan plus interest at the annual rate of 14%.

---

[14] **Observation:** Note that the unit of time in this problem is months. The unit of time doesn't matter as long as we use the same time unit for both **n** and **i** (number of months, monthly rate).

Example

Future Value of an Annuity

One of John's customers has just opened an Individual Retirement Account (IRA)[15] that pays 7% per year. He plans to deposit $2,000 per year for the next 25 years. How much will be in the account at the end of the 25 years?

Question: What is the future value of this annuity?

Solution steps:

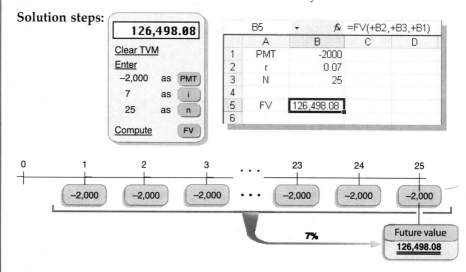

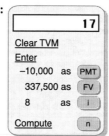

Answer: The customer's account will have a balance of $126,498.08 at the end of the 25 years.

Example

Length of an Annuity

certificate of deposit—a receipt for a bank deposit in which the depositor commits not to withdraw funds from the bank for a specified period of time in return for a better rate of interest

A young couple has asked John for some advice. They want to accumulate $337,500 to send their one-year-old quadruplets to college. They can afford to invest $10,000 per year. John suggests a **certificate of deposit** (or **CD**) that pays 8% interest. How long will it take for their account to total $337,500?

Question: What is the length of this annuity?

Solution steps:

[15] **Elaboration:**   Individual Retirement Accounts were enacted into law by the U.S. Congress to encourage people to provide for their own retirement and to supplement the Social Security system. IRAs get a very favorable tax treatment: the amount deposited each year can be deducted from income for tax purposes and neither it nor the interest earned becomes taxable until the money is withdrawn, presumably many years later. With a newer form of IRA, the Roth IRA, the deposit is made after paying income tax, but the interest earned is tax free.

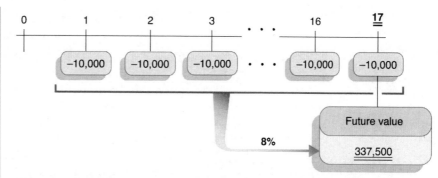

Answer: It will take the family <u>17 years</u> to reach their goal, exactly the time they have available.

Example

Interest Rate in an Annuity

John's bank normally makes personal loans at a 14% annual interest rate. Recently, however, the bank made a special offer to its customers: customers could borrow $10,000 to be repaid with 5 equal annual payments of $2,850. What interest rate is the bank offering on this loan?

Question: What is the interest rate in this annuity?

Solution steps:

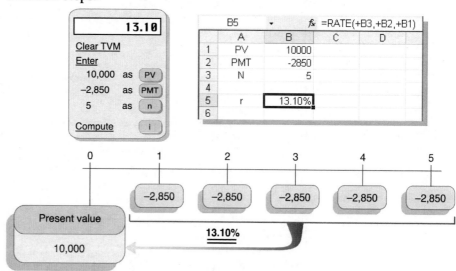

Answer: The loan carries an interest rate of <u>13.10%</u>.

Ordinary annuities vs. annuities due   All of the previous annuity examples were illustrations of what are referred to as **ordinary annuities** (also **annuities in arrears** or **END annuities**). In these annuities, the cash flow in each period comes at the end of that period. For example, in a typical loan, the borrower waits until the end of each period (month, quarter, year, etc.) to make a payment.

Some financial deals involving annuities, however, require payments at the beginning of each period. If you rent an apartment or lease a car, for example, you

ordinary annuity (annuity in arrears, END annuity)—an annuity in which the cash flows occur at the end of each time period

typically make your payments on the first of each month. These annuities are called **annuities due** (also **annuities in advance** or **BEGIN annuities**).

Since the timing of cash flows is critical to their worth, annuities due differ in present and future value from comparable ordinary annuities. Financial calculators and spreadsheets deal with this by providing a way to switch from an **END** setting to a **BEGIN** setting.[16] In the above examples the annuities were all ordinary annuities, and your calculator had to be set to **END** for you to get the correct answer. Now we look at both alternatives.

Example

Ordinary Annuity

Consider Sylvia Loeb, who is putting away money to pay for her retirement. Sylvia's plan is to deposit $2,500 at the end of each year into a bank account that pays 7% annual interest. She expects to make deposits for 30 years.

Question: How much will Sylvia have at the end of the 30 years?

Solution steps:

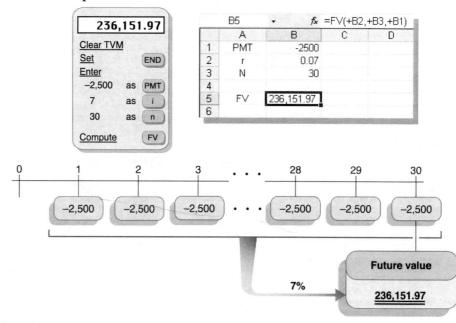

Answer: Sylvia will have $236,151.97 at the end of the 30th year.

Example

Annuity Due

Recently, a friend suggested to Sylvia that she make her deposits at the beginning of each year, rather than at the end of each year. In this way, the friend pointed out, each deposit could earn one year's extra interest.

Question: If Sylvia follows her friend's advice, how much will she have at the end of the 30 years?

---

[16] **Tip:**   Each financial calculator has its own method for switching between **END** and **BEGIN.** Time value functions in spreadsheet programs contain a **BEGIN/END** indicator. See your calculator manual or the calculator or spreadsheet appendix at the back of this book for specifics.

Solution steps:

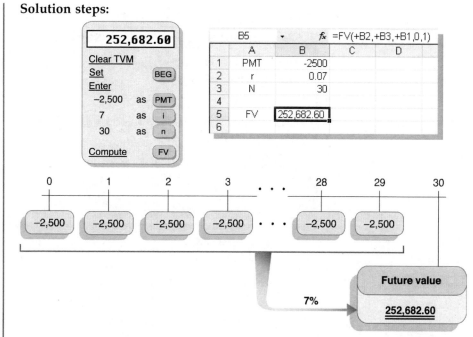

Answer: With beginning-of-year deposits, Sylvia will have $252,682.60 at the end of the 30th year.

Notice that if Sylvia makes her deposits at the beginning of every year, she accumulates $16,530.63 more than if she waited until the end of the year to make the deposits. The difference of $16,530.63 is exactly 7% of $236,151.97, reflecting one year's extra interest on all of her deposited money. Her friend was right!

2. The Growing Cash Stream

Van Hoffmann's close friend has given him a hot tip—buy the common stock of Techno-Industries, Inc., the new darling of Wall Street. Van understands that the stock's price is a present value, but he is having difficulty using time value techniques to calculate how much he should be willing to pay for each share. In particular, he is concerned that the annuity calculations he has just learned will not work here. For one thing, Van does not know how long the firm might remain in business—corporations like Techno-Industries are going concerns with no end-of-life in sight—yet annuities are defined in part by their finite length. For another, the cash flows Van expects to receive, the firm's dividend payments, are not likely to be constant year-in and year-out, yet annuity cash flows must be constant by definition.

growing cash stream—an infinitely long series of equally spaced cash flows in which each flow is greater than the previous one by a constant rate of growth

Van needs to learn about the **growing cash stream** relationship for present value. A growing cash stream is defined as an infinitely long series of equally spaced cash flows in which each is greater than the previous one by a constant rate of growth.

Example

Recognizing a Growing Cash Stream

The following set of cash flows fits the growing cash stream relationship. The rate of growth is 10%:

Cash flow 1: $10,000

Cash flow 2: $11,000 (10% more than $10,000)

Cash flow 3: $12,100 (10% more than $11,000)

Cash flow 4: $13,310 (10% more than $12,100)

etc., forever . . .

Even though a growing cash stream goes on forever, the present value of a growing cash stream has a simple form, one that does not require a financial calculator to solve. We already have the variable **r** for the interest rate, but we need a bit of new notation:

CF_1 = **Cash Flow #1,** the first cash flow in the stream coming one period after the time of the present value.

g = **growth rate** of the cash flows.

The present value of a growing cash stream is:

$$PV = \frac{CF_1}{r - g}$$

Example

Growing Cash Stream

Now we can help Van with his stock investment. Suppose Van forecasts that Techno-Industries will pay a $2.00 per share dividend in one year, and that the dividend payment will grow at a rate of 6% for the foreseeable future. Van wants a 16% annual rate of return on this investment.

Question: How much is Techno-Industries common stock worth to Van?

Solution steps:

$$PV = \frac{CF_1}{r - g} = \frac{\$2.00}{.16 - .06} = \$20.00$$

Answer: The stock is worth <u>$20.00 per share</u> to Van. If he buys it at that price and his forecasts come true, he will earn his desired 16% rate of return.

Note two things about this relationship. First, since we are working with an equation and not the time value part of the financial calculator, both rates (r and g) were used in their decimal form (.16 rather than 16%; .06 rather than 6%). Second, the relationship only works when the value of r is greater than the value of g. Otherwise the formula is not valid and it gives incorrect results.

3. The Perpetuity

perpetuity—an annuity that continues forever; also, a growing cash stream with a zero rate of growth

A special case of the growing cash stream is the **perpetuity.** A perpetuity is a growing cash stream with a growth rate equal to zero. This makes every cash flow in the perpetuity the same amount. Another way of looking at a perpetuity is as an annuity that goes on forever. In fact, the word *perpetuity* is a special finance word made up from the words ***perpetual annuity.***

When g = 0, the growing cash stream present value relationship reduces to:

$$PV = \frac{PMT}{r}$$

(since every cash flow is the same, there is no need to distinguish the first one by the notation CF_1 here. PMT—payment—will do just fine. It is still required, however, that the first payment occur one period after the time of the present value.)

Example

Perpetuity

Van Hoffmann is also looking at the preferred stock of Techno-Industries which pays a $12.00 annual dividend per share, with the next dividend due in one year. Since Van considers Techno-Industries' preferred stock to be a bit less risky than the company's common stock, he only requires a 15% rate of return on this investment.

Question: How much is Techno-Industries' preferred stock worth to Van?

Solution steps:

$$PV = \frac{PMT}{r} = \frac{\$12.00}{.15} = \$80.00$$

Answer: The stock is worth $80.00 per share to Van. If he buys it at that price and his forecasts come true, he will earn his desired 15% rate of return.

*J*ay Herman put the calculator and instruction manual back into his attaché case. The train was pulling into the central station, and passengers were getting ready to make the final part of their journey to work. Jay had practiced a variety of the sample problems in the instruction manual, and by now the concepts and the location of the calculator keys were becoming familiar.

Analysis of financial values began with cash flows. To bring cash flows together, it was necessary to do time value calculations. This meant organizing the cash flows carefully by when they were expected to occur, choosing the time value model that fit the pattern of the cash flows, entering them into the calculator, and solving for the unknown quantity.

Jay stood up and eased into the aisle, flowing with the crowd toward the platform. As he left the station, he found himself smiling. If the rest of financial analysis was like this, it was certainly going to be a lot of fun!

Summary of Key Points

■■ **Understand why the value of money depends on the time of its receipt or payment and, therefore, why money amounts can only be compared after they have been adjusted for time.** The value of money depends on *two* things, its amount and the time of its receipt or payment. A larger sum of money is more valuable than a smaller sum. Receiving money sooner and paying it later is more valuable than later receipt or earlier payment, as additional interest may be earned. Since almost every business deal involves a payment today (present value) in order to get greater receipts in the future (future value), there is a natural tradeoff between the two characteristics of how much and when. To analyze a business deal, it is necessary to perform time value of money calculations.

■■ **Calculate the present value and future value of cash flows, the interest rate that describes any pair of cash flows, and the length of time it takes to reach a financial goal.** The fundamental relationship of time value is the compound interest formula that relates a present value and a future value through a rate of interest that can be earned over a period of time. If we know three of the variables, we can solve for the fourth.

■■ **Analyze a set of uneven cash flows.** Uneven cash flows can be analyzed individually or can be entered into a financial calculator or spreadsheet program to be analyzed together.

■■ **Recognize when time value analysis can be simplified because the cash flows form a standard pattern.** Many time value problems involve multiple cash flows. When the flows do not form a pattern, we must analyze them individually. However, if cash flows are in the pattern of an annuity, a growing cash stream, or a perpetuity, we can use the relationships developed for these cash flow patterns to simplify our work considerably.

Questions

1. What is the relationship between a future value and a present value?

2. Some economists argue that people increase their savings when interest rates rise since they can earn more money. Suppose you were putting money away with the goal of raising $50,000 in five years. Would an increase in interest rates increase the amount of money you saved?

3. What is the relationship among an annuity, a perpetuity, and a growing cash stream?

4. A well-known advertisement by American Express urged travelers returning home to keep their travelers' checks rather than cash them in. The reason given was to have cash in an emergency, but could American Express have had any other reason for encouraging this behavior?

5. Why do airlines require that you pay for your ticket on the date you book your flight rather than the date you actually fly?

Problems

1. **(Basic future value)** If you invest $15,000 today at 9% annual interest, how much will you have in:

    a. 1 year? c. 5 years?
    b. 2 years? d. 10 years?

2. **(Basic future value)** How much will you have in 5 years if you invest $25,000 for a 5-year period at an annual interest rate of:

    a. 25%? c. 7%?
    b. 12%? d. 0%?

3. **(Basic present value)** You have been told you will receive $75,000 at some time in the future. In the meantime you can earn interest at an annual rate of 6%. How much is the $75,000 worth to you today if the time you must wait for its receipt is:

    a. 1 year? c. 5 years?
    b. 2 years? d. 10 years?

4. **(Basic present value)** You are due to receive $30,000 in 7 years. How much is it worth to you today if you can earn interest at an annual rate of:

    a. 25%? c. 7%?
    b. 12%? d. 0%?

5. **(Basic time period)** You have $10,000 today. How long will it take for you to double your money if you can earn interest at an annual rate of:

    a. 5%? c. 15%?
    b. 8%? d. 100%?

6. **(Basic time period)** If you can earn interest at an annual interest rate of 9%, how long will it take for $25,000 to grow to be:

    a. $30,000? c. $75,000?
    b. $40,000? d. $100,000?

7. **(Basic interest rate)** What annual interest rate does it take to make $45,000 grow to be $60,000 in:

   a. 3 years?
   b. 5 years?
   c. 10 years?
   d. 20 years?

8. **(Basic interest rate)** What annual interest rate, earned over 8 years, will make an initial $17,500 grow to be:

   a. $20,000?
   b. $25,000?
   c. $35,000?
   d. $50,000?

9. **(Present value of uneven cash flows)** Find the present value (as of today) of the following cash flow streams at an interest rate of 8%:

Year	Stream A	Stream B	Stream C
1	$1,000	$4,000	$5,000
2	2,000	2,000	4,000
3	3,000	3,000	3,000
4	4,000	1,000	2,000
5	5,000	5,000	1,000

10. **(Present value of uneven cash flows)** You wish to set aside a fund of money to provide for your elderly parents. You estimate you will need $25,000 at the end of each of the next 5 years and $15,000 at the end of each of the five years after that. What amount of money, deposited today, will provide these funds if you can earn at an annual interest rate of 6%?

11. **(Future value of an ordinary annuity)** If you save $5,000 at the end of each year for 15 years, how much will you have accumulated if you can earn at an annual interest rate of:

    a. 6%?
    b. 10%?
    c. 12%?
    d. 15%?

12. **(Future value of an ordinary annuity)** If you can earn at an annual interest rate of 8% per year, how much will you have accumulated if you save $3,000 at the end of each of the next:

    a. 5 years?
    b. 10 years?
    c. 15 years?
    d. 20 years?

13. **(Future value of an annuity due)** Redo Problem 11 assuming that you make your deposits at the beginning of each year.

14. **(Future value of an annuity due)** Redo Problem 12 assuming that you make your deposits at the beginning of each year.

15. **(Amount of an ordinary annuity)** How much must you pay at the end of each year to repay a $50,000, 14% annual interest rate loan if you must make:

    a. 10 payments?
    b. 15 payments?
    c. 20 payments?
    d. 30 payments?

16. **(Amount of an ordinary annuity)** How much must you deposit at the end of each of the next 10 years to accumulate $50,000 if you can earn interest at an annual interest rate of:

    a. 3%?
    b. 5%?
    c. 7%?
    d. 9%?

17. **(Amount of an annuity due)** Redo Problem 15 assuming that you make your payments at the beginning of each year.

18. **(Amount of an annuity due)** Redo Problem 16 assuming that you make your deposits at the beginning of each year.

19. **(Present value of an ordinary annuity)** You wish to create a bank account from which you can withdraw $10,000 per year at the end of each of the next 10 years. How much must you deposit today to provide these benefits if you can earn at a rate of:

    a. 5%?
    b. 12%?
    c. 16%?
    d. 20%?

20. **(Present value of an ordinary annuity)** You have asked your banker for a loan and stated that you are willing to repay the loan with annual end-of-year payments of $1,500. Your banker responded by informing you that the interest rate would be 12%. How much can you borrow if the loan is for a period of:

    a. 2 years?
    b. 5 years?
    c. 7 years?
    d. 10 years?

21. **(Present value of an annuity due)** Redo Problem 19 assuming that you make your withdrawals at the beginning of each year.

22. **(Present value of an annuity due)** Redo Problem 20 assuming that you make your loan payments at the beginning of each year.

23. **(Length of an ordinary annuity)** You have saved $250,000 and wish to retire today. For how many years can you draw $30,000, at the end of each year, if you can continue to earn interest at a rate of:

    a. 5%?
    b. 8%?
    c. 10%?
    d. 11%?

24. **(Length of an ordinary annuity)** You plan to make deposits into a retirement account and have set a goal of having $2 million in the account when you retire. You forecast you can earn interest at a 6% rate. How many years will it take for you to reach your retirement goal if, at the end of each year, you deposit:

    a. $10,000?
    b. $20,000?
    c. $30,000?
    d. $40,000?

25. **(Length of an annuity due)** Redo Problem 23 assuming that you make your withdrawals at the beginning of each year.

26. **(Length of an annuity due)** Redo Problem 24 assuming that you make your deposits at the beginning of each year.

27. **(Interest rate in an ordinary annuity)** An insurance fund advertises that if you invest $50,000 today, you will receive a fixed amount at the end of each of the next 20 years. What interest rate are they giving you if the annual amount is:

    a. $ 3,500?   c. $ 7,500?
    b. $ 5,000?   d. $10,000?

28. **(Interest rate in an ordinary annuity)** You have decided to start saving for your children's education and want to accumulate $250,000. You can afford to deposit $15,000 into your education fund at the end of each year. What annual interest rate must you earn if you need to reach your savings target in:

    a. 6 years?   c. 10 years?
    b. 8 years?   d. 12 years?

29. **(Interest rate in an annuity due)** Redo Problem 27 assuming that the fund pays you at the beginning of each year.

30. **(Interest rate in an annuity due)** Redo Problem 28 assuming you make your deposits at the beginning of each year.

31. **(Growing cash stream)** You have the opportunity to buy the stock of a company which is expected to pay a $3.50 dividend in one year and grow thereafter at a rate of 4%. If you require a 16% rate of return on this investment, how much is the stock worth to you?

32. **(Growing cash stream)** The stock of a company that is expected to pay a $1.75 dividend in one year and grow thereafter at an annual rate of 11% is currently selling for $35.00 per share. What rate of return does the market require on this security?

33. **(Perpetuity)** A certain preferred stock pays a $14.00 annual dividend. The next dividend is expected in one year. How much is the stock worth to you if you require a rate of return of:

    a. 10%?   c. 17%?
    b. 14%?   d. 20%?

34. **(Perpetuity)** You can buy a preferred stock that pays a $12.50 annual dividend, the next dividend due in one year. What rate of return does the stock offer if you can buy it for:

    a. $75.00?   c. $100.00?
    b. $90.00?   d. $120.00?

CHAPTER 4
MONEY RATES

*S*andra Maglen found herself nodding in agreement. The treasurer's point made perfect sense: her company had to do a better job of responding to conditions in the general economy. Sandra thought back to her economics classes in college and smiled as she remembered a favorite professor who was fond of pointing out how the macroeconomy affected the microeconomy. Perhaps she would write a letter to the professor to reestablish contact and to let him know that some of his teachings remained with her.

The treasurer went on, "The immediate issue is that the CFO received a call today from one of the major financial rating agencies saying that we've been put on a 'credit watch,' in part due to concerns about our exposure to foreign currencies. The boss fears that our ratings might slip. If that happens we would have to pay more to borrow. We can't be competitive if our costs rise like that. But the larger issue is that we shouldn't have gotten into this position in the first place. Let's see if we can come up with a strategy for avoiding these kinds of problems altogether."

Sandra and several others were asked to form a team to research and write a report identifying key factors affecting the interest rates the firm paid on its debt including potential losses from foreign exchange. The team agreed to collect their thoughts and materials and get together later that afternoon. Back at her desk, Sandra took her old college economics books off the shelf and blew off the dust. She leafed through several pages and began to recall that interest rates depend on a variety of factors. In another chapter, she found information on foreign exchange rates. She jotted down some thoughts and made a note to collect some recent economic data prior to the meeting.

Interest rates are prices—the price to rent money. Of all the prices in an economy, interest rates are perhaps the most important, since money is such a universal commodity. They have a profound effect on the functioning of an economy and all of its components, and upon a wide range of business decisions. Except where determined by government regulation, they are set in competitive markets by the forces of supply and demand.

Exchange rates are also prices—the price of one currency in terms of another. Like interest rates, exchange rates change with economic and political conditions. And, just as interest rates affect the value of all cash flows, the value of trade and investment that crosses borders depends crucially on the level of exchange rates.

The problem on which Sandra has been asked to work is one that all firms face. In addition to understanding the general level of interest rates, it is important to understand the structure of rates—why all borrowers do not pay the same rate to raise money (and, correspondingly, why lenders receive different returns on their investments). And, as Sandra is remembering from her textbook, an effective financial manager must be aware of exchange rate relationships and the positive and negative effects that variations in exchange rates can have on the firm. Every dollar lost to currency movements is one less dollar available to meet stakeholder needs.

Key Points You Should Learn from This Chapter

After reading this chapter you should be able to:

- Demonstrate the relationships between interest rates and present value and between present value and time to cash flow.
- Subdivide any interest rate into its components.
- Explain why interest rates differ by maturity of obligation.
- Understand how risks and taxes impact interest rates.
- Describe fixed and floating exchange rate systems and their variations.
- Express exchange rates as direct, reciprocal, and cross rates.
- Define the meaning of spot and forward rates.
- Identify how changes in exchange rates affect businesses dealing in multiple currencies.

Introductory Concepts—Interest Rates, Present Value, and Time

Interest rates play several important roles within the economy. They balance the supply of, and demand for, money—thus permitting the market for money to clear. In doing so they ration credit, providing it to those borrowers who can promise the highest rates of return and shutting out those with poor-yielding investments. In addition, governments, as major suppliers and demanders of money, use interest rates as a key component of economic policy, pushing rates lower to stimulate growth or raising them to slow inflation.

Interest rates are also critical for business decision making. As we saw in Chapter 3, every business decision involving money flows should be analyzed using time value of money calculations. But time value calculations require the use of an interest rate. As rates change, the value of business decisions changes as well. In particular, *interest rates and present values move in opposite directions*. As interest rates rise, the present value of future benefits declines, making investment alternatives less valuable. By contrast, as interest rates decline, present values rise and investment alternatives become correspondingly more valuable.

Example

The Inverse Relationship Between Interest Rates and Present Value

You can purchase an investment that will return $100,000 in five years. How much should you pay if you require a rate of return of 10%? 12%? 14%? 16%?

Question: What is the present value at each interest rate?

Solution steps:

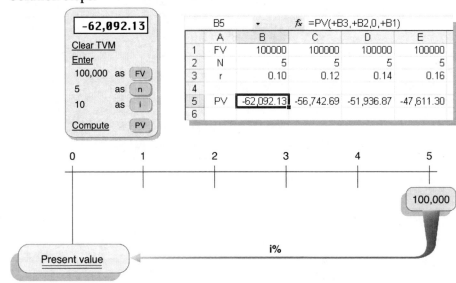

Answer:

Rate	i	Present Value	PV
10%		$ −62,092.13	
12		−56,742.69	
14		−51,936.87	
16		−47,611.30	

The present value declines when interest rates rise. With a fixed future value, the only way you can obtain a higher rate of return is to pay a lower amount.

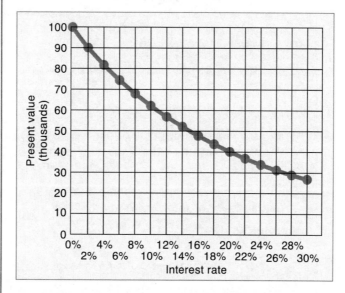

The graph shows the inverse relationship between interest rates and present values using the data of this example (future value = $100,000, n=5 years). Notice as the interest rate rises, present value declines.

A second important relationship involves present values and time: present values become more volatile as the time to receiving the cash flow increases.

Example

The Volatility of Present Value as Time to Cash Flow Increases

You can purchase an investment that will return $100,000 in one year, or a second investment that will return $1,586,309 in 30 years. Investors require a 10% rate of return from both investments.

Question: What is the present value of each investment?

Solution steps:

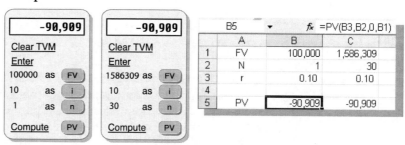

Answer: Both investments have a present value of <u>$90,909</u>.

Question: What happens to the present value of each investment if investors' required rate of return rises to 12%?

Solution steps:

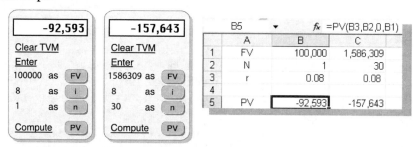

Answer: The present value of the one-year investment falls to $89,286 while the present value of the 30-year investment <u>falls much further</u> to $52,948.

Question: What happens to the present value of each investment if investors' required rate of return falls to 8%

Solution steps:

	-92,593			-157,643			B5		f_x =PV(B3,B2,0,B1)
	Clear TVM			Clear TVM			A	B	C
	Enter			Enter		1	FV	100,000	1,586,309
	100000 as	FV		1586309 as	FV	2	N	1	30
	8 as	i		8 as	i	3	r	0.08	0.08
	1 as	n		30 as	n	4			
	Compute	PV		Compute	PV	5	PV	-92,593	-157,643

Answer: The present value of the one-year investment falls to $92,593 while the present value of the 30-year investment <u>rises much further</u> to $157,643.

Financial managers study interest rates as they plan future business activity. They forecast the future level of rates to plan the level of their investment and financing actions. They forecast the speed with which rates might change to plan the timing of their investment and financing actions. Financial managers who anticipate and respond wisely to interest rates can add significant value to their organization.

The Components of Interest Rates

A particularly useful way to study interest rates is the model of the economist Irving Fisher.[1] In Fisher's model, any interest rate may be subdivided into three components: a pure rate of interest, a premium for inflation, and a premium for risk. As with other interest rate calculations, the proper formulation of this model requires multiplication by terms of the form $(1 + r)$ to ensure that the three effects "compound" upon each other:

$$\textit{Nominal rate} = (1 + \textit{pure rate})\,(1 + \textit{inflation premium})\,(1 + \textit{risk premium}) - 1$$
$$= (1 + r_p)\,(1 + r_i)\,(1 + r_r) - 1$$

---

[1] **Reference:**   Irving Fisher, "Appreciation and Interest," *Publication of the American Economics Association,* Aug. 1896.

Expanding the equation gives:

$$Nominal\ rate = r_p + r_i + r_r + r_p r_i + r_p r_r + r_i r_r + r_p r_i r_r$$

Because the last four (cross-product) terms are small relative to the first three terms, they are often omitted (with some loss of accuracy), and the model is written in the additive form:

$$Nominal\ rate = r_p + r_i + r_r$$
$$= pure\ rate + inflation\ premium + risk\ premium$$

Example

The Fisher Model—Multiplicative vs. Additive Form

Assuming that: the pure rate of interest (r_p) = .03
the inflation premium (r_i) = .05
the risk premium (r_r) = .06

then the full (multiplicative) Fisher-model gives:

$$Nominal\ Rate = (1 + r_p)(1 + r_i)(1 + r_r) - 1$$
$$= (1.03)(1.05)(1.06) - 1 = \underline{14.64\%}$$

while the additive model gives:

$$Nominal\ Rate = r_p + r_i + r_r = 3\% + 5\% + 6\% = \underline{14.00\%}$$

Even though the difference between the two calculations can be significant, the additive form of the model is often used due to its simplicity.

nominal rate of interest—a quoted rate of interest; in the context of the Fisher model, the rate of interest including the premiums for inflation and risk

The **nominal rate of interest** is the all-inclusive interest rate that is quoted with respect to any financial instrument. This is the same usage as in the time value of money, where the quoted rate is also called the *nominal rate*. In Fisher's model, the nominal rate is constructed from three components: a pure rate, a premium for inflation, and a premium for risk.

1. Components of the Fisher Model

pure rate of interest—the interest rate prior to inclusion of the premiums for inflation and risk

The **pure rate of interest** (r_p) is the starting point of Fisher's model. This is the rate of interest that would exist if there were no anticipated inflation or forecasted risk. Since it is rare for those conditions to exist, it is unusual to observe the pure rate of interest in practice. Nevertheless, the concept is useful as it permits us to separate out and focus on expectations of inflation and risk, two primary determinants of any particular interest rate.

inflation premium—the component of interest rates demanded by investors as compensation for anticipated inflation

purchasing power—the value of money measured by the goods and services it can purchase

The **inflation premium** (r_i) is the addition to interest rates demanded by investors as compensation for anticipated inflation. If investors anticipate no inflation over the life of an investment, the premium for inflation equals zero. However, if investors forecast a non-zero inflation rate, the inflation premium becomes non-zero as well. Investors must receive enough added return to protect the **purchasing power** of their money.

Example

Increasing Interest Rates to Protect Purchasing Power

Sandra Maglen has $1,000 and wishes to invest it to increase her purchasing power by 8% during the next year. She anticipates inflation to raise prices by 5% over that period.

Question: What rate of interest must she earn to achieve her goal?

Solution steps: Sandra needs to end the year with:

$$\$1,000 \ (1.05) = \$1,050$$

simply to stay even with price increases. To make her purchasing power grow by 8% as well, she must earn an additional 8%:

$$\$1,050 \ (1.08) = \$1,134$$

This is a 13.40% increase in her starting $1,000.

Alternatively:

$$\text{Required rate} = (1 + \text{rate prior to inflation}) \ (1 + \text{inflation premium}) - 1$$
$$= (1.08) \ (1.05) - 1 = .1340 = 13.40\%$$

Answer: With 5% inflation, Sandra must earn <u>13.40%</u> to achieve her 8% growth in purchasing power.

risk premium—the component of interest rates demanded by investors as compensation for risk

The **risk premium** (r_r) is the addition to interest rates demanded by investors as compensation for assuming the risk of an investment. If the investment is risk-free, the premium for risk equals zero. As the perceived risk of an investment rises, so too does the required risk premium.[2]

real rate of interest—the rate of interest excluding the premium for inflation

Real rate The rate of interest prior to considering inflation is called the **real rate of interest**. The real rate measures the increase to an investor's purchasing power. Disregarding the inflation premium, the Fisher model reduces to:

$$Real\ rate = (1 + pure\ rate)\ (1 + risk\ premium) - 1$$
$$= (1 + r_p)\ (1 + r_r) - 1$$

Example

The Real Rate of Interest

Investors are assessing the common stock of the Xerox company to determine what rate of return they should demand. They have concluded:

1. the pure rate of interest (r_p) = .03,
2. they will require an inflation premium (r_i) = .05, and
3. the uncertainties of the Xerox Company's future indicate a risk premium (r_r) = .06

We calculated with these data (on page 89) that investors would require a nominal rate of interest of 14.64%. However, their real rate of interest is only:

$$\text{real rate} = (1 + r_p)\ (1 + r_r) - 1$$
$$= (1.03)\ (1.06) - 1 = .0918 = \underline{9.18\%}$$

Although the investors will receive a 14.64% rate of return, their purchasing power will increase by only 9.18%.

NET Present Value
In the U.S., the agency responsible for keeping inflation down is the Federal Reserve at www.federalreserve.gov

---

[2] **Cross-reference:** We will study risk premiums and how they can be measured in Chapter 8.

risk-free rate of interest—the rate of interest excluding the premium for risk; it is the rate available on a risk-free investment

Risk-free rate   The rate of interest prior to considering risk is called the **risk-free rate of interest**. The yields on short-term securities issued by a strong and solvent government, and backed by the power of that government to tax, are generally considered to be examples of the risk-free rate.[3] Disregarding the risk premium, the Fisher model reduces to:

$$Risk\text{-}free\ rate = (1 + pure\ rate)(1 + inflation\ premium) - 1$$
$$= (1 + r_p)(1 + r_i) - 1$$

Example

The Risk-free Rate of Interest

Continuing the example,

If: the pure rate of interest (r_p) = .03, and
      the inflation premium (r_i) = .05

then the risk-free rate of interest is:

$$Risk\text{-}free\ interest\ rate = (1 + r_p)(1 + r_i) - 1$$
$$= (1.03)(1.05) - 1 = .0815 = \underline{8.15\%}$$

2. Interest Rates in Different Countries

Interest rates differ among countries (or more accurately, among currencies). Using the Fisher model, we can pinpoint the reasons for these differences.

First, there could be differences in the pure rate of interest among countries. These could stem from a variety of sources. Savings habits might differ because of cultural or economic reasons.[4] Attitudes toward borrowing might not be the same. Differences in banking systems might lead to differences in cash-on-hand requirements or differences in money creation. The access by foreigners to domestic funds might differ. Any of these factors could make the supply of or demand for loanable funds differ among countries and lead to different interest rates.

Second, the anticipated rates of inflation might differ among countries. Investors will require higher rates of interest to protect their purchasing power in countries with greater anticipated inflation rates.

---

[3] **Elaboration:**   Examples are U.S. government Treasury bills and U.K. government gilts.

[4] **Observation:**   For example, it has been observed that the savings rate in Japan is significantly higher than that in the United States. This increases the supply of loanable funds in Japan vis-à-vis the U.S. and contributes to a lower pure rate of interest.

FINANCE IN PRACTICE

Different Interest Rates Around the World

In its edition of June 1, 2011, the Financial Times reported the following interest rates for "benchmark government bonds," ten-year maturity bonds issued by governments around the world that are widely seen as indicators of the level of interest rates in their country of origin:

Country	Maturity Date	Yield
Australia	May 2021	5.23%
Belgium	September 2021	4.20
Canada	June 2021	3.07
Denmark	November 2019	3.03
France	April 2021	3.41
Germany	July 2021	3.03
Italy	September 2021	4.79
Japan	March 2021	1.16
Netherlands	July 2021	3.31
Spain	April 2021	5.37
United Kingdom	September 2020	3.31
United States	May 2021	3.05

Reference: Financial Times, June 1, 2011, page 21.

Third, risk levels might differ among comparable investments in different countries or currencies due to cultural or political issues, to the relative strengths of the governments and economies in question, or to other legal and social matters.

The Term Structure of Interest Rates

maturity—the time remaining until the expiration of a security

yield—the rate of return available from a security

term structure of interest rates—the relationship between a security's yield and maturity

Investors and financial managers have long been interested in the relationship between a security's **maturity** and its **yield**. In part, this is because they constantly face the choice of selling and/or buying alternative financial instruments with a wide range of maturities. At one end of the maturity spectrum are loans with a maturity of "overnight" or even one or two hours. At the other end are shares of stock whose lifetime is undefined, representing ownership in a going concern. In between are thousands of securities with every maturity imaginable.

The relationship between yield and maturity, all other factors held constant, is known as the **term structure of interest rates**.

To observe the term structure, it is necessary to have many securities that differ in maturity but not in any other way. The best selection of securities that fits this specification in the United States is U.S. Treasury issues—bills, bonds and notes. All are backed by the "full faith and taxing power" of the U.S. federal government, so there is no apparent risk differential.

Figure 4.1 is an excerpt from the daily quotations of U.S. Treasury issues on the Bloomberg website as of late 2010.[5] The Treasury borrows money to fund day-to-day government operations and the national debt by issuing bonds, notes, and

---

[5] **Reference:** www.bloomberg.com/markets/rates-bonds/government-bonds/us, November 1, 2010.

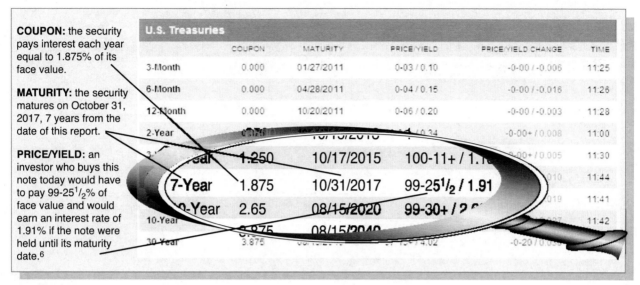

COUPON: the security pays interest each year equal to 1.875% of its face value.

MATURITY: the security matures on October 31, 2017, 7 years from the date of this report.

PRICE/YIELD: an investor who buys this note today would have to pay 99-25$\frac{1}{2}$% of face value and would earn an interest rate of 1.91% if the note were held until its maturity date.[6]

FIGURE 4.1

Through the Looking Glass: Prices and yields of U.S. Treasury securities. Each day *Bloomberg.com* reports information for a representative sample of Treasury securities.

bills. While there are a few other differences among them, the primary distinction is their maturity: bills are issued for 1 year or less, notes for 1 to about 10 years, and bonds for up to 30 years. It is popular in the investment community to call the Treasury bond with the longest maturity the "long bond."

yield curve—a graph of the term structure, most commonly of U.S. Treasury securities

Yields of the Treasury securities from Figure 4.1 are graphed in Figure 4.2, a graph popularly known as a **yield curve**.[7] While it is possible to draw a yield curve us-

FIGURE 4.2

Yields of U.S. Treasury securities, November 1, 2010. On that date the yield curve was normal, or upward-sloping.

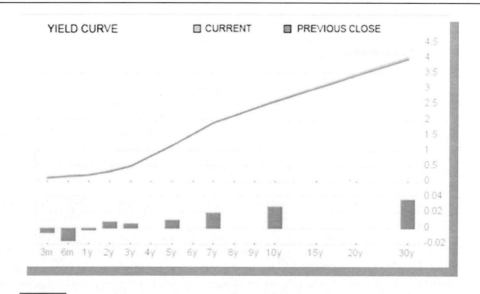

[6] **Observation and cross-reference:** This example illustrates the inverse relationship between interest rates (the bond's yield) and present values (the bond's price) discussed on pages 86–87. For this bond, the yield has risen from 1.875% to 1.91% and the price has responded by falling from 100% to 99-25½% of face value. We will study other characteristics of bonds in Chapter 6, and examine the relationship of bond prices and yields more closely in Chapter 9.

[7] **Reference:** www.bloomberg.com/markets/rates-bonds/government-bonds/us, November 1, 2010.

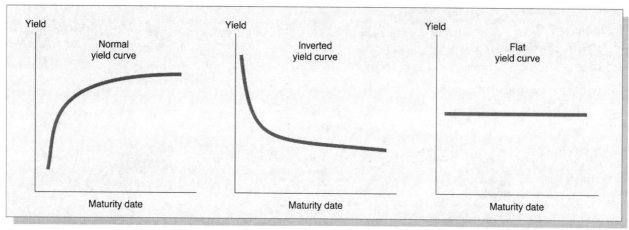

FIGURE 4.3
Yield curve shapes. The yield curve can slope upward (normal), downward (inverted), or be flat.

ing other securities, in the U.S. the term is most often applied to Treasury issues. In the more than 100 years that yield curves have been observed, their shape has either been upward sloping (up to the right), downward sloping (down to the right), or primarily flat, as illustrated in Figure 4.3. Of these, the upward-sloping yield curve has been the most common by far, so much so that an upward-sloping yield curve is commonly called a **normal yield curve** and a downward-sloping curve an **inverted yield curve**.

normal yield curve—an upward-sloping yield curve in which long-term rates exceed short-term rates

inverted yield curve—a downward-sloping yield curve in which short-term rates exceed long-term rates

Over the years, three theories have been developed to explain the shape of the yield curve. These are: (1) the expectations hypothesis, (2) the liquidity preference hypothesis, and (3) the segmentation or hedging hypothesis. All three have some logical and empirical support.

1. The Expectations Hypothesis

expectations hypothesis—a theory of the term structure focusing on investors' forecasts of future interest rates

According to the **expectations hypothesis**, the long-term rates we see today are (geometric) averages of today's short-term rates and the short-term rates investors expect in the future. An upward-sloping yield curve indicates that investors expect interest rates to rise, while a downward-sloping curve is a forecast of falling rates. The flat yield curve is typically seen as a transition state between a normal and an inverted curve, and vice-versa.

Economists have used the expectations hypothesis to explain how the shape of the yield curve changes with the business cycle. At the bottom of the cycle, the supply of resources exceeds demand. Investors' concerns about price increases are small, and the yield curve is slightly upward-sloping. As the economy expands, however, some resources become scarce, their price is bid up, and investors begin to expect further price increases. Incorporating this anticipated inflation into their yield requirements, investors produce an upward-sloping yield curve. When the economy crests and begins to contract, investors reverse their forecasts. Now they predict a drop in demand for resources and with it, an easing of inflationary pressures. Investors incorporate their forecast of declining inflation into their yield requirements—and the yield curve becomes inverted and remains downward-sloping until the next expansionary phase of the business cycle begins.

2. The Liquidity Preference Hypothesis

liquidity preference hypothesis—a theory of the term structure focusing on investors' loss of liquidity as maturities lengthen

A second theory of the term structure is the **liquidity preference hypothesis**. This theory points out that most Treasury securities are really not risk-free since they are price-sensitive to interest rates. Investors in Treasuries do avoid **default risk**. However, if the securities have a maturity longer than a few days, investors cannot escape **interest-rate risk**, the risk that interest rates will rise, reducing the bond's price. Should this happen, investors would lose some liquidity. Since long-term securities are more price-sensitive than short-term securities, long-maturity bonds are more risky than short-maturity bonds. Investors, preferring liquidity, will demand higher yields on the longer-term instruments. As a result, this theory claims it is impossible to construct a yield curve with securities that are identical in risk.

default risk—the risk that a borrower will delay or not make scheduled payments, or otherwise violate a loan agreement

interest-rate risk—the risk that interest rates will rise, reducing the value of securities

According to the liquidity preference hypothesis, all yield curves have a greater upward tilt (or lesser downward tilt) than they would otherwise have, since longer maturities demand a higher yield.

3. The Segmentation or Hedging Hypothesis

Both the expectations and liquidity preference hypotheses assume that investors are indifferent to the maturities of the bonds they hold: an investor who wishes a holding period of eight years, for example, has many, equally attractive, ways to reach that goal. The third explanation of the term structure, the **segmentation or hedging hypothesis**, discards that assumption. Investors are assumed to select maturities to **hedge**, or match the maturities of, specific liabilities. For example, the manager of a pension fund might select maturities based on when money will be needed to pay retirement benefits. As a result, all maturities are not substitutes for one another since investors have preferences for specific maturities. In this view, each maturity is a separate market, that is, the market for bonds is "segmented" by maturity. Each maturity market has its own supply and demand and hence its own equilibrium interest rate. The yield curve is simply a presentation of many separate interest rate determinations on one graph.

segmentation or hedging hypothesis—a theory of the term structure focusing on investors' desire for specific maturity instruments to hedge their liabilities

hedge—to balance liabilities with assets of equal amount and maturity

According to the segmentation or hedging hypothesis, yield curves can have any shape.

Other Interest Rate Structures

In addition to their term structure, interest differ by the risk of the underlying security and by how (really, by whom) the interest earned will be taxed. As a result, we also talk of the "risk structure of interest rates," and the "tax structure of interest rates."

1. The Risk Structure of Interest Rates

An important component of interest rates is the premium for risk. Investors generally require higher returns to take on greater risk. Thus any element of a security which adds risk raises the interest rate on that instrument. Among the common risk-adding elements are:

- Default risk—the possibility that a borrower will be unable to live up to the loan agreement. Sometimes default is not critical to value, as when a borrower fails to deliver a document called for under the agreement. Usually, however, default is serious and involves late or missing payments, reducing the time value of the payment stream.

- Interest-rate risk—the possibility that interest rates will rise, reducing the value of securities. Investors who needed their cash back prior to a security's maturity date would have to sell it in the market and take a loss. Interest rate risk is particularly severe in long-maturity securities and motivates investors to prefer shorter-maturity instruments.

reinvestment risk—the risk that interest rates will fall, limiting reinvestment opportunities

- **Reinvestment risk**—the possibility that interest rates will be low at the time an investment matures leaving investors with poor reinvestment opportunities. This motivates investors to prefer longer-maturity instruments so they can "lock in" a rate of return. Note that interest-rate risk and reinvestment risk have opposite effects.

marketability risk—the risk that a security will be difficult, hence costly, to sell

- **Marketability risk**—the projected difficulty of selling a security. An investor might have to take a loss to sell a security with poor marketability.

call risk—the risk that a lender will retire a security prior to maturity, taking a good earning opportunity away from an investor

- **Call risk**—the possibility that the issuer might take the security away. Many securities have a call feature giving the issuer the option to terminate the borrowing agreement prior to maturity. While investors are compensated for giving up the security, the compensation normally is insufficient to prevent a loss in value. Companies are motivated to call their debt when interest rates have fallen and they can refinance at a lower rate of interest. Investors can therefore lose a relatively high-earning security at just the time when interest rates have fallen and reinvestment opportunities are poor.

FINANCE IN PRACTICE

GM is Pushed to the Brink of Default

The "economic crisis" and recession of 2008 had a severe impact on the automobile industry. As consumer confidence fell and people lost their jobs the demand for new automobiles plummeted. This was compounded by the contraction of the credit markets where the automobile manufacturers' financing arms suddenly found it difficult to raise money to lend car buyers. Auto dealerships, many of which had been around for decades, were forced to close their doors.

General Motors, for years the world's largest automaker, saw its sales plummet 23% in 2008. Fearing that GM might go out of business leading to even more job losses and economic decline, the U.S. and Canadian governments fashioned a joint rescue package and lent GM billions of dollars under the condition that GM restructure to significantly lower its costs by June 1, 2009.

Although the "bailout" funds kept GM afloat, the company continued to lose money, and its sales fell a further 30% in 2009. In April 2009, when it became clear that GM would not reach its government-mandated cost targets, CFO Ray Young announced that the company had decided to default on its debt by not making $1 billion of payments due on June 1st. GM's hope was that by threatening to default it would convince its creditors to swap their bonds for shares of stock. That didn't happen, and on June 1st GM filed for bankruptcy protection. Although GM's sales decline leveled off later in 2009, by the end of the year Toyota had surpassed GM as the world's largest automobile manufacturer.

Issuer	Taxed by			
	Federal	Issuing state	Other states	Locality
U.S. government	X			
State or local government			X	
Corporation	X	X	X	X

FIGURE 4.4
Who taxes what? While government bonds escape some taxes, income from corporate bonds is taxed by all levels of government.

2. The Tax Structure of Interest Rates

Securities are not all taxed in the same way. In particular, while income from federal government securities (such as U.S. Treasury bonds) is subject to federal taxes, it is not taxed by state and municipal authorities. Conversely, income from bonds issued by state and local governments (municipal bonds or "munis") is not taxed by the federal system and typically not taxed by the issuing state or locality. (See Figure 4.4)

Investors are ultimately interested in their final, or after-tax, returns and would prefer not to lose a portion of their interest earnings to taxes. They are attracted to investments that are taxed at low rates and thus increase the demand for tax-advantaged securities relative to those without tax preferences. In response, the prices of tax-advantaged securities rise and their pre-tax yields fall, while the reduced demand for fully taxed securities lowers their prices and raises their pre-tax yields.[8] The pressure on prices continues until the average investor (that is, the investor in the average tax bracket) finds no remaining yield benefit from tax-advantaged securities. At market equilibrium, therefore, pre-tax yields have adjusted so that after-tax yields for the average investor-taxpayer on all securities of comparable risk and maturity are the same.

Example

Calculating After-Tax Yields

Sandra Maglen lives in Maryland. She pays federal income taxes at a marginal rate of 28% and state taxes at a marginal rate of 7%. As she examines various investment alternatives, she discovers the following:

If she purchases a bond yielding 8% issued by a corporation, her income would be taxed by both state and federal authorities at a total rate of 28% + 7% = 35%. After taxes she would keep:

$$8\% - 35\% \ (8\%) = 8\% \ (1 - .35) = 8\% \ (.65) = \underline{5.20\%}$$

If she purchases a U.S. Treasury bond yielding 8%, her income would be taxed only by the federal authorities at a rate of 28%. After taxes she would keep:

$$8\% - 28\% \ (8\%) = 8\% \ (1 - .28) = 8\% \ (.72) = \underline{5.76\%}$$

---

[8] **Reminder and cross-reference:**   Recall that we began this chapter by pointing out that interest rates and present values move in opposite directions. On pages 86–87 we illustrated how changing interest rates alter present values by examining the worth of a potential investment evaluated at alternative rates. In this example, the direction of the effect is the opposite (changing prices alter interest rates) but the relationship is precisely the same.

If she purchases a bond yielding 8% issued by the state of Virginia (or any other state or local bond <u>not</u> issued in Maryland), her income would be taxed only by the State of Maryland at a rate of 7%. After taxes she would keep:

$$8\% - 7\% \ (8\%) = 8\% \ (1 - .07) = 8\% \ (.93) = \underline{7.44\%}$$

However, if she purchases a state of Maryland bond yielding 8%, her income would not be taxed at all. She would keep the full <u>8%</u>.

◼ Exchange Rate Systems

(foreign) exchange rate—the value of one currency in terms of another

foreign exchange risk—the possibility of variation in exchange rates which makes uncertain the value of assets, liabilities, cash flows, and income denominated in a foreign currency

There are more than 150 currencies in the world. Unfortunately, the **rate of exchange** among them is not stable. This creates problems for any business that operates across borders; while $100 might buy £65 today, the same $100 might only buy £62 tomorrow—or it might buy £67 tomorrow. As a result of this **foreign exchange risk,** the value of all business denominated in foreign currencies takes on an added degree of uncertainty.

Early foreign exchange was based on a "gold standard," with gold and other precious metals serving as the common international currency. To trade internationally one needed access to gold; therefore local markets in gold effectively determined exchange rates. While the price of gold varied somewhat from place to place, it did not vary dramatically but remained within a "band" reflecting the cost of transporting it.[9] This system worked as long as the volume of international trade was small and not in excess of the available supply of gold. It continued until the mid-1940s.

Toward the end of World War II, the (about to be) victorious western nations gathered in Bretton Woods, New Hampshire, to grapple with forecasts of a dramatically increased postwar volume of international transactions and the need to restore financial stability to a highly destabilized world. Out of that meeting came a new system for international currency relationships.[10] Dubbed the "Bretton Woods system," the plan called for the U.S. dollar to supplement the supply of gold as the standard for foreign exchange. As a result, world trade would not be limited by the availability of gold and international trade would be freed from physical money. The United States would stand ready to buy or sell gold at the fixed price of $35 per ounce, and each country would price its currency in terms of dollars. Anyone receiving dollars could exchange them for gold; in fact the dollar was "as good as gold!"

fixed exchange rate system—a system in which exchange rates are kept constant by government policy

The Bretton Woods system was a **fixed exchange rate system** since each participating currency had a fixed relationship to every other currency through the dollar. This achieved the sought-after stability among currencies, and international investment and trade grew dramatically after the war. Governments were encouraged to pursue fiscal and monetary policies consistent with a stable currency.

[9] **Elaboration:**   As long as the price of gold was not too far out of line in any one location, it did not pay for traders to take advantage of the price discrepancy, since the cost of transportation outweighed the profit from the price differential.

[10] **Elaboration:**   The Bretton Woods conference also created an infrastructure to support the new international financial system including the World Bank, to provide resources to developing countries, and the International Monetary Fund, to serve as a central bank to governments in need of additional reserve currency.

couraged to pursue fiscal and monetary policies consistent with a stable currency. Businesses could forecast that exchange rates would remain constant and that there would be no foreign exchange risk. Assets were insulated from devaluation and liabilities from increasing. Income and cash flow were not dependent on the variability of exchange rates.

Although the Bretton Woods system was appealing, it had its flaws. While it called for stable currency relationships, it could not repeal the underlying economic forces that lead currencies to grow or decline in value. Fundamentally, exchange rates reflect the supply of and demand for each currency in comparison to the others, due to transactions between domestic entities and foreigners. These flows are summarized periodically in the national accounting data of each country as the country's **balance of payments.** For fixed exchange rates to remain stable, each country's balance of payments must be in balance, and this is rarely the case.

A country's balance of payments reflects the desire of foreigners to acquire its currency for investment and to pay for the country's exports, balanced by the desire of domestic individuals to spend their currency on foreign investment and imports. If inflows and outflows are not in balance, there will be a surplus or deficit in the balance of payments. For example, if Venezuela consistently imports more than it exports, it will have a deficit in its balance of payments. The foreign currency earnings from its exports will not fully pay for its imports, and the Venezuelan central bank will have to spend its holdings of reserve currencies (such as U.S. dollars) to pay for the remainder.[11] Foreigners will accumulate increasing amounts of Venezuelan bolivars, but there will be little they can buy with them. The value of the bolivar will decline relative to other currencies.

At first, the Bretton Woods system was able to deal with these economic imbalances. The United States ran a strong balance-of-payments surplus and returned foreign currency to various countries through business investment and government aid programs. It was the weaker countries of the world that occasionally had to adjust the value of their currencies against the dollar, and, with so much economic power residing in the United States, the other countries had little choice but to go along with the system. By the mid-1960s, however, conditions had changed. Other countries, now economically stronger, became less willing to devalue their currencies. When they found they had no choice but to adjust exchange rates, the changes typically were large and late. The United States began to have sizable and continuing deficits in its balance of payments,[12] and its holdings of gold fell to levels deemed too low to back the domestic currency, much less the currencies of the western world. In 1971 the United States announced that it would no longer convert dollars to gold on request, and the Bretton Woods system was dead. By March 1973, most of the western nations permitted their currencies to adjust freely in the marketplace.

Today we have a mixture of various exchange rate systems in the world. In theory, most countries follow a **floating exchange rate system,** in which their currencies adjust in value on a continuous basis in the public foreign exchange mar-

balance of payments—the net difference between money inflows and outflows for a country during a period of time

floating exchange rate system—a system in which exchange rates are allowed to change freely with market conditions

---

[11] **Elaboration:** The country could also print more of its own money or borrow to cover its obligations (and would have to if its reserve currency balances were insufficient to cover the deficit) but these actions would eventually lead to the same result.

[12] **Observation:** This was due in part to the resurgence of other economies leading to a decline in U.S. exports and a dramatic increase in imports and in part to the added outflows necessary to fight the war in Vietnam.

managed (dirty) float—a system in which government influences a floating exchange rate system through central bank intervention in the currency markets

pegged float—a system in which a currency is fixed against another which itself is free to float against other currencies

kets. However, almost all countries attempt to influence the value of their currencies on occasion by having their central bank enter the markets to buy or sell in large quantities (the so-called **managed** or **dirty float**), thus changing the balance between supply and demand. Other countries tie or **peg** the value of their money to another currency, either because the other currency is quite stable or because it plays an important economic role in their own currency's value. In a particularly interesting development, in 1999 the European Community (EC) launched the euro, a common currency intended to replace the individual currencies of the member nations. Seventeen of the EC states now use the euro as their currency.

■■ Foreign Exchange Market Quotations

NET Present Value
Go to
http://ec.europa.eu/euro to learn more about the euro

Figure 4.5 is a sample of exchange rate quotations taken from *The Wall Street Journal*.[13] The table lists countries with which the U.S. conducts significant trade. After each country name is the name of its currency. The numbers across the table are the exchange rates, the price of that currency against the U.S. dollar. For some currencies, 1-, 3-, and 6-month forward rates are given as well. We will refer back to Figure 4.5 as we explore these concepts and illustrate the relationships among various exchange rates.

direct exchange rate—the number of units of domestic currency required to purchase one unit of a foreign currency

1. Direct Rates

The first data column of Figure 4.5 is **direct rates** (also called "American" rates), the number of U.S. dollars required to purchase one unit of each foreign currency.

Example

Direct Exchange Rates
On the right-hand side of Figure 4.5 locate the entry for the U.K. As of the date of these quotations, it takes $1.6024 to purchase one British pound. On the left-hand side is the entry for Thailand. As of the date of these quotations, it takes $.03340 to purchase one Thai baht.

2. Reciprocal Rates

reciprocal exchange rate—the number of units of a foreign currency required to purchase one unit of domestic currency

The second data column of Figure 4.5 contains **reciprocal rates** (also called "European" or "Continental" rates), the number of units of each foreign currency required to purchase one U.S. dollar.

Example

NET Present Value
www.bloomberg.com/markets/currencies has up-to-date information on foreign exchange rates

Reciprocal Exchange Rates
Locate the entries for the U.K. and Thailand in Figure 4.5. As of the date of these quotations, it takes £.6241 to purchase one U.S. dollar and ฿29.940 to purchase one U.S. dollar.

Reciprocal rates get their name because they are indeed the reciprocals of their corresponding direct rates.

---

[13] *The Wall Street Journal*, November 1, 2010, page C8.

Currencies

U.S.-dollar foreign-exchange rates in late New York trading on Friday

Country/currency	Fri in US$	Fri per US$	US$ vs, YTD chg (%)	Country/currency	Fri in US$	Fri per US$	US$ vs, YTD chg (%)
Americas				Vietnam dong	.00005131	19490	5.5
Argentina peso*	.2529	3.9541	4.0	**Europe**			
Brazil real	.5886	1.6989	-2.5	Czech Rep. koruna	.05655	17.684	-4.2
Canada dollar	.9803	1.0201	-3.0	Denmark krone	.1866	5.3591	3.1
1-mos forward	.9797	1.0207	-2.9	Euro area euro	1.3919	.7184	2.8
3-mos forward	.9781	1.0224	-2.7	Hungary forint	.005124	195.16	3.3
6-mos forward	.9757	1.0249	-2.5	Norway krone	.1708	5.8548	1.0
Chile peso	.002044	489.24	-3.6	Poland zloty	.3508	2.8506	-0.6
Colombia peso	.0005437	1839.25	-10.0	Russia ruble‡	.0324	30.845	1.8
Ecuador US dollar	1	1	unch	Sweden krona	.1497	6.6800	-6.7
Mexico peso*	.0810	12.3472	-5.6	Switzerland franc	1.0162	.9841	-5.0
Peru new sol	.3573	2.799	-3.1	1-mos forward	1.0165	.9838	-5.0
Uruguay peso†	.04980	20.08	2.8	3-mos forward	1.0169	.9834	-5.0
Venezuela b. fuerte	.232851	4.2946	100.0				-5.0
Asia-Pacific				Turkey lira**	.6972	1.4343	-1
Australian dollar	.9797			UK pound	1.6024	.6241	0.9
China yuan	.149			1-mos forward	1.6020	.6242	0.9
Hong Kong dollar	.12			3-mos forward	1.6011	.6246	0.9
India rupee	.02256			6-mos forward	1.5995	.6252	
Indonesia rupiah	.0001119						
Japan yen	.012427	80.47		Bahrain			unch
1-mos forward	.012430	80.45	-13.6	Egypt pound*	.1732	5.7747	5.3
3-mos forward	.012438	80.40	-13.6	Israel shekel	.2750	3.6364	-4.1
6-mos forward	.012453	80.30	-13.6	Jordan dinar	1.4129	.7078	unch
Malaysia ringgit	.3214	3.1114	-9.1	Kuwait dinar	3.5578	.2811	-2.1
New Zealand dollar	.7624	1.3116	-4.8	Lebanon pound	.0006662	1501.05	-0.1
Pakistan rupee	.01164	85.911	1.8	Saudi Arabia riyal	.2667	3.7495	unch
Philippines peso	.0233	42.900	-7.2	South Africa rand	.1428	7.0028	-5.5
Singapore dollar	.7726	1.2943		UAE dirham	.2723	3.6724	unch
South Korea won	.0008893	1124.48					
Taiwan dollar	.03267	30.609					
Thailand baht	.03340	29.940		SDR††	1.5718	.6362	-0.3

*Floating rate †Financial §Government rate ‡Russian Central Bank rate **Rebased as of Jan 1, 2005
††Special Drawing Rights (SDR); from the International Monetary Fund; based on exchange rates for
U.S., British and Japanese currencies.
Note: Based on trading among banks of $1 million and more, as quoted at 4 p.m. ET by Reuters.

Country and currency: this quote is the value of the dollar against the currency of the U.K., the pound.

in US$: it costs $1.6024 to buy one pound. This is a "direct rate."

per US$: it costs £.6241 to buy one dollar. This is a "reciprocal rate."

1-mos forward: banks are willing to commit to a rate of $1.6020 for an exchange to take place 1 month from now.

3-mos forward: banks are willing to commit to a rate of $1.6011 for an exchange to take place 3 months from now.

6-mos forward: banks are willing to commit to a rate of $1.5995 for an exchange to take place 6 months from now.

FIGURE 4.5
Through the Looking Glass: Exchange rate quotations. Each number is the price of a foreign currency versus the U.S. dollar.

Example

Relating Direct and Reciprocal Exchange Rates

The direct rate in the U.S. for the British pound is $1.6024 per pound. Taking the reciprocal of $1.6024 gives:

$$1/(\$1.6024 \text{ per pound}) = £.6241 \text{ per dollar}$$

which is the reciprocal rate. The direct rate in the U.S. for the Thai baht is $.03340 per baht. Taking the reciprocal of $.03340 gives:

$$1/(\$.03340 \text{ per baht}) = ฿29.940 \text{ per dollar}$$

which is the reciprocal rate.

Even though direct and reciprocal rates are substitutes for one another, it is common to use the number greater than one, rather than the fractional number, when quoting exchange rates. (There are some exceptions to this rule based on convenience or tradition.) Often the quotation does not specify whether the quote is the direct or reciprocal rate; it is up to the reader/listener to fill in the remainder of the relationship.

3. Cross Rates

cross rate—the price of one foreign currency in terms of another, calculated via their relationships to a third currency

Figure 4.5 gives us the price of currencies in terms of the U.S. dollar, but not the relationship of the non-dollar currencies to each other. However, it is easy to calculate these other exchange rates. Any two foreign currencies may be related to each other if we have the relationship, direct or reciprocal, between each of them and a third currency. The process is either to multiply or to divide the two rates we have to eliminate the third currency. When an exchange rate is calculated in this way, we identify it as a **cross rate.**

Examples

Calculating Cross Rates

The dollar-pound exchange rate is $1.6024 per pound. The baht-dollar exchange rate is ฿29.940 per dollar.

Question: What is the baht-pound cross rate?

Solution steps: Since the common currency (dollars) is in the numerator of the first rate (<u>dollars</u>/pound) and in the denominator of the second rate (baht/<u>dollar</u>), multiply to cancel out the dollars:

$$1.6024 \ \frac{\text{dollars}}{\text{pound}} \times 29.940 \ \frac{\text{baht}}{\text{dollar}} = 47.976 \ \frac{\text{baht}}{\text{pound}}$$

Answer: The cross rate is <u>฿47.976 per pound</u>.

The baht-dollar exchange rate is ฿29.940 per dollar. From Figure 4.5, the Swiss franc-dollar exchange rate is CHF0.9841 per dollar.

Question: What is the baht-franc cross rate?

Solution steps: Since the common currency (dollars) is in the denominator of both rates (baht/<u>dollar</u> and francs/<u>dollar</u>), divide to cancel out the dollars:

$$\frac{29.940 \ \frac{\text{baht}}{\text{dollar}}}{0.9841 \ \frac{\text{francs}}{\text{dollar}}} = 30.424 \ \frac{\text{baht}}{\text{franc}}$$

Answer: The cross rate is <u>฿30.424 per franc</u>.

NET Present Value
The three-letter codes for currencies are available at several sites such as www.xe.com/iso4217.php

The dollar-pound exchange rate is $1.6024 per pound. From Figure 4.5, the dollar-euro exchange rate is $1.3919 per euro.

Question: What is the euro-pound cross rate?

Solution steps: Since the common currency (dollars) is in the numerator of both rates (<u>dollars</u>/pound and <u>dollars</u>/euro), divide to cancel out the dollars:

$$\frac{1.6024 \ \frac{\text{dollars}}{\text{pound}}}{1.3919 \ \frac{\text{dollars}}{\text{euro}}} = 1.1512 \ \frac{\text{euro}}{\text{pound}}$$

Answer: The cross rate is <u>€1.1512 per pound</u>.

Spot and Forward Rates

spot (exchange) rate—an exchange rate available for the immediate trade of currencies

forward exchange contract—a contract binding the parties to a future trade of currencies on a specified date and at a specified exchange rate, the forward rate

forward (exchange) rate—an exchange rate for a contract to be entered into today (forward exchange contract) but with the trade of currencies to take place on a specified future date

Exchange rates for transactions today are called **spot rates.** Each rate we have looked at so far was a spot rate—$1.6024 per pound, ฿29.940 per dollar, CHF0.9841 per dollar, $1.3919 per euro. To use these rates we would have to be ready to exchange our money for the other currency right away.[14] But it is also possible to sign a foreign exchange agreement providing for the actual exchange of currency to take place some time in the future. Such agreements are called **forward exchange contracts** and the rates quoted today are **forward rates.**

There is an active market for forward contracts in the major currencies. Referring back to Figure 4.5, we can find 1-month, 3-month, and 6-month forward rates for the U.S. dollar vs. the Canadian dollar, Japanese yen, Swiss franc, and British pound. Since many export-import transactions specify delivery and payment in 1 or 3 or 6 months, quotes are published for these periods. However, contracts are available for interim periods as well. It is difficult to obtain forward contracts for periods much longer than 180 days as banks are normally unwilling to guarantee an exchange rate very far in advance.

Example

Forward Exchange Rates

In Figure 4.5, locate the entry for the U.K. It currently takes $1.6024 to purchase one pound at spot. Immediately below are the forward rate quotes: $1.6020 for a 1-month forward contract, $1.6011 for a 3-month forward contract, and $1.5995 for a 6-month forward contract.

Look at the second column of the U.K. quote in Figure 4.5. It now takes £.6241 to purchase one U.S. dollar at spot. Immediately below are the forward rate quotes: £.6242 for a 1-month forward contract, £.6246 for a 3-month forward contract, and £.6252 for a 6-month forward contract.

Notice that the dollar-pound forward rates are not equal to the spot rate. In this example the dollar-pound forward rates decrease systematically as the contract period lengthens, while the pound-dollar forward rates increase with time. More advanced courses examine the forces which determine the pattern of forward rates. For now two observations are useful. First, the spot and forward rates taken together form somewhat of a mini-term structure, the relationship of the exchange rate to the maturity of the forward contract. Second, it is common to describe the relationship between the forward and spot rates using the concepts of forward discount and forward premium.

---

[14] **Elaboration:**   Common banking practice is to allow two days, the "settlement period," from the time of agreement until the currency must be delivered to the bank.

forward discount—the condition when forward rates are less than the spot rate, also the amount of the difference

forward premium—the condition when forward rates are greater than the spot rate, also the amount of the difference

To say that one currency trades at a **forward discount** relative to another is to say that a forward contract is cheaper to purchase than a spot contract. Conversely, when a currency trades at a **forward premium** relative to another currency, a forward contract is more expensive to purchase than a spot contract. In the above example, the pound is trading at a forward discount to the dollar since the dollar-pound forward rates are less than the spot rate. It is cheaper to purchase forward pounds with dollars than to purchase pounds at spot. Yet at the same time, the dollar is trading at a forward premium to the pound since the pound-dollar forward rates are greater than the spot rate. It is more expensive to purchase forward dollars with pounds than to purchase dollars at spot.

Forward rates have the same reciprocal rate characteristic as spot rates. Therefore, in comparing two currencies, it will always be true that if currency A is trading at a forward discount to currency B, then currency B will trade at a forward premium to currency A. As one forward rate rises the reciprocal forward rate must decline, and vice-versa.

Forward discounts and premiums are generally quoted in the foreign exchange markets in percentage terms on a nominal annual basis using the formula:

$$Forward\ discount\ or\ premium = \frac{forward - spot}{spot} \times \frac{12}{months\ forward}$$

In this relationship, the first term is the rate of discount (if negative) or premium (if positive) for the contract period. The second term annualizes the rate using the nominal (multiplicative) calculation.

Examples

Calculating Forward Discounts and Premiums

From Figure 4.5, the dollar-pound spot rate is ($/£)1.6024 and the 1-month forward rate is ($/£)1.6020.

Question: What is the percentage forward discount?

Solution steps:

$$Forward\ discount = \frac{1.6020 - 1.6024}{1.6024} \times \frac{12}{1}$$

$$= -0.000250 \times 12 = -.0030 = -0.30\%$$

Answer: The pound is trading at a 1-month forward discount (note that the result is negative) to the dollar of <u>0.30%</u>.

From Figure 4.5, the 6-month forward rate is ($/£)1.5995.

Question: What is the percentage forward discount?

Solution steps:

$$Forward\ discount = \frac{1.5995 - 1.6024}{1.6024} \times \frac{12}{6}$$

$$= -0.00181 \times 2 = -.0036 = -0.36\%$$

Answer: The pound is trading at a 6-month forward discount (note that the result is negative) to the dollar of <u>0.36%</u>.

From Figure 4.5, the pound-dollar spot rate is (£/$).6241 and the 1-month forward rate is (£/$).6242.

Question: What is the percentage forward premium?

Solution steps:
$$\text{Forward premium} = \frac{.6242 - .6241}{.6241} \times \frac{12}{1}$$
$$= 0.00016 \times 12 = .0019 = 0.19\%$$

Answer: The dollar is trading at a 1-month forward premium (note that the result is positive) to the pound of <u>0.19%</u>.

From Figure 4.5, the 6-month forward rate is (£/$).6252.

Question: What is the percentage forward premium?

Solution steps:
$$\text{Forward premium} = \frac{.6252 - .6241}{.6241} \times \frac{12}{6}$$
$$= 0.00176 \times 2 = .0035 = 0.35\%$$

Answer: The dollar is trading at a 6-month forward premium (note that the result is positive) to the pound of <u>0.35%</u>.

■ Business Exposure to Exchange Rates

Foreign exchange risk affects businesses in three ways: transaction exposure, translation exposure, and economic exposure.

transaction exposure— exposure to foreign exchange losses on day-to-day transactions due to adverse exchange rate movements

Businesses that engage in foreign trade face **transaction exposure.** Such companies regularly enter into contracts for the purchase of materials and for the sale of their products and services. Often there is a time lag between the analysis and pricing of a contract and the date of receipt or payment of the foreign exchange. If the relevant exchange rate moves against the firm during that time, the firm will suffer a loss. In Chapter 15 we look at methods for protecting the firm from transaction exposure.

translation exposure— exposure to reduction of accounting income and values due to adverse exchange rate movements

Translation exposure affects the accounting statements of the multinational firm. The various accounts of the firm must be consolidated to produce annual financial statements; amounts measured in foreign currencies must be translated to the firm's home currency for this purpose. FASB Statement No. 52, Foreign Currency Translation, requires that all balance sheet amounts denominated in a foreign currency be translated to home currency at the exchange rate prevailing on the statement date. This makes the home-currency values of foreign accounts subject to change with exchange rates. In addition, the changes to equity due to asset and liability revaluation must pass through the income statement as profit or loss. Other income statement items must be translated at the weighted-average exchange rate for the accounting period. A significant shift in exchange rates could eliminate a large part, or perhaps all, of a firm's reported profits. And while accounting profits are not cash flows and do not directly represent financial value, they typically give stakeholders important information as to the health and possible future direction of the firm. Accounting losses due to exchange rate movements could well accompany or precede real financial losses.

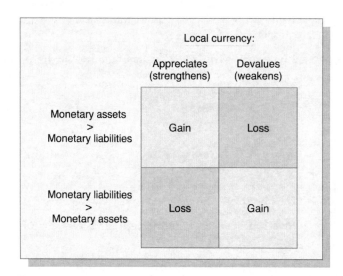

Local currency:

	Appreciates (strengthens)	Devalues (weakens)
Monetary assets > Monetary liabilities	Gain	Loss
Monetary liabilities > Monetary assets	Loss	Gain

FIGURE 4.6
Economic exposure. A company's risk from changing exchange rates depends on the balance of its monetary assets and liabilities.

economic exposure— exposure to a reduction in monetary asset values, an increase in monetary liabilities, or a reduction in cash flow due to adverse exchange rate movements

Firms are also subject to **economic exposure**, a term typically used to describe the risk of loss in the money value of assets, liabilities, and cash flows. A firm's assets and liabilities may be classified as monetary or nonmonetary.[15] If a monetary asset or liability is denominated in foreign currency, such as local accounts receivable and payable, then it is exposed to foreign exchange risk. As measured in a company's home currency, foreign-denominated monetary assets lose value when the foreign currency devalues (weakens), while foreign-denominated monetary liabilities become more costly if the foreign currency appreciates (strengthens). Nonmonetary assets and liabilities on the other hand, for example plant or some liabilities of service, are not denominated in money terms and are somewhat insulated from exchange-rate movements. Figure 4.6 shows that the effect on a firm of a shift in the exchange rate depends on the relationship of its monetary assets and liabilities. A firm anticipating a devaluation of the local currency would be wise to have many monetary liabilities and few monetary assets while a firm expecting the local currency to appreciate should follow the reverse strategy, insuring that its monetary assets exceed monetary liabilities.

All of a firm's future cash flows denominated in a foreign currency are likewise subject to loss of value. Every estimate of future flows, for whatever purpose, must be examined for the risk of foreign exchange loss. We will look at this issue in more depth when we study financial decision making later in the book.

*S*andra Maglen walked into the conference room and took a seat. Since the meeting that morning she had reread the sections in one of her textbooks dealing with interest rates and exchange rates. Shortly, the room filled up and the team began discussing the firm's rising cost of borrowing. Sandra waited for a lull in the conversation before she spoke.

---

[15] **Elaboration and tip:**   A monetary asset (such as cash) is defined by its money value, while a nonmonetary asset (for example, plant and equipment) is not. See your accounting textbook for a further review if you find it useful.

"The Fisher model identifies that interest rates consist of three components: pure, inflation, and risk. The pure rate of interest and investors' forecasts of inflation depend on the overall economy and have nothing to do with our company. That leaves risk. If the analysts at the rating agencies are concerned about our securities, they must be seeing an increased level of risk." Sandra then outlined several risks faced by her firm including the risks from foreign exchange exposure: transaction, translation, and economic.

The discussion quickly turned to what information the analysts might be looking at and to what company activities, if any, might be causing the increased risk perception. The team decided to work closely with the rating agencies to identify to management the most significant risk factors.

As the meeting came to a close, Sandra thought again about her former professor. She made herself a promise to write a letter that afternoon to share her experiences and to renew a relationship.

Summary of Key Points

■ **Demonstrate the relationships between interest rates and present value and between present value and time to cash flow.**   As an important component of present value calculations, interest rates help determine the financial worth of all decisions. Since higher interest rates increase the difference between present and future values, the worth of a forecasted future benefit declines as interest rates rise, and vice-versa. Present values become more volatile as the time to receiving a cash flow increases. When interest rates change, the present value of cash flows to be received far in the future changes by more than the present value of near-term cash flows.

■ **Subdivide any interest rate into its components.** The Fisher model decomposes interest rates into a pure rate, inflation premium, and risk premium. By examining each component, we obtain insight into various rates and learn why rates differ among investments and countries. We can also identify the risk-free rate of interest and the real rate of interest and relate them to the nominal rates we observe.

■ **Explain why interest rates differ by maturity of obligation.**   The term structure of interest rates is the relationship of rates to the maturity of securities. Three theories, each of which seems to be somewhat true, are offered to explain it. Expectations theory argues that the term structure reflects expectations of future interest rates, primarily due to forecasts of inflation. Liquidity preference theory points out that investors' liquidity decreases with maturity, making longer-term securities inherently more risky and requiring higher rates of return. The hedging/seg-

mentation theory argues that each maturity is a separate market and should be considered independent of the others.

■ **Understand how risks and taxes impact interest rates.**   Differences in yields often come from risk differences, since investors demand higher returns to take risks. Default risk is the probability of nonpayment. Interest-rate risk is the possibility of decline in value should interest rates rise. Reinvestment risk is the danger of being unable to continue to earn high rates should rates fall. Marketability risk is the likelihood that it will be costly to sell a security. Call risk is the chance that a security will be redeemed by its issuer prior to maturity. Differences in yields also come from tax differences. Although corporate bonds are taxed by all levels of government, the federal government does not tax municipal securities, and vice-versa. Investors ultimately receive returns after their personal taxes and take their personal tax rates into account when pricing securities.

■ **Describe fixed and floating exchange rate systems and their variations.**   The world has passed through several exchange-rate eras. Prior to World War II, an informal gold standard prevailed. This was expanded and formalized at Bretton Woods, and for over 25 years, exchange rates were fixed. But underlying economic forces ultimately made the Bretton Woods system unworkable, and it was scrapped in the early 1970s. Today most exchange rates are free to float with economic conditions, but governments often intervene in the currency markets. Common currencies, such as the Euro, and currencies pegged to stronger currencies are ways that countries are attempting to regain some of the stability of fixed rates in a floating-rate environment.

- ■■ **Express exchange rates as direct, reciprocal, and cross rates.** Exchange rates may be direct—dollars per unit of foreign currency; reciprocal—foreign currency per dollar; or cross—two currencies related via a third.

- ■■ **Define the meaning of spot and forward rates.** Spot rates are exchange rates for the immediate trade of currencies. Forward rates are for contracts to be signed today for the future trade of currencies. In general, forward rates are not equal to spot rates but exhibit a forward discount (lower than spot) or premium (greater than spot).

- ■■ **Identify how changes in exchange rates affect businesses dealing in multiple currencies.** Any firm that deals in more than its domestic currency faces foreign exchange risk through transaction exposure, translation exposure, and economic exposure. As exchange rates vary they change the value of the firm's assets, liabilities, and equity, as well as its income and cash-flow stream.

Questions

1. Why do securities prices rise when interest rates fall, and vice-versa?

2. What happens to a company's ability to raise funds when interest rates rise? when interest rates fall?

3. Why does the price of a a 30-year maturity bond vary more than the price of a 1-year maturity bond?

4. Identify the terms of the Fisher equation. What factors cause each term to take on its value?

5. Identify the following concepts:
   a. Nominal rate of interest
   b. Pure rate of interest
   c. Real rate of interest
   d. Risk-free rate of interest

6. Can you think of any examples in which you or some company has changed its behavior in response to inflation?

7. Why do American economists typically base the term structure of interest rates on U.S. Treasury securities?

8. Explain the term structure of interest rates using each of the three theories of term structure.

9. Why are interest-rate risk and reinvestment risk often considered opposite sides of a coin?

10. Assume the average investor is in the 28% marginal federal income tax bracket. If you were in the 15% tax bracket, would you prefer to invest in U.S. or state bonds? What if you were in the 31% tax bracket?

11. How could investors who own homes in more than one state use the concepts of this chapter to select which home should be their legal residence?

12. What was the Bretton Woods system? What were its strong points? Why did it ultimately break down?

13. Distinguish between a fixed exchange rate system and a floating exchange rate system.

14. What is meant by the terms:
    a. Managed float?
    b. Pegged float?
    c. Joint float?

15. What is the relationship between direct and reciprocal exchange rates?

16. What is a forward rate? Why might a business person be interested in it?

17. What pattern of forward rates characterizes a currency trading at
    a. A forward discount?
    b. A forward premium?

18. Identify:
    a. Transaction exposure
    b. Translation exposure
    c. Economic exposure

    What events might trigger each of these business risks?

Problems

1. **(Interest rates and present value)** Calculate the present value of $250,000 to be received 10 years from now at an interest rate of:
   a. 5%   c. 15%
   b. 10%   d. 20%

2. **(Interest rates and present value)** An investment promises to pay you $50,000 per year at the end of each the next 15 years. What is this investment worth to you today if you require a rate of return of:
   a. 8%?   c. 14%?
   b. 11%?   d. 17%?

3. **(Present value and time)** An investment promises to return $20,000 in 1 year while a second investment promises to return $186,350 in 30 years. Investors require an 8% rate of return from both investments.
   a. What is the present value of each investment?
   b. What happens to the present value of each investment if the required rate of return rises to 10%?
   c. What happens to the present value of each investment if the required rate of return falls to 6%?
   d. Why do the present values change this way?

4. **(Present value and time)** You are considering investing in one of two alternatives. The first promises to return $15,000 in 2 years while the second promises to return $203,287 in 25 years. Investors require a 12% rate of return from both investments.

   a. What is the present value of each investment?
   b. If the required rate of return falls to 10%, how will you gain?
   c. If the required rate of return rises to 14%, how much will you lose?
   d. Why do the present values change this way?

5. **(Fisher model)** The pure rate of interest is 3%, and investors demand an inflation premium of 4%. What interest rate should they demand if they require a risk premium of:

   a. 0%?   c. 5%?
   b. 2%?   d. 8%?

6. **(Fisher model)** The pure rate of interest is 3.5%, and investors require a 4% risk premium of a certain investment. What interest rate should they demand if they require an inflation premium of:

   a. 3%?   c. 9%?
   b. 6%?   d. 15%?

7. **(Using the Fisher model)** The rate of interest available on a certain security is 14%. If the pure rate of interest is 3.25%, what risk premium do investors demand if they require an inflation premium of:

   a. 2%?   c. 6%?
   b. 4%?   d. 8%?

8. **(Using the Fisher model)** The rate of interest available on a certain security is 17%. If the pure rate of interest is 3.75%, what inflation premium do investors require if they require a risk premium of:

   a. 0%?   c. 8%?
   b. 3%?   d. 11%?

9. **(Components of the interest rate)** The pure rate of interest is 3%, and investors require an inflation premium of 6% and a risk premium of 4% to invest in a certain security. What is the:

   a. Nominal rate of interest on the security?
   b. Real rate of interest on the security?
   c. Risk-free rate of interest on securities of this maturity?

10. **(Components of the interest rate)** The pure rate of interest is 3.5%, and investors require an inflation premium of 3% and a risk premium of 6% to invest in a certain security. What is the:

    a. Nominal rate of interest on the security?
    b. Real rate of interest on the security?
    c. Risk-free rate of interest on securities of this maturity?

11. **(International interest rates)** The interest rate on a ten-year U.S. Treasury bond is 7%, and the rate on a ten-year U.K. gilt (the British equivalent of a treasury bond) is 12%. If the pure rate of interest is 3.75% in each country, what is the difference in anticipated ten-year inflation rates between the U.S. and the U.K.?

12. **(International interest rates)** The expected return on a share of ExxonMobil stock in the U.S. is 17% while the rate of return expected on a share of Royal Dutch Shell stock in the Netherlands is 15%. If the pure rate of return is 3% in each country and the required risk premium is 8% for each company's stock, find the anticipated long-term inflation rate in each country.

13. **(After-tax yields)** A corporate bond is currently yielding 9%. What after-tax yield would you receive if you are in the:

    a. 15% federal tax bracket and 4% state tax bracket?
    b. 28% federal tax bracket and 6% state tax bracket?
    c. 33% federal tax bracket and 5% state tax bracket?
    d. 36% federal tax bracket but you live in state without an income tax?

14. **(After-tax yields)** A State of California bond is currently yielding 5.50%. What after-tax yield would you receive if you are in the:

    a. 28% federal tax bracket and, as a California resident, the 7% state tax bracket?
    b. 36% federal tax bracket and, as a New York resident, the 6% state tax bracket?
    c. 25% federal tax bracket and, as a Colorado resident, the 3% state tax bracket?
    d. 33% federal tax bracket and, as a Florida resident, you pay no state income tax?

15. **(After-tax yields)** Your income puts you in the 28% federal tax bracket, and as resident of Illinois, in the 4% state tax bracket. What after-tax yield would you receive on:

    a. An ExxonMobil Corporation bond yielding 10%?
    b. A U.S. Treasury bond yielding 5%?
    c. A State of New Jersey bond yielding 4%?
    d. A State of Illinois bond yielding 4%?

16. **(After-tax yields)** Your income puts you in the 33% federal tax bracket, and as resident of Kentucky, in the 3% state tax bracket. What after-tax yield would you receive on:

    a. A Bank of America Corporation bond yielding 9%?
    b. A U.S. Treasury bond yielding 6%?
    c. A State of Kentucky bond yielding 3.5%?
    d. A State of Oregon bond yielding 3.5%?

17. **(Reciprocal rates)** Find the reciprocal rate between the U.S. dollar and the Swiss franc (CHF) if the direct rate is:

a. $0.5902/CHF   c. $0.6200/CHF
b. $0.6010/CHF   d. $0.6475/CHF

18. (**Reciprocal rates**) Find the direct rate between the U.S. dollar and the euro if the reciprocal rate is:

a. EUR1.20/$ c. EUR1.04/$
b. EUR1.12/$ d. EUR0.96/$

19. (**Cross rates**) Find the cross rates between the Japanese yen, now trading at ¥132.20 per U.S. dollar, and:

a. The Bahrain dinar, now at $2.6525 per BHD.
b. The Canadian dollar, now at CAD0.6263 per U.S. dollar.
c. The South African rand, now at ZAR0.0883 per U.S. dollar.
d. The Peruvian new sol, now at $3.4778 per PEN.

20. (**Cross rates**) Find the cross rate between the euro, now trading at EUR1.1000 per U.S. dollar and:

a. The Hong Kong dollar, now trading at HKD7.7984 per U.S. dollar.
b. The British pound, now trading at $1.4490 per GBP.

c. The Thai baht, now trading at $0.02274 per THB.
d. The Kuwait dinar, now at KWD0.3071 per U.S. dollar.

21. (**Forward discount or premium**) Calculate the forward premium for the U.S. dollar priced in Swiss francs if the spot rate is CHF1.6543 per dollar and the forward rates are:

a. 30-day forward rate: CHF1.6549/$
b. 60-day forward rate: CHF1.6561/$
c. 90-day forward rate: CHF1.6585/$
d. 180-day forward rate: CHF1.6623/$

22. (**Forward discount or premium**) Calculate the forward discount for the Canadian dollar priced in U.S. dollars if the spot rate is USD0.6263 per Canadian dollar and the forward rates are:

a. 30-day forward rate: USD0.6258/CAD
b. 60-day forward rate: USD0.6248/CAD
c. 90-day forward rate: USD0.6233/CAD
d. 180-day forward rate: USD0.6207/CAD

PART II
RAISING
MONEY

In Part II we look at the process of raising money: how much a firm needs, in what forms it comes, and where to get it.

Chapter 5 looks at the process of financial planning and budgeting. Through this process, financial managers can estimate how much money their firm needs in the coming time period and why. After introducing specific item forecasting, we explore the percentage-of-sales method through an extended example. We identify how much money can come from internal sources and how much must be raised externally. Then we examine the impact of different external financing sources on the firm's balance sheet.

Chapter 6 describes the sources of financing available to the firm: short-term, intermediate-term, and long-term debt; and preferred and common equity.

Chapter 7 introduces the financial markets and the institutions that operate within them. We discuss the roles of these markets including how new securities are brought to market and traded. We also discuss how security prices are measured and how investors interpret security price behavior.

CHAPTER 5
FINANCIAL
PLANNING

*R*ichard Paulson left the vice president's office with a puzzled look on his face. He had been asked to prepare an analysis of how much financing his firm, the Jefferson Company, would need to raise in the financial markets in the coming year. He was to present his conclusions at a meeting of the executive committee in two weeks' time.

At first Richard thought the answer was obvious—the company would need enough money to pay for the construction of a new plant and the purchase of equipment that had been ordered for delivery in the coming year. But the more he thought about it, the more uncertain he became. There were other things the company had to pay for: labor, materials, operating costs, and so on. The Jefferson Company would surely need additional money to pay for those items. On the other hand, the company was expected to earn profits next year; some of this money ought to be available to help cover the firm's costs. Conceivably, not all of the firm's funding needs would have to come from outside sources. But Richard was sure this was only a part of the story. Perhaps there were other money flows he was overlooking.

As he returned to his desk, one thing was clear in Richard's mind. He would need a systematic way to organize the firm's resources and needs if he were to determine accurately the amount of financing his company required.

Few business firms are precisely self-sufficient, generating exactly as much cash as they need to spend. Many companies, especially those that are young and growing, need to acquire assets faster than they can generate the cash to pay for them. These businesses go to the financial markets to raise the additional funds they require. Other companies—especially older, more mature firms—find they have become "**cash cows**," with little or no need for outside financing.

cash cow—a firm that regularly generates more cash than it needs for operations and growth

To know which type of company the Jefferson Company is, Richard will have to study the firm's growth rate as well as its economic and financial structure. In this chapter we will look at techniques Richard can use to help his company plan for its future financial needs.[1]

Key Points You Should Learn from This Chapter

After reading this chapter you should be able to:

■ Describe the functions and limitations of planning and budgeting, including financial planning.

■ Recognize when specific-item forecasting is an appropriate financial planning technique.

■ Identify financial statement accounts that relate to sales and establish those relationships.

■ Use the percentage-of-sales technique to project a firm's financial statements.

■ Interpret pro-forma financial statements.

[1] **Observation:** The same concepts also apply to individuals. When you are young, you typically need to buy more assets than you can self-finance, and so you borrow. As you get older, your income rises but your need for assets declines until, eventually, you can repay your debts and accumulate money for your later years. As you read this chapter, you might find it interesting to apply the planning techniques that we discuss to your personal financial situation and begin a financial plan for yourself.

Introductory Concepts—The Role of Planning

All successful businesses plan for the future. Without effective planning, a firm drifts from day to day with no direction and a very low probability of survival. Planning significantly increases a firm's chances of success.

1. Planning

Planning begins with a corporate mission statement, a broad statement of purpose intended to underlie all the firm's activities. Mission statements frequently include beliefs about ethics, quality, the worth of people, and other fundamental convictions to guide all personal interactions and decision making. Without a clear and well-defined statement of mission and beliefs, a firm's employees are left to decide for themselves what actions are consistent with the interests and intentions of the firm. They are forced to base decisions on their own or others' subjective impressions of managements' philosophy or to give up trying to understand the firm's intentions and resign themselves to doing whatever seems to work. They very often end up working at cross purposes relative to others who make differing interpretations of the firm's mission.

The second step in planning is to focus on the firm's customers and other stakeholders: to identify them and to understand their expectations for the products and services they receive. Remember that a critical day-to-day goal of any firm is to exceed customer expectations. The firm cannot do this if it does not know who its customers are and what they want.

Once an organization has identified its goals and has learned from its customers what it takes to exceed their expectations, it devises a strategy for achieving them. To be effective, the strategy must place the firm in alignment—that is, consistent—with its internal culture and strengths and also with its environment. Next, the company develops operating plans consistent with its strategy and designed to move the firm toward its objectives. As with all aspects of the firm, strategies and plans must be continuously revised and improved as new information becomes available and as the firm and its environment change.

Traditionally, planning has been seen as the first, and most important, job of the manager.[2] Planning helps the organization establish its goals and identify the role of each organizational unit in achieving them. It sets activities in motion at the right time and in the right scale. It identifies the individuals within the organization who will do each task. It establishes benchmarks against which to test results. It enforces an objective rationality on the activities of the firm.

2. Budgeting

budget—a time-oriented statement of the financial resources allocated to carry out an organization's activities

A key tool of the planning process is the **budget,** the translation of the organization's plan into its dollar impacts. The common denominator of money forces the plan to be consistent with the accounting system and encourages managers to focus efforts on maximizing financial value. Budgets divide the firm's plan into time

---

[2] **Elaboration:** The other traditional roles of the manager have been organizing (establishing the structure of the organization, delegating and coordinating work, dealing with internal conflict), leading (providing motivation and reward, developing employees), and controlling (testing actual results against budgets, auditing performance, making changes).

units, permitting their use as performance standards. Managers use budgets to guide their planning process, to allocate resources, and to test performance against the plan. Deviation from budget is often taken as a signal that something is wrong and that corrective action is necessary.

As companies adopt modern management practices, emphasizing customer-focused quality, planning continues to be a necessary activity but the planning process tends to change. It becomes less of a top-down activity—a set of instructions from the boss—and more of a team-oriented one. Organization members at all levels participate earlier and more fully than they did in the past, as managers attempt to take advantage of the knowledge of those near the "bottom of the traditional organization chart."

Although necessary for managing an organization, budgets have long been recognized as having some unintended, and often damaging, side-effects. Individuals may be penalized for not making their budgets, even though the shortfall is due to events or conditions over which they have no control. Above-average performers often achieve their budget goals with ease and then produce no more. They fear they will be criticized as "rate-busters" by their peers or will be forced to achieve a higher budget next year. Below-average performers may produce poor-quality output as they rush or cheat to achieve the targets in their budgets. When compensation is tied to performance against budget, organizational members often become competitive instead of cooperative, failing to assist each other in reaching the firm's goals or even interfering with each others' efforts.

Recently, increased understanding of quality-management concepts has called attention to another type of problem with budgets, which only a few managers were fully aware of in the past. Budgets can lead managers to overreact to apparent changes in the environment. Some deviation from budget is inevitable: there is variation in the world, and it is impossible to predict the future with certainty. As a result, the firm will rarely, if ever, perform exactly on budget, so it is wrong for management to intervene in response to every variation.

An important part of managing is to separate special causes of variation from common causes of variation. Common causes produce problems that recur many times, for example, untrained workers who perform poorly day after day. Management should work on common causes of variation, studying them and removing them (in this case, by developing and using appropriate training).

Special causes, on the other hand, are one-time events which will not recur on a regular basis—for example, normally high-performing workers who do a poor job on a specific day when they are ill. Special causes deserve unique responses (in this case, perhaps, encouraging sick workers to go home for the day). There is no benefit to changing the firm in response to something that will not happen regularly or perhaps ever again. A management that is overly concerned with budgets as performance targets is susceptible to **tampering,** making changes in processes and systems in response to special causes. Such changes will tend to make the firm's performance worse, not better.

tampering—modifying a system in response to special causes of variation, further destabilizing the system's performance

3. Financial Planning

Financial planning is an important component of the firm's overall planning effort. To be effective in carrying out its operating plans, the firm must obtain and deploy financial resources as needed. Good financial planning permits the finance function to provide the appropriate money resources to the rest of the firm.

Tasks of financial planning Financial planning is designed to accomplish six tasks: (1) make assumptions explicit and shared, (2) identify actions consistent with health, (3) identify needed financial resources, (4) provide guidelines for external financing, (5) be a benchmark for results, and (6) assist in communicating with stakeholders.

1. *Make assumptions explicit and shared.* Financial planning forces assumptions about the firm's financial future to be made explicit and shared throughout the company. Arranging for wide participation in developing the plan improves its quality by separating realistic assumptions from unrealistic ones. It also contributes to a shared assessment of the firm's prospects and the steps necessary to achieve success; from a shared assessment, organization members can derive a shared commitment toward achieving the firm's goals.

2. *Identify healthy actions.* Financial planning identifies company actions that are consistent with financial health, and vice-versa. By locating courses of action that have a high probability of leading to financial success, financial planning provides important input to management's choices. By identifying impending financial problems, and often nonfinancial problems as well, it permits management to address issues early, before they have a serious effect on the firm. In addition, management can develop contingency plans to handle alternative economic scenarios.

3. *Identify financial resources.* Financial planning identifies the financial resources required for the firm to carry out its plans. In particular it identifies: (a) how much money the firm will need, (b) whether the money can be generated internally or will have to come from sources external to the firm, and (c) the timing of the firm's needs.

4. *Guide financing choices.* Financial planning provides guidelines in the choice of external funding sources. If the firm requires outside money, it might have the luxury of choosing from a variety of available sources. Financial planning generates some of the data necessary to make those choices.

5. *Benchmark results.* Financial planning serves as a benchmark against which to compare the firm's actual results. Of course, it is unrealistic to expect that actual performance will agree perfectly with the financial plan—too many unpredictable things happen. However, deviations from the forecast provide new information to help management understand the forces acting on the firm and to improve the planning process.

6. *Communicate with stakeholders.* Financial planning helps the firm communicate with its stakeholders, who must be partners in achieving the firm's goals.

NET Present Value
Among the organizations that provide financial planning services to businesses is SAS Institute, Inc. at
www.sas.com/solutions/financial/fms/index.html

Parts of the financial plan The financial plan consists of several parts, including (1) the long-run financial plan, (2) the capital budget, and (3) the operating or cash budget.

1. *The long-run financial plan:* This is a look at the firm's financial needs over the next several years. Five years is a commonly used planning horizon. The long-

"The animals are always the first to know."

run financial plan is designed to identify major financial trends the firm will face and permit an early start at large-scale, long-term financing.

2. *The capital budget:* This is an analysis of available long-term investment opportunities, testing each to see if it adds financial value to the firm.

3. *The operating or cash budget:* This is a short-run, more detailed look at the firm's money needs, usually over the next year. It is normally done on a monthly basis, although a shorter period (weekly or daily) might be appropriate if the insights from greater detail outweigh the costs of producing the more extensive plan.

pro-forma financial statement—a financial statement that projects a firm's condition or operating results into the future

Pro-forma financial statements A primary device used in financial planning is the preparation of **pro-forma financial statements.** These projected statements give management insight into many of the "what-if" questions they need to explore. They show what the firm would look like under each of the economic and competitive scenarios forecasted. They permit management to see the results of different decisions it might make. With the arrival of personal computers and spreadsheet programs, it is easier than ever to generate pro-forma statements.

Specific-Item Forecasting

specific-item forecasting—a forecasting technique in which each account on a firm's financial statements is projected without reference to the other accounts

One way to forecast financial variables is to project each financial statement account independent of the others. This approach is called **specific-item forecasting.** Each account is studied individually to determine the factors that produce its value. A relationship is then derived relating the account to its causal factors.

Example | **Establishing a Forecasting Relationship**

Luz Iluminata has been asked to forecast the cost of lighting a building. Looking at past records, she discovers that lighting costs consist of: (1) the cost of electricity, (2) the cost of light bulbs, and (3) the cost of replacing blown-out bulbs. In turn, these costs depend upon the number of bulbs in use; the life of each bulb; the power consumption of each bulb; and the prices of electricity, light bulbs, and maintenance services. Luz combines her findings into a formula relating lighting cost to the causal variables.

Specific-item forecasting is particularly appropriate for a firm whose financial statement accounts are not closely related to one another.

Example

Deciding to Use Specific-Item Forecasting

Helen Leonia runs a real-estate company that owns and rents space in a number of office buildings. As she examines the accounts on her income statement, she discovers:

Line Item	Depends on:
Rental revenue	Occupancy rate
Depreciation	Historical cost, GAAP rules
Maintenance	Level of service, age of buildings
Repairs	Type of tenant, weather
Salaries	Needs of management
Interest	Debt level, interest rates
Taxes	Net income, tax law

Helen concludes that specific-item forecasting is appropriate for her income statement since the accounts do not appear to be related to one another.

The advantage of specific-item forecasting is its flexibility. We can search for the relationship that best explains each variable we wish to forecast. The disadvantage is that we ignore relationships among the variables that, if taken into account, might improve our forecasting accuracy.

Forecasts That Relate to Sales

In Chapter 2 we saw that many financial ratios contain sales in their calculation. This is because the value of so many accounts depends on sales (and vice-versa). We can take advantage of this observation to improve our financial statement forecasting. If we believe that an account relates to sales, then it makes sense to study that relationship and incorporate it into our projections. By doing so we increase the internal consistency of our forecasts and hence the likelihood that they will be good predictors of the future.

Example

Accounts That Relate to Sales

Whenever the Washington Company makes a sale, it makes two related accounting entries. The first debits "cash" or "accounts receivable" and credits "sales" to record revenue. The second debits "cost of goods sold" and credits "inventory" to record expense. As a result, the balances of the cash, accounts receivable, inventory, and cost of goods sold accounts change whenever sales changes. They are related to sales.

While we might consider relating accounts to some other variable, none works as well as sales. Companies are in business to deliver products and services to their customers; sales demand is the outside force to which the firm must respond. A firm that faces high demand is justified in spending to acquire resources to produce additional products and services. A firm with declining demand is best advised to limit its spending on existing activities, or costs will exceed revenue and the firm will lose money. Rather, it must refocus its attention to identifying and meeting changing customer needs. To survive and prosper, the company must match its resources and commitments to the demand from its customers.

Of course, not everything relates to sales. Some accounts relate to other causal factors. For example, interest expense depends on the amount of money a firm has borrowed and the interest rate it must pay, neither of which will change automatically as sales changes. Other accounts, such as accumulated depreciation, depend primarily on history and accounting rules. Still others vary only if management chooses to change them—for example, bonds payable or common stock. We must be careful not to find connections to sales that do not exist.

For a forecast based on sales to be useful, we must: (1) start with a good sales forecast, (2) correctly identify the accounts that relate to sales, and (3) accurately establish the relationship of those accounts to sales.

1. Start with a Good Sales Forecast

Since so many accounts relate to sales, a good independent sales forecast is critical. A small error in the sales forecast can easily be magnified into a large error in the firm's pro-forma statements.

2. Identify Accounts That Relate to Sales

To produce a forecast containing relationships to sales, we must separate the firm's accounts into two broad categories: those that relate to sales and those that do not.

It is useful to ask three questions to help make this separation. First, *why is the firm spending this particular amount of money?* If the money is going to purchase a resource that is intimately associated with the production or sales process, and that needs to be acquired only if production or sales takes place, this amount relates to sales.

Example | **Identifying an Account as Related to Sales**

Adams Company uses a just-in-time inventory system, buying production materials only when it is ready to produce and sell. It concludes that the cost of materials is closely related to sales.

On the other hand, if the money is going for a resource not associated with the production or sales process, that would be acquired regardless of the firm's level of sales, this amount does not relate to sales.

Example | **Identifying an Account as Not Related to Sales**

Adams Company identifies the cost of power for heat and light in their office building as not related to sales since the amount they spend varies with the weather and utility rates and not with their volume of business.

Second, *what is the time horizon of the account?* Some assets, a plant for example, take time to acquire or to sell. In the short-run,[3] some costs are fixed simply because the firm cannot change them fast enough, even though it might wish to do so. In the long-run, by definition, no costs are fixed.

Example

Identifying an Account as Not Related to Sales Due to Time Horizon
One of Adams Company's product lines has become obsolete. Sales go to zero immediately, but it will take the firm two years to dispose of related machinery. The book value of this machinery will not fully respond to sales until two years have passed.

Third, *how will management respond to changes in sales?* If management views a change in sales as a temporary phenomenon, it will likely respond with temporary or variable resources. However, if it perceives a change in sales as permanent, management might commit to additional fixed resources.

Example

How a Management Decision Can Determine if a Cost Is Related to Sales
Adams Company is experiencing a 20% increase in orders this month, requiring additional usage of production machinery. Management could lease time on another firm's machinery, making the cost vary with sales. Alternatively, management could purchase new machinery, fixing the new cost independent of sales. Whether the additional cost is variable or fixed will depend on the choice management makes.

In Chapter 2 we saw that income statement accounts that change with sales are identified as *variable costs;* examples are: direct production labor, materials used in production, and commissions and bonuses based on sales. Income statement accounts that do *not* change with sales—such as production overhead, the base level of administrative salaries, and interest costs—are identified as *fixed costs.*[4]

spontaneous account—a balance sheet account whose value changes with sales without the need for specific management action

There is a comparable classification for the balance sheet. Accounts on the balance sheet that change with sales are termed **spontaneous accounts.** This is because their value responds to a change in sales automatically, or "spontaneously," without the need for specific management action. In general, the following accounts are spontaneous:

● Assets that support the firm's operations—operating cash, accounts receivable, inventories, prepaids, plant and equipment.

● Trade and institutional liabilities—accounts payable, accrued payables (wages payable, taxes payable).

● Earned equity—the income component of retained earnings.

discretionary account—a balance sheet account whose value does not change with sales but rather is set by a management decision

Balance sheet accounts that do *not* change with sales are called **discretionary accounts** since their value is solely up to the judgment or "discretion" of management. In general, the following accounts are discretionary:

---

[3] **Elaboration:**   You may recall that the economic definition of *short-run* is that period of time during which the firm faces constraints on its ability to change and cannot adjust its resources as desired. By contrast, the *long-run* is defined as that period of time long enough so that the firm faces no limitations on its choice or use of resources.

[4] **Cross-reference:**   Variable and fixed costs are introduced on pages 46-47.

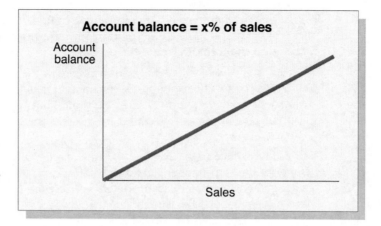

FIGURE 5.1
The percentage-of-sales relationship. The balance of an account is projected to remain a given fraction of sales.

- Assets unrelated to the firm's operations—marketable securities apart from the operating cash balance, investments in other companies.
- Contractual liabilities—bank notes payable, commercial paper, leases, term loans, bonds payable.
- Managed equity—common and preferred stock, treasury stock, the dividend component of retained earnings.

3. Establish the Relationship to Sales

Once an account is identified as varying with sales, we must specify the form of variation. While many relationships are possible, it is useful to develop the concepts of this chapter assuming that the most simple relationship holds: all accounts that change with sales do so in a strictly linear fashion.[5] This is the *percentage-of-sales relationship*. It is illustrated graphically in Figure 5.1.

Although percentage of sales is clearly a simplification in many cases, it provides a basic forecast that is typically quite useful. In particular, if sales is difficult to project, the use of more complex relationships may not materially improve the quality of the forecast. In addition, percentage of sales gives us a forecasting relationship that is easy to understand and build upon. For these reasons, percentage of sales is widely used, both within companies and by banks and other stakeholders who analyze the firm.

The Percentage-of-Sales Method Illustrated

The percentage-of-sales method consists of seven steps:

1. *Forecast sales.* Obtain a good sales forecast.
2. *Classify accounts.* Identify the variable and spontaneous accounts, the ones that vary with sales. Also identify the fixed and discretionary accounts as well as accounts that are connected to some other variable.

---

[5] **Cross-reference:** See Web Appendix 5A for a discussion of other possible relationships.

3. *Determine relationships.* Calculate the percentage-of-sales relationship for all variable and spontaneous accounts. For accounts that vary with some other variable, obtain that relationship as well.

4. *Project new values.* Calculate the anticipated value of each variable and spontaneous account by applying its percentage of sales to the new sales number. Also determine the value of those accounts that vary with other variables by applying the appropriate relationship determined in Step 3.

5. *Fill in the pro-forma income statement and balance sheet.* Insert the new values for all accounts calculated in Step 4. Transfer the values of all fixed and discretionary items unchanged, making the forecast independent of discretionary management actions. Use projected net income and dividends to calculate end-of-year retained earnings.

6. *Force the pro-forma balance sheet to balance.* Since each account is forecasted individually, we do not adhere to double-entry bookkeeping, and the pro-forma balance sheet likely will not yet balance. If liabilities plus equity exceed assets, we learn that the firm will bring in more resources than it has plans to use, and we balance the statement by adding a new asset called "excess cash." If assets exceed liabilities plus equity, we learn that the firm needs more assets than it has money for; in this case, we balance the statement by adding a new item on the right-hand side called "external financing needed."

7. *Produce the pro-forma cash flow statement.* Rearrange the numbers on the pro-forma income statement and on the beginning-of-year and end-of-year pro-forma balance sheets.

We illustrate the percentage-of-sales method by following Richard Paulson as he forecasts the 2012 pro-forma financial statements for the Jefferson Company. The numbers have been kept simple to focus on the process. Since we last left Richard, in the introduction to this chapter, he has read up on financial planning and forecasting and has chosen to use the percentage-of-sales method for his task. Richard begins with the financial statements in Jefferson's 2011 annual report:

THE JEFFERSON COMPANY
Income Statement
For the year ended December 31, 2011

Sales		$ 2,500
− Cost of goods sold		1,738
Gross profit		762
− Operating expenses	$550	
− Depreciation	40	
		590
EBIT		172
− Interest expense		18
EBT		154
− Tax expense		54
EAT		$ 100
− Dividends		33
Addition to retained earnings		$ 67

THE JEFFERSON COMPANY Balance Sheet December 31, 2011			
Cash	$ 100	Accounts payable	$ 150
Marketable securities	50	Accrued payables	200
Accounts receivable	150	Bonds payable	200
Inventories	200	Common stock	150
Plant, net	500	Retained earnings	300
Total assets	$1,000	Total liability and equity	$1,000

Richard follows the seven steps we discussed above:

Step 1—Obtain a Good Sales Forecast

Richard talks to his peers in marketing. Together they review the state of the economy and the competitive picture for the company's products. They conclude that the most likely number for 2012 sales is $3,000.

Step 2—Classify Accounts

Richard studies his company's accounts carefully. He examines past relationships and asks questions about the role of each account. He concludes:

a. Variable costs—all of cost of goods sold and $375 of operating expense will vary with sales.

b. Fixed costs—the remainder of operating expense ($175 in 2011) and all $40 of depreciation expense will not vary with sales.

c. Spontaneous accounts—cash, accounts receivable, inventories, net plant, accounts payable, and accrued payables will change with sales.

d. Discretionary accounts—marketable securities, bonds payable, and common stock will not change with sales.

Richard also discovers the following:

e. Bonds payable—$50 of the $200 of bonds payable falls due on December 31, 2012. The bonds carry a 9% interest coupon. (Richard notes that this explains the interest expense of $18 in 2011 since 9% of $200 = $18.)

f. Income taxes—the firm pays taxes on income at a flat 35% rate. (Richard notes that this explains the tax expense of $54 in 2011 since 35% of $154 = $54.)

g. Dividends—management's announced policy is to target a payout ratio of 1/3 of earnings after tax. (Richard notes that this explains the dividend of $33 in 2011 since 1/3 of $100 = $33).

Step 3—Determine Relationships

Richard studies the relationship of each variable cost and spontaneous account to sales. He concludes that 2011 was a representative year and, therefore, the relationships in the 2011 financial statements are appropriate to use. Using 2011 data, he calculates:

a. Variable costs:

Cost of goods sold/sales = $1,738/$2,500 = 69.52%
Operating expense/sales = $ 375/$2,500 = 15.00%

b. Spontaneous accounts:

Cash/sales = $ 100/$2,500 = 4.00%
Accounts receivable/sales = $ 150/$2,500 = 6.00%
Inventories/sales = $ 200/$2,500 = 8.00%
Net plant/sales = $ 500/$2,500 = 20.00%
Accounts payable/sales = $ 150/$2,500 = 6.00%
Accrued payables/sales = $ 200/$2,500 = 8.00%

Step 4—Project New Values

Richard next uses the sales forecast from Step 1 and the relationships from Step 3 to project 2012 values:

a. Variable costs:

Cost of goods sold = 69.52% of sales = 69.52% × $3,000 = $ 2,086
Variable operating expense = 15.00% of sales = 15.00% × $3,000 = $ 450

(Therefore, total operating expense = the variable component of $450 plus the fixed component of $175 = $625.)

b. Spontaneous accounts:

Cash = 4.00% of sales = 4.00% × $3,000 = $120
Accounts receivable = 6.00% of sales = 6.00% × $3,000 = $180
Inventories = 8.00% of sales = 8.00% × $3,000 = $240
Net plant = 20.00% of sales = 20.00% × $3,000 = $600
Accounts payable = 6.00% of sales = 6.00% × $3,000 = $180
Accrued payables = 8.00% of sales = 8.00% × $3,000 = $240

Richard also uses the other information he discovered to project the following:

c. Bonds payable—since $50 will be repaid in 2012, the end-of-year balance should be $200 − $50 = $150. However, since the repayment will not take place until December, the balance of debt throughout the year will remain $200 and interest expense should again be $18—just as in 2011.

Step 5—Fill in the Pro-Forma Statements

Richard now compiles his projections into a pro-forma income statement and balance sheet. He uses the same format as was used in 2011.

THE JEFFERSON COMPANY Pro-Forma Income Statement For the year ending December 31, 2012			Data obtained from:
Sales		$ 3,000	Step 1—forecast
− Cost of goods sold		2,086	Step 4a—projection
Gross profit		914	
− Operating expenses	$ 625		Step 4a—projection
− Depreciation	40		Step 2b—fixed cost
		665	
EBIT		249	
− Interest expense		18	Step 4c—projection
EBT		231	
− Tax expense (35%)		81	Step 2f—calculation
EAT		$ 150	
− Dividends		50	Step 2g—calculation
Addition to retained earnings		$ 100	

From the statement of retained earnings at the bottom of the pro-forma income statement, Richard discovers that $100 will be added to retained earnings in year 2012. This will increase the retained earnings balance to $300 + $100 = $400.

THE JEFFERSON COMPANY Pro-Forma Balance Sheet December 31, 2012		Data obtained from:
Cash	$ 120	Step 4b—projection
Marketable securities	50	Step 2d—discretionary
Accounts receivable	180	Step 4b—projection
Inventories	240	Step 4b—projection
Plant, net	600	Step 4b—projection
Total Assets	$ 1,190	
Accounts payable	$ 180	Step 4b—projection
Accrued payable	240	Step 4b—projection
Bonds payable	150	Step 4c—projection
Common stock	150	Step 2d—discretionary
Retained earnings	400	Step 5—pro-forma income statement
	$ 1,120	
External Financing Needed	70	Step 6—force a balance
Total liability and equity	$ 1,190	

Step 6—Force the Pro-Forma Balance Sheet to Balance

Richard's balance sheet does not balance! His projection shows that by December 2012, Jefferson Company will require $1,190 of assets to support sales of $3,000, an increase of $190 from December 2011. But spontaneous sources will provide only $120 of new money. (Accounts payable will increase by $30, accrued payables will increase by $40, and retained earnings will increase by $100, for a total of $170 of new financing. However, the firm will have to use $50 of this to refund its bonds payable. This will leave it with a net spontaneous increase in financing of $120, raising the liability-equity side of its balance sheet to $1,120.)

external financing needed— the amount of financing a firm must raise from outside sources to acquire the assets necessary to support its forecasted level of sales

Richard forces the balance sheet to balance by adding a "plug figure" to the side with the smaller amount, in this case the liability-equity side. This is the **external financing needed (EFN),** the financing the firm must raise from outside sources. For sales to grow to $3,000, the firm must acquire $190 of new assets. To do so it will need $190 of new financing, yet internal operations will only produce $120 of that amount. The extra $70 must come from outside, or external, sources.[6]

Richard is careful to write the EFN of $70 into his pro-forma balance sheet as a separate line and not to include it in any other account. Management must still decide how to raise the $70, and Richard does not want to assume any decision before it is made.

Although Richard found that his firm will need external funds in 2012, this is not always the case. As we will see in the next section, EFN typically comes with rapidly growing sales. Had Richard's sales forecast been much lower, he would have projected a smaller growth in assets, and spontaneous liabilities and equity would have been more than sufficient to pay for this. The plug figure to make the balance sheet balance would now be placed on the asset side and would be la-beled **excess cash.** Now, management's decision would be how best to use this cash that is not needed to support sales.

excess cash—the amount of spontaneous financing produced by a firm over and above what it needs to acquire the assets necessary to support its sales forecast

Step 7—Produce the Pro-Forma Cash Flow Statement

Richard can now produce a cash flow statement by rearranging the data of his pro-forma income statement and balance sheet:[7]

THE JEFFERSON COMPANY Pro-Forma Statement of Cash Flows For the Year ending December 31, 2012		Data obtained from:
CASH FLOW FROM OPERATIONS		
Received from customers	$2,970	Pro-forma statements[8]
Paid to suppliers and employees	(2,681)	Pro-forma statements[9]
Interest paid	(18)	New income statement
Income taxes paid	(81)	New income statement
Net cash provided by operating activities	190	

---

[6] **Observation:** The firm could also use some or all of its $50 of marketable securities to meet this need.

[7] **Tip:** If you feel the need for a review of the relationship among these three statements, see your introductory accounting textbook.

[8] **Calculation:** This is the projected sales of $3,000 less the $30 projected increase in accounts receivable—sales that will not be collected in 2012.

[9] **Calculation:** This is the projected cost of goods sold plus operating expenses ($2,086 + 625 = $2,711) plus the $40 projected increase in inventories—an additional payment—less the $70 projected increase in accounts and accrued payables—expenses that will not be paid in 2012.

```
CASH FLOW FROM INVESTMENTS
  Payment for purchase of
      property plant and equipment              (140)     Both balance sheets¹⁰
CASH FLOW FROM FINANCING
  External financing              70                      New balance sheet
  Repayment of long-term debt    (50)                     Both balance sheets¹¹
  Dividends paid                 (50)                     New income statement
Net cash used by financing activities          (30)
NET INCREASE (DECREASE) IN CASH                 20
Cash and equivalents, beginning of year        150
Cash and equivalents, end of year          $   170

RECONCILIATION OF NET INCOME TO CASH PROVIDED
      BY OPERATIONS
  Net income                              $   150         New income statement
    Add back: Depreciation                     40         New income statement
  Subtract increase in:
    Accounts receivable                       (30)        Both balance sheets
    Inventories                               (40)        Both balance sheets
  Add increase in:
    Accounts payable                           30         Both balance sheets
    Accrued payables                           40         Both balance sheets
Net cash provided by operations           $   190
```

Interpreting the Pro-Forma Statements

The pro-forma statements give important clues as to the future behavior and condition of the firm. From them, the financial manager can begin to learn how much financing the firm will need and why, and can get a first sense of which source(s) of financing might be a good choice. In addition, the financial manager can use the pro-forma statements to anticipate financial trends within the firm. In all cases, the objective is to be in a position to provide resources and financial guidance at an early stage so financial problems do not arise.

1. There Are Two Reasons Why Firms Need External Funds

As Richard prepared the pro-forma balance sheet, he discovered an external financing need (EFN) of $70: on December 31, the Jefferson Company would need

---

[10] **Calculation:** Plant is now $500. During 2012, depreciation will be $40, reducing plant to $460. If the account is to go up to $600, $140 of new plant must be purchased during 2012. The following T-account summarizes this:

```
                    Plant, net
Beginning balance    $500
Buy new plant         140   Depreciation    $40
Ending balance       $600
```

[11] **Calculation:** Subtract the beginning-of-year balance sheet number from the forecasted end-of-year number.

$70 of additional financing. The EFN was required because of the firm's *growth*. Projected growth in sales meant the firm would have to purchase additional assets, yet the company would be unable to generate sufficient funds internally. It would have to raise external money.

When he prepares his cash budget, Richard will see that the financing needs of his company go beyond the EFN of $70 due to the firm's *seasonality*. This need is independent of its growth.[12]

The insight that his firm needs financing for two distinct reasons prompts Richard to think about where the financing might come from. The cash budget points out that the seasonal cash requirements will be short-term in nature. Perhaps, muses Richard, a short-term financing source, such as a bank loan or commercial paper, would be appropriate for this. On the other hand, the EFN of $70 is due to the growth of the firm, a long-term trend. Richard wonders whether some long-term source of money, such as bonds or stock, might be appropriate to cover this part of Jefferson's needs.

2. The Cash-Flow Statement Gives Additional Clues to Funding

According to the pro-forma cash flow statement, the Jefferson Company will use cash for three major purposes other than operations in 2008: to pay dividends ($50), to purchase plant ($140), and to retire bonds ($50). These uses total $240 and are all long-term in nature. None will result in cash coming back to the firm in the near future.

Jefferson's sources of cash are projected to be from operations ($190) and external funds ($70). The funds from operations are long-term in the sense that management may choose to retain them forever. The external financing, however, may be either short- or long-term at management's discretion.

One reasonable financing strategy would be to hedge the balance sheet[13], matching the long-term uses of cash with long-term sources. Since there are $240 of long-term uses, roughly $240 of the sources, including most or all of the external funds, would then be long-term in character.

3. Financial (Ratio) Analysis Can Be Used to Examine the Results

Financial ratios can be used to test the pro-forma statements in the same way as they are used to evaluate past and present performance. In particular, ratios calculated from the pro-forma data can be compared to prior values of the same ratios to search for improvement or deterioration of the firm's condition.

---

[12] **Cross-reference and elaboration:** Richard prepares a cash budget consistent with his income statement and balance sheet forecasts in Web Appendix 5B. The line "Cumulative financing needed" on his cash budget shows that the firm's cash position is projected to be seasonal during the year—beginning with excess cash, then changing to a need which peaks at $152 in March, returning to excess cash during the summer, and reverting to a need for external financing in the last four months of the year.

[13] **Cross-reference and elaboration:** This risk management strategy is discussed in Chapter 15.

Not all ratios are useful for this test. For example, the gross margin ratio and the various asset turnover ratios define the percentage-of-sales relationships used to forecast gross profit and asset balances in the first place. These ratios calculated from the pro-forma statements should be exactly the same as ratios taken from the data used to obtain the percentage-of-sales figures. A change in these ratios indicates an error of calculation and not a company trend.

Certain ratios can be used to anticipate general trends within the business. These are the ratios that are not directly related to sales and therefore do not define the percentage-of-sales relationships used in constructing the pro-forma statements. Examples are times interest earned, net profit margin, and return on assets.

Example

Using Ratios to Test the Pro-Forma Statements for Trends		

Richard calculates the following ratios:

	2011 Actual	**2012 Pro-Forma**
Times interest earned	9.6 times	13.8 times
Net profit margin	4.00%	5.00%
Return on assets	10.0%	12.6%

If these changes are meaningful and not merely natural variation, and if the forecast comes to pass, the Jefferson Company will strengthen on all three of these dimensions in 2012.

Another group of ratios is particularly sensitive to how the firm chooses to finance its EFN.[14] They can be used both to look for trends in the company and to study the impact of the financing choice on the firm's structure.

Example

Using Ratios to Test the Choice of EFN Source			

Richard calculates the following ratios assuming an EFN of 70:

		2012 Pro-Forma: EFN Financed by:		
	2011 Actual	**Current Liabilities**	**Long-term Liabilities**	**Common Equity**
Current ratio	1.25	1.20	1.40	1.40
Quick ratio	0.75	0.71	0.83	0.83
Debt ratio	50.0%	49.6%	49.6%	43.7%
Return on equity	22.2%	27.3%	27.3%	24.2%

From the 2012 pro-forma balance sheet (page 125), current assets are forecasted to be 590 (120 of cash + 50 of marketable securities + 180 of accounts receivable + 240 of inventories) and current liabilities are forecasted to be 420 (180 of accounts payable + 240 of accrued payables) prior to determining the form of the EFN. If Jefferson finances its EFN using short-term liabilities, current liabilities will rise to 490 (420 + 70) and its current ratio will be:

$$590/490 = 1.20$$

If, on the other hand, Jefferson uses long-term liabilities or equity to finance its EFN, its current liabilities will remain 420 and its current ratio will be:

$$590/420 = 1.40$$

---

[14] **Observation:**   To the extent that the choice of financing impacts interest expense, the prior group of ratios will change as well.

Richard uses the same logic to get each of the other ratios above.

The Jefferson Company has a strong profitability (return on equity) which will improve no matter how the EFN is financed. Liquidity (current and quick ratios) is weak. It would weaken further with current liability financing but would improve if long-term money were used. Leverage (debt ratio) could be improved if equity financing were used; otherwise it would not be significantly changed.

4. Relationships Are Changing

In our example of the Jefferson Company, Richard used percentage relationships from the 2011 financial statements to project 2012. In doing so he assumed that the structure of the company would not change in any significant way. In today's environment, this assumption may well be incorrect.

As companies respond to the pressures of global competition, many are re-examining the way they conduct each part of their business. As they change their production methodologies and use of resources, the percentage relationship of virtually every account to sales may change. For example, the move toward just-in-time manufacturing systems dramatically reduces inventory balances, and inventory as a percentage of sales declines sharply. It also reduces the need for much factory space, reducing many overhead costs. The elimination of rework and inspection costs lowers cost of goods sold. As customers perceive higher quality, they are willing to pay more and revenue rises. These changes reduce the percentage relationship of costs to sales. As companies become progressively more skilled at continuously improving their work processes, relationship between sales and other financial accounts are likely to continue to change year after year.

Astute financial managers build these changes into their financial forecasts and budgets. They work with others throughout the organization to understand and be part of the improvements taking place. Correspondingly, they encourage others to help shape the financial forecasts. Doing so makes the forecasts more accurate and permits them to capture the dynamic nature of the business. Further, to the extent that the financial forecast truly reflects the aspirations of the company, predicting improvement may actually help make it happen!

CONTRIBUTING TO GLOBAL SUSTAINABILITY

Planning for Sustainability

Many companies are now preparing sustainability plans along with their traditional operational and financial plans. While sustainability plans differ from company to company, most plans share the following components: (1) an overarching goal for the sustainability plan that is consistent with the firm's vision and mission statements, (2) an analyisis of the firm's environmental and social impacts to determine which ones are most problematic and which offer the most opportunity for risk reduction, operational efficency, and increased sales, and (3) specific goals to be reached in the short- and long-terms including strategies for achieving the goals, how the company will measure progress, and who will be the responsible person in the firm to lead the effort.

*R*ichard Paulson put the finishing touches on his last transparency and sat back with a satisfied feeling. His presentation to the executive committee was the next day, and he was confident it would go well. He put the transparencies in order and began to practice what he would say.

Richard would start his presentation with the assumptions he had made from his interviews with others in the organization. Next, he would present his pro-forma financial statements for the coming year. He would highlight the external financing needs number and then show how that amount would vary over a range of alternative sales forecasts. Finally, he would show how the financial condition of the company would change if the sales forecast proved accurate.

As he thought back to the past two weeks, Richard was amazed at how much he had learned. He had been surprised at the extent to which his forecasts took advantage of accounting relationships and was certainly glad he had done well in his accounting courses. But he also had a new appreciation of the value of accounting information and how it could be used in financial planning.

Summary of Key Points

- **Describe the functions and limitations of planning and budgeting, including financial planning.** Planning begins with a mission statement: a statement of goals and beliefs to guide all activities of the firm. It focuses on customers and on exceeding their expectations. It leads to strategies that are aligned with the firm's culture, strengths, and environment. Although planning traditionally has been a job for managers, in modern management practice planning is becoming the responsibility of all members of the organization. The use of budgets, a key component of planning, is also changing. Whereas budgets traditionally have been targets for performance, today they are seen more as guides for planning and acquiring resources. Financial planning accomplishes six tasks. It (1) forces assumptions to be made explicit, (2) identifies actions that are consistent or inconsistent with financial health, (3) identifies the financial resources required to support the firm's plans, (4) provides guidance in the choice of financing sources, (5) becomes a benchmark against which to compare results so as to improve the planning process, and (6) helps the firm communicate with its stakeholders. A financial plan consists of a long-run financial plan, a capital budget, and an operating budget. An important technique used in financial planning is the construction of pro-forma financial statements, projections of the firm's future financial activity and position.

- **Recognize when specific-item forecasting is an appropriate financial planning technique.** Specific-item forecasting is a technique for estimating values independently of one another. It is particularly appropriate when the variables are not related through a central causal variable. A more commonly used forecasting technique is the percentage-of-sales method, in which many accounts are related to sales to ensure an internal consistency to the forecast.

- **Identify financial statement accounts that relate to sales and establish those relationships.** A percentage-of-sales forecast requires a good understanding of how the firm's financial accounts relate to each other. To identify which accounts relate to sales we ask: (1) why is this money being spent? (2) what is the account's time horizon? and (3) how will management respond to a change in sales? For those accounts determined to be spontaneous, we construct a relationship connecting the account balance to the level of sales.

- **Use the percentage-of-sales technique to project a firm's financial statements.** The percentage-of-sales technique consists of seven steps: (1) forecast sales, (2) classify accounts as variable and spontaneous, and fixed and discretionary, (3) determine relationships between the variable and discretionary accounts and sales, (4) project new values for all accounts, (5) fill in the pro-forma statements with the projected amounts, (6) force the pro-forma-balance sheet to balance with "external financing needed (EFN)" or "excess cash," and (7) produce the pro-forma cash flow statement.

- **Interpret pro-forma financial statements.** Pro-forma statements help the financial manager to separate needs caused by growth from needs caused by seasonality. The cash flow statement may be examined to see if sources and uses of cash match. Ratios may be calculated from the pro-forma income statement and balance sheet to gauge the future condition of the firm. As companies adopt quality-management methods, the relationships among the numbers on their financial statements are changing. Accurate forecasting requires that the financial manager work closely with others in the company to understand and be part of quality improvements and to incorporate them into financial forecasts.

Questions

1. What is the role of planning in management?
2. How can budgets hurt rather than help a firm?
3. Identify the six tasks that financial planning can help a firm to accomplish.
4. What is the distinction between specific-item forecasting and forecasts that relate to sales?
5. In the percentage-of-sales forecasting method, what is the significance of:

   a. Having a good sales forecast?
   b. Relating accounts to sales?

6. Identify the following concepts. What is their relationship to financial forecasting?

   a. Variable cost
   b. Fixed cost
   c. Spontaneous account
   d. Discretionary account

7. What is the relationship between external financing needed and excess cash?
8. A firm with a high growth rate typically requires external financing. In what other situations would a firm require external financing?
9. How is the use of total quality management changing financial forecasting relationships?

Problems

1. **(Percentage of sales—income statement)** Using the percentage-of-sales method, forecast the income statement of a company with the following data:

Sales last year	$8,000,000
Variable expenses:	
Cost of goods sold	$4,800,000
Operating expense	$1,760,000
Fixed operating expense	$ 750,000
Interest bearing debt:	
Average balance next year	$2,500,000
Average interest rate next year	10%
Tax rate	35%

   if the company's sales forecast for the coming year is:

   a. $8,000,000   c. $9,500,000
   b. $8,800,000   d. $10,000,000

2. **(Percentage of sales—income statement)** Using the percentage-of-sales method, forecast the income statement of a company with the following data and forecasts:

Sales last year	$3,000,000
Variable expenses:	
Cost of goods sold	$1,200,000
Operating expense	$ 960,000
Fixed operating expense	$ 200,000
Interest bearing debt:	
Average balance next year	$1,000,000
Average interest rate next year	12%
Tax rate	35%

   if the company's sales forecast for the coming year is:

   a. $3,400,000   c. $4,200,000
   b. $3,900,000   d. $4,500,000

3. **(Percentage of sales—spontaneous accounts)** A company had sales of $4,500,000 last year and ended the year with $450,000 of accounts receivable, $200,000 of inventory, and $300,000 of accounts payable—all of which are considered spontaneous accounts. Forecast the end-of-coming-year balances for these three accounts using the percentage-of-sales method if the sales forecast for the coming year is:

   a. $4,000,000   c. $5,000,000
   b. $4,500,000   d. $6,000,000

4. **(Percentage of sales—spontaneous accounts)** A company had sales of $1,500,000 last year and ended the year with $75,000 of accrued payables, which is considered a spontaneous account. Using the percentage-of-sales method, determine the level of sales that can be supported by the following end-of-coming-year accrued payables balances:

   a. $65,000   c. $90,000
   b. $75,000   d. $120,000

5. **(Percentage of sales—spontaneous accounts)** In the past, a company's collection period has been 45 days. Using the percentage-of-sales method, determine the end-of-coming-year level of accounts receivable that would accompany the following sales levels if accounts receivable were a spontaneous asset:

   a. $200,000   c. $800,000
   b. $400,000   d. $1,600,000

6. **(Percentage of sales—spontaneous accounts)** In the past, a company's accounts receivable turnover ratio has been 12 times, and the company does not expect this relationship to change in the coming year. Using

the percentage-of-sales method, determine the level of sales that can be supported by the following end-of-coming-year accounts receivable balances if accounts receivable were a spontaneous asset:

a. $100,000   c. $500,000
b. $250,000   d. $1,000,000

7. **(Percentage of sales—spontaneous and discretionary accounts)** A company had sales of $3,500,000 last year and forecasts sales of $4,000,000 in the coming year. It ended last year with $140,000 in its cash balance and with another $100,000 of marketable securities. Cash is considered a spontaneous asset. Forecast the end-of-coming-year balances of cash and marketable securities under each of the following alternatives:

a. 100% of the marketable securities balance is considered part of the company's operating cash and therefore spontaneous.

b. 70% of the marketable securities balance is considered part of the company's operating cash and therefore spontaneous. The remainder is considered discretionary.

c. 30% of the marketable securities balance is considered part of the company's operating cash and therefore spontaneous. The remainder is considered discretionary.

d. None of the marketable securities balance is considered part of the company's operating cash, but rather it is all considered discretionary.

8. **(Percentage of sales—spontaneous and discretionary accounts)** A company had sales of $10,000,000 last year and forecasts sales of $12,000,000 in the coming year. It ended last year with $250,000 in its cash balance and with another $175,000 of marketable securities. Cash is considered a spontaneous asset. Forecast the end-of-coming-year balances of cash and marketable securities under each of the following alternatives:

a. 100% of the marketable securities balance is considered part of the company's operating cash and therefore spontaneous.

b. 60% of the marketable securities balance is considered part of the company's operating cash and therefore spontaneous. The remainder is considered discretionary.

c. 25% of the marketable securities balance is considered part of the company's operating cash and therefore spontaneous. The remainder is considered discretionary.

d. None of the marketable securities balance is considered part of the company's operating cash, but rather it is all considered discretionary.

9. **(Percentage of sales—plant and equipment)** A company had sales last year of $16,000,000 and forecasts sales of $20,000,000 in the coming year. It ended the year with $5,000,000 of plant and equipment. Forecast the end-of-coming-year balance for plant and equipment under each of the following alternatives.

a. Plant and equipment is now at capacity and will be increased proportionally to sales.

b. Plant and equipment is now at capacity. New plant and equipment must be purchased in $750,000 increments.

c. Plant and equipment is now being used at 90% of capacity. New plant and equipment will be purchased in the exact amount needed.

d. Plant and equipment is now being used at 90% of capacity. New plant and equipment must be purchased in $750,000 increments.

10. **(Percentage of sales—plant and equipment)** A company had sales last year of $30,000,000 and forecasts sales of $40,000,000 in the coming year. It ended the year with $12,000,000 of plant and equipment. Forecast the end-of-coming-year balance for plant and equipment under each of the following alternatives.

a. Plant and equipment is now at capacity and will be increased proportionally to sales.

b. Plant and equipment is now at capacity. New plant and equipment must be purchased in $2,500,000 increments.

c. Plant and equipment is now being used at 90% of capacity. New plant and equipment will be purchased in the exact amount needed.

d. Plant and equipment is now being used at 70% of capacity. New plant and equipment must be purchased in $2,500,000 increments.

11. **(Percentage of sales—bonds payable)** A company listed bonds payable in its year-end balance sheet, of which $500,000 was reported as a current liability. Next year another $500,000 will become current. Forecast its end-of-coming-year balance of "bonds payable—current" and "bonds payable—long term" if this year's year-end balance of bonds payable—long-term is:

a. $500,000   c. $5,000,000
b. $2,500,000   d. $10,000,000

12. **(Percentage of sales—bonds payable)** A company listed bonds payable in its year-end balance sheet, of which $125,000 was reported as a current liability. Next year $75,000 will become current. Forecast its end-of-coming-year balance of "bonds payable—current" and "bonds payable—long term" if this year's year-end total balance of bonds payable is:

a. $250,000   c. $1,000,000
b. $500,000   d. $1,500,000

13. **(Percentage of sales—retained earnings)** A company reported $250,000 of retained earnings on its balance sheet last year. In the coming year it expects sales of $800,000. Forecast the end-of-coming-year balance of retained earnings if the company has a:

    a. Net margin ratio of 12% and a dividend payout ratio of 40%
    b. Net margin ratio of 8% and a dividend payout ratio of 15%
    c. Net margin ratio of 5% and a dividend payout ratio of 75%
    d. Net margin ratio of 8% and a dividend payout ratio of 100%

14. **(Percentage of sales—retained earnings)** A company reported $6,000,000 of retained earnings on its balance sheet last year. In the coming year it expects sales of $4,500,000. Forecast the end-of-coming-year balance of retained earnings if the company has a:

    a. Net margin ratio of 3% and a dividend payout ratio of 80%
    b. Net margin ratio of 7% and a dividend payout ratio of 25%
    c. Net margin ratio of 9% and a dividend payout ratio of 100%
    d. Net margin ratio of 14% and a dividend payout ratio of 40%

15. **(Percentage of sales—full projection)** A company published the following financial statements in its 2011 annual report:

Income Statement
For the year ended December 31, 2011

Sales		$ 70,000
− Cost of goods sold		45,000
Gross profit		25,000
− Operating expenses	$ 8,000	
− Depreciation	5,000	
		13,000
EBIT		12,000
− Interest expense		1,300
EBT		10,700
− Tax expense		3,745
EAT		$ 6,955
− Dividends		3,000
Addition to retained earnings		$ 3,955

Balance Sheet
December 31, 2011

Cash	$ 8,000
Marketable securities	2,000
Accounts receivable	10,000
Inventories	6,000
Plant, net	20,000
Total assets	$ 46,000
Accounts payable	$ 7,000
Accrued payables	3,000
Bonds payable	10,000
Common stock	15,000
Retained earnings	11,000
Total liabilities and equity	$ 46,000

Sales in 2012 are estimated to be $80,000. Forecast the 2012 income statement, balance sheet, and statement of cash flow assuming: (1) cost of goods sold and $5,000 of the operating expenses are variable; (2) depreciation and the remainder of operating expenses are fixed; (3) cash, accounts receivable, inventories, net plant, accounts payable, and accrued payables are spontaneous; (4) marketable securities, bonds payable, and common stock are discretionary; (5) $500 of bonds payable are current and will be repaid at the beginning of the year; and (6) the firm will maintain its 2011 dividend payout ratio in year 2012.

16. **(Percentage of sales—full projection)** A company-published the following financial statements in its 2011 annual report:

Income Statement
For the year ended December 31, 2011

Sales		$ 500,000
− Cost of goods sold		350,000
Gross profit		150,000
− Operating expenses	$ 75,000	
− Depreciation	20,000	
		95,000
EBIT		55,000
− Interest expense		20,000
EBT		35,000
− Tax expense		12,250
EAT		$ 22,750
− Dividends		10,000
Addition to retained earnings		$ 12,750

**Balance Sheet
December 31, 2011**

Cash	$ 25,000
Marketable securities	10,000
Accounts receivable	50,000
Inventories	85,000
Plant, net	200,000
Total assets	$ 370,000
Accounts payable	$ 60,000
Accrued payables	35,000
Bonds payable	140,000
Common stock	105,000
Retained earnings	30,000
Total liabilities and equity	$ 370,000

Sales in 2012 are estimated to be $650,000. Forecast the 2012 income statement, balance sheet and statement of cash flow assuming: (1) cost of goods sold, $30,000 of the operating expenses, and depreciation expense are variable; (2) the remainder of operating expenses is fixed; (3) cash, accounts receivable, inventories, net plant, accounts payable, and accrued payables are spontaneous; (4) marketable securities, bonds payable, and common stock are discretionary; (5) $10,000 of bonds payable are current and will be repaid at the beginning of the year; and (6) the firm will maintain its 2011 dividend payout ratio in 2012.

17. **(Evaluating the pro-forma statements)** Analyze the pro-forma statements you prepared for the firm of Problem 15, using those financial ratios that are not used in the percentage-of-sales projection by:

   a. Calculating ratios from the 2011 statements
   b. Calculating ratios from the year 2012 pro-forma statements assuming:

      (1) EFN is financed with current liabilities
      (2) EFN is financed with long term liabilities
      (3) EFN is financed with common equity

   c. Commenting on the direction of change of the ratios. Which financing alternative (if any) does the best job of improving the firm's financial ratios (or at least not degrading them too much) ?

18. **(Evaluating the pro-forma statements)** Analyze the pro-forma statements you prepared for the firm of Problem 16, using those financial ratios that are not used in the percentage-of-sales projection by:

   a. Calculating ratios from the 2011 statements
   b. Calculating ratios from the year 2012 pro-forma statements assuming:

      (1) EFN is financed with current liabilities
      (2) EFN is financed with long term liabilities
      (3) EFN is financed with common equity

   c. Commenting on the direction of change of the ratios. Which financing alternative (if any) does the best job of improving the firm's financial ratios (or at least not degrading them too much) ?

CHAPTER 6
FINANCIAL
INSTRUMENTS

*A*licia Vasquez chewed on the end of her pen as she glanced around the conference room. She recognized everyone there, a cross-section of her company's finance organization called together by the company's treasurer. In front of her on the table, full of her notes, was a pad with the emblem of the local university where she was finishing her business degree at night.

Alicia had recently joined the treasury group of a large multinational company. Because of the company's size, it was regularly approached by commercial and investment banks with recommendations for raising financing of all types. But the proposals were difficult to compare, and there was some concern in the group that the best recommendations were not always the ones accepted.

Alicia focused her attention toward the flip-charts at the corner of the room where the treasurer was finishing his presentation. "So, it seems to me that the first step in making better financing choices is to fully understand the various financial instruments we could issue. Some of their characteristics are easy to see, like whether they are debt or equity, or that some loans are for one year while others have a 30-year maturity. But other differences are less obvious, and I'm not sure we all are comfortable with them. Let's see if we can put together a summary of the major features of each financial instrument we might consider using"

As the meeting broke up, Alicia found herself thinking of how the company's problem was similar to the topics she was covering in her finance class at the university. She decided to bring her notes from the meeting to class later that week to see if that would help her learn more about the many financial instruments her company was considering.

In one sense, every source of financing is the same: it gives the firm the money it needs to finance its growth and operations. But in another sense, every source of financing is different. Each has its own legal form, maturity, and specific terms and conditions. These features define each *financial instrument*,[1] the general name given to the contract between the firm and its supplier of funds.

To make intelligent choices among financing alternatives, Alicia and her colleagues must understand their distinctive features. In this chapter we look at the most common financial instruments in turn to understand their characteristics. Later in this book we will see how financial managers select the financing sources that are best for their firms.

Key Points You Should Learn from This Chapter

After reading this chapter you should be able to:

■ Differentiate between debt and equity and identify how both are further classified.

■ Describe trade credit, accruals, and bank loans as sources of short-term debt, and identify two capital market alternatives to bank loans.

■ Describe term loans, leases, bonds, and floating rate notes as intermediate- and long-term debt sources.

■ Identify the characteristics of and rationale for issuing preferred stock.

■ Describe common stock including various measures of number of shares and value.

---

[1] **Cross-reference:** The term "financial instrument" first appeared along with its definition in Chapter 1 on page 6.

Introductory Concepts—Characteristics of Financing

There are several ways to classify the forms of financing available to a company.

debt—a loan

equity—investment in a business

The broadest form of classification is to separate financing sources into debt and equity. **Debt** is a loan, a legal obligation between the lender and the firm. In return for use of the money, the firm promises to repay the loan, typically with interest, over a specified period of time. **Equity** is an investment in the company and is represented by shares of stock. Unlike debt, equity promises no repayment. Rather, equity investors become the owners of the firm. They receive dividends if management chooses to pay them; in addition, the value of their shares changes daily in the stock market. If the firm does well, equity holders can receive a high return on their investment. On the other hand, if the firm does poorly, the equity holders could receive a poor rate of return or perhaps no return at all!

Debt can be further classified by maturity, the time period of the loan. If the loan is for one year or less, it is classified as "short-term." Debt with longer maturities is considered "intermediate-term" or "long-term." We have organized the portion of this chapter that discusses debt in this way. Other ways to classify debt are by legal terms and type of lender.

Equity is classified by ownership privileges. A major distinction is between "preferred stock" and "common stock." Preferred stockholders typically get a fixed dividend but not the right to vote for members of the board of directors. Common stockholders typically can vote for directors, but do not get a fixed rate of return. Different types of preferred and common stock differ by the specific ownership privileges they convey: the right to vote for board members, the dividends they receive, special claims on the performance of a part of the company, etc.

◼ Short-Term Debt

Short-term debt is loans with a maturity of one year or less. It is particularly attractive to financial managers because for most firms it is (1) easily available, (2) inexpensive, and (3) flexible.

Of all types of financing, short-term debt is typically the easiest to obtain. Accruals (wages payable, taxes payable, interest payable) are built into the firm's normal business arrangements and require no further effort to acquire. Many suppliers routinely extend trade credit without any special negotiation. Banks and finance companies compete to make short-term loans to companies of all sizes. In fact, for small firms, short-term debt may be the *only* source of financing available from sources outside the company.

Short-term debt is normally a low-cost source of financing relative to debt of longer maturities. Some short-term financing is actually free. For debt carrying an interest rate set in the public markets, short-term debt is usually cheaper than long-term debt since the yield curve is normally upward-sloping, with short-term rates lower than long-term rates.[2]

---

[2] **Cross-reference:**   The yield curve is discussed in Chapter 4, pages 93-94.

Short-term financing also provides a high degree of flexibility in that a company can change its level of funding quickly and easily as its needs change. In fact, most commercial bank lines of credit and related short-term debt sources are specifically designed with this feature in mind. By contrast, long-term debt financing is more difficult to obtain and often more difficult to repay.

1. Trade Credit

Trade credit is a company's accounts payable—the opportunity to purchase supplies and other resources without paying for them immediately. For some companies, especially small firms without good access to the capital markets, trade credit can represent a large percentage of their financing.

NET Present Value
Information on potential customers' credit histories is available from several sources such as Creditfyi at www.creditfyi.com

banker's acceptance—a promissory note which carries a bank's promise of payment

Legal arrangement   The legal arrangement encompasses whether there is a formal note or not and, if so, whether the note is backed by the buyer alone or by the buyer plus some financially stronger third party. An account payable is characterized by no formal legal agreement between the parties. The seller delivers goods or provides a service at the request of the buyer and follows up with an invoice asking for payment. If the buyer's creditworthiness is questionable, the seller might require the buyer to sign a formal promissory note upon shipment of the goods or provision of the service. This amount appears on the company's books as a "note payable." Compared to an open account, the note gives the seller a stronger legal position should the buyer not pay. For financially weak or unknown buyers—for example, newly formed firms or foreign companies—sellers often require that a third party—such as a parent company or a bank—guarantee payment. When the guarantee comes from a bank it is termed a **banker's acceptance,** a service banks regularly sell for a fee.

Terms of sale   Figure 6.1 lists common terms of sale from the most liberal to the most restrictive. Although called "terms of sale," they really define the terms of *payment*—when payment is due. They differ primarily in how much time a buyer has before payment must be received. Liberal terms of sale are appropriate when the buyer is reputable but financially weak; stricter terms are used in dealings with unknown customers or those with questionable reputations.

FIGURE 6.1
Terms of sale. The terms, which specify when payment is due, range from liberal (consignment) to highly restrictive (cash before delivery).

Terms	Payment is due
Consignment	Whenever the buyer resells the goods
Seasonal dating	After an agreed-upon date corresponding to a high point in the buyer's cash flow cycle
Monthly billing	Upon receipt of a monthly statement
Discount, net	By a specified date; however, a discount is offered for early payment
Net	By a specified date
Cash on delivery (COD)	When the goods are delivered
Cash before delivery	Prior to shipment of the goods

consignment—shipping goods to a buyer but not requiring payment until the goods are resold

At the liberal end of the scale is **consignment,** a practice often used when the buyer is financially quite weak. The seller ships goods to the buyer but retains title to them. In effect, the seller initially treats the buyer as a warehouse rather than as a customer. Payment for the goods becomes due only when the buyer resells the goods to its customer.

seasonal dating—invoicing several months' worth of shipments at a strong point in the buyer's seasonal pattern

In **seasonal dating,** all purchases made before a specified date are treated as if made on that date for billing purposes. For example, a seller might ship goods throughout the year but not send an invoice to the buyer until October 1. Seasonal dating is used when the customer's business is highly seasonal and the customer is only able to pay at certain points in its cash flow cycle (for example retail toy stores) or when selling high-cost items to financially weak but reliable customers (such as jewelry to small retail stores). It is also often used strategically, for example to support a customer's plans for expansion or when introducing a new product line.

Many companies use "monthly billing," a practice by which all sales made before a certain date (often the 25th of the month) are invoiced at month's end. Payment is due during the following month. This method is particularly appropriate when many transactions are made during the month. For example, professionals such as attorneys and consultants often bill monthly rather than send an invoice for every hour of work. Monthly billing is also the method used to bill customers using retail credit cards such as Discover, MasterCard, and Visa.

Traditionally, the most common terms of sale extended to other businesses have been "discount, net" and "net." Examples are "2/10, net 30" and "net 45." With terms of 2/10, net 30, full payment is due 30 days after the invoice date but a 2% discount is granted if payment is made by day 10. Net 45 asks for full payment 45 days after the invoice date with no discount offered for early payment.

The strictest terms of sale, used for high-risk customers or when no credit information about the buyer is available, are "cash on delivery (COD)" and "cash before delivery." With COD, goods are released from the shipper to the buyer only upon payment by cash or certified check. Cash before delivery requires the buyer to pay in full before the seller will ship the goods or perform the service.

Net credit We can combine trade credit extended (accounts receivable) and trade credit used (accounts payable) into a measure of a company's overall trade credit position:

$$Net\ credit = accounts\ receivable - accounts\ payable$$

If a company's accounts receivable balance is greater than its accounts payable balance, its net credit measure is positive and it is a net supplier of trade credit. Positive net credit is appropriate for large firms with good access to financial markets which can raise funds more cheaply than their customers and can support their customers by passing on the low financing cost through trade credit. It is inappropriate for small and financially weak firms.

If a company's accounts receivable balance is less than its accounts payable balance, its net credit measure is negative and it is a net user of trade credit. A negative net credit position is appropriate for small and financially weak firms which can finance through low-cost trade credit provided by strong suppliers. It is inappropriate for large firms with good access to financial markets.

2. Accruals

Accruals are a company's other payables: wages payable, interest payable, taxes payable, etc. They arise spontaneously because it is normal business practice to pay certain obligations at intervals even though they are incurred on a day-by-day basis (for example, wages—which are paid weekly, biweekly, or monthly even though they are earned every day). In general, accruals do not lead to higher payments and are therefore free sources of financing.

However, there may be hidden costs to some accruals. Perhaps employees would prefer to be paid at more frequent intervals and would reward the company with greater loyalty and productivity. Or perhaps a bank would reduce the firm's interest rate if payments were scheduled more frequently. There might be costs associated with a payable that offset the advantage of float. For example, suppliers may treat customers who pay quickly as "preferred customers," providing special treatment without charge. Companies must throughly analyze their accruals to determine if they are truly free or contain any of these or other hidden costs.

3. Bank Loans

NET Present Value
An example of a full service bank is the Chase unit of JPMorgan Chase at www.chase.com

Loans from commercial banks are an important way companies acquire short-term funds beyond those provided by trade credit and accruals. And for small firms, bank loans may be the only other financing alternative. A bank loan is discretionary financing since the amount and timing of the loan request is up to a firm's management.

Prenegotiated loans   It is normal for a firm's cash balance to vary significantly throughout the year.[3] Most companies use their cash budget to project a maximum need for external short-term funds and then negotiate with their bank the ability to borrow up to that amount.

Prenegotiated loans come in two forms: the line of credit and the revolving credit line (revolver). In a **line of credit,** the bank makes no commitment to its customer that money will be available and the bank does not have to honor any request for funds under the line. Most banks, however, treat a line of credit as a commitment unless the borrower is delinquent or has fallen significantly in creditworthiness. A familiar form of a line of credit is contained in a bank credit card (MasterCard, Visa). The cardholder can borrow up to the amount of the credit line as desired, but the bank reserves the right to cancel the card at its discretion.

line of credit—a relationship in which a bank offers to lend up to a specified amount for a given time period with no guarantee that funds will be available

Unlike a line of credit, a **revolving credit line** is legally binding. It contains a commitment that the bank will honor any request by the customer up to the limit of the line. In return for taking this additional risk, the bank normally charges a "commitment fee" on the unused portion of the facility.

revolving credit line—a line of credit containing a guarantee that funds will be available for the period of the line

Offering basis loans   The alternative to a prenegotiated loan is an **offering basis loan.** A familiar example is an automobile loan. There is no prior negotiation between the bank and borrower, and the loan proceeds are intended for a specific purpose.

offering basis loan—a short-term loan with no prenegotiation

---

[3] **Cross-reference:**   This is illustrated by the cash budget in Web Appendix 5B.

Loan pricing Banks quote interest rates on most loans relative to a base rate of interest. Within the United States the most common base rate is the **prime rate**, the rate charged to the most creditworthy customers on the shortest-term loans. Banks making U.S.-dollar denominated loans outside the United States most often use the **London inter-bank offering rate (LIBOR),** the rate at which the large British clearing banks lend to each other, as their base rate.

Since the banking industry is an oligopoly, the prime rate is set by a price leader, usually one of the large New York banks. To determine whether the prime rate should be changed, the price leader looks at comparable financing instruments whose rates are set in the marketplace (such as commercial paper) or at the cost of funds to the bank (e.g., CD rates, Fed funds, etc.). In most cases other banks quickly follow the leader and adopt the new prime rate, although sometimes the other banks disagree with the leader and force the leader to rescind the change. Differences among banks do not last long since their product (cash) has limited differentiation and since bank customers, many of whom maintain multiple banking relationships, can easily shift their borrowing to the bank with the lowest rates.

When a company applies for a bank loan, officers of the bank perform a **credit analysis** to assess the company's creditworthiness—its ability to repay the loan. The credit analysis reviews the firm's financial condition, the intended use of the loan proceeds, and the integrity of the company's management. Credit analysis quantifies the risks of making the loan—if the bank elects to proceed, the analysis specifies the premium over the reference rate to charge and indicates the need for any special terms and conditions in the loan contract.

The final loan quote is usually in the form of "base rate plus," for example, "prime plus 1" which identifies that the interest rate will be 1% above the prime rate. Should the prime rate change, the loan rate is reset accordingly.

Asset-based loans Banks want their loans to be repaid from the cash flows generated by their customers' operations. However, in cases where the borrower is not of the highest creditworthiness, banks often ask for a claim on some or all of the borrower's assets to give them a "second way out" of the loan. When this happens, we have an **asset-based loan.**

The property pledged to back the repayment of a loan is called **collateral.** If the loan is repaid, the bank's claim on the collateral expires. But if the borrower defaults, the bank can institute legal proceedings to claim the collateral, sell it, and use the proceeds to satisfy the loan obligation. The most common collateral for short-term lending is working capital assets: the accounts receivable and inventories financed by the loan.

The use of collateral is governed by the Uniform Commercial Code (UCC), the commercial law adopted in whole or in part by all 50 states. The borrower signs a security agreement, a standard document by which property is pledged as collateral. The agreement is then filed with the state government ("perfected"), after which it has legal force and the lender obtains a security interest in the pledged property. The state makes all security agreements public so other lenders can know the extent of pledged assets and so anyone who disputes the agreement can know of its existence.

Assignment is the normal way that accounts receivable are pledged as loan collateral. The borrower extends credit to its customers and then sends the invoices

CONTRIBUTING TO GLOBAL SUSTAINABILITY

Starbucks Expands a Loan Program for Small-Scale Coffee Farmers

In 2009, Starbucks joined in a partnership with two organizations that promote fair trade to increase the amount of money available for loans to small farmers of specialty coffee beans. The partnership, the "Small Farmer Sustainability Initiative" has the goals of improving the farmers' standard of living, increasing their environmental stewardship, and helping them survive economic cycles.

The project began with a three-year pilot program to educate farmers in Latin America, East Africa, and the Asia-Pacific region through existing Starbucks Farmer Support Centers in those coffee-growing areas. Phase two will include the expanded loan program as well as additional technical assistance and the development of a single audit system for farmers who wish to apply for both fair trade and Starbucks Coffee and Farmer Equity (C.A.F.E.) certification.

According to Dub Hay, Starbucks' Senior Vice President for Coffee and Tea, "Our business relies on increasing the production and sustainability of small-scale coffee farmers around the world. Currently, 85% of Starbucks coffee is grown on family farms with less than 12 hectares of land, so increasing their access to affordable loans and technical support will help them not only survive the current global ecnomic crisis, but will help them emerge as stronger business partners for the future."

Reference: Transfair USA press release, April 16, 2009.

and supporting information to the bank. The bank does a credit evaluation of the borrower's customers and accepts some or all of the receivables as collateral. In general, the bank will accept receivables only from firms with an established credit rating. Also, banks prefer large accounts (i.e., receivables from the sale of "big-ticket" items) to minimize administrative costs as a percent of the loan. The bank then advances some fraction of the accepted receivables as a loan to the borrower. Usually the borrower's customer is unaware of the agreement and is instructed to mail its payment to a lock box picked up by the bank. When a payment arrives, the bank takes the fraction advanced to the borrower plus interest and remits (or credits the borrower's demand account for) the rest. Should a receivable become uncollectible, the bank has recourse to the borrower.

factoring—selling accounts receivable

factor—a company that purchases accounts receivable

Factoring is similar to assignment except that the accounts receivable are *sold* to the bank. The bank has no further recourse to the borrower if a receivable becomes uncollectible. When acting in this capacity, the bank is known as a **factor.**[4]

NET Present Value
Pacific Business Capital Corporation, at www.pbcc.com, is a typical factoring company

The collateral value of inventory depends on its perishability, marketability, market prices, and cost of disposing the inventory if necessary. In general, raw material is acceptable collateral if it is a commodity, but work-in-process is rarely acceptable because it is difficult to sell. The worth of finished goods and merchandise as collateral depends on the product: for example, appliances, canned foods, building materials, and fuels are generally acceptable while clothing, fresh foods, and specialized products are not.

---

[4] **Elaboration:**   Throughout this section we have been referring to banks as if they were the only source of short-term loans. In fact, quite a few other organizations—some independent such as Credit Centers, Inc. and CIT, and some affiliated with industrial corporations such as GE Credit—make short-term loans, especially asset-based loans.

There are four common methods by which a lender secures its interest in inventory collateral: (1) a floating lien, (2) a chattel mortgage, (3) a trust receipt, or (4) a warehouse receipt. They differ by the degree of control over the inventory demanded by the lender.

1. A *floating lien* is a general claim to all inventory owned by the borrower, either now or in the future as long as any part of the loan remains outstanding. Because of its broad coverage, it is also known as a "blanket lien." A floating lien is the least restrictive claim on inventory. The borrower retains full control of the goods, and the lender must first locate and identify the inventory and then take legal possession should it be needed to satisfy a loan.

2. A *chattel mortgage* is a claim on specific items of inventory, usually identified by serial number. Inventory remains with the borrower, however the borrower cannot sell it without the lender's consent. This form of security is particularly suitable for low-turnover, easily identifiable items.

3. With a *trust receipt,* the inventory collateral and any proceeds from selling it must be held by the borrower in a legal trust for the benefit of the lender. For example, trust receipts are often used to finance an inventory of automobiles at a retail showroom (where the process is known as "floor planning"). The cars on the lot are effectively owned by the lender and can be sold only if the dealer "buys" them by placing the sale proceeds in the lender's name. As a result of this degree of control, the lender's permission is not required prior to each sale.

4. A *warehouse receipt* is the most restrictive form of an inventory claim. Under this system, goods serving as collateral must be separated from the borrower's other inventory and kept in a warehouse under the control of a third party. The lender advances funds against each inventory item upon obtaining a receipt from the warehouse manager certifying that the item is indeed in the warehouse. Goods can be released from the warehouse only with the lender's permission. A warehouse located on the borrower's property is termed a "field warehouse." This arrangement is appropriate when the inventory is difficult or costly to move or when the borrower needs access to the inventory for technical or marketing reasons. A lender concerned that goods might be removed from the warehouse without permission will often require that the pledged inventory be taken from the borrower and stored in a "terminal warehouse" located away from the borrower's facilities.

4. Capital Market Alternatives to Bank Loans

In 1933, the Glass-Steagall Act separated commercial banks and investment banks in the United States.[5] Subsequently, each sought ways to recapture some of the business lost to the other in the split-up. Two creations of investment banks to reenter the world of short-term lending are commercial paper (a substitute for an offering basis loan) and Euronotes (a substitute for a revolving line of credit).

commercial paper—short-term, unsecured notes issued by large corporations

Commercial paper is short-term, unsecured, negotiable promissory notes representing direct borrowing and lending between large corporations without the use

---

[5] **Historical note:**   Most of the provisions of the Glass-Steagall Act were repealed by the Financial Services Modernization Act of 1999.

FINANCE IN PRACTICE

A Classic Tale: Sometimes Even a Terminal Warehouse Isn't Enough

In the early 1960s, officers of the Allied Crude Vegetable Oil Company approached the Bank of America for an asset-based loan to finance an inventory of salad oil. Because the president of Allied, Angelo (Tino) DeAngelis, had a criminal record and was known to associate with organized-crime figures, the bank hired American Express Field Warehousing Company, a unit of American Express, to establish and manage a terminal warehouse facility. American Express Field Warehousing posted a 24-hour-per-day armed guard. However, even these precautions proved insufficient. Tino DeAngelis arranged for his associates to be hired as guards who then looked the other way while he removed the oil. He also bribed American Express inspectors not to take a physical inventory and modified the oil tanks so spot checks would make it appear as if the oil were still there.

The theft was ultimately discovered, and DeAngelis spent years in federal prison for the "Great Salad Oil Swindle." But the salad oil was never recovered. Bank of America and the lending syndicate lost over $200 million, and the resulting lawsuits and bad publicity nearly put American Express out of business.

of a commercial bank. It is typically issued at a discount to its face value, much like Treasury bills, and carries no interest coupon.

Commercial paper is arranged by investment bankers who bring together the issuer and buyer (lender) for a broker's fee. Because the issuer and buyer deal directly, the amount and maturity of each issue is tailored to the parties' needs rather than to any standard amount or time period. Maturities range from a few days to nine months, but are rarely longer since paper with maturity of 270 days or less does not have to be registered with the Securities and Exchange Commission.

To encourage lenders to buy commercial paper, the major investment banks maintain an active secondary market for high-quality paper. This guarantees that a lender can resell the paper if it needs to retrieve its funds prior to maturity. In addition, most issuers maintain a commercial-bank revolving-credit line to back the issue. Should the issuer be unable to refund the paper at maturity due to low cash flow or the inability to issue new paper ("roll over the issue"), it can obtain the needed funds by borrowing against the revolver.

Commercial paper has become very popular among large corporations for at least five reasons. (1) It is low-cost financing. The interest rate on paper is normally below the reference rate by 1/4% to 2%, since investment banks bear none of the costs or risks of intermediation. (2) There are no compensating balance or fee requirements (other than the commitment fee for a backup revolving credit line) to add to the effective cost of the issue. (3) There are no institutional restrictions on the size of the financing. By contrast, the amount a bank can lend to any one customer is limited both by law and prudence to prevent excessive exposure to that customer's risks. (4) The investment bank serves as a resource. It provides market-oriented advice which may be of help in other capital-market-related decisions. (5) There is prestige in the ability to issue commercial paper. Only the largest, most creditworthy firms can enter this market.

However, there are some disadvantages to commercial paper. Firms that issue paper reduce their business with banks, potentially weakening those relationships. The interest rate on commercial paper, determined in the open market, is more volatile than the prime rate, exposing issuers of paper to greater uncertainty in their cost of funds. Also, the market for paper is impersonal and cannot handle variations in the issuer's plans, such as a change in cash needs or the desire to extend the maturity of a loan in a bad market.

Nevertheless, most large corporations have found the advantages of commercial paper to be so significant that they now use it for much of their negotiated short-term debt. Today, the dollar amount of commercial paper outstanding rivals total bank lending. Banks that once specialized in lending to the largest corporations have seen much of that business evaporate and now lend primarily to middle-sized ("middle market") and small companies.

Euronotes—short-term, unsecured, standardized notes issued by large corporations and governments in the Eurodollar market

Euronotes are short-term, unsecured, promissory notes issued by corporations and governments in the Eurodollar market outside the United States. They are most commonly denominated in dollars, but also in other currencies such as euros. Like commercial paper, they are issued at a discount to face value. However, they tend to have standardized face values—typically multiples of $250,000—and standardized maturities of one, three, or six months.

Euronote facility—a contract for the issuance of Euronotes

Euronotes are commonly issued through a **Euronote facility,** a contract between a bank (or syndicate of banks)[6] and the borrowing organization. The contract provides that the borrower may issue a series of Euronotes with a predetermined interest rate (normally referenced to LIBOR), typically over a period of five to seven years. The bank commits to purchase all the notes as issued up to a specified maximum amount for resale to investors. In return, the borrower pays a commitment fee to the financial institution.

A Euronote facility provides the equivalent of a revolving line of credit guaranteed for the life of the contract. In addition, Euronote financing is usually cheaper than domestic borrowing for two reasons: (1) the facility is priced in relation to LIBOR and not the higher U.S. prime rate, and (2) since Euronotes are resold to the general investing public, they have broadened the market for corporate debt by offering investors the ability to buy the paper of top-quality credits previously held only by banks.

Intermediate- and Long-Term Debt

Financial accountants classify debt with a maturity longer than one year as long-term, but the real-world division between current and long-term is somewhat more arbitrary and awkward. A note that matures in 13 months would be classified as long-term on the balance sheet, but is not very different from a 12-month note and is clearly not long-term in any meaningful sense. To deal with this distinction, financial professionals have coined the term "intermediate-term debt" for the middle maturities. While the dividing line between the intermediate term and long term is a matter of some debate and opinion, most financial observers place it somewhere in the range of seven to ten years.

---

[6] **Observation:** Since Euronotes are created and sold outside the US, the Glass-Steagall Act did not apply. Both U.S. investment and commercial banks became active participants in this market.

1. Term Loans

Term loans are loans with a maturity greater than one year. The word *term*, a synonym for *maturity*, emphasizes the extended time frame. Term loans are made primarily by commercial banks and life insurance companies. However, while banks are specialists in credit analysis, life insurance companies generally are not. As a result, banks lend to companies of all sizes and financial conditions, while the insurance companies lend primarily to large, financially sound companies.

Term loans are particularly appropriate financing in three circumstances: (1) when used to purchase an asset with an intermediate-term life, (2) as a substitute for a line of credit for a company whose operating cycle is longer than one year, and (3) as a "bridge loan." Often a company wishes to acquire an asset with an intermediate-term life which will generate cash benefits and provide good collateral value over that lifetime and not beyond. Such an asset matches the payment and collateral requirements of a term loan. A company with an operating cycle longer than one year—for example, a construction company whose natural cycle is the business cycle—may find short-term financing *too* short-term. A term loan guarantees the availability of financing for more than a year and avoids the out-of-bank clean-up period common to short-term loans. When market conditions are unfavorable for long-term financing, a term loan is often used to finance the firm until a bond issue becomes less costly. In this use the term loan is a **bridge loan,** spanning the gulf between today's position and the future financing. Term loans are also used as a bridge when long-term needs are uncertain and the company is unwilling to commit long-term to an amount or maturity of debt.

2. Leases

A lease is a rental agreement in which the owner of an asset (the lessor) gives another party (the lessee) the right to use the asset in return for a series of payments. An early use of leasing was to make the monthly cost of real estate affordable. Many companies did not have the desire or cash to purchase the land and buildings they required, and banks were unwilling to make loans for the temporary use of someone else's property. As other benefits of leasing were discovered, leasing was extended to virtually all types of business assets. Recently, there has been an explosion in nonbusiness leases, in particular individuals leasing automobiles.

Several types of organizations are active as lessors. Manufacturers often lease their own products, as IBM did for many years with its mainframe computers. Some manufacturers set up leasing subsidiaries to purchase their products and provide them to customers via lease. The three domestic automobile manufacturers are examples: Chrysler through Chrysler Financial, Ford through Ford Motor Credit, and GM through General Motors Acceptance Corporation (GMAC).[7] Most major banks have a sister leasing company; examples are Citigroup Leasing and Chase Manhattan Leasing. Leasing is also provided by some financing companies unaffiliated with a manufacturer or bank—"independents" such as Comdisco and ITEL Leasing.

---

[7] **Recent developments:** In 2006, GM spun off GMAC as an independent company that then became Ally Financial, a bank holding company, in 2008. Chrysler Financial separated from the automaker in 2007 when DiamlerChrysler sold its Chrysler unit to Cerberus Capital Management.

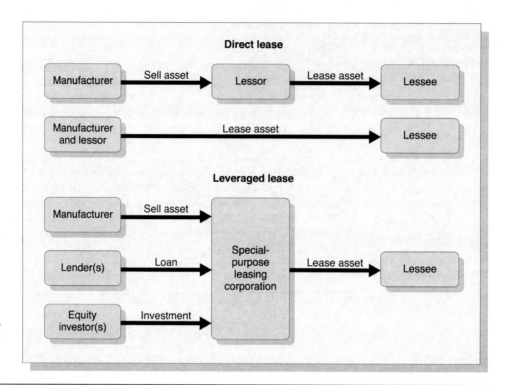

FIGURE 6.2
Direct and leveraged leases. In a leveraged lease, the lessor/investor leverages its position by borrowing to purchase the asset.

direct lease—a lease with only one investor, the lessor, who owns the leased asset

leveraged lease—a lease with both equity (the lessor) and debt investors

sale and leaseback—a transaction in which a company sells an asset to a lessor and then leases it back

full-service lease—a lease for an asset and also its operation and maintenance

net lease—a lease for an asset without any supporting services

Number of lessors   In some leases, called **direct leases,** the lessor manufactures or purchases the asset to be leased. Other leases are **leveraged leases,** in which the lessor invests only a portion of the cost of the asset and borrows the remainder, leveraging its investment position and increasing its rate of return. Figure 6.2 illustrates this difference. Leveraged leases are particularly popular for expensive assets with good collateral value such as airplanes, which can cost over $100 million apiece.

Previous ownership   Some leases are for equipment that is purchased directly by the lessor from its manufacturer or some other vendor. An alternative is the **sale and leaseback,** in which the lessor purchases the asset from the lessee and then leases it back to that company. A sale and leaseback is a way for a company to turn its investment in an asset into cash without losing the use of that asset. In recent years, several major New York banks have entered into sale and leaseback arrangements in which they have sold their headquarters office building to a lessor and then leased it back. The banks freed up millions of dollars to use for lending while retaining the use of the buildings.

Services purchased   Lessors use the term **full-service lease** when they provide both the use of an asset and its operation; the lessee's payment covers the cost of the asset itself and of operating and maintaining it. Mainframe computers and large-scale xerography equipment are examples of assets often obtained on full-service leases. The alternative is a **net lease,** a lease for the asset under which operating and maintaining the asset is the responsibility of the lessee. Automobile and aircraft leases are typically net leases.

operating lease—a lease providing temporary use of an asset

Nature of lease terms   An **operating lease** is similar to renting an apartment for a year—the lessee gains temporary use of the asset. The lease term is small relative to the life of the asset, and the lessee often can cancel the lease prior to its end. Lease payments represent only a fraction of the asset's worth. At the end of the lease, the asset generally returns to the lessor who may lease it to another party. Operating leases are used for assets required on a temporary basis such as office space, for assets subject to rapid obsolescence such as computers, and for assets that have short lives such as automobiles.

financial lease—a lease providing long-term use of an asset

A **financial lease** is similar to purchasing a house with a mortgage loan—the lessee gains use of the asset for or near its full life. The lease term is long relative to the life of the asset and rarely has a cancellation clause. Total lease payments are greater than the cost of the asset. At the end of the lease, the asset often becomes the property of the lessee, either automatically or for a nominal payment such as $1. Financial leases are generally used for assets required for long periods of time such as core plant and equipment.

Financial leases are of particular interest to financial managers because they are very similar to purchasing the asset using a term loan as financing. In both cases the company gets the use of the equipment over its full life. In both cases there is no way to cancel the acquisition of the asset. And in both cases the payments are greater than the asset's cost and may be seen as comprising the purchase price of the asset plus interest on the debt taken to procure it.

Financial accounting rules   Regardless of whether a lease is an operating or financial lease, the only transactions between lessee and lessor are the regular lease payments. As a result, there is a natural tendency to simply record each payment as an expense when it is made. Since the lessee does not own the asset, it does not appear on the lessee's books; neither is any obligation included in the lessee's liabilities. This accounting treatment makes sense for an operating lease in which there is no suggestion of ownership or any long-term obligation.

off-balance-sheet financing—financing that is not included in balance sheet liabilities

However, this simple accounting approach is inappropriate for financial leases since they duplicate the combination of a term loan and the purchase of an asset. Using this simple accounting approach, a company could use financial leases to hide both the existence of its leased assets and the associated payment obligations. When companies are able to raise funds without putting the liabilities on their balance sheet they are engaging in **off-balance-sheet financing.**

Examples

Off-Balance-Sheet Financing

Alicia Vasquez's company currently has $50 million of assets financed by $30 million of liabilities and $20 million of equity. Net income last year was $5 million. Alicia is wondering about the change to two financial ratios—return on assets and debt/equity—if $10 million of the assets financed by debt had been leased instead of purchased.

Question: Calculate the company's return on assets and debt/equity ratios at present.

Solution steps:

1. Return on assets (ROA) = net income/assets
   = $5 million/$50 million = 10%

2. Debt/equity ratio   = liabilities/equity
   = $30 million/$20 million = 1.5

Question: Recalculate these ratios assuming that $10 million of assets owned by the company and financed with $10 million of debt had been leased instead and could have been kept off the balance sheet.

Solution steps:

1. Calculate what assets and liabilities would have been:

   Assets = $50 million − $10 million = $40 million
   Liabilities = $30 million − $10 million = $20 million

2. Recalculate the ratios:

   Return on assets = $5 million/$40 million = 12.5%
   Debt/equity ratio = $20 million/$20 million = 1.0

Answer: If the debt and assets could be kept off the balance sheet, the company's <u>return on assets would increase from 10% to 12.5% and its debt/ equity ratio would decline from 1.5 to 1.0</u>.

Since off-balance-sheet financing can provide an inaccurate picture of a firm's financial condition, financial accounting rules have been designed to identify financial leases (also called *capital leases*) and require companies to treat them as if the firm had indeed taken a term loan and used the proceeds to purchase the asset. The asset appears on the lessee's books under a category called *leased assets* and is offset by a liability titled *obligations under capital leases,* representing the loan.

Benefits of a lease to the lessee   A company that obtains the use of an asset through a lease can obtain one or more of four benefits:

- Tax savings—A company that purchases an asset can reduce its taxes through depreciation and any other deductions and credits it is permitted to put on its tax return. However, the amount of the tax benefit depends on the firm's level of income. For example, a company with low income might be in a low tax bracket and get only a small tax reduction. By contrast, if a lessor in a high income tax bracket owns the asset, it can take full advantage of tax deductions in the current year and pass a portion of the savings along to the lessee in the form of lower lease payments. Leasing real estate provides another tax benefit: owned land cannot be depreciated while payments made to lease property are fully tax deductible.

- Cost savings—A lessor that regularly deals in a particular asset can often purchase it or maintain it for less than the lessee. The lessor can offer advice about the selection of the asset and can dispose of it more efficiently than the lessee at the end of its useful life.

- Risk avoidance—By leasing an asset on an operating lease instead of purchasing it, a lessee shifts the risk of obsolescence to the lessor. Obsolescence can be of two types: obsolescence of the asset itself due to a change in technology, or obsolescence of use in which the company's needs have changed and the asset is no longer useful. Either way, the lessee can return the asset to the lessor and not have to concern itself with disposal of the asset.

● Financing flexibility—Leasing is readily available for many assets without the need for a formal loan application or an extensive credit review. Unlike term loans, in which a bank might only lend 80% of the value of an asset, 100% financing is standard. There are rarely any protective covenants restricting the firm or its financial activities. In addition, many financial leases are structured with an annuity of lease payments, making the term loan embedded within them a fixed-rate loan. This provides companies the opportunity to acquire fixed-rate financing at rates that are often better than fixed-rate term loans.

Benefits of a lease to the lessor   For the lessor, a lease is the equivalent of a profitable loan. In an operating lease, the loan is a loan of property, and the lessor recoups some of the asset's cost. In a financial lease, the loan is one of money. The lessor makes or purchases the asset and is promised a series of payments that fully pay for the asset plus provide an acceptable rate of return. Also, the lessor has a superior position in bankruptcy compared with a bank that has made a collateralized loan, as it owns the asset and does not have to wait for legal authority to repossess it should the lessee stop making payments.

3. Bonds

A bond issue is a loan divided into uniform pieces or "bonds," designed to enable a company to raise funds from many lenders. Corporate bonds normally are in units of $1,000 each, municipals $5,000, and U.S. Treasurys $10,000 to $1,000,000. Thus a $10,000,000 corporate bond issue might be subdivided into 10,000 bonds, each with a $1,000 face value; and any one investor needs to lend only $1,000 to participate in the loan.

bond indenture—the formal agreement between a bond's issuer and buyer

The bond indenture   A **bond indenture** is the formal agreement spelling out the relationship between the lenders and the borrower, the organization that issues the bond. It specifies the bond's characteristics, collateral, and any restrictions placed on the company during the life of the financing.

trustee—a third party to a bond indenture, responsible for representing the bondholders to the issuing company

When bonds are held by the general public, it is normal for the issuer to appoint and pay a **trustee** to represent the interests of what can be a diverse and geographically separated group of investors. Most large commercial banks maintain a corporate trust department that offers this service. The trustee acts as an auditor, monitoring the issuer's activities against the requirements of the indenture and mailing to each bondholder an annual certification that the issuer is in compliance with the terms of the indenture. Should the issuer violate the indenture, the trustee can take action, legal if necessary, to protect the investor group.

mortgage bond—a bond with collateral

Bonds with collateral are called **mortgage bonds,** since the lenders receive a claim or mortgage on asset(s) of the borrower. A "first mortgage bond" has the most senior claim. If the company is unable to repay its debts and has to sell the collateral, first mortgage bondholders would receive their money before any other claim. Next in line are any "second mortgage bonds," "third mortgage bonds," etc. Some mortgages are "open-ended," meaning that any amount of additional debt of the same seniority may be issued using the same assets as collateral. Other mortgages are "limited open-ended" where a specified amount of additional debt of the same seniority may be issued using the assets as collateral, or "closed-ended," in which no additional debt of the same seniority may be issued against the named assets. Still other indentures have an "after-acquired clause" requiring that any new assets purchased by the company become additional collateral.

debenture—a bond with no collateral

A bond without collateral is a **debenture.** With a debenture, the lender's ability to be repaid depends on the firm's general financial strength, hence debentures are issued only by large, financially sound firms. Debentures often contain a "negative pledge clause" preventing both present and future assets from being pledged as collateral to any other lender, an action that would weaken the debenture holders' position should the issuer enter bankruptcy. Debentures may be "subordinated" to other financing, ranking below nonsubordinated debt in order of their claim to income and assets.

default—to breach a loan agreement

Bond ratings A borrower that violates one or more provisions of a bond indenture is said to be in **default.** There are two types of default. Financial default is the failure to make interest or principal payments on time. Technical default is the failure to comply with some other indenture provision—for example, maintaining ratios, insuring collateral, or providing information. Both types of default, however, can reduce a bond's value, either directly through changed cash flows, or indirectly through changed risk perceptions. When a company issues a bond, the interest rate it must pay depends in part on the risk of default perceived by investors. In an effort to sell their bonds at the lowest possible interest rate, many issuers hire a credit rating agency to evaluate the issue's default risk.[8]

NET Present Value Moody's is at www.moodys.com and S&P is at www.standardandpoors.com

The two major credit rating agencies for bonds are Standard & Poor's (S&P) and Moody's Investor Services. To establish their ratings they study a variety of factors which might provide clues to the issuer's future ability and willingness to meet its obligations. These include the issuer's business risk and stability of earnings, financial leverage, cash flow and interest coverage, and quality of management. Techniques used include financial ratio analysis, interviews with employees of the issuer and its key stakeholders, and a study of published information about the issuer and its industry. In general the agencies do not place much weight on collateral unless it is real property, due to the difficulty of predicting liquidation values.

The rating systems employed by S&P and Moody's are very similar and are listed in Figure 6.3. (Several of the classifications are further subdivided where finer distinctions are possible and worthwhile, such as category AA, which is divided into AA1, AA2, and AA3.) For both companies, a bond rated in any one of the top four categories is considered to be "investment grade," a bond with a sufficiently low probability of default to be legitimately considered a sound investment. Bonds rated below the first four categories are "speculative grade," too risky to be included in an investment portfolio.

In general there is a good correlation between bond ratings and yields, just as finance theory would predict. New bond issues rated highly by the agencies are

---

[8] **Elaboration:** Although sometimes the rating agencies will evaluate the default risk of a widely held bond on their own to make their rating books more complete, for the most part they only rate bonds when an issuer hires them to do so.

Moody's	S&P	Comment
Aaa	AAA	Highest grade obligation
Aa	AA	High grade; little difference from "triple-As"
A	A	Upper-medium grade; may be affected by changes in economic conditions
Baa	BBB	Medium grade; borderline between sound and speculative; good coverage under normal conditions but susceptible to downturns; lowest-quality commercial bank investment
Ba	BB	Lower medium grade; poor performance likely in downturns
B	B	Speculative; not desirable investments; small assurance of performance over long-term
Caa	CCC	Speculative (Moody's: may be in default)
Ca	CC	Speculative to a high degree; marked shortcomings (Moody's: usually in default)
C	C	Moody's: in default; S&P: an income bond with no payment
	D	S&P: in default

FIGURE 6.3

Bond ratings. Bonds in the first four categories are considered suitable for investment while those with lower ratings are described as speculative.

accepted in the financial markets as having a low risk of default and carry lower interest rates than bonds with lower ratings. However, the rating agencies generally lag the financial markets in analyzing changes to a bond's risk. Therefore, the ratings of seasoned issues tend to confirm what investors have already discovered about the bonds, rather than provide much new information. Figure 6.4 illustrates the relationship between bond ratings and yields for 30-year maturity, investment grade bonds.

In the 1980s, some investment professionals, most notably Michael Milken of the investment bank of Drexel, Burnham, Lambert, argued that the additional return from speculative grade bonds was high relative to the added risk making them an excellent investment opportunity. Known throughout the 1980s as **junk bonds,** speculative grade bonds were in great demand. Previously, all bonds were investment grade when issued and only became speculative grade if the issuer fell on hard times. However, in the 1980s, the demand for junk bonds grew to be so high—fueled in large part by Milken's success in publicizing his claims—that many companies came to market with bonds that were speculative to begin with.

junk bond—a speculative grade bond

FIGURE 6.4

Bond yields as a function of their ratings. As concerns about default risk increase, required yields increase as well.

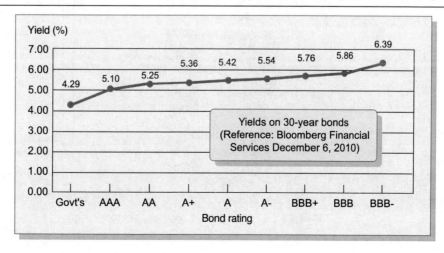

Yields on 30-year bonds (Reference: Bloomberg Financial Services December 6, 2010)

As long as business was booming, Milken's assertion held: the returns were high and few bonds defaulted. But by 1990 the economy had entered a recession, defaults on junk bonds had increased significantly, and the financial markets returned to the conventional wisdom that junk bonds were truly speculative.

International bonds   With the globalization of the financial markets, it is now possible for an issuer to raise funds in many currencies and in many countries. In general, a bond issued outside the borrower's home country is considered an **international bond.** It is useful to separate international bonds into three categories: (1) foreign bonds, (2) Eurobonds, and (3) multicurrency bonds.

international bond—a bond issued outside the borrower's home country

A **foreign bond** is a bond issued by a foreign borrower and denominated in the currency of the country in which it is issued. For example, a Swiss franc bond issued in Zurich by PepsiCo to fund its operations in Switzerland would be a foreign bond. Other than the fact that the issuer is not a Swiss company, this bond would be similar to other bonds issued in the Swiss capital markets. The issue would be denominated in Swiss francs, handled by Swiss investment bankers, offered to Swiss investors, and would trade in the Swiss bond markets.

foreign bond—a bond issued by a foreign borrower in the currency of the country of issue

A **Eurobond** is a bond denominated in a currency other than that of the country in which it is initially sold. Eurobonds are brought to market by a syndicate of investment bankers with global operations. The Eurobond market is an "off-shore" market, conducted outside the national boundaries of any one country.

Eurobond—a bond denominated in a currency other than that of the country in which it is sold

A **multicurrency bond** is a bond in which the principal, interest payments, or both are denominated in more than one currency. Three types of multicurrency bonds are: (1) multiple currency bonds, giving the lender the right to request that interest and/or principal be paid in any one of several specified currencies, (2) currency cocktail bonds, denominated in a currency unit based on a mix of currencies, and (3) dual currency bonds, in which interest payments are made in one currency and principal payments in another.

multicurrency bond—a bond denominated in more than one currency

"... and this is the office of our bond expert."

Retiring bonds Many bond issues remain in place for their full lifetime. On the maturity date the face value of each bond in the issue is paid to the bondholders and the bond issue ceases to exist. Other issues are retired early by being repurchased by the issuer, or converted to equity by the bondholder.

serial bond issue—a bond issue composed of bonds of many maturities

Some bond issues are structured as **serial bonds,** an issue consisting of bonds with different maturities. For example, in a 20-year issue of 10,000 bonds, 500 of the bonds might mature after one year, another 500 after two years, and so on, with the last 500 maturing at the end of the twentieth year. To identify the different maturities, each bond carries a serial number and the indenture specifies which bonds mature on which date. Other bond issues contain call options permitting the issuer to retire some or all of the bonds prior to their maturity date. The bonds are repurchased with cash on hand or cash accumulated in a **sinking fund**. Still other bonds contain a conversion option gives the bondholder the right to trade in the bond for shares of stock.

sinking fund—an account set up to accumulate the cash to retire debt

4. Floating-Rate Notes

Floating-rate notes (FRNs) are bonds issued for intermediate and long-term maturities with a variable rate of interest. They are primarily issued in U.S. dollars, but also in euros, U.K. pounds sterling, Canadian dollars, Hong Kong dollars, and SDRs. Although FRNs originated in the Eurocurrency markets, the FRN concept has spread to many domestic capital markets, including the United States, Switzerland, France, Italy, Belgium, and others.

The FRN has led to the creation of a family of similar securities including: (1) floating-rate certificates of deposit (FRCDs)—negotiable receipts for dollar-denominated bank deposits held in the United States; (2) Eurodollar floating rate certificates of deposit—FRCDs for dollar deposits outside the United States; and (3) floating/fixed-rate notes—convertible FRNs which may be exchanged for a traditional fixed-rate bond, either at the lender's option or automatically as provided at issue.

◼ Preferred Stock

preferred stock—stock with one or more features better than common stock and without any ownership claim

Preferred stock, also called *preference stock,* is stock that has no claim of ownership on the firm. In return, it has one or more features that are better than the comparable features of the company's common stock. Examples are a stated, unchanging dividend versus common stock's variable and uncertain dividend, and seniority to common stock in the event of bankruptcy or liquidation.

1. A Stock-Bond Hybrid

In concept and on the balance sheet, preferred stock resides between long-term debt and common equity (although as stock, it is often grouped with the owners' equity for reporting purposes). This location is appropriate for, in many ways, preferred stock is a hybrid between a bond and a share of stock.

Like a bond Among the characteristics of preferred stock that make it resemble bonds are the following:

- Preferred stock has a face value, also called *maturity value* and *par value*, representing the amount to be paid to the investor when the relationship is terminated. (Unlike bonds, that typically have face values of $1,000 or higher, the most common face value for preferred stock is $100 per share.)
- Preferred stock pays its holder a fixed amount each year which may be stated as a dollar amount or a percentage of face value.

Example

Preferred Stock Payment

Alicia Vasquez's father owns 200 shares of "$10 preferred stock" and also 100 shares of "11%, $100 face value preferred stock."

Question: How much does Mr. Vasquez receive in dividends each year from these two investments?

Solution steps:

1. The "$10 preferred stock" pays $10 per share per year.

$$200 \text{ shares} \times \$10 = \$2,000$$

2. The "11%, $100 face value preferred stock" pays 11% × $100 = $11 per share per year.

$$100 \text{ shares} \times \$11 = \$1,100$$

Answer: Mr. Vazquez receives $2,000 plus $1,100 or $\underline{3,100}$ in total.

- Preferred stock normally has no voting privileges.
- Preferred stock has priority above common stock in liquidation.
- Preferred stock may contain a call feature.
- Preferred stock may be convertible to common stock.
- A preferred stock issue may require a sinking fund for retirement. The sinking fund is often combined with a call feature so the firm has the ability to retire the issue at the lower of market price or call price.
- A preferred issue may contain indenture provisions—for example, a restriction on the firm's ability to issue senior claims or a requirement for a minimum level of liquidity.

Like common stock   Among the characteristics of preferred stock that make it resemble common stock are the following:

- Preferred stock rarely has a fixed maturity.
- The payment to investors in preferred stock is a dividend. It is paid at the discretion of the firm and is not tax-deductible.
- Some preferred issues permit preferred stockholders to vote in company affairs if an issue before the board of directors has a major effect on them or if the preferred dividend is not paid. Some issues give the preferred shareholders control over a fixed minority of seats on the board of directors.
- Preferred stock has priority after all debt in liquidation.

● The dividend on some preferred issues, known as *participating preferred stock*, can be increased if the firm has a particularly good year. Participating preferred stock may be "partially participating," where the extra preferred dividend is some fraction of the common dividend, or "fully participating" where any extra preferred dividend is equal to the dividend on the common stock.

Examples

Participating Preferred Stock

Mr. Vazquez's company has issued $12 *partially* participating preferred, requiring that if the common dividend exceeds $8.00 per share, the preferred dividend will rise by $0.50 for each additional $1.00 of common dividend.

Question: If a $10.00 per share common dividend is paid, what will happen to the preferred dividend?

Solution steps:

1. Determine the amount by which the common dividend exceeds the threshold of $8.00 per share:

$$\$10.00 - 8.00 = \$2.00$$

2. Add $0.50 per dollar of extra common dividend to the $12.00 preferred dividend:

$$\$12.00 + (2 \times \$0.50) = \$13.00$$

Answer: The preferred dividend will rise to <u>$13.00</u> per share.

Mr. Vasquez's company has also issued $9 *fully* participating preferred which pays a $9 per share dividend if the common dividend is $9 per share or less and pays a dividend equal to the common dividend if the latter is above $9 per share.

Question: If a $12 per share common dividend is paid, what will happen to the preferred dividend?

Answer: The preferred dividend will rise to <u>$12</u> per share to match the common stock dividend.

2. Cumulative Feature

Because preferred stockholders are concerned that the company's management may not pay the preferred dividend, most preferred stock has a protection built in known as the "cumulative feature." The cumulative feature prohibits payment of dividends on common stock if any preferred dividends have not been paid. A company that has not fully paid all preferred dividends is said to be *in arrears,* and the cumulative amount of preferred dividends owed is known as *arrearages.*[9]

Arrearages on preferred stock create (or confirm) problems for the company and its common stockholders as well as for the preferred stockholders. The company

---

[9] **Observation and cross-reference:** Recall that the word *arrears* first made an appearance in this book in Chapter 3, page 75, to describe an annuity in which cash flows come at the end of each period of time. In general, the word *arrears* implies *later in time,* which explains its use here.

may suffer a decline in its credit rating and a lessened ability to sell additional securities. Resumption of common dividends requires a large cash payment to the preferred shareholders, something that may be quite difficult for a cash-strapped firm. Common stockholders are prevented from receiving dividends as long as the arrearages remain outstanding, leading to a downward pressure on the market value of their stock. Preferred stockholders see their stock fall in price. Also, arrearages earn no interest; even if they are subsequently paid, the preferred shareholder has lost the time value of this money.

3. Advantages and Disadvantages of Issuing Preferred Stock

Preferred stock can be an attractive source of funds for many companies for several reasons: (1) Preferred financing preserves a company's debt capacity while raising funds in a manner similar to long-term debt. The preferred issue is fixed-rate financing, collateral is not required, and voting control is not diluted. (2) Preferred stock is accepted as equity by some regulatory authorities, permitting utilities and banks to maintain legally required equity levels without diluting their common stock. (3) Compared to common stock, preferred stock usually has a lower capital cost. (4) Preferred stock provides tax benefits to its holders, making it an attractive alternative to long-term debt for investors looking for steady income. 70% of dividends paid by one corporation to another are tax free. In addition, if preferred stock is acquired in a stock swap, any capital gain may be deferred until the preferred stock is sold, possibly years later.

There are also some important limitations to preferred stock: (1) Like dividends on common stock, preferred dividends are not tax-deductible to the issuing company, making the explicit cost of preferred stock capital high relative to debt. (2) Investors often see preferred stock as a particularly risky investment. The market price of preferred is volatile, swinging over a large range in response to interest rate fluctuations since preferred stock has an infinite life. Also, investors have no legal claim to preferred dividends, and historically many arrearages have not been paid in full. (3) A missed dividend could result in a strong negative reaction from creditors and stockholders, closing access to other financing.

Common Stock

common stock—ownership shares in a corporation

In a corporation, owners' equity takes the form of shares of **common stock.** Each share represents a fraction of the ownership of the corporation; for example, if a company has 1 million shares in the hands of its shareholders, each share owns one-millionth of the company.

The earliest companies depended on retained earnings or a few wealthy investors for their equity capital. The development of shares of stock permitted companies to raise equity funds from many investors, each contributing a relatively small amount of money, which significantly broadened companies' ability to raise funds.

NET Present Value
Full financial statements are available at
investor.shareholder.com/
jpmorganchase/annual.cfm

Figure 6.5 is the owners' equity section of the JPMorgan Chase & Company balance sheet published in the company's 2010 annual report. It shows that JPMorgan Chase has two types of stock outstanding: preferred and common stock. In addition, the statement shows that JPMorgan Chase has:

	2010	2009
Stockholders' Equity		
Preferred stock	$ 7,800	$ 8,152
Common stock ($1 par value; authorized 9,000,000,000 shares, issued 4,104,933,895 shares at both December 31, 2010 and 2009)	4,105	4,105
Capital surplus	97,415	97,982
Retained earnings	73,998	62,481
Accumulated other comprehensive income (loss)	1,001	(91)
Shares held in RSU Trust, at cost (1,192,712 shares and 1,526,944 shares at December 31, 2010 and 2009, respectively)	(53)	(68)
Treasury stock, at cost (194,639,785 shares and 162,974,783 shares at December 31, 2010 and 2009 respectively)	(8,160)	(7,196)
Total Stockholders' Equity	**$ 176,106**	**$ 165,365**

Source: Reprinted by permission of JPMorgan Chase & Co.

FIGURE 6.5
JPMorgan Chase & Company's owners' equity. The company has both preferred and common stock outstanding.

- Capital surplus, also known as "additional paid-in-capital"—money invested by common shareholders in excess of par value.

- Retained earnings—earnings reinvested in the business.

- Accumulated other comprehensive income (loss)—a second retained earnings account for "income" that is excluded from the income statement according to Generally Accepted Accounting Principles (GAAP). For JPMorgan Chase, these numbers come from the change in value of marketable securities held by the bank, the cost of cash-flow hedging activities, the change in the dollar value of the bank's foreign currency denominated investments (translation adjustment), and net losses assumed upon the acquisiton of Bear Sterns.

- Shares held in RSU Trust—JP Morgan Chase common stock held as Restricted Stock Units required for awards to key Bear Stearns executives under the Bear Stearns executive compenstation plan that existed before JP Morgan Chase aquired Bear Sterns in 2008.

- Treasury stock—shares repurchased by the company from investors.

You might find it interesting to refer back to this statement as you read further in the chapter about the characteristics of common stock.

1. Share Concepts

The common stock of a corporation may be subdivided into several groups. These are: (1) authorized shares, (2) issued shares, (3) outstanding shares, and (4) treasury shares. Figure 6.6 illustrates the relationship among these groups.

Authorized shares   Authorized shares are the maximum number of shares the firm has the legal authority to issue. When a company incorporates, it must spec-

FIGURE 6.6
Common stock share relationships. Some authorized shares are issued; issued shares remain outstanding unless repurchased for the corporate treasury.

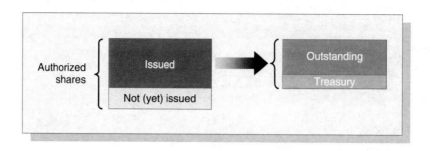

ify in its charter (the legal document of its corporate powers) the number of shares it plans to issue, now or in the future. By accepting the firm's charter, the state effectively authorizes the firm to issue up to this number of shares. Most companies do not immediately issue the full number of authorized shares but issue a lesser amount and reserve the remaining shares for subsequent issues. As long as the company stays within the limit of its authorization, it does not need to obtain state approval to issue additional shares. However, should the company desire to issue more shares than authorized, it must ask the state to amend its charter. All states require a stockholder vote before agreeing to such an amendment (since additional shares will dilute the shares already issued) but routinely approve the amended charter if stockholders agree.

Issued shares Issued shares are the number of shares the firm has distributed to investors. Management may elect to issue any amount from one to the full number of authorized shares. The number of unissued shares become those "authorized but not issued."

Outstanding shares Outstanding shares are the portion of the issued shares currently in the hands of investors. At any time, the company may repurchase some of the issued shares. Those remaining with shareholders are the outstanding shares.

Treasury shares Treasury shares are those issued shares no longer held by investors since they have been repurchased by the firm. They remain authorized and may be reissued again whenever management finds it appropriate to do so.

Example

Share Concepts

The end-of-year balance sheet in the JPMorgan Chase 2010 annual report discloses the following numbers about common stock:

Shares authorized:	9,000,000,000
Shares issued:	4,104,933,895
Treasury shares:	194,639,785

Question: How many shares were outstanding at the end of 2010?

Solution steps:

Shares outstanding = shares issued − treasury shares
= 4,104,933,895 − 194,639,785 = 3,910,294,110

Answer: There were 3,910,294,110 shares outstanding.

Earnings per share are calculated using the *average* number of outstanding shares.

Example

Earnings per Share

JPMorgan Chase reported net income applicable to common stock of $15,764,000,000 in 2010. While there were 3,910,294,110 shares outstanding at December 31, 2010, the *average* number of outstanding shares during 2010 was 3,956,000,000. Had all holders of options to buy the stock done so at the beginning of 2010, there would have been 3,977,000,000 shares outstanding on *average*.

Question: What was the company's primary and fully diluted earnings per share for 2010?

Solution steps: Earnings per share numbers are based on net income applicable to common stock

1. Primary EPS = net income/average shares outstanding
    = $15,764,000,000/3,956,000,000 = $3.98

2. Fully diluted EPS = net income/maximum average shares
    = $15,764,000,000/3,977,000,000 = $3.96

Answer: In 2010, JPMorgan Chase earned $3.98 per share, and $3.96 per share fully diluted.

2. Value Measures

The value of a share of common stock is measured in several ways: (1) par value, (2) book value, (3) market value, and (4) liquidation value.

par value—the minimum amount of money per share a shareholder is required to invest

Par value   When it refers to common stock, **par value** is a legal term representing the minimum capital contribution per share for which shareholders are liable. The concept was developed during the nineteenth century when a company's creditors looked to contributed capital as the firm's major source of funds for repaying its debts. Lenders felt more comfortable making a loan knowing the corporation could call on its shareholders for additional capital. Today, however, par value is not very relevant. Creditors have learned to look to operating cash flow as the source of funds for debt repayment. Further, par value is often set to a nominal (or zero) value so stockholders have fully met their capital requirement upon initial purchase of the stock. In fact, some states permit common stock to be issued without a par value.

Example

Par Value

The common stock of JPMorgan Chase has a par value of $1.00 per share. An investor who bought the stock from the company many years ago for $0.40 per share would be required to invest up to another $0.60 per share at the request of management. An investor who purchased a more recent issue at a price of $50.00 per share, however, would have no further obligation to invest.

Book value   Book value is the accounting measure of a share's worth: the value of owners' equity on the accounting records divided by the number of shares outstanding. By the fundamental accounting identity, owners' equity is equal to total assets less total liabilities. Thus, book value depends on the valuation rules (monetary versus nonmonetary, cash equivalent versus historical cost) and recognition (accrual) rules of Generally Accepted Accounting Principles for assets and liabilities. Since accounting asset values tend toward the conservative—using historical cost rather than market value for many numbers—while liabilities are usually carried at full value, book value is sometimes used by financial analysts as a lower limit when estimating the firm's worth.

Example

Book Value

JPMorgan Chase reported total stockholders' equity of $176,106,000,000 on December 31, 2010. There were 3,910,294,110 shares outstanding at that time.

Question: What was the company's book value per share on that date?

Solution steps:

Book value per share = total book value/shares outstanding

= $176,106,000,000/3,910,294,110 = $45.04

Answer: JPMorgan Chase's book value per share was $45.04.

Market value   Market value is the price of the firm's stock in the securities markets. In theory, it represents investors' aggregate judgment of the present value of all future benefits from the firm discounted at their required rate of return. Market value is the measure of shareholder wealth and is used to represent the value of the equity stakeholder in financial analysis and decision making.

Example

Market Value

JPMorgan Chase common stock closed at a price of $42.42 per share on December 31, 2010. There were 3,910,294,110 shares outstanding at that time.

Question: What was the total market value of JPM stock on that date?

Solution steps:

Total market value = share price × shares outstanding

= $42.42 × 3,910,294,110 = $165,874,676,146

Answer: The total market value of JPM stock was $165,874,676,146.

Liquidation value   Liquidation value is the amount left over for distribution to common shareholders in the event the firm terminates the business, sells its assets, and settles all prior claims. It is used primarily when a company is in or approaching bankruptcy and liquidation is expected.

*A*licia Vasquez walked out of her finance class talking animatedly to her classmates. There was a palpable excitement in her voice. Speaking faster than some of her friends could follow, she related her assignment at work and how she had taken advantage of that evening's class to learn more about the characteristics of various financial instruments.

Debt came in many versions, and equity was available in several forms. Among the differences between debt instruments were the debt's maturity, the extent of the lender's legal claim, and whether the debt would be included on the company's balance sheet. Key differences among equity instruments were voting power and the certainty of dividend payments. Alicia and her friends debated which of these features were the most important and what their impact would be both on a company and on its lenders and investors. The after-class discussion was so lively that an hour passed before anyone looked at a watch and the group finally said good-bye.

Alicia got into her car and tossed her books on the seat beside her. A well-chewed pen fell out of her notebook and onto the floor. Alicia laughed out loud as the pen caught her eye. "Well, that pen earned its keep today," she thought as she turned the key and backed out of the parking space. As she drove home, she began to look forward to going to work the next day and sharing her new insights with her colleagues.

Summary of Key Points

■ **Differentiate between debt and equity and identify how both are further classified.** Debt is a loan. Equity is investment in a company. Debt is classified by maturity, legal terms, and type of lender. Equity is classified by ownership privileges, in particular the right to vote for the board of directors and the certainty of dividend payments.

■ **Describe trade credit, accruals, and bank loans as sources of short-term debt, and identify two capital market alternatives to bank loans.** Trade credit can be in the form of an account payable, a note payable, or a third-party acceptance. A wide range of terms of sale—really terms of payment—are common, from the most liberal consignment to the most restrictive cash before delivery. Accruals—wages payable, taxes payable, interest payable, etc.—provide free financing since the delayed payment requires no increase in obligation. However, accruals can hide performance-related costs. Bank lines of credit and revolving credit lines are prenegotiated, while offering basis loans are not. Bank loans are normally priced relative to a base rate of interest: the prime rate in the United States and the London inter-bank offering rate (LIBOR) in the Euromarkets. For all but the most creditworthy customers, it is common for the bank to ask for accounts receivable or inventories as collateral. With factoring, the borrower sells its receivables to the bank. Capital market alternatives to bank loans are commercial paper and Euronotes. A Euronote facility guarantees that a firm can issue Euronotes up to a maximum amount for the length of the contract.

■ **Describe term loans, leases, bonds, and floating rate notes as intermediate- and long-term debt sources.**

Term loans are loans with maturities of greater than one year used to hedge intermediate-life assets, finance a long operating cycle, or serve as a bridge loan in an uncertain environment. An important distinction is between operating leases (short-term rentals), and financial leases (those that are very similar to the combination of a term loan and asset purchase). Financial leases must be accounted for as if a loan had been taken and the proceeds used to purchase the asset since the financial accounting profession is concerned about off-balance-sheet financing. Bonds are long-term debt instruments divided into uniform pieces for sale to many investors. Mortgage bonds are those with collateral; bonds with no collateral are termed debentures. To obtain lower interest rates, bond issuers often employ the services of credit rating agencies to evaluate and publicize the issue's risk of default. Those with low default risk are termed investment grade; bonds with greater risk of default are speculative grade or junk bonds. Many bonds are now issued in foreign countries and/or foreign currencies. Bonds end their lives by full payment at maturity, through periodic repayment of principal over the issue's lifetime, through the exercise of an option prior to maturity, or by default. Floating-rate notes are intermediate- and long-term, variable-rate bonds.

■ **Identify the characteristics of and rationale for issuing preferred stock.** Features such as its face value, fixed payment, lack of voting privileges, and priority above common stock, cause preferred stock to resemble a bond. However, other features such as lack of a fixed maturity, discretionary payment, and priority below debt, make preferred look like common stock. To prevent management from skipping the preferred dividend, most preferred stock issues have a cumulative feature preventing payment of a common stock dividend if the preferred dividend is in arrears.

■■■ **Describe common stock including various measures of number of shares and value.** Common stock is a corporation's owners' equity. A company arranges for the state to authorize shares, some of which are issued to the public. Those not repurchased for the company's treasury are identified as outstanding. Equity can be measured by its par value, book value, market value, and liquidation value.

Questions

1. Why is short-term debt an attractive source of financing to financial managers?

2. Why might a seller not be happy with an open account payable? What are the alternatives?

3. Under what conditions would a seller be willing to sell on consignment? on terms of cash before delivery? Under what conditions would a buyer be comfortable with each of these two extreme terms of sale?

4. What is net credit? What kind of company should have positive net credit? negative net credit?

5. Identify some of the hidden costs of accruals.

6. What are the differences among a line of credit, revolving credit line, and an offering basis loan?

7. What is a base rate of interest? What are the rates most commonly used for dollar-denominated loans?

8. What is collateral? Why do banks usually insist that it be part of a loan agreement?

9. What is the difference between assignment of receivables and factoring?

10. Why did investment banks create commercial paper and Euronotes? Distinguish between them.

11. Identify three conditions in which term-loan financing is particularly appropriate.

12. Identify the following lease concepts:
    a. Direct lease
    b. Leveraged lease
    c. Sale and leaseback
    d. Full service lease
    e. Net lease
    f. Operating lease
    g. Financial lease

13. Why do many companies find off-balance-sheet financing attractive? How might a company's investors —bondholders and stockholders—react?

14. Identify four benefits of a lease to the lessee and two benefits to the lessor.

15. Identify the following bond concepts:
    a. Indenture
    b. Trustee
    c. Mortgage
    d. Debenture
    e. Serial bond
    f. Sinking fund

16. What is the difference between technical default and financial default? Which is more critical to bondholders?

17. What is a junk bond? Why were junk bonds so popular in the 1980s? Why are they less popular today?

18. Distinguish between a foreign bond, Eurobond, and multicurrency bond. What are the advantages and disadvantages of each to both lender and borrower.

19. What is a floating-rate note?

20. Why is preferred stock often called a hybrid between bonds and common stock?

21. Is there any difference in value between cumulative and noncumulative preferred stock? Why, or why not?

22. Distinguish among the following common stock concepts:
    a. Authorized shares
    b. Issued shares
    c. Outstanding shares
    d. Treasury shares

23. What is the difference between primary and fully diluted earnings per share?

24. Distinguish among the following common stock concepts:
    a. Par value
    b. Book value
    c. Market value
    d. Liquidation value

Problems

1. **(Net credit)** A company has accounts receivable of $1 million. Calculate the company's net credit and whether it is a net supplier or net user of trade credit if its accounts payable equals:
    a. $600,000   c. $1,000,000
    b. $800,000   d. $1,200,000

2. **(Net credit)** A company has accounts payable of $4 million. Calculate the company's net credit and whether it is a net supplier or net user of trade credit, if its accounts receivable equals:
    a. $6 million   c. $4 million
    b. $5 million   d. $3 million

3. **(Off-balance-sheet financing)** A company currently has $100 million of assets financed with $50 million of debt and $50 million of equity. Net income last year was $10 million. Calculate the company's return on assets ratio and debt/equity ratio:

   a. Now
   b. Assuming the company had leased $5 million of its assets off the balance sheet
   c. Assuming the company had leased $15 million of its assets off the balance sheet
   d. Assuming the company had leased $25 million of its assets off the balance sheet

4. **(Off-balance-sheet financing)** A company currently has $400 million of assets financed with $250 million of debt and $150 million of equity. Net income last year was $20 million. Calculate the company's return on assets ratio and debt/equity ratio:

   a. Now
   b. Assuming the company had leased $25 million of its assets off the balance sheet
   c. Assuming the company had leased $50 million of its assets off the balance sheet
   d. Assuming the company had leased $75 million of its assets off the balance sheet

5. **(Preferred dividend)** A company has an outstanding issue of $100.00 par value preferred stock. It recently declared a $7.00 per share dividend on its common stock. How much will the company pay in annual per-share preferred dividends if the preferred is:

   a. "$12.00 preferred stock"?
   b. "14% preferred stock"?
   c. $10.00 partially participating preferred, requiring that the preferred dividend increase by $0.25 for every dollar the common dividend exceeds $5.00?
   d. $6.00 fully participating preferred, requiring that the preferred dividend increase to equal the common dividend if the latter exceeds $6.00?

6. **(Preferred dividend)** A company has an outstanding issue of $100.00 par value preferred stock. It recently declared a $12.00 per share dividend on its common stock. How much will the company pay in annual per-share preferred dividends if the preferred is:

   a. "$13.00 preferred stock"?
   b. "11% preferred stock"?
   c. $8.00 partially participating preferred, requiring that the preferred dividend increase by $0.60 for every dollar the common dividend exceeds $8.00?
   d. $8.00 fully participating preferred requiring that the preferred dividend increase to equal the common dividend if the latter exceeds $8.00?

7. **(Number of shares)** A company whose charter authorizes 10 million shares, has sold 6 million to the public. Of these, 5 million are in the hands of investors today.

   a. How many shares are issued?
   b. How many shares are authorized but not issued?
   c. How many shares are outstanding?
   d. How many shares are in the treasury?

8. **(Number of shares)** A company whose charter authorizes 40 million shares, has sold 25 million to the public. Of these, 7 million have been repurchased by the company.

   a. How many shares are authorized but not issued?
   b. How many shares are outstanding?
   c. How many shares are in the treasury?
   d. Could the company split its stock 2 for 1 without getting authorization for additional shares?

9. **(Share value)** At the end of last year a company had 12 million shares ($2.50 par value) outstanding and total owners' equity of $96 million. Net income in the past year was $25 million, and 11.5 million shares were outstanding on average during the year.

   a. What is the remaining obligation, if any, of a shareholder who purchased shares from the company at $1.00 per share?
   b. What is the remaining obligation, if any, of a shareholder who purchased shares from the company at $10.00 per share?
   c. Calculate the company's book value per share at year-end.
   d. Calculate the company's earnings per share for the year.

10. **(Share value)** At the end of last year a company had 25 million shares ($1.00 par value) outstanding, and total owners' equity of $100 million. Net income in the past year was $75 million, and 24 million shares were outstanding on average during the year.

   a. What is the remaining obligation, if any, of a shareholder who purchased shares from the company at $0.40 per share?
   b. What is the remaining obligation, if any, of a shareholder who purchased shares from the company at $40.00 per share?
   c. Calculate the company's book value per share at year-end.
   d. Calculate the company's earnings per share for the year.

CHAPTER 7
FINANCIAL
MARKETS AND
INSTITUTIONS

*A*lexandra McLean reached for one of the dozen books on the chair beside her desk, located the passage she was looking for, and wrote several notes on one of the 20 or so pieces of paper covering her desk. Replacing the book, she grabbed a second sheet of paper and wrote down another thought. After about 40 minutes of this, she sat back and surveyed her desk with a shake of her head. How would she make sense of all this information?

Alex was a vice president and lending officer at a large bank. Several years ago she had completed her bachelors degree with honors at a local university, and now she had been asked by the chair of the finance faculty to speak on financial markets and institutions at a session of the introductory finance class. Alex's problem was to organize the material in a way that would be interesting and useful to the students—all within one 90-minute class period.

Alex looked over her notes. One page was labeled "primary markets." Another was titled "secondary markets." There were several pages on investment and commercial banks, insurance companies, mutual funds, and other members of the "financial industry." Directly in front of her were notes about the way security prices behaved. She moved several of the pages around, cocked her head, and looked over the papers again. Slowly, the pattern was making sense. Alex took out a clean sheet of paper and sketched out a summary outline of the topics. She could see the class session beginning to take shape. One by one she reorganized the pages, turning them into the materials that would guide her during the class.

The financial markets provide the setting in which much financial activity occurs. Within these markets, individuals and companies obtain money for the present and save and invest for the future. Securities are issued and traded, loans are made and repaid, and risks are shared and shifted. Companies' prospects are analyzed and priced. Financial institutions—including investment and commercial banks, insurance companies, mutual funds, and pension and endowment funds—are key players in these markets, bringing savers and investors together and handling the transfer of billions of dollars daily.

As students of finance, we all struggle with the same problem facing Alex. The world of financial markets and institutions is a marvelously rich and complex one, with many participants and organizations providing a wide variety of financial products and services. The study of financial markets and institutions is legitimately a full course in itself. Like Alex's 90-minute class, this chapter can only hope to scratch the surface and provide a description of the most important players and concepts.

Key Points You Should Learn from This Chapter

After reading this chapter you should be able to:

- Describe seven roles of financial markets and institutions, three methods of channeling funds from net savers to net investors, and the difference between the money and capital markets.
- Discuss how newly created securities are issued, including the role of the investment banker, flotation costs, and private placement.
- Describe the nature of the secondary financial markets, including the securities exchanges and other trading mechanisms.
- Identify indexes that measure financial market activity; and compare technical analysis, fundamental analysis, the efficient market hypothesis, and the random walk as descriptions of security price behavior.
- Describe three types of financial intermediaries and five types of financial intermediation.

Introductory Concepts—The Functions and Functioning of Financial Markets and Institutions

Of all the roles played by the financial system, the movement of funds from individuals and companies with surplus resources to those in need of money is one of the most important. In this section, we look briefly at the roles played by financial markets and institutions, identify three ways in which funds move within the system, and draw the distinction between the money and capital markets.

1. Functions of Financial Markets and Institutions

Financial markets and institutions perform at least seven functions in the economic system. They are: (1) a payments mechanism, (2) a vehicle for savings, (3) a supplier of credit, (4) a storehouse of wealth, (5) a means of obtaining liquidity, (6) a mechanism for risk shifting, and (7) a vehicle for public policy.

Payments mechanism   Most payments for goods and services are made by checks or electronic transfers processed by the banking system.

Savings vehicle   Individuals use financial markets and institutions such as banks and stock brokers to move their savings into bank deposits, notes, bonds, and stocks.

Credit supplier   Financial institutions such as banks, as well as companies and individual investors operating in the financial markets, provide loans that permit companies and individuals to supplement their income and purchase assets.

Wealth storehouse   Most individuals and companies that have accumulated liquid capital use financial instruments traded in the financial markets to store their wealth.

Liquidity source   The many participants in the financial markets provide savers with the ability to convert most financial assets to cash if and when required.

Risk reducer   Financial intermediaries such as banks and insurance companies sell a wide variety of products to reduce the risk of exposure to financial and physical damages.

Policy vehicle   The federal government uses its ability to affect the financial markets to influence the stability and rate of growth of the economy.

2. Imbalances in Income and Expenses

Consider what a typical year in your life will look like from a financial point of view. Most likely, you will earn some money from a job, which may be supplemented by earnings from a bank account or other investments. From your income you will have to pay your living expenses: food, clothing, shelter, education, entertainment, etc. As we saw in Chapter 5, if you earn more than you spend, you face the decision of how best to deploy your excess cash. On the other hand, if you spend more than you earn, your problem is to obtain external financing to make up the deficit. The same is true for every other individual and business in the economy.

Accordingly, over any period of time, every individual, business, and government falls into one of three categories: (1) a **deficit-budget unit,** (2) a **balanced-budget unit,** or (3) a **surplus-budget unit.** A deficit-budget unit is one whose expenditures exceed its revenues; to make up the deficit it must acquire additional funds. A balanced-budget unit (a rarity) is one whose expenditures exactly equal its revenues; it is able to take Polonius's advice in *Hamlet* and: "neither a borrower nor a lender be." A surplus-budget unit is one whose revenues exceed its expenditures; it looks for ways to invest its excess funds.

It is normal for any individual or business to move back and forth between these three states. Individuals tend to be deficit-budget units in the early stages of their working lives when their income is relatively low and when they are starting families and acquiring assets. Later in life, individuals often switch over to be surplus-budget units as their income increases and their children grow up and leave home. As the external financing needs (EFN) model of Chapter 5 illustrated, companies tend to be deficit-budget units during periods of rapid growth and surplus-budget units when they reach a more mature stage.

3. Moving Funds from Surplus Units to Deficit Units

In a world with both surplus-budget units looking to invest funds and deficit-budget units looking to obtain them, it is natural that the financial markets have created mechanisms to channel funds from the former to the latter. It is common to classify these routes into three categories: (1) direct transfer, (2) semidirect transfer, and (3) indirect transfer or intermediation. Figure 7.1 illustrates these three paths. For simplicity, surplus-budget units are identified as "lenders" and deficit-budget units as "borrowers" in Figure 7.1, even though the transaction they engage in might not have the legal form of a loan.

Direct transfer   The simplest method for moving funds is direct transfer from lender to borrower. If you have ever borrowed money from a relative or friend, you have used this method. Some corporations and investment funds also use direct transfer. However, since this method requires both parties to know of and have access to each other, it is the least used of the three routes.

Semidirect transfer   Semidirect transfer involves the use of a professional **broker** to locate buyers and sellers and bring them together. Imagine trying to sell a house using direct transfer. The odds of your knowing a buyer with the desire and the money to buy your house when you want to sell it are minuscule. You could advertise in the local paper or put a sign on the lawn to attract passersby, but this might not bring in sufficient potential buyers. As a result, most people use a real-estate broker when they sell their houses. As Figure 7.1 indicates, in the financial markets this role is primarily played by investment bankers. Like direct transfer, the money and securities are exchanged directly by the lender and borrower. The broker does not handle the funds but simply earns a finder's fee.

(margin notes)

deficit-budget unit—an individual or business that spends more than it earns

balanced-budget unit—an individual or business that spends exactly what it earns

surplus-budget unit—an individual or business that spends less than it earns

broker—an individual or company that locates buyers and sellers and brings them together

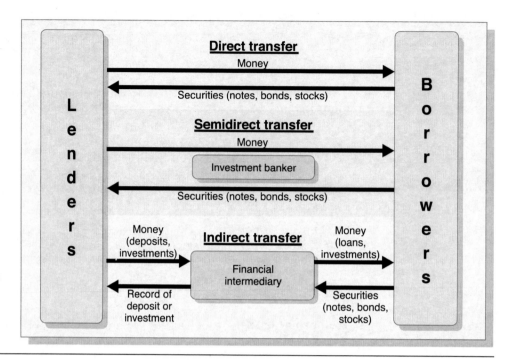

FIGURE 7.1

Methods of funds transfer. Money moves from lenders to borrowers in one of three ways: direct, semidirect, or indirect.

financial intermediary—an organization that takes funds from surplus-budget units and provides them to deficit-budget units

intermediation —moving funds through financial intermediaries

Indirect transfer   The third method of moving funds is through a **financial intermediary,** an organization that places itself between savers and investors. Because of the participation of intermediaries, this route is called **intermediation.** It is quite common for the needs of lenders and borrowers not to match. For example, suppose you had $1,000 you wished to invest for the next 60 days. What are the odds that you, or a broker hired by you, would find a deficit-budget unit with exactly that requirement for funds? Financial intermediaries solve this and other problems of mismatched needs by combining the loans of many lenders, repackaging the money in other forms, and then relending the funds to a variety of borrowers.

A commercial bank would be a typical financial intermediary represented in Figure 7.1. You could deposit your $1,000 in a savings account at a bank and be able to withdraw your funds in 60 days. The bank would combine your money with the deposits of other lenders and make loans of many different types to its customers—the deficit-budget units—in the amounts and for the periods of time they desire. Note that you never deal with the ultimate borrowers of your money—in fact you never even learn who those persons or organizations are. Both your needs and those of the borrower are met by the intermediary.

4. Money vs. Capital Markets

money markets—the markets for (debt) securities with maturity of one year or less

capital markets—the markets for securities with maturity greater than one year

The term **money markets** is used for the financial markets where debt securities with a maturity of one year or less trade. The **capital markets** are the markets for securities with maturity longer than one year, including intermediate and long-term notes, bonds, and stocks.

With its short-term focus, the primary function of the money markets is to help individuals and organizations manage their liquidity, i.e., their day-to-day cash

CONTRIBUTING TO GLOBAL SUSTAINABILITY

The Equator Principles

In June 2003, a group of ten large banks announced that they were adopting the Equator Principles, a new set of lending guidelines for project finance, commonly major industrial and infrastructure projects. The Principles apply to all projects over US$50 million and require the lending institutions to assess the environmental and social risks of the projects. For a loan to be made to a project that is likely to have major adverse impacts on the environment or vulnerable social gorups, the lender must complete an Environmental Assessment to include an analysis of resource use; protection of health, biodiversity, and cultural resources; use of dangerous substances; occupational heatlh and safety; socioeconomic impacts; energy use; and pollution. The borrower must prepare a corresponding Environmental Management Plan that addresses mitigation of the problems including action plans, monitoring, and risk management. The Environmental Assessment and Environmental Management Plan then become covenants in the financing agreement; should the borrower not comply with them, the financing is declared in default and the lenders can force compliance or terminate the agreement and request immediate repayment.

By the summer of 2011, 72 financial institutions had adopted the Equator Principles.

NET Present Value
Information about U.S. Treasury bill, bond, and notes can be found at
www.publicdebt.treas.gov/

position. Individuals use the money markets for short-term personal loans, cash advances against their credit cards, and to cover overdrafts against their checking accounts. Companies use the money markets to finance temporary working capital needs. Governments borrow heavily in the money markets as well; for example, the federal government sells the Treasury bills we discussed in Chapter 4 to balance its tax receipts and expenditures. And investors, both individuals and institutions, use funds from the money markets to finance the purchase of securities on margin, a topic we will cover in Chapter 8. In Chapter 6, we studied the common money market instruments used by businesses.

The capital markets provide intermediate and long-term financing for assets of comparable maturity. Individuals use the capital markets to finance the purchase of homes, automobiles, and other durable goods. Companies raise funds in the capital markets to build plant and equipment, to finance permanent working capital, and for mergers and acquisitions. Governments use capital market funds to build schools and highways and to finance their long-term deficits. In Chapter 6 we looked at the common capital market instruments that businesses use.

Although the maturities of the instruments traded and the functions of the money and capital markets are clearly distinct, in practice the distinction blurs quite a bit both in terms of the participants and the places where market activity takes place. Most individuals and organizations participate in both markets. For example, a commercial bank may make short-term and intermediate-term loans in the same day, the federal government may sell 90-day Treasury bills and 15-year Treasury bonds in the same week, or a family may take a one-month cash advance on its credit card and refinance its 30-year home mortgage in the same month. Also, both money market and capital market securities are often traded in the same location. For example, a commercial bank retail office may be the site of loan transactions of many maturities, and one-month Treasury bills trade along with the common stock of many companies on the "over-the-counter market."

Primary Financial Markets

primary financial markets— the markets for the initial issue of securities

The **primary financial markets** are the markets where securities are issued for the first time. For example, when China Hydroelectric Corporation, sold $96,000,000 of its common stock in January 2010, it did so in the primary markets. In 2010, U.S. corporations issued bonds worth $1.05 trillion, and more than 200 companies came to market for the first time with **initial public offerings** worth $42.9 billion.[1]

initial public offering (IPO)— the first public sale of a company's stock

1. The Investment Banker

NET Present Value
One well-known investment banking firm is Goldman Sachs at
www.gs.com

A key player in the primary markets is the investment banker, a specialist in the distribution of new securities. Most firms go to the capital markets infrequently and find it costly to develop the skills and resources needed to issue securities. Investment bankers have the expertise, contacts, and scale of operations to perform this function efficiently and at comparatively low cost.

Investment bankers provide a variety of services to companies issuing securities, including: (1) analysis and advice, (2) underwriting, (3) selling, and (4) market stabilization.

Analysis and advice As experts in the issuance of securities, investment bankers advise companies on the amount and timing of a new issue, the combination of features to include in the issue, how to price the issue, and the legal aspects of bringing the issue to market (although most of the detailed legal work generally is done by outside counsel who are specialists in the complex area of Securities and Exchange Commission (SEC) registration requirements).

For a publicly traded stock, it is typical for an issue of additional shares to be priced at slightly below market in order to attract new investors. For an initial public offering, however, there is no market price on which to base the offering price of the new issue, and the investment banker will conduct an analysis of the company, conditions in the stock market, and comparable firms to recommend a fair price. Either way, since market conditions change daily, the actual offering price normally is not finalized until the last moment.[2]

Underwriting Companies need to plan their cash flow and usually wish to avoid the risk of not knowing the proceeds of a security issue until after the fact. In response, investment bankers offer a service known as **underwriting** that ensures that the firm will receive a given amount from the sale. The investment banker purchases the issue at the agreed-upon price and then assumes the responsibility for reselling the issue to the public. Notice that when investment bankers assume this role, they go beyond the simple broker relationship between buyer and seller and act as intermediaries.

underwriting— guaranteeing the proceeds of a security issue by purchasing the issue at an agreed-upon price

The investment banker normally creates an underwriting group, or syndicate, to spread the risk of underwriting an issue. Within the syndicate, the firm's invest-

---

[1] **Reference:** The Securities Industry and Financial Market Association website (www.sifma.org).

[2] **Elaboration:** When 3Com Corp. spun off Palm, Inc., the manufacturer of the PalmPilot electronic organizer, in March of 2000, the offering price was reset from $14/share to $38/share in the days leading up to the IPO reflecting intense interest in the new security. The stock opened for trading at $150/share.

ment banker is known as the *originating house* and usually takes on the responsibility of lead underwriter or manager of the syndicate.

Selling   The investment banker puts together a selling group, consisting of the syndicate members plus up to several hundred additional securities dealers who actually place the securities with their customers. To further reduce the risk of underwriting, the selling group typically lines up buyers even before the offering is made. Since the SEC prohibits offering a security without a disclosure statement known as a **prospectus**, a preliminary prospectus, popularly known as a *red herring*, is used at this stage.

Market stabilization   The manager typically agrees to "make a market in" (buy and sell) the newly issued securities for a specified period after the issue date—normally 30 days—guaranteeing that the original investors can resell the securities if they desire.

Figure 7.2,[3] is an announcement of China Hydroelectric Corporation's public offering of $96,000,000 of common stock, popularly known as a *tombstone*. In addition to identifying the company and the number and type of securities, tombstones list the investment bankers who participated in the issue, in this case just Broadband Capital Management LLC.

prospectus—a booklet of data about a company that must be given to potential investors prior to soliciting any money

2. Flotation Cost

Flotation cost, the cost of issuing new securities, generally consists of two components: the spread, or investment bankers' fees; and administrative costs including registration of the issue with the SEC, legal fees, printing costs, trustee's fees, outside auditors' fees, and taxes.

Flotation costs vary with the risk of placing the issue—how difficult it will be for the investment banker to sell the securities. One factor is the riskiness of the security itself. In general it is more difficult to sell stock than bonds, so the flotation cost for stock is normally greater than that for bonds. For the same reason, large, stable firms pay lower flotation costs than small, speculative firms. Flotation costs also vary with the size of the issue. In general, large issues cost less to float on a percentage basis due to the ability to spread the fixed costs of the issue across many securities, the ease of selling better-known issues, and competition among investment bankers for major clients.

Example

Underwriting Spread
In advising a company on its planned security issue, its investment banker has proposed a spread equal to 4% of the issue's face value, subdivided as follows:

Managing underwriter's fee	0.60% of issue
Underwriting (risk) fee	1.40% of issue
Concession (selling) fees	2.00% of issue
	4.00%

---

[3] **Reference:**   Broadband Capital Management website; http://broadbandcapital.com/deals.php

FIGURE 7.2
A tombstone. These announcements of new security issues identify the amount of the issue, company, type of security, and the investment banker.

3. Private Placement

private placement—the sale of a new issue of securities directly to an investor

A **private placement** is the sale of a security issue directly to one or a small group of investors without going through the public markets. For example, a company might sell $10 million of its debt to a life insurance company rather than offering it to the general public. Both bonds and stock are privately placed, although the volume of debt transactions far exceeds that of privately placed equity.

Private placements are done both with and without the services of an investment banker. Large, experienced companies that are known to the private investment community often use private placements to avoid engaging a broker and paying flotation costs. However, smaller companies and those with less exposure to financial markets typically still require the services of an investment banker to locate investors and to provide advice about market conditions, timing, and how to structure the issue. Banks that assist companies in privately placing their debt like to advertise in the financial press to celebrate their success and to attract new customers. Figure 7.3[4] is the announcement of the private placement of $6.5 million of notes by the City of Winooski, Vermont.

Four advantages of private placements relate to: (1) speed, (2) privacy, (3) terms of the issue, and (4) size of the issue.

Speed   Compared to public offerings, private placements can be made far more quickly. There is no requirement for registration with the SEC, avoiding the time it takes to prepare and file extensive paperwork, and no mandated waiting period between filing and offering dates as there is with a public issue. In 1982, however, in response to concerns over long lead time, the time to issue securities to the public was lessened considerably when the SEC approved a system known as **shelf registration.** Under shelf registration, a company files the required paperwork for a public issue in advance of its intention to issue the securities. The company then can issue the securities in small batches via auction without further SEC authorization.

shelf registration—advance SEC approval to make small public security issues

Privacy   Because there is no public filing or announcement in a private issue, the company is not required to disclose any information to the public about its

---

FIGURE 7.3
Announcement of a private placement. The City of Winooski borrowed $6.5 million from Banknorth, N.A.

This announcement appears as a matter of record only.

$6,500,000

City of Winooski, Vermont

Winooski Downtown Redevelopment Project

Revenue Anticipation Note Series 2004

These notes were placed with

Banknorth, N.A.

The undersigned acted as Financial Advisor to the City

BITTEL FINANCIAL ADVISORS

May 26, 2004   Burlington, Vermont

---

[4] **Reference:**   Bittel Financial Advisors, LLC website: www.bitteladvisors.com/tombstones.asp.

operations, finances, or management. This can be appealing to companies concerned about competitors' potential use of the data or to wealthy stockholders and managers who might prefer not to make their financial status public.

Terms   In a private placement, the terms of the issue are tailored to the needs of the borrower and lender through direct negotiation. There is far less pressure to make the issue conform to the standard terms and forms preferred in the public markets.

Size   Private placement permits small issues to be sold without excessive flotation costs. For example, while a small public issue might be anything below $10,000,000 a small private issue could easily be as small as $100,000.

There are also some disadvantages to private placements. Privately placed securities tend to be difficult to resell since a public market for the issue has not been established. The lender, desiring to benefit from the issue for its full term, often insists on a covenant prohibiting refinancing at the borrowers' option. And even though flotation costs are typically lower than for a public issue, overall costs are usually higher since private lenders demand a higher interest rate and also often negotiate some form of "sweetener," such as warrants or a convertible feature.[5]

Secondary Financial Markets

secondary financial markets—the markets for trading existing securities

The **secondary financial markets** are the markets for the reselling or trading of previously issued securities. In this section we look at the functions of secondary markets and explore the exchanges and other mechanisms by which securities are traded.

1. Functions of the Secondary Markets

Five functions of the secondary markets are: (1) to permit trading, (2) to provide information, (3) to create continuity, (4) to protect participants, and (5) to improve the distribution of capital funds.

Permit trading   The secondary markets are places where a large number of buyers and sellers can come together. By centralizing the activities of many participants, the probability becomes very high that every buyer will find a seller and every seller will find a buyer quickly and for the same amount of securities. Participants can invest for the long term or, if so inclined, can speculate on future price movements of securities.

Provide information   Trading activities in the organized secondary markets are public and highly visible. The ticker tape reporting security trades—no longer a physical tape but now a computerized record—is made available to the public in real time. It is displayed in brokerage houses and on television channels, and is accessible to anyone by computer. In addition, fair and competitive price quotations are available for the asking.

---

[5] **Cross-reference:**   Warrants and convertibles are discussed in Web Appendix 6D.

Create continuity   With so many trades taking place, the secondary markets guarantee that securities are highly liquid and marketable. This not only makes it easy for investors to cash out of their positions, it also ensures that securities are good loan collateral, permitting trading on margin and enhancing individuals' and companies' ability to borrow.

Protect participants   The regulation of the secondary markets by the Securities and Exchange Commission and the rules of activity established by each exchange (which must be approved by the SEC) create a set of publicly known and accepted ground rules for trading activities. Security brokers and dealers must be licensed—a designation requiring the passing of examinations covering market procedures and securities law—and must act within a strict set of guidelines defining legal and ethical behavior. Market activities are supervised by regulatory authorities on a continuous basis in a further attempt to identify and eliminate any fraudulent activities.

Improve capital distribution   An active secondary market makes investors more willing to purchase securities in the primary market, since it becomes possible to resell the securities should an investor's needs or opinion of the investment change. In addition, to the extent that there are many participants in the secondary market, security prices reflect investors' consensus estimate of each firm's opportunities. An investor looking to invest new funds is more likely to direct the money to a company with good business opportunities when investment prices are realistic than if a company's opportunity set and security prices are disconnected.

2. The Security Exchanges

At the core of the secondary markets are the security exchanges, the places where buyers and sellers come together. Originally, security exchanges were central locations where brokers met in person to trade securities for themselves and their customers. Today, they are equally likely to be computer networks linking brokers and traders around the world. In what follows, we look first at the physical security exchanges and then at the NASDAQ market, the primary electronic exchange in the United States.

The physical exchanges   When most people think of the "bricks and mortar" securities markets, they think of the organized exchanges of national scope such as the New York Stock Exchange. This market is indeed central to stock trading in the United States, but there are other domestic stock exchanges as well. Some are regional in orientation, such as the Philadelphia Stock Exchange serving the east coast, the Chicago Stock Exchange, and the Pacific Stock Exchange in San Francisco. Others, such as the Boston Stock Exchange, are primarily local in orientation. Each of the regional and local markets primarily trades shares of companies in its geographical area, including some that are also listed on the New York and American exchanges.

There are, of course, security exchanges in each major financial center: London, Tokyo, Frankfurt, Paris, Milan, Toronto, Zurich, Hong Kong, etc., on which the securities of companies headquartered in that country trade. Until recently, it was

NET Present Value
The New York Stock Exchange website is www.nyse.com

NET Present Value
The London Stock Exchange website is www.londonstock exchange.com and the English language site of the Tokyo Stock Exchange is www.tse.or.jp/english

unusual for securities of a company to trade on an exchange outside its home country. However, there is currently a trend for multinational companies to list their shares on stock exchanges in more than one country, for example, British Petroleum, whose stock is traded both in London and on the New York Stock Exchange. This reflects the increasing desire of these companies to see themselves as global in all aspects: strategy, products, facilities, employees, and—in part through the international trading of their securities—ownership.

From its birth on Wall Street in 1792 until 2006, the New York Stock Exchange (NYSE) was a membership organization. Each membership was called a "seat" reflecting the original practice of members sitting in assigned seats as stocks were announced for trading in roll call fashion, one security at a time. In 1871, continuous and simultaneous trading began, and "seat" lost its literal meaning. Originally the number of seats increased or decreased as the number of members changed, but in 1868 the number of seats was fixed, and seats began to change hands in an open market, just like securities. Occasionally seats were added as increased activity required new participants, but from 1953–2006 the number remained constant at 1,366. In 2006, following the acquisition of Archipelago, an electronic stock exchange, the NYSE became a publicly-owned business, the NYSE Group.[6]

There are four types of members on the New York Stock Exchange: commission (or "house") brokers, independent brokers, registered competitive market makers (RCMMs), and specialists. Commission brokers are the individuals most associated with the exchange in the public's mind, the people who work for large broker-dealers and who execute trades for customers. Independent brokers, once called "$2 brokers" after an early commission rate, offer their services to other brokers rather than to the public, handling trades for small brokerage firms without a member on the floor and overflow business during periods of high activity. RCMMs offer their services to no one; they are wealthy individuals who own a seat to be part of the action on the exchange floor and to trade for their own account.

The fourth type of member is the "specialist," whose role is significantly different from the other three. Each specialist is located at a specific trading location on the floor and is responsible for the activity of one or more securities on the exchange. Specialists record all trades in their assigned securities and send the information to the ticker tape. They quote prices on request: the last trade and the current bid and asked prices. They are the "broker's brokers," accepting trading instructions from other brokers and executing them when an opposite party arrives. They are responsible for maintaining a continuous, orderly market by trading for their own accounts, becoming the opposite side to any unmatched trade.

listing—arranging for a company's securities to trade on a stock exchange

A company that wishes its securities to trade on an organized exchange must meet the exchange's **listing** requirements. Each exchange has its own standards, both for initial listing and for a company to remain listed. Although there are some complexities and flexibilities in its rules, the primary initial listing requirements of the New York Stock Exchange for domestic companies are given in Figure 7.4.[7] In addition each exchange requires listed companies to adhere to its rules of operation and all SEC requirements for listed companies.

---

[6] **Reference:** New York Stock Exchange website: www.nyse.com.
[7] **Reference:** New York Stock Exchange website: www.nyse.com.

Criterion	Requirement
Earning power	Earnings before taxes of at least $10 million over the last three years and $2 million in each of the two most recent years
Operating cash flow	At least $25 million aggregate over the last three years, each year positive
Market value of publicly held shares	At least $100 million with share price of at least $4.00
Shares outstanding	At least 1.1 million
Shareholders	At least 400 holders of 100 shares or more

FIGURE 7.4
Key New York Stock Exchange initial listing requirements. Only large, widely-held companies trade on the New York Stock Exchange.

NET Present Value
New York Stock Exchange listing requirements are at www.nyse.com/regulation/nyse/1147474807344.html

Since only large companies can meet the listing requirements, listing conveys some prestige and an enhanced reputation as a financially sound firm, a reputation that might lower the company's cost of capital. However, some companies, including Apple, Microsoft, and Intel, have chosen not to list on the organized exchanges due to the emergence of the NASDAQ system as an alternative to physical exchange trading.

NET Present Value
You can visit the Nasdaq at www.nasdaq.com

NASDAQ   NASDAQ (pronounced "NAZ-DAK") is the acronym of the National Association of Securities Dealers Automated Quotation system, a computerized network of some 500 securities dealers who offer to buy and sell ("make a market in") securities. Trading, quotations and settlement are provided by the computer network. Among the securities traded in the NASDAQ system are roughly half of all industrial stocks, all government bonds, and about 90% of corporate bonds. In the 1990s, the dramatic success of many technology-related and Internet companies listed on the NASDAQ increased NASDAQ's visibility, and it became widely identified as the exchange for "high-tech" and "dot.com" companies. In 2010, $20.4 trillion of securities were traded via the NASDAQ system.[8]

3. Other Trading Mechanisms

Although the vast majority of securities are traded on the exchanges, there are two other vehicles for trading: (1) institutional block trading and (2) trading through private computerized services.

Institutional block trading   Large blocks of securities are often traded directly through stockbrokers, usually by large institutional investors. Often it is difficult to buy or sell a large number of shares without moving the market price in an adverse direction. For example, a portfolio manager wishing to sell 50,000 shares of General Motors might be concerned that such an increase in the num-

---

[8] **Reference and elaboration:**   Nasdaq website. In 2000, the National Association of Securities Dealers spun off Nasdaq as a for-profit, shareholder-owned corporation. Nasdaq purchased the Boston Stock Exchange and the Philadelphia Stock Exchange in 2007, and in 2008 became NASDAQ OMX Group with the acquisition of OMX AB which owned seven northern European exchanges.

"Losses and failures and risk, oh my!"

ber of shares available for sale would drive down the price. Institutional block trades are handled much like a primary market issue. The broker locates buyers through its network of customers instead of finding them via the exchanges. It is only as a final step, when all the buyers have been located and confirmed, that the actual trade(s) are passed through the exchange floor to meet the broker's obligation to funnel trades to the exchanges of which it is a member.

NET Present Value
A typical ECN is TD Ameritrade at
www.tdameritrade.com

Electronic communications networks (ECNs)   These companies offer trading through their own computer systems. Some—including the Instinet unit of Reuters Group and Island—serve brokers and other securities-market professionals. Others, such as E*TRADE and TD Ameritrade are marketed to individual investors via the Internet. Trades are cheap, fast and anonymous. ECNs have become significant competitors to the traditional exchanges, so much so that in 2006 the New York Stock Exchange acquired the ECN Archipelago and repositioned it as its electronic market for emerging companies.

The Behavior of Financial Markets

Measuring and predicting the future of security prices, especially stock prices, has fascinated financial observers ever since the first securities were traded in Venice in the thirteenth century. Today, there are many ways to measure security price movements and four major schools of thought about how these prices change and can be forecasted.

1. Measuring the Markets

NET Present Value
Go to
http://quote.bloomberg.
com/markets/indexes for
current information on
stock market indexes in
the U.S. and around the
world

Investment professionals, securities exchanges, and the financial press have created a wide variety of devices to measure the performance of securities in the financial markets. The most visible of these measures are the various market indexes which attempt to capture the overall performance of a group of securities or of a financial market as a whole. Among the most popularly followed are:

● The Dow Jones indexes—based on the sum of the prices of a select number of New York Stock Exchange stocks representing sectors of the economy. There is the Dow Jones Industrial Average, an index of 30 large industrial stocks; the Dow Jones Transportation Average, an index of 20 transportation stocks; and the Dow Jones Utility Average, an index of 15 utility stocks. Dow Jones also publishes an index consisting of all 65 stocks that make up the three other averages.[9]

● The Standard & Poor's (S&P) indexes—based on the market value of a large number of New York Stock Exchange stocks representing sectors of the economy. Best known is the S&P 500, an index of 500 stocks drawn from across many industries.

● Composite indexes—a measure of the market value of all stocks traded on an exchange, such as the New York Stock Exchange Composite Index, and the NASDAQ Composite Index.

● Multimarket indexes—indexes that span several exchanges and markets such as the Russell 2000 Index and the Wilshire 5000 Index, broad indexes of the value of most exchange and NASDAQ stocks.

● Foreign indexes—indexes measuring the activity on major stock exchanges such as the Financial Times Stock Exchange 100 (abbreviated FTSE 100 and pronounced "Footsie 100") in London, the Nikkei 225 in Tokyo, the Xetra DAX in Frankfurt, the Hang Seng in Hong Kong, and others in each major financial market.

Figure 7.5 is taken from the "Market Data" summary in *The Wall Street Journal* which appears daily on the fourth page of the "Money and Investing" section.[10] Shown are graphs of the Dow Jones Industrial Average and the S&P 500 Index for the last three months. Not shown in Figure 7.5 but included in the daily summary is further information about other stock market indexes—both domestic and foreign—plus commodity prices, interest rates, foreign exchange rates, and mutual fund yields.

2. Models of Security Price Behavior

Four models of the way security prices are determined are widely discussed, debated, and followed in the financial markets: (1) technical theory and analysis, (2) fundamental theory and analysis, (3) the efficient market hypothesis, and (4) the random walk.

Technical theory and analysis   Technical theory argues that the price and not the value of a security is the foundation of investment decisions. Prices are the result of supply and demand interaction; and with the supply of a firm's stock fixed in the short run, it is investors' demand that sets prices. Demand is both ra-

---

[9] **Cross-reference:**   The 65 Dow Jones stocks appear in Figure 8.8 on page 209, where they are presented to illustrate the risk of companies in various industries.

[10] **Reference:**   *The Wall Street Journal,* December 15, 2010, page C4.

FIGURE 7.5
The Wall Street Journal Markets Data. Widely followed financial market indexes are reported daily.

tional and irrational, with rational forces in control of long-run movements in price and irrational forces in control in the short-run. Irrationality depends on human psychological behavior: most people follow the lead of others, hence prices move in trends. And, because human nature is consistent through the ages, trends (patterns of price movement) repeat themselves.

Perhaps the best known exponent of technical theory was the British economist John Maynard Keynes, who used technical methods to increase tenfold the worth of the endowment fund of his employer, Kings College of Cambridge University, during the depths of the Great Depression of the 1930s. Keynes likened investing to beauty contests of the times in which newspaper readers were asked to select, from pictures in the paper, the contestant that the judges would eventually pick as the winner. As Keynes pointed out, the decision depends on what the judges will do, not on which contestant the reader finds most beautiful. Similarly, Keynes argued, choosing stocks depends on what other investors will do, not on which securities an investor finds most attractive.

Fundamental theory and analysis   Fundamental theory takes a very different approach, arguing that every financial asset has a "true" or **intrinsic value** equal to the economic benefit of owning that asset. Skilled analysis of economic data will lead to the discovery of a security's intrinsic value. For a bond this would involve analysis of the issuer to determine risk of default and of interest rates to quantify interest rate and reinvestment risk. For a stock, fundamental analysis would include an examination of the company's products and growth potential, costs and earnings quality, business risks, etc.

Fundamental analysts attempt to purchase a security when it is selling for a price that is some "margin of safety" below its intrinsic value, to allow for a margin of error in the analysis. Then, they argue, the odds are in favor of the security's price rising to (or above) intrinsic value over the medium-to-long term.

The efficient market hypothesis   A capital market is efficient if it channels money accurately and quickly to those real investments that result in the greatest benefits to society. For this to be true, companies' security prices must accurately reflect their earnings opportunities. The importance of this market function has motivated economists and students of finance to study the capital markets extensively. However, researchers have found it difficult to measure directly the distributive power of the markets.

One fruitful line of study is an information arrival model, a model of stock price formulation that bears directly on efficiency and can be formulated in a way that lends itself to testing. In its simple form, the model is written out in Figure 7.6. At any point in time there exists a set of stock prices. There is no reason for these prices to change unless new, relevant information becomes available to market participants. However, new information arrives regularly, and once the new information is processed and its meaning understood, prices will change and a new equilibrium will be established.

The key issue for market efficiency is the time lag between the arrival of information in the marketplace and the establishment of revised stock prices. If the

intrinsic value—the true economic worth of an asset

FIGURE 7.6
The information arrival model. Stock prices change when new information reaches the capital markets.

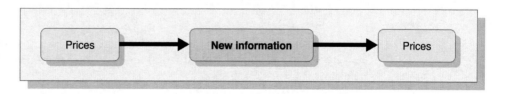

time lag is extended, the market is inefficient, with old prices existing long after the new information shows them to be no longer correct. However, if the time lag is short, the market is efficient; stock prices are adjusting quickly to the import of the new information, and there is little if any time during which they give wrong signals to investors.

For formal testing purposes, the premise that the capital markets are efficient with respect to their reaction to the arrival of new information has been formulated as the efficient market hypothesis:

Prices contain all relevant information.

If the hypothesis is true and stock prices react quickly to the arrival of new information, the markets are efficient—at least with respect to the incorporation of information into investment values. The hypothesis is further subdivided into three versions depending upon the amount of information under study.[11]

- *The weak form:* In this version of the hypothesis, all relevant information is defined to be past stock prices. Thus the hypothesis becomes "Prices contain all that can be known from the study of past prices." If the weak form is true, technical analysis, with its emphasis on the patterns and trends of stock price movements, is worthless for locating investment opportunities. Academic studies of commodities prices, comparisons of stock prices to computer-generated random numbers and the Brownian motion of gaseous atoms, tests for serial correlation between stock price movements, tests for patterns of stock price changes, and tests of investment rules based on price patterns have consistently supported the weak form.

- *The semistrong form:* This strangely named version of the hypothesis equates all relevant information to all public information. Thus the hypothesis becomes "Prices contain all that can be known from the study of all public information." If the semistrong form is true, fundamental analysis with its emphasis on economic analysis of public data is worthless. Early academic studies of stock market responses to leading economic indicators, income statement data release, stock splits, Fed discount rate changes, etc. have supported the semistrong form. More recently there have been some studies of inflation, takeover offers, etc. that point out some lack of efficiency with respect to public information. While substantially supporting the semistrong form of the hypothesis, the research results here are somewhat mixed.

- *The strong form:* In the strong form, all relevant information means *all* information, public or private. Thus the hypothesis becomes "Prices contain all that can be known—period!" If this form of the efficient market hypothesis is true, no amount of analysis can predict the movement of stock prices better than purely random selection. Academic studies of trading by stock exchange specialists and corporate insiders, individuals who might have inside information, have not supported this form of the hypothesis. It appears that private information is quite useful in stock price prediction.

In summary, many financial market practitioners argue that they are successful using technical and fundamental analysis to earn returns above the market aver-

---

[11] **References:**   An excellent summary of the efficient market hypothesis and early tests of all three forms is Chapter 4 of James H. Lorie and Mary T. Hamilton, *The Stock Market—Theories and Evidence* (Homewood, Il: Richard D. Irwin, 1973).

ages. Academics are split. The true believers of most of the research argue that it is impossible to use technical or fundamental analysis consistently to beat the market. Other academics accept at least some of the more recent research as showing that there are areas of inefficiency in the financial markets. All agree that: (1) originality of analysis and better-than-average insight on a regular basis, kept secret from other analysts, should lead to a superior investment record, and (2) tests of efficiency have been done primarily on New York Stock Exchange stocks due to the availability of data. Other markets, served by fewer stock analysts and with less widely circulated data, may well be less efficient.

The efficient market hypothesis gives rise to a fascinating paradox. In its semistrong form, the hypothesis argues that fundamental analysis is worthless, yet it is the existence of many fundamental analysts, disseminating new information quickly and analyzing voluminous data, that most likely accounts for the measured efficiency of the market.

random walk—a process in which successive changes are independent of each other

The random walk   The movement of stock prices has been characterized by some academics as a **random walk.** This is an attempt to quantify the concept of the efficient market hypothesis in statistical terms. The random walk is a stronger statement than the efficient market hypothesis due to the quantification.

The concept of the random walk is that successive percentage price changes of a given security appear to be independently drawn from a single probability distribution (representing the set of possible percentage price changes)—much like rolling a pair of dice produces a set of random numbers drawn from the distribution of possible results of dice rolls.

Financial Intermediaries

Financial intermediaries separate surplus budget units and deficit budget units, permitting each to enter into their desired financial transaction without the need to find a counterparty on their own. In this section we identify three classes of intermediaries and five types of intermediation.

1. Classes of Intermediaries

Financial intermediaries can be grouped into three classes: (1) deposit intermediaries, (2) contractual intermediaries, and (3) investment intermediaries.

Deposit intermediaries   Deposit intermediaries include commercial banks, savings and loan associations, mutual savings banks, and credit unions. They take deposits from lenders and make loans to borrowers. In return they collect interest and principal repayments from the borrowers and return the lenders' deposits with interest earned.

Contractual intermediaries   Contractual intermediaries include insurance companies—both life, and property and casualty—pension funds, and endowment funds. They take premiums and contributions from their customers and contributors and invest the proceeds, making loans to governments and corporations.

In return, the earnings and principal of their investment portfolio are used to pay insurance claims, pay retirement benefits, or support the endowed institution.

NET Present Value
One of the largest mutual fund intermediaries is Fidelity Investments at www.fidelity.com

Investment intermediaries   Investment intermediaries are primarily mutual funds. They aggregate money from investors and purchase many kinds of investment portfolios, providing each investor the ability to own a piece of a broadly diversified portfolio. They manage the portfolios for their investors and return the money when requested.

2. Types of Intermediation

Financial intermediaries provide five kinds of separation between lending and borrowing: (1) amount intermediation, (2) risk intermediation, (3) maturity intermediation, (4) portfolio mix intermediation, and (5) information intermediation.

Amount intermediation   Intermediaries serve lenders and borrowers who have and need different amounts of money. For example, a commercial bank aggregates deposits of all sizes from its many depositor-lenders and then makes loans of different amounts to its many customer-borrowers.

Risk intermediation   Intermediaries serve lenders and borrowers with different attitudes toward and perceptions of risk. For example, a property and casualty insurance company collects premium money from its customers and assumes risks associated with loss to the insured assets. It lends the money to governments and corporations by buying bonds with quite different levels of risk and uses some of the proceeds to compensate its customers for the losses that occur.

Maturity intermediation   Intermediaries serve lenders and borrowers with different maturity needs. For example, a savings and loan association takes in short-term deposits and provides money to homebuyers in the form of mortgage loans of up to 30 years.

Portfolio mix intermediation   Intermediaries serve lenders and borrowers who desire to change the combination of investments they are holding. For example, a mutual fund takes deposits from its investors and provides each with a share of ownership in a broadly diversified investment portfolio.

Information intermediation   Intermediaries serve borrowers and lenders with different access to information. For example pension funds construct retirement packages based on sophisticated actuarial analyses not easily available to many workers. Mutual funds base their investment decisions on extensive data collection and analyses most investors would not have the time or the skills to accomplish.

*A*lexandra McLean spoke animatedly and pointed to a diagram she had drawn on the blackboard. Her class at the local university had just ended, and she found herself surrounded by a half-dozen eager students with lots of questions. The class had gone by quickly—too quickly—both because she had brought much more material to class than the time allowed and because she had genuinely enjoyed the experience.

Alex had opened the class by relating several of her recent experiences in designing loan packages tailored to the needs of her customers. She talked about the different ways her customers could raise financing and discussed the benefits of each. Then she presented some of the important characteristics of the primary and secondary financial markets. For the remainder of the class, she led the group in a discussion of financial intermediation and the role of her bank in bridging the needs of its various depositors and borrowers, always coming back to her perspective of the importance of understanding and meeting her customers' financing needs.

As the last student left the classroom, the chair of the finance faculty walked up to Alex from the back of the room where he had observed the class. "That was a fabulous presentation," he said. "Judging from the students' level of attention and questioning you were a big hit!"

"It was a really great experience," Alex replied with a smile. "Your students are excellent." She looked at the blackboard thoughtfully. "They taught me something as well. I live in the financial markets every day, and think I know a lot about them. But so much is going on out there that it really is important to step back every once in a while to review the roles that financial markets and institutions play and the ways they operate."

Summary of Key Points

■ **Describe seven roles of financial markets and institutions, three methods of channeling funds from net savers to net investors, and the difference between the money and capital markets.** Financial markets and institutions serve as a conduit for the movement of money from surplus-budget economic units to deficit-budget economic units. They do so by providing mechanisms for making payments, vehicles for savings, supplies of credit, investments in which to store wealth, sources of liquidity, mechanisms for shifting and reducing risk, and vehicles for government economic policy. Funds move from net savers to net investors through direct transfer when the parties know each other, semidirect transfer using the services of a broker, or indirect transfer with the funds passing through a financial intermediary. We separate the financial markets into the money markets and capital markets based on maturities of the instruments traded.

■ **Discuss how newly created securities are issued, including the role of the investment banker, flotation costs, and private placement.** New securities are sold in the primary markets. Public issues are normally brought to market by an investment banker who can provide advice, underwriting, selling, and market stabilization services. Private placements, with or without the services of an investment banker,

have the advantages of faster speed to market, greater privacy, more-tailored terms, and fewer limitations on the amount of the issue. Flotation costs, the costs of bringing a new security issue to market, include the investment banker's spread and all administrative costs.

■ **Describe the nature of the secondary financial markets, including the securities exchanges and other trading mechanisms.** Previously issued securities trade in the secondary markets. These markets bring buyers and sellers together, provide information to investors, create continuity of trading which enhances investors' liquidity, protect market participants through regulation, and improve capital distribution in the economy. The exchanges include the physical exchanges, such as the New York Stock Exchange, where brokers and traders come together in person, and the electronic exchanges, such as the NASDAQ computer network. Other trading mechanisms are block trading among financial institutions, and computerized trading services.

■ **Identify indexes that measure financial market activity; and compare technical analysis, fundamental analysis, the efficient market hypothesis, and the random walk as descriptions of security price behavior.** Among the many indexes that capture financial market activity are market indexes, supply-demand indicators, opinion indicators, and measures of relative strength. Charts are widely used to make security price and other data visual and to look for trends. Technical analysis looks at these trends to predict future security prices. Fundamental analysis looks at economic and business information to calculate a security's true or intrinsic value. By contrast, the efficient market hypothesis—in its weak and semistrong forms—concludes that security prices react so quickly to new information that technical and fundamental analysis are useless in making investment decisions. If the strong form of the efficient market hypothesis is true, even inside information does not give investors an edge over other market participants. The random walk attempts to quantify security price movements in statistical terms.

■■ **Describe three types of financial intermediaries and five types of financial intermediation.** Financial intermediaries are commonly grouped into: (1) deposit intermediaries—banks and thrift institutions, (2) contractual intermediaries—insurance companies and pension and endowment funds, and (3) investment intermediaries—primarily mutual funds. They separate lenders and borrowers, enabling funds to flow when the individual parties differ in: (1) the amount of money they wish to move, (2) the risks they wish to take, (3) the time over which they wish to invest, (4) the mix of their investment portfolios, and (5) their access to investment information.

Questions

1. Identify seven functions of financial markets and institutions.
2. What is the difference among a deficit-budget unit, a balanced-budget unit, and a surplus-budget unit? Is it possible for an individual or company to be one of the three in one year and another in the next?
3. Distinguish among direct transfer, semidirect transfer, and indirect transfer. Which financial organizations play an important role in each?
4. In what ways are the money markets and capital markets different? In what ways are they similar?
5. Distinguish between the primary financial markets and secondary financial markets.
6. Identify four services provided by investment bankers in helping companies issue securities.
7. How does underwriting work?
8. Describe what the components of a $1 million flotation cost might be.
9. What are the differences between a public security issue and a private placement?
10. What is shelf registration? Why was it created? What do you think is its impact on the way companies issue securities?
11. Identify five functions of secondary financial markets.
12. Why did British Petroleum list its stock on the New York Stock Exchange when it was already trading in London?
13. Why do you think Microsoft chose not to list its securities on a physical exchange?
14. What are the differences between the Dow Jones indexes and the Standard & Poor's indexes?
15. Contrast technical analysis and fundamental analysis as methods for finding good stock investments.
16. Describe the three forms of the efficient market hypothesis.
17. Why does:
    a. The weak form of the efficient market hypothesis invalidate technical analysis?
    b. The semistrong form of the efficient market hypothesis invalidate fundamental analysis?
18. Why is it possible to earn above-normal rates of return in the stock market if you have inside information? What does this suggest about laws regulating the investment activities of corporate officers?
19. What is the random walk? What is its relationship to the efficient market hypothesis?
20. Identify three classes of financial intermediaries. In what way(s) do they differ?
21. Identify five types of intermediation. Describe a situation in which you might wish to use each one.

PART III

RISK VS.

RETURN

In Part III we study the interrelationship of risk and return, the framework used in finance theory for evaluating financial managing decisions.

Chapter 8 elaborates on risk. We define risk, describe reactions to it, establish the relationship of risk to financial value, and identify the three primary sources of risk. We then develop two models that relate risk to the rate of return required by investors: a total risk model for a stand-alone investment and a portfolio risk model, the capital asset pricing model (CAPM), for an asset held as part of a diversified portfolio.

Chapter 9 is devoted to valuation, how time value and risk can help us determine the worth of various financial instruments. We identify the value of a security as a present value that is independent of investors' holding periods. We distinguish between value and price. Then we study the valuation of bonds, preferred stock, and common stock.

Chapter 10 examines the cost of capital, the rate of return a company must earn to satisfy its investors. We present the process of calculating a cost of capital: determining investors' required rates of return, calculating the cost of a capital source, integrating the cost of each capital source to produce an overall cost of capital, and producing a cost of capital schedule. We then illustrate each step as it applies to a company financed by bonds, preferred stock, and common stock.

CHAPTER 8

RISK

AND ITS

MEASUREMENT

*C*ecilia Moreira stared at the open door to her office and reflected on what had just happened. Not more than one minute ago, Carl Leonel, one of her best employees, had stormed out of her office in an extremely distraught state of mind. It was clear that Carl would not be very productive today, and Cecilia wondered how this incident would affect Carl's willingness to contribute to the organization in the future.

Cecilia was the CFO of a small company that provided service to customers seven days a week. Last week, Cecilia's boss had circulated a memo "informing" certain employees that they would have to report to work on alternate Saturdays. As the father of a small child, Carl felt he could not afford to work on Saturday. More important, he was enraged at what he considered a cavalier attitude toward employees' personal lives by the company's management.

Cecilia thought back to last week, to a meeting with the company's investment bankers in which the topic was the market profile of the company's stock. At issue was the high amount of risk investors felt they were taking and how that risk level raised the rate of return the investors demanded. Cecilia understood that if investors required a higher level of return, it would be more difficult to raise money and the price of the company's stock would be depressed.

Cecilia remembered something Carl had said when he objected to working on Saturday: "Why are they making it so risky to be employed here?" As she mulled over how to respond to Carl's concerns, Cecilia wondered whether the risk Carl was feeling was in any way connected to the risks the investment bankers were concerned about.

Cecilia is dealing with one of the most fundamental issues in finance, how to understand risk and the effects of risk on a company's operations and value. Over the years, finance theorists have developed a comprehensive theory of risk as it affects the shareholder—how to define it, measure it, and estimate its impact on stock price. Today we are beginning to understand that each stakeholder of the firm faces risks and that all of these risks must be successfully addressed if the firm is to succeed and prosper.

In this chapter we define risk and identify why it is important. We then identify different types of risk and learn what events cause them. We also draw upon basic concepts in probability and statistics to measure risk and to reach important conclusions about the relationship of risk to the financial value of the firm.

Key Points You Should Learn from This Chapter

After reading this chapter you should be able to:

- Define *risk* and know why it is important to the financial manager.
- State the relationship between risk and financial value.
- Describe the three primary sources of risk faced by a firm.
- Measure the risk of a single security held by itself and relate this level of risk to investors' required rate of return.
- Measure the risk of a security held in a diversified portfolio and relate this level of risk to investors' required rate of return.

Introductory Concepts—What Is Risk and Why Does It Matter?

Risk is the chance that something will come out worse than planned. If we cross the street, our plan is to get to the other side safely. The risk is the chance that we might be injured in the process. The same concept is true in finance. For example, if we invest in the common stock of a company, we anticipate a fair rate of return on our investment. The risk is that we may earn less than anticipated.

Different streets have different levels of risk. The likelihood of injury in crossing a back country road is much less than that of crossing a busy urban freeway. Similarly, in finance, different investments have different levels of risk. A deposit in a federally insured bank account that pays a fixed, stated rate of interest has much less risk than an investment in a biotech startup company.

risk seeker—an individual willing to pay to assume additional risk

Social scientists have identified three possible attitudes toward risk. Some people find risk something that increases value. Such people are called **risk seekers,** and they look for opportunities to add risk to their activities. In fact, risk seekers are willing to pay more for something if it contains an element of risk. Gambling in Las Vegas, bungee jumping, and taking mind-altering drugs are examples of activities that are pursued by risk seekers. In each case, the individuals (or their money) are safer if they avoid the activity. In each case, they pay for the opportunity to be in the risky situation. In each case, the thrill from the risk itself is an important part of the reward from the activity.

risk averter—an individual willing to pay to avoid risk

Other people dislike risk and find that it reduces value. These people are called **risk averters.** Risk averters look for opportunities to subtract risk from their activities. They stay away from risky situations and buy insurance when risk cannot be avoided. In financial markets, they insist on an increased rate of return on their invested money as compensation for the risks they take.

risk neutral—indifferent to risk

Of course, it is possible that some people are indifferent to risk. For them risk is irrelevant, and they will make decisions without taking risk into consideration. We call these people **risk neutral.**

When it comes to money, most people hold a combination of all three attitudes. For small amounts of money, they act as risk seekers and are willing to take small risks. For example, many people enjoy buying a lottery ticket, even though with the state taking its percentage off the top, they stand to win less on average than they pay for the ticket. The risk of losing is high, but the amount of money at risk is very low. In this case the added excitement from the possibility of winning—however tiny—more than compensates for the small added cost.

For slightly larger amounts of money, people tend to become risk neutral. They might, for example, purchase tickets to a play without ever thinking that the risk of not enjoying the production should lower the ticket price.

However, as the amount of money at risk increases further and becomes a significant fraction of a person's total wealth, almost all people become risk averters. For example, there are few of us who will gamble everything we own on a lottery ticket or move a long distance to take a job with an organization we know nothing about. Now the potential for significant loss dominates our thinking and outweighs any thrill from the risk.

Calvin and Hobbes

by Bill Watterson

At the level of a business, large amounts of money are at risk. As a result, it is reasonable that the key stakeholders of a business—customers, suppliers, employees, creditors, and investors—act as risk averters, a conclusion borne out by research into human and financial market behavior. If each stakeholder of the firm is a risk averter, then each will demand some form of compensation to assume risk. And in each case, the demand for that compensation will drain value from the firm and leave it worse off.

- For customers, the risk of poor product or service quality reduces the price they are willing to pay. Over time it also reduces the amount they are willing to purchase, which further lowers the firm's revenues.

- For suppliers, the risk of an unstable relationship increases the prices they charge the firm. They build in protection against the possibility that their investment in tooling up might not be fully recouped. They are less willing to work with an unpredictable customer or invest additional time and money, which further increases the firm's costs.

- For employees, the risk of job changes and termination increases the wage the company must pay to attract and hold its staff. And as Cecilia Moreira found out at the beginning of this chapter, employees who feel at risk tend to reduce their willingness to contribute to the firm in general.

- For creditors, the risk of default increases the interest rate they must earn on loans to the company. They further protect themselves by writing restrictive loan agreements that limit the firm's operating and financial freedom.

Each of these risks—as seen by customers, suppliers, employees, and creditors—reduces the firm's profitability and adds uncertainty to its cash flow stream. For the firm's investors, the risk of lower and less-predictable income raises the rate of return they demand from the firm, increasing the firm's "cost of capital"[1] and reducing its stock price.

---

[1] **Cross-reference:** Cost of capital is the subject of Chapter 10.

Risk and Financial Value

In Chapter 4 we introduced the Fisher interest rate equation:[2]

Nominal rate = (1 + pure rate) (1 + inflation premium) (1 + risk premium) − 1
            $= (1 + r_p) (1 + r_i) (1 + r_r) − 1$

which, since the risk-free rate is the combination of the pure rate and the inflation premium, could also be written in the following form:

Nominal rate = (1 + risk-free rate) (1 + risk premium) − 1
            $= (1 + r_f) (1 + r_r) − 1$

The Fisher equation illustrates the impact of risk on the rates of return investors require. If an investment is perceived as being risky, investors will ask not only for the risk-free rate, the interest rate appropriate for a risk-free investment, but also for a risk premium.

Example

How Risk Increases Nominal Rates

Investors are currently demanding a rate of return of 5% on a U.S. Treasury bill considered risk-free.

Question: What rate of return will investors require from an investment in Beatriz Industries stock if the appropriate risk premium is 7%?

Solution steps: Using the Fisher equation:

Nominal rate $= (1 + \text{risk-free rate}) (1 + \text{risk premium}) − 1$
        $= (1 + r_f) (1 + r_r) − 1 \; = \; (1.05) (1.07) − 1$
        $= .1235 = 12.35\%$

Answer: Investors will require a rate of return of <u>12.35%</u>.

The level of risk estimated by investors will determine the value of the risk premium (r_r) and hence the required rate of return.

Example

How a Higher Risk Premium Leads to a Higher Required Rate of Return

Investors are still demanding a rate of return of 5% on a U.S. Treasury bill considered risk-free. However, because of recent setbacks, investors now see Beatriz Industries (BI) stock as a riskier investment.

Question: What rate of return will investors require from an investment in BI stock if the appropriate risk premium has risen to 8%?

Solution steps: Using the Fisher equation:

Nominal rate $= (1 + \text{risk-free rate}) (1 + \text{risk premium}) − 1$
        $= (1 + r_f) (1 + r_r) − 1 \; = \; (1.05) (1.08) − 1$
        $= .1340 = 13.40\%$

Answer: Now investors will require a rate of return of <u>13.40%</u>.

---

[2] **Cross-reference:** The Fisher model is discussed on pages 88–92.

As financial value is the present value of the benefits investors expect to receive, financial value declines as interest rates go up.

Examples

How Financial Values Decline With Higher Interest Rates

Investors estimate that Beatriz Industries (BI) will produce a perpetuity of benefits of $5.00 per year for each common share.

Question: What was the value of BI stock when investors demanded a risk premium of 7%.

Solution steps: With a 7% risk premium, investors required a 12.35% rate of return. Using the perpetuity model:

$$\text{Value} = \text{PV of perpetuity} = \text{PMT} / \text{r}$$
$$= \$5.00 / .1235 = \$40.49 \text{ per share}$$

Answer: BI stock was worth <u>$40.49 per share</u>.

Question: What happened to the value of BI stock when investors raised their required risk premium to 8%.

Solution steps: With a 8% risk premium, investors now require a 13.40% rate of return. Using the perpetuity model:

$$\text{Value} = \text{PV of perpetuity} = \text{PMT} / \text{r}$$
$$= \$5.00 / .1340 = \$37.31 \text{ per share}$$

Answer: The increase in perceived risk lowered BI's stock price from <u>$40.49 to $37.31, a decline of $3.18, or 7.85%</u>.

In summary, then, when investors perceive a high level of risk, they require a high rate of return, and the firm's financial value is reduced. Other things equal, a firm's value can be increased by reducing the risks to which investors are exposed.

◼◼ Sources of Risk

Figure 8.1 identifies the forces which create risk in a firm's financial results. As the figure reveals, each firm faces three primary sources of risk.

environmental risk—
unexpected changes outside the firm that impact its operations

The first source of risk is **environmental risk,** which comes from events outside the firm. This includes scientific discoveries, ecological and social changes, shifts

FIGURE 8.1
Sequence of risks. Variability from the environment is magnified by the firm's process variability, which is further magnified by the firm's financing mix.

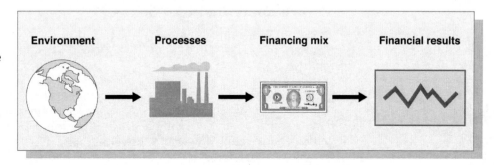

in the business and economic climate, actions of competitors, technological advances, revaluation of currency prices, political limitations such as restrictions on transferring currency or other resources from one country to another, etc. While the firm typically cannot influence these forces, it can prepare for them so that if they occur, plans are in place to minimize their negative impact. In addition, good strategic planning often finds ways to position the firm to take advantage of these events.

process risk—unnecessary variability caused by systems within the firm that are out of control

The second source of risk is **process risk,** which comes from unnecessary variability within the firm itself. This includes problems due to out-of-control production operations as well as complications caused by dissatisfied customers, employees, and suppliers. If the firm's internal processes are functioning well, the only variability is the small amount of natural variation found in all processes. By contrast, poorly functioning processes vary greatly in their output and tend to magnify any problems due to changes in the environment.

business risk—the total variability of a firm's operating results

Taken together, the combination of environmental risk and process risk is known as **business risk** in that it describes the variability of the operating results of the business. In financial terms, business risk is variability in the firm's operating profit stream.

financial risk—the increased variability in a firm's financial results caused by its financing mix

The third source of risk, known as **financial risk,** comes from the financing mix the firm chooses. A firm that finances with debt adds the magnification of leverage to its profit and cash flow. For creditors, financial risk is the risk of default on the debt. For stockholders, leverage magnifies any variability in the firm's operating profit and cash flow, a topic explored more fully in Chapter 14.

NET Present Value
To learn more about the risks faced by a business visit the International Risk Management Institute website at www.irmi.com

These three risk factors cascade, one upon the other. Risks from the environment are magnified by risks due to faulty processes, and that result is then further magnified by the leverage built into the financing mix. The stability of the firm's financial results reflects the combination of these three risk sources.

Measuring Risk—The Total Risk Model

Since risk creates variability in a firm's financial results, it is common to use elementary statistical concepts to measure risk. In this section we look at the risk of a single asset taken by itself. In the next section, we acknowledge that most assets are not held alone but rather as part of a portfolio of assets, and we look at risk in that context.

1. Probability Distributions

To say that something is uncertain is to say that we cannot predict its outcome precisely. However, if we can identify possible outcomes and identify the probability of each outcome occurring, we can apply some elementary concepts in probability and statistics to the problem.

probability distribution—a listing of all possible results of some activity showing the chance of each result taking place

A **probability distribution** is a listing of possible outcomes along with the chance that each will occur. For example, if we flip a fair coin, there is a 50% chance of getting heads and a 50% chance of getting tails. The probability distribution for this event is therefore:

FINANCE IN PRACTICE

A Classic Tale: Excessive Financial Risk at Pan Am

The airline industry is characterized by high debt levels. Large amounts of money are required to purchase and maintain an up-to-date fleet, and the planes serve as excellent collateral for borrowing. However, the industry also has a high degree of environmentally caused business risk since the demand for both business and leisure air travel is very sensitive to the economy. In Pan American's case, the combination of high financial risk piled upon high business risk proved fatal. Each time the economy turned down, Pan Am's cash flow dried up. Throughout the 1970s and 1980s, Pan Am raised cash to stay aloft by selling its assets—the Intercontinental Hotel chain, its headquarters building in New York City; its Pacific routes, the Boston–New York–Washington shuttle, and its Latin American routes. Finally, there was nothing left to sell, and the once proud carrier that "opened the world" to air travel crash landed, a victim of excessive financial risk.

Outcome	Probability
Heads	50% = .50
Tails	50% = .50
	100% = 1.00

The probabilities of all outcomes taken together must add up to 100% (or 1.00) if we are including every possible outcome.

A probability distribution for the returns from an investment looks much the same. Each outcome, usually shown as a rate of return, is listed along with its probability. Often there is a third column describing the underlying economic conditions which lead to each outcome. Consider, for example, an investment in common stock. In general, the better the economy, the more likely the company is to prosper, leading to increased dividends and a higher stock price, hence to high rates of return. Conversely, the worse the economy, the less likely the company is to prosper, leading to reduced dividends and a lower stock price, therefore to low rates of return.

Suppose you are considering an investment in the stock of one of two companies, AMR Corporation (American Airlines) and Con Edison (the New York City–area utility). AMR's performance is very dependent on economic conditions which influence the volume of business and leisure travel. By contrast, Con Edison's business is relatively stable as demand for gas and electricity depends on population trends and the weather and is somewhat independent of the business cycle.

Example

Probability Distributions for Two Investments

Investors have simplified their forecasts of the economy to five possibilities—boom, good times, average times, bad times, and recession—and have constructed the following probability distributions for returns from investing in AMR and Con Edison:

State of the Economy	Probability of This State of the Economy	Rate of Return from	
		AMR Corp.	Con Edison
Boom	10% = .10	75%	30%
Good times	20 = .20	40	20
Average times	40 = .40	20	12
Bad times	20 = .20	−10	5
Recession	10 = .10	−40	−10
	100% = 1.00		

From the example we see that investors estimate a 10% chance of a boom, in which case Con Edison should do well (a 30% rate of return) and AMR should do very well (returning 75%). Investors also estimate a 10% chance of a recession, in which case both companies are expected to do poorly, although AMR (a 40% loss) is expected to fare worse than Con Edison (down 10%). Because AMR is so much more dependent on the economy than Con Edison, its performance is estimated to vary much more widely, both in a boom and in a recession.

2. Expected Value

Looking a bit further at the numbers in the above example, it appears that AMR is expected to provide a higher rate of return than Con Edison. It is useful to have one number that captures the average anticipated level of returns; a common measure used for this is the **expected value** of the probability distribution.

expected value—the weighted average of the forecasted rates of return from an investment

The expected value of a probability distribution is calculated by multiplying each forecasted outcome by the probability of its occurrence and summing the results.[3]

Example

Expected Values of Two Investments

Working with the probability distributions for returns from investing in AMR and Con Edison:

State of the Economy	Probability (1)	AMR Corp.		Con Edison	
		Return (2)	Product (1) × (2)	Return (3)	Product (1) × (3)
Boom	.10	75%	7.5%	30%	3.0%
Good times	.20	40	8.0	20	4.0
Average times	.40	20	8.0	12	4.8
Bad times	.20	−10	−2.0	5	1.0
Recession	.10	−40	−4.0	−10	−1.0
	1.00		17.5%		11.8%

The expected rate of return from an investment in AMR stock is 17.5% and from Con Edison stock is 11.8%

3. Graphing Probability Distributions

It is common to illustrate probability distributions by graphing them. Figure 8.2 shows probability distributions for both AMR Corp. and Con Edison.

While it is convenient to estimate probability distributions as if there were only a few states of the economy that could take place, in reality there are many possi-

---

[3] **Cross-reference:** Formulas for expected value and the other statistical calculations discussed in this chapter are given in the Summary of Mathematical Formulas at the end of the book.

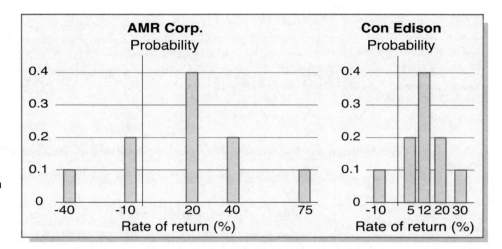

ble states of the economy—a continuum of possibilities. Figure 8.3 extends the probability distributions of AMR Corp. and Con Edison to be continuous distributions by filling in probabilities for the remaining possible rates of return. This produces smooth curves. As is true of all probability distributions, the sum of all the probabilities must equal 1.00, hence the total area under each curve equals 1.00. With an infinite number of possible rates of return, this means that the probability of any one particular rate of return occurring is infinitesimally small.

4. Variance and Standard Deviation

From Figures 8.2 and 8.3, we can see that the probability distribution for Con Edison is quite a bit narrower than the distribution for AMR Corp. This means there is less of a chance that Con Edison's rate of return will deviate far from its expected value than will that of AMR. In particular, there is a smaller chance that Con Edison's rate of return will be significantly below its expected value—precisely the concept of risk discussed earlier in the chapter.

variance—a measure of the variability of rates of return

It is common to use the concepts of variance and standard deviation to measure the width of a probability distribution, and as a result, variance and standard deviation are used in finance to measure the risk of financial returns. The **variance** (written as σ^2) of a probability distribution is a measure of how far each possible outcome deviates from the distribution's expected value. It is calculated by: (1) ob-

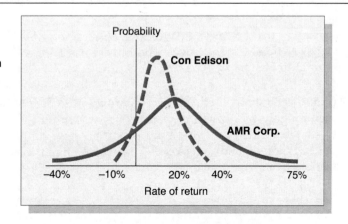

taining the deviation of each outcome by subtracting the expected value, (2) squaring the deviations to eliminate any difference between positive and negative deviations, and (3) calculating a weighted average of the results using the probabilities as weights in the same way as we calculated the expected value. The **standard deviation** (σ) is the square root of the variance and has the virtue that its unit of measure is rate of return (whereas variance is measured as "rate of return squared," an awkward concept).

standard deviation—the
square root of the variance

Example

Variance and Standard Deviation of Two Investments

Working with the probability distributions for returns from investing in AMR and Con Edison:

1. AMR Corp. (expected return = 17.5%)

State of the Economy	Probability (1)	Return (2)	Deviation (3) = (2) − 17.5	Deviation² (4) = (3)²	Product (1) × (4)
Boom	.10	75%	57.5%	3306.25	330.625
Good times	.20	40	22.5	506.25	101.250
Average times	.40	20	2.5	6.25	2.500
Bad times	.20	−10	−27.5	756.25	151.250
Recession	.10	−40	−57.5	3306.25	330.625
	1.00				916.250

and $\sqrt{916.250} = 30.27\%$

The variance of AMR's expected returns is 916.250 and the standard deviation is 30.27%.

2. Con Edison (expected return = 11.8%)

State of the Economy	Probability (1)	Return (2)	Deviation (3) = (2) − 11.8	Deviation² (4) = (3)²	Product (1) × (4)
Boom	.10	30%	18.2%	331.24	33.124
Good times	.20	20	8.2	67.24	13.448
Average times	.40	12	.2	.04	.016
Bad times	.20	5	−6.8	46.24	9.248
Recession	.10	−10	−21.8	475.24	47.524
	1.00				103.360

and $\sqrt{103.360} = 10.17\%$

The variance of Con Edison's expected returns is 103.360 and the standard deviation is 10.17%.

The calculations confirm our visual observations that Con Edison stock has less risk than AMR stock since Con Edison has a much lower variance and standard deviation.

If the distribution of returns for a security is estimated to be normal (bell-shaped), then roughly 68% of the probability lies within plus-or-minus one standard deviation from the expected value, about 95% lies within plus-or-minus two standard deviations, and well over 99% lies between plus-or-minus three standard deviations.

Example	**Interpreting the Standard Deviation of Returns**

Con Edison's expected return is 11.8% and its standard deviation is 10.17%. This tells us that investors are forecasting that the probability is 68% that the rate of return on Con Edison stock will fall between:

$$11.8\% - 10.17\% = 1.63\%$$

and

$$11.8\% + 10.17\% = 21.97\%$$

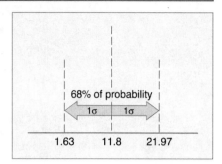

By contrast, AMR's expected return is 17.5% and its standard deviation is 30.27%. This tells us that investors are forecasting that the probability is 68% that the rate of return on AMR stock will fall between:

$$17.5\% - 30.27\% = -12.77\%$$

and

$$17.5\% + 30.27\% = 47.77\%$$

Again, these numbers point out how much riskier AMR stock is compared to Con Edison stock.

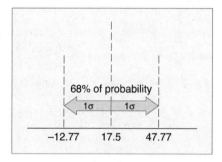

5. The Capital Market Line (CML)

capital market line (CML)—a graph of investors' required rate of return as a function of an asset's total risk

It is common to summarize the risk-return relationship for a single asset using the **capital market line (CML).** The CML, illustrated in Figure 8.4, shows the relationship between the expected return and *total risk* from investing in a single asset. At the left of the graph are assets with no risk, which return the risk-free rate. Further to the right on the graph lie the risky assets. The graph's upward slope reflects investors' risk aversion as they insist on higher rates of return to compensate for taking on riskier investments.

FIGURE 8.4

The capital market line (CML). For an individual asset, investors' required rate of return increases with *total risk* (σ).

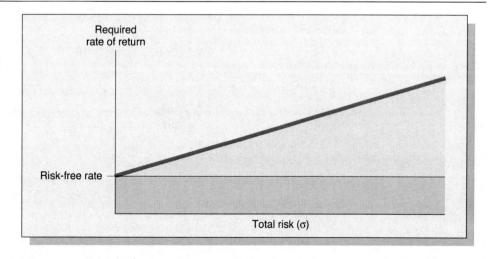

The equation of the CML is that of a straight line:

$$\textit{Required rate of return} = r_f + \textit{(slope)} \times \sigma$$
$$= r_f + \textit{(market price of total risk)} \times \sigma$$

market price of total risk—
the additional return
demanded by investors to
take on one unit of total
risk

where the slope is the **market price of total risk,** the added return required per unit of standard deviation. Note that the CML is consistent with the Fisher model:[4]

$$\textit{Nominal rate} = r_f + \textit{risk premium}$$
$$= r_f + \textit{(market price of total risk)} \times \sigma$$

For a single asset, the risk premium equals the market price of total risk multiplied by σ, the total risk of the investment.

■■ Measuring Risk—The Portfolio Risk Model

So far we have treated each investment as if it were the only one owned by an investor. However, most investors do not put all their eggs in one basket. Rather, they spread their money across several investments. Intuitively, this makes sense. An investor who holds only one security is particularly vulnerable to any setback in that investment. An investor who holds several securities, on the other hand, has spread the risk; low returns from one security are often offset by higher returns from the others, and a poor performance by one security is far less of a concern. In this section, we look at the risk and return of a portfolio of investments.

1. The Concept of a Portfolio

portfolio—a group of
investments held at the
same time

diversify—to spread your
money across several
investments, i.e., to
purchase a portfolio

A **portfolio** of investments is simply a group of investments held together. If you have $5,000 to invest, and you choose to buy $1,000 worth of each of five securities, you own a five-security portfolio. When you purchase a portfolio, you have chosen to **diversify** your investments.

A portfolio is characterized by the investments included in it and also by the amount invested in each security. As we will see, the securities in which more is invested play a larger role in the portfolio's performance than those with little invested. In the above example you elected to invest an equal amount in each of the five securities, and they will all contribute equally to the portfolio's risk and return. By contrast, had you chosen to invest $3,000 of your $5,000 in one security and $500 in each of the four others, you would be holding a quite different portfolio, and the $3,000 security would dominate the portfolio's performance.

2. Portfolio Returns

The rate of return from a portfolio is simply the weighted average of the returns from each security in the portfolio where the weights reflect how much money is invested in each security.

---

[4] **Elaboration:** On page 89 we wrote the Fisher model in expanded form as:
$$\textit{Nominal rate} = r_p + r_i + r_r + r_p r_i + r_p r_r + r_i r_r + r_p r_i r_r$$
Regrouping the terms gives:
$$\textit{Nominal Rate} = (r_p + r_i + r_p r_{i)} + r_r \,(1 + r_p + r_i + r_p r_i)$$
$$= r_f + \textit{risk premium}$$

Example

Rate of Return from a Portfolio

Cecilia Moreira owns a portfolio consisting of $3,000 worth of AMR stock and $7,000 worth of Con Edison stock.

Question: What is the expected rate of return from Cecilia's portfolio?

Solution steps: Calculate the weighted average rate of return given that 30% of her money is invested in AMR and the other 70% in Con Edison.

Security	Expected Return	Percent of Portfolio	Product
AMR	17.5%	30%	5.25%
Con Edison	11.8	70	8.26
			13.51%

Answer: The portfolio has an expected return of 13.51%. Since Cecilia has more than half (70%) of her money in Con Edison, the portfolio's expected return is closer to that investment's 11.8% expected return than it is to AMR's expected return of 17.5%.

Since the expected return from a portfolio is an average, it will always lie somewhere in the middle of the expected returns from each security that makes up the portfolio (13.51% lies between 11.8% and 17.5%). *It is impossible to produce higher expected returns by investing in a portfolio!*

3. Portfolio Risk

The real benefit from a portfolio lies in its risk-reducing ability, because, unlike the expected return, the risk of a portfolio is <u>not</u> simply the weighted average of the risks of its components. Rather, the standard deviation of a portfolio is almost always lower than the weighted average of the standard deviations of the component securities. To illustrate, suppose Cecilia Moreira is thinking of "investing" $1,000 in the flip of a coin.[5] If heads comes up she earns 40% and gets back $1,400 (her initial $1000 plus $400). If tails comes up she loses 20% or $200 and only retrieves $800 as shown in the table below. This is certainly a risky "investment" (with expected return of 10% or $100 and standard deviation of 30% or $300). There is a 50% chance Cecilia will lose money.

Outcome	Probability	Payoff
Heads	.50	40%($1,000) = $400
Tails	.50	−20%($1,000) =−$200

Suppose, instead, Cecilia elects to diversify and invest $500 in each of two coin flips instead. The possible outcomes from this "two-investment portfolio" are:

Outcome			Payoff		
Coin 1	Coin 2	Probability	From Coin 1	From Coin 2	Total
Heads	Heads	.25	40%($500) = $200	40%($500) = $200	$400
Heads	Tails	.50	40%($500) = $200	−20%($500) = −$100	$100
Tails	Heads		−20%($500) = −$100	40%($500) = $200	
Tails	Tails	.25	−20%($500) = −$100	−20%($500) = −$100	−$200

---

[5] **Observation:** A foolish thing to do, perhaps, but the beginning of a very good illustration of the portfolio risk reduction effect.

This portfolio has the same 10% (or $100) expected rate of return as the single-flip "investment," but the standard deviation is lower: 21.213% (or $212.13).[6] There is now a 50% chance that Cecilia will earn the expected $100 return, and only a 25% chance she will lose money. She has reduced her risk without giving up any expected return!

The amount of risk reduction that comes from combining investments into a portfolio depends on the relationship among the investments. In the coin flip example, the two investments (coin flips) were independent of each other—the result of the first flip had no bearing on the outcome of the second. In statistical terms, there was zero correlation between the flips. The statistical measure known as the **correlation coefficient** (written as r) captures this idea. r can range from +1 (perfect correlation: the two investments move together in perfect synchronization), through zero (no relationship: the two investments are completely independent of one another, like the coin flips), to −1 (perfect negative correlation: when one investment goes up the other always goes down by the same amount, and vice versa). If r = 1, the portfolio is no different than each of its components and risk is not reduced. Since it is rare to find perfectly correlated investments, most pairs of investments can be combined to reduce risk. And, the lower the correlation between the investments in a portfolio, the more they tend to move in opposite directions and the greater the risk reduction.

correlation coefficient—a measure of the relationship between the returns from two investments

Example

Risk of a Portfolio with Correlation Coefficient of +1

Five years ago, Carl Leonel invested in a portfolio of two stocks that were perfectly positively correlated (r = +1). He invested an equal amount of money in each. The returns from this investment were:

Year	Stock A	Stock B	Carl's Portfolio
2006	30%	30%	30%
2007	10	10	10
2008	−20	−20	−20
2009	50	50	50
2010	10	10	10
Average return	16%	16%	16%
Standard deviation	23.3%	23.3%	23.3%

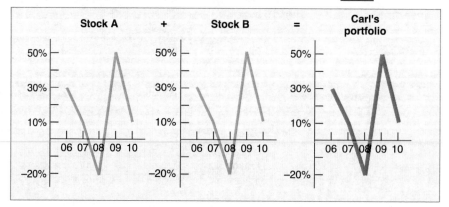

---

[6] **Observation:**   We have not illustrated the calculation of the expected return or standard deviation of Cecilia's investments. Interested students are invited to check our numbers using the formats on pages 198 and 200.

Since the two stocks moved precisely with one another, Carl's portfolio performed no differently than each of the individual stocks, and the portfolio had the same standard deviation as each stock. <u>Diversification did not reduce risk.</u>

Example

Risk of a Portfolio with Correlation Coefficient Between −1 and +1

Five years ago, Carl Leonel invested in a second portfolio of two stocks that were somewhat positively correlated (r = +0.757). He invested an equal amount of money in each. The returns from this investment were:

Year	Stock A	Stock C	Carl's Portfolio
2006	30%	19%	24.5%
2007	10	38	24.0
2008	−20	−28	−24.0
2009	50	33	41.5
2010	10	18	14.0
Average return	16%	16%	16%
Standard deviation	23.3%	23.3%	<u>21.9%</u>

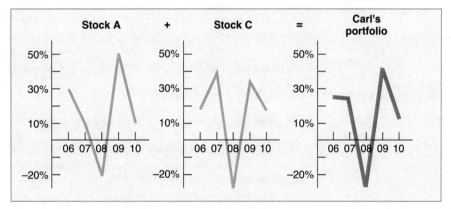

Since the two stocks did not move precisely with one another, Carl's portfolio had a lower standard deviation than each stock. <u>Diversification reduced risk.</u>

Example

Risk of a Portfolio with Correlation Coefficient of −1

Five years ago, Carl Leonel invested in a third portfolio of two stocks that were perfectly negatively correlated (r = −1). He invested an equal amount of money in each. The returns from this investment were:

Year	Stock A	Stock D	Carl's Portfolio
2006	30%	2%	16%
2007	10	22	16
2008	−20	52	16
2009	50	−18	16
2010	10	22	16
Average return	16%	16%	16%
Standard deviation	23.3%	23.3%	<u>0%</u>

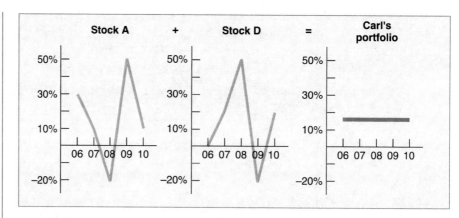

Since the two stocks moved precisely opposite to one another, the upswings in one stock were cancelled out by the downswings from the other. <u>Diversification completely eliminated risk.</u>

Both U.S. federal and state law recognize the risk reducing benefits from a portfolio and require most financial institutions to hold a diverse portfolio of investments. Insurance companies, for example, must spread their investments among many securities, and banks can lend no more than a small portion of their assets to any one borrower. The many available **mutual funds** make it possible for every investor, even one with a small amount of money to invest, to own a share of a broadly diversified portfolio.

mutual fund—a pool of money from many investors that is invested in a portfolio of securities

4. Systematic and Unsystematic Risk

Total risk may be decomposed into two components: systematic risk and unsystematic risk. This division is important because diversification affects each component differently. In this section we identify these two components of total risk and begin the discussion of how investors can use diversification to reduce them.

All investments are tied in some way to the overall economy. When employment rises, or inflation goes down, or the dollar falls against foreign currencies every investment is affected in some way. The variability caused by these environmental risk sources is known as **systematic or systemic risk** because it is due to the overall economic system.

systematic (systemic) risk—the variability in an investment's rate of return caused by factors that impact all investments

Systematic risk is what causes investments to be correlated. For example, a weaker dollar helps exporters so they all will do better if the dollar declines in value. At the same time, importers will fare worse as the falling dollar increases the price of foreign goods. A portfolio of the stocks of exporters would have a high degree of correlation, as would a portfolio composed only of the stocks of importers. A portfolio of some importers and some exporters would have a much lower correlation. In the same manner, companies in a given industry have a high degree of correlation since they tend to be affected similarly by economic events. As a result, a portfolio of only steel manufacturers would not be very diversified.

unsystematic (idiosyncratic) risk—the variability in an investment's rate of return caused by factors that only impact that investment

Unsystematic or idiosyncratic risk is the variability that is not shared by other companies. Much of a company's unsystematic risk comes from the variability in its internal processes—variability specific to that firm. Other sources of unsystematic risk are product successes and failures, patent and other legal issues, and

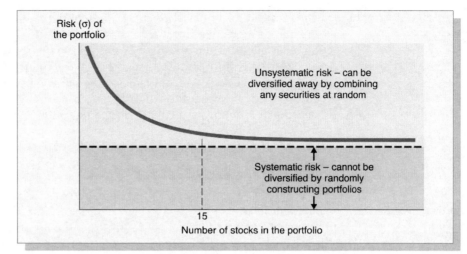

FIGURE 8.5
How unsystematic risk can be diversified away by naive diversification. Any portfolio of 15 or more securities has virtually no unsystematic risk.

personnel problems such as management shakeups and strikes. Since, by definition, the unsystematic risk of one company is unrelated to the unsystematic risk of other companies, there is no correlation between changes in rates of return due to these factors. This means that in *any* portfolio of securities, unsystematic movements tend to cancel each other out and lower risk—in the same way as Cecilia Moreira's two-coin-flip portfolio reduced her risk.

naive diversification—the construction of a portfolio at random

Figure 8.5 shows what happens when portfolios of various size are constructed at random, a process known as **naive diversification.** Small portfolios (at the left side of the graph) have both systematic and unsystematic risk. In larger portfolios, unsystematic risk is diversified away as the unsystematic movements in each security's returns are offset by the unsystematic movements of the others. By the time the portfolio has grown to about 15 securities, most of the unsystematic risk has been eliminated. By contrast, systematic risk cannot be diversified away by naive diversification. Rather, we must combine securities that have a low correlation with each other; random combinations of securities will not necessarily have the low correlations required to reduce systematic risk.

Figure 8.6 points out that, compared to a portfolio composed only of domestic investments, an internationally diversified portfolio has less systematic risk, per-

FIGURE 8.6
International naive diversification. Since economies are not perfectly correlated, diversifying internationally permits further risk reduction.

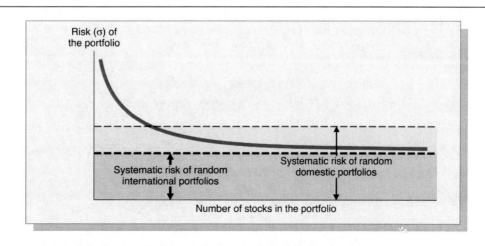

mitting much greater naive diversification. In the same way that the returns from companies in a given industry tend to be more highly correlated than returns from companies chosen from a variety of industries, the securities of companies from one country are more highly correlated than an international selection of investments. This is because all companies in a country are affected by that country's economy while the economies of different countries may not be highly correlated. In the global economy, systematic risk comes only from those factors that have a consistent impact on more than one economy.

5. Beta

characteristic line—the relationship of an investment's rate of return to the overall rate of return available in the market

It is useful to have a measure of systematic risk, the way each firm responds to changes in the overall economy. Figure 8.7 shows the **characteristic lines** of three investments, a plot of the rate of return from the investment versus the rate of return available from investing in the economy as a whole. For convenience, the rate of return from the economy is typically measured by a major stock market index, such as the Standard & Poor's 500 stock index, and is called the **market return.** A low-risk investment has a characteristic line with a gradual slope, indicating that its rate of return is not too sensitive to changes in the economy. An average-risk investment has a characteristic line with a slope of 1 (a 45-degree line) and moves up and down at the same rate as the economy. A high-risk investment has a characteristic line with a steep slope, indicating that it is particularly sensitive to changes in the economy.

market return—the rate of return from the economy, commonly measured by a major stock market index

beta—the numerical relationship between the returns from an investment and the returns from the overall market

The slope of an investment's characteristic line is known as that investment's **beta.** Beta equals 1 for an average-risk investment, which means that the investment's rate of return closely follows the market. If the market moves up by 5%, an average-risk investment will also move up by 5%; if the market moves down by 5%, the investment will move down by 5%. A high-risk investment has a beta greater than 1: a 5% increase in the market will cause this investment to rise by more than 5%, while a 5% market decline will push this investment down by more than 5%.

FIGURE 8.7
The characteristic lines of three securities with different betas. Beta, the slope of the line, measures how the security's rate of return responds to stock market movements.

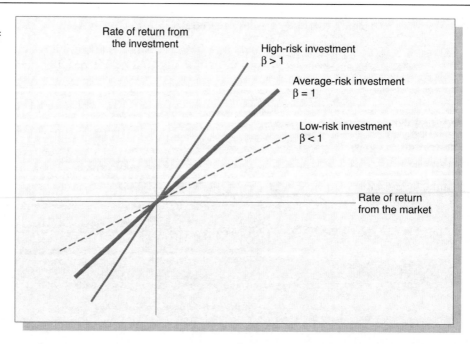

The Stocks that Make Up the Dow Jones Averages and Their Betas

30 Industrials		20 Transportations		15 Utilities	
Alcoa	1.86	Alexander & Baldwin	1.38	AES	1.55
American Express	1.47	AMR	1.63	American Electric Power	.69
AT&T	.50	C.H. Robinson Worldwide	.70	Centerpoint Energy	.72
Bank of America	1.40	Con-way	.99	Consolidated Edison	.51
Boeing	1.36	CSX	1.63	Dominion Resources	.67
Caterpillar	1.85	Delta Air Lines	1.08	Duke Energy	.45
Chevron	1.02	Expeditors International	.96	Edison International	.82
Cisco	1.28	FedEx	1.16	Exelon	.85
Coca-Cola	.47	GATX	1.36	FirstEnergy	.77
Du Pont	1.42	Hunt Transportation	.88	Nextera Energy	.66
ExxonMobil	.92	JetBlue Airways	1.38	Nisource	.85
General Electric	1.50	Kansas City Southern	2.04	PG&E	.58
Hewlett-Packard	1.07	Landstar System	.80	Public Service Enterprises	.79
Home Depot	1.05	Norfolk Southern	1.41	Southern Company	.43
IBM	.84	Overseas Shipholding Group	1.88	Williams Companies	1.66
Intel	1.05	Ryder System	1.63		
Johnson&Johnson	.45	Southwest Airlines	1.01		
JPMorgan Chase	1.31	Union Pacific	1.35		
Kraft Foods	.38	United Continental Holdings	1.73		
McDonald's	.37	United Parcel Service	1.01		
Merck	.64				
Microsoft	.82				
Minnesota Mining (3M)	.94				
Pfizer	.69				
Procter & Gamble	.42				
Travelers	.63				
United Technologies	1.06				
Verizon	.35				
Wal-Mart	.42				
Walt Disney	1.22				

Reference: Bloomberg, June 1, 2011

FIGURE 8.8
Beta coefficients of the Dow Jones stocks. Most Transportations are aggressive while most Utilities are defensive. The betas of the Industrials are distributed around the market average beta of 1.00.

A low-risk investment has a beta less than 1, and a 5% change in the market will cause this investment to change by less than 5%. (Of course, no stock follows the market precisely—betas measure average responses to market movements over time.) Because it rises by a greater amount than the market when stock prices are rising, an investment with a beta above 1 is called an **aggressive security** and is sought after in an up market. By contrast, an investment with beta less than 1 moves by a smaller amount than the market and is known as a **defensive security** because it tends not to lose much of its value in a down market.

aggressive security—an investment with a beta greater than 1

defensive security—an investment with a beta less than 1

Industrial stocks in general tend to have values of beta that are distributed around the market average of 1. Securities of companies which are quite sensitive to condition of the economy, for example airlines like AMR, have high betas. Stocks of companies that are less influenced by the state of the economy, like Con Edison, have low betas. Figure 8.8 illustrates these points by listing the betas of the stocks that make up the Dow Jones industrial, transportation, and utility averages, three widely followed indexes of stock market performance constructed from groups of securities. The transportation stocks often have a beta greater than 1, reflecting their relatively high level of risk. The utilities, by contrast, have low betas which indicate their relative stability. In between are the betas of the industrial stocks which represent a broad cross-section of industries.

NET Present Value
Betas can be found at Yahoo by going to
http://finance.yahoo.com
Enter the ticker symbol of the stock and click the GET QUOTES button, then click on "Key Statistics" under "COMPANY" in the left-hand menu bar.

If a portfolio is sufficiently diversified so that all unsystematic risk has been eliminated, the only risk remaining is the systematic—the risk connected with the overall economy. As a result, for a well-diversified portfolio, its beta measures its risk. The beta of a portfolio, much like the expected return of a portfolio, can be calculated by taking the weighted average of the betas of its component investments. Adding another security changes the portfolio beta by the amount invested in the new security multiplied by the new security's beta. Therefore, beta captures the marginal risk of adding a security to a well-diversified portfolio. *When investors diversify, beta becomes the appropriate measure of the risk of an investment.*

6. Alpha

alpha—the extra return from an investment above that of the average security of the same risk

There is a second attribute of an investment's characteristic line that is of interest to investors: where it intersects the Y-axis. This value, known as the **alpha** of the investment, is the rate of return from the investment when the return from the overall market equals zero. More important, the greater an investment's alpha, the greater the return from the investment no matter what the overall market is doing.

Figure 8.9 shows the characteristic lines of three investments that differ only by their alpha. Since they all have the same slope, or beta, all three investments have the same systematic risk. The thickest line is the average security of this risk class with alpha equal to zero. Lying above the thick line is the charactersitc line of an

FIGURE 8.9
The characteristic lines of three securities with different alphas. Alpha, the Y-intercept of the line, measures how the security's rate of return differs from the average security of the same risk.

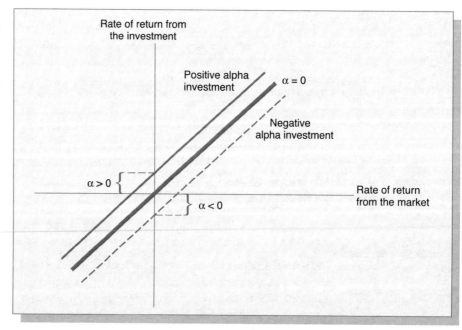

investment with positive alpha. Note that for any level of market return, the return from this investment exceeds that of the average security. Below the thick line is the characterstic line of an investment with negative alpha. This investment yields a lower return than the average security for any level of market return.

If the only reason for differences in the rate of return from invesetments were differences in their systematic risk as measured by beta, all investments would have alpha equal to zero in an efficient market. Investors would arbitrage away non-zero alphas. Positive alpha securities with their higher return would be demanded by investors who would bid up their price and lower their rate of return. Investors would avoid negative alpha investments, and their price would fall thereby increasing their rate of return. However, since positive and negative alphas do exist, either the financial markets are not efficient in recognizing and removing these abnormal returns or there are other factors beyond systematic risk that are determining the returns of these investments.

Investments with positive alpha are very attractive to investors. They have the same risk (beta) as the average investment yet they provide a higher rate of return. As a result, no matter what level of risk investors desire to take, they are always "seeking alpha."

7. The Security Market Line (SML)

security market line (SML)—
a graph of investors'
required rate of return as a
function of an asset's
portfolio (systematic) risk

It is common to summarize the risk-return relationship for a portfolio or for an asset held in a portfolio by using the **security market line (SML),** as shown in Figure 8.10. The SML illustrates the relationship between the expected return from investing in an asset and its *portfolio risk*. At the left of the graph are assets with no risk, which return the risk-free rate. Further to the right lie the risky assets. The graph's upward slope reflects investors' risk aversion as they insist on higher rates of return to compensate for taking on riskier investments.

Since the market average beta is 1.00, investments with betas equal to 1 reflect the risk of the market as a whole and would be expected to provide a rate of return equal to that of the market in general, a rate known as the "rate of return on the market portfolio." This point is illustrated by the dotted lines on the graph.

FIGURE 8.10

The security market line (SML). For an asset held as part of a portfolio, investors' required rate of return increases with *portfolio risk* (β).

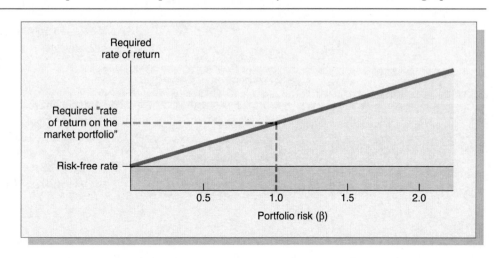

The equation of the SML is that of a straight line:

$$Required\ rate\ of\ return = r_f + (slope) \times \beta$$
$$= r_f + (market\ price\ of\ portfolio\ risk) \times \beta$$

market price of portfolio risk—the additional return demanded by investors to take on one unit of portfolio risk

where the slope is called the **market price of portfolio risk,** the added return required per unit of beta. In Figure 8.10, investors' required rate of return rises from the risk-free rate (r_f) to the required rate of return on the market portfolio (r_m) as beta goes from zero to one. Since the slope of a straight line is $\Delta y / \Delta x$, the market price of portfolio risk must be:

$$\frac{\Delta y}{\Delta x} = \frac{r_m - r_f}{1 - 0} = r_m - r_f$$

which is the difference between the rate of return currently required on an average risk stock or portfolio and today's risk-free rate. Including this detail, the SML can be written:

$$Required\ rate\ of\ return = r_f + (r_m - r_f)\,\beta$$

Like the capital market line, this equation is also consistent with the Fisher model:

$$Nominal\ rate = r_f + risk\ premium$$
$$= r_f + (r_m - r_f)\,\beta$$

Here, the risk premium equals the market price of portfolio risk ($r_m - r_f$) multiplied by β, the portfolio risk of the investment.

Example

Using the Security Market Line to Obtain Required Rates of Return

AMR stock has a beta of 1.35, and Con Edison has a beta of .75. The risk-free rate is 5% and market price of portfolio risk is 8.5%.

Question: What is the required rate of return on a stock of average risk, on AMR stock, and on Con Edison stock?

Solution steps:

1. Average-risk stock—Recall that the average-risk stock has a beta of 1:

$$Required\ rate = r_f + (market\ price\ of\ portfolio\ risk) \times \beta$$
$$= 5\% + 8.5\% \times 1.00$$
$$= 5\% + 8.5\% = 13.50\%$$

2. AMR stock:

$$Required\ rate = r_f + (market\ price\ of\ portfolio\ risk) \times \beta$$
$$= 5\% + 8.5\% \times 1.35$$
$$= 5\% + 11.475\% = 16.475\% \approx 16.48\%$$

3. Con Edison stock:

$$Required\ rate = r_f + (market\ price\ of\ portfolio\ risk) \times \beta$$
$$= 5\% + 8.5\% \times 0.75$$
$$= 5\% + 6.375\% = 11.375\% \approx 11.38\%$$

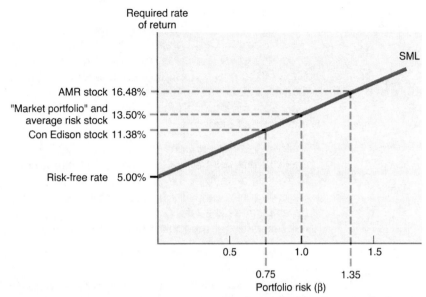

Answer: Investors will require a rate of return of 11.38% on the low-risk Con Edison stock, 13.50% on the average-risk stock, and 16.48% on the high-risk AMR stock.

Earlier we pointed out that an investor can eliminate unsystematic risk through naive diversification by simply constructing any portfolio of 15 or more investments. Since naive diversification is so easy and costless, the financial markets provide no added return to those who take on unsystematic risk. Eliminating systematic risk, on the other hand, is not costless but requires combining assets that do not respond in tandem to economic forces, the concept captured by beta. A low-beta investment, with its low correlation with the economy, tends to reduce the systematic risk of a portfolio, as opposed to a high-beta investment which can add risk. Accordingly, low-beta securities are highly desirable and sell at high prices and low rates of return. High-beta securities are risky, and investors insist on much higher rates of return as compensation.

As we shall explore more fully in the next chapter, investors use the required rate of return on an investment as an important input in setting an investment's market price. The security market line relationship, relating required rates of return to beta, thus also tells us something about the appropriate price for an asset that is likely to be held in a portfolio in the capital markets. As a result, finance theorists have given this model the name **capital asset pricing model (CAPM)**.

capital asset pricing model (CAPM)—the finance model relating asset prices and rates of return to the asset's beta, its impact on the risk of a well-diversified portfolio

The security market line differs from the capital market line in that the CML relates return to total risk while the SML relates return to portfolio risk. The CML is the appropriate model to use when evaluating assets that will not be held in a portfolio, for example, when evaluating the worth of a small business fully owned by its founder who owns few other investments. The SML is the appropriate model to use when valuing a publicly traded security, one that most likely appears in many investment portfolios. This insight, that the correct measure of investment risk depends on the context in which investments are held, is one of the important discoveries of modern financial theory.

*C*ecilia Moreira hung up the phone. She had just finished giving the good news to Carl Leonel. Earlier that day she had convinced her company's president to withdraw the memo that had so enraged Carl and to empower a team of the affected employees to work on a better solution to the problem. Carl was clearly relieved, and Cecilia also felt a lot better. As she reflected on Carl's complaint, she found herself a bit more comfortable with the issues the incident had triggered.

Risk comes from uncertainty, from not knowing what will happen. When people predict there will be risk, they increase their demands on the firm. The concept is the same whether the subject is rates of return provided to stockholders, product quality delivered to the customers, or the job environment as perceived by employees like Carl. An important role of managing is to reduce perceived risk levels to get the most from every contributor to the company's success.

For investors holding portfolios of securities, the relationship between Carl and the company was not very important. It was part of their unsystematic risk and was easy to diversify away. To Carl, on the other hand, his job was his only financial resource and not simply one component of a larger portfolio. Carl had no way to "diversify away" his on-the-job risk.

Cecilia made a note to examine the systematic and unsystematic risk of her company's stock. She was certain that this would help her understand and then address the risk levels the company's stockholders were seeing. She sat back and smiled as she recognized how her understanding of finance had broad applicability throughout the company.

Summary of Key Points

■ **Define** *risk* **and know why it is important to the financial manager.** Risk is the chance that an outcome might turn out to be worse than expected. It is important to financial managing because the firm's stakeholders are risk averters when it comes to investments of large amounts of time, energy, and money; they require additional compensation for assuming a greater amount of risk. As a result, high risk levels are costly—value can be added to the firm and all its stakeholders by keeping risk levels low.

■ **State the relationship between risk and financial value.** The Fisher model of interest rates identifies risk premiums as an important component of rates. Financial values, the present values of expected future cash flows, are inversely related to interest rates. Accordingly, a firm that exposes its stakeholders to high risks must produce higher rates of return to adequately reward its stakeholders.

■ **Describe the three primary sources of risk faced by a firm.** There are three sources of risk for the business firm. Environmental risk comes from changes external to the business—economic, ecological, social, technological, attitudinal, etc. Process risk results from unnecessary variability inside the firm. Combined, environmental risk and process risk are known as *business risk*. The   third risk is financial risk, the added variability of the firm's profit and cash flow stream due to the firm's financing mix.

■ **Measure the risk of a single security held by itself and relate this level of risk to investors' required rate of return.** Risk can be measured using basic statistical concepts. Forecasts of future events are translated into probability distributions. The expected value of the distribution measures the amount of return and, for a single investment, standard deviation measures the risk. The capital market line summarizes the return-risk relationship for a single asset.

■ **Measure the risk of a security held in a diversified portfolio and relate this level of risk to investors' required rate of return.** Many investments are held as part of diversified portfolios. While the expected value of returns from a portfolio is an average of the expected values of the individual components, the standard deviation is not. Rather, it depends on the correlation between the returns from the portfolio's investments, and this enables portfolios to reduce investment risk. A high degree of positive correlation results in little risk reduction while a low or negative correlation permits much of the risk to be eliminated. At the extreme, investments with a perfect negative (–1) correlation can be combined to eliminate all of the risk. The capital asset pricing model shows that risk can be subdivided into the systematic and the unsystematic. Unsystematic (or idiosyncratic) risk, the variability of each investment that is not related to any other, can be eliminated with naive diversification (any combination of assets will suffice) and therefore carries no added rate of return. Systematic (or systemic) risk, the variability related to broad economic factors, affects all investments and is not so easily eliminated. To measure systematic risk, we calculate an investment's beta, the way in which its returns change with the economy. Since reducing systematic risk requires finding low-beta investments, beta is the relevant risk variable for investments held in diversified portfolios. The security market line provides the relationship of required rates of return to beta.

Questions

1. What is risk? Give an example of a risk faced by each of the following stakeholders:

   a. Customers
   b. Employees
   c. Suppliers
   d. Governments
   e. Neighbors
   f. Lenders
   g. Investors

2. If risk is the chance of loss, why is the standard deviation used as a risk measure when it measures variation both below and above the expected value?

3. Are you risk averse, risk neutral, or a risk seeker? Is your answer absolute or can you think of circumstances where you might have each of these attitudes?

4. Give an example of each of the following risks faced by the firm:

   a. Environmental risk
   b. Process risk
   c. Financial risk

5. What is a portfolio? Why do people diversify their investments? Why is it better to diversify across countries than only within one country?

6. Under what circumstance would the risk of a portfolio be the same as the riskiness of its component parts?

7. Why is it not too useful to diversify by buying the stocks of five companies in the same industry?

8. Why is naive diversification called *naive*? What does it do?

9. Comment on the accuracy of the following assertion: "It is easy to diversify away unsystematic risk, but it is impossible to eliminate systematic risk."

10. Even though the unsystematic risk within one company does not affect the risk of a holder of a large portfolio, it may still be relevant to that investor. Why?

11. What is the beta of a security? Connect it to the following concepts:

    a. Low-risk security
    b. Average-risk security
    c. High-risk security
    d. Aggressive security
    e. Defensive security

12. Why do transportation stocks have high betas while utilities have low betas?

13. What is the alpha of a security? Why do investors "seek alpha"?

14. Identify the:

    a. Capital market line
    b. Security market line

    Distinguish between them. When should each be used?

15. How would the security market line change if:

    a. Investors' forecast of inflation changed?
    b. Investors' level of risk aversion changed?

16. The AT&T company sponsors a well-known "Collegiate Investment Challenge," in which students simulate managing a $500,000 stock portfolio and compete to see who can produce the highest-value portfolio by the end of the game. What portfolio of stocks is likely to be the winning one?

Problems

1. **(Required rates of return)** U.S. Treasury bills currently return 4.5%. Determine the required rate on an investment with a risk premium of:

   a. 2%   c. 7%
   b. 4.5%   d. 9.5%

2. **(Required rates of return)** U.S. Treasury bills currently return 5%. Determine the risk premium investors are demanding if their required rate of return is:

   a. 5%   c. 10%
   b. 7.5%   d. 12.5%

3. **(Probability distributions of returns)** Investors have made the following forecast about the returns from investing in securities issued by two companies:

State of the economy	Probability of this state of the economy
Boom	15% = .15
Good times	25 = .25
Average times	35 = .35
Bad times	20 = .20
Recession	5 = .05
	100% = 1.00

State of the economy	Rate of Return from	
	Company A	Company B
Boom	50%	25%
Good times	30	20
Average times	20	15
Bad times	−5	5
Recession	−25	0

a. Graph each probability distribution.
b. Calculate the expected return of each distribution.
c. Calculate the standard deviation of each distribution.
d. In terms of total risk, which security is riskier? How do you conclude this?

4. **(Probability distribution of returns)** Investors have made the following forecast about the returns from investing in securities issued by two companies:

State of the economy	Probability of this state of the economy
Boom	5% = .05
Good times	20 = .20
Average times	50 = .50
Bad times	15 = .15
Recession	10 = .10
	100% = 1.00

State of the economy	Rate of Return from	
	Company C	Company D
Boom	25%	50%
Good times	20	30
Average times	15	20
Bad times	5	−5
Recession	0	−25

a. Graph each probability distribution.
b. Calculate the expected return of each distribution.
c. Calculate the standard deviation of each distribution.
d. In terms of total risk, which security is riskier? How do you conclude this?

5. **(The capital market line)** The risk free rate of interest is 4% and the market price of total risk is 0.5.

a. Write the equation of the capital market line.
b. What is the required rate of return on a security with a standard deviation of 5%?
c. What is the required rate of return on a security with a standard deviation of 10%?
d. What is the required rate of return on a security with a standard deviation of 15%?

6. **(The capital market line)** The capital market line is given by:

$$\text{Required rate} = .06 + 0.4\,\sigma$$

a. What is the risk-free rate of interest?
b. What is the value of the market price of total risk?
c. What is the required rate of return on a security with a standard deviation of 12%?
d. What is the standard deviation of a security with a required rate of return of 14%?

7. **(Rate of return on a portfolio)** A portfolio has been constructed from the following securities:

Security	Expected return	Amount invested
K	15%	$5,000
L	9	3,000
M	20	2,000

a. What is the expected rate of return from this portfolio?
b. If Security L is sold, what will be the expected return of the remaining two-stock portfolio?
c. If the investor buys $10,000 of Security N, with expected return of 12%, and adds it to the portfolio, what will be the expected return of the resulting four-stock portfolio?
d. If the investor sells $2,000 of Security K, what will be the expected return of the remaining three-stock portfolio?

8. **(Rate of return on a portfolio)** A portfolio has been constructed from the following securities:

Security	Expected return	Amount invested
P	5%	$40,000
Q	18	25,000
R	15	35,000

a. What is the expected rate of return from this portfolio?
b. If Security Q is sold, what will be the expected return of the remaining two-stock portfolio?
c. If the investor buys $50,000 of Security S, with expected return of 10%, and adds it to the portfolio, what will be the expected return of the resulting four-stock portfolio?
d. If the investor sells $20,000 of Security R, what will be the expected return of the remaining three-stock portfolio?

9. **(Risk of a portfolio)** Stocks T, U, and V have provided the following returns to investors over the past five years:

Year	Stock T	Stock U	Stock V
2006	15%	15%	5%
2007	−10	−10	30
2008	20	20	0
2009	35	35	−15
2010	5	5	15

a. What was the average annual rate of return on each stock?

b. What would have been the average rate of return on a portfolio composed of 50% of Stock T and 50% of Stock U?

c. What would have been the average rate of return on a portfolio composed of 50% of Stock T and 50% of Stock V?

d. Which securities are positively correlated? negatively correlated?

10. **(Risk of a portfolio)** You are thinking of investing half of your money into each of two stocks, both of which have a 50%–50% chance of earning 25% or earning only 5%.

a. What is the expected rate of return from each stock?

b. What is the standard deviation of returns from each stock?

c. What is the standard deviation of your planned portfolio?

d. Why have you lowered your risk by investing in the two securities instead of just one?

11. **(Beta)** ABC Transport has a beta of 1.3 while Central Gas and Power has a beta of .70

a. Which stock is aggressive?

b. Which stock is defensive?

c. If the market rose by 20%, what would happen to the value of each on average?

d. If the market fell by 10%, what would happen to the value of each on average?

12. **(Beta)** Classify the following stocks as aggressive, average, or defensive and identify if its beta is less than 1, equal to 1, or greater than 1:

a. Stock rises by 30% in response to a market rise of 20%.

b. Stock rises 10% in response to a market rise of 10%.

c. Stock falls 15% in response to a market decline of 20%.

d. Stock falls 10% in response to a market decline of 10%.

13. **(Beta of a portfolio)** ABC Transport has a beta of 1.3 while Central Gas and Power (CGP) has a beta of .70. What is the beta of a portfolio of these two securities if the amount of each is:

a. 20% ABC, 80% CGP?

b. 40% ABC, 60% CGP?

c. 60% ABC, 40% CGP?

d. 80% ABC, 20% CGP?

14. **(Beta of a portfolio)** A portfolio manager currently holds a diversified portfolio of 30 stocks. The amount invested in each stock is $10,000, and the portfolio beta is 1.05. What would happen to the portfolio beta under each of the following scenarios?

a. Another stock is added to the portfolio: amount $10,000, beta 1.05.

b. One of the stocks with beta 1.05 is sold.

c. Another stock is added to the portfolio: amount $10,000, beta 1.50.

d. One of the stocks with beta 0.75 is sold.

15. **(The security market line)** The risk-free rate of interest is 7%, and the risk premium for a stock with beta of 1 is 6%. XXX stock has a beta of 0.85, and YYY stock has a beta of 1.2.

a. What is the equation of the SML?

b. Draw the SML.

c. What is the required rate of return on XXX stock?

d. What is the required rate of return on YYY stock?

16. **(The security market line)** The pure rate of interest is 3%, investors demand a 5% inflation premium on long-term investments, and the risk premium for a stock with beta of 1 is 7%. ZZZ stock has a beta of 1.35.

a. What is the required rate of return on ZZZ stock?

b. Suppose investors increase their inflation premium to 6%. What is the new required rate of return on ZZZ stock?

c. Now suppose investors increase their risk premium for a stock with beta of 1 to 8% (the inflation premium is still 5%). What is the new required rate of return on ZZZ stock?

d. Now suppose investors decrease their estimate of ZZZ's beta to 1.25 (the inflation premium is still 5%, and the risk premium is still 7%). What is the new required rate of return on ZZZ stock?

CHAPTER 9

THE VALUE

OF SECURITIES

"I know it's difficult to forecast stock prices." Steve Payne listened carefully as the CFO of his firm continued. "But in order to raise money for the company at the cheapest cost, we have to have a pretty good sense of whether our stock price is relatively low or high. Otherwise, we'll never know the right time to sell new shares."

Steve was a recent business school graduate working in the company's finance group. Because of its rapid rate of growth in recent years, his company found itself making frequent trips to the financial markets to raise funds through bond and stock sales. Steve had been assigned to participate on a team modeling the value of the firm's securities. He looked around the room; every member of the team was present. Steve returned his attention to the CFO, who was still speaking.

"If we can sell shares when our stock price is at a relative high, we don't have to sell so many shares to raise our target amount of money. This means less dilution for existing shareholders." The CFO concluded his remarks with encouragement for the team.

As the CFO left the room, Steve joined the other members of his team to brainstorm an approach to the problem. He looked forward to getting to know the other team members. Most of all, he felt comfortable that he could apply what he had learned in his finance courses to this assignment.

The problem Steve's team is grappling with is one of the most fundamental in finance. Every company that raises funds from outside investors must make decisions about the timing of security issues. A financial manager who can consistently raise money when security prices are relatively high can save the business a lot of money.

The value of a company's securities is of considerable importance to financial managers for other reasons as well. Recall from our discussion of the goal of the firm in Chapter 1 that when a company successfully exceeds the expectations of its customers and other stakeholders, it will grow and prosper. This will increase the value of the firm, hence the value of its securities, rewarding existing investors. New investors will be attracted to the firm, further increasing the demand for its securities and putting additional upward pressure on their prices. And, since the long-term financial goal of the firm is to maximize the wealth of its shareholders through a high stock price, understanding the valuation of securities is an important part of understanding the financial results of publicly-owned companies.

Key Points You Should Learn from this Chapter

After reading this chapter you should be able to:

- Discuss why the value of a security is a present value and is independent of how long an investor plans to hold it.
- Describe the difference between value and price.
- Calculate the value and yield of traditional and zero-coupon bonds.
- Calculate the value and yield of preferred stock.
- Calculate the value and rate of return of common stock.

Introductory Concepts—What Is Value?

The ability to place a value on money flows is one of the most important jobs of financial managers. Most business decisions have a financial impact, and financial managers serve as a key resource, helping others in the firm understand the money value of alternative courses of action. Financial managers are also responsible for the firm's relationship to investors; in this capacity they must understand how the firm's decisions affect the value of its bonds and stock.

NET Present Value
The American Society of Appraisers at www.appraisers.org is a professional organization of experts in valuation

Any set of cash flows may be valued, regardless of their source. In this chapter we examine the cash flows leaving the firm to service its securities—stocks and bonds. In later chapters we will use the same concepts to value the cash flows from the firm's internal investments.

The basic valuation model used in this chapter is the present value model: a security's value is the present value of the cash flows its holder expects to receive. The interest rate used to calculate the present values must be the rate the investor needs to earn to justify buying the series of cash flows. As we saw in Chapter 4, this rate must take into account the overall level of interest rates as well as the riskiness of the cash flows.[1] We call this rate, which differs for each investment, the **required rate of return.** Investors who pay the calculated value and receive the anticipated cash flows will indeed earn their required rate of return.

required rate of return—the minimum acceptable rate of return on an investment which will appropriately compensate the investor for time and risk

Example

Finding the Value of a Cash Flow

Steve Payne is considering the purchase of a note which promises one payment: $1,000 in exactly one year. He anticipates receiving the $1,000 on schedule, and requires a 15% return if he is to make this investment.

Question: What is the value of this note to Steve?

Solution steps: Calculate the present value of the anticipated cash flow:

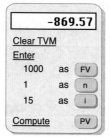

Answer: The note is worth $\underline{\$869.57}$ to Steve. If he pays this amount and receives the $1,000 in one year, he will earn his required rate of return of 15%.

Check on answer:

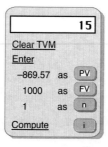

---

[1] **Cross-reference:** For review, refer back to the Fisher model of interest rates on pages 88–91.

An important concept which applies to all the financial instruments in this chapter is that the value of a security is independent of how long the investor actually plans to hold it. We will take advantage of this insight to simplify our modeling by calculating values as if each security is held until its maturity date (forever, in the case of a perpetual security). The reason is straightforward. To sell a security prior to its maturity date requires finding another investor. That investor, using the same valuation process, will be willing to pay an amount equal to the present value of the remaining cash flows, the same value the original investor would receive by not selling. Therefore, investors will forecast that they will receive the same cash benefits no matter how long they hold the security.

Examples

Value Does Not Depend on Holding Period

Steve is looking at another note, which pays $500.00 at the end of each of the next two years. He again anticipates that the issuer will pay on schedule and requires a 15% return on his money.

Question: What is the value of this note to Steve if he plans to hold it for the full two years?

Solution steps: Calculate the present value of the anticipated cash flows:

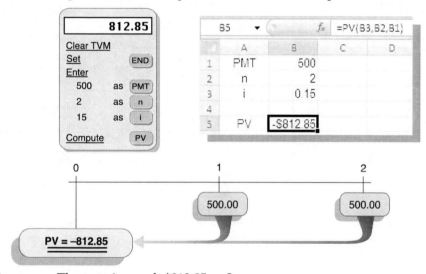

Answer: The note is worth $812.85 to Steve.

Question: What would the note be worth to Steve if he planned to sell it immediately after receiving the first $500 in one year.

Solution steps: Steve will receive the first $500 payment plus the market value of the note when he sells it in one year.

1. Find the market value of the note in one year. This will be the value of the note to investors at that time, the present value of the second $500 to be received in another year:

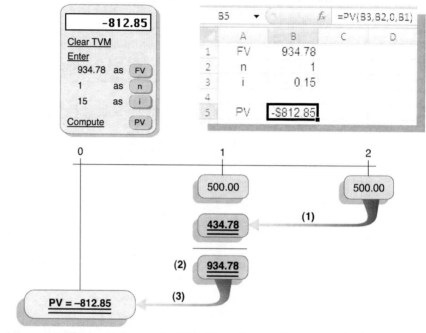

2. Summarize the cash flows Steve anticipates: in one year he expects to receive the first $500 payment plus $434.78 from selling the note = $934.78.

3. Calculate the present value of Steve's anticipated cash flows:

Answer: The note is worth $\underline{\$812.85}$ to Steve, *the same value he calculated assuming he held it until maturity!*

Value vs. Price

There is an important distinction between value and price. In this chapter we discuss *value*, what something is worth. *Price* refers to what something sells for. We know from our everyday experience that not all things carry a price equal to their value. In fact, in many cases, price and value differ considerably. For example, air is free, yet it is invaluable to life. By contrast, precious gems are priced well above their value to many people.

For securities, the relationship of price to value depends upon the level of efficiency of the financial marketplace. If the market is efficient, so that a security's price reflects all information about that company, then price equals value. Academic studies of the security markets have generally found a high degree of efficiency.[2] However, not all markets have been extensively studied, and there are many investors who believe there are significant inefficiencies in some markets. They look for companies with prices substantially different from value to purchase securities when they are "undervalued" and sell them when they are "overvalued." These investors fall into two groups:[3]

1. Technical analysts—those who believe that mass psychology (fear, greed, exuberance, etc.) is a significant factor in the setting of prices. They study investors' behavior and trends of security prices to detect investors' attitudes. Technical analysts predict price movements as continuations or reversals of these trends. They generally pay little attention to value but buy, sell, or hold based on their predictions of price movements.

2. Fundamental analysts—those who believe that security prices tend to oscillate around their values. At any particular time, however, a security's price could differ significantly from its value due to faulty or incomplete examination of economic and other information by security analysts. Fundamental analysts study company, industry, economic, and political data looking for clues to value that other analysts have missed. They avoid predicting price movements other than to assert that mispriced securities will eventually be priced correctly as other analysts discover the insights they have unearthed.

The more the future cash flows from an investment are uncertain, the more opportunity there is for price to diverge from value.[4] Investors have a much easier time forecasting the future cash flows from a bond—which specifies the cash flows it promises to pay—than from a share of common stock, where future cash flows depend upon the firm's future economic performance. As a result, price is generally close to value for notes and bonds. Technical and fundamental analysts pay most of their attention to stocks.

Bond Valuation

NET Present Value
One place to learn more about bonds is the Securities Industry and Financial Markets Association at www. investinginbonds.com

traditional bond—a bond that returns a fixed periodic interest payment plus a fixed principal value at maturity

coupon— the amount of cash interest paid annually by a bond

The cash flows from a bond anticipated by investors are the regular (coupon) interest payments plus the payment of the face, or maturity, value promised in the bond indenture.

1. Traditional Bond

A **traditional bond** has both an interest **coupon** and a face value. Interest is normally paid at six-month intervals, however, in this book we make all bond interest payments annual for simplicity. As we saw in Chapter 6, corporate bonds typically have a maturity value of $1,000, and a bond's coupon rate multiplied by its face value defines the annual interest payment.

---

[2] **Cross-reference:**   Security market efficiency is discussed in Chapter 7, pages 183–185.

[3] **Cross-reference:**   We discussed these two approaches to investing in Chapter 7, pages 181–183.

[4] **Observation and cross-reference:**   And, as we saw in Chapter 8, there will be more risk and investors will require a higher rate of return.

An investor who buys a traditional bond purchases two cash flow streams: the interest payments—which form an annuity, and the face value—a single future value at the bond's maturity date. Therefore, the present value of a traditional bond is:

$$\text{Price of bond} = \text{PV of interest annuity} + \text{PV of face value}$$

Example

Value of a Traditional Bond

Steve Payne is considering the purchase of a traditional bond issued by Lydan Corporation that has a $1,000 face value, a 12% coupon, and matures in 25 years. He anticipates that Lydan will make payments on schedule, and he requires a 12% rate of return if he is to make this investment.

Question: What is the value of this bond to Steve?

Solution steps:

1. Identify the cash flows Steve anticipates receiving: With a 12% coupon, the bond pays 12% of $1,000 = $120 per year. He will also be paid the bond's $1,000 face value when it matures 25 years from now.

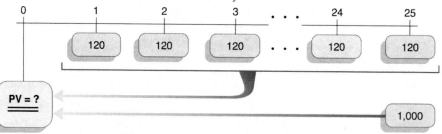

2. Calculate the present value of these cash flows:

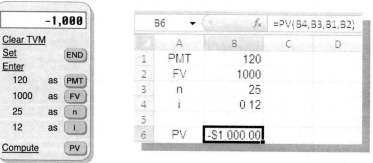

Answer: The bond is worth $1,000 to Steve, its face value.

Because this bond carries an interest coupon exactly equal to Steve's required rate of return, it is worth precisely its face value to him. And if the consensus of investors is that 12% is the appropriate required rate of return, the bond will be a **par bond**, priced at its face value as well. However, if a bond pays a coupon different from investors' required rate of return, it will sell at either a **discount** from, or a **premium** to, its face value.

When investors require a rate of return greater than a bond's coupon, the bond will sell at a discount.

par bond—a bond with a price equal to its face value

discount bond—a bond with a price less than its face value

premium bond—a bond with a price greater than its face value

Example

Bond Selling at a Discount

Investors have revised their opinion of the Lydan Corporation bond (perhaps they perceive greater risk) and now require a 14% rate of return.

Question: What is the new price of this bond?

Solution steps: Recalculate the bond's present value at a 14% rate:

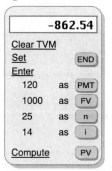

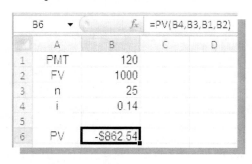

Answer: The bond is now selling for $862.54, a discount of ($1,000−862.54 =) $137.46 from its face value.

When investors will accept a rate of return lower than a bond's coupon, the bond will sell at a premium.

Example

Bond Selling at a Premium

Investors have again revised their opinion of the Lydan Corporation bond (perhaps the risk they perceive has declined) and now require a 10% rate of return.

Question: What is the new price of this bond?

Solution steps: Recalculate the bond's present value at a 10% rate:

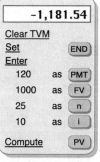

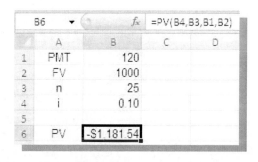

Answer: The bond is now selling for $1,181.54, a premium of ($1,181.54 − 1,000.00 =) $181.54 above its face value.

Even when investors' required rate of return does not vary, the price of a discount or premium bond will change over time. With each passing year, investors are closer to receiving the bond's maturity value. As a result, a bond's present value is less affected by the discounting process (fewer periods of discounting) as it ap-

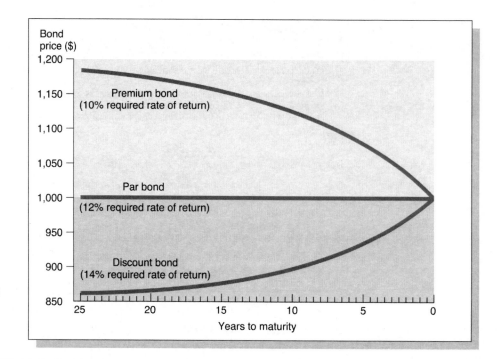

FIGURE 9.1

Price change of Lydan bonds over time (assuming investors' required rate of return remains constant). A bond's price converges on its face value as it approaches maturity.

proaches its face value. Thus, the prices of all bonds converge on maturity value as the years go by. Figure 9.1 summarizes this pattern.

Example

Change in a Bond's Price as It Approaches Maturity

Investors still require a rate of return of 10% per year from the Lydan Corporation bond. Last year, with 25 years until maturity, they priced it at $1,181.54 (previous example). One year has now passed.

Question: What is the new price of this bond?

Solution steps: Recalculate the bond's present value now that it has only 24 years of life remaining:

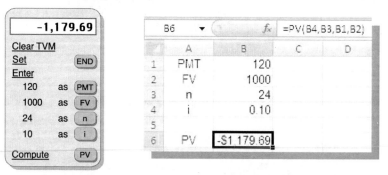

Answer: The bond's price has declined to $1,179.69, a reduction of ($1,181.54−1,179.69) = $1.85.

2. Zero-Coupon Bond

zero-coupon bond—a bond which makes no cash interest payments

Zero-coupon bonds have no coupon, only a final maturity value. Since there are no cash interest payments, we value "zeros" by discounting the bond's face value.

Example

Value of a Zero-Coupon Bond

Steve is also considering the purchase of a $1,000 face value, zero-coupon bond that matures in 18 years. He requires a 13% rate of return to make this investment.

Question: What is the value of this bond to Steve?

Solution steps:

1. Steve will receive only one cash flow from this bond: its face value when it matures 18 years from now.

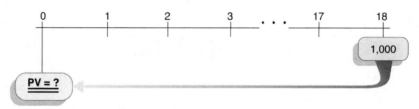

NET Present Value
You can learn more about zero-coupon bonds at http://invest-faq.com/articles/bonds-zeros.html

2. Calculate the present value of this cash flow:

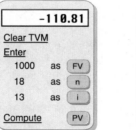

Answer: The bond is worth $110.81, a deep discount from its face value.

deep discount bond—a bond with a price significantly less than its face value

When a bond sells at a price significantly below its face value, it is said to be selling at a **deep discount.** Zero-coupon bonds with more than a few years remaining until maturity must sell at a deep discount since the entire return has to come from the difference between their price and maturity value.

3. Yield-to-Maturity

yield-to-maturity—the rate of return an investor would earn from a bond if it were purchased at today's price and held until its maturity date—provided it made all promised payments

So far, we have been calculating a bond's value given its promised cash flows and investors' required rate of return. However, we can reverse the calculation. Given the bond's promised cash flows and its price, we can calculate the rate of return an investor who paid today's price would earn. If we consider all the bond's promised cash flows—from today until its maturity date—the rate of return we calculate is called the bond's **yield-to-maturity** (YTM).

Example

Calculating Yield-to-Maturity

A bond issued by the Gary Corporation has a $1,000 maturity value, an 8% coupon, and is due to mature in ten years. It currently sells for a price of $885.[5]

Question: What is the yield-to-maturity of this bond?

Solution steps:

1. Identify the cash flows promised by this bond: With an 8% coupon, the bond will pay 8% of $1,000 = $80 per year for the next 10 years. It will also pay its $1,000 maturity value 10 years from now.

2. Calculate the interest rate embedded in these cash flows:

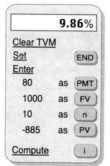 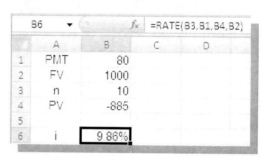

Answer: The bond's yield to maturity is <u>9.86%</u>.

4. Holding-Period Yield

If investors' required rates of return change, the price of a bond would change as well and the lucky (or unlucky) investor who held the bond would receive a yield quite different from the expected yield. The actual rate of return investors receive, incorporating all the cash flows they experience, is called their **holding-period yield.** This rate can only be determined after an investor sells the bond and all the investor's cash flows are known.

holding-period yield—the rate of return an investor actually earns from an investment

Example

Holding-Period Yield

Steve Payne bought the Gary Corporation bond for $885. He planned to hold it for several years anticipating a yield-to-maturity of 9.86%. However, interest rates fell during the next year, and investors reduced their required rate of return to 9.25%. Steve sold the bond after holding it for one year.

Question: What was Steve's holding-period yield?

Solution steps:

1. Calculate the bond's price at the time Steve sold it (the bond now has 9 years of life remaining):

---

[5] **Elaboration:** This price would be quoted in the financial press and by bond traders as $88\frac{1}{2}$, meaning 88.5% of maturity value.

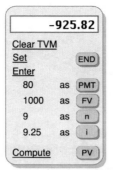

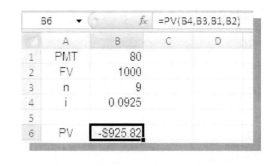

2. Calculate the interest rate Steve received by analyzing the cash flow he experienced during the one year he held the bond:

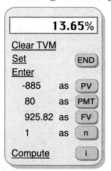

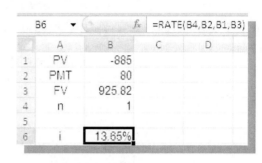

Answer: Because interest rates fell, the bond's price rose quickly. Steve did not realize his anticipated 9.86% rate of return. Instead he did much better, earning a holding-period yield of <u>13.65%</u>.

5. Bond Quotations

Figure 9.2 is an excerpt from *The Wall Street Journal*'s daily quotation of the most active (prior day's trading volume) investment grade corporate bonds.

FIGURE 9.2

Through the Looking Glass: New York Stock Exchange bond quotations. Each day *The Wall Street Journal* reports price and yield information.

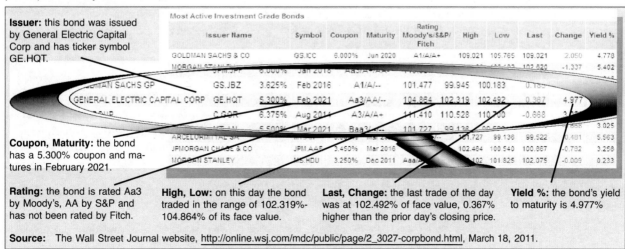

◼◼ Preferred Stock Valuation

The cash flows from preferred stock anticipated by investors are the dividends the stock promises to pay.

1. Fixed-Rate Preferred Stock

NET Present Value
You can learn more about preferred stock at http://invest-faq.com/ articles/stock-preferred.html

Fixed-rate preferred stock promises a fixed dividend, usually paid every quarter (three months).[6] Also, it is normal that preferred stock has no set maturity but promises its dividend flow for as long as the firm is in existence. If we can view the business as a "going concern," the dividend flow may be projected as a perpetual annuity of benefits. Accordingly, the appropriate present value model is the perpetuity model.

The payment is the dividend, typically represented by "D_p". The interest rate is the rate of return required from this stock by investors, represented by "r_p", where the subscript "p" stands for *preferred*. For preferred stock, therefore, the present value model is written:

$$Value = PV = \frac{D_p}{r_p}$$

Example

Value of Fixed-Rate Preferred Stock

Central Maine Power Co. preferred stock pays an annual dividend of $7.88 per share. Today the market demands an 8.385% yield on this stock.

Question: What is the value of this stock?

Solution steps: Apply the model for the present value of a perpetuity:

$$Value = PV = \frac{D_p}{r_p}$$

$$= \frac{\$7.88}{.08385} = \$93.98$$

Answer: The stock is worth $93.98 per share to investors and will sell for this amount.

The preferred stock valuation model can be solved for rate of return, given the periodic dividend and the market price. Rearranging the algebra gives:

$$Yield = r_p = \frac{D_p}{market\ price}$$

Example

Yield of Fixed-Rate Preferred Stock

JPMorgan Chase Corporation has an outstanding issue of preferred stock which pays an annual dividend of $2.08 per share. Today the market price of this stock is $26.50.

Question: What is the yield on this stock?

---

[6] **Simplification:**   As with bonds, we will illustrate preferred stock calculations with annual dividend payments for simplicity.

Solution steps: Apply the model for the yield of preferred stock:

$$r_p = \frac{D_p}{\text{market price}}$$

$$= \frac{\$2.08}{\$26.50} = 7.8491\%$$

Answer: The stock yields 7.85%.

2. Variable-Rate Preferred Stock

Variable-rate preferred stock provides corporate treasurers the opportunity to purchase a high-yielding, tax-advantaged, marketable security.[7] Variable-rate preferred stock adjusts its dividend with changes in interest rates to maintain a relatively constant value. As interest rates can change every day, the dividend is reset at least as frequently as once per week. As a result, the value of this stock never strays much away from its face value, typically $100 per share.

Common Stock Valuation

The cash flows from common stock are the dividends the stock promises to pay. Unlike preferred stock, however, common stock dividends may vary considerably from quarter to quarter—there is no promise that the dividend will remain constant or even be paid at all. In addition, the dividend stream may continue for a long time since the firm is a going concern. All this makes it very difficult to forecast the future dividends of any business, hence place a value on its common stock.

1. The Dividend-Growth Model

To simplify the common-stock valuation problem, it is usual to assume that future dividends will grow according to some pattern. By far the simplest and therefore easiest pattern to work with is constant growth. By assuming that a company's dividends will grow forever at a constant rate, we can use the growing cash stream present value model to value the firm's stock. When the growing cash stream model is used for this purpose, it is typically referred to as the "dividend-growth model."[8] Recall that the growing cash stream model has the form:

$$\text{Present value} = \frac{CF_1}{r - g}$$

The first cash flow is the first dividend to be received one period from now, written as "D_1". The interest rate is investors' required rate of return, represented by

---

[7] **Elaboration and cross-reference:**   The high yield is due to the greater risk of the preferred stock compared to other marketable securities—refer back to the Fisher model, Chapter 4, pages 88-91. The tax advantage is the result of the law that makes 70% of dividends paid from one corporation to another tax free, as discussed in Web Appendix 2E.

[8] **Elaboration and cross-reference:**   It is also widely known as the "Gordon model" or the "Gordon-Shapiro model" after the finance professors who suggested this application and wrote extensively about it. The model was introduced in Chapter 3 , pages 77–78.

"r_c", where the subscript "c" stands for *common* stock. "g" is the rate of growth of dividends anticipated by investors. For common stock, therefore, the present value model is written:

$$Value = PV = \frac{D_1}{r_c - g}$$

Normal practice is for corporations to pay dividends on a quarterly basis, however we will continue to assume annual payments for simplicity.

Example

Value of Common Stock—Constant Growth

Coca Cola common stock pays an annual dividend of $1.76 per share. Investors expect the company's dividend to grow at a rate of 11.5% as far into the future as they can forecast. Today the market demands a 14% rate of return from Coca Cola stock.

Question: What is the value of this stock?

Solution steps: Apply the dividend-growth model:

$$Value = PV = \frac{D_1}{r_c - g}$$

$$= \frac{\$1.76}{.14 - .115} = \frac{\$1.76}{.025}$$

$$= \$70.40$$

Answer: The stock is worth $70.40 per share to investors and will sell for this amount.

The dividend-growth model uses dividends—cash flow to investors—as the basis for value. But what about a company that does not pay a dividend? According to the model, the value of a nondividend-paying firm should be zero, yet many companies retain all their earnings and are not worthless. The reason is that the value of a company may not depend primarily on the amount of its dividend payment.[9] Rather, value stems from the ability to earn money. Dividends are the result of earnings. To value a company that pays little or no dividends, many investment analysts apply the dividend-growth model to the company's earnings numbers or to its cash flow.[10]

It would be unusual for any company to grow at a constant rate forever—economic, technological, and competitive conditions are far too variable. Therefore the dividend-growth model is only an approximation to the value of a share of stock. The best we can hope for is that the growth rate we forecast is an adequate summary of the *average* growth rate of the company. Nevertheless, the advantage of simplifying our calculations often outweighs the disadvantage of the approximate nature of our answer.

2. The Rate of Return from Common Stock

The dividend-growth model may be rearranged to solve for r_c, the forecasted rate of return from holding common stock:

$$Rate\ of\ return = r_c = \frac{D_1}{stock\ price} + g$$

While this model holds precisely only if we forecast constant growth, it shows that the return from an investment in common stock can be decomposed into two parts. The first term (D_1 / stock price) is the stock's expected **dividend yield**, the return coming in the form of regular cash payments and the equivalent of a bond's current yield. The second term (g) is the expected growth rate of the company's dividend stream and translates into the stock's capital gains yield.

dividend yield—the portion of a stock's rate of return coming from dividend payments

Example

Rate of Return on Common Stock—Constant Growth

Reconsider the Coca Cola common stock example. Investors anticipate a $1.76 dividend which is expected to grow thereafter at a rate of 11.5%. The stock currently sells for $70.40 per share.

Question: Subdivide the stock's rate of return into the dividend yield and the capital gains yield.

Solution steps: Calculate the two yields:

Dividend yield = D_1 / price = $1.76 / $70.40 = 2.5%
Capital gains yield = g = 11.5%

Answer: The stock's 14% rate of return comes in the form of a <u>2.5% dividend yield</u> plus a <u>11.5% capital gains yield</u>.

---

[9] **Cross-reference:**   We will explore the dividend decision of the firm in some depth in Chapter 16.
[10] **Cross-reference:**   We pursue this idea further in Chapter 17.

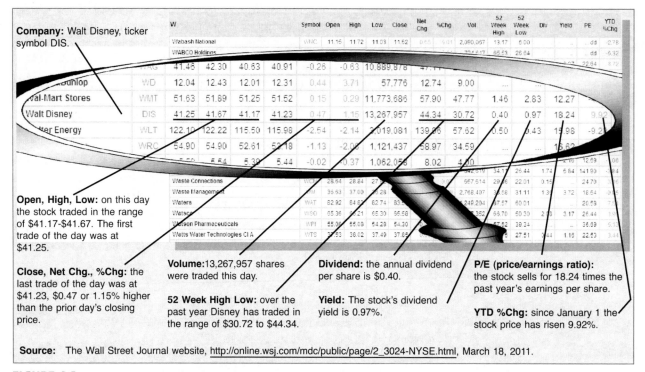

Company: Walt Disney, ticker symbol DIS.

Open, High, Low: on this day the stock traded in the range of $41.17-$41.67. The first trade of the day was at $41.25.

Close, Net Chg., %Chg: the last trade of the day was at $41.23, $0.47 or 1.15% higher than the prior day's closing price.

Volume: 13,267,957 shares were traded this day.

52 Week High Low: over the past year Disney has traded in the range of $30.72 to $44.34.

Dividend: the annual dividend per share is $0.40.

Yield: The stock's dividend yield is 0.97%.

P/E (price/earnings ratio): the stock sells for 18.24 times the past year's earnings per share.

YTD %Chg: since January 1 the stock price has risen 9.92%.

Source: The Wall Street Journal website, http://online.wsj.com/mdc/public/page/2_3024-NYSE.html, March 18, 2011.

FIGURE 9.3

Through the Looking Glass: New York Stock Exchange stock quotations. Each day *The Wall Street Journal* reports summary price and trading information for the securities of listed companies.

NET Present Value
Stock quotations are available at many financial websites such as *The Wall Street Journal*'s site:
www.wsj.com

3. Stock Quotations

Figure 9.3 is taken from *The Wall Street Journal*'s daily quotations of stocks traded on the New York Stock Exchange as of March 2011.

*S*teve Payne looked up at the flip-charts taped to the wall. The dividend-growth model was written on one of them. Steve's company had historically paid a regular dividend, so the team had begun its work with that classic stock valuation formula.

The value of the company's stock could be modeled as the present value of the dividends anticipated by investors. This made sense and was consistent with the method of valuing any security. But that word anticipated had given the team a lot of trouble. Who were the relevant investors? What was their required rate of return? And how could the team learn what dividends they anticipated?

Steve waited for a chance to speak. "My sense is that our task here is a lot like many of the analyses I've seen in finance. At first, the tough part appears to be learning to use the various models. But pretty soon it becomes apparent that the real work is in getting good data to put into the models. Nevertheless, these present value relationships do an excellent job in pointing us in the direction we should be looking to find the information we need."

Summary of Key Points

- **Discuss why the value of a security is a present value and is independent of how long an investor plans to hold it.** Financial value comes from receiving cash, and any security can be seen as a stream of anticipated future cash flows. Time value of money analysis—in particular, present value—is the technique for finding today's value of a future cash flow stream. In this chapter we looked at the present value of the cash flows anticipated by investors in bonds and stocks. The value of any security can be found by calculating the present value of the security's cash flows assuming that the first investor holds it until maturity—or forever in the case of perpetual bonds and stock. This is because investors who expect to sell a security prior to its maturity date forecast a sale price equal to the present value of the remaining cash flows—an even trade—resulting in the same present value as if they hold on until maturity.

- **Describe the difference between value and price.** This chapter is primarily concerned with *value*, the worth of a security to any one investor. The *price* of a security will reflect the consensus forecast of future cash flows and the overall rate of return required by investors. In efficient markets, investors process information quickly and price tends to equal value. However, many observers of the investment scene believe that price and value diverge regularly and meaningfully.

- **Calculate the value and yield of traditional and zero-coupon bonds.** Bonds can be valued by calculating the present value of the cash flows investors expect, using their required rate of return as the discount rate. The appropriate present value model depends on the cash-flow structure of the bond. The calculation may be reversed to calculate a bond's yield-to-maturity or holding-period yield.

- **Calculate the value and yield of preferred stock.** Like bonds, fixed-rate preferred stock can be valued by calculating the present value of the cash flows investors expect, using their required rate of return as the discount rate. The appropriate present value model is the perpetuity model since preferred stock promises a constant dividend with no maturity date. The calculation may also be reversed to calculate the stock's yield given its market price. Variable-rate preferred stock maintains a constant value since the dividend adjusts to market conditions.

- **Calculate the value and rate of return of common stock.** Common stock can also be valued by calcu-

lating the present value of the cash flows investors expect, using their required rate of return as the discount rate. The appropriate present value model is the growing cash stream model since common-stock dividends may be forecasted to grow with the firm. Reversing the calculation produces the stock's rate of return, which may be decomposed into dividend yield, the portion coming from cash distributions, and capital gains yield, the portion coming from growth in value.

Questions

1. What determines investors' required rate of return from a bond or stock?

2. What is the relationship of the value of a security to the holding period of investors? Why is this so?

3. Distinguish between the value of a security and its price. Under what conditions would value equal price?

4. What is the philosophy of technical security analysts? What is the philosophy of fundamental security analysts?

5. Identify the following:
   a. Traditional bond
   b. Par bond
   c. Discount bond
   d. Premium bond
   e. Zero-coupon bond

6. What happens to the value of a discount bond as it approaches its maturity date? What happens to the value of a premium bond as it approaches its maturity date?

7. If a zero-coupon bond never pays an interest coupon, how do investors earn anything?

8. Identify the following:
   a. Yield-to-maturity
   b. Holding-period yield

9. According to the dividend-growth model, a stock that pays no dividends is worthless! Discuss this statement.

Problems

1. **(Traditional bond)** The Chevron Corporation has outstanding an issue of $1,000 face value, 8 1/2% coupon bonds which mature in 15 years. Calculate the value of one bond to an investor who requires a rate of return of:

   a. 7%   c. 10%
   b. 8.5%   d. 11.5%

2. **(Traditional bond)** Alcoa, Inc. has outstanding an issue of $1,000 face value, 10.95% coupon bonds which
   mature in 26 years. Calculate the value of one bond
   to an investor who requires a rate of return of:

   a. 10%   c. 15%
   b. 11%   d. 18%

3. **(Bond price over time)** 3M Corporation has outstanding an issue of $1,000 face value, 8 1/2% coupon
   bonds which mature in 15 years. Today, investors require a 14% rate of return.

   a. Calculate the price of these bonds today.
   b. Calculate the price of these bonds 5 years from now
      if market interest rates do not change.
   c. Calculate the price of these bonds 5 years from now
      if investors' required rate of return declines to 11%.
   d. Calculate the price of these bonds 14 years from
      now assuming investors' required rate of return:
      (1) declines to 10%.
      (2) remains at 14%.
      (3) increases to 18%.

4. **(Bond price over time)** General Electric Corporation
   has outstanding an issue of $1,000 face value, 11 3/4%
   coupon bonds which mature in 20 years. Today investors require a 10.5% rate of return.

   a. Calculate the price of these bonds today.
   b. Calculate the price of these bonds 7 years from now
      if market interest rates do not change.
   c. Calculate the price of these bonds 14 years from
      now if market interest rates do not change.
   d. Calculate the price of these bonds 20 years from
      now if market interest rates do not change.

5. **(Bond prices and maturity)** AT&T, Inc. has two
   $1,000 face value bond issues outstanding with an 8
   5/8% coupon. One issue matures in 16 years and the
   other matures in 35 years.

   a. Calculate each bond's price if investors require a
      rate of return of 8 5/8%.
   b. Calculate each bond's price if investors require a
      rate of return of 5%.
   c. Calculate each bond's price if investors require a
      rate of return of 12%.
   d. Comment on the pattern of price changes you ob-
      serve.

6. **(Bond prices and maturity)** Compare the 9 5/8%
   coupon bonds of ExxonMobil Corp. which mature in
   8 years with those of Verizon Corp. which mature in
   29 years. Both have a $1,000 face value.

   a. Calculate each bond's price if investors require a
      rate of return of 9 5/8%.
   b. Calculate each bond's price if investors require a
      rate of return of 6%.

c. Calculate each bond's price if investors require a
   rate of return of 13%.
d. Comment on the pattern of price changes you observe.

7. **(Zero-coupon bond)** Allied Chemical Corporation
   has outstanding an issue of $1,000 face value zero
   coupon bonds which mature in ten years. Calculate
   the value of one bond to an investor who requires a
   rate of return of:

   a. 9%   c. 13%
   b. 11%   d. 15%

8. **(Zero-coupon bond)** Motorola Corporation has outstanding an issue of $1,000 face value zero coupon
   bonds which mature in 18 years. Calculate the value
   of one bond to an investor who requires a rate of return of:

   a. 8%   c. 15%
   b. 12%   d. 18%

9. **(Yield-to-maturity)** Proctor & Gamble has outstanding an issue of $1,000 face value, 12 5/8% coupon
   bonds which mature in 14 years. Calculate the bond's
   yield-to-maturity if its current market price is:

   a. $ 875   c. $1,000
   b. $ 950   d. $1,080

10. **(Yield-to-maturity)** Citigroup has outstanding an is-
    sue of $1,000 face value, 8.45% coupon bonds which
    mature in 16 years. Calculate the bond's yield-to-ma-
    turity if its current market price is:

    a. $ 800   c. $1,150
    b. $1,000   d. $1,300

11. **(Holding-period yield)** Assume you purchase one
    Proctor & Gamble bond of Problem 9, hold it for five
    years, and then sell it for $975. For each of the four
    purchase prices given, calculate your holding-period
    yield.

12. **(Holding-period yield)** Assume you purchase one
    Citigroup bond of Problem 10, hold it for two years,
    and then sell it for $1,200. For each of the four pur-
    chase prices given, calculate your holding-period
    yield.

13. **(Preferred stock value)** McDonald's Corp. pre-
    ferred stock pays an annual dividend of $5 per share.
    Calculate the value of one share to an investor who
    requires a rate of return of:

    a. 6%   c. 12%
    b. 9%   d. 15%

14. **(Preferred stock value)** Ohio Edison preferred
    stock pays an annual dividend of $7.36 per share. Cal-
    culate the value of one share to an investor who re-
    quires a rate of return of:

a. 5%   c. 11%
b. 8%   d. 14%

15. **(Preferred stock yield)** Calculate the yield of the McDonald's Corp. preferred stock of Problem 13 if its market price per share is:

    a. $ 30   c. $ 85
    b. $ 65   d. $100

16. **(Preferred stock yield)** Calculate the yield of the Ohio Edison preferred stock of Problem 14 if its market price per share is:

    a. $ 60   c. $100
    b. $ 80   d. $120

17. **(Common stock—constant growth)** The common stock of the Kellogg Company pays an annual dividend of $2.12 per share. Calculate the value of one share to an investor who requires a 14% rate of return and who forecasts that Kellogg's dividends will grow at a constant annual rate of:

    a. 0%   c. 7%
    b. 4%   d. 10%

18. **(Common stock—constant growth)** The common stock of the Seagrams Company pays an annual dividend of CAD2.12 (Canadian dollars) per share. Cal-culate the value of one share to an investor who requires a 12% rate of return and who forecasts that Seagrams' dividends will grow at a constant annual rate of:

    a. –5%   c. 5%
    b. 0%   d. 15%

19. **(Common stock—rate of return)** The stock of the CocaCola Corporation recently paid an annual dividend of $1.08 per share. Investors anticipate the company's dividend will grow at a 10% rate for the foreseeable future. Calculate the stock's dividend yield, capital gains yield, and total rate of return if one share of Gillette stock is currently selling for:

    a. $45   c. $75
    b. $60   d. $90

20. **(Common stock—rate of return)** The stock of the JCPenney Corporation recently paid an annual dividend of $2.64 per share. The stock is currently selling for $50 per share. Calculate the stock's dividend yield, capital gains yield, and total rate of return if investors anticipate the company's dividends will grow for the foreseeable future at a rate of:

    a. –2%   c. 7%
    b. 0%   d. 12%

CHAPTER 10
THE COST OF
CAPITAL

*S*arah Liddel refilled her coffee cup and returned to the conference table. The director of financial analysis for her company was pointing to a flip-chart in the corner of the room. "I've put the Irving Fisher interest rate model up on this chart. Remember that all interest rates are composed of pure, inflation, and risk factors. It is important that we understand each component of the rates of return demanded by our investors if we are to come up with a meaningful number."

As a new member of her company's financial analysis staff, Sarah was part of the group responsible for bringing a finance perspective to the analysis of the firm's investment decisions. Today, the group was meeting to update the calculation of the firm's cost of capital.

The meeting had begun with a review of the current state of the financial markets presented by the chief economist of the firm's bank. This led to a discussion of the level and structure of interest rates and forecasts of where rates might be in 3, 6, and 12 months. Now the group was talking about ways to measure investors' perceptions of the riskiness of the firm's securities.

Sarah raised her hand. "I'm still not sure how we should handle the fact that we raise money from a variety of sources—we've already talked about banks, long-term creditors, and stockholders, just for starters. I can't believe that all of them want the same rate of return from us. In fact, if the modeling we're doing is correct, they should want different rates of return. After all, they hold financial instruments that differ in maturity and risk. How do we put it all together?"

Sarah's question points out a fundamental financial dilemma all companies face. A proposed use of funds adds value to a firm if it generates benefits in excess of the requirements of the company's stakeholders. Yet, every firm has multiple stakeholders, and they each have their own requirements. Which stakeholders' requirements should be used to test whether a proposed use of money is acceptable? Fortunately, finance theory provides a practical solution to Sarah's concern, recommending that a firm first meet the needs of its noninvestor stakeholders and then test the remaining cash flows against the cost of capital, a single rate integrating the requirements of all financial investors.

The cost of a firm's capital, like the cost of the other resources it uses, is a significant determinant of its ability to be competitive. A company that can raise low-cost capital has an important edge over its competition. When its capital costs are low, a company can price aggressively and still be profitable. It can plow more funds into research and development and into other product and service improvements. And by generating high rates of return it can increase the benefits it provides to all of its stakeholders. Accordingly, a key part of the financial manager's responsibility is to minimize capital costs, a job that begins with a thorough understanding of where the firm's cost of capital comes from and how it is constructed.

Key Points You Should Learn from This Chapter

After reading this chapter you should be able to:

- Discuss the meaning of the cost of capital and how the establishment of a cost of capital affects management decision making.
- Describe the process of calculating a cost of capital.
- Determine an investor's required rate of return.
- Explain why the cost of a capital source may differ from the investor's required rate of return.
- Calculate the cost of financing with bonds, preferred stock, and common stock.
- Integrate the cost of a firm's capital sources to produce its cost of capital.
- Graph a firm's cost of capital schedule.

Introductory Concepts—The Nature of the Cost of Capital

cost of capital—the minimum rate of return a firm must earn on new investments to satisfy its creditors and stockholders

The **cost of capital** is an interest rate—the minimum interest rate a firm must earn on its investments to add value for its stakeholders. It is closely related to investors' required rates of return, a concept we explored in the last chapter, but it goes beyond the requirements of investors to include other costs of raising money that investors do not see.

1. The Cost of Capital Is an Incremental Cost

In economic terms, the cost of capital is a firm's opportunity cost.[1] Every time a company invests money, it makes a choice. By accepting one investment, it forgoes the opportunity to invest elsewhere. One "alternate investment" is for the company to return the funds to its investors and let them put the money into some other earning opportunity. Investors will demand this if the firm cannot do better than they can elsewhere. Accordingly, the firm must earn a rate of return above this opportunity cost to satisfy its investors.

The cost of capital concept is incremental in nature. Every new investment opportunity requires management either to raise new money or to reinvest money already within the firm, money that otherwise could be returned to investors. Either way, by making an investment, the firm is asking investors to forgo some other investment opportunity that could earn at today's level of interest rates. *The cost of capital is thus always calculated using the rates of return investors would require today to provide new funds to the firm.*

---

[1] **Cross-reference:**   The concept of an opportunity cost was introduced in Chapter 2, page 46.

2. The Effect of the Cost of Capital on the Organization

Establishing a cost of capital provides a powerful signal to members of an organization as to what is acceptable financial behavior. It states loudly and clearly that an investment idea that cannot better that benchmark will be rejected out of hand. Individuals hoping to get approval for their proposals will be motivated to spend time recasting their work into a form that can be tested against the cost of capital. Done properly, this can be a healthy discipline. Done poorly, it can lead to much destructive behavior.

If the cost of capital analysis is too tightly managed by the finance function, it can place too much authority in the hands of finance. This can lead finance to adopt a "judge and jury" role, making decisions about ideas on which it is often not well qualified to pass judgment. This also erects barriers between business departments and works against cooperative teamwork within the organization.

At the other extreme, if the cost of capital is not used under the guidance of those with financial expertise, it is in danger of being used incorrectly by those hoping to have their pet projects approved. Numbers will be twisted to look good and lose all their meaning in the process.

The cost of capital typically will differ among the various parts of the organization. Each unit of a company has its own risks, different from the other parts of the business. Accordingly, each unit has its own beta and requires its own risk premium. Further, the different parts of a business often provide access to individualized funds, sources of money not available to other units of the organization. To the extent a business unit can obtain low-cost funds, it lowers its cost of capital vis-à-vis the rest of the organization. The wise financial manager works closely with the various parts of the business to foster an understanding about the cost of capital so it is not used or seen as a tool of arbitrary discrimination.

Properly used, the cost of capital becomes a shared understanding of the financial requirements of the business—a guide helping everyone within the organization grasp what is needed for successful financial performance.

The Process of Calculating a Cost of Capital

The calculation of a cost of capital proceeds through five steps:

1. *Identify the sources of capital the firm will use.* Only these sources enter the cost of capital calculation; the firm has no obligation to people or organizations that are not its stakeholders. In Chapter 2 we saw that financial leverage ratios are often used to test the wisdom of the firm's financing decisions. We will continue the analysis of financing choice in Chapter 14, where we examine the mix of debt and equity. In Chapter 15, we will study the mix of debt maturities. In this chapter we will assume that the firm has already made these decisions.

2. *For each source of financing the firm plans to use, determine the required rate of return demanded by the supplier(s) of those funds.* The cost of capital begins here

since its purpose is to test potential uses of funds to see if they produce the returns investors want. Where the investor is a professional, such as a banker or a private investor, we only need to ask. However, if we are raising funds from many investors in the public markets, it is impossible to learn investors' required rate of return by asking. First, it is difficult to phrase the question in a way that conveys precisely the correct meaning to each respondent. Second, it is unlikely that investors would give the desired answer; rather they might ask for a much higher rate of return in the hopes of motivating management to do better. Third, we would have to ask all potential investors. As a result, we use other means to estimate investors' required rate of return for publicly issued securities.

cost of a source of funds— the rate a firm must earn from the use of funds to provide the rate of return required by that investor

flotation costs—the total amount paid to third parties in order to raise funds

3. *Convert each required rate of return to the **cost of that source of funds.*** Since we plan to use the cost of capital to qualify the firm's potential investments, we need a number that captures all the benefits and obligations the firm will experience if it raises these funds. The cost of a source of capital is found by adjusting investors' required rate of return by the effects of flotation costs and income taxes. **Flotation costs,** the costs associated with issuing a security, add to the cost of capital by requiring a company to earn not only the investors' required rate of return, but also enough to cover these extra costs. By contrast, whenever the cash paid to investors is a legitimate deduction on a firm's tax return—interest payments, for example—the government effectively reduces the cost of that source of capital by reducing the firm's tax payments.

4. *Integrate the various capital costs into one overall cost of capital for the firm.* The typical company raises money from a variety of sources, each with its own cost. Yet we want to produce a single number that the firm can use to test the adequacy of the returns on investments it might undertake. We use the relative proportion of each financing source to produce a "weighted-average" cost of capital.

5. *Extrapolate the cost of capital into a cost of capital schedule, projecting how the cost of capital will change with the amount of financing the firm attempts to acquire.* In general, firms use the least-expensive financing sources first, and, when these run out, turn to more-expensive sources of money. As a result, a company that needs to raise large amounts of funding will find its cost of capital rising.[2]

Figure 10.1 summarizes this process. In Figure 10.1, we introduce the notation used to represent these concepts. "r" stands for investors' required rate of return, and "k" stands for the cost of that source of capital. The subscripts are "d" for debt, "e" for equity, and "w" for the weighted-average. As needed, we will introduce additional subscripts to denote more specific forms of debt and equity: "b" for bonds, "ps" for preferred stock, "cs" for common stock, and "re" for retained earnings.

In the remainder of this chapter we will learn how to perform each of the five steps in turn.

---

[2] **Alternate point of view:**   We have shown this pattern in Figure 10.1 in the graph of the cost of capital schedule by drawing a line that starts off horizontal and then curves up as capital costs increase. However, there is some evidence that as large firms raise an increasing amount of money, the cost of capital declines before it increases due to economies of scale in raising funds.

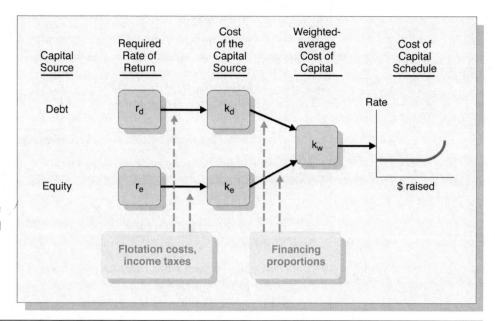

FIGURE 10.1
The process of calculating a cost of capital. Required rates of return first are converted into "costs" by incorporating flotation and income tax effects and then are combined by taking a weighted average.

Determining Required Rates of Return

Professional investors normally quote their required rate of return when asked. Sometimes the quotation is uncomplicated and gives the required rate of return directly.

Example

A Quotation That Directly Gives the Required Rate of Return

A loan officer at the First Finance Bank offers a $10 million ordinary interest loan for one year at a fixed annual rate of 12%. 12% is r_{bnp}, the bank's required rate of return on these "bank notes payable."

More often, the quotation contains sufficient complexity to require further analysis.

Example

A Quotation That Does *Not* Directly Give the Required Rate of Return

A loan officer at the Second Finance Bank offers a $10 million ordinary interest loan for one year at a fixed annual rate of 10% plus a 2% origination fee and a 15% compensating balance requirement.[3]

Question: Is r_{bnp}, the bank's required rate of return, equal to 10%?

Answer: r_{bnp}, the bank's required rate of return on this loan, is not simply the 10% rate quoted by the bank since the fee and balance requirement complicate the loan's cash flows. We must solve for the interest rate embedded in this quotation.

---

[3] **Elaboration and cross-reference:** A loan origination fee is paid to the lender at the time the loan is taken. A compensating balance is a noninterest-bearing deposit that must be kept at the bank as long as the loan remains outstanding.

If we are not dealing with a professional investor, we must use other means to calculate investors' required rate of return. One way is to infer their required rate from their behavior, in particular from the price they set on the firm's securities. As we saw in Chapter 9, investors use their required rate of return as the discount rate to set security prices. By doing the calculation in reverse we can use the price we observe to derive the required rate of return.

Price observed
required rate of return

Example

Inferring the Required Rate of Return from Security Prices

Investors have set a price of $950 on the $1,000 face value bonds of the Maggileo Company. The bonds have an 9.00% annual coupon and mature in seven years.

Question: What is r_b, the rate of return required by bond investors?

Solution steps:

1. Identify the cash flows promised by this bond. With an 9.00% coupon, the bond pays 9.00% of $1,000 = $90 per year, for 7 years. It will also pay its maturity value 7 years from now.

	Year 0	Years 1–7	Year 7
Price/par	($950)		$1,000
Interest		$90	

2. Calculate the interest rate embedded in these cash flows:

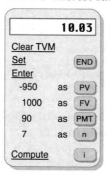

Answer: Investors' required rate of return from these bonds, r_b, is their yield to maturity of <u>10.03%</u>.

The required rate of return on common stock traded in the capital markets may also be estimated as the risk-free rate of interest plus an appropriate risk premium by using the capital asset pricing model presented in Chapter 8.

Example

Deriving the Required Rate of Return on Common Stock from

The common stock of the Land Company has a beta of 1.25. U.S. Treasury bonds currently yield 6.50%, and the market price of portfolio risk is estimated to be 7.3%.

Question: What is r_{cs}, the required rate of return of investors in this stock?

Solution steps: Apply the capital asset pricing model:
$$r_{cs} = r_f + (\text{market price of portfolio risk}) \times \beta$$
$$= 6.50\% + (7.3\%) \times 1.25$$
$$= 6.50\% + 9.13\% = 15.63\%$$

Answer: Investors require an <u>15.63%</u> rate of return from Land Company stock.

Calculating the Cost of a Capital Source

The cost of a source of financing, like investors' required rate of return, is an interest rate. And, like the required rate of return, it is typically found by organizing the cash flows associated with the financing and solving for the embedded rate of interest. It differs from the required rate of return in that it is more inclusive. While the required rate of return calculation looks only at the cash flows between the investor and the firm, the cost-of-a-capital-source calculation adds in the other cash flows the firm experiences as a result of taking the financing. Thus, while the required rate of return describes the *cash flows experienced by the investor,* the cost of a capital source describes the *cash flows experienced by the firm.*

There are two cash flows that arise from taking on financing which are experienced by the firm but not by investors: flotation costs and corporate income taxes.

1. Flotation Costs

NET Present Value
Goldman Sachs at <u>www2.</u>
<u>goldmansachs.com</u> is an investment bank providing assistance to businesses in raising funds

Flotation costs include all amounts paid to third parties to arrange the issue of securities: underwriting fees, selling fees, legal fees, printing costs, filing fees, etc. Some sources of financing—bank loans, for example—can be obtained without flotation costs. Others—for example, the public sale of bonds or stock—typically require investment banking and legal assistance. If flotation costs must be paid, the cost of that source of funds will be greater than investors' required rate of return.

Examples

How Flotation Costs Raise the Cost of a Capital Source

Maggileo Company's investment banker has advised the firm that it would be possible to sell at face value a new issue of $100 preferred stock with a $13 annual dividend and that they would charge 6% of face value to underwrite the issue.

Question: What is r_{ps}, the required rate of return of investors willing to purchase this new preferred stock issue?

Solution steps: Solve for the interest rate *investors* will experience if they buy this preferred stock. (Recall that preferred stock is a perpetuity.)

1. Organize the investors' cash flows:

	Year 0	Years 1–∞
Buy stock at face value	($100)	
Receive dividend		$13
Net cash flows	($100)	$13

2. Solve for the interest rate using the model for the present value of a perpetuity:

$$\text{Rate} = \frac{D_{ps}}{\text{price}} = \frac{\$13}{\$100} = 13.00\%$$

Answer: Investors require a 13.00% rate of return to invest in Maggileo Company's proposed preferred stock issue.

Question: What is k_{ps}, the cost to Maggileo Company of this preferred stock?

Solution steps: Solve for the interest rate *the firm* will experience if it issues this preferred stock.

1. Organize the firm's cash flows *including flotation cost* (6% of the planned $100 face value = $6 per share):

	Year 0	Years 1–∞
Sell stock at face value	$100	
Pay dividend		($13)
Pay flotation cost	(6)	
Net cash flows	$ 94	($13)

2. Solve for the interest rate using the model for the present value of a perpetuity:

$$\text{Cost} = \frac{D_{ps}}{\text{net proceeds}} = \frac{\$13}{\$94} = 13.83\%$$

Answer: The cost, k_{ps}, to Maggileo Company of this new preferred stock capital is 13.83%. This is greater than investors' required rate of return of 13.00%. If Maggileo Company issues the preferred stock, it will have to earn 13.83% from investing the proceeds both to pay the flotation cost and to return 13.00% to its investors.[4]

2. Corporate Income Taxes

The tax law of each country determines which expenses are deductible for tax purposes and which are not. In most countries, including the United States, deductible expenses include production, operating, and interest expenses but do not include principal amounts on loans or dividends, both of which are paid after taxes. A financing source that permits additional tax deductions lowers the firm's taxable income, reducing the taxes it must pay. The firm can use this "released" money for partial payment of its obligation to the investors—in effect the government provides a subsidy to the firm. As a result, a financing source that permits a company to increase its tax deductions will have a cost less than investors' required rate of return.

---

[4] **Elaboration:** Another way to look at the effect of flotation costs is to notice that, while each investor pays $100 for a share of the new preferred, Maggileo Company only receives $94. With less than the full amount to invest, each dollar has to earn at a higher rate of return to bring in the required $13 annual dividend.

Examples

How the Corporate Income Tax Lowers the Cost of a Capital Source

Maggileo Company can privately place an issue of $1,000 face value, 30-year bonds. The bonds would carry a 8.75% interest coupon paid annually and would be purchased by the investor at par. Since the issue would be privately placed, there would be no flotation cost. Maggileo is in the 35% marginal income tax bracket.

Question: What is r_b, the required rate of return of the investor willing to purchase this new bond issue?

Solution steps: Solve for the interest rate *investors* will experience if they buy this bond issue.

1. Identify the cash flows promised by this bond. With an 8.75% coupon, the bond pays 8.75% of $1,000 = $87.50 per year for 30 years. It will also pay its maturity value 30 years from now. The price is par value or $1,000 per bond.

	Year 0	Years 1–30	Year 30
Lend / get back principal	($1,000)		$1,000
Receive interest		$87.50	

2. Calculate the interest rate embedded in these cash flows:

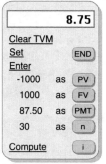 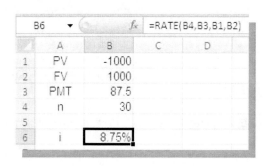

Answer: The investor requires an <u>8.75%</u> rate of return to buy Maggileo Company's proposed bond issue.

Question: What is k_b, the cost to Maggileo Company of this bond financing?

Solution steps: Solve for the interest rate *the firm* will experience if it issues these bonds.

1. Calculate the tax savings from deducting interest payments:

$$\text{Tax savings} = 35\% \times \$87.50 = \$30.63.$$

2. Organize the firm's cash flows *including the tax savings:*

	Year 0	Years 1–30	Year 30
Receive / repay principal	$1,000		($1,000)
Pay interest		($87.50)	
Tax savings		30.63	
Net cash flows	$1,000	($56.87)	($1,000)

3. Calculate the interest rate embedded in these cash flows:

5.69		
Clear TVM		
Set	END	
Enter		
1000	as	PV
-56.87	as	PMT
-1000	as	FV
30	as	n
Compute	i	

B6	f_x =RATE(B4,B2,B1,B3)			
	A	B	C	D
1	PV	1000		
2	PMT	-56.87		
3	FV	-1000		
4	n	30		
5				
6	i	5.69%		

Answer: The cost, k_b, to Maggileo Company of this new bond capital is <u>5.69%</u>. This is <u>less than investors' required rate of return</u> of 8.75%. If Maggileo Company issues the bonds, it will only have to earn 5.69% from investing the proceeds to be able to return 8.75% to its investor. The remainder of the 8.75% return will come from the cash redirected from tax payments to the investor.[5]

 Figure 10.2 identifies in summary form how long-term financing sources are affected by flotation costs and income taxes. In general, if a security is sold to the public the firm will incur flotation costs. Income taxes will be reduced for debt financing since interest payments (but not dividends) are tax-deductible. Notice that all four combinations are possible: a financing source can result in both flotation costs and tax reductions (publicly placed debt), flotation costs but no tax reductions (publicly placed preferred and common stock), tax reductions but no flotation costs (privately placed debt), or neither flotation costs nor tax reductions (retained earnings and privately placed preferred and common stock).

The Cost of Various Capital Sources

Every prospective entry on the right-hand side of a firm's balance sheet represents a possible source of financing. While they differ in many respects—different investors, different maturities, different degrees of flexibility, different claims, different risk exposures, etc.—each financial source used by the firm makes up one piece of its overall cost of capital. Financial managers must evaluate each of these funding sources and determine first the required rate of return, and then the cost of each. Nevertheless, the primary funding sources for many companies are the long term sources: bonds, preferred stock and common stock. As a result, we consider these three sources in the remainder of this chapter.

Since the calculation of the cost of a funding source is an extension of the calculation of the required rate of return (adding in the cash flows for flotation costs and corporate income taxes), we illustrate these two steps in combination in the examples of this section. In each case we will follow a two-step process:

---

[5] **Elaboration:** A simplified method to calculate the after-tax cost of financing when payments to the investor are tax-deductible is to multiply the (pre-tax) required rate of return by (1 − the tax rate). In this case:
$$k_b = r_b \times (1 - .35) = 8.75\% \times (.65) = \underline{5.69\%}$$

Financing source		Flotation cost	Reduced corporate income tax
Long-term debt (bonds)	Private placement		X
	Public issue	X	X
Preferred stock	Private placement		
	Public issue	X	
Common equity	Retained earnings		
	Private placement		
	Public issue	X	

FIGURE 10.2
Summary of additional cash flows. Public issues incur flotation costs while interest on debt reduces corporate income taxes.

1. Calculate investors' required rate of return by studying the market price and the cash flows anticipated by investors in an existing security of comparable risk and maturity to the proposed new issue.

2. Calculate the cost of the funding source by laying out the cash flows the firm would experience if it were to issue new securities to give investors the required rate of return determined in step 1.

1. Bonds

Bonds have an explicit cost due to their interest obligation, however, the interest is tax-deductible which lowers the cost of bond financing. If sold to the general public, a new issue will most likely have flotation costs as well. The tax treatment of flotation costs depends on the tax law; in the U.S., flotation costs on debt instruments must be capitalized and amortized over the life of the issue.[6] Thus, there is a second small tax subsidy for debt with flotation costs.

Examples

The Cost of Bonds

Land Company has $100,000 face value of outstanding bonds consisting of 100 $1,000 face value bonds with a 12.00% annual coupon. The issue will mature in 20 years and is currently selling for 102.5 ($1,025 per bond). Land's investment banker has advised that it would require a 4% underwriting fee to place a new 20-year issue of comparable risk. Land is in the 35% marginal tax bracket.

Question: What is r_b, the required rate of return of Land's bond investors?

Solution steps: Use the outstanding bond to calculate investors' required rate of return by solving for the interest rate *the investors* will experience if they buy the bond today:

1. Identify the cash flows of this bond. It will cost $1,025. With a 12.00% coupon, the bond will pay 12.00% of $1,000 = $120 per year for 20 years. It will also pay its face value 20 years from now.

	Year 0	Years 1–20	Year 20
Lend / get back principal	($1,025)		$1,000
Receive interest		$120	

---

[6] **Accounting review:**   This means flotation cost must be treated just like a machine subject to straight line depreciation with a zero salvage value. The company cannot deduct the flotation cost when the bond is issued but must spread it out evenly, deducting a small amount each year.

2. Calculate the interest rate embedded in these cash flows:

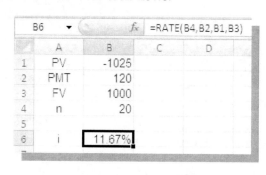

Answer: Investors require an <u>11.67%</u> rate of return, r_b, from Land's existing bonds.

Question: What is k_b, the cost to Land of a new issue of bond financing if the interest coupon on the new bonds is set so they will sell at par value?

Solution steps: Solve for the interest rate *the firm* will experience on the proposed new issue:

1. Since investors now require a yield of 11.67%, a new issue would have to carry a coupon of 11.67% × $1,000 = $116.70 per year to sell at par.

2. Calculate flotation costs and tax savings:

> Flotation cost = 4% × $1,000 = $40 per bond
>
> Tax saving from deducting interest each year
> = 35% × $116.70 = $40.85
>
> Tax saving from deducting flotation cost:
>   Amount deducted each year
>   = $40/20 years = $2.
>   Tax saving each year = 35% × $2 = $0.70

3. *Include flotation costs and income taxes in the cash flows:*

	Year 0	Years 1–20	Year 20
Receive / repay principal	$1,000		($1,000)
Pay interest		($116.70)	
Pay flotation cost	(40)		
Tax savings-interest		40.85	
Tax savings-flotation		.70	
Net cash flows	$ 960	($ 75.15)	($1,000)

4. Calculate the interest rate embedded in these cash flows:

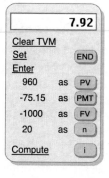

Answer: The cost of this financing, k_b, is <u>7.92%</u>. Land must invest the money to earn at least 7.92%.

2. Preferred Stock

Because preferred stock pays a dividend and not interest, payments to investors are not tax deductible. In addition, under United States tax law flotation costs on a stock issue may not be deducted on the firm's tax return. As a result, in the U.S. preferred stock receives no tax subsidy at all.

Example

The Cost of Preferred Stock

Land Company has $25,000 of outstanding preferred stock, consisting of 250 shares, each with $100 face value and currently selling for $87.50. The stock pays an annual dividend of $11.00 per share. Land's investment banker has advised that it would charge a 6% underwriting fee to place a new issue of comparable risk.

Question: What is r_{ps}, the required rate of return of Land's preferred stock investors today?

Solution steps: Use the outstanding preferred stock to calculate investors' required rate of return by solving for the rate *the investors* will experience:

1. Organize the investors' cash flows:

	Year 0	Years 1–∞
Buy stock	($87.50)	
Receive dividend		$11.00

2. Apply the model for the present value of a perpetuity:

$$\text{Rate} = \frac{D_{ps}}{\text{price}} = \frac{\$11.00}{\$87.50} = 12.57\%$$

Answer: Investors require a <u>12.57%</u> rate of return, r_{ps}, from Land's existing preferred stock.

Question: What is k_{ps}, the cost to Land of a new issue of preferred stock financing if the dividend on the new stock is set so it will sell at par value?

Solution steps: Solve for the rate *the firm* will experience on the proposed new issue:

1. As investors now require a 12.57% yield from Land Company preferred stock, a new issue would have to carry a dividend of 12.57% × $100.00 = $12.57 to sell at par.

2. Calculate flotation costs:

$$6\% \times \$100.00 = \$6.00 \text{ per share}$$

3. *Include flotation costs in the cash flows:*

	Year 0	Years 1–∞
Sell stock	$100.00	
Pay dividend		($12.57)
Pay flotation cost	(6.00)	
Net cash flows	$ 94.00	($12.57)

4. Solve for the interest rate using the model for the present value of a perpetuity:

$$\text{Cost} = \frac{D_{ps}}{\text{net proceeds}} = \frac{\$12.57}{\$94.00} = 13.37\%$$

Answer: The cost, k_{ps}, to Land Company of this new preferred stock capital is <u>13.37%</u>. Land must earn at least 13.37% on the money to justify its preferred stock financing.

3. Common Equity

A company that wishes to increase its common equity financing can do so in either of two ways. <u>First,</u> it can simply retain earnings. The earnings of a firm represent the residual increase in value not claimed by other stakeholders. By electing not to pay this as a dividend, management forces shareholders to increase the amount they have invested in the firm. Alternatively, management may choose to sell new shares of stock. These may be sold to existing shareholders or, more usually, to new investors.

Regardless of the source of new equity, the required rate of return is the same. Investors see no difference between the money they paid in and the money that management (re)invested for them. As a result, there is only one required rate of return for both retained earnings and for a new common stock issue. In addition, common stock financing, like preferred-stock financing, gets no tax subsidy, since neither its dividends nor flotation costs may be deducted on the firm's tax return.

However, there is a difference in the cost of these two common equity sources due to flotation costs. Notice that there are no flotation costs associated with retained earnings—a firm does not have to pay third parties to keep what it already has. By contrast, it is normal to use the services of an investment banker to sell a new stock issue. As a result, *the difference in flotation costs is the only distinction between the cost of retained earnings and the cost of a new common stock issue.*

Examples

The Cost of Common Equity   Returned earnings

Land Company has 10,000 shares of common stock outstanding currently selling for $25.00 per share. The stock recently paid a $1.70 per share dividend, and investors forecast that the firm will grow at an 8% annual rate for the foreseeable future. Land expects to retain $20,000.00 in the coming year. Should it require additional equity financing, it will sell shares of stock to the public; its investment banker has advised that it would require a 7% underwriting fee to place any new issue.

Question: What is r_{cs}, the required rate of return of Land's common stock investors today?

Solution steps: Use the outstanding common stock to calculate investors' required rate of return by solving for the rate *the investors* will experience:

1. Forecast the next dividend by incorporating the 8% growth rate:

$$D_1 = \$1.70 \, (1.08) = \$1.836$$

2. Apply the dividend-growth model:

$$\text{Rate} = \frac{D_1}{\text{Price}} + g = \frac{\$1.836}{\$25.00} + .08 = .0734 + .08 = .1534 = 15.34\%$$

Answer: Investors require a <u>15.34%</u> rate of return, r_{cs}, from Land's existing common stock.

Question: What is k_{re}, the cost to Land of retaining additional earnings?

Answer: $k_{re} = r_{cs} = \underline{15.34\%}$. With no flotation cost nor tax subsidy, *the cost of retained earnings always equals investors' required rate of return.*

Question: What is k_{cs}, the cost to Land of a new issue of common stock?

Solution steps: Solve for the rate *the firm* will experience on the proposed new issue:

1. Calculate the net proceeds to Land of a new stock issue.

   Flotation cost = 7% × $25.00 = $1.75 per share.
   Net proceeds = $25.00 − 1.75 = $23.25 per share.

2. Apply the dividend-growth model:

$$\text{Rate} = \frac{D_1}{\text{net proceeds}} + g = \frac{\$1.836}{\$23.25} + .08 = .0790 + .08 = .1590 = 15.90\%$$

Answer: The cost, k_{cs}, to Land of a new stock issue is <u>15.90%</u>. Land must earn a return on these funds of at least this amount to satisfy its common stock-holders.

The required rate of return and cost of common stock we calculated using the dividend-growth model are necessarily rough estimates. Unlike bonds and preferred stock, which specify their future cash flows, common stock does not. While we see the market price investors set on common stock, we can only guess at the future cash flows they forecasted and used to calculate that price. If we guess correctly, our estimates of the required rate of return and cost of common stock will be good; if we guess incorrectly we could be far off the mark.

Because it is difficult to obtain a precise figure for the cost of common equity, two other approaches are commonly used to confirm the accuracy of our calculations, (1) the capital asset pricing model, and (2) the "bond-yield-plus" model.

Capital asset pricing model   Earlier in this chapter we used the capital asset pricing model to estimate investors' required rate of return on Land Company stock. The number we obtained there, 15.63% is sufficiently close to our number above, 15.34% to give us some comfort.

Bond-yield-plus model   Another device for estimating the required rate of return on common stock is to calculate the required rate for a company's bonds and add a further risk premium. Common stock should be a riskier investment than bonds and should therefore yield a higher rate of return. From historical evidence, the appropriate incremental risk premium for many companies seems to be in the neighborhood of 4%. Applying this logic to the required rate of return we calculated for Land Company's bonds:

$$r_{cs} = r_b + \text{about } 4\% = 11.67\% + \text{about } 4\% = \underline{\text{about } 15.67\%}$$

This technique produces a number that is similar to the other two, further increasing our comfort level. It is likely that the required rate of return on Land's common stock is somewhere in the 15–16% range.

Calculating the Overall Cost of Capital

Land Company raises capital from various sources. If the funds could be kept in separate bundles—so that the money raised from bondholders was never mixed with the money raised from bankers or with the money raised from stockholders, etc.—then Land could use the cost of each funding source as the minimum rate of return it must earn using that money. For example, money with a 10% cost would be invested to earn more than 10%, while money with a 14% cost would have to earn more than 14%. However, the funds raised from various sources quickly get mixed together within a business; it is nearly impossible to look at any one dollar and identify its source. In addition, firms often undertake costly investment projects which require funding from more than one source. As a result, it is appropriate for Land to calculate and use a single number for its cost of capital.

weighted-average cost of capital (WACC)—a synonym for "cost of capital" emphasizing the method by which it is constructed

Land's overall cost of capital resources will be a composite of the cost of each capital source. To calculate this number we take a weighted average of the cost of each source of funding used by the firm. The resulting number is commonly known as the **weighted-average cost of capital (WACC),** reflecting its method of construction. It is also known as the **marginal cost of capital (MCC)** to emphasize its use as a marginal cost; that is, it measures the cost to the firm of raising its next dollar of capital where that dollar is composed of funding from various sources.

marginal cost of capital (MCC)—a synonym for "cost of capital" emphasizing its use as a measure of the marginal cost of capital funds

target capital structure—the percentage mix of financing sources management plans to use in the future

The weights used in calculating the WACC should be taken from the firm's **target capital structure,** management's plan for raising funding in the future. Recall that the WACC is intended to be an incremental figure, the cost of raising the *next* dollar of financing. We took care in calculating the cost of each capital source to look at today's requirements of investors. We must take equal care to ensure that our calculation combines these funds in a mix that reflects management's most up-to-date plans.[7]

Example

Calculating the WACC

Land Company's management has announced a target capital structure consisting of 40% bond financing, 10% preferred stock financing, and 50% common equity financing.

---

[7] **Elaboration:** Sometimes an analyst outside the firm does not know management's target capital structure yet must still approximate the firm's cost of capital. In this case it is usual to assume that the firm is currently at its target capital structure and take the weights from the mix of funds on the firm's most recent balance sheet. When doing this, analysts typically use the market value of each balance sheet item rather than its book value in order to reflect current market conditions and to avoid the incompatibilities of the financial accounting system.

Question: What is Land's WACC?

Solution steps: Construct a spreadsheet of funding costs[8] and proportions (the target capital structure) and calculate the weighted average:

Funding Source	Cost	Proportion	Cost × Proportion
Bonds	7.92	40%	3.168
Preferred stock	13.37	10	1.337
Common equity	15.34	50	7.670
		100%	12.175% ≈ 12.18%

Answer: Land has a WACC of 12.18%. If each of Land's investments earn this amount or more, the proceeds will be sufficient to give all investors their required rate of return.

Producing the Marginal Cost of Capital Schedule

cost of capital schedule—a graph showing how a firm's cost of capital will increase with the amount of capital it attempts to raise

break point—a point on the cost of capital schedule where the firm's cost of capital increases

Notice that the cost figure used for common equity in Land Company's WACC calculation (above) was 15.34%, the cost of retained earnings. Land faced a choice of using retained earnings or issuing new stock, costing 15.90%, to increase its equity financing. By selecting retained earnings first, Land's financial manager chose the cheaper source of funding. It will always be to a firm's advantage, other things equal, to select the cheapest financing alternatives first. The firm should turn to more expensive capital only after the cheaper sources of financing are exhausted.

If a firm attempts to raise a large amount of capital at any one time, it will eventually exhaust its cheaper sources of financing. As it substitutes more expensive capital for the cheaper funds, its cost of capital will rise. The summary picture of this process is the **cost of capital schedule,** a graph showing the firm's cost of capital as a function of the amount of new financing that it raises. Item by item, each component of the cost of capital will have to be replaced by a more expensive source; its cost will go up, and the weighted average will go up as well. Each time this happens, we have reached a **break point** in the cost of capital schedule.

To locate the break points in a firm's cost of capital schedule, we need two pieces of information: how much of the cheaper source of financing can be raised before it runs out, and what proportion of the total financing mix comes from that source. If management sticks to its target capital structure, the amount of financing newly raised from every source always equals its proportion of the total new financing. The following equation restates this point:

Amount of money from each source = its proportion × total new financing

Rearranging gives the form we use to calculate the break points:

$$Total\ new\ financing = \frac{amount\ of\ money\ from\ each\ source}{its\ proportion}$$

[8] **Cross-reference:** Land's funding costs are carried forward from the previous examples in this chapter: bonds on pages 249–251, preferred stock on pages 251–252, and common equity on pages 252-253.

Example

> ## Finding a Break Point in the Cost of Capital Schedule
>
> Land Company forecasts it will retain $2 million of new earnings in the coming year. Common equity is 50% of the target capital structure.
>
> **Question:**   How much total financing can Land raise before it will have used up its new retained earnings and will have to turn to the more expensive new stock issue?
>
> **Solution steps:**
>
> $$\text{Total new financing} = \frac{\text{amount from this source}}{\text{its proportion}}$$
>
> $$= \frac{\$2,000,000}{.50} = \$4,000,000$$
>
> **Answer:**   Land can raise a total of <u>$4 million</u> of new financing (of which 50% will be the $2 million of new retained earnings and the other 50% will be a mix of the remaining financing sources) before it will exhaust its supply of retained earnings.

After the break point we recalculate the WACC, substituting the higher-priced new stock issue for the cheaper retained earnings.

Example

> ## Recalculating the WACC After the Retained Earnings Break Point
>
> If Land Company raises more than $4 million of total new capital it will have to substitute newly issued stock with cost of 15.90% for retained earnings which cost 15.34%.
>
> **Question:**   What is Land's WACC after the break point?
>
> **Solution steps:**   Redo the spreadsheet making the substitution on the "common equity" line:
>
> | Funding Source | Cost | Proportion | Cost × Proportion |
> |---|---|---|---|
> | Bonds | 7.92 | 40% | 3.168 |
> | Preferred stock | 13.37 | 10 | 1.337 |
> | Common equity | **15.90** | 50 | **7.950** |
> | | | 100% | 12.455% ≈ 12.46% |
>
> **Answer:**   Land WACC goes up from 12.18% to <u>12.46%</u>.

Figure 10.3 is the cost of capital schedule for the Land Company as far as we have gone in this chapter. We have found two costs of capital separated by one break point. However, it is likely that there will be additional break points on the cost of capital schedule as Land studies its other sources of financing to predict when they will run out and have to be replaced with more expensive sources.

*S*arah Lidell listened intently to her peers as the meeting continued. After her earlier questioning, the group had begun an animated discussion of integrating the various components of the firm's cost of capital. By this point, Sarah felt she had a good grasp of how to construct that number.

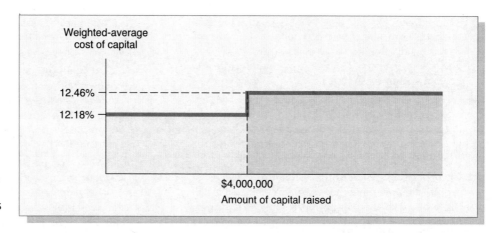

FIGURE 10.3
Cost of capital schedule for the Land Company. The first $4 million of new funds would have a cost of capital of 12.18%; additional funds would cost 12.46%.

The cost of capital was a combination of the rates of return required by all the company's financial investors. It was obtained by calculating a weighted average of the cost of each financial source, using the proportion of each source in the firm's financing mix as the "weights." The costs were derived by adding flotation costs and income tax reductions (if any) to each investor group's required rate of return.

As the meeting wound to a close, Sarah began to wonder some more about the needs of the nonfinancial stakeholders: the firm's employees and customers for example. Might it be possible to include their requirements into some kind of expanded cost of capital calculation, perhaps transforming it into a "cost of all resources" analysis? If so, what would such an analysis look like? And how might it be used? Sarah smiled as she realized she was asking important questions about the future of finance theory.

Summary of Key Points

■ **Discuss the meaning of the cost of capital and how the establishment of a cost of capital affects management decision making.** The cost of capital is the minimum rate of return a firm must earn on its new investments to meet the financial requirements of its investors. It is the firm's opportunity cost, capturing the requirement that the firm must earn more than investors' alternate opportunities. The cost of capital is an incremental concept measuring the cost of raising the next dollar of funds. As such it is always calculated with the most current information about investor needs and market conditions. Because the cost of capital can be an important determinant of what activities are supported within the firm, it must be used wisely in a collaborative team-oriented manner.

■ **Describe the process of calculating a cost of capital.** We construct the cost of capital for a firm in five steps: (1) select financing sources, (2) determine investors' required rates of return, (3) incorporate flotation costs and income taxes into the analysis to fully describe

the firm's experience, (4) combine the various capital sources by taking a weighted average, and (5) project how the cost of capital will increase if the firm attempts to raise large amounts of money. The final output of the process is the cost of capital schedule, a graph projecting the firm's cost of capital as a function of its fund-raising plans.

■ **Determine an investor's required rate of return.** Required rates of return can be obtained from professional investors by asking. When investors cannot give a meaningful quote, we infer required rates from market data. This is commonly done using cash-flow-based models and statistical risk models.

■ **Explain why the cost of a capital source may differ from the investor's required rate of return.** The cost of a capital source includes the effects of flotation costs and income tax flows associated with the financing. Flotation costs raise the cost of financing above investors' required rate of return while the corporate income tax lowers the cost of debt financing.

■ **Calculate the cost of financing with bonds, preferred stock, and common stock.** The cost of a financing source is calculated by organizing the cash flows the firm will experience due to the financing, including any flotation costs and income tax savings. The cost of the capital source is the interest rate embedded within those cash flows.

■■ **Integrate the cost of a firm's capital sources to produce its cost of capital.**   When the cost of each capital source has been determined, they are combined into a weighted-average cost of capital, using the firm's target capital structure as the weights.

■■ **Graph a firm's cost of capital schedule.**   The cost of capital schedule shows how a firm's capital costs will rise as it raises more and more money. Each time a firm exhausts a capital source, it must turn to more expensive financing. This causes a break in the cost of capital schedule, and the firm's WACC rises. There is one break for every increase in capital costs.

Questions

1. In what sense is the cost of capital an opportunity cost? An opportunity cost to whom?

2. Distinguish between an investor's required rate of return and the cost of that source of funding.

3. Why does flotation cost raise the cost of capital while the federal income tax lowers capital costs?

4. Why are estimates of the cost of capital more accurate for bond financing than for common stock financing?

5. Is it possible that there could be sources of financing that have a zero cost?

6. For what funding sources:
   a. are flotation costs applicable?
   b. are flotation costs never applicable?
   c. is the federal income tax subsidy applicable?
   d. is the federal income tax subsidy never applicable?

7. What is the difference between the cost of retained earnings and the cost of financing through the sale of common stock?

8. What weights should be used in calculating the weighted-average cost of capital?

9. What is meant by a *break point* in the cost of capital schedule? What causes a break point to happen?

10. Why do we often draw the cost of capital schedule as upward sloping? Under what circumstances might it be downward sloping?

Problems

1. **(Bonds)**   A company has an outstanding issue of $1,000 face value bonds with a 9.5% annual coupon and 20 years remaining until maturity. The bonds are currently selling at a price of 90 (90% of face value).

An investment bank has advised that a new 20-year issue could be sold for a flotation cost of 5% of face value. The company is in the 35% tax bracket.
   a. Calculate investors' required rate of return today.
   b. What annual coupon would have to be placed on the new issue in order for it to sell at par?
   c. Calculate the flotation cost and tax savings from the proposed new issue.
   d. Calculate the cost of the new bond financing.

2. **(Bonds)**   A company has an outstanding issue of $1,000 face value bonds with a 8.75% annual coupon and 10 years remaining until maturity. The bonds are currently selling at a price of 82.50 (82.50% of face value). The company wishes to sell a new bond issue with a 30-year maturity. Their investment bank has advised that (1) the new 30-year issue could be sold for a flotation cost of 3% of face value, and (2) current yield curves indicate that 30-year maturity bonds yield a nominal 75 basis points (0.75%) more than 10-year maturity bonds on average. The company is in the 35% tax bracket.

   a. Calculate investors' required rate of return today.
   b. What annual coupon would have to be placed on the new issue in order for it to sell at par?
   c. Calculate the flotation cost and tax savings from the proposed new issue.
   d. Calculate the cost of the new bond financing.

3. **(Preferred stock)**   A company has an outstanding issue of $100 face value fixed-rate preferred stock with an annual dividend of $10 per share. The stock is currently selling at $75 per share. An investment bank has advised that a new preferred-stock issue could be sold for a flotation cost of 8% of face value. The company is in the 35% tax bracket.

   a. Calculate investors' required rate of return today.
   b. What annual dividend rate would have to be placed on the new issue for it to sell at par?
   c. Calculate the flotation cost and tax savings from the proposed new issue.
   d. Calculate the cost of the new preferred-stock financing.

4. **(Preferred stock)**   A company has an outstanding issue of $100 face value fixed-rate preferred stock with an annual dividend of $18 per share. The stock is currently selling at $110 per share. An investment bank has advised that a new preferred-stock issue could be sold for a flotation cost of 6% of face value. The company is in the 35% tax bracket.

   a. Calculate investors' required rate of return today.
   b. What annual dividend rate would have to be placed on the new issue for it to sell at par?
   c. Calculate the flotation cost and tax savings from the proposed new issue.
   d. Calculate the cost of the new preferred-stock financing.

5. **(Common equity—dividend-growth model)** Today, you looked at *The Wall Street Journal* and a stock prospectus to read about a company whose stock you follow. You discovered the following:

Closing stock price:	$14.00 per share
Earnings announcement:	$3.00 per share
Earnings five years ago:	$2.00 per share
Dividend payout ratio:	40.0% of earnings
Flotation cost for a new stock issue:	7.5% of market price

Based on the above data:

a. Calculate the company's annual growth rate of earnings for the past five years.
b. Calculate the anticipated dividend one year from now, assuming no change in growth rate.
c. Calculate investors' required rate of return from the company's common stock.
d. Calculate the company's cost of retained earnings and cost of a new stock issue.

6. **(Common equity—dividend-growth model)** A company's common stock is currently selling for $24.00 per share. The company recently paid an annual dividend of $1.60 per share, and investors forecast that the dividend will grow to $3.30 in 10 years. An investment bank has advised that a new issue could be sold for a flotation cost of 7% of face value.

a. Calculate the annual dividend growth rate forecast for the company.
b. Calculate the dividend anticipated in one year.
c. Calculate investors' required rate of return from the company's common stock.
d. Calculate the company's cost of retained earnings and cost of a new stock issue.

7. **(Common equity—capital asset pricing model)** Today, you looked at *The Wall Street Journal* and the *Value Line Survey* to read about a company whose stock you follow. You discovered the following:

Treasury bond yield:	7.75%
Company's beta:	1.3

Calculate investors' required rate of return from this stock if the market price of portfolio risk is:

a. 6.5%?   c. 8.3%?
b. 7.2%?   d. 9.5%?

8. **(Common equity—capital asset pricing model)** Treasury bonds currently yield 8.5%, and the market price of portfolio risk has been estimated to be 8.3%. Calculate investors' required rate of return from a stock with beta coefficient of:

a. 0?   c. 1.0?
b. .75?   d. 1.25?

9. **(Common equity—bond-yield-plus-premium model)** A company's stock's historical return has

been 4% above its long-term bond yield. What would this relationship predict for investors' required rate of return from the stock if the bond yield were:

a. 9%?   c. 15%?
b. 12%?   d. 18%?

10. **(Common equity—bond-yield-plus-premium model)** A company's stock's historical return has been 5% above its long-term bond yield. What would this relationship predict for investors' required rate of return from the stock if the bond yield were:

a. 8%?   c. 13%?
b. 11%?   d. 16%?

11. **(Weighted average cost of capital—weights)** A company has the following right-hand side of its balance sheet:

Bonds payable	$100,000
Preferred stock (250 shares)	25,000
Common stock (100,000 shares)	75,000
Total Liabilities + Equity	$200,000

Bonds payable are currently priced at 85 (85% of face value) in the market, preferred stock is selling at $110 per share, and common stock is selling at $5 per share. Management has announced that it is targeting a capital structure composed of 40% debt and 60% equity. Of the equity, 15% is to be preferred stock with the remainder common stock. Calculate the weights to be used in the weighted-average cost of capital calculation if the weights are based on:

a. The company's book values
b. The company's market values
c. Management's target capital structure
d. Which of the above three alternatives is best? Why?

12. **(Weighted average cost of capital—weights)** A company has the following right-hand side of its balance sheet:

Bonds payable	$250,000
Preferred stock (1000 shares)	100,000
Common stock (200,000 shares)	400,000
Total Liabilities + Equity	$750,000

Bonds payable are currently priced at 115 (115% of face value) in the market, preferred stock is selling at $70 per share, and common stock is selling at $20 per share. Management has announced that it is targeting a capital structure composed of 65% debt and 35% equity. Of the equity, 10% is to be preferred stock, with the remainder common stock. Calculate the weights to be used in the weighted average cost of capital calculation if the weights are based on:

a. The company's book values
b. The company's market values
c. Management's target capital structure

d. If management's target weights were not known, which of the other two weighting schemes would you use? Why?

13. **(Weighted-average cost of capital—calculation)**   A company has the following capital costs and target capital structure:

	Cost	Proportion
Bonds payable	9.0%	35%
Preferred stock	15.5	20
Common stock	17.5	45
Total Liabilities + Equity		100%

Calculate the company's weighted-average cost of capital under each of the following scenarios:

a. It is calculated correctly.
b. The financial manager accidently omits the preferred stock from the calculation.
c. The financial manager accidently treats the preferred stock as if it were the same as common stock.
d. The financial manager accidently weighs each financing source equally.

14. **(Weighted-average cost of capital—calculation)**   A company has the following capital costs and target capital structure:

	Cost	Proportion
Bonds payable	8.25%	50%
Preferred stock	11.0	10
Common stock	13.5	40
Total Liabilities + Equity		100%

Calculate the company's weighted-average cost of capital under each of the following scenarios:

a. It is calculated correctly.
b. The financial manager accidently omits the bonds payable from the calculation.
c. The financial manager accidently treats the preferred stock as if it were the same as bonds payable.
d. The financial manager accidently weighs each financing source equally.

15. **(Cost of capital schedule—one break point)** A company plans to raise new capital as follows:

	Cost	Proportion
Bonds payable	9.0%	35%
Preferred stock	15.5	15
Common stock (retained earnings)	17.5	50
Total Liabilities + Equity		100%

The firm forecasts it can retain $1 million of new earnings. If it requires additional common equity, it will sell a new issue of common stock at a cost of 18.5%.

a. Calculate the company's WACC using new retained earnings as the equity source.
b. Locate the break point in the cost of capital schedule due to running out of new retained earnings.
c. Calculate the company's WACC after it substitutes the new stock issue for retained earnings.
d. Draw the cost of capital schedule.

16. **(Cost of capital schedule—one break point)** A company plans to raise new capital as follows:

	Cost	Proportion
Bonds payable	7.5%	30%
Preferred stock	10.0	10
Common stock (retained earnings)	11.5	60
Total Liabilities + Equity		100%

The firm forecasts it can retain $4 million of new earnings. If it requires additional common equity, it will sell a new issue of common stock at a cost of 13.0%.

a. Calculate the company's WACC using new retained earnings as the equity source.
b. Locate the break point in the cost of capital schedule due to running out of new retained earnings.
c. Calculate the company's WACC after it substitutes the new stock issue for retained earnings.
d. Draw the cost of capital schedule.

17. **(Cost of capital schedule—multiple break points)** The firm of Problem 15 also forecasts the following: (1) if it sells more than $250,000 of bonds, the cost of bond financing will rise to 10.0%, and (2) if it sells more than $400,000 of preferred stock, the cost of preferred-stock financing will rise to 16.5%.

a. Calculate the break point caused by running out of the cheaper bond financing.
b. Calculate the break point caused by running out of the cheaper preferred-stock financing.
c. Calculate the WACC in each interval.
d. Redraw the cost of capital schedule.

18. **(Cost of capital schedule—multiple break points)** The firm of Problem 16 also forecasts the following: (1) if it sells more than $6 million of bonds, the cost of bond financing will rise to 9.0%, and (2) if it sells more than $5 million of common stock, the cost common stock financing will rise to 15.0%.

a. Calculate the break point caused by running out of the cheaper bond financing.
b. Calculate the break point caused by running out of the cheaper common stock financing.
c. Calculate the WACC in each interval.
d. Redraw the cost of capital schedule.

PART IV

ADDING

VALUE

In Part IV we look at how financial managers can add value to their firms.

Chapter 11 examines capital budgeting, selecting value-adding investments in long-term assets. We identify the data that should enter the analysis and then demonstrate how to organize and analyze the data.

Chapter 12 shows how the techniques of capital budgeting can be adapted to the analysis of investments in permanent current assets, the base level of a firm's current resources. We illustrate this process with decisions involving the firm's balances of cash and accounts receivable.

Chapter 13 explores financial processes, the day-to-day work of financial managing. We define and identify the nature and functioning of these processes and show how their performance is measured. Then we discuss how financial processes can be improved and give examples of significant financial process improvement.

Chapter 14 discusses leverage and the optimal mix of debt vs. equity financing. We review why a firm's financing choice might affect its value. We describe four theories that attempt to explain the optimal debt-equity mix and look at practical approaches to the financing mix decision.

Chapter 15 is devoted to risk management. After introducing hedging and showing how it can be used to reduce financial risks, we describe the four-step sequence of making working capital decisions and apply hedging to two of the four steps.

CHAPTER 11
CAPITAL
BUDGETING

*R*ick Daniel stared at the computer screen and shook his head. The numbers did not seem to make sense. How could an investment with such obvious potential have such a low value?

Rick was an analyst in the corporate finance group of a large corporation. He had been assigned the task of evaluating the proposed purchase of a new kind of machinery which promised to reduce dramatically the cost of producing the company's highest-volume product. From his classes in finance, Rick knew that the proper method of analysis began with a complete summary of the incremental cash flows from accepting the project. But when he put the numbers into his spreadsheet program, the resulting calculations did not seem to be at all correct.

Puzzled, Rick printed out his spreadsheet and took the page to one of the group's senior analysts for advice. The analyst first looked at Rick's mathematics. Next, the analyst questioned Rick about his assumptions: where the numbers came from and how Rick had decided which numbers to include in the analysis. Rick took notes as he answered each question.

When he returned to his desk, Rick reviewed his notes. He had written a list of leads to follow up—leads that could improve his numbers and analysis. As he began to prioritize his follow-up actions, Rick thought back to his introductory finance course and realized that it was time to do a thorough review of the basics of capital budgeting.

A key part of the job of financial managing is to advise senior management of the value of potential uses of the firm's money. One important use is investment in long-term plant and equipment, the resources economists call a firm's "capital." As Rick Daniel is rediscovering, understanding whether a proposed capital expenditure is wise requires careful attention to researching and analyzing every consequence of the proposed change.

Finance as a discipline has been a pioneer in developing techniques for the analysis of long-term investment alternatives. Yet financial people have been widely blamed for many companies' lack of attention to long-term investment. While this may seem contradictory, there is much truth to both observations. Poor application of finance theory can easily lead to poor managerial judgments. In this chapter we will explore the methodology of evaluating investment projects as well as the pitfalls that can lead to myopic, short-term decision making.

Key Points You Should Learn from This Chapter

After reading this chapter you should be able to:

- Discuss the importance of capital budgeting to business success.
- Identify the data used in capital budgeting.
- Organize cash flow data for capital budgeting analysis.
- Use the techniques of net present value (NPV) and internal rate of return (IRR) to judge the worth of a capital project.

Introductory Concepts—The Importance of Capital Budgeting

capital budgeting—the process of discovering, evaluating, and deciding whether to pursue investments in long-term assets

capital budget—a financial plan showing a firm's intended outlays for long-term assets

Capital budgeting is the widely used term for the process of evaluating potential investments in long-term assets. The cash budget (presented in Web Appendix 5B) is the projection of the firm's day-to-day—or at least month-to-month—cash flow needs for the next year. Here we look at the **capital budget,** the parallel plan for spending money to acquire long-term resources.

Capital budgeting is important to any firm that makes significant use of plant and equipment, land, and other long-term assets. For one thing, long-term assets may make up 50% or more of the total assets of a company. Thus, capital budgeting may be the technique used to qualify the acquisition of a large amount of the firm's resources. Second, the decision to acquire—or not to acquire—capital resources has a major impact on the financing of the firm. Expenditures on assets require the company to make parallel and integrated decisions about where and in what form to raise funds. In addition, the effects of capital budgeting decisions stay with the firm for a long time. The wise acquisition of long-term assets can often be the difference between a business that is competitively strong, with opportunities for growth and market penetration, and a business that is weak and uncompetitive.

Even for the financial manager of a firm with little investment in capital assets, capital budgeting is an important technique to know and use well. As we will see in subsequent chapters, the techniques of capital budgeting are not only applicable to long-term asset decisions, they can be easily extended to deal with many

FINANCE IN PRACTICE

Manufacturing Returns to the United States

In May 2011, Yamaha Motor Corporation, the large Japanese manufacturer of musical instruments, audio products, semiconductors, and sports vehicles, announced that it would be shifting production of some all terrain vehicles (ATVs) from Japan to a plant in Georgia, the first step in eventually transferring the majority of the company's worldwide ATV manufacturing to the United States by 2013.

Throughout the 1990s and 2000s, the United States lost manufacturing jobs as many companies outsourced production to countries where labor was much cheaper than in the U.S., particularly China. However, China's rapid emergence as a developing nation has led to elevated living standards and increased wages making manufacturing there more expensive. China's growing purchasing power is also increasing the value of its currency, the Yuan, further adding to the cost of doing business there. And, at the same time, the recent recession has resulted in greater labor flexibility and lower wage rates in the United States.

"If the trend plays out, I think you'll see manufacturing growing and expanding in the U.S.," says Michael Zinser, one of the authors of a 2011 Boston Consulting Group study of international manufacturing. "China is no longer expected to be the default low-cost manufacturing location for those companies who are looking to supply the U.S. market. As a result of the changing economics, you're going to see a lot more products 'Made in th USA' in the next five years."

Reference: PRN/Newswire, Yamaha Motor Corp., U.S.A. press release, May 18,2011; Ben Forer, "Manufacturing in America: US Set for a 'Manufacturing Renaissance'," ABC News/ Money, May 13, 2011.

choices affecting current assets as well. In addition, the logic we develop in this chapter is of considerable use in other, nontraditional, areas where finance-trained people are becoming more frequently involved. Often, when working with a team drawn from throughout the organization, the incremental thinking of this chapter is the finance person's greatest contribution.

Identification of Data

To make sound capital budgeting decisions, it is necessary to keep eight data rules in mind. The first seven identify numbers to *include* in the analysis and the last specifies what to *exclude:* (1) Use cash flow numbers only. (2) Use incremental numbers only. (3) Include changes in every functional area of the business. (4) Include changes across the full life cycle of the product or service. (5) Include forecasted inflation in the cash flow estimates. (6) Consider the impact of the decision on quality and sustainability. (7) Consider the options implicit in the decision. (8) Do not contaminate the numbers with the firm's financing flows.

1. Use Cash Flow Numbers Only

Since financial value comes from cash flows, it is important to measure the impact of a decision in cash flow terms. In particular, we avoid accounting revenue and expense numbers. The amount and timing of these figures are highly dependent on financial accounting rules which are made by people and change from time to time. There are alternative treatments for a single event within financial accounting; as a result, the same economic event can be described in several different ways. By concentrating on cash flows, we avoid the risk of distorting business decisions because of the selection among accounting alternatives.

Financial accounting might require the business to recognize income at one point in time, even though the associated cash flows take place over a much longer period. Alternatively, the financial statements might spread revenues or expenses over several time periods even though the cash flow was received or paid in one lump sum. Perhaps the most common example is depreciation expense:

Example

Using Cash Flow and Not Depreciation Expense
Three companies are considering the purchase of the identical machine for $100,000. All three would depreciate it over five years to zero salvage value on their financial statements; but Company A would use straight-line depreciation, Company B would use sum-of-the-years-digits depreciation, and Company C would use double-declining-balance depreciation.
Question: What figure should each firm use in its capital budgeting analysis for the cost of the machine?
Answer: <u>All three should use the same number: $100,000 at the date of purchase</u>. This is the cash they must give up to acquire the machine. The differences between the three depreciation conventions are arbitrary and have nothing to do with the cost of the asset.

2. Use Incremental Numbers Only

As we discussed in the opening pages to this part of the book, incremental decisions are made by ignoring cash flows that do not change with the decision. One type of cash flow that cannot change with the decision, and therefore is a good example of a number that should not be included in capital budgeting analysis, is a sunk cost—a cash flow that took place in the past.

Example

Using Incremental Numbers and Not Sunk Costs
A firm has spent $10 million over the years to purchase plant and equipment. It is presently considering a proposal to spend $100,000 for another machine.
Question: Which figure should the firm use in its capital budgeting analysis for the cost of the machine?
Answer: <u>$100,000</u>. The decision to purchase the new machine involves this amount only. The $10 million is a sunk cost and cannot be changed by saying yes or no to the purchase of the new machine.

3. Include Changes in Every Functional Area of the Business

Capital budgeting projects can change cash flows throughout the business. While some changes will be obvious, others may be quite subtle and not immediately visible. Traditional cost accounting—grouping costs by functional area, cost center, profit center, etc.—is often inadequate to point out the financial interconnections throughout the organization. The analyst must adopt an activity-based approach, searching across all functional areas of the firm for cash flows that will change. Not to do so would be to miss some of the incremental cash flows from accepting the proposal.

Example

Using Activity-Based and Not Local Numbers
A firm is considering a change to its product which would reduce production costs by $0.50 per unit but add $0.75 per unit to warranty service costs.
Question: Which figure should the firm use in its capital budgeting analysis for the per-unit cash flow change?
Answer: <u>−$0.25 per unit</u> ($0.50 − 0.75). While the impact on warranty service costs may not be immediately visible to those who attempt to lower production costs, its impact is real. It doesn't pay to save $0.50 in the factory only to lose $0.75 in the service department.

4. Include Changes Across the Full Life Cycle of the Product or Service

Just as financial analysts must search across all functional areas of the firm, so too must they examine the entire life span of the activity for which a change is proposed. Traditional cost accounting often fails to provide sufficient information due

"It may not be the best investment decision, but hey, we won't know
for three years and I just got promoted to the L.A. office."

life-cycle numbers— numbers which cover the full life-span of some activity and which are not limited to any time period

to its focus on period-by-period reporting. The analyst must adopt a **life-cycle** approach considering all changes which might occur during the life span of the activity to be altered. Not to do so would be to miss some of the incremental cash flows from accepting the proposal.

Example

Using Life-Cycle and Not Single-Period Numbers

A firm is considering a change that would reduce production costs by $2.00 per unit but result in production machinery wearing out faster: new machinery would have to be purchased in three years instead of five.

Question: Which figure should the firm use in its capital budgeting analysis for the cash flow change?

Answer: <u>A figure that includes both the $2.00 and the cost to replace the machinery earlier</u>. While the replacement of machinery is still in the future, the earlier replacement date translates into a more costly expenditure when time value of money is taken into account. The two effects must be balanced against one another.

5. Include Forecasted Inflation in the Cash Flow Estimates

Inflation can create a tangible change to cash flows. If left out, future cash flow estimates will tend to be understated.

While the example below illustrates including inflation in *revenue* forecasts, it is likely that the company's *costs* for the new product will increase as well due to the same inflationary forces. The impact of inflation must be included in *all* cash flow projections, whether they are forecasts of inflows or outflows.

Example

Using Nominal and Not Real Numbers

A firm is considering whether to market a new product. It expects to sell 500 units of the product in each of the next three years. It would price the product at $1,000 per unit in the coming year. Inflation is forecasted to be 8% per year for each succeeding year, and management believes it could increase its prices with the general level of prices over that period.

Question: Which figures should the firm use in its capital budgeting analysis for receipts from the sale of the new product?

Solution steps: Year 1: Receipts = 500 units × $1,000 = $500,000

Year 2: Price = $1,000 (1.08) = $1,080
Receipts = 500 units × $1,080 = $540,000

Year 3: Price = $1,080 (1.08) = $1,166
Receipts = 500 units × $1,166 = $583,000

Answer: $500,000 for the first year, then $540,000, then $583,000. The economic environment will allow the firm to increase its prices which will bring in additional cash flow. Ignoring inflation and using $500,000 for each year's receipts would understate the benefits from this product.

6. Consider the Impact of the Decision on Quality and Sustainability

Capital budgeting proposals that affect the quality of a firm's products and services or the risks and/or opportunities from sustainability, will typically result in changes to cash flows well beyond what is immediately apparent. These quality- and sustainability-related cash flows can easily be large and far outweigh the obvious cash flow changes. An estimate of them must be included in the analysis.

Example

Including Quality- and Sustainability-Related Cash Flows

A firm is considering the installation of new energy-efficient lighting in its retail stores. The team working on the project has researched the cost of installation and savings from the more efficient bulbs. Beyond the hard numbers, there is a shared feeling among the team members that the new lighting will better show off the merchandise and communicate the firm's commitment to sustainability, and this will lead to increased customer satisfaction, hence generate more repeat sales and attract new customers.

Question: Which figures should be used in the capital budgeting analysis?

Answer: The analysis must include an estimate of the quality- and sustainability-related benefits as well as the cost of the lighting. Increased sales would produce new cash inflows which should not be ignored. Further, if the system were *not* installed, the firm might lose customers; a second incremental benefit of the new system is retaining the business of those customers who might otherwise go elsewhere. To estimate the value of new sales and existing customers retained, the analysts might interview members of the company's sales and marketing staff. They might also interview members of other companies that have installed similar lighting systems.

FINANCE IN PRACTICE

Real Options and Climate Change

One of the difficulties of reacting to climate change is the uncertainty surrounding the way it will affect any particular ecosystem. In 2010, a team of analysts from the World Bank evaluating development efforts in Vietnam found that the incorporation of real options analysis into local investment decisions could lead to significantly better choices.

The team looked at investments in houses, dykes, and community shelters in areas subject to floods and cyclones, weather events whose frequency and severity are affected by climate change. They discovered that each investment contained real options since the structures could be adapted to meet future climate conditions. By incorporating the value of these options into their analyses, the team was able to recommend more flexible designs that could be constructed initially at a lower cost than originally planned and could be modified at a later date should future weather conditions warrant.

Reference: Leo Dobes, "Notes on applying 'real options' to climate change adaptation measures, with examples from Vietnam," Centre for Climate Economics & Policy working paper, The Australian National University, November 2010.

7. Consider the Options You Get if You Make the Decision

Capital budgeting proposals are often rejected because the future benefits from the investment are not easily quantifiable. This is especially true in research and development, where it is difficult to know what products or services will emerge from the R&D or what the marketplace will look like in the future. Yet if a firm rejects all such R&D efforts while its competitors push ahead, it could find itself at a severe disadvantage in the future.

One way to deal with this dilemma is to view accepting investments whose returns are speculative as the equivalent of purchasing a call option.[1] The firm spends some amount today (the option premium) to develop its knowledge, technology, expertise, etc., in return for the right (capability) to enter the market at some future date.

8. Do Not Contaminate the Numbers of Any One Project with the Firm's Financing Flows

The techniques for evaluating capital budgeting projects (discussed later in this chapter) test each potential investment against the firm's cost of capital. Since the role of the cost of capital is to bring the company's financing cash flows into the decision, we exclude financing flows from the description of the investment project itself. Otherwise we would be "double-counting," incorporating the financing flows twice.

---

[1] **Cross-reference:**   Options are discussed in Web Appendixes 6D and 9B. The option valuation model can be used in capital budgeting to calculate the present value of future benefits where management expects at some future date to have the choice to proceed or terminate the investment.

Example

> **Omitting Financing Flows from the Description of the Investment Project**
>
> A firm is considering an investment project which would cost $100 today and return $115 in exactly one year. It will finance the project with capital costing 10% (it will cost $10, due in one year, to finance the $100 investment).
>
> **Question:**   Should the $10 financing cost be included in the project's cash flows?
>
> **Answer:**   <u>No!</u> The cost of capital <u>does not enter</u> the <u>analysis at this stage</u>. Do not deduct the $10 financing cost from the $115 to produce a $105 net return. Since the next step in evaluating the project will be to test its cash flows against the firm's 10% cost of capital, deducting the $10 would result in using the 10% number twice in the analysis.

Organizing the Data

In the remainder of this chapter we will use cash flow spreadsheets to organize the data for each capital budgeting problem. This is the same approach we used when we calculated the cost of each source of capital in Chapter 10. Recall that our spreadsheet summarizes cash flows by the date they are forecasted to occur, making it easy to do the required time value of money calculations.

The cash flows most often changed by capital budgeting decisions can be conveniently grouped into four categories: cash flows from (1) purchasing a new asset, (2) selling an existing asset, (3) changes in operations resulting from the asset purchase and/or sale, and (4) changes in the working capital required to support a new asset or no longer required when an asset is sold. These categories are summarized in Figure 11.1.

Some of Figure 11.1 is self-explanatory—for example, the first line which identifies the cash outflow when a new asset is purchased. Other cash flow treatments require an understanding of basic accounting and tax rules—for example the calculation of the tax impact of changes to depreciation expense.[2] The last category—changes to supporting working capital—might require a bit more explanation. Often an investment in long-term assets triggers an accompanying change in related current assets (different inventory levels, changed receivable levels if sales is projected to change, etc.). These working capital changes involve cash flows and must be included in the capital budgeting analysis. However, there is no standard pattern for these flows. Sometimes the additional working capital must be acquired along with the long-term asset—for example, an inventory of spare parts for a new machine. At other times, working capital is added in increments over the long-term asset's life—for example, additional accounts receivable as a new plant produces sales growth over time. On occasion, the new working capital becomes a permanent part of the company's resources; while in other cases, some or all of

---

[2] **Cross-reference and recommendation:**   Depreciation for corporate tax returns is done using the MACRS (modified accelerated cost recovery system) as described in Web Appendix 2E. The same rules apply to business assets owned by proprietorships and partnerships. See your accounting textbook if you desire further review of depreciation or of other accounting calculations such as the gain or loss when an asset is sold.

Category	Cash flow	Treatment
Cash flows from purchasing an asset	Initial cost	Cash outflow when purchased
	Tax savings due to depreciation	Cash inflow (reduced outflow) each year depreciation may be taken
	Terminal value	Cash inflow when the asset is sold (adjusted by tax if a capital gain or loss is reported)
Cash flows from selling an existing asset	Sale price	Cash inflow when sold
	Tax on sale	Cash outflow if a gain on sale is reported; cash inflow (reduced outflow) if a loss on sale is reported
	Tax savings forgone due to no longer being able to depreciate the asset	Cash outflow (increased taxes) each year depreciation would have been taken if the asset were not sold
	Terminal value forgone from no longer having the asset to sell on its original termination date	Cash outflow (lost cash inflow)
Cash flows from operations	Changed receipts or payments from having the new asset and/or not having the old asset	Cash inflows and/or outflows over the lifetime of the new and/or old asset(s)
	Taxes paid or saved as changed receipts and payments enter the tax return as changes to income	Cash inflows and/or outflows over the lifetime of the new and/or old asset(s)
Cash flows from the investment in supporting working capital	The cost of acquiring additional working capital when a new asset is purchased	Cash outflow when the asset, and hence the supporting working capital, is purchased
	The cash from selling working capital no longer required when an asset is sold	Cash inflow when the asset, and hence the supporting working capital, is sold

FIGURE 11.1

The most common changes to cash flows in capital budgeting analyses. The cash flows have been grouped into four categories for convenience.

it can be sold or recaptured when the underlying long-term asset is no longer needed. Because there are so many possibilities, financial analysts study capital budgeting proposals carefully to estimate the amounts and timing of their working capital requirements. But this level of detail is beyond the scope of this book. Accordingly, we have adopted the simplification that the working capital requirements of capital budgeting proposals may be summarized, whenever they appear, with only two cash flows:

● A cash outflow to represent the purchase of supporting working capital when a long-term asset is acquired

● A cash inflow of equal amount, representing the recovery of the investment in supporting working capital when the long-term asset is sold and the working capital is no longer needed.

In spreadsheet form, capital budgeting cash flows may be organized as shown in Figure 11.2.

Cash flows in all four categories are illustrated in the following examples:

	Year 0	Years 1-n	Year n
Buy asset	(Cost)		
Tax—new depreciation		Reduced taxes	
Terminal value			Recovery
Sell asset	Sale price		
Tax—gain/loss on sale	Tax in/outflow		
Tax—lost depreciation		(Increased taxes)	
Lost terminal value			(Lost recovery)
Operating cash flows		Changed in/outflows	
Tax—changed income		Tax on above	
Supporting working capital	(Investment)		Recovery
Net cash flows			

FIGURE 11.2

Cash flow spreadsheet for capital budgeting decisions. The spreadsheet organizes the data into four categories of cash flows and by the time of the cash flow.

Example

Organizing Cash Flow Data for Capital Budgeting

A real estate company is considering the purchase of a parcel of land for $1,000,000. Management forecasts it would hold the land for five years, during which time there would be no receipts or costs associated with the property. At the end of the five years, the land would be sold for a price forecasted to be $1,500,000. The firm is in the 35% income tax bracket.

Question: Organize the cash flows for this capital budgeting analysis.

Solution steps:

1. The purchase and sale price for the land are given. We must calculate the tax the company will pay when it sells the land:

$$\text{Gain on sale} = \$1,500,000 - 1,000,000 = \$500,000$$
$$\text{Tax on gain} = 35\% \times \$500,000 = \$175,000$$

2. Construct a cash flow spreadsheet:

	Year 0	Year 5
Buy the land	($1,000,000)	
Sell the land		$1,500,000
Tax—gain on sale		(175,000)
Net cash flows	($1,000,000)	$1,325,000

Answer: This project will require the firm to pay $1,000,000 at its inception in return for a forecasted $1,325,000 in five years.

Example

Organizing Cash Flow Data for Capital Budgeting

A manufacturing company is considering the purchase of a machine to reduce waste in its production process. The machine would cost $110,000, have a ten-year life, and be depreciated for tax purposes to a $10,000 salvage value using the straight-line[3] method. The company forecasts that the machine would save

---

[3] **Elaboration and cross-reference:**   Although the U.S. tax code requires businesses to use the "modified accelerated cost recovery system (MACRS)" to depreciate assets on their tax returns, we use the straight-line method throughout this chapter to keep the illustrations simple and manageable. See Web Appendix 11A for further discussion of the worth of accelerated depreciation.

the firm $33,000 in each of the ten years of its life and that it could be sold for its $10,000 salvage value at the end of the ten years. The firm is in the 35% income tax bracket.

Question: Organize the cash flows for this capital budgeting analysis.

Solution steps:

1. The purchase and sale price for the machine are given as is the annual savings. We must calculate the tax benefits from depreciating the machine and the tax obligations from reporting higher income due to the annual operating savings:

$$\text{New depreciation} = (\$110{,}000 - 10{,}000)/10 = \$10{,}000/\text{year}$$
$$\text{Tax benefit} = 35\% \times \$10{,}000 = \$3{,}500/\text{year}$$
$$\text{Tax on operating savings} = 35\% \times \$33{,}000 = \$11{,}550/\text{year}$$

2. Construct a cash flow spreadsheet:

	Year 0	Years 1–10	Year 10
Buy the machine	($110,000)		
Tax—new depreciation		$ 3,500	
Terminal value			$10,000
Operating cash flows		33,000	
Tax—changed income		(11,550)	
Net cash flows	($110,000)	$24,950	$10,000

Answer: This project will require the firm to pay $110,000 at its inception in return for a forecasted annuity of benefits of $24,950 per year for ten years plus a single cash benefit of $10,000 at the end of the tenth year.

Example **Organizing Cash Flow Data for Capital Budgeting**

A transportation company is considering the replacement of several trucks to reduce down-time, thus providing better on-time delivery service. The existing trucks were purchased three years ago for $75,000 and are being depreciated over their eight-year life to a $15,000 salvage value using the straight-line method. They could be sold today for $35,000. New trucks would cost $100,000, have a five-year life, and be depreciated for tax purposes to a $20,000 salvage value, also using the straight-line method. The company forecasts that the new trucks would reduce operating costs by $5,000 per year; in addition, increased customer satisfaction would add $20,000 per year to cash revenues. As long as the new trucks are around, the company must carry an increased inventory of spare parts costing $2,500. At the end of the five years, the new trucks would be sold for $25,000. The firm is in the 35% income tax bracket.

Question: Organize the cash flows for this capital budgeting analysis.

Solution steps:

1. The purchase and sale price for the new trucks are given, as are the sale price of the old trucks, the annual operating benefits, and the required increase to working capital assets. We must calculate the various tax effects:

New trucks:

New depreciation = ($100,000 − 20,000)/5 = $16,000/year

Tax benefit due to new depreciation = 35% × $16,000
= $5,600/year

Book value when sold = accounting salvage value = $20,000

Projected gain on sale = $25,000 − 20,000 = $5,000

Tax obligation due to gain on sale = 35% × $5,000 = $1,750

Old trucks:

Depreciation/year = ($75,000 − 15,000)/8 = $7,500

Tax obligation due to lost depreciation = 35% × $7,500
= $2,625/year

Current book value = $75,000 − (3 × $7,500) = $52,500

Loss on sale = $52,500 − 35,000 = $17,500

Tax benefit due to loss on sale = 35% × $17,500 = $6,125

Operating cash flows:

Tax obligation on cost saving = 35% × $5,000 = $1,750/year

Tax obligation on new revenues = 35% × $20,000 = $7,000/year

2. Construct a cash flow spreadsheet:

	Year 0	Years 1–5	Year 5
Buy the new trucks	($100,000)		
Tax—new depreciation		$5,600	
Terminal value			$25,000
Tax—gain on sale			(1,750)
Sell the old trucks	35,000		
Tax—loss on sale	6,125		
Tax—lost depreciation		(2,625)	
Lost terminal value			(15,000)
Operating cash flows			
Cost savings		5,000	
Tax—cost savings		(1,750)	
New cash revenue		20,000	
Tax—new revenue		(7,000)	
Supporting working capital	(2,500)		2,500
Net cash flows	($ 61,135)	$19,225	$ 10,750

Answer: This project will require the firm to pay a net $61,375 at its inception in return for a forecasted annuity of benefits of $19,225 per year for five years plus a single cash benefit of $10,750 at the end of the fifth year.

Reaching a Decision

The cash flow spreadsheet for a capital budgeting project gives a summary of the project's projected cash flows organized by when they are expected to occur. In this form the data are perfectly arranged for evaluation using time value of money tools. The use of time value analysis is necessary since long-term asset investments, by their very nature, involve cash flow changes at a variety of points in time—from the project's inception into the future—and, as we originally saw in Chapter 3, it is impossible to compare cash flows unless they are adjusted for time.

There are two widely used methods of applying time value analysis to a table of cash flows: (1) net present value and (2) internal rate of return. Both reduce the cash flow data to a single number. Both test that number against the firm's weighted-average cost of capital to determine if the investment project returns an amount sufficient to give investors their required rate of return. If so, the company should accept the proposed investment as it will add value for the firm's stakeholders; if not, the proposed investment should be rejected since to accept it would reduce the firm's worth.[4]

In what follows, we look further at these two methods and apply them to the four investments for which we developed cash flow spreadsheets on the previous pages.

1. Net Present Value (NPV)

net present value—the present value of all benefits from a proposed investment less the present value of all costs, using the weighted-average cost of capital as the discount rate

The **net present value** of a series of cash flows is the difference, or net, between the present value of all benefits and the present value of all costs. Alternatively, since cash inflows are written with a positive sign while cash outflows are treated as negative, net present value is simply the sum of the signed present values of all the cash flows. By combining the benefits and costs of a proposed project, NPV performs a (time-value-of-money adjusted) cost-benefit analysis.

The interest rate used to calculate net present value must be the cost of capital appropriate for the investment project. By using the cost of capital to discount future cash flows to their present value, NPV tests those flows to see if they represent a growth in value in excess of "the rate the firm must earn on new investments to return to investors their required rate of return."

NET Present Value (This time the subject really is "Net Present Value"!) A website with further information on the concept of NPV is www.investopedia.com/terms/n/npv.asp

When net present value is positive, benefits exceed costs and the proposal should be accepted. When net present value is negative, the reverse is true: costs are greater than benefits and the proposal should be rejected.

---

[4] **Elaboration and observation:**   Net present value (NPV) is the theoretically correct method, calculating the projected value added to the company from undertaking the proposed project. But internal rate of return (IRR) is a perfect substitute for NPV in many cases. Where this is so, many finance professionals prefer IRR since they find it easier to communicate and understand ("The proposed investment earns a 30% rate of return"). IRR, a rate of interest, is easily compared to other interest rates in the economy, especially the company's cost of capital. NPV on the other hand, a dollar amount, may seem like a more abstract concept ("The proposed investment would add $5,000 to the company's value measured in today's dollars"), and is more difficult to relate to the cost of financing the proposed capital budgeting project. See Web Appendix 11C for a discussion of those cases where IRR breaks down.

Examples

Calculating Net Present Value

In considering the land investment on page 272, the real estate company produced a cash flow spreadsheet with the following summary numbers:

	Year 0	Year 5
Net cash flows	($1,000,000)	$1,325,000

The company's weighted-average cost of capital is 12%.

Question: What is the proposal's net present value?

Solution steps:

1. Since the outflow takes place at "year 0," its present value is its face value of $1,000,000.

2. Calculate the present value of the benefit:

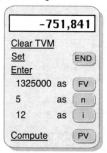 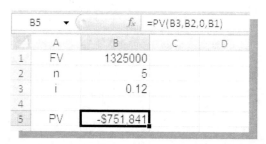

(The negative sign indicates that $751,841 is the fair price to *pay* today for a benefit of $1,325,000 to be received in five years if the goal is to earn 12%. In this context, however, since we are evaluating a *benefit*, we ignore the negative sign and treat the $751,841 as a positive amount: the equivalent today to receiving $1,325,000 in five years.)

3. NPV = present value of benefits − present value of costs
   = $751,841 − 1,000,000 = −$248,159

Answer: This project's net present value is −$248,159.

Question: Should the firm accept this proposal?

Answer: No! NPV is negative. To accept would be to give away $1,000,000 in return for future benefits worth only $751,841. The firm would lose $248,159 of value if it accepted the proposal.

Notice that net present value measures the change in value to the firm from accepting a proposal. This is always true and reinforces the decision rule that positive-NPV proposals are to be accepted while negative-NPV proposals should be rejected. In the previous example, the real estate firm's value would be reduced by $248,159 if the proposal were accepted.

Examples

Calculating Net Present Value

In considering the waste reduction investment on pages 272–273, a company produced a cash flow spreadsheet with the following summary numbers:

	Year 0	Years 1–10	Year 10
Net cash flows	($ 110,000)	$ 24,950	$ 10,000

The company's weighted-average cost of capital is 10%.

Question: What is the proposal's net present value?

Solution steps:

1. Since the outflow takes place at year 0, its present value is its face value of $110,000.

2. Calculate the present value of the benefits:

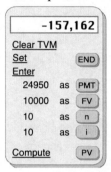

	A	B	C
1	PMT	24950	
2	FV	10000	
3	n	10	
4	i	0.1	
5	PV of benefits	-157,162	
6	PV of costs	110,000	
7	NPV	47,162	

B5 f_x =PV(B4,B3,B1,B2)

3. NPV = present value of benefits − present value of costs
   = $157,162 − 110,000 = $47,162

Answer: This project's net present value is $47,162.

Question: Should the firm accept this proposal?

Answer: Yes! NPV is positive.

By setting the calculator and spreadsheet to **END,** we have adopted the usual convention: to assume that all cash inflows during a year come at the end of that year. This simplifies the NPV calculation. It is a conservative assumption as it tends to reduce the worth of investments by treating benefits during the year as coming later in time. Normally, the error introduced by this assumption is small; however, if NPV calculates very close to zero, it might be worthwhile to place the cash flows more precisely within the year and recalculate NPV.

Examples | **Calculating Net Present Value**

In considering the replacement of trucks on pages 273–274, a transportation company produced a cash flow spreadsheet with the following summary numbers:

	Year 0	Years 1–5	Year 5
Net cash flows	($61,375)	$19,225	$10,750

The company's weighted-average cost of capital is 10%.

Question: What is the proposal's net present value?

Solution steps:

1. Since the outflow takes place at year 0, it's present value is its face value of $61,375.

2. Calculate the present value of the benefits:

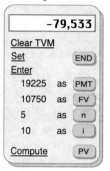

	A	B	C
		B5	f_x =PV(B4,B3,B1,B2)
1	PMT	19225	
2	FV	10750	
3	n	5	
4	i	0.1	
5	PV of benefits	-79.553	
6	PV of costs	61.375	
7	NPV	18,178	

3. NPV = present value of benefits − present value of costs
    = $79,553 − 61,375 = $18,178

Answer: This project's net present value is $18,178.

Question: Should the firm accept this proposal?

Answer: Yes! NPV is positive.

2. Internal Rate of Return (IRR)

The **internal rate of return** of a capital budgeting proposal is the anticipated interest rate returned by the investment project. Mathematically it is the discount rate at which the project's net present value is equal to zero, that is, the rate that makes the present value of the project's benefits exactly equal to the present value of the project's costs. Since it includes all benefits and costs in its computation, IRR, like NPV, performs a complete, time-value-of-money-adjusted, cost-benefit analysis.

It is not necessary to use the weighted-average cost of capital in the calculation of internal rates of return, since IRR is itself an interest rate. However, to use IRR as a decision tool, a proposed project's IRR must be compared to the cost of capital appropriate for that project. If the IRR exceeds the cost of capital, the investment project provides a rate of return in excess of that needed to compensate investors and the proposal should be accepted. Conversely, if the IRR is less than the cost of capital, the project does not earn a high enough rate of return and the proposal should be rejected.

Examples

Calculating Internal Rate of Return

In considering the land investment on page 272, the real estate company produced a cash flow spreadsheet with the following summary numbers:

	Year 0	Year 5
Net cash flows	($1,000,000)	$1,325,000

The company's weighted-average cost of capital is 12%.

Question: What is the proposal's internal rate of return?

Solution steps: Calculate the interest rate that connects the cash flows:

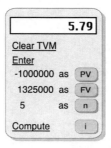

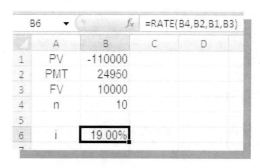

Answer: This project's internal rate of return is <u>5.79%</u>.

Question: Should the firm accept this proposal?

Answer: <u>No! The project's IRR of 5.79% is less than the 12% cost of capital.</u> The firm must earn 12% on its funds—this investment does not achieve that rate of return.

Examples

Calculating Internal Rate of Return

In considering the waste reduction investment on pages 272–273, a company produced a cash flow spreadsheet with the following summary numbers:

	Year 0	Years 1–10	Year 10
Net cash flows	($110,000)	$24,950	$10,000

The company's weighted-average cost of capital is 10%.

Question: What is the proposal's internal rate of return?

Solution steps: Calculate the interest rate that connects the cash flows:

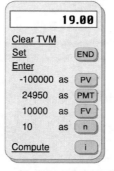

Answer: This project's internal rate of return is <u>19.00%</u>.

Question: Should the firm accept this proposal?

Answer: <u>Yes! The project's IRR of 19% exceeds the 10% cost of capital.</u>

Examples

Calculating Internal Rate of Return

In considering the replacement of trucks on pages 273–274 a transportation company produced a cash flow speadsheet with the following summary numbers:

	Year 0	Years 1–5	Year 5
Net cash flows	($61,375)	$19,225	$10,750

The company's weighted-average cost of capital is 10%.

Question: What is the proposal's internal rate of return?

Solution steps: Calculate the interest rate that connects the cash flows:

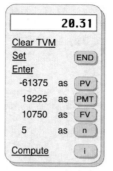

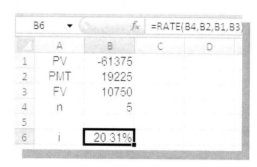

Answer: This project's internal rate of return is <u>20.31%</u>.

Question: Should the firm accept this proposal?

Answer: <u>Yes! The project's IRR of 20.31% exceeds the 10% cost of capital.</u>

3. Choosing the Appropriate Cost of Capital

Correct decisions using the NPV and IRR techniques require an accurate measure of the cost of capital. Financial managers need to keep two things in mind as they select the number to be used in any capital budgeting analysis: (1) a company's cost of capital changes as financial market conditions change and (2) the appropriate cost of capital for a proposed investment project is dependent on that project's risk.

IMPROVING FINANCE'S PROCESSES

Evaluating Investments in Customer Service at Polaroid

The Customer Service group at Polaroid Corporation, the consumer electronics company that pioneered instant photography, uses an innovative version of internal rate of return to evaluate investments in customer service. Prior to using the model, the group found it difficult to convince senior management that investments in service quality would provide an acceptable rate of return, generating sufficient new cash inflows to offset the costs of providing the additional service. Now the group constructs a cash flow model that explicitly identifies customer behaviors that, if changed, would increase cash inflows. Incremental outflows are the costs of the enhanced service. For each service initiative, values are calculated for the change(s) in behavior that would yield the company's minimum required IRR (its cost of capital). For example, the behavior change examined for a decision to provide pre-sale customer support was the percentage of leads that would subsequently become sales. The behavior change for a proposal to provide immediate replacement of defective cameras was the number of film packs the customer would purchase each month. Now when a proposed investment is presented to management, attention is immediately drawn to the most critical variables. Management can use forecasts of customer reactions to make the investment decisions. Customer groups can be segmented to provide the optimal service level to each. And unlike previous analyses, the new system is easy to understand and communicate to top management.

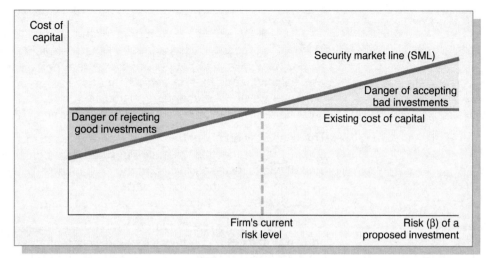

FIGURE 11.3

The appropriate cost of capital for a proposed investment project is a function of the project's beta. The existing cost of capital is valid only at the firm's current risk level.

Changing conditions   A company's cost of capital changes regularly. As we saw in Chapter 10, the calculation of the cost of capital begins with the rates of return required by the company's suppliers of funds, each of which incorporates the general level of interest rates and a premium for risk as delineated by the Fisher model we studied in Chapter 4. The cost of capital is then assembled by incorporating flotation costs, income tax effects, and the mix of financing used. As interest rates fluctuate, as risk perceptions shift, as flotation costs change, and as different tax rates affect the company, the cost of capital adjusts accordingly.

Risk appropriate   A company's cost of capital can also differ for each capital budgeting project it considers since the risk premium its investors will demand depends on the risk of the project itself. The capital asset pricing model (CAPM) tells us that when an asset is held as part of a well-diversified portfolio, the relevant measure of its risk is its beta—the relationship of that asset's returns to the returns available from the economy as a whole. Each investment a company makes becomes one asset in the portfolio of assets held by the company and, through its securities, held by the company's investors.

The relationship between beta and the appropriate rate of return is captured by the security market line (SML),[5] which is drawn in Figure 11.3. Also on the graph is the company's existing cost of capital, calculated without reference to the betas of proposed capital budgeting projects and hence shown as a horizontal line. Notice that the existing cost of capital is the correct rate to apply to a proposed capital budgeting investment only at one level of risk: the firm's current risk level where the two lines cross. To the left of that intersection, the proposed project is less risky than the firm; the existing cost of capital is too stringent a test and its use runs the risk of rejecting good projects. To the right of the intersection of the two lines, the proposed project is more risky than the firm; the existing cost of capital is too lenient a test and its use runs the risk of accepting poor projects.

---

[5] **Cross-reference:**   The capital asset pricing model is developed in Chapter 8, pages 202–213. The security market line is introduced on pages 211–213.

*R*ick Daniel put down the advanced finance text and turned back to his spreadsheet. He had just finished rereading several chapters on capital budgeting. He was happy to discover that he had remembered most of it but was equally happy that he had located several ideas that could be applied to his current task. One chapter in particular, on how to search methodically for good data, had confirmed some of the senior analyst's suggestions.

The cash flow numbers had been entered into the appropriate columns of the spreadsheet, reflecting estimates of when those cash flows would occur. The cost of capital was realistic. And the spreadsheet program was correctly calculating the project's net present value and internal rate of return. The problem seemed to be with the completeness of the data.

As he returned the text to his bookshelf, Rick thought back to his finance class on capital budgeting and remembered a statement his professor seemed to emphasize: "After a while, the NPV and IRR calculations become routine; getting good data is the difficult part of the job." Rick smiled wryly as he realized that his current problem was teaching him just how true that statement was.

Summary of Key Points

■■ **Discuss the importance of capital budgeting to business success.**   Capital budgeting is the process of evaluating potential long-term investments. Due to their long-term nature, investments in these assets have a major impact on the firm's ability to compete. The techniques of capital budgeting are applicable to other incremental decisions and form an important component of the financial manager's skills.

■■ **Identify the data used in capital budgeting.**   There are eight rules which specify the data that should and should not enter into capital budgeting analysis: (1) use cash flow numbers only, (2) use incremental numbers only, (3) include changes in all functional areas, (4) include changes across the life cycle, (5) include forecasted inflation, (6) consider quality and sustainability impacts, (7) consider the options implicit in the decision, and (8) leave the financing flows out.

■■ **Organize cash flow data for capital budgeting analysis.**   It is useful to organize the data of a capital budgeting decision with a cash flow spreadsheet that summarizes cash flows by time of occurrence. This makes the data ready for analysis using time-value-of-money methods.

■■ **Use the techniques of net present value (NPV) and internal rate of return (IRR) to judge the worth of a capital project.**   Net present value (NPV) compares the present value of the proposal's benefits to the present value of its costs to determine which is greater. The NPV number measures the value added to (or subtracted from) the firm by going ahead with

the investment. When NPV is positive, benefits exceed costs and the project should be accepted. When NPV is negative, costs exceed benefits and the project should be rejected. A project's IRR is its anticipated rate of return. When a project's IRR exceeds the appropriate cost of capital, the project should be accepted as it returns more than the minimum amount required to satisfy investors. When a project's IRR is less than the cost of capital, the project should be rejected as the return is insufficient to meet investors' needs. The cost of capital used to evaluate each proposed project must reflect current market conditions and be adjusted to match the risk of the project.

Questions

1. Why does capital budgeting analysis pay attention only to cash flows?

2. What is a sunk cost? Why is it ignored in capital budgeting?

3. What would happen to a capital budgeting analysis if inflation were omitted from the cash flow estimates?

4. What is meant by the "option" inherent in a capital budgeting decision?

5. A financial analyst included the interest cost of the debt used to buy new machinery in the cash flows from a capital budgeting project. Is this correct or incorrect? Why?

6. What function does a cash flow spreadsheet play in capital budgeting analysis?

7. What is the meaning of:

   a. Net present value?
   b. Internal rate of return?

   In what ways are they the same; how do they differ?

8. Why is the net present value of a capital budgeting project equal to zero when its internal rate of return is used as the discount rate?

9. True or false (and why?): The NPV technique uses the firm's cost of capital in its calculation, but the IRR technique does not. Therefore, the cost of capital is relevant only if capital budgeting projects are evaluated using NPV.

10. What is the danger of applying one cost of capital to all proposed capital budgeting projects?

Problems

1. **(Identifying cash flows)** An analyst has prepared the following data as part of a proposal to acquire a new machine:

Cost to purchase machine	$40,000
Cost to install machine	1,000
Cost of new electric wiring	2,000
First-year depreciation of machine	4,000
Sales tax on purchasing machine	3,000
Economic salvage value of the machine	10,000
Accounting salvage value of the machine	8,000

   a. Which of the above figures should enter the capital budgeting analysis?
   b. What figure should enter the capital budgeting analysis as the investment at year zero?
   c. Which of the above figures should not enter the capital budgeting analysis?
   d. Will any of the items you list in part c have a later impact on the firm's cash flows? If so, what?

2. **(Identifying cash flows)** A company is considering switching from accelerated to straight-line depreciation on its GAAP financial statements to reduce its depreciation expense and boost income.

   a. What effect will this change have on the firm's reported income?
   b. What is the financial value of this decision?
   c. Suppose the company made the same switch on its tax returns. Now what is the financial value of this decision?
   d. Given your answers to parts a–c, why do many companies make this change in choice of depreciation method?

3. **(Identifying incremental cash flows)** An analyst has prepared the following data as part of a proposal for an addition to the firm's plant:

Cost to build addition	$ 500,000
Book value of existing plant	7,000,000
Cost for new machinery	200,000
Cost of new electric wiring	30,000
Amount spent on study to date	2,000
Increase to working capital to support machinery	60,000
Interest on loan to finance the addition	40,000

   a. Which of the above figures should enter the capital budgeting analysis? Why?
   b. Which of the above figures should not enter the capital budgeting analysis? Why?
   c. Suppose that $15,000 of working capital currently in use elsewhere within the company could perform double duty by supporting this facility as well. How would this change your answers to parts a and b?
   d. Suppose the land under the plant would have been sold to a real estate developer for $1,500,000 if the addition were not built. How would this change your answers to parts a and b?

4. **(Identifying incremental cash flows)** Last week, your firm bought a fleet of trucks for $200,000 to begin a delivery service business. Today, someone came up with the idea to use the trucks to sell ice cream to suburban children door to door. Converting the trucks would cost $75,000. You have been asked to work on this capital budgeting project.

   a. What is the role of the $200,000 in your analysis?
   b. What is the role of the $75,000 in your analysis?
   c. What other information would you need to know about the trucks before making this decision?
   d. What information not about the trucks would you need to know before making this decision?

5. **(Identifying nominal numbers)** A company is considering an investment that would cost $25,000 and return a net after-tax cash flow of $8,000 per year in each of the next five years.

   a. Assume these figures include inflation forecasts. What numbers should enter the capital budgeting analysis?
   b. Now assume the above figures do *not* include inflation, forecast to be 6% per year. What numbers should enter the capital budgeting analysis?
   c. Why must the cash flows used in capital budgeting contain the impact of inflation?
   d. What would be the bias if the impact of inflation were left out?

6. **(Identifying nominal numbers)**   A company is considering an investment that would cost $70,000 and return a net after-tax cash flow of $10,000 per year in each of the next seven years.

a. Assume these figures include inflation forecasts. What numbers should enter the capital budgeting analysis?

b. Now assume the above figures do *not* include inflation, forecast to be 9% per year. What numbers should enter the capital budgeting analysis?

c. Why does inflation affect only one of the numbers above and not the other?

d. Does inflation appear anywhere else in the capital budgeting analysis? If so, where?

7. **(Organizing cash flows)** Judy Entrepreneur is considering the purchase of a machine for $100,000; the machine would be depreciated to a $20,000 salvage value over an eight-year period using the straight-line method. During its life, the machine would improve Judy's annual cash earnings by $25,000 per year. The firm expects to sell the machine for its $20,000 salvage value at the end of the eight years. The firm's federal tax rate on income is 35%. Calculate the incremental cash flows from:

a. The purchase of the machine
b. The depreciation of the machine
c. The operation of the machine
d. The sale of the machine

8. **(Organizing cash flows)** Joe Businessperson is considering the purchase of a machine for $650,000. The machine would be depreciated to a $50,000 salvage value over a nine-year period using the straight-line method and would bring in incremental cash income of $80,000 in each year. However, the firm expects to sell the machine for $60,000 at the end of the nine years. The firm's federal tax rate on income is 35%. Calculate the incremental cash flows from:

a. The purchase of the machine
b. The depreciation of the machine
c. The operation of the machine
d. The sale of the machine

9. **(NPV, IRR)** A company can invest $200,000 in a capital budgeting project that will generate the following forecasted cash flows:

Years	Cash flow
1–4	$75,000

The company has a 14% cost of capital.

a. Calculate the project's net present value.
b. Calculate the project's internal rate of return.
c. Should the firm accept or reject the project?
d. At what cost of capital would the firm be indifferent to accepting or rejecting this proposal?

10. **(NPV, IRR)** A company can invest $3 million in a capital budgeting project that will generate the following forecasted cash flows:

Years	Cash flow
1–16	$275,000

The company has an 8% cost of capital.

a. Calculate the project's net present value.
b. Calculate the project's internal rate of return.
c. Should the firm accept or reject the project?
d. At what cost of capital would the firm be indifferent to accepting or rejecting this proposal?

11. **(NPV, IRR)** A company can invest $200,000 in a capital budgeting project that will generate the following forecasted cash flows:

Year	Cash flow
1	$110,000
2	150,000
3	120,000
4	200,000

The company has a 10% cost of capital.

a. Calculate the project's net present value.
b. Calculate the project's internal rate of return.
c. Should the firm accept or reject the project?
d. What is the value added to the firm if it accepts this proposed investment?

12. **(NPV, IRR)** A company can invest $1,600,000 in a capital budgeting project that will generate the following forecasted cash flows:

Year	Cash flow
1	$500,000
2	720,000
3	300,000
4	600,000

The company has a 13% cost of capital.

a. Calculate the project's net present value.
b. Calculate the project's internal rate of return.
c. Should the firm accept or reject the project?
d. What is the value added to the firm if it accepts this proposed investment?

13. **(Organizing cash flows, NPV, IRR)** A company is evaluating the purchase of Machine A. The new machine would cost $120,000 and would be depreciated for tax purposes using the straight-line method over an estimated ten-year life to its expected salvage value of $20,000. The new machine would require an addition of $30,000 to working capital. In each year of Machine A's life, the company would reduce its pre-tax costs by $40,000. The company has a 12% cost of capital and is in the 35% marginal tax bracket.

a. Identify the incremental cash flows from investing in Machine A.
b. Calculate the investment's net present value (NPV).
c. Calculate the investment's internal rate of return (IRR).

d. Should the company purchase Machine A? Why or why not?

14. **(Organizing cash flows, NPV, IRR)** A company is evaluating the purchase of Machine X to improve product quality. The new machine would cost $1,000,000 and would be depreciated for tax purposes using the straight-line method over an estimated seven-year life to its expected salvage value of $125,000. The new machine would require an addition of $100,000 to working capital. In each year of Machine X's life, the company would increase its pre-tax receipts by $400,000. The company has an 11% cost of capital and is in the 35% marginal tax bracket.

a. Identify the incremental cash flows from investing in Machine X.
b. Calculate the investment's net present value (NPV).
c. Calculate the investment's internal rate of return (IRR).
d. Should the company purchase Machine X? Why or why not?

15. **(Organizing cash flows, NPV, IRR)** This problem follows Problem 13. It is now five years later. The company did buy Machine A, but just this week Machine B came on the market; Machine B could be purchased to replace Machine A. If acquired, Machine B would cost $80,000 and would be depreciated for tax purposes using the straight-line method over an estimated five-year life to its expected salvage value of $20,000. Machine B would also require $30,000 of working capital but would save an additional $20,000 per year in pre-tax operating costs. Machine A's salvage value remains $20,000, but it could be sold today for $40,000.

a. Identify the incremental cash flows from converting to Machine B.
b. Calculate this investment's net present value (NPV).
c. Calculate this investment's internal rate of return (IRR).
d. Should the company convert to Machine B? Why or why not?

16. **(Organizing cash flows, NPV, IRR)** This problem follows Problem 14. It is now four years later. The company did buy Machine X, but just today Machine Y came on the market; Machine Y could be purchased to replace Machine X. If acquired, Machine Y would cost $750,000 and would be depreciated for tax purposes using the straight-line method over an estimated three-year life to its expected salvage value of $150,000. Machine Y would require $160,000 of working capital but would add an additional $300,000 per year to pre-tax receipts. Machine X's salvage value re-

mains $125,000, but it could be sold today for $100,000.

a. Identify the incremental cash flows from converting to Machine Y.
b. Calculate this investment's net present value (NPV).
c. Calculate this investment's internal rate of return (IRR).
d. Should the company convert to Machine Y? Why or why not?

17. **(Adjusting the cost of capital for risk)** A company with a 13% cost of capital is evaluating four independent potential capital budgeting proposals with the following forecasted internal rates of return (IRRs) and betas:

Proposal	IRR	Beta
A	12%	.85
B	10	1.00
C	16	1.10
D	14	1.25

The market price of risk is 8.5%, and the risk-free rate of interest is currently 4%.

a. Write the equation of the security market line (SML).
b. Calculate the required rate of return on each investment according to the SML.
c. Which projects would be accepted by using the existing cost of capital?
d. Which projects would be accepted by using a risk-adjusted cost of capital for each project based on the SML?

18. **(Adjusting the cost of capital for risk)** A company with a 14% cost of capital is evaluating four independent potential capital budgeting proposals with the following forecasted internal rates of return (IRRs) and betas:

Proposal	IRR	Beta
W	15%	1.40
X	19	1.15
Y	11	.90
Z	12	.65

The market price of risk is 8%, and the risk-free rate of interest is currently 5%.

a. Write the equation of the security market line (SML).
b. Calculate the required rate of return on each investment according to the SML.
c. Which projects would be accepted by using the existing cost of capital?
d. Which projects would be accepted by using a risk-adjusted cost of capital for each project based on the SML?

CHAPTER 12

INVESTING IN

PERMANENT

WORKING CAPITAL

ASSETS

*M*arie Kaye stared through the window that was the front wall of her office and shook her head slowly. Outside were row after row of desks. She glanced at her watch; it was 7:30 A.M. Monday morning. Soon the desks would be occupied by the clerks who processed the company's accounts receivable—at last count there were 43 clerks in the department.

Marie had recently been appointed controller of her company. Among her responsibilities were customer billing and collection of outstanding accounts, areas that had proved quite problematic. Customers routinely complained that invoices were difficult to understand, sometimes even incorrect, and responded by withholding payment. Marie had recently added 10 clerks to the department in an effort to correct the problems and reduce the company's collection period, which was well above the industry average, yet little progress had been made. Even with the additional staff, every clerk remained busy all day and many had to work overtime to clear their desks.

Last week Marie had attended a professional meeting, at which she talked to the controllers of several competitors and similar companies in other industries. She was surprised to learn that some companies she considered comparable to hers operated their billing and receivables function with fewer than 10 employees and had far fewer outstanding accounts. She made some notes about assembling a team to tackle the problem and vowed to go in first thing Monday morning to get an early start.

Marie looked at her watch again; it was 7:45. She was eager for the work day to begin so she could discuss the problem with her colleagues and put together the team.

Working capital management involves day-to-day dealings with the firm's stakeholders: customers, suppliers, employees, bankers, etc. In fact, many stakeholders' primary experience with the company is through its working capital activities. To manage these resources, financial managers must understand how their work affects stakeholders and, in turn, how stakeholder actions affect them. Marie is discovering that successful working capital management requires not only good application of finance theory, but also the use of quality-management information and tools to ensure that stakeholder needs are being met.

Working capital management provides an excellent opportunity for financial managers to add value to their organizations. In many companies, fully half of the investment in assets—and up to 90% of the effort of the finance organization—are in the current accounts. In this chapter we examine the nature of working capital, how to add value by investing in permanent working capital, and how an awareness of quality-management issues can further improve the worth of these decisions.

What You Should Learn from This Chapter

After reading this chapter you should be able to:

- Separate working capital into permanent and temporary components.
- Organize permanent working capital data into cash flow terms.
- Describe the components of a firm's cash balance and analyze decisions involving accelerating cash in transit.
- Analyze proposed changes to a firm's permanent accounts receivable balance.

Introductory Concepts—Types of Working Capital

Working capital is the term commonly used to summarize the financial resources available for a firm's day-to-day operations. These must be liquid resources, available as cash (or convertible to cash) when required. Working capital includes cash and marketable securities—the most liquid of resources—and also the somewhat less liquid resources of accounts receivable, inventories, and prepaid expenses. Each is necessary for the firm to conduct its business, yet each is costly to maintain. One concern of financial managers is that their companies maintain adequate, but not excess, working capital.

A primary use of current resources is to pay debts as they fall due. The funds available for day-to-day operations may be considered the amount left over after resources have been allocated to pay current liabilities. As a result, working capital is normally represented as the difference between current assets and current liabilities:[1]

$$Working\ capital = current\ assets - current\ liabilities$$

1. Permanent Vs. Temporary Working Capital

Our examination of working capital in this chapter is organized by balance sheet account—cash, accounts receivable, etc.—since each account has its own characteristics. However, it is useful and important first to divide working capital in a different way: into "permanent" working capital and "temporary" working capital, a distinction that cuts across all the working capital accounts. We do this because permanent working capital decisions are analyzed differently from decisions to make temporary adjustments in working capital balances. In this chapter we look primarily at permanent working capital; temporary working capital is treated in Chapter 15.

In Figure 12.1, we graph a typical firm's balance sheet over time. The lines slope upward, representing a growing firm, but the picture would be equally valid if the company were unchanging or declining in size. On both sides of the equal sign, the bottom area represents the long-term: long-term assets on the left and long-term liabilities and equity on the right. Above the first dividing line are the current accounts—current assets and current liabilities—and each of these is subdivided into a permanent and a temporary component.

Permanent working capital is the base level of working capital, the amount required independent of daily, seasonal, or cyclical variations in business activity. It is made up of permanent current assets and permanent current liabilities. The firm needs its permanent working capital on a continuous basis. Even though a company's cash, accounts receivable, inventory, etc. turn over more frequently than once per year, and therefore are considered current assets by accounting, there will be some minimum *level* of each of these resources required at all times. It is impossible to operate without cash for liquidity. Extending trade credit, hence creating accounts receivable and payable, is normal practice in most industries. Some amount of inventory is a requirement for both merchandising and manu-

---

[1] **Elaboration:**   An alternative usage is to let *working capital* equal only a firm's current assets and use the term *net working capital* to represent current assets minus current liabilities.

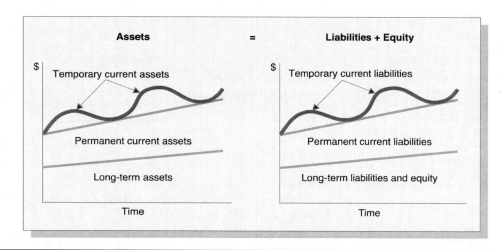

FIGURE 12.1
Levels of assets and claims across time for a growing firm. Current assets and liabilities can be divided into a permanent level plus temporary fluctuations.

facturing. Therefore, *even though permanent working capital appears on the accounting books in the current accounts, which suggests that it is short-term in nature, it is really a long-term requirement.*

temporary working capital—increases to working capital due to fluctuations in business activity

Temporary working capital is the amount above the base level which results from variations in business activity. It is caused by three simultaneous processes. First, the business cycle increases and decreases the resource needs of all businesses over a multiyear time period. Second, most firms are seasonal, having an annual cycle of activities. Third, daily events impact resource needs since revenues and expenses, and cash inflows and outflows, rarely balance on a day-to-day basis. Receivables and collections follow the pattern of sales. Expenses and payments, on the other hand, are often tied to the day of the month. In contrast to permanent working capital, temporary working capital is short-term in nature.

Organizing and Analyzing Permanent Working Capital Data

Decisions about the level of permanent working capital are made in the same way as capital budgeting decisions—we identify incremental cash flows, organize them using a cash flow spreadsheet, and apply time value of money analysis. There is only one difference between the two analyses, and it is minor: while plant and equipment have a finite life, working capital can be around for the entire life of an organization. Whenever we do not know how long the change will continue, we make the assumption that the company is a "going concern" with infinite life.

1. Cash Flow Spreadsheet for Permanent Working Capital Decisions

Figure 12.2 is a generic cash flow spreadsheet for permanent working capital. Notice that it is identical to the cash flow spreadsheets we used for capital budgeting[2] except that there is no column for "year n," the last year of the investment's life. Rather, the right-hand column is labeled "years 1–∞," representing all

---

[2] **Cross-reference:**   The cash flow spreadsheet for capital budgeting decisions was introduced on page 271.

FIGURE 12.2
Cash flow spreadsheet for permanent working capital decisions. The right-hand column is labeled "Years 1–∞" since these changes often have an indeterminate life.

	Year 0	Years 1–∞
Investment	(Cost) or recovery	
Operating cash flows		Changed in/(out)flows
Tax—changed income		Tax on above
Net cash flows		

years from the first year of change to the end of the company's existence. As with the spreadsheet for capital budgeting, this column would have to be separated into several columns if the cash flows from the proposed change differed from year to year. This simplified spreadsheet is intended to illustrate the form of permanent working capital decisions; we will provide more detail as we examine specific working capital items later in this chapter.

Because changes to permanent working capital are treated as having an indefinite life, the appropriate time value model to apply to the ongoing cash flows is the perpetuity (perpetual annuity) model.[3] Recall that for a perpetuity:

$$PV = \frac{PMT}{r}$$

and, rearranging the algebra, the interest rate embedded in a perpetuity, which for a permanent working capital decision is the internal rate of return, is:

$$r = \frac{PMT}{PV}$$

Examples

The Value of Permanent Working Capital Cash Flows

A proposed change to permanent working capital promises the following cash flows:

	Year 0	Years 1–∞
Investment	($50,000)	
Operating cash flow		$10,000
Tax (35%)		(3,500)
Net cash flows	($50,000)	$ 6,500

Question: What is the net present value of this decision if the firm's cost of capital is 10%?

Solution steps:

1. Since the outflow takes place at year 0, its present value is its face value of −$50,000.

---

[3] **Cross-reference:** The model for the present value of a perpetuity first appears on pages 78–79.

2. Use the perpetuity model to calculate the present value of the ongoing cash flows:

$$PV = PMT/r = \$6,500/.10 = \$65,000$$

3. NPV = present value of benefits − present value of costs

$$= \$65,000 - 50,000 = \$15,000$$

Answer: The proposed investment has a net present value of $\underline{\$15,000}$.

Question: What is the internal rate of return of this decision?

Solution steps: Use the perpetuity model to calculate the rate of return in the cash flows, letting the year 0 outlay be the value of the variable PV:

$$r = PMT/PV = \$6,500/\$50,000 = 13.00\%$$

Answer: The proposed investment has an internal rate of return of $\underline{13.00\%}$.

Question: Should this proposed investment be pursued?

Answer: $\underline{\text{Yes!}}$ Its NPV is greater than zero and its IRR exceeds the firm's cost of capital.

2. Net Annual Benefit

The assumption that the ongoing cash flow change will continue indefinitely at a constant level is troubling to many people—it is, after all, difficult to predict next year's cash flows much less flows many years into the future. As a result, some analysts prefer to use a third rearrangement of the perpetuity model:

$$PMT = r \times PV$$

net annual benefit (NAB)— the amount by which the annual benefit from an investment exceeds the amount required to cover the firm's cost of capital

and calculate **net annual benefit (NAB).** With this technique, we calculate the cash flow required each year to support the money invested and test this number against the actual benefit provided. If net annual benefit is positive, we accept the proposed project; we reject the proposal if net annual benefit is negative.[4]

Example

| **Net Annual Benefit** | | |

A proposed change to permanent working capital promises the following cash flows:

	Year 0	**Years 1–∞**
Net cash flows	($50,000)	$6,500

Question: What is the net annual benefit of this decision if the firm's cost of capital is 10%?

---

[4] **Elaboration:** In investments with an initial cash flow followed by a perpetuity, such as those in this chapter, net annual benefit will *always agree* with net present value. When one is positive, the other will also be positive, etc. Therefore, they are perfect substitutes for each other. See Web Appendix 12A for a demonstration of why this must be true.

Solution steps:

1. Use the perpetuity model to calculate the annual benefit required given the amount of the initial investment:

$$PMT = r \times PV = .10 \times \$50,000 = \$5,000$$

2. NAB = actual annual benefit − required annual benefit

$$= \$6,500 - 5,000 = \$1,500$$

Answer: The net annual benefit is <u>\$1,500</u>. Each year, this investment returns the \$5,000 required to support the \$50,000 capital investment *plus* an additional \$1,500 which adds to the value of the firm.

Permanent Cash

The line "cash" on a firm's balance sheet refers to money held in any of several forms. These include coins and currency, demand (checking) deposits, and time (savings) deposits. Some companies also include marketable securities with their cash balance. Because there are so many varieties of "cash," this balance sheet line is often labeled "cash and cash equivalents."

Business organizations hold cash for several reasons. Perhaps the most obvious is to pay for the operating and capital resources required to run the business. Like individuals, firms hold cash for their transactions needs and also hold extra cash as a precaution in case their spending needs unexpectedly increase.[5] There are also other, less obvious reasons why firms hold cash. Large deposit balances often reduce the fees and other charges levied by banks for services such as processing of checks, credit checking, currency conversion, and letters of credit. A high cash balance raises a firm's current and quick ratios,[6] making it appear more solvent to potential creditors. Holding (or electing not to hold) cash in a particular location or currency can also minimize currency movements, thereby reducing costs and risks: the cost of excessive foreign exchange transactions, the cost of taxes on money transfers, the risk of limitations on cash movement, and the risk of expropriation due to adverse political events.

1. Cash Allocation

A company's treasury function allocates its cash (1) among the various possible types and (2) among different currencies.

Types of cash   Coins and bills are kept for retail transactions and petty cash, although this amount is usually held to a minimum since it earns no interest and is exposed to theft. The appropriate local balance differs among each business location due to the nature and volume of business conducted. It also differs among

---

[5] **Cross-reference and elaboration:**   The transactions, precautionary, and speculative motives for holding cash were first described by John Maynard Keynes. Unlike individuals, businesses are not thought to hold a significant amount of cash for speculative purposes.

[6] **Cross-reference:**   The current and quick ratios are discussed in Chapter 2, page 38.

countries due to differences in financial customs: the frequency of credit card use, the method by which workers are paid (cash or check), the convenience and cost of the local banking system, and the significance of the underground economy.

Additional cash is kept in the form of demand (checking) deposits, which commonly earn a low or zero rate of interest and are also held to a minimum level. Analytically, a firm's optimal checking balance is a complex function of several variables. Generally the balance increases with (1) volume of transactions including regular (payroll, purchases, taxes, dividends) and irregular (capital expenditures, debt retirement) flows and (2) variability of cash flows. It decreases with (1) efficiency of cash management and (2) access to financial markets. Sometimes a firm holds a larger deposit balance than its analysis recommends because of the requirements of a loan agreement.

Extra cash beyond the minimum required for currency and demand deposits is normally invested to earn interest in bank time deposits or marketable securities.

Different currencies   Companies operating multinationally also must decide how much cash to maintain in each currency. The minimum requirement is to keep enough cash for local operating and investment needs. Beyond that amount, company treasurers must consider several additional issues. Cash is kept away from any country in which local political intervention could block the firm's ability to convert it and/or remove it. Cash is held in currencies that are expected to increase in value and not in those that are expected to depreciate. One loss of value comes from the fees incurred in exchanging currencies, so foreign exchange transactions are typically kept to a minimum. Cash is also often moved to currencies where investments earn the highest interest rates.[7]

When a company does business in several currencies, it commonly "nets out" all accounts receivable and accounts payable among its units. Thus, if Subsidiary A owes $100 to Subsidiary B, and Subsidiary B owes $120 to Subsidiary A, the two units will settle by B paying $20 to A. This reduces currency movements and exchanges, keeping their cost down.

Finance professionals debate the benefits of managing cash from a centralized treasury department versus spreading out cash management responsibilities to a firm's operating units. In general, centralized cash management lessens the likelihood that one unit is holding excess cash while another is short and must borrow. One central account can serve as the precautionary balance for multiple locations. Borrowing costs are lowered as borrowing is done on a larger scale. Larger and more frequent transactions provide treasury personnel increased experience and expertise. On the other hand, decentralized cash management reduces the number of times cash is moved among units. This lowers the transaction costs associated with currency movements and exchange. It also permits individual units to establish and maintain better relationships with local financial institutions.

---

[7] **Elaboration and cross-reference:**   The only way to benefit from moving cash into a high-interest-rate currency is to take the risk that the money can be exchanged back without loss of value. While an aggressive treasurer will move cash balances among countries to benefit from high interest rates and/or anticipated exchange rate movements, many treasurers choose not to expose their companies to these risks.

2. Managing Cash in Transit

receivables float—the dollar amount of incoming checks that have been mailed but have not yet been collected

Every dollar (or pound, or euro, etc.) of operating cash flowing through a company follows a similar path, diagrammed in Figure 12.3. The process begins when a customer mails a check to the company, initiating a period of **receivables float** during which "the check is in the mail." Some days later, the company receives the check and deposits it in its bank. Now the money is "in the company's control," and can be withdrawn and invested to earn interest. Later, when the company must pay a supplier, it writes a check; although it usually does not deposit the amount back into its bank account until just before the check clears. The period between writing a check and the check clearing can be divided into a period of **payables float** and a period during which the cash is sitting in the bank waiting to be paid out.

payables float—the dollar amount of outgoing checks that have been written but have not yet been covered by bank deposits

Receivables float cannot earn interest (although payables float normally does), nor is it usual for money sitting in a demand account waiting to be paid out to earn much interest. These amounts represent idle funds that cannot be used elsewhere, money that has an opportunity cost determined by the firm's cost of capital.

Example

The Cost of Idle Funds in Transit

It takes five days on average for customers' checks, averaging $50,000 per day, to reach a company. Once received, the money is invested to earn interest until required for payments to suppliers. Deposits, averaging $40,000 per day, are made to cover the company's checks one day before they clear. The company has a cost of capital of 12%.

Question: What is the annual cost of these idle funds?

Solution steps:

1. Multiply the number of idle days by the average daily cash flow to obtain the total sum of idle money:

$$\text{Idle money} = (5 \text{ days} \times \$50,000) + (1 \text{ day} \times \$40,000)$$
$$= \$290,000$$

2. Multiply the total idle money by the cost of capital:

$$\$290,000 \times 12\% = \$34,800$$

Answer: The annual cost of idle funds is $\underline{\$34,800}$. $290,000 is tied up in transit and cannot be used elsewhere, requiring the firm to raise another $290,000 at an annual cost of $34,800.

FIGURE 12.3
Operating cash flow into and out from a company. Customers mail checks to the firm, and the money is then used to make payments to suppliers.

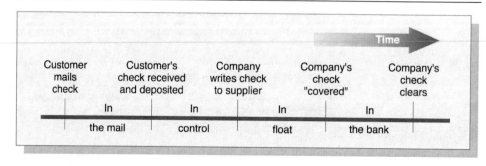

SERVING FINANCE'S CUSTOMERS

No Missed Cash Deliveries at Corning, Incorporated

The Treasury Division of Corning, Incorporated, the large multinational glass and ceramic products manufacturer, evaluates its performance in meeting its customers' requirements with a set of measurements the company calls Key Results Indicators (KRIs). For the Cash Management group, one KRI is the number of times Treasury fails to deliver the exact amount of cash needed by a company unit where and when required. Corning Treasury's goal is to have a KRI of zero—no missed cash deliveries.

NET Present Value
More information about the use of lockboxes can be found at the National Check Fraud Center website: www.ckfraud.org/lockbox.html

lock box—a post office box to which customers mail their payments

concentration banking—the practice of instructing customers to mail payments to a local bank which then forwards the payment electronically

electronic funds transfer—the computerized exchange of money between bank accounts

NET Present Value
A company offering a wide range of electronic funds transfer services is NPSGlobal at: www.npsglobal.com

Because idle funds in transit are costly, financial managers attempt to reduce receivables float by accelerating collections and reduce idle "in-bank" funds by delaying disbursements. Accelerating collections translates to speeding up or eliminating the mail. One way to do this is by instructing customers to mail payments to a **lock box,** a post office box used only for customer checks. A messenger from the company's commercial bank empties the lock box at regular intervals and takes the checks directly to the bank for deposit; the checks avoid the delay of being delivered to the company which then has to take them to the bank. Companies doing business in widely spread locations often also use **concentration banking,** in which customers mail their checks to a local lock box. There they are picked up by a local bank which then "concentrates" the funds by forwarding them electronically to the company's bank. With concentration banking, the time mail takes to travel long distances is avoided since all mail delivery is local.

Another way is to request that customers make payments by **electronic funds transfer** in which money is transferred directly from the customer's bank to the company, thereby avoiding the mail altogether (and increasing the liklihood of being paid). At first glance it would seem that customers would balk at such a system since they benefit from keeping their money for the period of float. However, in addition to eliminating receivables float in its entirety, direct electronic transfer eliminates the majority of the costs of a mail-based system: invoicing, paper, postage, handling, reconciliation of accounts, and the cost of rework when an error occurs. In many cases, the savings to both parties exceeds the cost of the float and can be shared between the parties.

A decrease in funds in transit is a permanent reduction to the firm's working capital needs and is analyzed using the perpetuity technique introduced earlier in this chapter. Interestingly, the change shows up on the accounting books not as a decrease to cash, but as a decrease in the accounts receivable balance since money owed the company is being collected more rapidly.

Example

Accelerating Collections

A company receives cash inflows of $1,000,000 per day from customers scattered across North America. For an annual fee of $300,000, its bank has proposed to implement a lock box/concentration banking system which would cut receivables float from an average of five days to two days. The company's cost of capital is 12% and it is in the 35% tax bracket.

Question: What is the value of the proposed system? Should it be implemented?

Solution steps:

1. Calculate the receivables float that can be eliminated:

   Float now $= 5$ days $\times$ \$1,000,000 $=$ \$5,000,000
   Float with new system $= 2$ days $\times$ \$1,000,000 $=$ \$2,000,000
   Reduction in float   \$3,000,000

2. Organize the cash flows: The company will pay \$195,000 each year after taxes to free up \$3,000,000.

	Year 0	Years 1–∞
Investment—float eliminated	\$3,000,000	
Operating cash flow—fee		(\$300,000)
Tax (35%)		105,000
Net cash flows	\$3,000,000	(\$195,000)

3. Calculate the value of the system using any of the three variations of the perpetuity model:

   a. NPV:

      PV of benefits $=$ \$3,000,000 since all benefits come at year 0
      PV of costs $=$ PMT$/r =$ \$195,000$/.12 =$ \$1,625,000
      NPV $=$ \$3,000,000 $-$ 1,625,000 $=$ \$1,375,000

   b. IRR:[8]

      IRR $= r =$ PMT$/$PV $=$ \$195,000$/$\$3,000,000 $=$ 6.50%

   c. NAB:[9]

      Annual cost of float $= r \times$ PV $= .12 \times$ \$3,000,000 $=$ \$360,000
      Annual cost of the proposed system $=$ \$195,000
      NAB $=$ \$360,000 $-$ 195,000 $=$ \$165,000

Answer: The proposal has an NPV of $\underline{\$1,375,000}$, an IRR of $\underline{6.50\%}$, and an NAB of $\underline{\$165,000}$. Since NPV and NAB exceed zero (and IRR is less than the cost of capital for this "opposite project") the system <u>should be implemented</u>.

Delaying disbursements is normally done by waiting until the last permissible date to make a payment. For example, if a company is given payment terms of "net 30 days" in which it is expected to pay 30 days from the invoice date, it will wait the full 30 days before it writes and mails its check. However, as with receivables, there are costs to maintaining an accounts payable system geared to

---

[8] **Elaboration and cross-reference:**   Notice that this is an "opposite project," in which a cash inflow is followed by cash outflows. In this case, the accept signal for the IRR measure is an IRR less than the cost of capital. Refer to Web Appendix 11C for further explanation.

[9] **Elaboration:**   Since this is an opposite project, the words describing the costs and benefits reverse from the example given on pages 291–292. There is a cash inflow projected for year 0, representing the money currently invested; when we multiply this by the cost of capital, we get the annual cost of having this money tied up ("annual cost of the float"). The year 1–∞ flow represents the cost of freeing up the receivables float, hence the "annual cost of the proposed system." The net annual benefit reflects the exchange: in each year paying the cost of the proposed system to avoid the cost of float.

payment on the last day. Some companies are finding that these costs exceed their earnings from payables float, making it cost effective to pay suppliers as early as the date an order is placed.

Permanent Accounts Receivable

Accounts receivable represent money owed to the firm by its customers. Many large retailers (Walmart, Target, Macy's, etc.), and companies that sell to other businesses extend credit themselves. They obtain data about each customer's financial condition, determine whether the customer is creditworthy, establish the customer's credit line—the maximum amount of credit the company is willing to extend, send the customer regular invoices, and then monitor the customer's performance in paying when due. Some large companies do the same but through a wholly owned finance subsidiary: examples are Sears through Sears Roebuck Acceptance Corporation, IBM through IBM Credit Corporation, and General Electric through GE Credit Corporation.

Small retailers, on the other hand, tend to avoid accounts receivable. Rather, they sign on with one or more of the national credit card organizations (Discover, Master Card, Visa). Customers can make purchases without cash, but it is the card company that extends the credit. The merchant is paid quickly by the card company, which then collects from the customer. Should the customer take longer than one month to pay, it is the card company that collects the interest.[10]

Whether a company sells for cash or chooses to extend credit depends on the nature of the customer and the nature of the product. Many business customers will pay for their purchases only when presented with an invoice and then only with a check, both to avoid holding currency and to ensure an adequate paperwork trail. Selling to these firms requires extending credit. At the retail level, large and expensive products—automobiles, refrigerators, etc.—tend to be sold on credit. They are easy to identify, making good loan collateral. Also, many customers cannot afford them unless they can pay over an extended period of time.

SERVING FINANCE'S CUSTOMERS

Paying Suppliers Upon Placing an Order at Motorola

In response to complaints from suppliers about slow payment of invoices, Motorola's finance department studied the company's accounts payable process. The analysis found that 1% of Motorola's expenditures accounted for fully 50% of its vendor-related paperwork. In response, Motorola scrapped its existing purchasing system and signed long-term commitments with suppliers of low-cost, high-volume goods, such as toilet paper and pencils. Vendors were told they had to perform at high quality levels to keep Motorola as a customer. In return, Motorola started paying those vendors by attaching a check to the purchase order and now pays by electronic transfer. Today, Motorola saves much more in reduced administrative costs than the value of the payables float.

---

[10] **Observation:**   Of course, virtually all large retailers also accept these credit cards.

Figure 12.4 is a cash flow spreadsheet for permanent accounts receivable decisions. It is an expanded version of Figure 12.2, listing the investment and operating cash flows common to accounts receivable decisions. There are three potential changes to the amount the firm has invested in its accounts receivable process, four potential changes to annual operating cash flow, and a potential change to income taxes. Where the numbers may be calculated by a formula, the relationship is given in the cash flow columns.

The potential changes in investment are:

● The change in the money invested in accounts receivable itself, calculated by taking the projected change in accounts receivable and multiplying it by a variable cost percentage to remove the profit portion.

● The changed value from receiving profits earlier or later, calculated as the daily profit flow (sales/day × contribution percentage) multiplied by the change, if any, in the collection period.

● The change in other working capital, such as inventory and cash, which is not calculated by a standard formula.

The potential changes in operating cash flows are:

● The change in profits, calculated as the change in sales multiplied by the firm's contribution percentage.

● The change in bad debt losses, calculated as the change in sales multiplied by the percent that become bad debts.

● The change in discounts granted, calculated as the discount percentage multiplied by the sales affected by the discount.

● The change in administrative costs, which is not calculated by a standard formula.

The change in taxes is the net change to operating cash flows multiplied by the firm's marginal tax rate.

FIGURE 12.4

Cash flow spreadsheet for permanent accounts receivable decisions. The spreadsheet organizes the data into three changes to the level of investment, four changes to operating cash flows, and the change to taxes.

	Year 0	Years 1–∞
Investment		
Accounts receivable	$\Delta AR \times$ variable cost %	
Changed collection period	(sales/day $\times$ contribution %) $\times \Delta CP$	
Other working capital		
Operating cash flows		
Contribution from sales		Δsales $\times$ contribution %
Bad debts		Δsales $\times$ % bad debts
Discounts		discount % $\times$ affected sales
Administrative costs		
Tax—changed income		Tax on above
Net cash flows		

A firm that extends credit to its customers must make three decisions that define its credit policy: (1) credit standards—who is an acceptable credit customer, (2) payment date—when is the customer expected to pay, and (3) price changes—what discounts may be taken for early payment and what finance charges will be added if payments are late. Each variable affects the level of the firm's permanent accounts receivable. We look at each in turn.

1. Credit Standards

NET Present Value
A discussion of credit scoring systems can be found at the Federal Trade Commission website:
http://www.ftc.gov/bcp/menus/consumer/credit/reports.shtm

To qualify acceptable credit customers, companies create scoring systems based on data about the customer's financial condition, stability, and past payment performance. Business customers are asked to provide financial statements and supporting data which are used for ratio and other financial analysis. Individuals are asked to fill out a form in which they report their income and their financial, employment, and family status. When available, information is obtained from credit reporting agencies, such as Dun & Bradstreet for businesses and Experian for individuals. A common system is to divide credit applicants into three groups. Those with the highest scores receive credit immediately, those with the lowest scores are rejected for credit, and those in the middle are investigated further before a decision is made.

Extending credit to riskier customers increases sales, and hence profits, but adds to administrative costs and exposes the firm to additional bad debts. Contracting credit reduces these costs but also reduces sales and profits.

Example

Credit Standards

Marie Kaye's company currently extends credit to applicants scoring 150 or more points on its credit qualification scale. Marie is interested in the value of extending credit to applicants who score 145–149 points. She has prepared the following forecasts:

a. Sales to the new customers will total $20,000,000 per year

b. The new customers will pay in 90 days on average (assume a 360-day year for convenience)

c. 5% of the new sales will become bad debts and will not be collected

d. No discounts will be offered to the new customers

e. Administering the additional accounts will cost $100,000 per year.

Marie's company has variable costs equal to 70% of sales, is in the 35% marginal income tax bracket, and has a 12% cost of capital.

Question: Should the company extend credit to these customers?

Solution steps:

1. Calculate the incremental cash flows:
   a. Incremental investment:

(1) From the concept of the collection period ratio,[11] (90 days/360 days) = 1/4 of the new sales will be outstanding as receivables at any time:

$$1/4 \times \$20,000,000 = \$5,000,000$$

Of this, 70% represents the company's cost, the amount the company invested to create the receivables:

$$70\% \times \$5,000,000 = \$3,500,000$$

(2) Existing customers are not changing their payment habits.

(3) There is no change anticipated to other working capital.

b. Incremental operating cash flows:

(1) Contribution margin = (1 − 70%) = 30%, so contribution from new sales:

$$30\% \times \$20,000,000 = \$6,000,000$$

(2) New bad debt losses:

$$5\% \times \$20,000,000 = \$1,000,000$$

(3) No discounts are being offered to these customers.

(4) Incremental administrative costs are given as $100,000

c. Income taxes will increase (an outflow) by:

$$35\% \,(\$6,000,000 - 1,000,000 - 100,000) = \$1,715,000$$

2. Organize the cash flows into a cash flow spreadsheet:

	Year 0	Years 1–∞
Investment		
Accounts receivable	($3,500,000)	
Operating cash flows		
Contribution from sales		$6,000,000
Bad debts		(1,000,000)
Administrative costs		(100,000)
Taxes on changed income		(1,715,000)
Net cash flows	($3,500,000)	$3,185,000

3. Calculate the value of the proposal using any of the three variations of the perpetuity model:

a. NPV:

PV of costs = $3,500,000 since all costs come at year 0
PV of benefits = PMT/r = $3,185,000/.12 = $26,541,667
NPV = $26,541,667 − 3,500,000 = $23,041,667

b. IRR:

IRR = r = PMT/PV = $3,185,000/$3,500,000 = 91.00%

c. NAB:

Required annual benefit = r × PV = .12 × $3,500,000 = $420,000
Actual annual benefit = $3,185,000
NAB = $3,185,000 − 420,000 = $2,765,000

---

[11] **Cross-reference:**   Financial ratios are presented in Chapter 2 and summarized at the end of the book. The collection period ratio appears on page 39.

Answer: The proposal has a NPV of $23,041,667, an IRR of 91.00%, and a NAB of $2,765,000. Since NPV and NAB exceed zero and IRR is greater than the cost of capital, credit should be extended to these new customers. In fact, the return is so attractive that Marie should consider analyzing the value of extending credit to potential customers scoring even lower on her company's credit qualification scale.

2. Payment Date

The invoice sent to a customer identifies when payment is due with terms such as net 30 (payment due in 30 days) or net 45 (payment due in 45 days). Permitting payment at a later date increases a company's investment in accounts receivable and slows its collection of profits but might encourage customers to increase their purchases. Shortening the time for payment, on the other hand, reduces the investment in receivables and accelerates profit collection but may reduce sales.

Example

Payment Date

Marie Kaye's company has a product line with sales of $7,800,000. She is curious about the impact of changing payment terms from net 60 to net 30 as customers are not paying their bills until the seventy-fifth day on average. Marie has prepared the following forecasts:

a. Customers will pay more quickly, reducing the collection period to 40 days (assume a 360-day year for convenience)

b. Her company will be able to reduce its idle cash balance by $25,000, freeing that money for other use

c. Some customers will take their business elsewhere and $600,000 of sales will be lost.

Marie's company has variable costs equal to 70% of sales, is in the 35% marginal income tax bracket, and has a 12% cost of capital.

Question: Should the payment date be changed?

Solution steps:

1. Calculate the incremental cash flows:

   a. Incremental investment:

   (1) From the collection period ratio, the accounts receivable balance is currently

   $$(75 \text{ days}/360 \text{ days}) \times \$7,800,000 = \$1,625,000$$

   If the change is implemented, the accounts receivable balance will decline to

   $$(40 \text{ days}/360 \text{ days}) \times \$7,200,000 = \$800,000$$

   a change of

   $$\$1,625,000 - 800,000 = \$825,000$$

   Of this, 70% represents the company's cost, the amount the company invested to create the receivables:

   $$70\% \times \$825,000 = \$577,500$$

(2) The customers who do not leave will speed up their payments. Daily profit flow from these customers is

$$30\% \times (\$7{,}200{,}000/360) = \$6{,}000$$

and if collected $(75 - 40 =)$ 35 days earlier, adds value of:

$$\$6{,}000 \times 35 \text{ days} = \$210{,}000$$

(3) Other working capital: idle cash will decline by $25,000

b. Incremental operating cash flows:

(1) Contribution lost from departing sales:

$$30\% \times \$600{,}000 = \$180{,}000$$

(2) Bad debts are not forecast to change.

(3) No discounts are being offered to these customers.

(4) Administrative costs are not forecast to change.

c. Income taxes will decrease (an inflow) by:

$$35\% \times \$180{,}000 = \$63{,}000$$

2. Organize the cash flows into a cash flow spreadsheet:

	Year 0	Years 1—∞
Investment		
Accounts receivable	$577,500	
Changed collection period	210,000	
Other working capital	25,000	
Operating cash flows		
Contribution from sales		($180,000)
Taxes on changed income		63,000
Net cash flows	$812,500	($117,000)

3. Calculate the value of the proposal using any of the three variations of the perpetuity model:

a. NPV:

PV of benefits = $812,500 since all at year 0
PV of costs = PMT/r = $117,000/.12 = $975,000
NPV = $812,500 − 975,000 = ($162,500)

b. IRR:

IRR = r = PMT/PV = $117,000/$812,500 = 14.40%

c. NAB:

Annual cost of the existing investment = r × PV
= .12 × $812,500 = $97,500
Annual cost of the proposed investment = $117,000
NAB = $97,500 − 117,000 = ($19,500)

Answer: The proposal has a NPV of (\$162,500), an IRR of 14.40%, and an NAB of (\$19,500). Since NPV and NAB are less than zero (and IRR is greater than the cost of capital for this "opposite project"), payment terms should not be shortened.

"I'm sorry that we can't extend credit, but our collection terms are net 30 and Zorgon 12 is three light years from here."

3. Price Changes

Discounts are often offered to business customers for early payment, such as in the terms 2/10, net 30, which gives the customer a choice: take a 2% discount (pay 98%) within ten days, or pay 100% by the thirtieth day. Granting discounts reduces a company's investment in accounts receivable and speeds up its collection of profits at the cost of the discount foregone. Eliminating existing discounts increases the investment in receivables and slows profit collection but does not give away profit dollars.

A second form of price change occurs when interest is added to an overdue account balance. This is identical to transforming the receivables balance into a loan.

Example

Discounts

Marie Kaye's company has another product line with sales of $9,000,000 on terms of net 60. Customers pay on time, so the average collection period is 60 days. Marie is interested in the effect of offering a 2% discount by changing payment terms to 2/10, net 60. She has prepared the following forecasts:

a. Eighty percent of the customers will take the discount and pay on the tenth day (assume a 360 day year for convenience)

b. The other 20% of customers will continue to pay on the sixtieth day.

Marie's company has variable costs equal to 70% of sales, is in the 35% marginal income tax bracket, and has a 12% cost of capital.

Question: Should the company offer the discount?

Solution steps:

1. Calculate the incremental cash flows:

 a. Incremental investment:

(1) From the collection period ratio, the accounts receivable balance is currently

$$(60 \text{ days}/360 \text{ days}) \times \$9,000,000 = \$1,500,000$$

If the change is implemented, the collection period will become

$$(80\% \times 10 \text{ days}) + (20\% \times 60 \text{ days}) = 20 \text{ days}$$

and the accounts receivable balance will decline to

$$(20 \text{ days}/360 \text{ days}) \times \$9,000,000 = \$500,000$$

a change of

$$\$1,500,000 - 500,000 = \$1,000,000$$

Of this, 70% represents the company's cost, the amount the company invested to create the receivables:

$$70\% \times \$1,000,000 = \$700,000$$

(2) On average, customers will speed up their payments. Daily profit flow is

$$30\% \times (\$9,000,000/360) = \$7,500$$

and if collected $(60 - 20 =)$ 40 days earlier, adds value of:

$$\$7,500 \times 40 \text{ days} = \$300,000$$

(3) There is no change anticipated to other working capital.

b. Incremental operating cash flows:

(1) Sales is not forecasted to change.

(2) Bad debts are not forecasted to change.

(3) Customers taking the discount purchase

$$80\% \times \$9,000,000 = \$7,200,000$$

If they take a 2% discount they will reduce their payments by

$$2\% \times \$7,200,000 = \$144,000$$

(4) Administrative costs are not forecasted to change.

c. Income taxes will decrease (an inflow) by:

$$35\% \times \$144,000 = \$50,400$$

2. Organize the cash flows into a cash flow spreadsheet:

	Year 0	Years 1–∞
Investment		
Accounts receivable	$ 700,000	
Changed collection period	300,000	
Operating cash flows		
Discounts		($144,000)
Taxes on changed income		50,400
Net cash flows	$1,000,000	($ 93,600)

3. Calculate the value of the proposal using any of the three variations of the perpetuity model:

a. NPV:

PV of benefits = \$1,000,000 since all come at year 0
PV of costs = PMT/r = \$93,600/.12 = \$780,000
NPV = \$1,000,000 − 780,000 = \$220,000

b. IRR:

IRR = r = PMT/PV = \$93,600/\$1,000,000 = 9.36%

c. NAB:

Annual cost of the existing investment = r × PV
= .12 × \$1,000,000 = \$120,000
Annual cost of the proposed investment = \$93,600
NAB = \$120,000 − 93,600 = \$26,400

Answer: The proposal has a NPV of \$220,000, an IRR of 9.36%, and a NAB of \$26,400. Since NPV and NAB exceed zero (and IRR is less than the cost of capital for this "opposite project"), the discount should be offered.

"*Hey*, how about a break for lunch," one member of the team asked, looking toward Marie Kaye. Marie glanced at her watch; it was almost 1:00PM! After what had seemed like an eternity waiting for the day to begin, the morning had flown by. Marie had invited members of her staff to brainstorm the company's accounts receivable problems, and there was no shortage of volunteers. Everyone had made important contributions during the morning's discussion, and by now the walls of the conference room were covered with the team's notes.

Marie had begun the meeting with a review of the company's receivables policy: credit standards, payment date, and discount terms. She had put her staff's most recent cash flow analyses on the table, and after a general discussion of incremental analysis techniques, breakout groups had reviewed the assumptions and calculations. There was general agreement that the company's policy was reasonable, given the assumptions that had been made about customer behavior.

But it quickly became apparent that the group did not understand the behavior of their customers: why they were not paying as they had been forecasted to do. Part of the problem seemed to be with the format of the invoices since customers complained they were difficult to understand (even though they made perfect sense to everyone in the room), and the team made plans to form a joint controller/customer task force to work on the issue. Part of the problem was the errors in some invoices, and another task force was formed to trace the billing process to discover where and why errors arose.

As Marie left the room and walked toward the company's cafeteria, she felt a strong sense of accomplishment. She was having fun blending the traditional skills of financial analysis with the team-based work of quality management, and more than ever she was convinced of the need to combine the two to do her new job well.

SERVING FINANCE'S CUSTOMERS

Reducing Billing "Contentions" at Southern Pacific

When a survey of customers identified billing accuracy as the finance process with which they were most dissatisfied—fully 13% of all bills were objected to as wrong, "contentions" in the jargon of the industry—the controller's office at Southern Pacific Rail Corporation began a project to improve the process. Quality-improvement teams improved the data flow from marketing to billing, realigned the billing group to be more consistent with the marketing organization's structure, constructed a common pricing database, and studied how to simplify the railroad's pricing structure. Customers active in quality management joined with Southern Pacific in the effort. Today, contentions have been significantly reduced, and since the reduction in contested invoices represents millions of dollars of receivables per day, the company's cash flow has improved dramatically.

Summary of Key Points

▇▇ **Separate working capital into permanent and temporary components.** Working capital represents a company's liquid resources available for daily use. Some is permanent, a base level required on an ongoing basis. The remainder is temporary, the changes around the base level due to the business cycle, seasonality, and the vagaries of day-to-day transactions.

▇▇ **Organize permanent working capital data into cash flow terms.** Permanent working capital decisions are analyzed using a cash flow table and the perpetuity time value of money model.

▇▇ **Describe the components of a firm's cash balance and analyze decisions involving accelerating cash in transit.** Cash includes coins and bills, demand deposits, and time deposits, and may be held in various currencies. Traditionally, companies have accelerated collections and delayed disbursements so cash in transit does not remain idle. Today, there is a trend toward using electronic payment systems to further speed up collections and reduce processing costs. Excess cash is moved to marketable securities to earn interest.

▇▇ **Analyze proposed changes to a firm's permanent accounts receivable balance.** A firm establishes its permanent accounts receivable balance through its decisions about credit standards, payment date, and price changes: discounts for early payment and interest added to overdue balances. Decisions are incremental, testing each proposed alternative and accepting changes that have a positive NPV or NAB or

an acceptable IRR. Accounts receivable will change temporarily in response to specific customers' needs and circumstances.

Questions

1. What are the two usages for the term *working capital?*

2. Distinguish between permanent working capital and temporary working capital. Why is the difference important to financial managers?

3. In what ways is the cash flow spreadsheet used to organize the data for permanent working capital asset decisions similar to and different from the cash flow spreadsheet used in capital budgeting?

4. What is a project's "net annual benefit"? Why is this measure used in evaluating permanent working capital asset decisions?

5. Are you comfortable with the assumption that permanent asset decisions are truly permanent—that is, their effects continue forever? Why or why not?

6. Discuss how a corporate treasurer allocates the firm's cash balance. What are the factors taken into account in making the allocation?

7. What is "float"? Why is it of concern to the financial manager? Discuss the advantages and/or disadvantages to receivables float and payables float.

8. How does a lock box-concentration banking system impact a firm's float?

9. When does a company move cash from its noninterest-bearing demand account to marketable securities?

10. What are the three components of a firm's credit policy? What does each entail?

11. What special considerations enter the credit granting decision when the customer is paying in a foreign currency?

Problems

1. **(Calculating working capital)** A company's current asset balance is $500,000. Calculate its working capital and current ratio if its current liabilities equal:

    a. $200,000   c. $500,000
    b. $350,000   d. $650,000

2. **(Calculating working capital)** A company's working capital equals $2,000,000. Calculate its balance of current liabilities and its current ratio if the company's current assets equal:

    a. $6,000,000   c. $4,000,000
    b. $5,000,000   d. $3,000,000

3. **(Changes to working capital)** A company has current assets of $1,500,000 and current liabilities of $800,000. Calculate the change to the company's working capital and current ratio from the following transactions (treat each case separately):

    a. Collecting $100,000 of accounts receivable
    b. Paying $100,000 of accounts payable
    c. Purchasing $100,000 of plant and equipment for cash
    d. Selling $100,000 of common stock

4. **(Changes to working capital)** A company has current assets of $5,000,000 and current liabilities of $2,000,000. Calculate the change to the company's working capital and current ratio from the following transactions (treat each case separately):

    a. Purchasing $500,000 of inventory on credit (accounts payable)
    b. Recording $500,000 of depreciation
    c. Moving $500,000 from cash to marketable securities
    d. Recognizing $500,000 of receipts in advance as being earned

5. **(Perpetuity analysis)** A company with a 11% cost of capital is considering an investment that would cost it $300,000 today in return for a perpetuity of benefits of $45,000.

    a. Calculate the project's NPV
    b. Calculate the project's IRR
    c. Calculate the project's NAB
    d. Should the investment be accepted? (Interpret your results from parts a, b, and c.)

6. **(Perpetuity analysis)** A company with a 9% cost of capital is considering scaling back its operations. $1,750,000 would be released from investment in current assets, but the firm would forgo a perpetuity of benefits of $250,000.

    a. Calculate the project's NPV
    b. Calculate the project's IRR
    c. Calculate the project's NAB
    d. Should the investment be accepted? (Interpret your results from parts a, b, and c)

7. **(Funds in transit)** It takes three days on average for customers' checks, averaging $75,000 per day, to reach a company. Also, the company makes deposits averaging $60,000 to its bank account one day before its checks clear. The company has a 12% cost of capital.

    a. What is the amount of idle money
        (1) In the mail?
        (2) In the bank?
    b. What is the total amount of idle money in transit?
    c. What is the annual cost of the funds
        (1) In the mail?
        (2) In the bank?
    d. What is the total annual cost of the idle funds?

8. **(Funds in transit)** It takes six days on average for customers' checks, averaging $200,000 per day, to reach a company. Also, the company makes deposits averaging $160,000 to its bank account one-half day before its checks clear. The company has a 10% cost of capital.

    a. What is the amount of idle money
        (1) In the mail?
        (2) In the bank?
    b. What is the total amount of idle money in transit?
    c. What is the annual cost of the funds
        (1) In the mail?
        (2) In the bank?
    d. What is the total annual cost of the idle funds?

9. **(Accelerating collections)** A company receives cash inflows of US$6 million per day from customers in North America. Checks take six days on average to arrive, but a large commercial bank has proposed to implement a lock box-concentration banking system for a $3 million annual fee which would cut the time a check is in receivables float to an average of three days. The company's marginal tax rate is 35%. What is the value of the proposed system to the company, and should it be implemented, if the company's cost of capital is:

    a. 8%?   c. 12%?
    b. 10%?   d. 15%?

10. **(Accelerating collections)**   A company with a 12% cost of capital receives cash inflows from customers throughout the United States and Canada. Checks take 5 days on average to arrive, but a large commercial bank has proposed to implement a lock box-concentration banking system for a $250,000 annual fee which would cut the time a check is in receivables float to an average of 1 1/2 days. The company's marginal tax rate is 35%. What is the value of the proposed system to the company, and should it be implemented, if the company's daily cash inflows average:

   a. $150,000?   c. $450,000?
   b. $300,000?   d. $600,000?

11. **(Credit standards)**   A company is considering extending credit to a group of customers who have not previously met the company's credit standards. The company forecasts that the new customers would purchase $80,000 per year, would pay in 75 days on average (assume a 360-day year), and would default on 8% of their purchases. It would cost $5,000 per year to administer the new accounts. The company's variable costs average 80% of sales, it is in the 35% marginal tax bracket, and it has a 9% cost of capital.

  a. Calculate the incremental cash flows from accepting this proposal.
  b. Organize your cash flows from part a into a cash flow spreadsheet.
  c. Calculate the proposal's NPV, IRR, and NAB.
  d. Should credit be extended to the new customers?

12. **(Credit standards)**   A company is considering withdrawing credit from a group of customers who are not paying on time. These customers purchase $200,000 per year, pay in 120 days on average (assume a 360-day year), and default on 15% of their purchases. The company would save $15,000 in administrative costs per year and could reduce its idle cash balance by $5,000 if it terminated these accounts. The company's variable costs average 60% of sales, it is in the 35% marginal tax bracket, and it has a 13% cost of capital.

  a. Calculate the incremental cash flows from accepting this proposal.
  b. Organize your cash flows from part a into a cash flow spreadsheet.
  c. Calculate the proposal's NPV, IRR, and NAB.
  d. Should credit be withdrawn from these customers?

13. **(Payment date)**   A company with annual sales of $5,000,000 is considering changing its payment terms from net 30 to net 45 to accommodate customers who are having difficulty in paying their bills. The com-

pany forecasts that customers would respond by: (1) paying on day 50 rather than on day 40 as at present (assume a 360-day year), (2) increasing their purchases by $100,000 per year, and (3) reducing their bad debts to 1.4% of sales from 1.5% of sales. The company also forecasts that its idle cash balance would increase by $50,000 but administrative costs would be reduced by $20,000. The company's variable costs average 75% of sales, it is in the 35% marginal tax bracket, and it has a 11% cost of capital.

  a. Calculate the incremental cash flows from accepting this proposal.
  b. Organize your cash flows from part a into a cash flow spreadsheet.
  c. Calculate the proposal's NPV, IRR, and NAB.
  d. Should the company lengthen its payment terms?

14. **(Payment date)**   A company with annual sales of $22,000,000 is considering changing its payment terms from net 40 to net 30 to encourage customers to pay more promptly. The company forecasts that customers would respond by paying on day 30 rather than on day 45 as at present (assume a 360-day year) but would decrease their purchases by $400,000 per year. The company also forecasts that its idle cash balance would decrease by $100,000 and administrative costs would be reduced by $50,000. The company's variable costs average 65% of sales, it is in the 35% marginal tax bracket, and it has a 12% cost of capital.

  a. Calculate the incremental cash flows from accepting this proposal.
  b. Organize your cash flows from part a into a cash flow spreadsheet.
  c. Calculate the proposal's NPV, IRR, and NAB.
  d. Should the company shorten its payment terms?

15. **(Discounts)**   A company with annual sales of $2,500,000 on terms of net 30 and a collection period of 40 days (assume a 360-day year) is considering offering its customers terms of 2/15, net 30. The company forecasts that 60% of the customers would take the discount and pay on day 15 while the remaining 40% would pay on day 35 on average. Customers are also expected to increase their purchases by $100,000, and the company forecasts that its idle cash balance would decrease by $60,000. The company's variable costs average 75% of sales, it is in the 35% marginal tax bracket, and it has a 10% cost of capital.

  a. Calculate the incremental cash flows from accepting this proposal.
  b. Organize your cash flows from part a into a cash flow spreadsheet.

c. Calculate the proposal's NPV, IRR, and NAB.

d. Should the company offer the discount?

16. **(Discounts)** A company with annual sales of $900,000 on terms of 2/10, net 30 is considering eliminating the discount and simplifying its terms of sale to net 30. Only 25% of customers take the discount and pay on day 10 (assume a 360-day year), the rest pay on day 30 on average. The company forecasts that if the discount were eliminated, its collection period for all sales would become 30 days, its idle cash balance would increase by $1,000, and administrative costs would decrease by $3,000. The company's variable costs average 70% of sales, it is in the 35% marginal tax bracket, and it has a 10% cost of capital.

a. Calculate the incremental cash flows from accepting this proposal.

b. Organize your cash flows from part a into a cash flow spreadsheet.

c. Calculate the proposal's NPV, IRR, and NAB.

d. Should the company eliminate the discount?

CHAPTER 13

IMPROVING

FINANCIAL

PROCESSES[1]

$\mathcal{B}$ ill Librasco was getting into the flow of his argument now. Looking at Jan Baxter and Hamid Allarani with a smile, he started what they all called a "patented Librasco lecture." "Look, I know we have to get more done with less in finance just as in the rest of the company. But quality management is not what we need. It may be a good idea to do that stuff elsewhere in the company, I really don't know, but we can't do it in finance.

"First, we don't produce widgets here. We produce decisions, and advice, and consultation . . . and we catch some errors and make sure other departments don't get sloppy. But the finance department is not a factory and finance people aren't like factory workers. Even if we could figure out a way to apply a few of the concepts and tools here, we couldn't get our people to use them. We are more skeptical, better educated, and more professional—not the type of folks who do that kind of stuff.

"And, we don't have the time. We have more important things to do than go to classes on how to 'empower' a team to move the water cooler to a place that makes everyone happier. For example, our boss took it in the ear last night about the increase in receivables. I have to be on the phone most of today to collect some of the overdue bills. Now that's worth a lot to the company! So, let's not waste our time trying to get finance people to do something impossible that they don't want to do and that would be trivial even if they did it."

---

[1] **Acknowledgment:** This chapter draws heavily on the work of members of the Juran Institute whose assistance is gratefully acknowledged.

As Bill took a deep breath, Jan and Hamid laughed and applauded quietly. When Bill started laughing too, Jan turned to Hamid and said, "You win again. I thought he'd be a quick learner because he's so smart. But you were right; all through this conversation he's been using his brains to prove it can't be done, rather than trying to figure out how it can be done." Turning away, with a twinkle in her eye, she said to Hamid: "Let's go find someone to work with who isn't as smart as Bill and hasn't yet figured out why it can't be done."

They had taken only half of a step to leave before Bill said, "Okay, you two. You've hooked me again. What are the details of the project you want me to volunteer for this time! But make it brief, I really do have to collect some receivables to get the heat off our boss."

The project Bill will eventually volunteer for will be one that many other financial managers have been undertaking in the last few years: to figure out how to accomplish a great deal more useful work with fewer resources. However, Bill and others will not be excited about the opportunity to improve finance's processes until they realize that finance has processes and that improving processes is an excellent way to do more with less.

This chapter looks first at recognizing and understanding financial processes. We will follow Bill, Jan, and Hamid as they investigate how a focus on processes can help their company with its receivables problem. Then we will see how the team can improve the process in which the receivables problem is embedded.

Key Points You Should Learn from This Chapter

After reading this chapter you should be able to:

- Define a work process and distinguish the tasks of managing and improving financial processes from the other financial managing tasks.
- Identify financial processes involving external and internal customers or suppliers.
- Use two concepts to describe the nature of financial processes and five steps to describe how a financial process transforms inputs into outputs.
- Identify five concepts useful in measuring process performance.
- Describe three key factors in achieving revolutionary rates of quality improvement in financial processes and the rest of the organization and describe the Juran model of process improvement.
- Describe three sets of quality-management tools used to improve financial and other processes and one systematic approach for improving financial and other processes.
- Describe two examples in which quality-management tools and approaches have been used to improve financial processes.

311

Introductory Concepts—Financial Processes

Bill Librasco is not alone in being slow to recognize that finance has processes of its own. However, when he thinks for a moment about the definition of a process, he may discover many financial processes around him: billing, cash management, making investment decisions, writing checks, closing the corporate books, and even collecting accounts receivable.

work process—a series of work activities intended to produce a specific result

We will define a **work process** as "a series of work activities intended to produce a specific result." A somewhat more rigorous definition is: "a series of definable, predictable, and repeatable work activities, consisting of people, equipment, procedures, and material, organized to produce a specific result."[2] We will use the words *process* and *work process* interchangeably. Each company has a number of major business processes, such as order fulfillment and working capital management, and many subprocesses that make up each major business process, such as the invoicing, shipping, and collections subprocesses of the order fulfillment process. When effectively designed and integrated these processes and their component subprocesses produce an effective **business system**: "a collection of integrated work processes that constitute an entire business organization."[3]

business system—the set of integrated and overlapping work processes that constitute an entire business organization

Figure 13.1[4] illustrates a business (or any other) process. The process is composed of a series of activities and subprocesses with inputs from a supplier and outputs to a customer. The dotted lines show two sets of feedback loops. The larger ones, on the left and right of the diagram, are labeled "customer requirements and satisfaction." They represent information about what customers actually want and how satisfied they are with the products and services provided by the process— how well the process meets or exceeds customer requirements. The second, smaller feedback loops in the diagram are labeled "results." These are the actual products or services provided by the process.

NET Present Value
For more definitions of process- and quality-related terms, visit the American Society for Quality glossary web page:
www.asq.org/glossary

Figure 13.1 calls attention to two important outcomes of a process: the actual products and services produced and the satisfaction (or dissatisfaction) the products and services create when used by the customer. Recently, many financial managers have become less willing to assume that finance's processes are producing exactly the services and financial products their customers need and are much more willing to investigate how effective those products and services are in meeting the needs of finance's customers.[5]

Although Bill does not recognize it, financial processes are similar to production processes, marketing processes, research and development processes, personnel

---

[2] **Reference:**   *American Express Quality Leadership Glossary.* (New York: American Express Company, Sept. 1992), page 6.

[3] **Reference:**   A rich discussion of the business and other organizational systems is given in Steven Cavaleri and Krzysztof Obloj, *Management Systems: A Global Prospective* (Belmont, Calif.: Wadsworth, 1993), page 13.

[4] **Source:**   Adapted, with adjustments, from *Business Process Quality Management* (Wilton, Conn.: The Juran Institute, 1993). Used with permission.

[5] **Elaboration:**   The feedback loops in Figure 13.1 can be interpreted in terms used by some influential quality-management professionals. The customer requirements part of the customer requirements and satisfaction feedback loop is called "the voice of the customer." The feedback loop dealing with the results of the process is called "the voice of the process." The extent to which these two voices coincide determines customer satisfaction. See William W. Scherkenbach, *Deming's Road to Continual Improvement* (Knoxville, Tenn.: SPC Press, 1991).

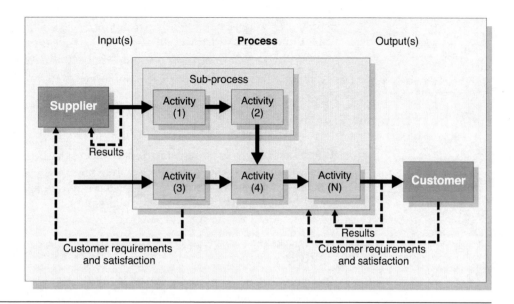

FIGURE 13.1

A business process. Process activities transform inputs from suppliers into outputs for customers.

processes and even legal processes. The similarity of these processes, once recognized, provides a useful vehicle for helping members of different departments and functions work together on shared process problems. It also makes a uniform language for describing and understanding processes possible and useful.

In addition, finance's processes, purposes, and members are similar enough to those of the rest of the company to enable it to use the same quality-management approaches that work elsewhere in the organization, even though finance does have its own unique aspects. Therefore, process improvements achieved in other parts of the organization may provide useful models for finance, as financial managers are increasingly expected to achieve the same high level of process performance as is found in operations and other parts of the enterprise.

In Chapter 1, we discussed five major financial management tasks. Three emphasize analysis and decision making: (1) obtaining financing and selecting long-term investments, (2) managing day-to-day financial flows, and (3) balancing the risks and returns faced by the firm and its stakeholders. One emphasizes study, analysis, and advice: (4) serving as a resource about financial markets and sources of financing. The fifth task also involves considerable study, analysis, and decision making, but it emphasizes two new dimensions—operations and improvement: (5) operating and improving financial processes.

Although improving its own processes has always been an important part of finance's work and a key way to do more with less, it has frequently not been given high priority by finance and other organizational members. This low priority came about in part because many finance people, like Bill, were not aware of the processes around them, so they were not likely to think in terms of improving them. It also came about because few finance members had the tools to make significant, sustainable improvements in financial and other processes.

Finance professionals are involved in two other tasks that support the five listed. These tasks—"distributing" the tools of finance and working on cross-functional teams—are so deeply embedded in finance's other tasks that they are not likely to be thought of as distinct activities. As a result they are easily overlooked. We mention them separately because they are becoming increasingly visible and important as finance strives to increase its contributions to the total organization.[6]

Recognizing Financial Processes

If Jan and Hamid decide to start Bill's "process education" by looking for places where finance has its own processes, they might well start where we started with this book. Figure 1.1 on page 4 suggests a whole set of financial processes involving external customers and suppliers.

1. Processes with External Customers or Suppliers

Wherever money or financial data are exchanged between the organization and its outside stakeholders, a financial process exists. These processes involve: (1) customers, (2) suppliers, (3) governments and local communities, (4) lenders, and (5) investors.

Financial processes with the organization's ultimate external customers include such activities as preparing, issuing, and collecting bills; extending credit; and providing cost estimates. Financial processes with the organization's external suppliers include verifying the accuracy of invoices and paying the bills, arranging for credit from suppliers or perhaps extending credit to them, and evaluating bids and cost estimates. Financial processes with governments include paying taxes, providing financial information, and reporting on compliance with regulations. Financial processes with local communities include contributing to educational, charitable, environmental and social activities. Financial processes with lenders include borrowing, servicing and repaying debt, arranging stand-by credit facilities, and obtaining trade financing. Financial processes with equity investors include paying dividends; issuing, transferring, and retiring equity shares; and reporting to shareholders and analysts on the organization's past and likely future competitive and financial performance.

2. Processes with Internal Customers or Suppliers

In addition to financial processes involving external customers and suppliers, finance is also involved in a great many processes whose customers and suppliers are members of the organization—internal customers and suppliers. For one set of processes, the customers are the organization's employees. For a second set of processes, the customers and suppliers are units of the organization that need finance's contributions to conduct the organization's business.

Financial processes directed toward the organization's employees include the calculation and payment of normal compensation, commissions, overtime, and special incentive bonuses; withholding and payment of employee-related taxes, dues,

---

[6] **Cross-reference:**   These two supporting tasks are discussed briefly in Web Appendix 13A.

insurance, and health care costs; investment in and management of pension funds; and payment of retirement benefits.

Financial processes are also a part of almost all of the internal management processes used to conduct the organization's business. These activities include investment project evaluation, sales planning and budgeting, long-range and strategic planning, human resource budgeting, internal auditing, working with outside auditors, and setting and measuring objectives.[7]

Understanding Financial Processes

Once a process becomes visible, there are a series of useful concepts for describing it and for understanding how it functions—including its "results." In this section, we divide these concepts into two categories: (1) concepts for describing the nature of a process, and (2) concepts for describing what a process does. Later in this chapter, we will discuss ways of measuring the performance of financial and other processes, and ways to improve them.

1. Describing the Nature of a Process

The concepts "process boundary" and "adding value" are helpful in recognizing that a process exists and in seeing the nature of a specific process. Another useful concept, "supplier-processor-customer" roles, recognizes that each member of a process is a "supplier" to the next step in the process, a "customer" of the preceding step, and a "processor" who (hopefully) adds value.[8]

When Bill's team members start thinking of the "receivables problem" as occurring in a financial process, they will very quickly find themselves asking, "Where does the receivables process begin and where does it end?" They are asking about the boundaries of the process.

process boundary—the line separating a process from other business activities

The **boundary of a process** is the conceptual line drawn for a specific purpose that distinguishes what is part of the process from what is not part of it. The phrase, *for a specific purpose,* is very important in understanding the concept of process boundary. For most processes, the boundary can be drawn in many logical places. Should we consider the process of collecting a receivable to begin with picking up the phone to call the customer about an overdue account? Or should it begin with reviewing the entire pile of overdue accounts to decide which one to call? Or perhaps we should go back much, much further and start where the invoice is sent to the customer, or even before the sale is made. The answer is frequently not obvious, and *the purpose for which the process is being defined is the key to drawing the boundary.*

"Gee," said Hamid. "When we started to draw the process boundaries around collecting receivables, I thought the answer was clear. The process starts when the customer fails to pay on time. But now that does not seem at all like a good way to look at things. The more we try to draw a picture of the collectibles process, the further back I want to go."

---

[7] **Cross-reference:**   Web Appendix 13A provides a figure showing some of the processes involving internal customers and suppliers.

[8] **Cross-reference:**   This concept is illustrated and discussed more fully in Web Appendix 13A.

adding value—making the output of a process worth more for its customers

Adding value is a phrase used to describe those activities performed within a process that make the resulting product or service of greater value to the process customer. If we define our receivables collection process to begin far enough back to include issuing the invoice, then one value-added step is easy to spot. Correctly calculating the cost of the products shipped and generating a simple, easy-to-read invoice add value for final customers by simplifying their work. Well-prepared invoices allow customers to make payment without having to obtain clarification about ambiguous invoice items or corrections of erroneous ones. They avoid delays required to resolve errors and clarify confusions.

2. Process Mapping—Describing What a Process Does

NET Present Value
Proccess mapping resources are available at many websites such as: www.processmaps.com/ mapping.html

Processes convert inputs into outputs, hopefully adding value as they do. One approach to describing a process, called "process-mapping", involves developing a flow chart of the process . Developing a process map consists of five steps: (1) describing the product or service produced, (2) specifying the customer(s), (3) specifying the suppliers and their inputs, (4) describing each task within the process, the sequences of tasks, and who performs each one, and (5) describing the characteristics of satisfactory inputs and outputs of the process. These steps are described briefly below for the process investigation stimulated by Bill Librasco's "receivables collection problem."[9]

Describing the product or service If Bill's team focuses very narrowly on the activity of collecting the overdue receivables, the team might describe the products of the collection process as either "a deposited payment for the invoice" or a "written-off invoice." In some situations, that narrow a focus may be appropriate. However, a focus that takes a more encompassing view of the process—with process boundaries that include more activities—is frequently more useful.

If they take a broader view, the team might see the process as producing "payments for sales." In this perspective, the process includes issuing the original invoices, collecting most of them on time without incident, and dealing with some that are not paid in a timely manner. Overdue receivables would be viewed as some form of "defect" requiring **rework,** a frequently used term in studying and improving processes.[10]

rework—an activity performed to correct an error or omission in an earlier stage of a work process

Specifying customer(s) Customers of the collection process could include many individuals and entities. In describing the process, Bill's team will certainly identify the actual buyer of the product or service who, hopefully, pays the invoice. The treasury function of Bill's company is also a customer when it deposits the check received in payment. Other customers could include a supplier in a new role. For example, the salesperson who made the sale may receive information on how smoothly or roughly the payment process went. The credit analyst who keeps records on payment performance and makes decisions on extending credit on future sales would be another customer.

---

[9] **Cross-reference:** A richer description is provided in Web Appendix 13A with additional process maps.

[10] **Cross-reference:** Rework is described more fully in Web Appendix 13A.

As they kept trying to describe the collection process, Jan started agreeing more and more with Hamid about the process boundaries: "I find that I keep wanting to add new internal customers to the process as we understand it better—treasury, sales, credit. And I keep seeing how our external customers differ. Not all customers who have not paid are the same. There are many reasons for not paying, and some of them seem to be our fault."

Identifying suppliers and inputs   By asking the question, "Who are the suppliers?" the team may start identifying others not included within the original process boundaries. For example, the team might decide that the sales department should be shown as a process supplier—because accurate sales information is necessary for preparing accurate invoices. That thought might then lead to the decision that it is desirable to include the group that prepares the invoice and also to include the treasury function, which receives and deposits payment for the invoice. If the team chooses to include these new actors in the process it is studying, it will be taking a step toward a more encompassing process definition—looking at a sales payment or an order fulfillment process rather than at an overdue invoice collection process. Figure 13.2 suggests what a fairly early stage of mapping the receivables collection process might look like.[11]

Describing tasks   As the team continues describing the process, it may keep discovering steps, actors, and products within the process that it had not anticipated. Each activity performed within the process must be described, including identifying who performs the activity and the order in which it is performed.

Describing satisfactory inputs and outputs   One satisfactory input might be an accurately completed statement of sales information prepared by the salesperson and forwarded to finance's invoicing department on the day of sale. The team might identify three satisfactory products of the sales payment process. One

FIGURE 13.2
The collection process expanded. The sales and invoicing departments are suppliers, and treasury is another customer of the process.

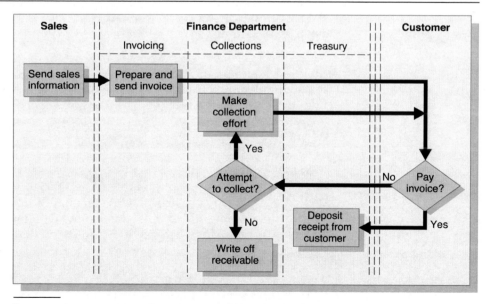

---

[11] **Cross-reference:**   Web Appendix 13A includes illustrations from a still earlier stage and a later stage of the mapping process.

would be a clearly written, accurate invoice showing the exact items shipped and the date of shipment with agreed terms of sale. The second would be a shipping confirmation—showing when the items were shipped—that arrives at the customer's purchasing office by EDI or by fax within 30 minutes of actual shipment. The third would be a check in the proper amount arriving at the corporate billing office within the time specified in the terms of sale.

Measuring Financial Process Performance

In addition to developing a diagram of the sales payment process, Bill's team will also want to collect data on the performance of the process. We will look briefly at five frequently measured process performance dimensions: effectiveness, efficiency, cycle time, stability, and capability.[12]

Bill's team may find it useful to distinguish between performance measures that focus on the effectiveness of the process (is it "doing the right things?") and those that deal with the efficiency of the process (is it "doing things right?"). The first type of measure captures how well the process satisfies its customers—the people or organizations the process is intended to serve. The second type of measure looks at how well the process uses resources.

1. Measures of Process Effectiveness

There are two dimensions of process effectiveness: conformance to specifications, the performance of the process in producing what it is supposed to produce and conformance to (customer) requirements, meeting and exceeding customer expectations—producing what the customer wants. Obviously, the latter measure is the more important one, but the former is also necessary and important.

Measures of conformance to specifications determine whether the process is doing what it is intended to do. Are invoices on time? Were investment projects evaluated with the correct cost of capital? Have financial forecasts used the agreed-upon set of assumptions about economic growth rates and inflation?

Measures of customer satisfaction—conformance to requirements—seek to determine how well a product or service meets or exceeds customer expectations. These measures are often based on customer surveys, which ask questions about reactions to the company's products and services.

2. Measures of Process Efficiency

Measures of process efficiency assess the success of the process in meeting customer needs at low cost. Indicators of process efficiency include the total resources used in achieving a specific result, the amount of time in which useful work is actually done (value added time) divided by total time to complete the process, and many others. Most such measures are logical and traditional in the sense of dividing easily recognized outputs by easily recognized inputs.

---

[12] **Cross-reference:** A more extensive discussion of these five measures appears in Web Appendix 13A which discusses two additional measures that are also important but by their nature difficult to measure (adaptability and robustness).

3. Cycle Time—A Powerful Measure

The concept of cycle time (the time from start to finish of an activity) was introduced in Chapter 2.[13] Cycle time is a particularly powerful measure because it is frequently tied closely to effectiveness, efficiency, or both.

4. Process Stability

process stability—the variation in the output of a process

natural variation—the random variation inherent in any process

Process stability refers to the extent to which a process exhibits low variation in its output. The concept of variation is one of the cornerstones of the global quality revolution.[14] Even when processes are running smoothly and are said to be "in control" or stable, they continue to demonstrate **natural variation** in their outputs. However, when a process is not running smoothly—when it is not stable—additional variation occurs from special events.

common causes of variation—factors that cause natural variation in a stable process

special causes of variation—factors that cause excessive variation and make a process unstable

The natural variation in outputs of a stable process is said to come entirely from **common causes**—factors inherent in the process. A normal number of clerical errors in calculating invoice dollar amounts, which lead in turn to delays in payment, would be an example of a common cause. Special events, like a new, improperly trained invoicing clerk who calculates invoice values from an out-of-date price list would be an example of a **special cause.** The resulting errors could well lead to an increase in late payments.

Many firms do not understand the distinction between common causes of variation and special causes. As a result, much more management time is devoted to finding and correcting errors arising from special causes rather than to reducing common cause variation, i.e., improving the process.

5. Process Capability

process capability—how well a process functions under normal operating conditions

Process capability refers to the extent to which a process will yield the intended output under normal operating conditions. A major impact of the global quality revolution on finance, as well as on all other parts of companies, is in the definition of process capability. Processes once considered adequate or good or even excellent are now considered inadequate (no longer capable). A company fully satisfied with a book-closing process requiring ten days may consider the process wholly inadequate when it discovers other companies are closing their books in two days, two hours, or even two minutes at lower costs with fewer errors.

6. Finance's Role in Measuring Process Performance

Finance members have two major involvements with process performance measures. First, in some companies they have started collecting data from their own internal and external customers on finance's performance in meeting their needs. Second, as the "custodian of the numbers" used in running the business, finance

---

[13] **Cross-reference:** See Chapter 2, page 49.

[14] **References:** Good references on variation are: Myron Tribus, "The Germ Theory of Management," ms. undated; Brian L. Joiner and Marie A. Gaudard, "Variation, Management, and W. Edwards Deming." *Quality Progress* (1990) pages 29–37, and William W. Scherkenbach, *Deming's Road to Continual Improvement* (Knoxville, Tenn.: SPC Press, 1991).

is beginning to play a vital role in collecting and reporting data from external and internal customers of other parts of the organization.

Systematic Process Improvement

Jan Baxter and Hamid Allarani exchanged amused glances as Bill Librasco collapsed into his chair but kept talking with his usual passion. "I don't know what you two are smiling about. We have been trying for two weeks to get the CFO and her staff to listen to what we have to say about the accounts receivable problem, but I don't think we have moved them one step forward. They simply do not see that the problems come from the process. First they blamed the manager and the department, then our customers, and then the sales force. Who knows who they will blame next. They simply can't see that accounts receivable is a process like any other process. Even the back-of-the-envelope study we did gives good hints on how to improve the process dramatically. If the IRR is less than 200%, I'll push a peanut with my nose from the CFO's office to the water cooler. Ah, come on now, what are you two laughing at? I'm serious."

Hamid looked at Bill and said: "Hey, don't be so pessimistic. We made good progress the last few months. The whole team learned a lot about the receivables situation, you have become a quality champion—or perhaps I should say a "quality fanatic"—and our boss did promise to go to that seminar on quality in finance. I think she has learned a lot more than you realize. That's not so bad for slipping this extra work into all our regular responsibilities. Look, we even learned that we only need four and a half hours of sleep at night!"

A month later, when their boss returned from the finance and quality-management seminar, Jan said to Hamid and Bill, "I don't know whether to celebrate or panic."

Their boss, the company's CFO, had really been turned on by the seminar. She "rewarded" the team with a new assignment, one to be added to their already large collection of individual responsibilities. The new task was wide open: "Get Finance started in quality management." No other guidance. No other directions. And no indication, as of yet, of what resources would be available.

"Ohhhhh boy," said Hamid to his friends, exhaling slowly, "Now we've really done it. Where do we start?"

NET Present Value
A good place to learn more about how quality management can improve financial and other processes is at the research page of the Juran Institute website: www.juran.com/research/back_articles.html

There are a variety of ways Hamid's team could "get started in quality management." The team could start learning and using the statistical and process improvement tools that are widely used by companies that have achieved rapid improvements in quality. It could study selected financial processes in other organizations and attempt to adapt the more promising approaches to its own company. It could start an inquiry into finance's mission in the total organization with the intent of developing a new mission statement. One way many quality experts recommend starting is by improving a highly visible process important to the organization—especially a process with a history of chronic problems that traditional approaches have not solved. Achieving major improvements in a visible, important, and troublesome process can demonstrate to the organization the value of managing for quality. The receivables problem from the previous chapter might be just such a project.

1. Three Keys to Revolutionary Rates of Improvement

One hallmark of the global quality revolution is the repeated success of many organizations in achieving revolutionary rates of quality improvement—not just 5% or 10% reductions in costs or defects, and not merely shortening cycle time from 30 days to 28. Financial executives in companies with such achievements talk of successes such as a 50% reduction in costs, ten times improvement in quality in two years, doubling market share, and cutting cycle time from eight days to four hours. These dramatic improvements come from many sources. Three very important ones are (1) internal projects, (2) external borrowing, and (3) broad organizational changes.

Internal projects Systematic, team-based quality-improvement projects are seen by many managers and quality experts as the single most important key to revolutionary rates of quality improvement. The extent to which team-based quality-improvement projects contribute to dramatic rates of improvement is a function of three factors: (1) number of teams, (2) project importance combined with team effectiveness, and (3) spread of team results.

The first factor is simply the number of teams in place. The greater the number of teams, the greater the opportunity to discover or invent improved processes. The second factor has two components: the importance of each project and the effectiveness of the team in executing its work. The third factor is the extent to which each project can be spread—"replicated"—throughout the organization.[15]

External borrowing The second major source of revolutionary rates of quality improvement is adopting and adapting improvements from other organizations. All companies that have made dramatic improvements in quality have also made significant progress in defeating one of the major barriers to organizational improvement—the "NIH syndrome." NIH stands for "not invented here," an all too common attitude that rejects the successes of other companies, or even other departments within the same company, because they were not developed by one's own organizational unit. Major new opportunities for improvement occur when organizations become aggressive in adopting others' useful ideas. Companies, like the textile company Milliken Corporation, refer to adopting good ideas from others as "stealing shamelessly" and are proud of their ability to bury NIH as a company attitude.

Competitive benchmarking, a quality-improvement tool, discussed later in this chapter, is used to make such borrowing a systematic part of managing.

Broad organizational changes Changes that align the individual elements of the organization with emerging modern management practices can also make major contributions to improved organizational performance. Such changes are also necessary to support and sustain the two sources of improvement just discussed. The transition from traditional management methods to modern customer-focused, quality-based management practices involves many changes

---

[15] **Cross-reference:** These factors are discussed in more detail in Web Appendix 13A.

throughout an organization. These changes include increased participation of employees in decision making, greater commitment to developing and using valid data, breaking down barriers that weaken effective collaboration among organizational departments, and many others.

The secret to the success of this type of contribution is to have a reasonably clear vision of what the emerging management system looks like so individuals and parts of the organization can be supported in moving toward that vision. Improvements in this realm are usually "opportunistic" in the good sense of opportunism—seeing an unpredictable opportunity to move the organization forward and acting in a timely way when that opportunity arises. Jan, Hamid, and Bill made just such a contribution when they talked their boss into attending the finance and quality-management seminar. The training from that seminar helped her to align her knowledge, values, and priorities with the organizational requirements for sustaining rapid improvement. Her open invitation "to get started in quality management" provides another such opportunity.

2. A Model of Process Management and Improvement

As Bill, Hamid, and Jan's team continues its inquiry into process improvement, having a fuller understanding of process management and improvement methods will be useful. Figure 13.3 presents a widely used model of process-management activities that is receiving increasing attention from financial managers. This diagram has been called the "Juran Breakthrough Cycle" and the "Juran Trilogy." It suggests how the quality-related costs of a process can be brought down over time. The cycle has three parts focused on process quality: quality planning, qual-

FIGURE 13.3

The Juran Trilogy. Quality planning, quality control, and quality improvement combine to improve work processes.

Source: The Juran Institute. Used with permission.

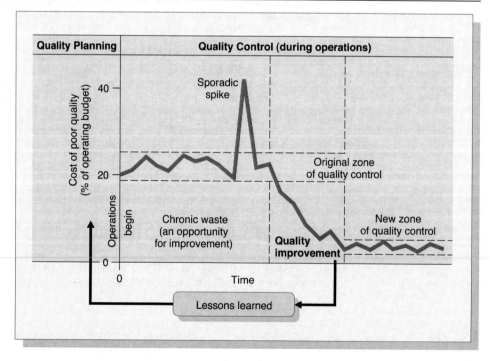

ity control, and quality improvement. The vertical dimension (y-axis) is the cost of poor quality, the cost to the company of known and unknown errors from weaknesses in the process. The horizontal dimension (x-axis) is time. The vertical axis could also be used to record the number of defects or errors in a process, such as the number of payroll checks incorrectly written or the amount of accounts receivable overdue more than 30 days. The figure is normally drawn so that downward movement over time indicates improvement.

Quality planning The first activity in achieving excellent financial processes is quality planning—creating processes that will be able to meet established goals under a wide range of operating conditions. Most financial (and other organizational) processes in use today were not originally designed with quality in mind. Rather, they simply grew over time, being modified as new demands were placed on them and with patchwork changes made when they seemed not to work very well. Such processes often present opportunities for dramatic improvements in customer satisfaction; reductions in cycle time, defect rates, and costs; and increased work enjoyment for the organizational members who work in them.

Quality control Juran describes the next stage—using Figure 13.3 as his illustration—in terms familiar to any of us who have struggled to function in a system that doesn't work very well:

> Following the planning, the process is turned over to the operating forces. Their responsibility is to run the process at optimal effectiveness. Due to deficiencies in the original planning, the process runs at a high level of chronic waste. That waste was planned into the process, in the sense that the planning process failed to plan it out. Because the waste is inherent in the process, the operating forces are unable to get rid of the chronic waste. If it does get worse (sporadic spike), a fire fighting team is brought in to determine the cause or causes of this abnormal variation. Once the cause(s) has been determined, and corrective action is taken, the process again falls into the zone defined by the "quality control" limits.[16]

In many companies, the large area of chronic waste has become accepted as normal, a cost of doing business. As long as sporadic spikes do not occur too often, the performance of the process is considered satisfactory. A major impact of the quality revolution has been the discovery that the large area of chronic waste in Figure 13.3 is not inevitable—that it can be removed, producing enormous positive impacts on market share, revenue, costs, and profitability.

Quality improvement The third stage of the breakthrough cycle is quality improvement. In this stage, systematic approaches of the types discussed in this chapter are used to achieve dramatic improvements in the process. The chronic waste that had become accepted by managers and nonmanagers alike as "the best we can do, given the way things are around here" is eliminated. The starting point is to begin seeing the chronic waste as no longer inevitable and acceptable. We will use the term *project-by-project-improvement* to refer to the organizationwide use of numerous teams working on continuous improvement projects.

---

[16] **Reference:** J. M. Juran, "The Quality Trilogy." *Quality Progress,* Aug. 1986, page 20.

3. Organizational Transformation

Organizational transformation refers to the large and small changes in all components of an organization as it moves from one state to another. Many of the changes in financial managing practices described in this book are part of this process of organizational transformation. As American and other companies adjust to a world of increasing competitiveness, all parts of the organization experience new pressures for change. The changes occurring in finance are also occurring in the other functional areas of the organization—accounting, marketing, human resources, legal, and so on.

Process Improvement Tools

Three sets of quality-management tools used by some innovative finance departments can be readily identified: quantitative-statistical-analytical tools; behavioral tools; and competitive benchmarking. These organizations also adopt a team-based systematic quality improvement process.

1. Quantitative-Statistical-Analytical Tools

Figure 13.4 presents the summary of how to achieve performance excellence through systematic quality improvement identified in the application for the Malcolm Baldrige National Quality Award. One of these particularly close to the heart of most financial managers is "measurement, analysis, and knowledge management" which demands a strong commitment to gather and use data for analysis and decision making rather than to rely too heavily on opinion and judgment. And, central to gathering and using data well are a set of quantitative-statistical-analytical tools some of which are listed in Figure 13.5. These seven are frequently called the "seven classical tools of statistical process control."[17]

FIGURE 13.4
Criteria for Performance Excellence through systematic quality improvement. All seven criteria must be in place for a company to achieve Baldrige Award-level quality.

Source: 2011-2012 Criteria for Performance Excellence, Baldrige Performance Excellence Program, page iv.

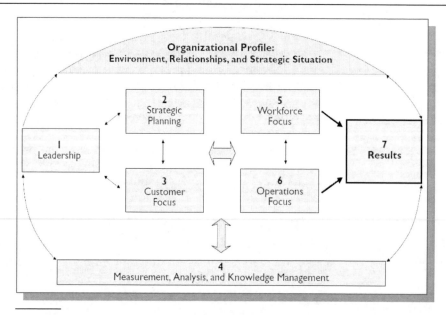

[17] **Cross-reference:** The "seven classical tools" are discussed further in Web Appendix 13B.

FIGURE 13.5
The seven classical tools of statistical process control. These tools form the basis for gathering and analyzing process data.

- Bar charts and histograms
- Pareto charts
- Scatter diagrams
- Run charts
- Control charts
- Cause-and-effect (also called Ishikawa or fishbone) diagrams
- Flow charts

For our work in financial managing at this stage, it is not necessary for most readers to learn how to use these tools or even to learn their names and nature if they are not already familiar with them. However, it is important to remember four things about the basic tools in Figure 13.5. First, all are fairly simple to learn and use. The most difficult requires roughly eighth-grade arithmetic skills for full mastery. Second, in most organizations that have made great progress in quality improvement, virtually all organizational members are familiar with the tools and are able to use them. Third, these tools are used repeatedly to improve organizational processes, products, and services; to communicate about problems, opportunities, and improvements; and to accomplish myriad daily tasks. Using these tools becomes simply a part of everyday work to get the job done.

The fourth thing to remember may be the most important of all for individuals studying finance. Although these tools do not require sophisticated mathematical skills, some of them do use numbers intensively. Many people are quite uncomfortable with mathematics whereas individuals interested in financial managing are much less likely to have such fears and to suffer from what John Allen Paulos called "innumeracy" in his best-selling book with that title.[18] Because of their comfort with numbers, financial managers are well placed to play leading roles in adopting these tools and in teaching them to others. Therefore, it is quite important that students of finance get to know these tools and their potential for contributing to a company's financial health and success.[19]

2. Behavioral Tools

Examples of behavioral tools are listed in Figure 13.6.[20] Again, it is not necessary to master these tools at this time, but, like the basic quantitative tools, a few things

FIGURE 13.6
Selected behavioral tools of quality management. These tools enable employee development and participation in quality improvement.

- Brainstorming
- Nominal group technique
- Task-force management processes
- Self-directed, self-managing, and self-leading work teams
- Active listening
- QIT (quality-improvement team) processes
- Business process reengineering techniques

[18] **Reference:** John Allen Paulos, "Innumeracy: Mathematical Illiteracy and its Consequences." New York: Vintage Books, 1990.

[19] **Cross-reference:** Web Appendix 13B also lists some additional analytical tools that are being adopted by many organizations. Some are fairly sophisticated analytical tools. Others are specialized planning and analysis tools.

[20] **Cross reference:** The behavioral tools are discussed further in Web Appendix 13C.

FIGURE 13.7
A quality storyboard process. The process has six steps.

1. Identify a project.
2. Establish the project.
3. Diagnose the cause.
4. Remedy the cause.
5. Hold the gains.
6. Replicate results and nominate new projects.

are important to remember. First, these behavioral tools are learned by virtually all organizational members. Second, they are widely used in daily work in companies making rapid progress in quality improvement.

Points one and two are directly parallel to the first two points about the quantitative tools, but points three and four are not. Third, unlike the basic quantitative tools, many of these behavioral tools are not easy to use. They require a new way of thinking, new ways of behaving as individuals, and new ways of working with others and in teams. These new ways are frequently different from our old ways that have become comfortable habits for ourselves and that we have often assumed "work just fine, thank you." And fourth, individuals interested in financial managing may not have any special advantages in learning to use these behavioral tools. All of them are conceptually fairly easy to understand, like the nominal group technique and effective task-force management processes. And all are within the intellectual and interpersonal capabilities of virtually every organizational member. But most require the development of considerable interpersonal skills for effective use and considerable personal behavioral discipline to continue their use over and over again. In the "heat" of day-to-day managing, it is easy to forget to use these behavioral tools. Ironically, successes with them in the past may create a temptation to take a shortcut or to forget to use them in the future. Yet, in spite of these difficulties, many organizations and many financial managers have made major progress in adopting these tools.

3. Competitive Benchmarking

NET Present Value
A good discussion of benchmarking may be found at the American Society for Quality website:
asq.org/learn-about-quality/benchmarking/overview/tutorial.html

Competitive benchmarking is a term used in quality management to describe the activity of discovering and achieving outstanding products, services, and processes. It involves identifying a superb example of a process, service, or product; setting that example as a standard to be matched or exceeded; and then doing so.[21]

Competitive benchmarking has become a widely used tool in companies committed to quality management. Motorola's success in shortening the time required to close its corporate books each month is described later in this chapter. However, closing the books is only one of many financial processes Motorola has improved dramatically. As a result of these successes, many activities of Motorola's finance function have become the competitive benchmark for other companies.

---

[21] **Cross reference:** The competitive benchmarking process of Xerox—one of the American leaders in developing this process—is summarized in Web Appendix 13A.

IDENTIFY PROJECT	ESTABLISH PROJECT		CURRENT STATUS		
	SELECT TEAM	VERIFY MISSION	RECENT MINUTES	CURRENT ACTIVITIES	CAN YOU HELP?

		DIAGNOSE CAUSE			
ANALYZE SYMPTOMS	CONFIRM OR MODIFY MISSION	FORMULATE THEORIES	TEST THEORIES		IDENTIFY ROOT CAUSE(S)

		REMEDY CAUSE			
EVALUATE ALTERNATIVES	DESIGN REMEDY	DESIGN CONTROLS	DESIGN FOR CULTURE	PROVE EFFECTIVENESS	IMPLEMENT

FIGURE 13.8
Quality storyboard. Progress on each step of a quality project is tracked and displayed.
Source: The Juran Institute. Used with permission.

4. A Systematic Process

Companies pursuing revolutionary rates of quality improvement use teams following a systematic step-by-step process. In pursuing their goal of delighting customers, some teams place more emphasis on reducing errors, some on eliminating unnecessary steps, and some on reducing the time required to complete activities, but each emphasis supports the other two.

The philosophy behind these team-based approaches is that: "Truly revolutionary improvement requires: (1) identifying . . . the most important opportunities, (2) assembling the right team to make the improvement, (3) realizing the maximum benefit from each quality improvement project, and (4) completing each project as quickly as the particular problem will permit."[22]

For smaller projects, many companies have found it useful to record and display the progress of each team on a "quality storyboard." Figures 13.7 and 13.8 show one such multistep quality-improvement process and the storyboard that is used with it. Larger projects are also attacked in team-based ways, but the process might be called a task-force project, "process reengineering," or "business process quality management."

The quality storyboard process shown in Figure 13.8 shows four of the six steps noted in Figure 13.7. There are many versions of this storyboard approach. Some,

---

[22] **Reference:** *Quality Improvement Storyboard* (Wilton, Conn.: The Juran Institute) 1992, page 1.

like the one in Figure 13.7, involve as few as 6 steps while others have as many as 12. Teams using this process give their members formal roles, such as team leader, facilitator, timekeeper, and scribe (recorder of the team's work). The progress of the team is usually recorded regularly on the storyboard, which is displayed in a prominent place. The storyboard in Figure 13.8 records progress on the first four steps and allows space to include some additional information.[23]

Examples of Improvements in Financial Processes

Throughout this book we have presented examples of ways finance has used quality approaches to serve its customers better and to improve its processes. For example, in Chapter 2 we described how Southern Pacific used quality initiatives to identify cost-saving improvements, and in Chapter 12 we discussed Corning's use of Key Results Indicators to improve cash deliveries. In this section we present two more examples of improvements in financial processes in somewhat greater detail than most of the other examples.[24]

"Which tie says, 'Here's the man responsible for positive cash flow from an outmoded operation in a depressed industry'?"

---

[23] **Reference:** We illustrate and discuss each step in a quality improvement process for a financial process in Web Appendix 13A.

[24] **Cross-reference:** A third example, reengineering Ford's account payable process is described in Web Appendix 13D.

1. Closing the Books at Motorola[25]

NET Present Value
Motorola is at:
www.motorola.com

In the early 1980s, the finance function of Motorola, the large manufacturer of electronic and communications equipment, recognized the need to join the company's progress in improving quality at a revolutionary rate. The pilot application in finance was the process of closing the corporate books each month—consolidating the financial statements from all units of the company.

As the project began, the monthly close averaged 9 working days. As a result, an updated forecast for the coming month was not available until 11 or 12 working days into the month. The monthly operating committee meeting to review the prior month's activities and the current month's plan was typically held a week later. Management was getting information for last month with the next already two-thirds over. And, many people in the Motorola financial function around the world worked very hard at the end of every month to provide this information.

To improve this business process, Motorola set the ambitious goal of reducing the closing time to 4 days by the first quarter of 1990 and 2 days by the end of 1992. As David Hickie, at that time senior vice president and assistant chief financial officer, pointed out,

> If you tell people to close the books in 7 days instead of 8, they will figure out how to do it very easily. They will work a little overtime over the weekend. If you say do it in 6 days, they will work on Sunday. But they would not change what they were doing. When we told them to do it in 4 days and that we would not let them use the weekend as a crutch, they had to look at a fundamental change in the process.

In examining the closing process, Motorola found that much of the cycle time was absorbed correcting erroneous journal entries, waiting for data from overseas units, and entering and correcting data in a headquarters computer. Efforts to improve these situations reduced monthly journal entry errors from roughly 8,000 to 2. Overseas data were forwarded directly to the United States rather than through three intermediate locations that routinely approved the data after considerable delay. Bringing back in-house the data-entry activity that was performed by an outside contractor sped up data entry and contributed to reducing errors.

Commenting on the improved process, Ken Johnson, vice president and corporate controller, identified the advantages of closing the books quickly.

> In addition to the cost savings, the early close frees up several hundred finance people for each day removed from the process. They can devote their attention to more important things than just preparing the numbers—like helping our people run the business.

Within two years, Motorola's finance organization had reduced monthly closing time from 9 days to 2 days. Motorola was able to report that speeding up the monthly close from the sixth to fourth day had saved the company $20 million per year. Motorola estimated a further $10 million annual savings was realized when it achieved a 2-day close.

---

[25] **Reference:** James A.F. Stoner and Frank M. Werner, *Finance in the Quality Revolution* (Morristown, N. J.: Financial Executives Research Foundation, 1993), pages 68–70.

2. "Distributing" Credit Analysis to Solectron's Salespeople[26]

Solectron, twice winner of the Malcolm Baldrige National Quality Award and now part of Flextronics International, Inc, is a contract manufacturer of electronic sub-assemblies, a rapidly changing, highly competitive business with very narrow profit margins. Contract manufacturers perform assembly and manufacturing operations for other companies. They compete not only with each other but also with the manufacturing operations of their own customers. Their success depends on their ability to produce at lower costs, greater speed, higher quality, or some combination of these three.

Over the years Solectron developed an effective team-based process for identifying promising customer prospects, evaluating them, and making decisions on their suitability. Finding a way to improve a step that used to come relatively late in the prospect identification process has added to finance's contribution to the entire process. That step involves the decision on the creditworthiness of the prospect and the amount of credit the prospect would be eligible to receive.

In Solectron's early days, there was no formal procedure for checking a customer's creditworthiness. The company was small and did not have appreciable financial resources to extend to customers. In addition, early customers tended to be well-established companies or were identified as prospects through personal contacts and were well known to management. By its second decade in business, however, Solectron had grown to the point where extension of credit was becoming increasingly important and appropriate as it expanded its customer base.

By then, finance had developed an internal credit matrix, a fairly elaborate and traditional credit analysis process similar to commercial bank systems. Unfortunately, the system proved quite cumbersome. Since few members of the sales force had finance skills or desired to take time away from selling, credit analysis was done within the finance organization. Salespeople lost considerable time as they contended for the attention of the company's sole analyst, lobbied for credit approval, and were forced to wait for the credit decision. It was difficult to be responsive to prospects. A negative decision meant that the time invested with a potential customer was wasted, leaving the sales staff, and very likely the rejected prospect, angry and frustrated.

Myron Lee, financial manager with credit responsibility, introduced a simplified process. Finance started dividing potential customers into three groups: "A customers," those who are large and financially healthy and for whom no credit check is required; "B customers," the middle-sized prospects for which it is important to check credit; and "C customers," those that are financially weak and are not to be pursued unless a special strategic rationale exists. Salespeople are free to pursue A customers without further financial review. For B customers, the salesperson now fills out a credit scoring sheet developed by Myron and his colleagues. The form uses easily obtainable data and is simple to fill out. A potential customer's score translates directly into the credit line Solectron is willing to extend.

[26] **Reference:**   James A.F. Stoner and Frank M. Werner, *Finance in the Quality Revolution* (Morristown, N.J.: Financial Executives Research Foundation, 1993), pages 100–102.

The new process empowers the sales staff to make preliminary credit decisions and eliminates the frustration of the prior system. Salespeople know how finance will react before approaching a customer and no longer waste time selling to unacceptable credit risks. Because it is so easy to understand, the form itself teaches the sales staff how and why finance makes the credit decision. Finance staffers are seen as a support system and are no longer the "bad guys" who interfere with sales. By distributing some of his skills to the sales force, Myron Lee eliminated much of his routine work and freed himself to devote more time to supporting strategic marketing decisions.

*H*amid, Jan, and Bill were only three of the dozen individuals who worked on the receivables cross-functional QIT (quality-improvement team) in the previous 11 months. They were also the lowest three in terms of the organization's formal hierarchy. Yet, their boss and all of the other team members recognized that in some sense it was uniquely "their project." And the achievements of the team and of the other organizational members who contributed to the project's success were, in a special way, an acknowledgement of their initiative in "getting started on quality in finance."

In that 11 months, the team had put remedies in place that cut overdue receivables by more than 80%. Changes included many "upstream" activities like more precise specification of sales contracts, less frequent partial shipments, and more timely completion of the service manuals that were part of many sales agreements. There were also changes in more traditional finance responsibilities, including easier to read invoices, more accurate invoice information, and the beginnings of electronic invoicing and payment arrangements with a few of the more sophisticated customers.

By far the most amusing discovery by the team was that 40% of the "overdue receivables" were not overdue at all—they were simply the result of customers deciding not to pay invoices for partial shipments: a legitimate decision even though the items left out of partial shipments were almost always minor items that did not inconvenience the customer and that carried very low price tags. However, awaiting payment was a wise financial decision for the customer—it provided free financing of the purchase, sometimes for as long as six months!

As the team met for the last time to celebrate its successes, Jan grinned at Bill and said, "Well, Quality Champion, now that you don't have to spend so much time on the telephone collecting overdue receivables, I wonder if you'd care to volunteer to find some ways to measure the revenue-increasing benefits of high quality?"

Bill just smiled.

Summary of Key Points

■ **Define a work process and distinguish the tasks of managing and improving financial processes from the other financial managing tasks.** A work process is a series of work activities intended to produce a specific result. As organizations adopt modern customer-focused quality-management practices, their finance members spend more time working in teams to improve financial and other organizational processes. In addition, members of finance continue to work on the traditional and continuing financial management tasks: (1) obtaining financing and selecting long-term investments, (2) managing short-term financial flows, (3) balancing risk and returns in daily and longer-term decisions, and (4) serving as a company resource about financial markets and sources of financing.

■ **Identify financial processes involving external and internal customers or suppliers.** Financial processes focused outside the formal boundaries of the organization include processes for handling transactions with (1) customers, (2) suppliers, (3) government, (4) creditors, and (5) shareholders. Financial processes focused on internal customers include (1) processes related to employees, and (2) processes involving other management activities. Financial processes also are part of almost all of the interanal management processes used to conduct the organization's business.

■ **Use two concepts to describe the nature of financial processes and five steps to describe how a financial process transforms inputs into outputs.** The boundary of a process is the conceptual line drawn for a specific purpose that distinguishes what is part of the process from what is not part of it. *Adding value* is a phrase used to describe those activities performed within a process that make the resulting product or service of greater value to the ultimate and final consumer of the product or service. Describing a process involves (1) describing the product or service produced by the process, (2) specifying the customer(s) of the product or service, (3) identifying suppliers who provide inputs to the process and specifying what inputs they provide, (4) describing each of the activities performed within the process and identifying who performs those activities, and (5) describing the characteristics of satisfactory inputs to the process and satisfactory products or services produced by the process.

■ **Identify five concepts useful in measuring process performance.** Process performance can be measured in terms of effectiveness, efficiency, cycle time, stability, and capability. The key measurement of effectiveness is customer satisfaction—how well a product or service meets or exceeds customer expectations. Efficiency measures the ability of a process to meet customer needs at low cost. Cycle time measures seek to report the length of time that elapses between the start of an activity and its completion. Measures of process stability indicate the extent to which a process exhibits low variation, arising only from random causes built into the process rather than from identifiable, sporadic shocks to the process. Process capability refers to the extent to which a process will yield the intended output under normal operating conditions.

■ **Describe three key factors in achieving revolutionary rates of quality improvement in financial processes and the rest of the organization and describe the Juran model of process improvement.** Revolutionary rates of quality improvement arise from: (1) team-based projects, (2) borrowing from other organizations, and (3) other organizational changes. Team-based contribution is a function of the number of teams, the importance and success of the projects they undertake, and the extent to which successful projects are replicated throughout the organization. Contribution from borrowing from other organizations requires eliminating the NIH syndrome. Broad changes that align the organization with modern quality-management methods offer additional opportunities for improvement and are necessary for supporting and sustaining the first two sources of rapid improvement. The Juran Breakthrough Cycle describes systematic quality improvement as quality planning, quality control, and quality improvement. This cycle can be applied to major business processes (macroprocesses) or portions of such processes (microprocess or subprocesses). Organizational transformation refers to the systematic change of so many aspects of an organization, including its financial systems, that the resulting organization differs dramatically from its original state.

■ **Describe three sets of quality-management tools used to improve financial and other processes and one systematic approach for improving financial and other processes.** Financial managers and other organizational members use: (1) a set of statistical, quantitative, and analytical tools (including Pareto charts, control charts, and cause and effect diagrams); (2) a set of behavioral techniques or tools (including brainstorming, nominal group technique, and business process reengineering); and (3) competitive benchmarking to improve financial and other organizational processes. Almost all companies making dramatic improvements in quality use some form of team-based systematic quality-improvement process. Such processes consist of a series of 6 to 12 clearly defined sequential steps. Team members fulfill roles such as leader, facilitator, time-keeper, and scribe. Team progress is frequently charted and communicated through a quality storyboard.

■ **Describe two examples in which quality-management tools and approaches have been used to improve financial processes.** (1) Motorola reengineered its process for closing its worldwide corporate books each month, reducing errors and rework, reducing the time required from nine days to two, and saving more than $30 million per year. (2) Solectron redesigned its credit approval process to enable sales representatives to determine whether a potential customer would eventually receive credit at the very beginning of the customer prospecting task rather than late in the process. By doing so, the company avoids wasting customer development efforts, speeds credit approval, and avoids disappointing the sales staff and rejected customers.

Questions

1. Why are the collections activities of a company considered a process? What is the benefit of thinking of it in this way?

2. What is the relationship of a work process to a business system?

3. Name five finance processes with *external* customers or suppliers. For each, identify at least one supplier and one customer.

4. Name five finance processes with *internal* customers or suppliers. For each, identify at least one supplier and one customer.

5. What is a process boundary? Identify the process boundary of the payroll process. Explain the purpose of drawing the boundary as you did.

6. Why is cycle time one of the most important measures of quality performance?

7. "All processes have natural variation." Comment on this statement.

8. Distinguish between common causes and special causes of variation.

9. What three factors influence the impact of team-based quality-improvement projects on the rate of companywide improvement? Why is each of the three important?

10. Describe the three components of Juran's "Quality Trilogy."

11. Describe a process from your own experience that performed poorly because quality was not planned in from the beginning.

12. Can you think of a situation in your own experience in which poor quality was intentionally planned into a process, product, or service?

13. What are the "seven classical tools of statistical process control"?

14. Identify seven behavioral tools used in quality management.

15. What is competitive benchmarking? Identify an example of an excellent process, product, or service you think might be good enough to benchmark.

16. Describe six steps in a typical quality storyboard process. Pick a finance process and describe how each of the steps could be applied to a process improvement project.

17. What do the two examples of improvements in finance processes (Motorola and Solectron) have in common? How do they illustrate the concepts of this chapter?

18. How could this chapter be improved to make it more valuable to you?

CHAPTER 14

SELECTING THE BEST

DEBT-EQUITY MIX

*D*ebbie Curtis looked again at the figures on the screen of her computer and shook her head slowly. She now had five sets of figures, and each was quite different from the others. "How to proceed?" she thought.

Debbie was assistant chief financial officer of her company, a business that was growing and in need of new capital funds. She was in the process of contacting several investment banks and other advisors for recommendations on what form the new financing should take.

Debbie's problem was that each person she called gave her another point of view. One investment banker told her that her firm could benefit from greater financial leverage and should issue long-term debt. Another pointed out the company's strong stock price and recommended a sizeable equity issue. An analyst at a large investment fund reminded her that her company's debt ratio was not in line with the industry—perhaps her company should attend to that. But a distinguished professor at the nearby university told her that her firm's choice of financing wasn't very important, so the firm could raise its money any way it found most convenient. There seemed to be no agreement on what was right for her company.

In an effort to sort through the conflicting recommendations, Debbie had constructed pro-forma financial statements for each recommendation using the spreadsheet program on her computer. The differences among the pro-forma statements were significant. As she looked at the computer screen again, she found herself wondering just what was the best financing mix for her firm.

debt-equity mix—the combination of debt and equity financing employed by a firm

capital structure—the combination of long-term debt and equity financing employed by a firm, often used as a synonym for *the debt-equity mix*

The **debt-equity mix** refers to the composition of the right side of a company's balance sheet—in particular, how much of the firm's financing comes from borrowing (debt) and how much is contributed by stock investors (equity). It is also called the firm's **capital structure,** where *capital* refers to long-term financing, even though most firms include some short-term debt in their financing mix.

Financial theorists disagree on the importance of the debt-equity mix to the value of the firm. On the one extreme are the "traditionalists," who say that it is important to get the mix of funds just right to generate high value for investors. On the other extreme are Professors Modigliani and Miller, both Nobel laureates in economics, who argue that if it were not for imperfections in the financial markets, the debt-equity mix would play no role at all in establishing the value of the firm. In between are a full spectrum of financial theorists and practitioners for whom the debt-equity mix decision carries some degree of importance. In this chapter we will meet them all. Debbie will have to understand the competing views on the debt-equity mix decision if she is to help her firm make a reasoned choice.

Key Points You Should Learn from This Chapter

After reading this chapter you should be able to:

- Define operating and financial leverage and describe their relationship to fixed costs.
- Discuss why a company's financing choice might affect the market value of its securities.
- Describe four theories that attempt to explain the optimal mix of debt and equity financing.
- Describe how companies approach the debt-equity mix decision in practice.
- Explain why the debt-equity mix differs by industry.

Introductory Concepts—Leverage

Leverage is magnification. We are all familiar with common examples of leverage in the physical world: a screwdriver that magnifies the force of a hand to turn a screw, a crowbar that magnifies the force of an arm to lift a heavy weight, a power braking system that magnifies the force of a foot to stop a car. An automobile or bicycle transmission, with its multiple gears to magnify the engine's or rider's power, is a particularly sophisticated form of leverage, adjusting the amount of magnification as needed to meet road conditions.[1]

In business, leverage is also magnification. But instead of the magnification taking a physical form, business leverage deals with the magnification of profits. Rather than a crowbar or screwdriver or gear, the lever in a business is its fixed costs. And, instead of some physical force pressing against the lever, in business it is changing sales that pushes the firm toward higher or lower profitability.

We introduced the nature of variable and fixed costs in Chapter 2.[2] The same concepts hold here. A variable cost is one that changes with changes in sales, while a fixed cost is one that remains constant as the level of sales varies. Although it is likely that most costs are neither totally variable nor totally fixed, we will continue to make the convenient assumption that all costs can be classified as either fixed or variable.

1. Two Types of Fixed Costs: Operating and Financial

Fixed costs come in two varieties: operating and financial. Figure 14.1 is an income statement with its top half in managerial form.[3] The top half of the statement (lightly shaded) is the operating half. It begins with sales and ends with EBIT, and records operating revenues and expenses. In this half of the statement, fixed operating costs—those incurred in the production and delivery of the firm's products and services—are identified directly. The bottom half of the statement (more darkly shaded) is the financial half. It begins with EBIT and includes the division of earnings after taxes (EAT) by the number of outstanding common shares to produce earnings per share (EPS). This half of the statement details how operating earnings (EBIT) are distributed: to creditors (interest), to the government (taxes), and to shareholders (earnings per share).[4] The fixed financing cost is interest, which must be paid regardless of the level of earnings,[5] and it arises when a company elects to finance with debt.

---

[1] **Observation:** In British business English, leverage is referred to as *gearing*, a usage based on this form of physical magnification.

[2] **Cross-reference:** Chapter 2, pages 46–47.

[3] **Explanation:** Rather than the GAAP cost categories of "cost of goods sold" and "operating expenses," this form of the income statement groups operating costs by their behavior—variable or fixed—making it easier for financial analysts to project costs should revenues change.

[4] **Observation and cross-reference:** We have omitted dividends paid to preferred shareholders from Figure 14.1 to avoid complexity in the illustration. The income statement of a company that pays a preferred dividend is presented in Web Appendix 14B in both statement and algebraic form.

[5] **Observation:** Corporate debt often carries a "variable interest rate," making interest costs a function of the level of interest rates. With respect to a company's profitability, however, interest costs are fixed since they are not tied to sales or EBIT.

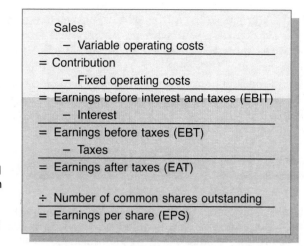

FIGURE 14.1
A simplified income statement in managerial form. The statement can be divided into an operating half and financial half, each with fixed costs.

Choosing between fixed and variable operating costs   Often a company has limited choice over its fixed operating costs. Some firms' resources are heavily weighted toward capital equipment because of the technology of their industries and they have no viable variable cost alternatives. For example, it is hard to imagine how a steel mill could replace a foundry with a more variable cost resource such as temporary labor. Other companies are characterized by costs that are primarily variable and have no practical fixed cost alternatives. An example is the hairdressing industry, where the personal skill of the practitioner and the relationship between hairdresser and customer cannot easily be replaced by machinery. On the other hand, some companies face a choice of operating resources that permits them to choose between variable and fixed costs. For example, a computer may be built in an automated factory with fixed assembly costs or it may be constructed by piecework laborers, making assembly costs quite variable.

Choosing between fixed and variable financing costs   Unlike the choice between fixed and variable operating costs, there are typically no technological barriers that prevent a firm from financing with different mixes of debt and equity. However, there often are practical limitations. Small firms rarely have good access to the capital markets. They cannot sell stock easily and often cannot place long-term debt. Their sole sources of external financing are through banks, insurance companies, etc., and their financing choices are limited to short- and intermediate-term debt. Larger firms do have good capital market access and can select more freely between debt and equity financing. To the extent a company can finance with either debt or equity funds, it can determine its level of fixed financing costs by its debt-equity mix.

2. Two Types of Leverage: Operating and Financial

operating leverage— magnification of changes in operating earnings (EBIT) in response to changes in sales that is caused by the existence of fixed operating costs in the firm's cost structure

Since there are two types of fixed costs, there are also two types of leverage. **Operating leverage** is caused by the fixed costs of operations and is the magnification in the operating (top) half of the income statement—how EBIT responds to a change in sales as diagrammed in Figure 14.2. When a company's sales change,

NET Present Value
Leverage is explained
further at
www.referenceforbusiness.
com/encyclopedia/ Kor-
Man/Leverage.html

its EBIT changes as well, but the amount of the change depends on the firm's operating leverage. In a firm with no operating leverage (no fixed costs), profits change at the same rate as sales. For example, if a firm with no fixed operating costs experiences a 10% sales increase, its EBIT will be up by 10% as well. A firm with operating leverage (with fixed costs) will find its EBIT changing by more than the change to sales. For this type of firm, a 10% sales increase will lead to a greater-than-10% increase in EBIT.

FINANCE IN PRACTICE

The Blurring of Fixed and Variable Operating Costs

Traditionally it has been easy to identify which operating costs were variable and which were fixed. Labor resources were the variable costs because labor, not too highly skilled, could be hired or laid off as needed. One worker was very much like another, and there was little cost to the business if there were turnover in the workforce. Capital resources were the fixed costs since it was often difficult to add or reduce plant and machine capacity at will. Plant took a while to build and place on-line. It was not easy to sell off unused plant and equipment since there was not a good market for those resources.

Today it is far more difficult to identify a type of operating cost with a type of resource. In many cases, labor is now a relatively fixed cost of operations while plant and equipment has become a variable cost. Several trends are behind this shift:

1. As business has moved toward the use of higher technology, the typical worker brings a much greater degree of skill to the workplace than in the past. In fact, for many companies, the knowledge, skill, and capability of their employees is now their most critical resource. It is more difficult than in the past to lay off workers and then rehire comparable employees.

2. Training is expensive, and the cost of training new workers can exceed the cost savings from reducing staff in a downturn.

3. Insights gained from companies pursuing quality management have convinced many companies that the improvement in productivity and quality of output from a work force that knows its jobs are safe more than compensates for the inability to reduce staff in periods of slow business activity.

4. Improvements in leasing have made many kinds of capital resources available to businesses on a temporary basis.

5. Modular plant and multipurpose equipment have been designed so that resources that are unneeded in one area of the business can be redeployed elsewhere.

6. Advances in transportation and communications have lessened the importance of having all capital resources in one location, thus broadening the market for unused plant and equipment.

7. The concept of the "virtual corporation," a fluid series of joint ventures with other companies, means highly complex resources can be obtained and released quickly as required.

In today's environment, financial managers can no longer rely on broad classifications such as "labor" and "capital" to assess which operating costs are variable and which are fixed. Rather, each element of cost must be studied to understand its overall role in the firm's production resource mix.

FIGURE 14.2
The operating half of the income statement. Operating leverage is the responsiveness of EBIT to changes in sales.

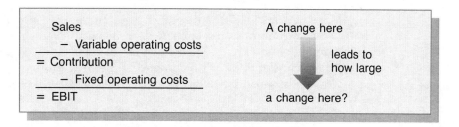

financial leverage— magnification of changes in earnings per share (EPS) in response to changes in EBIT that is caused by the existence of fixed financing costs (interest obligations) in the firm's cost structure

Financial leverage is caused by fixed financing costs and is the magnification in the financial (bottom) half of the income statement—how earnings per share responds to a change in EBIT as sketched in Figure 14.3. In a firm with no financial leverage (no interest costs), EPS changes at the same rate as EBIT. For example, if a firm financed solely with equity experiences a 10% increase in its EBIT, its per-share earnings will be up by 10% as well. By contrast, a firm financed partly with debt (and, therefore, responsible for interest costs) will find its earnings per share changing by more than the change to EBIT. For this kind of firm, a 10% increase to EBIT would lead to a greater-than-10% increase in its EPS.[6]

Financing Choice Might Change a Company's Value

A company's financial leverage affects both the returns and risk it provides to its stakeholders. Returns change due to the magnification of profits. Risk changes because magnified profits are more volatile. As a firm adds to its debt, increasing its financial leverage, it becomes increasingly sensitive to changes in its level of operating profits (EBIT). Small increases in EBIT produce large increases in earnings per share (EPS). And, small decreases in EBIT produce large decreases in earnings per share.

For high amounts of debt, all stakeholders are exposed to the increased risk—a firm that is having trouble making interest payments will also have trouble making other payments and providing a stable environment for its stakeholders. For low amounts of debt, the increased risk from leverage is felt primarily by the company's stockholders since they bear the residual variability of the firm's income stream. For this reason, and because corporate finance theory has been derived with the goal of shareholder wealth maximization, the issue of leverage is usually evaluated from the point of view of the firm's stockholders.

FIGURE 14.3
The financial half of the income statement. Financial leverage is the responsiveness of EPS to changes in EBIT.

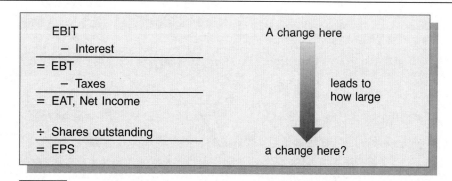

---

[6] **Cross-reference:**   For a discussion of the impact of leverage on the income statement in more detail and three useful financial ratios that measure the amount of magnification, see Web Appendix 14A.

The best debt-equity mix will depend on the way in which investors react to the risk and return issues contained in financial leverage. As customers of the firm, investors deserve the highest value for their participation in the business. Management should select the financing mix that produces the risk-return combination most satisfying to the financial markets, hence that produces the highest value for the firm's securities.

1. How Financial Leverage Changes Returns and Risk

To understand these ideas better, Debbie Curtis constructs the bottom half of her company's income statement for two levels of debt. First, she assumes that interest costs are $20,000 and that there are 8,000 shares outstanding. For the second case, she assumes the company has used more debt and, correspondingly, less equity, so that interest costs are $30,000 and there are 7,000 shares outstanding.

Examples

The Impact of Financial Leverage on Returns and Risk

Debbie's company has EBIT of $100,000 and is in the 35% tax bracket.

Question: Construct the bottom half of the company's income statement for Debbie's two cases.

Solution steps:

	Case 1	Case 2
EBIT	$ 100,000	$ 100,000
− Interest	20,000	30,000
= EBT	80,000	70,000
− Taxes	28,000	24,500
= EAT	$ 52,000	$ 45,500
÷ Number of shares	8,000	7,000
= EPS	$ 6.50	$ 6.50

Question: Repeat the analysis for EBIT of $80,000.

Solution steps:

	Case 1	Case 2
EBIT	$ 80,000	$ 80,000
− Interest	20,000	30,000
= EBT	60,000	50,000
− Taxes	21,000	17,500
= EAT	$ 39,000	$ 32,500
÷ Number of shares	8,000	7,000
= EPS	$ 4.88	$ 4.64

Question: Repeat the analysis for EBIT of $120,000.

Solution steps:

	Case 1	Case 2
EBIT	$ 120,000	$ 120,000
− Interest	20,000	30,000
= EBT	100,000	90,000
− Taxes	35,000	31,500
= EAT	$ 65,000	$ 58,500
÷ Number of shares	8,000	7,000
= EPS	$ 8.13	$ 8.36

Answer: For EBIT of $100,000, both financing plans produce the same EPS of $6.50. However, when EBIT changes, <u>EPS changes by a greater amount</u> when there is $30,000 of interest (down to $4.64, up to $8.36), than when there is only $20,000 of interest (down to $4.88, up to 8.13).

EBIT-EPS analysis—a graph showing how EPS responds to EBIT for various financing alternatives

Figure 14.4, produced from the data of this example and referred to as an **EBIT-EPS analysis,** summarizes Debbie's findings.

2. Finding the Indifference Point

indifference point—the level of EBIT that produces the same EPS regardless of the debt-equity mix

On the right-hand side of the graph of Figure 14.4, EPS is higher if Debbie's company uses a debt level with $30,000 of interest costs. On the left-hand side, EPS is higher if interest costs are $20,000. It will be important for Debbie to locate the **indifference point** at which the two lines intersect. At this level of EBIT, the two financing alternatives produce the same value of EPS, in this case, $6.50. To find this point, we use the algebraic representation of the bottom half of the income statement as given below,[7] fill in the numbers for each alternative, and then equate the two since we are looking for the point where EPS is equal.

$$EPS = \frac{(EBIT - interest) \times (1 - tax\ rate)}{number\ of\ shares}$$

Example

Finding the Indifference Point

Debbie Curtis wishes to locate the point at which the two lines in Figure 14.4 intersect.

Question: What is the indifference point between these two alternatives?

FIGURE 14.4

An EBIT-EPS analysis showing the effect of financial leverage on earnings per share. As a company's interest costs increase, its EPS becomes more volatile, rising and falling by greater amounts.

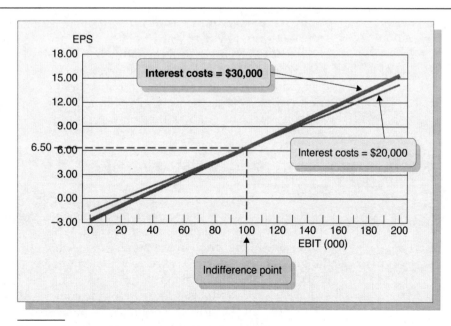

---

[7] **Cross-reference:**   This equation is derived in Web Appendix 14B.

Solution steps:

1. Write the algebraic representation of the bottom half of each income statement for each alternative:

$$\text{Alternative 1: EPS} = \frac{(\text{EBIT} - 20{,}000)(1 - .35)}{8{,}000}$$

$$\text{Alternative 2: EPS} = \frac{(\text{EBIT} - 30{,}000)(1 - .35)}{7{,}000}$$

2. Equate and solve for EBIT:

$$\frac{(\text{EBIT} - 20{,}000)(1 - .35)}{8{,}000} = \frac{(\text{EBIT} - 30{,}000)(1 - .35)}{7{,}000}$$

$$7{,}000(\text{EBIT} - 20{,}000) = 8{,}000(\text{EBIT} - 30{,}000)$$

$$7{,}000(\text{EBIT}) - 140{,}000{,}000 = 8{,}000(\text{EBIT}) - 240{,}000{,}000$$

$$1{,}000(\text{EBIT}) = 100{,}000{,}000$$

$$\text{EBIT} = 100{,}000$$

Answer: Earnings per share will be the same at <u>EBIT of $100,000</u>.

3. Summarizing the Effects of Leverage

To the right of the indifference point (EBIT > $100,000) higher levels of debt increase earnings per share. To the left of the indifference point (EBIT < $100,000) higher debt levels depress earnings per share. And on both sides, risk rises along with debt since debt increases the volatility of EPS. As we have seen throughout this book, high return with low risk is the return-risk combination that provides the highest financial value. Debbie Curtis summarizes what she has learned about financial leverage in this framework:

If EBIT is forecast to be *less than* the indifference point of $100,000, it is best to *avoid debt* since low debt leads to higher profits with less risk. However, if EBIT is forecast to be *greater than* the indifference point of $100,000, there is a *tradeoff between risk and return.* Higher debt increases profits but also increases risk; lower debt reduces risk but also reduces profits. In this case there is no clear financing strategy—the best debt-equity mix will be the one that gives investors the combination of returns and risk they most prefer.

How Investors React to Financial Leverage

The study of how investors react to alternative debt-equity combinations is typically done by looking for the mix that minimizes the company's cost of capital. This is because the minimum cost of capital corresponds precisely to the maximum value of the firm. The reason is straightforward. In Chapter 9 we saw that the price of any security is inversely related to investors' required rate of return: as required rates of return fall, security prices rise, and vice versa. The weighted-average cost of capital is a measure of the combined required rates of return of all investors in the firm. Accordingly, as the cost of capital falls, the combined value of all the firm's securities rises.

There are several ways a firm's cost of capital can be lowered, thereby raising the company's value. One, not under the control of the financial manager, is if the general level of interest rates falls due to a declining pure rate of interest or, more likely, due to falling inflation expectations. The others *are* manageable. The financial manager can be diligent in raising money from those investors who perceive the least amount of risk, hence have lower required rates of return than other investors. The cost of any financing source can be kept down by minimizing flotation costs and by maximizing opportunities for tax deductions. Finally, the cost of capital can be reduced by selecting the mix of debt and equity that produces the lowest weighted-average cost, the subject of this chapter.

In the discussion that follows, we present competing theories of how investors react to various debt-equity combinations. Each is illustrated with a graph showing how the cost of debt (k_d), the cost of equity (k_e), and the resulting weighted-average cost of capital (k_w) change as the financing mix is varied from 100% equity and no debt to 100% debt and no equity. To keep the graphs easy to read, we have assumed that the firm uses only one type of debt and one type of equity. In every case, the minimum value on the weighted-average cost of capital line indicates the optimal debt-equity mix: the mix that maximizes the value of the firm.

1. The Traditional Approach

In the 1950s Professor David Durand summarized prevailing thought about the debt-equity mix and identified three approaches to the issue. The first two, the "net income approach" and the "net operating income approach" seemed illogical in both their assumptions and conclusions and were dismissed by most financial managers. The third philosophy, which Durand called the "traditional approach," made assumptions and reached conclusions deemed much more reasonable and was widely accepted. The three approaches differ primarily in their assumptions about how investors react to increased levels of debt.[8]

The net income approach This approach assumes that neither creditors nor stockholders perceive that increased borrowing adds to their risks, so the firm's cost of debt and cost of equity remain constant regardless of its level of debt. Figure 14.5 summarizes this point of view. The lines for the costs of debt (k_d) and equity (k_e) are drawn horizontally to indicate that they are not changing as the financing mix goes from all equity to all debt. However, since the cost of debt is typically less than the cost of equity, the weighted-average cost of capital (k_w) declines as cheaper debt is substituted for the more expensive equity. The minimum cost of capital, corresponding to maximum value, is reached at the far right-hand side of the graph. As a result, the net income approach concludes that the best financing mix is 100% debt and no equity.

---

[8] **Elaboration:** The net income and net operating income approaches get their names from the way the value of the firm's stock is calculated. Under the net income approach, the value that belongs to shareholders is priced directly by taking the present value of the firm's projected *net income,* using the cost of equity as the discount rate. Under the net operating income approach, we first evaluate the company's total income stream by taking the present value of the firm's projected *net operating income* (EBIT) using the weighted-average cost of capital as the discount rate. Then, since EBIT is claimed by all investors, we subtract the value of the company's debt—the remainder must be the value of the firm's stock.

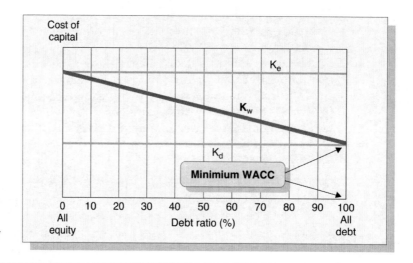

FIGURE 14.5
Capital costs under the net income approach. The optimal debt-equity mix is 100% debt.

The net operating income approach   Like the net income approach, this approach also assumes that creditors do not react to increased debt levels. Stockholders do find a higher debt ratio more risky, but their required rate of return increases to precisely cancel out the advantage of cheaper debt, making the firm's cost of capital constant regardless of its debt-equity mix. Figure 14.6 summarizes this point of view. The line for the cost of debt (k_d) is drawn horizontally to indicate it is not changing as the debt-equity mix goes from all equity to all debt. The line for the cost of equity (k_e) slopes upward, capturing stockholders' increasing required rate of return. The weighted-average cost of capital (k_w) remains constant (horizontal)—as the financing mix is changed to include more debt, the cheaper debt is exactly offset by the increasing cost of the remaining equity. Since there is no low point on the cost of capital line, there is no financing mix that maximizes the firm's value. The net operating income approach concludes that the debt-equity mix is irrelevant. Value comes only from the firm's operating income (EBIT), and any financing mix is as good as any other.

FIGURE 14.6
Capital costs under the net operating income approach. The debt-equity mix is irrelevant since no one mix produces a lower cost of capital, hence higher value, than any other.

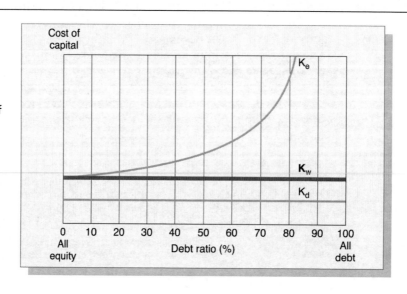

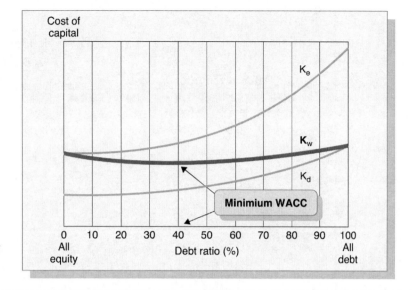

FIGURE 14.7

Capital costs under the traditional approach. The optimal debt-equity mix includes some debt and some equity.

The traditional approach   This approach assumes that both creditors and stockholders perceive that increased borrowing adds to their risks. As a firm increases its debt ratio, both its cost of debt and cost of equity increase. Figure 14.7 summarizes this point of view. The lines for the cost of debt (k_d) and the cost of equity (k_e) are now both drawn with an upward slope. The weighted-average cost of capital (k_w) first declines as cheaper debt is substituted for more expensive equity and then increases, swept up by the rising k_d and k_e. The cost of capital reaches a low point, and the firm's value reaches its maximum, in the middle of the graph. Accordingly, the traditional approach concludes that the best debt-equity mix is somewhere in the middle, a function of the rate at which the risks perceived by investors increase.

Example

The Traditional Approach to the Optimal Debt-Equity Mix

Debbie Curtis is experimenting with the traditional approach as a guide to the best way to finance her company. She has made the following forecasts of how the financial markets would react to alternative mixes of financing:

Debt Ratio	Cost of Debt	Cost of Equity
0%	5.0%	11.0%
10	5.0	11.0
20	5.0	11.2
30	5.3	11.6
40	5.7	12.2
50	6.2	13.2
60	6.8	14.8
70	7.8	16.8
80	9.0	19.2
90	10.4	22.0

Question: What is the optimum debt-equity mix?

Solution steps:

1. Calculate the weighted-average cost of capital for each mix:

Debt Ratio	Debt Proportion × Cost	+	Equity Proportion × Cost	=	WACOC
0%	0% × 5.0%	+	100% × 11.0%	=	11.00%
10	10% × 5.0	+	90% × 11.0	=	10.40
20	20% × 5.0	+	80% × 11.2	=	9.96
30	30% × 5.3	+	70% × 11.6	=	9.71
40	40% × 5.7	+	60% × 12.2	=	**9.60**
50	50% × 6.2	+	50% × 13.2	=	9.70
60	60% × 6.8	+	40% × 14.8	=	10.00
70	70% × 7.8	+	30% × 16.8	=	10.50
80	80% × 9.0	+	20% × 19.2	=	11.04
90	90% × 10.4	+	10% × 22.0	=	11.56

2. Locate the lowest weighted-average cost of capital: The cost of capital reaches a minimum value of 9.60% at a debt ratio of 40%.

Answer: The optimal debt-equity mix is <u>40% debt and 60% equity</u>. At that mix, the weighted-average cost of capital is minimized, hence the value of the firm is at a maximum.

2. Modigliani-Miller Theory

NET Present Value
You can learn more about Professors Modigliani and Miller at:
www.nobelprize.org/
nobel_prizes/economics/
laureates

In the late 1950s, Professors Franco Modigliani and Merton Miller (we'll refer to them as "MM") stunned the finance community by publishing a "proof" that, under certain circumstances, the conclusion of the net operating income approach was in fact correct: there is no optimal financing mix. Although MM's conclusions were the same as those of the net operating income approach, the way they reached their conclusions was very different.

Perfect market assumptions   MM began their analysis by making some simplifying assumptions, in particular, that the financial markets were uncomplicated and without any imperfections. Specifically, MM assumed:

1. Unlimited borrowing and lending is available to both companies and investors at one common interest rate. Individual borrowing to purchase stock is secured by the shares purchased, and the borrowers' liability is limited to the value of the shares. Should a company default on its debt, its creditors would seize the remaining assets and the company would suffer no further loss of value (there are no bankruptcy costs).

2. Firms can be grouped into "equivalent risk classes," groups of companies with the same business risk.

3. Securities trade in perfect capital markets in which every participant is a "price taker," too small to influence prices directly; no transactions costs (brokerage, flotation, transfer taxes, etc.) exist; complete and free information is available to all traders; and securities are infinitely divisible.

4. No taxes are paid on corporate income.

5. Shareholders are indifferent to receiving their returns in the form of dividends or capital gains, and ordinary income and capital gains are taxed at the same rate.

The MM argument   The net effect of assumption 1 is that personal borrowing and lending has the same cost and risk as corporate borrowing and lending. MM argued that if individuals could borrow and lend in the same way as corporations, they would not pay a higher stock price for corporations to do the borrowing or lending for them. What matter to investors are the total return and risk from their investment position, including the impact of corporate borrowing plus the impact of any borrowing or lending they do themselves. Should a company's level of debt be different than desired, each investor could personally borrow or lend to add to or undo any undesired corporate borrowing themselves. For example, if a company borrowed more than an investor thought prudent, that investor could lend (to the government, for example, by investing in Treasury bills) to offset the corporate debt. On the other hand, if a company borrowed less than an investor thought wise, the investor could **buy the stock on margin,** using borrowed funds to help pay for the stock thereby adding more debt to the investment position. Through the use of this **homemade leverage** investors could exactly duplicate corporate leverage, producing the same changes to returns and risk. Accordingly, investors would not care about the debt-equity mix chosen by any corporation.

buying stock on margin— purchasing stock using borrowed money for part of the purchase price

homemade leverage— borrowing by stock investors to leverage their investment portfolio

Assumptions 2 and 3 ensure that two companies with the same operating earnings (EBIT) cannot have different stock prices. By assumption 2, investors can identify companies that have the same business risk. Should two companies with the same earnings stream and the same business risk have different stock prices, investors would arbitrage between them, simultaneously selling the higher-priced stock and purchasing the lower-priced security, leaving their risk-return exposure unchanged while pocketing the difference in price. Assumption 3 guarantees that this would be an easy and costless procedure.

Assumptions 4 and 5 complete the MM argument. If there are no corporate income taxes, the tax system cannot create a value difference between debt and equity financing by allowing companies to deduct some payments to investors (interest) while not others (dividends). If investors are indifferent to the form of their returns, management cannot make the company more valuable to investors by directing the firm's returns into interest versus dividends and capital gains.

Corporate income taxes   Of all MM's assumptions, finance theorists consider the assuming away of corporate income taxes the one most at odds with the real world. Several years after their pathbreaking analysis, MM rederived their conclusions incorporating corporate income taxes. Not surprisingly, they found that in the United States, where interest payments are deductible but dividends are not, a firm can reduce its tax bill by tilting its financing mix toward debt. MM concluded that as long as a firm was profitable and would otherwise pay taxes, the best financing mix was to use as much debt as possible to reduce taxes by as much as possible. MM had revised their prescription for the debt-equity mix from the improbable conclusion of the net operating income approach to the even more improbable conclusion of the net income approach!

3. The Miller (Personal Tax) Model

In 1976, Merton Miller presented another version of the MM model which incorporated personal income taxes. In doing so, he relaxed the assumption that investors are indifferent to the form of their returns. Miller pointed out that: (1) creditors receive the majority of their returns as interest payments while stockholders' returns are far more likely to be in the form of capital gains, and (2) in the United States, interest is taxed at a higher rate than capital gains for two reasons. First, interest is lumped in with other income and taxed at the investor's marginal tax rate while capital gains receive a preferential lower rate. Second, interest is taxed when received while capital gains are not taxed until the security is sold, often many years later. Therefore, to minimize their personal taxes, investors would prefer to see a firm issue equity rather than debt. Miller concluded that the personal tax system's favoring of equity offset some or all of the corporate tax system's favoring of debt financing, and he returned to the original MM conclusion: the debt-equity mix was (essentially) irrelevant to the firm's value.

When Professor Miller studied personal taxes in 1976, long-term capital gains were taxed at only 40% of the taxpayer's marginal rate, so the difference he identified was quite significant for all taxpayers. Today, long-term capital gains do not receive such favorable treatment—they are taxed at a flat rate of 5% or 15%[9] which translates to 33% to 60% of the taxpayer's marginal tax rate. The result: in today's tax environment personal taxes still play an important but somewhat smaller role in the financing mix decision.

4. Compromise Theory

In the years since MM's contributions, finance theorists have been exploring the importance of each of MM's perfect market assumptions—how necessary each assumption is for the MM conclusions to hold. In effect, they have been searching for a compromise between the extreme results of MM and the more intuitively appealing conclusions of the traditional approach. Today, the majority opinion seems to be that there are three significant "imperfections" in the financial environment which tip the financing mix decision toward either equity or debt. These are: (1) the corporate income tax as considered by MM, (2) the costs of corporate bankruptcy, and (3) agency costs.

Corporate income taxes As MM pointed out, the corporate income tax favors debt financing. Interest payments are tax-deductible while dividends are not. A firm that borrows is rewarded with lower income tax payments while a firm that uses equity financing sees no comparable tax reduction.

bankruptcy—the condition of being unable to make payments on debt

Bankruptcy costs The costs associated with **bankruptcy** favor equity financing. MM simplified their analysis by assuming that there are no costs if a firm defaults on its debt. In practice, this is rarely true. When a firm defaults, it generally experiences one or more of the following costs: (1) fees paid to attorneys to control the legal damage; (2) court costs if a legal declaration of bankruptcy is sought to keep creditors at bay; (3) lost sales due to skeptical customers; (4) poor performance by pessimistic employees who spend part or all of their work time looking for other work; (5) impaired long-run viability from management decisions that sacrifice the long run to raise short-run cash; (6) interruptions of busi-

---

[9] **Elaboration and cross-reference:** Taxpayers in the 10% and 15% marginal tax brackets pay 5% on long-term capital gains. Taxpayers in higher marginal tax brackets pay 15%. Refer to Web Appendix 2D for more information on the U.S. personal income tax system.

ness process flow if creditors seize assets; (7) deterioration, obsolescence, and/or vandalism of plant and inventories due to suspension of business activities; and (8) sale of assets at less than full market value to satisfy creditors. Both creditors and stockholders perceive this risk which rises with increased debt levels.

Agency costs   Agency costs also favor equity financing.[10] At high levels of debt, management faces a more difficult task in balancing and aligning the needs of the firm's investment stakeholders. Creditors, concerned that management might act contrary to their best interests, typically impose loan covenants on the firm which restrict management's financial freedom and which must be monitored, usually at the firm's expense. All investors, observing these added costs and management issues, forecast lower EBIT and greater risk as more debt is taken on.

The compromise   Summarizing these effects, the impact of leverage on the value of a firm is often written as follows:

$$V_{levered} = V_{unlevered} + CT - BC - AC$$

where:

$V_{levered}$ = the value of a firm with leverage

$V_{unlevered}$ = the value of the same firm if it had no debt financing

CT = the added value from the corporate tax effect

BC = the reduction in value from the bankruptcy cost effect

AC = the reduction in value from the agency cost effect

Figure 14.8 depicts the conclusions of the compromise theory. As the firm begins to take on debt, the first impact comes from the corporate tax subsidy which lowers the cost of debt (k_d) and pushes down the cost of capital (k_w). With further borrowing, both the cost of debt (k_d) and cost of equity (k_e) lines rise due to the increased risk perceptions from estimates of bankruptcy and agency costs pushing the cost of capital (k_w) line back up. The weighted-average cost of capital (k_w)

FIGURE 14.8

Capital costs under the compromise approach. The cost of capital first falls, due to the corporate income tax effect, and then rises as bankruptcy and agency costs become significant.

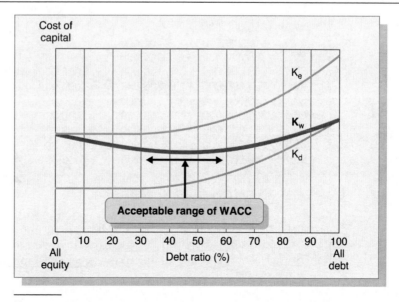

[10] **Cross-reference:**   Agency costs are discussed more fully in Chapter 17.

first declines and then rises. While there is a minimum cost of capital, and hence a corresponding maximum value of the firm, the k_w line is shallow at the bottom, and the precise minimum point is difficult to find. Instead, it is more useful to identify an **acceptable range** within which the cost of capital is at or near its minimum. Any debt-equity mix within the acceptable range is close enough to the optimum so that the cost of being more precise exceeds the possible added value.

acceptable range—the set of debt-equity mixes that produce a weighted-average cost of capital at or near its minimum value

Example

Compromise Theory

Debbie Curtis has estimated the unlevered value of her firm ($V_{unlevered}$) to be $50,000,000, and has also estimated the corporate income tax effect (CT), bankruptcy cost effect (BC), and agency cost effect (AC) for alternative mixes of financing:

Debt Ratio	CT	BC	AC
0%	$ 0	$ 0	$ 0
10	1,700,000	0	200,000
20	3,400,000	0	500,000
30	5,100,000	1,000,000	900,000
40	6,800,000	3,000,000	1,400,000
50	8,500,000	6,000,000	2,000,000
60	10,200,000	10,000,000	2,800,000
70	11,900,000	15,000,000	3,800,000
80	13,600,000	21,000,000	5,000,000
90	15,300,000	28,000,000	6,400,000

Question: What is the acceptable range of the debt-equity mix?

Solution steps:

1. Use the compromise theory relationship to calculate the value of the firm at each possible debt ratio:

$$V_{unlevered} \quad + \quad CT \quad - \quad BC \quad - \quad AC \quad = \quad V_{levered}$$

Debt Ratio	Value of the Firm									
0%:	$50,000,000	+	0	−	0	−	0	=	$50,000,000
10:	$50,000,000	+	1,700,000	−	0	−	200,000	=	$51,500,000
20:	$50,000,000	+	3,400,000	−	0	−	500,000	=	**$52,900,000**
30:	$50,000,000	+	5,100,000	−	1,000,000	−	900,000	=	**$53,200,000**
40:	$50,000,000	+	6,800,000	−	3,000,000	−	1,400,000	=	**$52,400,000**
50:	$50,000,000	+	8,500,000	−	6,000,000	−	2,000,000	=	$50,500,000
60:	$50,000,000	+	10,200,000	−	10,000,000	−	2,800,000	=	$47,400,000
70:	$50,000,000	+	11,900,000	−	15,000,000	−	3,800,000	=	$43,100,000
80:	$50,000,000	+	13,600,000	−	21,000,000	−	5,000,000	=	$37,600,000
90:	$50,000,000	+	15,300,000	−	28,000,000	−	6,400,000	=	$30,900,000

2. Locate the greatest value. The value of Debbie's firm reaches a maximum of $53,200,000 at a debt ratio of 30%.

Answer: From her calculations, Debbie determines the optimal debt-equity mix to be <u>30% debt and 70% equity</u>. However, recognizing the uncertainty in her estimates, she identifies the <u>acceptable range from 20% debt to 40% debt</u>.

Notice that Figure 14.8 looks very much like Figure 14.7, the one for the traditional approach. The only difference, in fact, is how we arrived at our conclusions. In a sense, finance theory has come full circle in its view of the debt-equity mix. We began with the traditional approach, which identified an optimal combination of debt and equity; moved to MM theory, which concluded that any debt-equity combination was okay; then moved on to "MM with corporate taxes," with its call for 100% debt; next flirted with Miller's personal tax theory, which returned us to the original MM position of financing irrelevance; and now have the compromise theory, which once again claims that an optimal combination of debt and equity exists for each company. We anticipate that in the coming years financial managers will see further developments as academics and practitioners make new contributions to the theory, as the government continues to tinker with the income tax code, and as quality-management and sustainability approaches to the alignment of the firm, its managers, and its stakeholders suggest new factors to consider and/or provide new insights into agency and bankruptcy costs.

Setting the Capital Structure in Practice

Because the theories of the debt-equity mix offer conflicting advice and because it is difficult to forecast the numbers required by the compromise theory, most financial managers seem to supplement the theories with other, more practical methods of making the financing mix decision. In this section we look at two of the more widely used: (1) a collection of techniques summarized by the acronym FRICTO and (2) a pattern of financing choice called the "pecking-order approach."

1. The FRICTO Approach

FRICTO—an acronym (flexibility, risk, income, control, timing, other) summarizing practical considerations in setting the debt-equity mix

FRICTO is an acronym for the words: flexibility, risk, income, control, timing, and other. The FRICTO approach assumes the financial manager is concerned about the form of the next financing issue. Although theory suggests the firm should stick closely to its target capital structure by issuing a mix of debt and equity every year, to do so would be very expensive in practice. It is far more common for a company to fund itself only with debt in some years and only with equity in others. FRICTO helps financial managers sort through the practical issues surrounding this choice. Each concept addresses one of the important effects of the financing mix decision on the firm's value and financial health.

Flexibility   Flexibility refers to the freedom to raise funds in the form of debt or equity whenever desired. A firm in need of funds but with limited financing choices is often at the mercy of the financial markets. For example, restrictive covenants on existing debt or a high debt load relative to the firm's cash flow often close off further debt financing, leaving equity as the only alternative. Each time a firm obtains funding, it must be careful not to limit its opportunities the next time around. In fact, a well-planned sequence of funding creates more, not less, opportunities for future financing.

Flexibility comes from proficient financial planning, identifying the amounts and timing of future security issues. It is increased by good communication with existing and potential investor stakeholders, so that bankers and capital market participants understand the company's financial strategy. Flexibility is further maintained by avoiding a debt-equity mix near the high end of (or above) the acceptable range—when a company's debt-equity mix is considered to be high, it can be difficult or quite costly to issue additional debt.

Risk   As we have seen in this chapter, the risk associated with the debt-equity mix has three components. One is the added volatility of the earnings stream that comes from financial leverage. Another is the danger of bankruptcy that comes from committing to fixed interest payments. The third is the risk from the overhead built into the firm's management because of agency considerations—for example, the potential loss of control that comes from loan documents that give lenders power over the firm's assets and actions if it defaults on its debt.

Risk can be quantified by a variety of measures, including financial leverage ratios such as the debt ratio, the funded debt ratio, the debt/equity ratio, times interest earned, and fixed charge coverage; the ratios that capture the magnification of leverage: degree of operating leverage, degree of financial leverage, and degree of total leverage; and the firm's levered beta.[11]

Financial managers must monitor the stability of the firm's earnings stream and the likelihood of default or bankruptcy, communicating with financial market par-

---

[11] **Cross-reference:**   Financial leverage ratios are discussed in Chapter 2, page 42; degree of leverage measures are presented in Web Appendix 14A; and the levered beta appears in Web Appendix 14C.

ticipants to ensure that the firm is not perceived as excessively risky. This is done by keeping leverage ratios within accepted norms and by conducting an ongoing dialog with lenders, analysts, bankers, debt rating agencies, etc., to inform them of the firm's financial plans.

Income Income refers to the ability of financial leverage to magnify the firm's earnings per share and reminds the financial manager to do the EBIT-EPS analysis of Figure 14.4.

Control If the firm finances by selling additional common shares, ownership of the firm is **diluted.** While the new financing may enable the company to earn sufficient additional income to restore earnings per share, investors have no way to restore their lost voting control other than by buying a proportionate share of the new issue.

dilute—to reduce the percentage of a firm owned by each common share by increasing the number of shares outstanding

In a company in which no single shareholder owns a significant number of shares, control is normally not a relevant issue. However, for the major shareholders of a **closely held firm,** dilution might represent a severe cost. Fortunately in this case, the financial manager can speak directly with those shareholders to learn their preferences and incorporate them into the financing mix decision.

closely held firm—a company in which a small number of shareholders own a significant percentage of the outstanding common stock

Timing Market conditions often favor the issue of one type of security or the other. When interest rates are at a historical low, debt issues become attractive. When stock prices are at a historical high, equity issues are favored. Financial managers must remain on top of financial market conditions to sequence debt and equity issues at the most favorable rates.

Other This category refers to a potpourri of miscellaneous considerations. Examples are: limits on debt or outstanding shares in the firm's charter, government regulations, the ability to use assets as collateral to reduce interest costs, the speed with which funds are needed, the amount of funds required, and the impact of the features of a new security issue on those currently outstanding.

2. The Pecking-Order Approach

Studies of how companies raise funds in practice have shown that a large number ignore the recommendations of all the debt-equity mix theories. Instead, many seem to follow a consistent pattern year after year, financing first with retained earnings, next with the easier-to-obtain forms of borrowing such as payables and bank debt, then with more complex debt forms such as bond issues, and last with issues of common stock. Professor Stewart Myers has labeled this pattern the **pecking-order approach.**

pecking-order approach—a pattern of financing in which a company raises funds in the same sequence each year

Since observing this phenomenon, Myers and other finance theorists have proposed several possible explanations. One suggestion is that the pecking order is the path of least resistance, the easiest way for financial managers to obtain funds. Retained earnings and payables are available with little or no effort, but it requires much more work to raise money in the public markets. However, it is difficult to believe that so many financial managers would choose financing that consistently ignores opportunities to add value to their companies just because it is easy.

Two other explanations do have a theoretical basis. First, the sequence of financing in the pecking-order approach is consistent with increasing flotation costs—from zero for retained earnings and payables, through moderate flotation costs for debt issues, through higher flotation costs for stock issues. Using the pecking-order approach keeps flotation costs to a minimum—important if flotation costs are a significant part of the cost of capital.

A second, theoretically-based explanation attempts to show why selling stock is last in the pecking order. Financial managers may want to avoid stock sales because the announcement of a stock issue tends to depress the stock's price by sending a negative signal to investors. This has been explained by the **asymmetric information hypothesis,** which studies financial behavior by observing that management typically knows more about the company than investors. In this application of the hypothesis, the argument is that management only wants to sell stock when it is at a relatively high price. This minimizes dilution since fewer shares will have to be sold to raise a given amount of money. However, investors realize that management is better informed than they are and treat a stock issue as "signaling" important new information: if management is willing to sell shares at this price, the stock could well be overvalued. In response, investors bid down the company's stock price.

In companies where the financial manager follows the pecking-order approach, the debt-equity mix is an accident of how much financing is needed each year. In years where the firm requires little funding, the money will come from retained earnings and the mix will tilt toward equity. If more funding is needed, the firm will borrow and the mix will tilt back toward debt. And if large amounts of new financing are required, the firm will have to issue common stock and the mix will tilt back toward more equity.

asymmetric information hypothesis—a theory that explores the ramifications of management having better information about a company's prospects than investors

FIGURE 14.9
Debt ratios of selected U.S. industries. Industries with good collateral, stable EBIT, or seasonal needs finance with high amounts of debt.

Source: Leo Troy, *Almanac of Business and Industrial Financial Ratios,* 42nd (2011) Edition. (Chicago, CCH, 2010.)

Industry	Average debt ratio	Comment
Airlines	77.2%	Make extensive use of debt to finance aircraft
Commercial banks	88.1	Highly stable EBIT due to regulation
Real estate lessors	57.0	Property used for collateral
Furniture stores	69.2	Representative retailers
Grocery stores	67.6	
Drug stores	57.7	
Furniture wholesalers	66.7	Representative wholesalers
Grocery wholesalers	45.2	
Pharmaceutical wholesalers	65.2	
Furniture manufacturers	62.8	Representative manufacturers
Grain milling	73.4	
Pharmaceutical manufacturing	61.2	
Regulated investment companies (mutual funds)	5.6	Funding is overwhelmingly from investors' deposits; charter typically prohibits borrowing to leverage investments

Typical Capital Structures

Capital structures differ significantly by industry. Figure 14.9 reports the industry-average debt ratios for representative industries in the United States.

*D*ebbie Curtis walked back into her office and turned on the computer. She loaded her spreadsheet program and looked again at her stock price model. Over the past week she had improved her figures several times to incorporate her new insights into the effects of financing on stakeholder value.

Debbie now understood why she had received such conflicting advice—the debt-equity mix decision was one of the least well understood in all of finance. If all the perfect market assumptions of Modigliani and Miller were correct, it wouldn't matter how her firm raised its money since the financing mix would not change the firm's value. But it was more likely that the financial markets were not perfect. The tax treatment of interest and stakeholders' concerns about the costs associated with bankruptcy and agency were very real and could change the company's worth. What was clear to Debbie was the need to understand the reactions of all the firm's stakeholders to the returns and risks from each financing alternative. And, it would require a lot of judgment to quantify those reactions.

Debbie reviewed her calculations once more and ranked the financing alternatives in order of their estimated impact on the company's value. Then she began to write her report for the CFO. She outlined the theoretical issues and then organized her analyses and observations using the FRICTO framework. As she printed out her results, a colleague stuck his head into her office and asked how she was doing. "I think it came out well," she replied. "There's no clear answer, but I sure have plenty to tell the CFO tomorrow."

Summary of Key Points

■ **Define operating and financial leverage and describe their relationship to fixed costs.** Operating leverage is the magnification of operating profits (EBIT) in response to changes in a firm's sales. Financial leverage is the magnification of earnings per share (EPS) in response to changes in a firm's operating profits (EBIT). Both are caused by the existence of fixed costs in the firm's cost structure. Operating fixed costs come from commitments to productive resources—human or technological. Financial fixed costs come primarily from interest on debt financing. Control over operating fixed costs is often limited due to technological constraints. While small companies typically have little choice about their financial leverage due to their inability to access the financial markets, larger firms can choose between debt and equity financing.

■ **Discuss why a company's financing choice might affect the market value of its securities.** Through its choice of financing, a company can modify the pattern of risk and return it provides to its stakeholders. As a firm's financial leverage rises, the behavior of its EPS changes: at high levels of EBIT, EPS is increased while at low EBIT levels, EPS is decreased. It is important to locate the crossover, or indifference, point. High financial leverage also adds volatility to a firm's EPS stream. A firm with EBIT below the indifference point should avoid debt financing—at this level of EBIT low leverage produces higher returns and lower risk. A firm with EBIT above the indifference point must weigh the tradeoff from adding leverage: greater returns but also greater risk. The best financing mix will be the one that produces the most value for the firm's stakeholders.

▪▪▪ **Describe four theories that attempt to explain the optimal mix of debt and equity financing.** The traditional approach studies how investors perceive the risks of increased debt, concluding there is an optimal financing mix. MM show that if financial markets are "perfect," the financing mix decision is irrelevant to firm value; adding corporate income taxes, MM conclude that the optimal financing mix is 100% debt. Miller shows that personal income taxes partially offset the effects of the corporate income tax. Compromise theory focuses on "imperfections" in the financial markets, concluding that there is an optimal financing mix due to the corporate income tax, bankruptcy costs, and agency costs.

▪▪▪ **Describe how companies approach the debt-equity mix decision in practice.** Some firms use the acronym FRICTO (flexibility, risk, income, control, timing, other) to organize their analysis of the debt-equity mix. Others appear to use the pecking-order approach, in which they consistently finance first with retained earnings, then debt, then stock sales.

▪▪▪ **Explain why the debt-equity mix differs by industry.** Values of the debt-equity mix vary widely among companies in different industries, due primarily to the level of operating leverage and the stability of the industry's sales and EBIT. Often stability is due to government regulation.

Questions

1. In what way is business leverage similar to physical leverage?

2. Distinguish between operating leverage and financial leverage.

3. How much choice does a firm have over its operating leverage? over its financial leverage?

4. Describe the way in which earnings per share responds to changing EBIT in a firm with:
   a. No fixed financing costs
   b. Some fixed financing costs

5. How does a firm's financial leverage affect:
   a. Its profitability?
   b. Its level of risk?

6. A firm is considering two alternative capital structures and has calculated its profitability at various EBIT levels under each structure. What should the firm do if its projected EBIT is:
   a. Below the indifference point?
   b. Above the indifference point?

7. Compare and contrast the net income approach, net operating income approach, and traditional approach to the optimal debt-equity mix. Which assumptions do you find reasonable? unreasonable?

8. What role does each of MM's assumptions play in their theory of the debt-equity mix?

9. Describe "homemade leverage."

10. Is Professor Miller's personal tax model relevant in today's tax environment?

11. What are the variables that enter compromise theory? What is the effect of each on the optimal debt-equity mix?

12. Define the meaning of each letter of *FRICTO,* and give an illustration of each.

13. What is meant by the *pecking-order approach*? Give three explanations why it is an observed phenomenon.

Problems

1. **(Magnification)** A firm has sales of $5 million of which 45% are variable costs. Fixed operating costs are $1 million but the firm has no debt and therefore no interest expenses. The firm is in the 35% tax bracket and has 1 million shares outstanding.
   a. Calculate the company's EBIT and EPS.
   b. Calculate EBIT and EPS if sales goes up by 5% and if sales goes down by 5%.
   c. For each case of part b, by what percent did EBIT and EPS change?
   d. Compare the results of part c for EBIT and EPS.

2. **(Magnification)** A firm has sales of $5,000,000 of which 65% are variable costs. There are no fixed operating costs, but interest expense totals $750,000. The company is in the 35% tax bracket and has 1,000,000 shares outstanding.
   a. Calculate the company's EBIT and EPS.
   b. Calculate EBIT and EPS if sales goes up by 5% and if sales goes down by 5%.
   c. For each case of part b, by what percent did EBIT and EPS change?
   d. Compare the results of part c for EBIT and EPS.

3. **(Leverage, returns, and risk)** A company with EBIT of $1,000,000 is considering two financing alternatives. The first would have interest expense of $250,000 and 200,000 outstanding shares, whereas the

second would have interest expense of $350,000 but only 150,000 shares outstanding. The company is in the 35% federal income tax bracket.

a. Construct the bottom half of the income statement for each financing alternative.
b. Repeat part a if EBIT rises to $1,100,000.
c. Repeat part a if EBIT falls to $900,000.
d. What do you observe about the behavior of EPS?

4. **(Leverage, returns, and risk)** A company with EBIT of $8,000,000 is considering two financing alternatives. The first would have interest expense of $2,250,000 and 1,000,000 outstanding shares, whereas the second would have interest expense of $4,000,000 but only 800,000 shares outstanding. The company is in the 35% federal income tax bracket.

a. Construct the bottom half of the income statement for each financing alternative.
b. Repeat part a if EBIT rises to $9,200,000.
c. Repeat part a if EBIT falls to $6,800,000.
d. What do you observe about the behavior of EPS?

5. **(Indifference point)** A company is considering two debt-equity mixes. Under Plan A its annual interest costs will be $500,000 and it will have 400,000 shares of common stock outstanding. Under Plan B its annual interest costs will be $800,000, but it will only issue 250,000 common shares. The company pays taxes at a 35% rate.

a. Sketch a graph of EPS versus EBIT for EBIT in the range of zero to $3,000,000. Your graph should have two lines on it, one for Plan A and one for Plan B.
b. Locate the indifference point between Plans A and B.
c. What is the firm's EPS at the indifference point?
d. On which side of the indifference point is EPS higher under Plan A? Plan B?

6. **(Indifference point)** A company is considering two debt-equity mixes. Under Plan X its annual interest costs will be $2,000,000 and it will have 250,000 shares of common stock outstanding. Under Plan Y its annual interest costs will be only $1,200,000, although it would issue 450,000 common shares. The company pays taxes at a 35% rate.

a. Sketch a graph of EPS versus EBIT for EBIT in the range of zero to $6,000,000. Your graph should have two lines on it, one for Plan X and one for Plan Y.
b. Locate the indifference point between Plans X and Y.
c. What is the firm's EPS at the indfference point?
d. On which side of the indifference point is EPS higher under Plan X? Plan Y?

7. **(The traditional approach)** A company has gathered the following data about its cost of capital:

Debt ratio	Cost of debt	Cost of equity
0%	4.0%	10.5%
10	4.0	11.0
20	4.0	11.6
30	4.2	12.4
40	4.5	13.6
50	4.9	15.3
60	5.4	17.8
70	6.2	21.5
80	7.5	26.0

a. What is the relationship between the cost of capital and the optimal debt-equity mix?
b. Calculate the cost of capital at each debt ratio.
c. Which debt-equity mix is optimal?
d. According to the traditionalists, why do the cost of debt and cost of equity exhibit the above patterns?

8. **(The traditional approach)** A company has gathered the following data about its cost of capital:

Debt ratio	Cost of debt	Cost of equity
0%	3.5%	9.0%
10	3.5	9.0
20	3.5	9.2
30	3.5	9.6
40	3.7	10.2
50	4.0	11.4
60	4.5	13.0
70	5.2	15.2
80	6.2	18.2

a. Calculate the cost of capital at each debt ratio.
b. Which debt-equity mix is optimal?
c. Calculate the increase in the cost of debt and the cost of equity for each 10% increase in the debt ratio. Explain the pattern you discover.
d. Calculate the difference between the cost of debt and the cost of equity at each debt ratio. Explain the pattern you discover.

9. **(Compromise theory)** The stock of a company with no debt has a market value of $35,000,000. Its investment bankers have helped it gather the following information, where:

CT = present value of federal income taxes saved from deducting interest expenses
BC = present value of bankruptcy costs
AC = present value of agency costs

Debt ratio	CT	BC	AC
0%	$ 0	$ 0	$ 0
10	1,000,000	0	200,000
20	2,000,000	1,000,000	400,000
30	3,000,000	2,000,000	700,000
40	4,000,000	4,000,000	1,100,000
50	5,000,000	7,000,000	1,600,000
60	6,000,000	11,000,000	2,200,000
70	7,000,000	16,000,000	2,900,000
80	8,000,000	22,000,000	3,700,000

a. Calculate the value of the firm at each debt ratio.
b. Which debt-equity mix is optimal?
c. Locate the acceptable range.
d. Why do the CT numbers increase at a constant rate while the BC and AC numbers increase at an increasing rate?

10. **(Compromise theory)** The stock of a company with no debt has a market value of $80,000,000. Its investment bankers have helped it gather the following information, where:

CT = present value of federal income taxes saved from deducting interest expenses

BC = present value of bankruptcy costs

AC = present value of agency costs

Debt ratio	CT	BC	AC
0%	$ 0	$ 0	$ 0
10	3,000,000	0	1,000,000
20	6,000,000	0	1,500,000
30	9,000,000	4,000,000	2,200,000
40	12,000,000	8,000,000	3,100,000
50	15,000,000	14,000,000	4,200,000
60	18,000,000	22,000,000	5,500,000
70	21,000,000	32,000,000	7,000,000
80	24,000,000	44,000,000	8,700,000

a. Calculate the value of the firm at each debt ratio.
b. Which debt-equity mix is optimal?
c. Locate the acceptable range.
d. Why are there agency costs at a 10% and 20% debt ratio while bankruptcy costs remain at zero?

11. **(Changing the capital structure)** A company with $10 million in assets currently has $3 million of debt financing. The cost of this debt is 5%, and the company's cost of equity is now 12%. The company's treasurer has suggested borrowing another $2 million and using the proceeds to retire an equivalent amount of common stock. The new debt would have a cost of 6.5%, and the treasurer estimates the company's stockholders would respond to the change in financing mix by raising the cost of equity to 14%.

a. Calculate the company's debt ratio now and after the proposed change.
b. Calculate the cost of debt after the change (assume it is the weighted average of the two debt issues).
c. Calculate the company's weighted-average cost of capital now and after the proposed change.
d. Should the company alter its debt-equity mix as suggested by the treasurer?

12. **(Changing the capital structure)** A company with $50 million in assets currently has $40 million of debt financing as a result of a recent leveraged buyout. The cost of this debt is 10%, and the company's cost of equity is now 19%. Now the company's management wishes to take the company public again by selling $15 million of equity and using the proceeds to retire an equivalent amount of debt. The treasurer estimates the company's stockholders would respond to the change in financing mix by reducing the cost of equity to 12%.

a. Calculate the company's debt ratio now and after the proposed change.
b. Calculate the company's weighted-average cost of capital now and after the proposed change.
c. Now assume the company used this opportunity to call its debt and replace it with new debt with a cost of 6%. Calculate the company's weighted-average cost of capital after the proposed change.
d. Should the company alter its debt-equity mix, and if so, should it refund its debt?

CHAPTER 15

MANAGING RISK

*C*lif Carlton finished writing on the flip-chart and turned back to the conference table. "My concern is that our cash and accounts receivable balances are becoming more variable. They have always been seasonal, but recently they have been fluctuating over a wider range on a weekly basis. And since we expanded our overseas business last year, the problem has become worse. Not only do we have more rapidly changing current asset balances, but the currencies we hold are changing almost as quickly. Yet we've been slow to respond to these changes."

Clif was treasurer of a medium-sized transportation company. Among his responsibilities were selecting and obtaining the firm's liabilities. Recently he had become concerned about changing patterns of the company's cash flows and balance sheet accounts, and he had called today's meeting to address his concerns. Around the table were members of each finance group that reported to him—domestic cash management, international cash management, investment management, and financial planning and research—but he had also invited several colleagues from other areas of the company who could contribute to the discussion or might be affected by the alternatives his group would consider.

Clif continued his remarks. "I'm convinced it's time to rethink our hedging strategy. With rapidly changing asset balances, our risk exposure is constantly changing as well. I'm not convinced that our existing policies are up to the job of dealing with that. We also need to look again at the mix of debt financing we use and how that affects the company's risk posture. Let's put together a team to study the way our business has changed and recommend whether new approaches are required."

Clif is concerned about financial risk management, using financial managing methods and products to reduce the financial risks faced by his company. As Clif's team re-examines the company's hedging strategy, it will find itself studying how well the company uses these risk management techniques in both its overall financing strategy and its day-to-day operations. Modern finance has developed powerful tools for limiting risks. Used wisely, they can enable a company to be involved in business activities that might otherwise be far too risky to take on.

However, financial risk management has an important role to play even in companies that normally shun risky ventures. Like Clif's firm, every company is exposed to potential losses from many of its business activities. Some risks, such as product liability, involve the firm's customers. Other risks are employee-related, for example the risk of on-the-job injury. The possibility of fire, theft, or damage to property poses yet another risk. In this chapter we look at the way financial risk management is used to address two types of risk that arise from the firm's financial transactions: (1) the risk of being unable to repay and refinance debt, and (2) the risk of losses due to fluctuations in interest and foreign exchange rates. The first is addressed by matching the maturities of assets and liabilities across the balance sheet, the second through the use of financial insurance contracts and derivative securities. These two activities are worth investigating for another reason as well. As we will see, they are the third and fourth steps in a four-step process of managing a company's working capital that begins with the incremental decisions about permanent working capital we discussed in Chapter 12.

Key Points You Should Learn from This Chapter

After reading this chapter you should be able to:

- Discuss how hedging can reduce financial risks.
- Describe the four-step sequence of working capital decisions.
- Discuss how companies set their debt maturity mix.
- Relate how temporary working capital arises in the current accounts.
- Discuss the basics of hedging against foreign currency and interest rate movements.

Introductory Concepts—Hedging

Suppose a professional basketball player's contract specifies that he will get a $200,000 bonus if his team wins the championship. In effect the player faces some financial risk: depending on the outcome of the season, he could receive a bonus payment of either $0 or $200,000. One way the player could deal with this risk would be to make a $100,000 bet against his team winning the championship. If the team wins, he would receive the $200,000 bonus but would have to pay the $100,000, for a net take of $100,000. If the team loses, he would get no bonus but would receive the $100,000 from the bet. Effectively, the bet would change his risky position into a riskless one: either way he would get $100,000.

Of course, it would be wrong (and illegal!) for a basketball pro to bet against his own team. Fortunately, however, betting of this kind is not illegal in business. Consider, for example, the problem of a farmer who grows corn. The farmer's financial position is quite risky since the amount of money the crop will bring in will depend on corn prices at harvest time. The risk is that corn prices will fall. One way for the farmer to obtain protection is to "bet against himself" by selling futures contracts that require the farmer to deliver a set amount of corn at a specified price, contracts whose value is tied to the price of corn. If corn prices fall, the futures position will increase in value, offsetting the loss, since the contracts would be cheaper to fulfill. Cereal manufacturers are in a position precisely opposite to that of the farmer, running the risk that corn prices will rise. They can reduce their risk by purchasing the futures contracts so that if corn prices rise, their loss will be offset by the increased value of owning contracts which fix (limit) the price they have to pay.[1]

hedging—balancing a risky financial position with an opposite position to cancel out the risk

Each of these examples is an illustration of **hedging,** offsetting a financial risk with an equal and opposite position so that changes in the value of the two positions cancel each other out. While many financial risk positions can be addressed with hedging, in this chapter we concentrate on two: balancing assets and liabilities, and balancing cash inflows and outflows.

SERVING FINANCE'S CUSTOMERS

Risk Management at Corning, Incorporated

Corning, Incorporated's treasury has redefined the scope of its financial risk management activities. In addition to the hedging conducted by domestic and international cash management professionals, another group, known formally as "Risk Management and Prevention," looks at the potential for financial loss from product liability claims. The group defines Corning's operating units as its customers. Once seen simply as a buyer of insurance, today the group includes both finance specialists and Ph.D. scientists who work together to identify, assess, and reduce the customer units' risk exposure. The goal is to drive down avoidable litigation costs, those that would not have happened if Corning made no errors, to a tiny fraction of total litigation costs. As a result of its innovative use of quality-management approaches, the Risk Management and Prevention group within Corning, Incorporated's treasury is recognized within the profession as world class.

---

[1] **Acknowledgment:**   These examples were suggested by Professor Robert G. Schweback of the University of Wyoming.

In this book, we first encountered the concept of hedging in Chapter 4, when we looked at the "segmentation or hedging hypothesis" for explaining the yield curve.[2] That theory supposes that bond investors choose the maturities of the bonds they buy based upon when they will need the cash back. They do so to lock in a known dollar value at a specified time and ensure that cash will be available as needed. The hedging we examine in this chapter is done for the same reasons: to guarantee values and to improve a company's liquidity.

By hedging across the balance sheet, financial managers ensure that the correct amount of cash will be available to pay each of the firm's liabilities when they fall due and that there will be financing for every asset.

Example

Hedging Across the Balance Sheet

Belleco Resources recently issued $10 million of 20-year bonds to finance its investment in an off-shore oil platform. Cash from the oil platform project will be used to pay the bonds' interest and principal. Belleco's treasurer chose 20 years as the bonds' maturity to match the forecasted 20-year life of the platform.

By hedging individual cash flows, financial managers ensure that every receipt can be efficiently used and that there is a known cost to every obligation.

Example

Hedging a Cash Flow

Belleco Resources has an obligation to pay ¥1.5 million to a Japanese supplier in 30 days. To guarantee the exchange rate, which might fluctuate during the next month, Belleco's treasurer has entered into a forward exchange contract with its bank.[3]

Notice that while hedging reduces risk, it also takes away the opportunity to benefit from favorable results. The basketball player gave up the possibility to receive $200,000 by hedging his bonus. The farmer gave up the opportunity to sell his crop at a higher price had corn prices risen. The cereal producer lost the chance to purchase the corn at a lower price had prices fallen. Hedging eliminates variability, upward changes as well as downward changes.

To further understand the benefits of hedging, it is useful to consider what happens when financial managers do not hedge. Whereas hedged receipts are promptly used, unhedged receipts become excess cash, over and above the firm's needs. Although this money can be invested, it often earns interest at a lower rate than better-planned investments. Unhedged obligations force a company to obtain funds for their payment in today's markets. The money might carry a high interest rate, or, if in another currency, might only be available at a foreign exchange rate less favorable than could have been obtained with prior planning.

NET Present Value
A website with extensive coverage of hedging and financial risk management is: www.finpipe.com/hedge.htm

Throughout this chapter we study how risk management activities can *reduce* financial risks. However, it is quite possible to use the insights, tools, and instruments of financial risk management to speculate in risky situations, effectively *increasing* a company's risk exposure in the hope of greater returns. Although some

---

[2] **Cross-reference:**   The segmentation or hedging hypothesis appears on page 95.

[3] **Cross-reference:**   Forward exchange rates, the quotes for forward exchange contracts, were introduced in Chapter 4, pages 103–104.

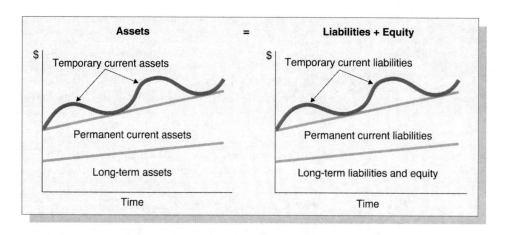

FIGURE 15.1

Levels of assets and claims across time for a growing firm. Current assets and liabilities can be divided into a permanent level plus temporary fluctuations.

treasurers engage in this kind of speculation, most do not, treating it as not supportive of the company's activities and as a business they do not want to be in. Accordingly, we have not looked at the speculative side of financial risk management in this chapter.

The Four-Step Sequence of Working Capital Decisions

Working capital is put in place in a sequence with four steps, much like a set of building blocks. As we consider this process, it is useful to recall the concepts of permanent and temporary working capital, a distinction we made in Chapter 12.[4]

1. Permanent and Temporary Working Capital Revisited

Recall from Chapter 12 that permanent working capital is the base level of current accounts, the amount that remains in place regardless of variations in business activity. Temporary working capital is the remainder, the additions to working capital that come from cyclical, seasonal, and daily fluctuations. Figure 15.1, a repeat of Figure 12.1, illustrates the division of both current assets and current liabilities into permanent and temporary portions.

2. The Four Steps in Establishing Working Capital Balances

There are four steps in setting a company's working capital levels:

1. Put the permanent current assets into place.

2. Use attractive short-term financing opportunities as permanent current liabilities.

3. Add additional permanent debt, if needed, to hedge the maturities of the balance sheet.

4. Respond to temporary working capital needs and opportunities.

---

[4] **Cross-reference:** The distinction between permanent and temporary working capital appears throughout Chapter 12, but it is explicitly discussed on pages 288–289.

However, since business and financial market conditions regularly change, the process is not quite as neat and linear as our description makes it sound. It is common for each step to be revisited regularly and for the four steps to be rethought on an ongoing basis.

Figure 15.2 illustrates the four steps. In addition, the figure illustrates another important point. At the same time that working capital opportunities are being analyzed, two other financial managing balance-sheet-related activities are taking place. In Chapter 11 we studied capital budgeting, the evaluation and selection of noncurrent asset investments. Chapter 14 was devoted to setting the debt-equity mix. Both analyses are done in parallel to working capital decisions, and

FIGURE 15.2

The four steps in working capital decisions. In order, the steps involve: (1) permanent current assets, (2) low-or-no-cost permanent current liabilities, (3) other permanent debt, and (4) temporary working capital.

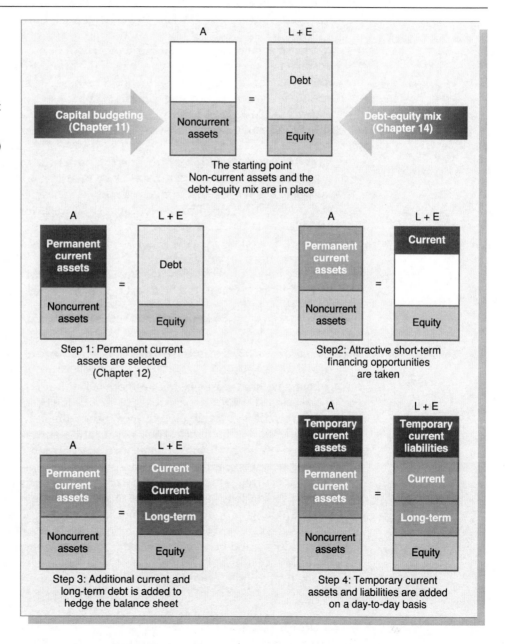

there is some amount of interaction between all of them. However, to simplify our presentation, we will assume that these other two decisions have already been made as we enter the four working capital steps. The top of Figure 15.2, which shows a balance sheet containing some amount of noncurrent assets and with a target split between debt and equity financing, will therefore be our starting point for considering working capital.

The four steps are described further below:

First: set the permanent current asset balances   In Chapter 12 we discovered that investments in permanent current asset balances are analyzed in much the same way as long-term assets.[5] For each opportunity to adjust permanent current assets we estimate incremental cash flows, establish a cost of capital appropriate for the level of risk, and apply time value of money calculations. A company should invest in all permanent working capital assets that produce a positive net present value. Accordingly, the appropriate level for the permanent component of each current asset is the amount that produces a positive NPV, and a company's total permanent working capital asset balance becomes the sum of these figures. Step 1 of Figure 15.2 builds on the starting point by adding in a balance of permanent current assets.

Second: use attractive short-term financing opportunities as the first permanent current liabilities   A company should use short-term payables for financing whenever the interest rate is favorable and the supplier is happy with the relationship. The rate of interest on most institutional payables (wages payable, taxes payable) is typically zero, hence it benefits a company to use as much of this financing as is available. For trade credit (accounts payable), an interest rate must be calculated, and the company should take this credit when the effective interest rate is below market levels. The total of these low-or-no-cost current liabilities becomes the first part of the firm's permanent current liability balance. Step 2 of Figure 15.2 builds on Step 1 by adding in a balance of low (or no) cost permanent current liabilities.

Third: add additional current liabilities and long-term debt to hedge the balance sheet   Steps 1 and 2 establish current asset and current liability balances without reference to one another. But from the point of view of hedging, it makes sense for the two current portions of the balance sheet to be related. Current assets, those expected to produce cash in the near term, are a primary means of paying current liabilities. The current ratio—current assets divided by current liabilities—used by financial analysts to measure the overall relationship of the current accounts, captures this concept.[6] At the same time, it is prudent for the firm's noncurrent assets—expected to be around for many years—to be financed primarily with long-term funds. In this step, the financial manager adds appropriate amounts of permanent current liabilities and long-term debt to move the balance sheet toward the desired relationship between the current assets and current liabilities, and between noncurrent assets and long-term financing. The "debt-maturity mix," the split between short- and longer-term debt financing employed by the firm, results from these choices. This is shown in Step 3 of Figure 15.2.

---

[5] **Cross-reference:**   This insight is presented on pages 289–292, and is illustrated throughout the remainder of Chapter 12.

[6] **Cross-reference:**   The current ratio is discussed in Chapter 2, page 38.

Fourth: respond to temporary working capital needs and opportunities   Cyclicality, seasonality, and day-to-day events require a company to take on additional, temporary working capital assets and provide opportunities for temporary working capital financing. These issues are handled on a day-to-day basis as they arise. Step 4 of Figure 15.2 adds temporary current assets and liabilities to the balance sheet to illustrate these changes.

Example

The Four-Step Working Capital Sequence

The treasurer of Belleco Resources has determined the following:

- Investment opportunities in current assets totalling $36 million are available with positive net present values when evaluated at the appropriate risk-adjusted cost of capital.

- The company's payroll and tax systems create wages payable and taxes payable totalling $8 million. No interest or other payments are required to support these payables.

- A sensitivity analysis of Belleco's liquidity indicates the need for a minimum current ratio of 1.8 times.

- Daily fluctuations in working capital balances are anticipated throughout the coming year.

Question: How should the working capital balances be set?

Solution steps: Belleco's treasurer follows the four-step process:

1. "Set the permanent current asset balances." Invest the $36 million in working capital assets.

2. "Use attractive short-term financing opportunities as the first permanent current liabilities." Make the $8 million of institutional payables the first portion of permanent current liabilities since they have zero cost.

3. "Set the split between current liabilities and long-term financing."

   a. With $36 million of permanent current assets and a minimum current ratio of 1.8 times, the target number for Belleco's total permanent current liabilities can easily be determined:

   $$\text{Current assets/current liabilities} = 1.8$$

   so:

   $$\text{Current liabilities} = \$36 \text{ million}/1.8 = \$20 \text{ million}$$

   b. Since $8 million of permanent current liabilities is already in place from Step 2, add another $12 million of short-term debt.

4. "Respond to temporary working capital needs and opportunities." Use the methods discussed later in this chapter, including investment in marketable securities and the hedging of cash flows, to reduce day-to-day risks as working capital levels deviate from the permanent balances throughout the year.

In the remainder of this chapter we look in more detail at the third and fourth steps in this process: achieving a desired level of working capital by setting the split between current and long-term financing, and making use of temporary working capital.

The Debt Maturity Mix

debt maturity mix—the
blend of debt maturities
used by a firm

The term **debt maturity mix** refers to the relative amounts of each maturity of debt in a company's capital structure. It is important to include all maturities in the analysis, as each can play a role in hedging the company's assets. However, since the balance sheet divides liabilities into "current" and "long-term," it is common and convenient to think of the debt maturity mix as referring to these two categories. When a company hedges its balance sheet as the third step in setting its working capital balances, it sets its debt maturity mix.

1. The Risk-Return Tradeoff

By setting its debt maturity mix, a company establishes an important part of its risk-return posture. A firm can normally lower its financing costs by weighting its debt maturities toward the short term since yield curves have historically been upward-sloping, with current liabilities costing less than long-term debt. However, a company's liquidity goes down, hence its risk goes up, as its current liabilities increase relative to its current assets. The initial step in setting the debt maturity mix is evaluating this classic risk-return tradeoff.

Example

The Risk-Return Tradeoff in the Debt Maturity Mix

Rumat Industries is considering three alternative approaches to setting its debt maturity mix. Strategy A is aggressive, emphasizing short-term debt. Strategy C is conservative, emphasizing long-term debt. Strategy B lies between the other two. Rumat's treasurer has organized the following data (in millions of dollars) to use in the analysis:

● The company has $1,000 of assets of which $400 are current.

● $400 of liabilities will be obtained. If Strategy A is adopted, $300 of this will be current; $200 under strategy B; and $100 under Strategy C.

● EBIT is forecasted to be $200, and Rumat is in the 35% income tax bracket.

● The yield curve is currently upward-sloping: the interest rate on bank notes is 6%, and long-term debt yields 10%.

Question: What will Rumat's balance sheet and the financial half of its income statement look like under each strategy?

Solution steps:

1. Organize the asset, liability, and equity data into a balance sheet format. Note that with $1,000 of assets and $400 of liabilities, owners equity will equal $600 under each alternative.

		Strategy A	**Strategy B**	**Strategy C**
Assets:	Current	$ 400	$ 400	$ 400
	Noncurrent	600	600	600
	Total	$ 1,000	$ 1,000	$ 1,000
Liabilities:	Current	$ 300	$ 200	$ 100
	Long-term	100	200	300
Equity:		600	600	600
	Total	$ 1,000	$ 1,000	$ 1,000

2. Construct the financial half of Rumat's income statement under each alternative:

a. Calculate interest expense under each alternative (from the yield curve data equal to 6% of current liabilities plus 10% of long-term liabilities):

$$\text{Strategy A: } (6\% \times \$300) + (10\% \times \$100) = \$28$$

$$\text{Strategy B: } (6\% \times \$200) + (10\% \times \$200) = \$32$$

$$\text{Strategy C: } (6\% \times \$100) + (10\% \times \$300) = \$36$$

b. Organize the information of the income statements:

	Strategy A	Strategy B	Strategy C
EBIT	$200	$200	$200
− Interest	28	32	36
EBT	172	168	164
− Taxes (35%)	60	59	57
EAT	$112	$109	$107

Question: What will Rumat's return and liquidity risk look like under each alternative as measured by its return on equity and current ratios?

Solution steps:

$$\text{Return on equity} = \text{EAT/owners equity}$$
$$\text{Current ratio} = \text{current assets/current liabilities}$$

	Strategy A	Strategy B	Strategy C
Return on equity	$\dfrac{112}{600} = \underline{18.7\%}$	$\dfrac{109}{600} = \underline{18.2\%}$	$\dfrac{107}{600} = \underline{17.8\%}$
Current ratio	$\dfrac{400}{300} = \underline{1.33}$	$\dfrac{400}{200} = \underline{2.00}$	$\dfrac{400}{100} = \underline{4.00}$

Answer: Rumat's rate of return and liquidity move in opposite directions. While Strategy A increases Rumat's rate of return, it reduces the firm's liquidity. Strategy C provides a high degree of liquidity at the cost of a lowered rate of return. Strategy B lies in the middle.

2. Using Hedging to Reduce Risk

Currently, finance theory offers no clear formula for finding the best debt maturity mix. However, the technique of hedging can be used to reduce a company's repayment and liquidity risks. If this can be done at low cost, it is possible to improve the firm's risk-return posture. In this section we look at three strategies for using hedging to set the debt maturity mix: (1) individual asset/liability hedging, (2) maturity-range hedging, and (3) maturity-range hedging with deviations.

Individual asset/liability hedging This approach is the ultimate application of hedging: the financial manager attempts to offset each liability with an asset of identical size and maturity. This would ensure that every cash flow could be used fully and every liability would have a cash flow to pay it when due. A financial company with many discrete liabilities, such as a bank or insurance company, can often come close to this ideal. For a nonfinancial firm such as a manufacturing company, with a small number of individual items on the right-hand side of the balance sheet, this approach is both impractical and very costly. Nevertheless, the concept of hedging individual assets and liabilities serves as a useful starting point for further analysis.

Maturity-range hedging   With this approach, the overall *level* of assets with a given range of maturities is matched with a similar level of liabilities and/or equity with the same maturity range. Figure 15.3 illustrates this approach. Maturity-range hedging would have the firm set the following relationships among its balances:

> Current liabilities = current assets
>
> Long-term liabilities and equity = noncurrent assets

We can improve upon maturity-range hedging by allowing for permanent current assets. Since, as we saw in Chapter 12, permanent current assets are treated as having an infinite (long-term) lifetime, a more consistent use of maturity-range hedging is to set:

> Current liabilities = temporary current assets
>
> Long-term liabilities and equity = permanent current assets
>   plus noncurrent assets

This approach is illustrated in Figure 15.4.

Deviations from maturity-range hedging   Some companies elect to move away from precise maturity-range hedging, especially if they are small or if their asset needs are unpredictable. Small firms find it difficult and costly to issue long-term securities; they tend to deviate from the hedging goal by weighting their financing toward short and intermediate sources. And, the more unpredictable a company's asset levels, hence its financing needs, the more difficult it is to hedge.

However, many larger companies deviate from maturity-range hedging by choice. Some firms choose to have a higher level of current liabilities than maturity-range hedging would prescribe. They finance some portion of their permanent current assets and possibly even some of their noncurrent assets with short-term sources,

FIGURE 15.3
Maturity-range hedging. The level of current assets is matched by a similar level of current liabilities.

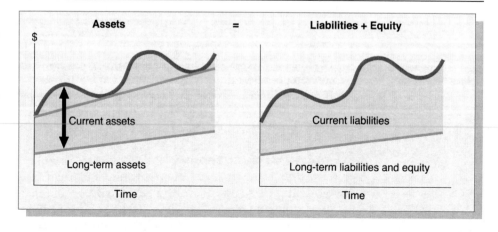

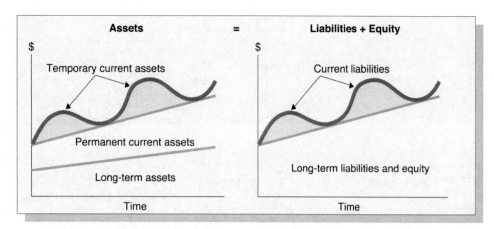

FIGURE 15.4
Improved maturity-range hedging. Long-term financing is used for permanent current assets as well as noncurrent assets; current liabilities finance temporary current assets.

as Figure 15.5 illustrates. This strategy has three effects: (1) Since yield curves normally slope upwards, additional short-term debt usually reduces financing costs. (2) Offsetting this saving is a possible increase to the administrative costs and fees associated with obtaining debt since high levels of short-term financing imply more frequent debt contract renewals. (3) It is relatively easy to adjust the level of short-term financing (as compared to long-term debt or equity), especially bank borrowing. With a high level of current debt, the firm can more exactly match its financing to its needs.

Other companies elect to use a lower level of current liabilities than maturity-range hedging would dictate. Thus they finance some portion of temporary current assets with long-term sources. This strategy has four effects. (1) The company's risk of near-term bankruptcy is reduced. Lower current liabilities means less debt coming due in the near future. This removes pressure from the firm to have the liquidity necessary to repay this debt. (2) The company faces less exposure to changing interest rates. Whereas short-term debt maturities mean regular renewal at changing interest rates, long-term debt maturities typically lock in the cost of debt financing so the firm can more easily plan its long-term capital budget. (3) The company will generally have a better credit rating, since having a small amount of current debt—which implies more working capital and better liquid-

FIGURE 15.5
Increased current liabilities. Current liabilities finance temporary current assets plus some permanent current assets.

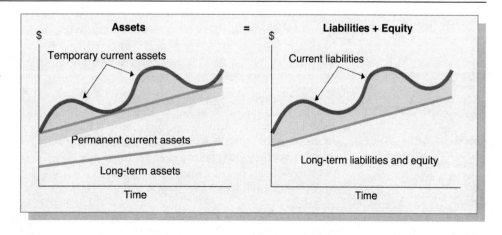

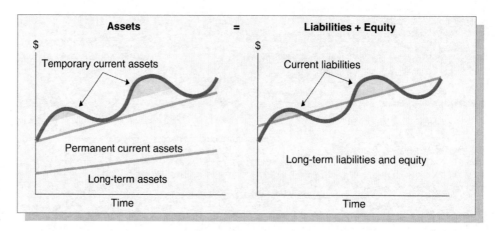

FIGURE 15.6
Decreased short-term debt. In this strategy, current liabilities finance only a portion of temporary current assets.

ity ratios—is seen as a conservative financing strategy. (4) When temporary current assets drop below the level of long-term financing, the firm has extra funds which, practically, cannot go toward reducing debt. The most common use for these funds is marketable securities that earn at a rate lower than the cost of debt. Thus, the firm loses money on these excess funds. Figure 15.6 illustrates this approach.

Temporary Working Capital

In this section we look more closely at the nature of the temporary balances in each of the working capital accounts: cash, marketable securities, accounts receivable, inventory, and payables. Then we point out some dangers of poor temporary working capital management.

1. Temporary Cash

It is common for a firm's cash balance to rise above its target minimum amount. Inflows and outflows of cash are rarely equal on a day-to-day basis. When a company sells a major asset or raises capital funds by selling bonds or stock, it usually has excess cash for some period of time until the money is spent. Companies often accumulate cash when planning for a large expenditure, such as a major asset acquisition or debt principal repayment. A treasurer who expects interest rates to rise or stock prices to fall might find it attractive to raise cash in today's market environment, even if the money could not be used fully for some time.

2. Marketable Securities

marketable security—an investment with a ready market that may be sold easily to obtain its value in cash

When the cash balance rises above target, the excess is normally invested to earn interest. Treasurers look for **marketable securities,** low-risk, highly liquid investments that may be resold easily without loss of principal. Among the alternative investment choices for excess U.S. dollar funds are U.S. Treasury securities (bonds, notes, and bills),[7] federal agency issues, state and local bonds, banker's accep-

---

[7] **Cross-reference:** U.S. Treasury obligations first appeared in Chapter 4, pages 92–96, in our discussion of the yield curve.

Treasury bills	Maturities of 91 days (13 weeks), 182 days (26 weeks), 364 days (52 weeks). Sold on discount basis. New issue weekly: auction every Monday with bills sold to highest bidders (lowest yield). Small buyers can buy at average bid price.
Treasury notes	Maturities of one to seven years. Sold on coupon basis. Shorter maturities are bearer bonds; longer maturities are registered.
Treasury bonds	Maturities over five years. Sold on coupon basis; registered.
Federal agency issues	Maturities of one month to 15 years with 2/3 less than one year. Guaranteed by specific agency, not a general obligation of the Treasury. Issued by "government agencies" (the public has no ownership interest) and "government-sponsored enterprises" (some public ownership).
State and local bonds	Maturities of more than one year. Income exempt from federal taxes and local taxes in state and/or city of issue. Rated by rating agencies; AAA-rated bonds very safe.
Banker's acceptances	Drafts accepted by banks for later payment. Obligations of the bank. Maturities of one to six months.
Negotiable certificates of deposit (CDs)	Large denomination term borrowing by banks. Maturities between a few days and 18 months. Banks encourage secondary market to help primary issuance.
Repurchase agreements (Repos)	Borrowing by selling securities and simultaneously agreeing to repurchase them at a specified date. Maturities very short; most frequent maturity: overnight.
Commercial paper and Euronotes	Short-term unsecured borrowings of large corporations. Maturities of less than nine months—tailored to parties' needs.
Money market mutual funds	Pooled money owning a portfolio of money market securities. Company can write checks directly on the fund to convert the investment back to cash. Particularly suitable for small firms that cannot afford to manage a portfolio of marketable securities themselves.
Variable-rate preferred stock	Seventy percent of dividends are tax-free to corporations. Variable interest rate means the stock always sells close to par value, thus avoiding the interest rate risk that would accompany such a perpetual-life issue.

FIGURE 15.7

Marketable securities. Characteristics of the more common investments used by companies to earn interest on temporary excess cash.

NET Present Value
Information about U.S. Treasury securities can be found at:
www.treasurydirect.gov

tances, negotiable certificates of deposit, repurchase agreements, commercial paper, Euronotes, money market mutual funds, and variable-rate preferred stock. Figure 15.7 summarizes some of the key characteristics of each of these investment instruments.

A firm with significant inflows of temporary cash might find itself holding a portfolio of marketable securities. In Chapter 8 we looked at the dynamics of a portfolio and discovered that systematic risk can be reduced by diversifying the portfolio to lower its beta.[8] For a portfolio of marketable securities, however, diversification of this kind is not possible. In practice, the primary systematic factor affecting the risk of marketable securities is the level of interest rates—when rates rise, marketable securities fall in value together, and vice versa. As a result, the risk of one security does not offset that of another, and a portfolio of many marketable securities has much the same risk as a large holding of only one. This does not mean that financial managers should ignore the mix of marketable securities. Securities should be selected based on their maturity dates to hedge the timing of future cash needs. This ensures that the company will receive known face values from redeeming the securities rather than having to sell them in the market and receive uncertain future market values.

Because there is a cost to buying and selling marketable securities—the banker's or broker's fee plus the administrative cost of managing the transaction—it is not always efficient to invest every dollar of excess cash in marketable securities. Web Appendix 15A presents several models that attempt to find an optimal cash-marketable securities policy.

3. Temporary Accounts Receivable

A company's balance of accounts receivable will vary about its base level when its sales vary due to the business cycle or to seasonality or when special terms of payment are negotiated with individual customers. Customers applying for credit are evaluated against a set of criteria often summarized as the "five Cs":

NET Present Value
More on extending and managing credit can be found at the website of the National Association of Credit Management:
http://www.nacm.org

- **Character** Does the credit applicant honor obligations?
- **Capacity** Does the applicant have the ability to pay?
- **Capital** Does the applicant have sufficient financial strength to withstand reverses and still make payments?
- **Collateral** Does the applicant have assets that can be seized and sold to provide cash in case of lack of payment?
- **Conditions** What outside factors, such as a downturn in economic activity, might alter the situation and make repayment difficult? What is the probability of each downside scenario, and what is the effect of each scenario on the applicant?

If an exchange of currency is taking place, other considerations enter the credit decision: the choice of currency in which to denominate the transaction and the impact of changing foreign exchange values on the payment terms. As recipient of the payment, the seller will prefer the sale to be denominated in the stronger currency, whereas the buyer will prefer to pay with the weaker currency. If the buying firm's currency is the stronger of the two, there is a tendency for the seller to be generous with payment terms to keep the amount denominated in the strong currency as long as possible. Conversely, if the selling firm's currency is the stronger, the tendency is to shorten terms in order to move the money to the stronger currency as quickly as possible. The relative bargaining power of the parties and the extent to which they have created alignment in their relationship, cou-

---

[8] **Cross-reference:** Diversification and its implications are discussed in the second half of Chapter 8, beginning on page 202.

FINANCE IN PRACTICE

The Global Recession Leads to Excessive Working Capital

Even though the global economy inmproved in 2010, the effects of the worldworld recession appear to be lingering in the form of increased levels of working capital. An analysis of 2,000 companies in the United States and Europe recently prepared by Ernst & Young, the large accounting and consulting firm, concluded that these companies have US$1.1 trillion in unnecessary working capital, just less than 7% of their annual sales and roughly equal to the Gross Domestic Product of South Korea.

Although more efficient working capital management would free up money that could be used elsewhere, in many cases one company's gain is another's loss. Last year, for example, European pharmaceutical companies reduced their working capital by 6%, primarily due to more aggressive collection of accounts receivables. However, as their receivables declined, so did the accounts payable of their customers, increasing the customers' working capital by the same amount.

Source: Ernst & Young news release, "US$1 trillion plus still tied up in working capital despite modest improvements," May 31, 2011.

pled with their exchange-rate forecasts, usually determines the outcome of this negotiation. Also, one or both parties might favor the other's currency for cash flow reasons. The seller might need the buyer's currency to meet local payment obligations or to retire debt. The buyer might have a supply of the seller's currency obtained from foreign revenues or borrowing.

4. Temporary Inventory

Companies adjust their finished goods and merchandise inventories about the permanent base level in response to seasonal manufacturing or selling peaks. They tend to accumulate raw materials when price increases are anticipated, either domestically or because of a change in foreign exchange rates. They also stock up when price or exchange controls are forecasted that would limit the company's future ability to acquire materials.

When a commodity is a critical raw material, companies often buy large amounts in advance of their needs to lock in a price. This can be through direct purchase or by buying forward contracts, futures, or options to guarantee a price for later delivery. Examples are grain for cereal producers or fuel for airlines.

5. Temporary Payables

When productive resources are purchased on credit, accounts payable will rise and fall with inventories. Wages payable will vary during seasonal peaks. Accounts payable will vary around its base level due to the same factors that affect accounts receivable.

Special terms of payment might be negotiated with individual suppliers when the volume or riskiness of the customer's business differs from the company's norms or when one party can raise funds more cheaply than the other due to financial strength or superior financial market access. As part of a customer-supplier alignment, a financially strong buyer often shortens the payment period to aid a weaker supplier while a financially strong supplier can extend credit for a longer period of time. Also, the same foreign currency considerations discussed above under accounts receivable apply to the buyer as the other party to the transaction.

6. Poor Temporary Working Capital Management

Although temporary working capital may appear to be a small part of a company's resources, poor temporary current working capital management can lead to financial distress. This is because a firm's liquidity is intimately connected to its working capital balances. When working capital is out of control, it is easy for a company to become illiquid and be unable to pay its bills.

Hedging Temporary Working Capital Flows

The time lags between the receipt and payment of cash and the need to convert currencies expose the firm to financial market risks. What interest rate will be available next month between the payments for production and sales and the collection of the resulting accounts receivable? What will the exchange rate be in 90 days when a large inflow denominated in a foreign currency is expected to arrive? Because of its ability to reduce or eliminate these exposures, hedging is used extensively to stabilize the value of many cash obligations and receipts.

Since the purpose of hedging an obligation is to ensure that the correct amount and type of money is available when needed, one technique is to invest in an asset that pays back the required amount of cash on the due date of the obligation.

Example

Hedging a Liability
Suppose you have a $5,000 tuition bill to pay next September. You could guarantee you will have the money when you need it by investing in a $5,000 face value certificate of deposit that matures on September 1.

Other common ways to hedge are to use forward contracts and derivatives.

1. Forward Contracts

forward contract—a contract binding the parties to a future transaction on a specified date and at a specified price or rate

One way to eliminate risk is to pay another party to assume it. A **forward contract** is an agreement committing the parties to enter into an exchange at a specified future date at a specified price. Because the price at which the exchange will take place is specified, forward contracts insulate the company from changes in prices or rates between the date the contract is signed and the date of the exchange.

We introduced the concept of forward foreign exchange contracts in Chapter 4.[9] These contracts are available for periods of a few days to about one year and are widely used to hedge cash flows from day-to-day transactions with foreign customers and suppliers.

[9] **Cross-reference:** See pages 103–105.

Example

Using a Forward Exchange Contract

Your company has placed an order with a British supplier which requires a payment of £20,000 in 30 days when the goods are expected to arrive. You could hedge that obligation by entering into a forward exchange contract and depositing the present value of the contractual amount at your bank. In return for your deposit, the bank will provide the £20,000 in 30 days.

forward rate agreement (FRA)—a contract binding the parties to a future loan on a specified date, for a specified period, and at a specified interest rate

Forward contracts known as **forward rate agreements (FRAs)** are also available on interest rates and are used to lock in a borrowing or lending rate for a future time period.

Example

Using a Forward Rate Agreement

Your company expects to receive $30,000 from customers during the first week of next month; however, the money will not be required to cover accounts payable for another 20 days. Rather than wait and invest the money at the floating rate available next month, you could guarantee the rate the money will earn by purchasing a forward rate note today for that 20-day period.

The primary suppliers of forward contracts are commercial banks. This might make it appear that banks are assuming huge risks—all the risks offloaded by the companies that enter into the forward contracts. However, this is not the case. Each bank is also engaged in hedging, in this case to offset its exposures. For example, if a bank commits to provide Swiss francs to one customer in 90 days, it looks to enter another 90-day contract in which it commits to purchase the same number of Swiss francs at the same price. It can then simply deliver the francs from one customer to the other, without having to exchange currencies. While it is difficult, if not impossible, to offset each exposure with a precisely opposite contract, it is possible to net out the bank's exposure across all forward contracts to a substantial degree. (Notice that this is much like the maturity-range hedging we looked at earlier in this chapter: it is difficult to hedge individual assets and liabilities, but it is very possible to hedge ranges of maturities.) By balancing its foreign exchange "book," the bank nets out its own risks while it reduces the risks faced by its customers.

Although forward contracts can eliminate the risk of future price and rate changes, they do not eliminate all risks. Forward contracts are a commitment; the firm must go through with the exchange. If a company enters into a forward contract to hedge an anticipated receipt that never comes, the company must honor the contract, even if there is now a high cost to obtaining the money.

2. Derivatives

derivative—a contract whose value is defined by a financial market rate or the price of a financial instrument

Derivatives are contracts whose value changes with the price of a specified ("underlying") security, money rate, or economic index. Because their value is driven by the underlying economic variable, they are particularly useful for hedging the risk of being exposed to that variable. Some derivatives, such as futures and options, come in relatively standard forms and are traded on the organized securities exchanges. Others are custom-designed to meet the specific needs of investors and financial managers.

"Tell me again, how were you able to reduce our financial risk so quickly?"

Puts and calls on common stock,[10] the oldest form of derivatives, have been around for a long time. However, the increased volatility of interest and exchange rates stemming from the oil price shocks of the early 1970s and the subsequent liberalization and globalization of world trade made financial managers eager to find new risk management opportunities. Formalized trading of options began in the mid-1970s, and the number of types and uses for derivatives exploded dramatically during the 1980s. In the year 2010, for example, some $994 trillion of futures and options on agricultural products, commodities, weather events, interest rates, currencies, and stock indexes changed hands on the exchanges of the CME Group: The Chicago Merchantile Exchange, Chicago Board of Trade, and New York Merchantile Exchange.[11]

When used for hedging, derivatives are purchased or sold to create an exposure that is equal and opposite to the risk to be hedged. In this way, the movement of one cancels out the other.

Example

Using Derivatives to Hedge Temporary Working Capital
Belleco Resources expects to accumulate an inventory of petroleum over the next three months and sell it at the end of that period. Belleco's treasurer is concerned, however, that spot oil prices will decline over the three-month period, reducing the value of the inventory. To hedge this risk, the treasurer has sold futures contracts whose value is tied to the price of oil and which commit Belleco to deliver the oil in three months. Should the price of oil decline, the contracts would increase in value (since they would be cheaper to fulfill) and would offset Belleco's loss of inventory value.

[10] **Cross-reference:** Puts and calls, the basic types of options, are introduced in Web Appendix 6D.
[11] **Reference:** CME Group 2010 Annual Report, CME Group website.

Four basic types of derivatives are (1) options, (2) futures, (3) swaps, and (4) synthetic securities.

Options   Options represent a right to purchase or sell some asset at a prespecified price and within a certain time. Exchange-traded options are available on common stocks, stock indexes such as the Standard & Poor's 500 index, interest rates, major international currencies, futures contracts, and commodities.

future—an exchange-traded standardized forward contract

Futures   Like a forward contract, a **future** is also a contract committing the parties to enter into an exchange at a specified future date at a specified price. However, unlike forward contracts, which are tailored to the needs of the parties, futures contracts are standardized so they can be traded on the securities exchanges. As with options, futures are available for common stocks, stock indexes, interest rates, currencies, and commodities.

swap—an exchange of financial obligations

Swaps   A **swap** is an exchange of obligations between two parties, for example a dollar loan for a pound sterling loan. It permits a company to trade away a risky exposure for one considered less risky. Swaps are individually arranged by commercial or investment banks which maintain an active resale market for swap contracts, allowing a company to get out of a swap it previously entered or assume the obligations of an existing swap arrangement.

synthetic security—an artificial security constructed from real securities and derivatives

Synthetic securities   **Synthetic securities** are securities constructed from a combination of real securities and derivatives. Sometimes the new security's cash flow pattern is the same as an already existing security; other times the pattern is something brand new. When they recreate the pattern of cash flows of an already existing security, their purpose is to get around regulatory, tax, or accounting limitations, or to make that cash flow pattern available to a market participant who otherwise would find it unavailable. New cash flow patterns create new hedging opportunities, as well as new investment and financing opportunities, for financial managers.

Clif Carlton walked into the conference room with a big smile on his face and tossed the stack of computer reports on the table. "Nice job, gang," he said, provoking the usual mock protest from one team member who kept insisting that he had no desire to be part of a gang. "We're making great progress in getting our risk exposure under better control."

Three months had elapsed since Clif first called the team together. In that time, the team had studied the company's increasing risk exposure, met with the company's bankers, and laid out a strategy for improving the firm's risk management activities.

The team began its work with a look at the maturities of the company's assets and liabilities. A comparison with past balance sheets identified that the company's asset maturities had changed over the past five years but no comparable changes had been made to the firm's liability structure. The team identified the

FINANCE IN PRACITICE

Southwest Airline's Fuel Hedging Strategy

In the late 2000s the global financial crisis turned into a global recession, and profits in the airline industry plummeted as leisure travel was postponed and business travel was drastically curtailed. After making profits of $15.0 billion in 2006 and $19.9 billion in 2007, the world's airlines lots $8.9 billion in 2008. Southwest Airlines, however, remained in the black; while the four largest US airlines (American, Delta/Northwest, United/Continental, and US Airways) lost a combined $19.2 billion in 2009, Southwest turned a profit of $178 million.

The primary reason for Southwest's success was its program of fuel hedging. Aircraft fuel typically accounts for 30-35% of the cost of running an airline. In 2008, forecasting rising fuel prices, the low cost carrier used petroleum futures to lock in a price of $51 per barrel for more than 70% of the fuel it expected to use that year. Its competitors, not anticipating a significant price increase, only hedged 20-30% of their anticipated fuel purchases at a price of about $100 per barrel. When crude oil prices soared to $145 per barrel in July 2008, Southwest had a significant cost advantage over its competitors who were now paying 2-3 times as much for fuel.

The price of crude oil fell significantly toward the end of 2008 reaching $36.51 in January 2009, and for several months Southwest lost money on its fuel hedges. However, as CFO Laura Wright pointed out, the savings from lower fuel costs were far more beneficial to the company than the losses on the futures contracts. And, by March 2009, the price of crude had risen again above $51 per barrel and continued to rise thereafter. As this is written in mid-2011, the price of a barrel of crude oil is again above $100, and Southwest Airlines is once again in a very strong financial position compared to its competitors.

References: Air Transport Association website; http://airlines.org/Economics/DataAnalysis/Pages/AnnualResultsWorldAirlines.aspx; Bloomberg Professional Service; Peter Pae, Hedge on Fuel Prices Pay Off, Los Angeles Times, March 30,2008; New York Mercantile Exchange website: http://www.nyse.tv/crude-oil-price-history.htm.

mismatched maturities and then invited the company's investment bankers to join them in a discussion of how to adjust the company's financing. Together, they recommended a moderate increase in intermediate-term borrowing plus the refinancing of one bond issue, a transaction that had just been completed this past week.

Next the team turned its attention to improving how the company hedged its daily cash flows. After passing around two books and countless magazine articles taken from the company library, they attended a seminar on financial derivatives, sponsored by their commercial bank. On returning to the office, they made a modest proposal to begin testing some of the newer derivative products. Clif had approved the experiment enthusiastically, and the early results were quite encouraging.

Clif looked around the room, and it was clear he was genuinely pleased. "Last month when I was over at our bank, their risk management specialists walked me through the exposure book they maintain to be sure their interest rate and currency risks are as fully hedged as possible. It seems to me we're well on the way to running our own little 'bank' a whole lot better than we used to."

Summary of Key Points

■ **Discuss how hedging can reduce financial risks.** Hedging is balancing a risky financial position with an opposite position to cancel risk. It includes offsetting assets and liabilities with equal amounts and maturities. Hedging balance sheet aggregate numbers ensures that cash will be available to pay liabilities as they fall due. Hedging individual cash flows guarantees that receipts can be used efficiently and that obligations have a known cost.

■ **Describe the four-step sequence of working capital decisions.** Current account balances are the result of a four-step decision process: (1) permanent current asset alternatives with positive NPV are accepted, creating the permanent current asset balance, (2) current liabilities with a low or zero interest rate are taken, creating the first portion of the permanent current liability balance, (3) additional debt is divided among maturities to hedge the balance sheet; the short-term portion completes the current liability balance, and (4) temporary current assets and liabilities are taken as they arise naturally in day-to-day operations.

■ **Discuss how companies set their debt maturity mix.** The debt maturity mix is a product of the third step of the working capital sequence. Debt maturities are selected to hedge the balance sheet, establishing a risk-return position between debt costs and liquidity risk. While financial institutions can hedge individual assets and liabilities, nonfinancial companies hedge maturity ranges. Because of their long-term presence, permanent current assets are included with noncurrent assets for this analysis. Some companies elect to deviate from maturity-range hedging to reach a preferred combination of risk and return.

■ **Relate how temporary working capital arises in the current accounts.** Temporary cash comes from imbalances in cash inflows and outflows, and from large dollar transactions. Marketable securities permit the firm to earn interest on otherwise idle excess cash. Temporary accounts receivable often represent the tailoring of the firm's receivables policy to its customers. Temporary inventory reflects business seasonalities or large-scale commodities purchases. Temporary payables follow the production cycle and arise for the same reasons as temporary accounts receivable.

■ **Discuss the basics of hedging against foreign currency and interest rate movements including the use of derivative securities.** Companies use forward contracts and derivative securities to deal with exchange and interest rate positions. Forward contracts guarantee that the other party, often a commercial bank, will provide an agreed-upon price, or interest rate, or exchange rate at some future date. Derivative securities—options, futures, swaps, and synthetic securities—move in value opposite to the firm's exposure, creating a gain (or loss) that balances out any loss (or gain) suffered by the firm due to price or rate movements.

Questions

1. Why does hedging reduce risk?

2. What is the difference between hedging across the balance sheet and hedging individual cash flows?

3. What are the four steps in putting working capital on the balance sheet?

4. Why are the "attractive short-term financing opportunities," described in the second step of the four-step process, considered before other debt financing?

5. How is the current ratio used in setting the debt maturity mix? Can you think of any other financial measures that also could be used in this analysis?

6. Why is the debt maturity mix normally simplified to short- versus long-term debt? What, if anything, is lost in making this simplification?

7. What role does the debt maturity mix play in the firm's overall risk-return posture?

8. Distinguish between individual asset/liability hedging and maturity-range hedging. What type of company can do each?

9. What role do permanent current assets play in maturity-range hedging?

10. Why do companies deviate from maturity-range hedging?

11. What factor(s) enter the decisions about the composition of a portfolio of marketable securities?

12. Which financial instruments are most commonly used as marketable securities?

13. What is meant by the "five Cs"?

14. Some financial professionals consider forward contracts to be another kind of derivative security. Why do you think this is so?

15. How does a forward contract work as a hedging device?

16. How does a derivative security work as a hedging device?

17. A new finance student was overheard making the following statement: "In efficient financial markets, all hedging devices should be perfect substitutes!" Discuss.

18. Draw a flow chart of the four-step working capital process.

Problems

1. **(Four-step sequence)** A company with $2 million of low-cost current financing opportunities wishes to target a current ratio of 2.5. How much additional short-term financing should it raise if its permanent current asset balance is:

   a. $10 million?   c. $5 million?
   b. $8 million?   d. $2 million?

2. **(Four-step sequence)** A company with $25 million of permanent current assets has $4 million of low-cost current financing opportunities. How much additional short-term financing should it raise if its target current ratio is:

   a. 1.8?   c. 2.4?
   b. 2.0?   d. 2.8?

3. **(Debt-maturity mix)** A company has $25 million of current assets and another $25 million of noncurrent assets. It forecasts an EBIT of $5 million and is in the 35% income tax bracket. Currently the yield curve is normal; bank notes carry a 7% interest rate, and the company can issue long-term bonds at 12%. The company has set a target debt ratio of 40%. For each of the following debt maturity mixes: (1) construct the company's balance sheet, (2) construct the financial half of its income statement, and (3) evaluate its risk and return using the return on equity and current ratios.

   a. 20% of the debt is current, 80% long-term
   b. 40% of the debt is current, 60% long-term
   c. 60% of the debt is current, 40% long-term
   d. 80% of the debt is current, 20% long-term

4. **(Debt-maturity mix)** A company has $400 million of assets of which $250 are current assets. It forecasts a basic earning power ratio of 15% and is in the 35% income tax bracket. Currently the yield curve is normal; bank notes carry a 5% interest rate, and the company can issue long-term bonds at 10%. The company has set a target debt ratio of 50%. For each of the following debt maturity mixes: (1) construct the company's balance sheet, (2) construct the financial half of its income statement, and (3) evaluate its risk and return using the return on equity and current ratios.

   a. 20% of the debt is current, 80% long-term
   b. 40% of the debt is current, 60% long-term
   c. 60% of the debt is current, 40% long-term
   d. 80% of the debt is current, 20% long-term

PART V
RETURNING VALUE TO SHARE-HOLDERS

Chapter 16
Dividend Policy

Chapter 17
Increasing Share Price

In Part V we look at how shareholders receive value from their investment in a company.

Chapter 16 examines dividend theory and practice. We review how shareholders get their returns and describe five classes of dividend theories. Then we discuss patterns of dividends and how they are paid.

Chapter 17 explores the linkage between a company's actions and its share price. We review four financial managing techniques that can add value to a firm. Then we describe techniques used by shareholders and financial analysts to value a company's stock. We identify two important barriers to good financial managing: the agency barrier and the finance theory barrier. Finally we look at how companies communicate their activities to the financial community.

CHAPTER 16

DIVIDEND POLICY

*B*ob Woods looked up from his pad of paper but continued to scribble furiously, making notes of everything the CFO said. Bob was a new member of the finance organization of his company. As part of his training, he had been invited to join a team to recommend a new dividend policy to the board of directors at their next meeting. The CFO had just finished outlining the company's past dividend practice and was turning to the current policy issue.

"It seems as if everybody has their own idea about what our dividend should be. You all know that the son of our founder sits on the board and lives on the dividends we pay him. He would love to see the dividend raised. Some other board members have strong feelings about keeping continuity in our payout policy. So, if they have their way, not only can't we pay less than last quarter, we can't pay so much that the dividend becomes unsustainable and we might have to reduce it later. Now the president talks about reducing the dividend because of the taxes it forces our shareholders to pay. On the other hand, the chairman believes we must be more aggressive in distributing our profits to shareholders. As for me, sometimes I wonder why we pay a dividend at all. If we retained the money we could avoid raising other funds with all the costs and problems that entails."

After the CFO's presentation, the team got into an animated discussion over how to approach the problem. Bob found the talk fascinating—there certainly were conflicting opinions about what to do. But he was bothered by the sense that he hadn't heard any solid basis for making the decision, only a collection of observations and "gut feelings." As he left the meeting, Bob headed to the company library to read all he could about dividend policy.

The problem Bob and his colleagues are grappling with is a difficult one for most financial managers because there is no single comprehensive theory to guide a company's dividend payments. The situation is quite similar to the debt-equity mix and debt maturity mix decisions, described in Chapters 14 and 15: there are conflicting points of view over what dividend payment stream maximizes the value of a firm to its stockholders, as well to any other stakeholders who might be affected by the decision. Bob's team will have to balance a variety of ideas to arrive at a policy appropriate for his company.

dividend policy—a company's plan for the level and pattern of its dividend payments

In this chapter we look at the theoretical and practical considerations financial managers face in establishing a corporation's **dividend policy.** We use the word *policy* intentionally because it is not enough to decide solely on the next dividend. Both theory and practice tell us that the pattern of dividend payments is as important a consideration as the amount of each payment.

Key Points You Should Learn from This Chapter

After reading this chapter you should be able to:

■ Explain how shareholders get their returns.

■ Describe five classes of theory that attempt to identify a company's optimal dividend policy.

■ Discuss seven practical considerations in setting a firm's dividend.

■ Describe the mechanics of how dividends are declared and paid.

Introductory Concepts—Does It Matter How Shareholders Get Their Returns?

A **dividend** is any direct payment from a firm to its stockholders. Dividends may be paid in cash, but they may also be in the form of stock or other noncash distributions. This includes stock splits and stock dividends, as well as spinoffs of units of the business. An alternative to cash dividends is the repurchase of common shares.

Dividends are one of the two methods by which stockholders receive value from their investment (the other is via capital gains—*if* the price of their shares goes up). Dividends put cash or other valuable paper into the hands of investors, money that can be spent or reinvested. Other things equal, then, investors should prefer to receive high and regular dividends. But are other things equal?

In Chapter 9, we applied the growing cash stream model—renamed the *dividend-growth model* for this application—to common stock. We assumed a constant rate of dividend growth to simplify the mathematics and calculated the value of a share as the present value of the firm's dividend stream. We concluded that a stock's market value depends on the upcoming dividend (D_1), investors' required rate of return from the common stock (r_c), and the firm's rate of growth[1] (g):

$$Stock\ value = PV\ of\ dividend\ stream = \frac{D_1}{r_c - g}$$

This relationship is consistent with our earlier observation: other things equal, a higher dividend produces a higher stock value. In fact, if investors do not change their growth forecast or required rate of return, the value of a share will rise by the same proportion as the increase in the dividend.

Examples

A Dividend Increase, Other Things Equal

Yesterday, investors forecast that the Dolan Company would pay a $4.00 per share dividend one year from now, and would increase the dividend at the rate of 6% per year. Investors require a 15% rate of return.

Question: What was the value of one share of Dolan's stock yesterday?

Solution steps: Use the dividend-growth model:

$$Stock\ value = \frac{D_1}{r_c - g} = \frac{\$4.00}{.15 - .06} = \frac{\$4.00}{.09} = \$44.44$$

Answer: Dolan's stock was worth $\underline{\$44.44\ per\ share}$.

In today's newspaper, Dolan's CFO was quoted as saying that the company expects to pay a dividend of $4.40 per share next year.

---

[1] **Observation:**   Strictly speaking, g is the growth rate of the firm's dividend stream, the cash flow that is being evaluated in this present value model. However, in estimating a value for g, many analysts also look at the growth rate of the variables that underlie the firm's ability to pay a dividend, such as sales and earnings, especially if the company's dividend stream has been low (or zero) or erratic, making future dividends difficult to forecast.

Question: What will Dolan's share value be after the announcement if investors do not change their growth forecast or their required rate of return?

Solution steps:

$$\text{Stock value} = \frac{D_1}{r_c - g} = \frac{\$4.40}{.15 - .06} = \frac{\$4.40}{.09} = \$48.89$$

Answer: The value of one share of Dolan's stock will <u>rise by 10%, from $44.44 to $48.89</u> in response to the 10% rise in the next estimated dividend.

Even if investors change their growth forecast or required rate of return, increased dividends could lead to an increase in a stock's value. This would occur if stockholders' required rate of return (r_c) declines or the growth rate (g) anticipated by investors increases. However, if raising the dividend reduces investors' forecasts of the firm's growth rate or increases their required rate of return, increasing the dividend could depress the value of the company's stock.

Example

A Dividend Increase, Other Things *Not* Equal

In response to Dolan Company's announcement of a dividend increase, investors do not modify their 15% required rate of return. However, they conclude that the company will have less money to reinvest in the business and reduce their growth forecast to 4% per year.

Question: What will happen to Dolan's share value?

Solution steps: Use the dividend-growth model:

$$\text{Stock value} = \frac{D_1}{r_c - g} = \frac{\$4.40}{.15 - .04} = \frac{\$4.40}{.11} = \$40.00$$

Answer: The value of Dolan's stock will <u>fall from $44.44 to $40.00</u>. Rather than add to shareholders' wealth, the dividend increase reduced value.

The critical question about dividends then is whether—and if so, how—a dividend paid today changes investors' forecasts of future dividends or their required rate of return. The combination of dividends and investors' reactions that produces the highest value for shareholders will define a company's optimal dividend policy.

Dividend Theories

Finance thinkers have identified many factors that might affect investors' reaction to dividends. Unfortunately, there is little theory to join them into a coherent picture. In fact, the various arguments are downright contradictory in many respects. In the discussion below we present these factors grouped under five headings: (1) theories that argue for the payment of dividends, (2) theories that argue against the payment of dividends, (3) a theory that concludes that dividends are irrelevant since they have nothing to do with the value of the firm, (4) theories that argue that any dividend is acceptable as long as the company is consistent, and (5) a theory that argues against setting a dividend policy in the first place.

1. Theories That Argue for the Payment of Dividends

These theories claim that the benefits from dividends exceed any offsetting changes in investors' forecasts of growth or required rates of return.

Risk-reduction theories   These three theories argue that the payment of a dividend reduces investors' perceived risk, reducing their required rate of return. The cash from the dividend and the reduced risk combine to increase the value of a share of stock.

- Resolution of uncertainty: Payment of a dividend resolves some of investors' uncertainty about their returns. This is because dividends are more difficult to forecast, hence riskier, the further they are into the future.[2] In the context of the present value model, investors apply a lower required rate of return to evaluate current dividends than to evaluate future dividends. As a result, paying current dividends reduces investors' net (averaged over time) required rate of return, yielding a higher stock value.

- Information transmittal: Dividends, especially changes in dividends, convey useful data to investors permitting better predictions of the company's future performance. For example, an increase in the dividend often signals management's confidence that the firm can support a higher payout while an unchanging dividend when earnings rise suggests a cautious management attitude. Note that only firms with truly good prospects can credibly raise their dividends, or else the dividend signal would quickly backfire as investors discovered that management was bluffing. For the announcement of a dividend increase to send a meaningful signal, the higher dividend must be sustainable. Improved information lowers investors' uncertainty, reducing their risk and lowering their required rate of return. A company that does not pay a dividend forgoes this opportunity to communicate with the financial markets.

- Liquidity: Dividends increase investors' liquidity by converting a portion of their investment value into cash. By contrast, investors who need cash but receive their returns in the form of stock price appreciation, risk having to sell some of their shares in what could turn out to be poor market conditions. Payment of dividends permits investors to manage their liquidity better, reducing the risk of their investment position and, correspondingly, reducing their required rate of return.

Market imperfection theories   Financial markets are imperfect if the law does not treat all investors equally. These two theories argue that investors find the shares of companies that pay dividends particularly attractive due to regulatory or tax law and are willing to accept a lower rate of return. Investors increase the demand for dividend-paying shares raising their value.

- Legal restrictions: Some institutional investors can only acquire shares of stock if they pay dividends. For example, life insurance companies are restricted by the laws of most states to invest only in securities that pay interest or divi-

---

[2] **Elaboration:**   This argument is sometimes called the "bird in the hand" theory after the old, familiar proverb. In this context: "$1 in the hand is worth $2 still inside the corporate bush."

dends. Other investors, such as endowment funds, are often prohibited by their charters from touching the fund's principal and depend on dividends for income.

● Tax preferences: Two provisions of the tax code make dividend-paying stocks particularly attractive to investors. First, corporate investors benefit from the rule that 70% of the dividends paid by one corporation to another are tax-free. For an investor corporation in the 35% bracket, intercompany dividends are taxed at an effective rate of only (35% × 30% =) 10.5% raising the after-tax rate of return. Second, a company that does not pay dividends risks a tax penalty if the Internal Revenue Service determines it has "improperly accumulated" retained earnings. Paying a regular dividend lessens the chance of running afoul of the IRS.[3]

Efficiency theory   Financial market efficiency is enhanced when investors have the freedom to direct new investment dollars to the best available opportunities. This theory argues that investors prefer firms that pay dividends since this permits them to reinvest their earnings where they desire. By contrast, a company that retains earnings limits its shareholders' opportunities, forcing them to reinvest only in that company. Investors are willing to pay a premium (accept a lower rate of return) for reinvestment flexibility, a premium that directly increases the value of dividend-paying stocks.

2. Theories That Argue Against the Payment of Dividends

These theories argue that adverse changes to investors' forecasts of growth or required rates of return outweigh any benefits from paying dividends.

Supply-demand theory   When the supply of a company's stock goes up, its price faces downward pressure. A company in need of additional equity can avoid selling shares of its stock by not paying dividends and retaining its earnings instead. Figure 16.1, a traditional supply-demand graph, illustrates how selling new

FIGURE 16.1

Supply-demand theory. Dividends should be avoided because they force companies to sell new shares, increasing their supply and lowering their price.

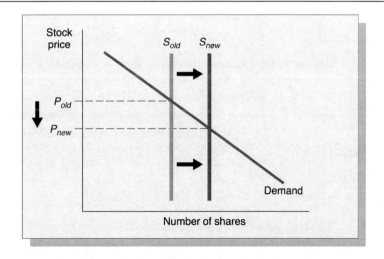

---

[3] **Cross-reference:**   See Web Appendix 2E for more detail about these provisions of the corporate tax code.

shares can lower a company's stock price. S_{old} (old supply) and S_{new} (new supply) represent the number of shares outstanding before and after a new stock issue. The intersection of the supply and demand curves determines the market equilibrium price, which declines from P_{old} to P_{new}. Effectively, to attract new stockholders—people who previously chose not to invest in the company—the stock must provide a higher rate of return; and the market price of the new shares, and therefore the market price of *all* shares, must fall.

Market imperfection theories These financial market imperfections are "frictions," costs arising from the payment of dividends that remove value from the firm and its shareholders. Each one either reduces after-tax dividends today or lowers investors' forecast of future growth. A company can avoid these costs by not paying dividends.

- Processing costs: Banks charge a fee for transferring the funds.

- Flotation costs: In Chapter 10 we saw that flotation costs make the cost of external equity greater than the cost of retained earnings. Since companies that pay dividends eventually substitute external equity for the earnings they are not retaining, they raise their cost of capital. But high company value is consistent with minimizing the cost of capital, as we saw in Chapter 14.[4] This problem is especially acute for firms needing limited amounts of new equity financing as small stock issues are particularly costly to sell.

- Tax differences: Dividends are effectively taxed twice, once as corporate income and once as personal income to the investor.[5] Firms that do not pay dividends do not expose their shareholders to this double taxation. By contrast, capital gains are taxed only once to the investor, are not taxed until the security is sold, and are taxed at a lower rate (0% versus 10% or 15%; and 15% versus 25%, 28%, 33%, or 35%).[6]

Control theory Reliance on external sources of equity financing results in the continued dilution of each shareholder's percentage ownership. For some investors, dilution translates to lower future dividends. For others, dilution means added risk—and a higher required rate of return—as it reduces their influence on the firm. A company can minimize dilution by not selling new shares, hence by retaining its earnings and not paying dividends.

Sustainable growth theory Sustainable growth refers to the ability of a firm to grow without selling additional common shares. As a company grows, it typically needs additional financing, and the new money must come from both debt and equity sources if the firm is to maintain a target debt-equity mix. However, retained earnings is the sole source of equity financing for small or financially weak companies that cannot (and for larger companies that choose not to) access the equity markets. A company that cannot sell new shares yet pays a dividend limits its growth potential. In response, investors lower their forecast of future growth, reducing the value of the firm's stock.

---

[4] **Cross-reference:**   Chapter 10, pages 252–253; Chapter 14, pages 342–343.

[5] **Cross-reference:**   See Web Appendix 2E.

[6] **Elaboration:**   These lower rates are for long-term capital gains, gains on securities held for more than one year, realized in 2008-2012. From 2013 forward the long-term capital gains and ordinary income tax rates change to 10% versus 15%; and 20% versus 28%, 31%, 36%, or 39.6%.

SERVING FINANCE'S CUSTOMERS

Reducing the Dividend at Bank of America

During the mid-2000s, Bank of America enjoyed healthy growth and rewarded its shareholders by raising its dividend from 10¢/share in March 2003 to 64¢/share in September 2007. But the financial crisis forced the bank to turn to the U.S. Government for help. As a condition of the "bailout", the government required the bank to reduce its dividends to conserve cash; BofA complied by halving the dividend to 32¢/share in December 2008 and then reducing it to 1¢/share in March 2009.

In March 2011, the Federal Reserve announced that the large banks that had received federal assistance could begin to increase their dividends providing they passed "stress tests" to see if they had recovered sufficiently to withstand another recession. Bank of America promptly submitted a request to raise its dividend for the second half of 2011, but the Fed rejected the bank's request concluding that it was not yet healthy enough to survive another economic downturn.

3. A Theory That Concludes Dividends Are Irrelevant

In Chapter 14 we met Professors Modigliani and Miller (MM), who proved that if the capital markets were "perfect" a firm's value would be independent of its debt-equity mix.[7] MM have made a similar argument for dividends, concluding that the dividend decision also does not affect the value of the firm's stock.

MM begin by assuming the same perfect market conditions used in their proof of the irrelevance of financing choice. They show that payment of a dividend decreases shareholders' value by exactly the amount of the dividend. The sum of the remaining market value and the dividend is constant regardless of the amount of the dividend, thus the dividend does not change shareholders' wealth.

Examples

Modigliani-Miller Dividend Theory

The Dolan Company is financed only with equity. Stockholders require a 15% rate of return and forecast a perpetuity of earnings after taxes (EAT) of $600. Dolan's policy is to pay out 100% of its EAT as dividends at year end.

Question: What is the market value of Dolan's stock on January 1?

Solution steps: Use the dividend-growth model with growth equal to zero (which is the same as the perpetuity model):

$$\text{Stock value} = \frac{D_1}{r_c - g} = \frac{\$600}{.15 - .00} = \$4,000$$

Dolan is considering a change to its 100% payout ratio.

Question: What will Dolan's stock be worth on December 31 if the dividend is $0, $200, $400, or $600?

Solution steps: To the January 1 value of $4,000, add this year's income and subtract the dividend:

---

[7] **Cross-reference:** See pages 342-343

Possible dividend	$0	$200	$400	$600
Value, January 1	$4,000	$4,000	$4,000	$4,000
+ EAT this year	600	600	600	600
− Dividend	0	200	400	600
Value, December 31	$4,600	$4,400	$4,200	$4,000

Question: How much total value will Dolan's stockholders have on December 31 if the dividend is $0, $200, $400, or $600?

Solution steps: Add the stock value and the dividend:

Possible dividend	$0	$200	$400	$600
Stock value, December 31	$4,600	$4,400	$4,200	$4,000
+ Dividend	0	200	400	600
Total shareholder value	$4,600	$4,600	$4,600	$4,600

Answer: <u>Dolan's shareholders will have $4,600 of total value regardless of the company's dividend</u>. The effect of the dividend is only to split shareholders' value between cash (from the dividend) and stock.

MM rely on their proof of financing irrelevance to claim that their conclusion holds for any firm, regardless of its debt-equity mix, and not just for the all-equity firm in the above example. They also show that the company's choice of dividend cannot reduce the worth of investors who would have preferred a different payout since these investors can easily reallocate their value between cash and stock. Investors who want a larger dividend can create it personally by simply selling some shares—a process called **homemade dividends,** while investors who prefer a lower dividend can reinvest some or all of the dividends they received. With perfect financial markets, these reallocations would take place with no loss in value due to brokerage costs, taxes, etc.

homemade dividends— selling shares of stock to augment a company's dividends

4. Theories That Argue for Consistency

These theories conclude that a firm's dividend policy does not matter as long as the firm is consistent in its payout.

clientele—a group of investors with a similar preference for dividends

Clientele theory   A **clientele** is an investor group with a distinct dividend preference. For example, a clientele of retired senior citizens might desire high and regular dividends for income while a clientele of high-income professionals might prefer not to receive dividends since they would be taxed at high marginal rates. This theory argues that investors will naturally gravitate toward those firms whose dividend policies meet their needs. Over time, a company's shareholders will reflect its dividend policy; there is no need to craft a dividend policy in advance to meet the needs of any particular shareholder group. Any dividend payout policy is acceptable as long as it is consistently maintained.

Market imperfection theories   These financial market imperfections prevent MM's homemade dividend process from being costless. Investors who receive a dividend different from what they prefer cannot easily reallocate their investment between cash and stock. To prevent placing shareholders in the position of having to reallocate their investment, a company should establish and maintain an announced, consistent dividend policy.

- Indivisibility of securities: Investors who hold a stock that does not pay dividends but who prefer income must sell an integral number of shares. However, this may not yield the amount of income desired. Investors who hold a stock that pays dividends but who prefer share value must buy an integral number of shares. But this may not match the amount of the dividend received. For companies with a low share price this is not a significant problem, but where share price is high, buying or selling the right amount of stock can be problematic. Consider, for example the stock of Berkshire Hathaway, Inc., which in February 2011, sold for over $131,000 per share.

- Brokerage costs: The cost to buy or sell a small number of shares is high relative to the amount of the transaction. Investors selling a few shares for income will pay excessive brokerage fees which could be avoided entirely if a dividend were paid. Investors buying a few shares with an unwanted dividend will also pay excessive brokerage fees which could be avoided entirely if no dividend were paid.

5. A Theory That Argues Against Setting a Dividend Policy

Each theory we have discussed so far in this chapter began with the assumption that it is useful to look at a company's dividend policy as a variable for the financial manager to optimize. This theory turns the subject upside down. Dividends are one-half of the decision of how to dispose of a firm's earnings after taxes (EAT). The other half is retained earnings. This theory argues that the dividend is not the important decision, rather it is the retained earnings decision that should be optimized. The dividend should merely be the residual result of the decision to retain or not to retain earnings.

According to the residual approach, a company should arrive at its dividend as follows:

1. Determine the total need for new financing from the operating and capital budgets.
2. Determine how much new financing should be equity, using the target debt-equity mix.
3. Use retained earnings to the greatest extent possible since it is the cheapest and most convenient source of new equity.
4. Make the dividend payout
   a. 100% of earnings after taxes (EAT), if no new equity funds are needed,
   b. the earnings not required for new investments, if EAT is more than sufficient to finance new equity needs, or
   c. zero, if equity needs exceed EAT.

Examples | **Residual Theory of Dividends**

The Dolan Company has determined it will require $850 million of new financing in the coming year. Its target debt ratio is 40%.

Question: How much of the new financing should come from equity to maintain the target debt-equity mix?

Solution steps: 40% of the new financing should come from debt, so 60% should come from equity.

$$60\% \times \$850 \text{ million} = \$510 \text{ million}$$

Question: What should Dolan's dividend be if it uses the residual theory of dividends and its EAT is $400 million? $600 million?

Solution steps: Compare EAT to the equity needed:

1. If EAT = $400 million. Retain all $400 million since the $510 million of equity needed exceeds EAT. Nothing is left for a dividend.
2. If EAT = $600 million. Retain $510 million and pay out the remaining $90 million.

Answer: <u>If EAT is less than the $510 million of equity needed</u>, retain it all and <u>pay a dividend of $0. If EAT exceeds $510 million</u>, retain $510 million and <u>pay out the difference</u>.

The residual theory of dividends is very much at odds with the prescription of those theories that argue for consistency of dividend payments. A firm adhering to residual theory will appear to be following an irregular dividend pattern since EAT and capital needs will vary from year to year. As a result, residual theory is not used by many financial managers.

Dividends in Practice

Given the conflicting advice of the various dividend theories, most companies use a combination of theory and practical guidelines to establish their dividend policy. Perhaps the most commonly followed rule is to maintain stability of dividend payments. A company's stage in its life cycle also plays an important role in its dividend policy. Other considerations are the availability of cash to pay the dividend, alternative uses for the cash, access to banks and financial markets to replace the cash used for dividends, shareholder preferences if ascertainable, and legal or charter restrictions on dividend payments.

1. Stability of Payments

Several of the theories identify that stability is a value-adding strategy. Stability lowers the volatility of investors' cash flows, reducing the risk of that component of their rate of return. Maintaining a stable dividend during a temporary downturn in earnings conveys management's optimism to investors and could limit a drop in stock price. Some investors look to dividends for current income and will pay more for a predictable dividend. Regular dividends attract institutional investors increasing the demand for a stock, and hence its price.

There are three common approaches to achieving stability of dividend payments: (1) maintaining a stable payout ratio, (2) maintaining a stable dollar dividend, and (3) maintaining a stable dollar dividend plus a year-end dividend bonus.

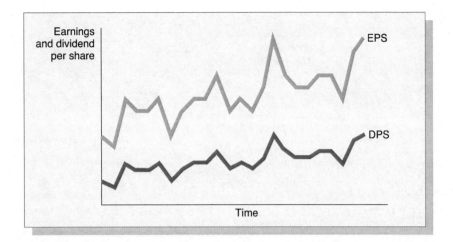

FIGURE 16.2
Stable payout ratio.
Dividends are a fixed
percentage of earnings.

Stable payout ratio   Recall that the payout ratio equals dividends divided by earnings. Under this approach, per-share dividends are kept equal to a fixed percentage of earnings per share (EPS). Of course, if followed exactly, this approach will produce a stable dividend only if EPS is stable. Figure 16.2 shows the more common scenario in which fluctuating EPS leads to a fluctuating dividend stream. As a result, financial managers who target a stable payout ratio rarely use the current quarter's or year's earnings as the basis for the dividend. Rather, they apply this method with a time lag; for example, dividends might be set equal to a percentage of average earnings over the last several years.

Example

Stable Payout Ratio

The Dolan Company reported the following earnings per share (EPS) over the past 12 quarters (three years).

Quarter	EPS	Quarter	EPS
1	$1.00	7	$1.30
2	1.20	8	1.40
3	1.30	9	1.70
4	1.25	10	1.80
5	1.45	11	2.00
6	1.50	12	2.10

Question: What quarterly dividend per share (DPS) should Dolan have paid to maintain a stable payout ratio of 40%?

Solution steps: Multiply each EPS figure by 40%:

Quarter	DPS	Quarter	DPS
1	$0.40	7	$0.52
2	0.48	8	0.56
3	0.52	9	0.68
4	0.50	10	0.72
5	0.58	11	0.80
6	0.60	12	0.84

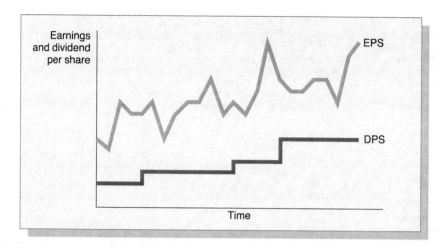

FIGURE 16.3
Stable dollar dividend.
Dividends are kept
constant for a while and
are changed when the
overall level of earnings
changes.

NET Present Value
A company that has paid
a stable dollar dividend is
ExxonMobil; information
is at:
www.exxonmobil.com/
corporate/investor_
dividend.aspx

Stable dollar dividend   Under this approach, dividends are set equal to a fixed dollar amount, independent of the precise value of EPS. As Figure 16.3 illustrates, when EPS trends upward, the dividend is increased in a series of steps. Should EPS drop, the dividend would be maintained as long as possible. The result is a much smoother pattern of dividends than with the stable payout ratio approach. Investors are insulated from some of the variability of EPS and receive the benefits of a less volatile cash stream.

Example

Stable Dollar Dividend

The Dolan Company reported the following earnings per share (EPS) over the past 12 quarters (three years):

Quarter	EPS	Quarter	EPS
1	$1.00	7	$1.30
2	1.20	8	1.40
3	1.30	9	1.70
4	1.25	10	1.80
5	1.45	11	2.00
6	1.50	12	2.10

Question: What quarterly dividend per share (DPS) should Dolan have paid to maintain a stable dollar dividend, beginning at $0.40 in quarter 1 and increasing to 40% of EPS whenever EPS reached a level 20% above its value at the last dividend change?

Solution steps: Proceed quarter by quarter as in the following table. Calculate the change to EPS in each quarter relative to its value the last time dividends were raised and reset the dividend if EPS is up by at least 20%. For example, in quarter 5:

1. EPS was $1.45.

2. The last time the dividend was changed was in quarter 2 when EPS was $1.20.

3. $1.45 represents a 20.8% increase over $1.20 (a change of $0.25, which equals $0.25/$1.20 = 20.8%).

4. Since 20.8% is above the 20% threshold, the dividend should be reset.
5. The new dividend will be 40% × $1.45 = $0.58.

Quarter	(1) EPS	(2) EPS When Dividend Last Changed	(3) Percentage Change to EPS	(4) Reset the Dividend?	(5) Dividend
1	$1.00				$0.40
2	1.20	$1.00	20.0%	Yes	0.48
3	1.30	1.20	8.3	No	0.48
4	1.25	1.20	4.2	No	0.48
5	**1.45**	**1.20**	**20.8**	**Yes**	**0.58**
6	1.50	1.45	3.4	No	0.58
7	1.30	1.45	−10.3	No	0.58
8	1.40	1.45	−3.4	No	0.58
9	1.70	1.45	17.2	No	0.58
10	1.80	1.45	24.1	Yes	0.72
11	2.00	1.80	11.1	No	0.72
12	2.10	1.80	16.7	No	0.72

Stable dollar dividend plus a year-end bonus payment   This method attempts to combine the best features of the stable payout ratio and stable dollar dividend approaches. The quarterly dividend is held constant throughout the year. At year end, the company pays a "bonus dividend" if appropriate. There are four advantages to this approach.

"It's from our cartoon department. They say there's absolutely nothing funny about dividends."

1. Dividends appear stable to investors since they do not fluctuate from quarter to quarter.

2. The company can use the year-end bonus to reward stockholders in a particularly good year without committing to a higher regular dividend.

3. The sum of the four quarterly dividends is less than the planned annual payout. Should earnings decline, the firm has the flexibility to decrease its annual dividend without losing quarterly stability, by simply reducing or eliminating the bonus dividend.

4. The year-end bonus can be adjusted to keep the annual payout proportional to earnings if the company wishes to maintain a constant payout ratio.

Example

Stable Dollar Dividend with Year-End Bonus

The Dolan Company reported the following earnings per share (EPS) over the past 12 quarters (three years):

Quarter	EPS	Quarter	EPS
1	$1.00	7	$1.30
2	1.20	8	1.40
3	1.30	9	1.70
4	1.25	10	1.80
5	1.45	11	2.00
6	1.50	12	2.10

Question: What regular and bonus dividend per share (DPS) should Dolan have paid to maintain a stable dollar dividend plus year-end bonus if the regular quarterly dividend is set to 40% of first quarter EPS and the year-end bonus is calculated to bring the annual payout ratio up to 40%?

Solution steps:

Year 1 (quarters 1–4):

1. Quarterly dividend = 40% × $1.00 = <u>$0.40</u>
2. Bonus:

$$40\% \text{ of annual EPS} = 40\% \,(\$1.00 + 1.20 + 1.30 + 1.25)$$
$$= 40\% \times \$4.75 \qquad = \quad \$1.90$$
$$\text{Less: regular dividend paid} = 4 \times \$0.40 = \quad \underline{1.60}$$
$$\underline{\$0.30}$$

Year 2 (quarters 5–8):

1. Quarterly dividend = 40% × $1.45 = <u>$0.58</u>
2. Bonus:

$$40\% \text{ of annual EPS} = 40\% \,(\$1.45 + 1.50 + 1.30 + 1.40)$$
$$= 40\% \times \$5.65 \qquad = \quad \$2.26$$
$$\text{Less: regular dividend paid} = 4 \times \$0.58 = \quad \underline{2.32}$$
$$\underline{-\$0.06}$$

Dolan would <u>not pay a bonus dividend in this year</u> since its regular quarterly dividend payments have distributed more than 40% of EPS.

Year 3 (quarters 9–12):

1. Quarterly dividend = 40% × $1.70 = $\underline{\$0.68}$
2. Bonus:

$$40\% \text{ of annual EPS} = 40\% (\$1.70 + 1.80 + 2.00 + 2.10)$$
$$= 40\% \times \$7.60 \qquad = \quad \$3.04$$
$$\text{Less: regular dividend paid} = 4 \times \$0.68 = \quad \underline{\quad 2.72}$$
$$\underline{\$0.32}$$

2. Company Maturity

A second practical consideration in setting a dividend policy is the position of a company in its life cycle. Companies pass through a series of stages as they grow and mature. Each stage is characterized by different needs and access to cash, hence different pressures on retaining earnings. Each stage is also characterized by different growth rates, hence different abilities to produce returns for investors in the form of capital gains. Both factors affect dividend policy. We look briefly at three of these stages below: (1) birth, (2) rapid growth, and (3) maturity.

Birth   At birth, few companies are able to pay dividends. Almost all companies begin their lives in a cash-poor position, requiring every dollar they can get their hands on to survive and grow. At this stage, firms generally have poor access to external resources since they are unknown and have not yet established successful financial histories. Their equity financing is normally from their founder(s) or venture capitalists—investors who intimately understand the company's need to conserve every bit of its cash and who are willing to postpone receiving dividends in the hope of much larger returns later.

Rapid growth   During rapid growth, most companies choose not to pay a dividend. As described in Chapter 5, when companies grow quickly they need significant infusions of cash to acquire assets. At the same time, rapid growth may now be providing their stockholders with a high rate of return in the form of capital gains, mitigating the need for dividends. If a firm in this stage pays a dividend at all, it tends to be quite modest.

Maturity   At maturity, companies tend to pay moderate to high dividends. As companies mature, their rate of growth settles down. They can no longer generate high returns for investors through stock price appreciation and must use dividends to provide stockholders with a reasonable rate of return. They no longer need large amounts of new cash to expand their asset base and often do not have good internal uses for all the money they earn. At the extreme, a profitable company that ceases to grow may pay out all its earnings as dividends.

3. Other Practical Considerations

In addition to a desire for stability and stage in life cycle, several other practical concerns shape a company's dividend policy.

Availability of cash To pay regular dividends, a company must have sufficient cash on hand each quarter. A firm with a predictable and stable cash flow finds it easier to commit to regular dividend payments than one whose cash flow is uncertain or erratic.

Alternative uses for cash Closely connected to the availability of cash is the lack of competing uses for the money. Companies that regularly have a large selection of attractive investment opportunities or consistently need funds to repay debt principal may have difficulty finding the cash for dividends.

Access to banks and financial markets Companies that can obtain funds easily can pay dividends without worrying too much about securing replacement financing if needed. Such companies also typically pay low flotation costs when they issue stock, which keeps down the cost differential between external equity and retained earnings. If investors in these companies accept a wide range of debt-equity mixes, the firm can borrow as required to maintain its dividend and a higher dividend can be sustained.

Shareholder preferences To the extent the financial manager can determine them, the firm's dividend policy can be directly responsive to shareholders' tax positions and control preferences. This is possible in closely held companies where there are few key shareholders and is difficult if the company's stock is widely held.

Legal or charter restrictions Provisions of a company's charter, contracts it has entered, or the law can place boundaries around a company's dividend policy. Most state corporation laws have a "capital impairment rule" that limits dividends to the sum of a firm's retained earnings and/or an "insolvency rule" that prohibits insolvent firms (those with negative equity) from paying dividends. Loan agreements are often written to limit or prohibit dividend payments to prevent money that should be used for debt service from leaving the firm. In the other direction, recall the provision of the federal tax code that subjects excess retained earnings to a special "improper accumulation" penalty.

How a Dividend Is Paid

date of declaration—the date a company's board of directors votes to pay a dividend

date of record—the date a company determines who will receive a dividend

payment date—the date a dividend is paid

The decision to pay a dividend is typically a regular agenda item on a company's board of directors' quarterly meeting. If the board votes to pay or "declares" a dividend, that date is identified as the **date of declaration.** The board also establishes two other dates that define the remaining mechanics of paying the dividend. The first is the **date of record,** the date on which the company will look at its list of shareholders to determine who will receive the dividend. The second is the **payment date,** on which dividend checks will be mailed.

Figure 16.4 is the McDonald's Corporation web page on which the company reports its history of dividends and stock splits.[8] The data for the most recent dividend is in the third paragraph: the dividend was in the amount of $0.61 per share,

---

[8] **Reference:** McDonald's Corporation website:
http://aboutmcdonalds.com/mcd/investors/stocks_and_dividends/dividend_and_split_informat ion.html, March 24, 2011.

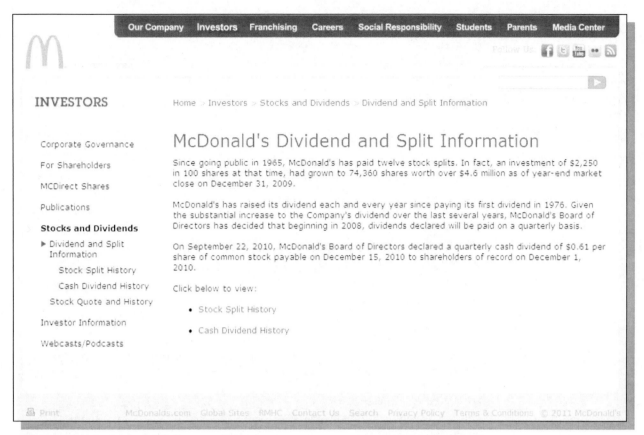

FIGURE 16.4
Announcement of a dividend. The announcement specifies the amount of the dividend as well as the date of declaration, record date, and payment date.

had been declared on September 22, 2010, and was paid on December 15 to shareholders whose name appeared on the company's records at the close of business on December 1.

There is a fourth date relevant to dividend payments. It could take several days for information about stock transactions to make its way to a company. Suppose some investors bought McDonald's stock on November 30. Would their names reach the company by December 1 so they would be eligible for the December 15 dividend? To protect investors and assure them that they will (or will not) get the next dividend, each stock exchange establishes an **ex-dividend date,** usually 2–3 business days prior to the date of record. For the McDonald's dividend, the ex-dividend date was Monday, November 29. Investors who purchased the stock before November 29 were assured by the New York Stock Exchange that their name would reach the company by December 1, in time to be included in the company's records and receive the next dividend. At the beginning of the trading day on November 29, McDonald's stock went "ex-dividend"; an investor who purchased the stock after that point did not receive the next dividend—rather it was paid to the former stockholder.

ex-dividend date—the date by which stock must be purchased to receive the next dividend

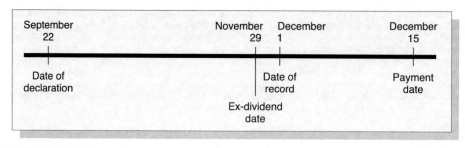

FIGURE 16.5
McDonald's dividend timetable. Four dates define the payment of a dividend.

The four dates for the McDonald's dividend are diagrammed on a time line in Figure 16.5.

*B*ob Woods looked at his watch and was surprised at how much time had passed. He had spent the last several hours in a comfortable chair in the back corner of the company library reading all he could about dividend policy. Bob stood up and stretched, then placed some books back on the shelf and gathered up his notes. As he returned to his office, Bob mulled over what he had learned.

Dividend policy was an area in which finance theory gave very mixed signals. Some theories argued that the payment of dividends added value to shareholders while others claimed that dividends lowered stock values. Professors Modigliani and Miller were convinced that dividends had nothing to do with value. The other theories were in conflict as well: one argued for stable payments while another made dividends the unstable residual of the retained earnings decision.

Dividend practice seemed a bit more settled than the theory since there was broad agreement that stability of payments was of value. Yet there were different ways to achieve stability, and they all seemed so contradictory.

Back in his office, Bob rewrote his notes, organizing his findings into a series of pros and cons and matching them with the opinions expressed in that morning's meeting. He had the sense that a pattern of ideas was emerging. After reading through his notes one more time, Bob went down the hall to seek out other members of the team and test out his new insights.

Summary of Key Points

■■■ **Explain how shareholders get their returns.** Shareholders' returns come in the form of dividends (direct distributions from the corporation) and capital gains (increased stock value). The dividend growth model shows the relationship between current dividends, investors' required rate of return, and investors' growth forecast and identifies the tradeoffs financial managers face in planning a dividend policy.

■■■ **Describe five classes of theory that attempt to identify a company's optimal dividend policy.** Dividend theories may be classified into five categories: (1) theories that conclude that dividends add value, (2) theories that conclude that dividends reduce value, (3) MM theory which concludes that dividends have nothing to do with value, (4) theories that conclude that consistency adds value, and (5) residual theory which turns our attention away from dividends and toward retained earnings. The theories all improve our knowledge of dividend policy, yet are wildly contradictory in their advice.

■ **Discuss seven practical considerations in setting a firm's dividend.** One important consideration is stability of payments. Three approaches to stability are a stable payout ratio, a stable dollar dividend, and a stable dollar dividend plus a year-end bonus payment. A second factor is where the company is in its life cycle. Other practical considerations are the availability of cash, alternative uses for the cash, access to banks and financial markets, shareholder preferences regarding taxes and control, and legal or charter restrictions on dividend payments.

■ **Describe the mechanics of how dividends are declared and paid.** When a board of directors declares a dividend, it determines the amount to be paid and sets a date of record and a payment date. In response, the relevant stock exchange establishes an ex-dividend date, the last day to buy the stock and receive the coming dividend.

Questions

1. Why do we talk of a dividend *policy* and not just a dividend in this chapter?

2. Under what circumstances does a dividend increase raise the value of a corporation's stock?

3. How can the payment of a dividend reduce investors' risk?

4. What market imperfections enter into the planning of a corporation's dividend policy?

5. "If all companies paid dividends the financial markets would be more efficient!" Comment on this assertion.

6. What conditions must be true for MM's dividend irrelevance theory to be correct?

7. What is a homemade dividend?

8. What is a clientele? Describe three groups of investors who might form a clientele.

9. The consistency theories and the residual theory of dividends reach opposite conclusions. What are those conclusions, and why are they so different?

10. Can a stable payout policy ever produce a stable dollar dividend? Under what condition(s)?

11. What is the relationship of a company's dividend policy to its stage in its life cycle?

12. In today's environment, which of the practical considerations that guide corporations' dividend policies are most important?

13. Distinguish among the following events:

a. Declaration date
b. Ex-dividend date
c. Date of record
d. Payment date

Problems

1. **(Dividend-growth model)** Investors who require a 14% rate of return forecast that a company will pay a dividend of $2.00 one year from now. What will the value of a share of stock be if investors forecast an annual growth rate of:

a. 0%?   c. 8%?
b. 4%?   d. 12%?

2. **(Dividend-growth model)** Investors forecast that a company will pay a dividend of $4.00 one year from now, which will grow thereafter at an annual rate of 4%. What will the value of a share of stock be if investors require an annual rate of return of:

a. 8%?   c. 14%?
b. 11%?   d. 17%?

3. **(Dividend-growth model)** A company is thinking of announcing an increase in its next dividend from $1.50 to $1.65. Currently investors forecast a 6% growth rate and have a 12% required rate of return. Calculate:

a. The value of one share of the company's stock today.
b. The value of a share after the announcement if investors do not change their growth forecast or their required rate of return.
c. The value of a share after the announcement if investors lower their growth forecast to 5% but do not change their required rate of return.
d. The value of a share after the announcement if investors do not change their growth forecast but increase their required rate of return to 14%.

4. **(Dividend-growth model)** A company is thinking of announcing an increase in its next dividend from $1.00 to $1.10. Currently investors forecast an 8% growth rate and have a 13% required rate of return. Calculate:

a. The value of one share of the company's stock today.
b. The value of a share after the announcement if investors do not change their growth forecast nor their required rate of return.
c. The value of a share after the announcement if investors lower their growth forecast to 6% but do not change their required rate of return.

d. The value of a share after the announcement if investors lower their growth forecast to 6% and decrease their required rate of return to 10%.

5. **(Risk reduction)** A company is considering the following two dividend policies for the next four years:

Policy A	Policy B
$1.00	$0.00
1.00	0.00
1.00	2.50
1.00	2.50

a. How much total dividends per share will a stockholder receive under each policy?

b. If investors see no difference in risk between the two policies and apply a discount rate of 12% to both, what is the present value of each dividend stream?

c. Now suppose investors see Policy B as the riskier of the two. They apply a 12% discount rate to Policy A but a 16% rate to Policy B. What is the present value of each dividend stream?

d. Why might investors see Policy B as riskier?

6. **(Risk reduction)** A company is considering the following two dividend policies for the next four years:

Policy X	Policy Y
$3.00	$2.00
3.00	4.00
3.00	2.50
3.00	4.00

a. How much total dividends per share will a stockholder receive under each policy?

b. If investors see no difference in risk between the two policies and apply an 11% discount rate to both, what is the present value of each dividend stream?

c. Suppose investors see Policy Y as the riskier of the two. They apply an 11% discount rate to Policy X but a 14% rate to Policy Y. What is the present value of each dividend stream?

d. Now suppose investors apply an 11% discount rate to Policy X but a 17% rate to Policy Y. What is the present value of each dividend stream?

7. **(Taxation)** Among the stockholders of the Dolan company are Dorothy, a widow in the 15% marginal federal income tax bracket; Josh, a successful young businessman in the 36% bracket; and Kateco, a corporation in the 35% bracket. Dolan's financial managers are considering the effect of either paying a dividend of $2.00 per share on March 1 or retaining the income, in which case they forecast that their share price will rise by the same $2.00 on or about March 1.

a. Calculate the after-tax benefit of the dividend and the capital gain to Dorothy.

b. Calculate the after-tax benefit of the dividend and the capital gain to Josh.

c. Calculate the after-tax benefit of the dividend and the capital gain to Kateco.

d. What is the message from this exercise for Dolan's financial managers?

8. **(Taxation)** Among the stockholders of the Dolan company are Edwin, a retired businessman in the 15% marginal federal income tax bracket; Sylvia, a rich widow in the 39.6% bracket; and Ernco, a corporation in the 35% bracket. Dolan's financial managers are considering whether to increase the dividend by $1.00 per share.

a. Calculate the after-tax benefit of the proposed dividend increase to Edwin.

b. Calculate the after-tax benefit of the proposed dividend increase to Sylvia.

c. Calculate the after-tax benefit of the proposed dividend increase to Ernco.

d. How should Dolan's financial managers react to the tax consequences of increasing the dividend if they believe the company's shareholders are primarily corporations?

9. **(Residual theory)** A corporation forecasts it will require $3 million of new financing in the coming year. Its target debt ratio is 30%, and it plans to use the residual theory to determine its dividend.

a. How much new financing should come from debt and how much from equity to meet the target debt ratio?

b. What should the corporation's dividend be if its earnings after taxes (EAT) is $1 million?

c. What should the corporation's dividend be if its EAT is $2 million?

d. What should the corporation's dividend be if its EAT is $3 million?

10. **(Residual theory)** A corporation forecasts it will require $800,000 of new financing in the coming year. Its target debt ratio is 50%, and it plans to use the residual theory to determine its dividend.

a. How much new financing should come from debt and how much from equity to meet the target debt ratio?

b. What should the corporation's dividend be if its earnings after taxes (EAT) is $600,000?

c. What should the corporation's dividend be if its EAT is $400,001?

d. What should the corporation's dividend be if its EAT is $200,000?

11. **(Dividends in practice)** On the basis of the following (admittedly very limited) information, recommend a dividend policy—high, moderate, or low payout ratio—for the following companies:

    a. Growth rate: 2%, target cash balance: 2% of total assets

    b. Growth rate: 2%, target cash balance: 15% of total assets

    c. Growth rate: 15%, target cash balance: 2% of total assets

    d. Growth rate: 15%, target cash balance: 15% of total assets

12. **(Dividends in practice)** On the basis of the following (admittedly very limited) information, recommend a dividend policy—high, moderate, or low payout ratio—for the following companies:

    a. Growth rate: 3%, good access to financial markets

    b. Growth rate: 3%, poor access to financial markets

    c. Growth rate: 12%, good access to financial markets

    d. Growth rate: 12%, poor access to financial markets

13. **(Stability)** A company predicts the following quarterly earnings per share for the next three years:

Quarter	EPS	Quarter	EPS
1	$1.00	7	$1.30
2	1.20	8	1.40
3	1.30	9	1.70
4	1.25	10	1.80
5	1.45	11	2.00
6	1.50	12	2.10

What quarterly dividend per share (DPS) should the company pay if it follows:

a. A stable payout ratio of 50%?

b. A stable dollar dividend beginning at $0.50 in Quarter 1 and increasing to 50% of EPS whenever EPS reaches a level 15% above its value at the last dividend change?

c. A stable dollar dividend plus a year-end bonus if the regular quarterly dividend is set to 50% of first quarter EPS and the year-end bonus is calculated to bring the annual payout ratio up to 50%?

d. How well do each of these three methods achieve the goal of a stable dividend?

14. **(Stability)** A company predicts the following quarterly earnings per share for the next three years:

Quarter	EPS	Quarter	EPS
1	$2.00	7	$3.00
2	2.50	8	3.50
3	2.00	9	3.50
4	2.75	10	3.80
5	3.00	11	4.00
6	3.10	12	4.50

What dividends should the company pay if it follows:

a. A stable payout ratio of 40%?

b. A stable dollar dividend beginning at $0.80 in Quarter 1 and increasing to 40% of EPS whenever EPS reaches a level 25% above its value at the last dividend change?

c. A stable dollar dividend plus a year-end bonus if the regular quarterly dividend is set to 40% of first quarter EPS, and the year-end bonus is calculated to bring the annual payout ratio up to 40%?

d. Why might a financial manager prefer the plan of part c to those of parts a and b?

CHAPTER 17

INCREASING

SHARE PRICE

*B*ill Lin looked at his computer screen one more time and frowned. In one window was his company's stock price, virtually unchanged for the last six months. In another window were excerpts from recent analysts' reports which were not very enthusiastic about the firm's performance. To Bill, it just made no sense. Since becoming Senior Financial Manager at a medium-sized software company, he had worked hard to apply what he had learned in his business school finance classes. His manager, the company's CFO, had given him good feedback about his work. "Good financial decisions should lead to an increased stock price," he thought, yet the financial markets did not seem to be responding to the good things he was doing within the firm.

Bill was a graduate of a well-known technical university. After working for several years as a computer programmer, he had earned an M.B.A. degree so he could move into the business side of his company. Bill remembered from his finance classes that the financial objective of the firm was to maximize shareholder wealth—his company's stock price, and that was done by smart financial decision making. He had made smart financial decisions, yet his company's stock price was not responding. "How could this be possible?," he said to himself, running his hand through the tuft of hair growing from his forehead.

Bill took out a sheet of paper and, drawing on his computer programming background, started sketching a flowchart of how company actions turned into stock price movements. On the left of the chart were boxes with financial managing activities. On the right was a big box in which he had written 'stock price'. "But what goes in between?," he mused. "What connects financial managing to stock price?" As he left work that day, Bill promised himself that he would spend time over the next few days learning how to complete his flowchart.

The problem Bill Lin is grappling with is shared by all financial managers. While a company's financial managers can do many things to add value to their firm, management does not set the price of the company's shares. Nevertheless, management is expected to increase the firm's share price. What is the linkage between financial managing and share price? How can this linkage be identified, acted upon, and strengthened? How can financial managing that adds to share price be encouraged and rewarded?

We begin this chapter on the left-hand side of Bill Lin's flowchart with a brief review of key financial managing concepts for adding value that we encountered earlier in this book. Then we help Bill with the middle of his flowchart by examining how analysts and investors evaluate the firm. Next we explore two important barriers to value-adding financial managing and look at management and reward systems designed to overcome these problems. Finally, we look at the importance of communicating internal business activities to the financial community

Key Points You Should Learn from This Chapter

After reading this chapter you should be able to:

- State the relationship between good financial managing and a company's stock price.
- Identify four key financial managing techniques for adding value to a firm.
- Describe techniques used by the financial community to place a value on common stock.
- Identify the agency barrier to good financial managing, and discuss techniques for minimizing agency costs.
- Identify the finance theory barrier to good financial managing, and describe the nature of "value based management" systems.
- Describe how companies communicate value-adding activities to their shareholders and the investment community.

Introductory Concepts—How Can Management Make Share Price Go Up?

We have learned in this book that the financial objective of the firm is to maximize the wealth of its owners. We have also learned that for a company traded in the public financial markets, owners' wealth comes from a combination of dividends and increased share price. In Chapter 16 we studied how dividend policy affects owners' wealth. In this chapter we look how good financial managing can increase a firm's share price.

There is a problem, however. While a company's management can do many things to add value to a firm, management does not directly control the price of the company's stock. Rather, share price is determined outside the firm by the decisions of investors. To understand how financial managers can increase share price, therefore, we first have to recall how investors decide what a share of stock is worth.

NET Present Value
Perhaps the most well-known proponent of fundamental theory is Warren Buffet, chairman of Berkshire Hathaway, Inc., whose widely-read annual letters to shareholders, summarizing his philosophy, can be found at:
www.berkshirehathaway. com/letters/letters.html

In Chapter 7 we discussed characteristics of the financial markets and introduced several theories of stock price behavior.[1] They provide important clues to the answers Bill Lin is searching for. Technical theory focuses on the psychology of investors and concludes that short-run stock price movements are not very much connected to a firm's business activities. Fundamental theory is based on economic value; a firm's stock price should be close to the present value of the future cash flows it is expected to produce. The efficient market hypothesis looks at the availability of information to investors and argues that stock price movements track the arrival to investors of meaningful information.

From these theories Bill can reach three important conclusions:

● From technical theory he can learn not to be too concerned about short-run stock price movements that seem unconnected to his company's activities. There is little that financial managing can do to influence these price fluctuations, and they do not truly create shareholder value.

● From fundamental theory he can see that the true way to add value is to improve the present value of firm's anticipated future cash flows.

● From efficient market theory he can see the importance of promptly and accurately informing the financial markets about value-adding activities going on within the company.

So, good financial managing, directed at increasing shareholder wealth, involves taking steps to increase the present value of future cash flows and to communicate these activities to the investment community.

Financial Managing Activities That Add Value

In this book we have encountered four major financial managing activities that can increase the present value of a company's future cash flows, hence add value. The starting point for increasing shareholder wealth is to understand and to do these activities well.

---

[1] **Cross-reference:**   These stock-price behavior theories appear on pages 181-185.

1. Invest in Positive NPV Projects

In Chapters 11 and 12 we saw that financial managers could increase the present value of future cash flows by investing in positive net present value (NPV) projects. The NPV of a proposed investment project is the difference between the present values of the forecasted incremental benefits and incremental costs from accepting that project. A positive NPV means that benefits are expected to exceed costs, and the amount of the NPV is the anticipated added value to the company.

The same logic can be applied to any kind of investment, for example, the acquisition of another company, the decision to spend more on advertising, or an investment in educating and training employees. If the net present value of the investment is positive it will add value to the firm.

Finding and evaluating positive NPV projects is an ongoing, never-ending activity. New investment possibilities arise every day, and each presents an opportunity to add value.

2. Improve Processes

In Chapter 13 we saw that financial managers could increase future net cash flows, and hence their present values, by improving processes both within the finance function and elsewhere in the organization. Better functioning processes lead to greater customer satisfaction and higher quality products and services which often translate into increased revenues. Better functioning processes reduce costs by reducing waste and unnecessary work, by decreasing the need for investment in assets (such as plant and inventories), and by speeding up cash flows. And, better functioning processes improve employee morale, increasing their contributions to customer satisfaction, quality, and future process improvements.

Like the evaluation of potential investments, improving processes is ongoing and never ending. There is virtually always a better way to do any activity, and each successful process improvement adds value to the firm.

3. Raise Low Cost Money

In Chapter 10 we studied the cost of capital. We saw that each source of money has a cost, the rate the firm has to earn on that money to return to investors their minimum acceptable rate of return. The cost of each capital source is a function of investors' required rate of return, flotation costs, and income tax reductions. Therefore, financial managers can reduce the cost of financing by (1) seeking investors with the lowest required rate of return, (2) minimizing flotation costs (for example, by using retained earnings for new equity rather than issuing additional shares of common stock), and (3) maximizing the tax deductions from financing.

In Chapter 14 we saw that financial managers could further reduce their company's cost of capital by selecting the best mix of debt and equity financing. Since security prices are present values, and since the cost of capital is the combined discount rate of all its investors, reducing a company's cost of capital increases the firm's value. Compromise theory concludes that there is an "acceptable range" for the debt-equity mix that minimizes a firm's cost of capital. When a company maintains its financing mix within that range, it adds to its stock market value.

4. Reduce Risk

In Chapter 4 we encountered the Fisher model which taught us that risk was an important component of interest rates. Then, in Chapter 8, we saw that investors taken as a whole are risk averters. Accordingly, greater perceived risk drives up investors' required rates of return, and they lower security prices. Conversely, lowered risk increases security prices. Other things equal, the financial manager can increase value by lowering the risks taken by the company's investors.

In Chapter 15 we discussed methods of reducing risk. Hedging across the balance sheet matches asset and liability maturities so financing is available for the time period necessary to meet asset needs. Hedging temporary working capital flows matches cash inflows and outflows by timing and currency so that inflows can be used efficiently and outflows can be made quickly and at the lowest cost.

Evaluating a Firm

Translating a company's activities into a reasonable stock price is simple in concept. Finance theory tells us that the price of a share of stock is the present value of all the cash flows the company will generate in the future. And, modern financial calculators and spreadsheet programs make doing this calculation easy for all of us. However, while simple in concept, placing a value on a company's stock is quite difficult in practice. The major problem is that it is very hard to forecast the firm's future cash flows.

1. The Dividend-Growth Model

In Chapter 9, we used the growing cash stream present value model to introduce common stock valuation.[2] This model is written as:

$$Value = PV = \frac{D_1}{r_c - g}$$

where D_1 is the next dividend investors anticipate receiving, g is the growth rate of the dividends into the future, and r_c is investors' required rate of return. In this use, we often call the model the "dividend-growth model." By using dividends in the model, we focus on the cash flows seen by investors. By assuming that the company's dividends will grow forever at a constant rate, we avoid the difficulty of forecasting every dividend the company will pay infinitely far into the future. In fact, this model forms the basis for much of the work of investment analysts.

Clearly, however, this model is a simplification. Some companies grow at rates greater than their cost of equity capital ($g > r_c$) invalidating the model.[3] No company can be expected to grow at a constant rate forever. And, of course, not all companies pay dividends. Accordingly, investment analysts who use this model typically modify it to describe more accurately the company they are evaluating.

---

[2] **Cross-reference:** The growing cash stream model first appears in Chapter 3, pages 77-78. It is used in Chapter 9 to evaluate common stock on pages 231-233.

[3] **Reminder:** The growing cash stream model is valid only if r > g.

Supernormal-growth companies To apply the dividend-growth model to a company growing at a rate greater than investors' required rate of return, analysts remind themselves that such a high growth rate cannot last forever. The period of supernormal growth will end some day after which the company's growth rate will become more "normal," much closer to the growth rate of the economy as a whole. Analysts apply the dividend-growth model only to the latter period of normal growth and calculate the present value of the first (high-growth) period year by year without the aid of a simplifying model.

Variable-growth companies To apply the model to a company with a growth rate that is forecast to vary from low to high and back again, analysts typically estimate an average growth rate number that summarizes the variable growth rates. Alternatively, they predict growth rates for groups of years and use a spreadsheet program to handle the present value calculations.

Non-dividend-paying companies Efforts to apply the dividend-growth model to firms that do not pay dividends have evolved through three stages: first using earnings, then cash flow from operations, and, most recently, free cash flow:

- Early attempts to apply the dividend-growth model to non-dividend-paying firms involved using earnings as a substitute for dividends. Analysts pointed out that earnings captured the economic performance of a company, and that firms that did pay dividends paid them from their earnings. They reminded themselves of the argument of Professors Modigliani and Miller that a company's value does not depend on paying dividends and concluded that evaluating earnings was very similar, if not identical, to evaluating dividends.

- As the finance insight that value comes from cash flow became more widely understood, analysts turned away from accounting earnings and began to use cash flow from operations in the model.

- Today, most analysts use **free cash flow** as the input to the growing cash stream model, regardless of whether the firm pays dividends or not. A company's free cash flow is its cash flow from operations minus cash that is reinvested in the company (to increase working capital and long-term assets). Written out as a formula:

free cash flow—the cash flow distributed by a firm to its investors, equal to the firm's cash flow from operations less cash reinvested in the company

free cash flow = cash flow from operations − cash flow reinvested

Notice that this is the cash flow equivalent to the accrual accounting relationship:[4]

dividends = earnings − earnings retained

Free cash flow is exactly equal to the cash distributed by the company to its investors, regardless of whether the cash is paid out as dividends or in some other form such as share repurchases.[5]

---

[4] **Elaboration:** This relationship comes from rearranging the equation that says the amount a company adds to its retained earnings each year equals its earnings less the portion paid to shareholders in the form of dividends:

earnings − dividends = earnings retained

[5] **Observation:** Some analysts include interest and debt repayments in free cash flow in which case the dividend-growth model calculates the combined value of the company's debt and equity. They then subtract the market value of the debt to estimate the company's equity value.

Example

Growing Cash Stream Model Using Free Cash Flow

Investors expect Zena Corp. to generate cash flow from operations of $5.00 per share in the coming year (after payment of all interest and debt principal obligations). Of this amount, Zena Corp. is expected to reinvest $1.50 in growing its assets to meet future sales targets.

Question: How much free cash flow per share will Zena Corp. produce in the coming year?

Solution steps:
Free cash flow = cash flow from operations – cash flow reinvested
= $5.00 – 1.50 = $3.50

Answer: Zena Corp. will produce free cash flow of $\underline{$3.50}$ per share in the coming year.

Question: If investors expect free cash flow to grow at an annual rate of 5% and require a 12% rate of return what is the value of one share of Zena Corp. stock?

Solution steps: Use the dividend-growth model substituting free cash flow for dividends:

$$\text{Value} = \text{PV} = \frac{D_1}{r_c - g} = \frac{\$3.50}{.12 - .05} = \frac{\$3.50}{.07} = \$50.00$$

Answer: Zena Corp. stock is worth $\underline{$50.00}$ per share.

2. Inputs to Stock Valuation

As they develop the inputs to their stock valuation models, security analysts look at a wide variety of information—some quantitative and some qualitative—about the economy, the industry, and the firm. Among the most commonly studied data besides financial statements are:

Economy data   Analysts look for and obtain forecasts of broad economic data that they think will impact the company. For example, bank profits are sensitive to interest rates, companies with significant international business are affected by foreign exchange rates, and the sales of consumer durables such as appliances and automobiles depend significantly on consumer sentiment.

Industry data   Analysts study industry trends to see if demand for the industry's products and services is growing or declining. They look at the industry's ability to innovate and respond to changing markets. They search for new industries, products, and services that could emerge as competitors.

Market position   Analysts examine the position of each company within the industry looking for strengths and weaknesses. They compare the company to its peers to see where it stands with regard to product competitiveness, brand recognition, intellectual capital, reputation for innovation and quality, etc.

Risk exposure   Analysts look at the company's risk exposure: business risk, financial risk, regulatory risk, etc. They examine the division between systematic and unsystematic risk to determine how sensitive the company is to overall economic factors vs. local company events.

Backlog   Analysts look the company's backlog of orders to see if they have confirmed business in the future. This is particularly important when evaluating companies with long manufacturing lead-times, such as aircraft manufacturers, that need to book orders years in advance of delivery.

Management   Analysts study the record of the company's management looking for visionary leadership, evidence of sound and credible strategic planning, use of systematic quality management, understanding of sustainability challenges, ability to meet objectives, depth and breadth of skills, etc.

Quality of earnings   Earnings quality is the probability that a company's earnings will repeat and grow into the future. It is the summary of all the analyst's qualitative judgments. High quality earnings have a sound basis, and will likely repeat or grow. Low quality earnings, on the other hand, reflect special circumstances and will most likely not be maintained. Since past earnings is the starting point for estimating future earnings and cash flows, earnings quality is an important summary input to estimating the value of a company's common stock.

3. Ratio-Based Models

multiplier—a number used to estimate the value of common stock by multiplying an accounting performance figure

As an alternative to the dividend-growth present value model, or as a check on the results of the model, analysts often use **multipliers**, numbers applied to key accounting performance figures, to estimate the value of common stock. Among the most commonly used accounting performance figures are net income (earnings); cash flow from operations; earnings before interest and taxes (EBIT); and earnings before interest, taxes, depreciation, and amortization (EBITDA). Multipliers effectively are financial ratios and are derived from studying comparable firms.

Example

Using Multipliers to Value Common Stock	

Zena Corp.'s most recent income statement and cash flow from operations is:

Sales	$ 5,000,000
– Cost of goods sold	3,000,000
Gross profit	2,000,000
– Operating expenses	800,000
EBITDA	1,200,000
– Depreciation and amortization	300,000
EBIT	900,000
– Interest expense	200,000
– Taxes	200,000
Net income	500,000
Cash flow from operations	1,300,000

From studying the economy, the industry, and the company, analysts have concluded that the following multipliers are appropriate for Zena Corp. stock:

Earnings multiplier	25
Cash flow from operations multiplier	10
EBIT multiplier	15
EBITDA multiplier	11

Question: What is the total value of Zena Corp.'s owners' equity?

Solution steps: Apply each multiplier:

Earnings x multiplier = $500,000 x 25 = $12,500,000
Cash flow x multiplier = $1,300,000 x 10 = $13,000,000
EBIT x multiplier = $900,000 x 15 = $13,500,000
EBITDA x multiplier = $1,200,000 x 11 = $13,200,000

Answer: Zena Corp.'s equity is worth <u>between $12.5 and $13.5 million</u>.

Question: What is the value of one share of Zena Corp. stock if there are 260,000 shares of common stock outstanding?

Solution steps: Divide the estimated total market value by the number of outstanding shares:

Low estimate: $12,500,000 ÷ 260,000 = $48.08
High estimate: $13,500,000 ÷ 260,000 = $51.92

Answer: Zena Corp. Stock is worth <u>between $48.08 and $51.92 per share</u> (consistent with the $50.00/share price from the dividend-growth model).

When applying a multiplier to earnings, it is common first to modify the reported earnings number to obtain **normalized earnings.** This calculation removes the impact of one-time events, such as a strike, a legal settlement, or the closing of a plant. It also removes the impact of any accounting procedure the analyst considers inappropriate or misleading. The goal is to produce an earnings number that represents the repeatable economic activity of the company.

normalized earnings—
earnings that reflect the true earning power of a company

Example

Normalized Earnings

Although Zena Corp.'s earnings per share last year was $1.92, Janet Lehr, an analyst at one major brokerage house feels that 7¢ of the company's earnings were due to non-repeatable events.

Question: What figure would Janet calculate for Zena Corp.'s normalized earnings?

Solution steps: Remove the non-repeatable amount:

Reported earnings – non-repeatable amount = $1.92 – 0.07 = $1.85

Answer: Janet calculates normalized earnings of <u>$1.85</u> per share.

Question: What figure would Janet estimate for Zena Corp.'s per-share value, assuming she agrees that the earnings multiplier should be 25?

Solution steps: Value = earnings x mutiplier = $1.85 x 25 = $46.25

Answer: Janet estimates Zena Corp.'s value to be <u>$46.25</u> per share.

Since multipliers are derived by studying other companies, they are used to estimate a company's *value*, what its stock price *should be*. However, it is possible to calculate a multiplier from a company's current share price. When the earnings multiplier is calculated this way is called the price earnings (or "P/E") ratio.

Price/earnings ratio = stock price/earnings per share

Example

Price/Earnings Ratio

Zena Corp.'s earnings per share last year was $1.92, and the company's stock is currently selling for $55.00 per share.

Question: Calculate Zena Corp.'s price/earnings ratio.

Solution steps:

P/E ratio = stock price/earnings per share = $55.00/$1.92 = 28.6

Answer: Zena Corp.'s stock is selling for <u>28.6</u> times earnings.

As another check on common stock valuation, analysts often calculate a firm's market/book ratio:

Market/book ratio = stock price/book value per share

Book value per share is total equity divided by the number of shares of common stock outstanding. This ratio compares stock price, the value of a company's equity in the market, to the accountants' value for the same equity. Since accounting values are designed to err on the conservative side ("lower of cost or market"), this ratio usually is above 1.0 for a well-regarded firm.

Barriers to Shareholder Wealth—The Agency Problem

Recently, finance academics and practitioners have devoted attention to describing and removing an important barrier to effective shareholder wealth maximization: the differences in motives between a corporation's stockholders and its professional managers. These insights are summarized under the title *agency theory*.

1. Background to Agency Theory

In agrarian societies prior to the Industrial Revolution, business dealings were quite simple. Most transactions were exchanges between farmers, shopkeepers, craftsmen, etc. Transactions were carried out face to face between parties who often knew each other personally. There was little need to be concerned about whether other parties to a transaction would fulfill their obligations.

With the arrival of the Industrial Revolution, much of this changed. To produce new and often complex products, a variety of labor and material resources had to be brought together. Transactions grew more complicated, many involving relationships between persons who did not know each other. Today, the number, variety, and complexity of goods and services demanded by consumers are immense. It is commonplace for a business to be operating in dozens of locations around the world, producing hundreds of different products, requiring thousands of raw materials and tens of thousands of employees. It is no longer possible to rely on personal relationships to ensure that all these transactions occur as desired. It would be very costly to engage in and monitor so many independent transactions; rather, a more formal structure of relationships is required.

The world of business in advanced economies is dominated by corporations. Corporations exist because they provide the formal structure necessary to organize complex transactions and, in doing so, reduce the cost of doing business. As Ronald Coase, the winner of the 1991 Nobel Prize in economics, has written[6], firms are formed whenever the cost of making individual transactions exceeds the additional costs of operating within a business. Consider what you would do if you had to arrange for the education of a child. You could enter into separate transactions with each teacher, with suppliers of instructional materials, with a landlord for classroom space, with a caterer for lunch, etc.; but you would probably find it easier to contract with a school to provide all the services. Even with all its internal overhead costs, it is cheaper—in terms of money and effort (and headaches!)—to employ the school. As a result, schools exist to deliver educational services. In the same manner, all corporations exist to deliver products and services cheaply and efficiently.

2. The Agency Problem

As useful as corporations are, their existence does introduce a new problem into the maximization of owners' wealth. Recall that shareholders employ professional managers to run the business. Borrowing from legal terminology, we can identify shareholders as a corporation's **principals** and the firm's professional managers as the shareholders' **agents.** It is quite possible that the goals of the agents, who make the day-to-day decisions about the direction and activities of the firm, might differ from the goals of the principals. If so, the manager-agents might not act in the best interests of the shareholder-principals to maximize owners' wealth. This is the **agency problem.**

The agency problem arises from a variety of sources. The six problems discussed below are frequently cited.

The time horizon problem   Because managers spend a relatively short time in any one position, they have a tendency to slight the long term, favoring decisions that pay off during their tenure on the job over those with longer-term payoff, for which they might receive no recognition. They are motivated to ignore good opportunities that do not produce measurable returns in the short term and to accept poor opportunities that do well in the short term but ultimately reduce owners' wealth. This is especially true if some portion of managers' compensation is based on the current year's profits. The manager-agents look good and receive raises and promotions, but at the expense of the shareholder-principals.

principal—a person who employs another to act in his/her behalf

agent—a person who acts on behalf of and by the authority of another

agency problem—the possibility that an agent will not act in the best interests of his/her principal

---

[6] **Reference and observation:** Ronald Coase, "The Theory of the Firm," *Economica* 4(1937), pages 386–405. Note how long it can take for excellent research to be honored—Coase published in 1937 but was not honored by the Nobel committee until 1991!

The compensation problem   Managers typically have considerable influence over their salaries independent of the "fair" value of their compensation. It is not uncommon to hear of executives who vote themselves large bonuses or other forms of compensation that have no connection to their firm's performance. The manager-agents are well paid, but at the expense of the shareholder-principals.[7]

The perquisite problem   Managers often add to their earnings by increasing their **perquisites ("perqs")**, the nonmonetary forms of their compensation. They arrange for luxurious offices, company cars, and company-paid vacations. They carry company-paid credit cards which permit them to eat well and regularly attend plays, the opera, or the symphony. The manager-agents increase their overall compensation, but at the expense of the shareholder-principals.

perquisite ("perq")— compensation in a form other than money

The information problem   Managers are insiders, privy to detailed knowledge about all facets of the firm's operations. Shareholders, on the other hand, are dependent on managers for their knowledge of the firm. As a result, managers can limit the information received by shareholders. This **information asymmetry** allows managers to make decisions without having to be fully accountable to the firm's owners. The manager-agents can get away with making decisions that favor their own interests at the expense of the shareholder-principals.

information asymmetry— the condition in which a firm's manager-agents know more about the firm than its shareholder-principals

The risk-preference problem   Managers' attitudes toward risk may differ from shareholders' attitudes. Managers are often unwilling to take on risky opportunities that have a good chance of benefiting the firm's owners. If the opportunity succeeds, the managers will get little of the benefit; but if the opportunity fails, they may lose their jobs. Or the reverse might be true: a manager might take excessive risks not in the shareholders' best interests in the hope of obtaining a large bonus. The manager-agents make decisions that protect or enrich themselves at the expense of the shareholder-principals.

The retained earnings problem   Managers may choose to maintain an excessively high level of cash in the business to provide a cushion against a poor economic environment. In this way they avoid being blamed for any cash shortages that might otherwise develop. They retain a higher degree of the firm's earnings than necessary and pay a lower dividend. The manager-agents protect themselves against poor times, but at the expense of the shareholder-principals.

In each of these cases, the agency problem arises because the managers' best interests are not consistently the same as the owners' best interests. The company's owners suffer an **agency cost**, a reduction in their wealth. By contrast, the agency problem does not exist in a proprietorship, for in that case the manager is the owner—increased management compensation is simply a change in the form of the owner's wealth. Questionable management decisions may turn out to be mistakes, but they are not mistakes motivated by an agent's opportunity to take advantage of a principal.

agency cost—the reduction in a principal's wealth when an agent does not act in the principal's best interests

---

[7] **Reference:**   This issue was discussed in detail in Graef S. Crystal's book *In Search of Excess* (New York: W.W.Norton, 1991).

3. Viewing Relationships as Contracts

contract—an agreement between parties specifying each party's role in the relationship

Recently a comprehensive theory of agency has been developed in finance.[8] Each relationship within the firm and between the firm and outsiders is seen as a **contract,** an agreement covering each party's rights and responsibilities. Some contracts are explicit, such as those between the firm and its suppliers, which are in written form and specify each facet of the relationship. Other contracts are implicit, not in written form but understood through verbal agreement and common business behavior, such as the amount of work per day a nonhourly employee owes the firm. Contracts often include terms that specify penalties for nonperformance, for example, lending agreements that stipulate that the lender can claim some of the firm's assets should the firm default on its promise to pay. Agency theory sees the firm as a **nexus of contracts,** a series of many such agreements between every party within and outside the business.

nexus of contracts—an interconnection of many contracts

One advantage of viewing the firm as a nexus of contracts is that it encourages us to focus on the relationships between the various parties within a business. The concept of a contract provides a framework for delineating each relationship, for discovering whether the parties to that relationship are working together in the best interests of the firm, and for examining what the parties are doing to align their goals.

4. Minimizing Agency Costs

The shareholder-principals of a corporation will want to minimize agency costs, since each dollar of agency cost saved is one more dollar available to them. In response, two broad methods of controlling agency costs have become well established: incentives[9] (the carrot) and threats (the stick).

Incentives   The most common incentives are those that attempt to connect managers' compensation directly to increases in shareholder wealth. There are three variations on the theme.

NET Present Value
Microsoft is a company that uses stock options as part of its executive compensation package. To learn more see the company's website: www.microsoft.com/investor/reports/ar10/10k_fr_not_19.html

- Salary and bonus plans—These approaches base the agent-managers' compensation on objectives that are negotiated at the beginning of the year. Salary plans tie managers' salaries to their achievements. Bonus plans pay managers a base salary plus a bonus based on the company's financial performance.

- Stock-related incentives—These approaches reward managers with company stock to sharpen their focus on shareholder wealth. In the typical plan, a manager cannot cash out until some time has passed to maintain the manager's involvement for the longer term.

- Dividend units—This approach gives managers a bonus based on future dividends, tying compensation to the cash benefits shareholders receive.

---

[8] **Reference:**   The seminal work in agency theory is: Michael C. Jensen, and W. H. Meckling, "Theory of the Firm: Managerial Behavior, Agency Costs and Ownership Structure," *Journal of Financial Economics* 3(1976), pages 305–360.

[9] **To delve further:**   Web Appendix 17A describes the incentive approaches in more detail along with the agency problem each addresses and the conditions required for their success.

Threats   A variety of oversight and control techniques exist at various levels in most corporations to prevent manager-agents from acting other than in the shareholders' best interests. These include the following mechanisms.

- The firm's internal planning and control systems—Planning makes public what is expected of everyone within the corporation, creating a benchmark against which to measure results. Knowing that their actions are subject to scrutiny by their senior management, managers are more careful about doing what is expected of them.

- Corporate governance—A corporation's board of directors exists to monitor and control the company's management. Knowing that their actions are subject to the scrutiny of the board of directors—which has direct responsibility for protecting shareholder interests—managers are more careful about developing and executing plans that will maximize shareholders' wealth.

- The market for corporate control—A corporation not acting in the best interests of its shareholders will experience a decline in stock price as investors perceive the firm to have less value. This makes it an inviting target for outsiders or frustrated managers who can buy enough shares to win control of the company, throw out board members and managers unresponsive to shareholder interests, and install new directors and managers more willing to act for the shareholders.

5. Problems with the Traditional Methods of Minimizing Agency Costs

The problems of using these well-established methods of reducing agency costs have long been recognized. Three broad problem areas stand out.

Dependence on financial measures   Traditional incentive-oriented methods of dealing with agency costs often use profits or stock price as their measure of performance. Managers are encouraged to improve financial metrics over the time horizon most advantageous to them, which may not be in the best interests of shareholders.

Conflictual premise   Traditional threat-oriented methods of dealing with agency costs emphasize the conflicts described by agency theory. In doing so they ignore areas of shared interests between principals and agents and discourage the development of win/win approaches to solving the agency problem.

Reliance on the vertical organizational structure   Traditional approaches to dealing with the agency problem focus on contracts made between senior managers and their subordinates, following the vertical structure of the firm. However, the work of the organization and the relationships crucial for a firm's success are more likely to be horizontal, crossing departmental and functional lines. Building rewards on vertical relationships may discourage collaboration in horizontal relationships.

■■ Barriers to Shareholder Wealth—Ignoring Finance Theory

Finance theory tells us that the value created by a company is the present value of its free cash flow, the cash distributed by the firm to its investors. Yet many managers and security analysts persist in using financial accounting measures (for example, earnings per share) for financial decision making and to evaluate a company's success. When managers ignore finance theory in this way, they create another barrier to effective shareholder wealth maximization.

1. The Problem

As we have seen in this book, accounting performance measures are inadequate for good financial decision making. There are several reasons for this:

● Accounting numbers are not consistent over time. Since GAAP rules often permit choices of accounting methods (for example LIFO vs. FIFO), there are multiple ways to measure the same economic event. And, since the rules change over time as new accounting standards are introduced, accounting income can change its meaning from year to year.

● Accounting numbers do not equal cash flow. GAAP uses an accrual system in which revenues enter the books when a product or service is delivered, regardless of whether the company has already collected the cash (a receipt in advance), collects cash at the time of sale, or collects the cash at a later date (an account receivable). Expenses are matched against revenues or time periods, regardless of whether they are already paid for (a prepaid expense), paid for at the same time, or paid for later (an account payable).

● Accounting numbers rarely take time value of money into account. Income this year is seen as the same as income in future years.

● Accounting numbers do not include a cost of capital. As a result, they cannot report whether the company's profits represent a rate of return sufficient to satisfy the firm's investors.

FIGURE 17.1
Comparison of the Stern Stewart & Co. and HOLT/LCRT systems of value based management. Although both are based on finance theory, they differ in approach.

Issue	Stern Stewart &Co.	HOLT/LCRT
Finance theory approach	NPV / NAB	IRR
Goal: number to maximize in the financial markets	Market Value Added (MVA)	Total Shareholder Return (TSR)
Number to maximize internally	Economic Value Added (EVA)	Total Business Return (TBR), Cash Flow Return on Investment (CFROI)
Changes from accrual accounting to cash	Only if the change is material and can be clearly communicated to employees and investors	Adjust for inflation, remove depreciation, 40-year fade
Implementation	Throughout many organizations, connected to compensation systems	Strategic planning, money management
Characteristic	Usability	Accuracy

2. Value Based Management

value based management—
a system of management
emphasizing adherence to
finance theory

Recently, finance consultants and academics have suggested new measures and methods for financial managing designed to overcome the limitations of accounting and to be more consistent with the prescriptions of finance theory. Together, these measures and methods are known as **value based management**. Although several approaches to value based management are currently in use, they all share the same key underlying concepts: focus on shareholder value as the goal of the firm, evaluate free cash flow instead of accounting income when making management decisions, and incorporate a cost of capital when deciding whether the firm's performance is adequate.

Professor Alfred Rappaport was among the first to propose that value based management be used for financial managing.[10] Today, two approaches to value based management are particularly popular among many financial executives: (1) the Economic Value Added (EVA[TM])[11] approach developed by the consulting firm Stern Stewart & Co., and (2) the Cash Flow Return on Investment (CFROI) approach developed by HOLT Value Associates, now part of Credit Suisse First Boston, and further developed by Life Cycle Returns, Inc. as Life Cycle Returns Technology (LCRT). The two approaches follow the same overall logic: create a new and improved financial measure that (1) eliminates the problems of accrual accounting, (2) can be managed inside the company, and (3) if maximized should maximize shareholder wealth in the financial markets as well. However, they differ significantly in their details. A comparison of the two approaches is given in Figure 17.1.

NET Present Value
For more on the Economic Value Added approach to value based management, go to the Stern Stewart website:
www.sternstewart.com

Economic Value Added The Stern Stewart approach is to maximize a number called Market Value Added (MVA). This is the difference between a company's current stock market value and the amount invested by shareholders:

$$MVA = market\ value - invested\ capital$$

MVA is the amount by which management has increased the net present value of the company. If MVA is positive, management has added value to the firm; a negative MVA means management has destroyed value.

The way to increase MVA is to manage and increase Economic Value Added (EVA), Stern Stewart's newly developed internal financial measure. EVA is calculated as:

$$EVA = NOPAT - k_w\ CAPITAL$$

where

● NOPAT is Net Operating Profit After Tax. The calculation of NOPAT begins with the firm's net income, the accounting measure of profit for equity investors. After-tax interest expense is then added back to obtain net *operating* income after tax, the income available to provide returns to all invested money, both debt and equity. Finally, a series of adjustments are made to bring the number closer to cash flow. Stern Stewart has identified some 160 possible adjustments, but recommends that the firm only make those that are material in size and can easily be explained to employees and investors.

---

[10] **Reference:** Professor Rappaport summarized his recommendatons in *Creating Shareholder Value: The New Standard for Business Performance*. New York: The Free Press, 1986.

[11] **Elaboration** Stern Stewart & Co. trademarked the abbreviation EVA[TM].

FINANCE IN PRACTICE

Economic Value Added at Whole Foods

Whole Foods Market, the natural foods supermarket chain, is an enthusiastic user of the EVA system of value based management. The company dedicates a page within its website to EVA on which it writes:

> We use Economic Value Added ("EVA") as a basis for our business decisions and for determining incentive compensation. ... We believe that one of our core strengths is our decentralized culture, where decisions are made at the store level, close to the customer ... and that EVA is the best financial framework that team members can use to help make decisions that create sustainable shareholder value.

> We use EVA extensively for capital investment decisions, including evaluating new store real estate decisions and store remodeling proposals. ... The EVA decision-making model also enhances operating decisions in stores. ... We believe that focusing on EVA improvement encourages continuous improvement of our business.

> Over 750 leaders throughout the Company are on EVA-based incentive compensation plans, of which the primary measure is EVA improvement. EVA-based plans cover our senior executive leadership, regional leadership and the store leadership team (store team leaders and assistant store team leaders) in all stores. ... We expect EVA to remain a significant component of our compensation structure throughout the Company in the coming years.

Reference: Whole Foods Market website: http://www.wholefoodsmarket.com/company/eva.php, June 6, 2011.

- k_w is the company's cost of capital.
- CAPITAL is the total amount of money that lenders and investors have given to the firm adjusted to a cash figure in the same manner as NOPAT.

Since the product of k_w and CAPITAL is the amount required to meet the needs of investors, a positive value for EVA means NOPAT exceeds investors' requirements and management has added value during the year. A firm with a positive EVA year after year will increase its Market Value Added since MVA is the present value of all future EVAs.

Notice that EVA is a measure of net annual benefit (NAB), a concept we encountered in Chapter 12 as we studied decisions to invest in permanent current assets. There we defined NAB as "the amount by which the annual benefit from an investment exceeds the amount required to cover the firm's cost of capital."[12] Effectively, EVA is the net annual benefit produced not by a single investment but by the entire company.

Stern Stewart recommends that EVA replace accounting numbers in management planning and capital allocation decisions. To motivate performance they have de-

---

[12] **Cross-reference:**   This definition appears on page 291. The use of net annual benefit is introduced on pages 291–292 and illustrated throughout the remainder of Chapter 12.

SERVING FINANCE'S CUSTOMERS

The Best At Creating Share-holder Wealth

Each quarter year, EVA Dimensions ranks 3,000 U.S. companies by Market Value Added (MVA). For the year ending March 2011, the ten top ranked companies were:

Rank	Company	MVA ($millions)	2011 EVA ($millions)
1	Apple	$269,175	$11,736
2	Exxon Mobil	254,108	21,458
3	Altria Group	163,981	9,704
4	Microsoft	147,686	16,007
5	Google	139,822	5,922
6	Intl Business Machines	136,534	4,705
7	Oracle	134,648	5,787
8	Coca-Cola	121,914	5,070
9	Wal-Mart Stores	113,114	8,969
10	Philip Morris International	112,612	5,601

Source: EVA Dimensions, LLC. Reprinted with permission.

signed a system that ties a portion of middle and senior managers' compensation to EVA.[13]

NET Present Value
For more on the Cash Flow Return on Investment approach to value based management, go to the Credit Suisse Holt website:
www.creditsuisse.com/investment_banking/holt/en

Cash Flow Return on Investment The HOLT/LCRT approach is to maximize a number called Total Shareholder Return (TSR). This is the cumulative rate of return earned by shareholders over a period of time. Unlike MVA and EVA which are based on net present value and net annual benefit, Total Shareholder Return is an internal rate of return calculation.

The way to increase TSR is to manage and increase Total Business Return (TBR), HOLT/LCRT's newly developed internal financial measure. TBR is the overall internal rate of return the company will achieve in the future, the combination of the rates of return from existing assets and the rates of return from the firm's planned growth in assets. HOLT/LCRT call each of these rates of return on assets a Cash Flow Return on Investment (CFROI) to emphasize its use of free cash flows.

A company's CFROI on existing assets is the overall (weighted average) rate of return on its present investments. The calculation of this CFROI is done like the capital budgeting analysis we saw in Chapter 11 (if the firm is subject to significant inflation, HOLT and LCRT recommend that the analysis be done in real terms to remove any distortions caused by changing price levels):

● Estimate the average life of the firm's assets and expected free cash flows from those assets over their life. Also, project a "terminal value" for the firm at the end of the time period by assuming the company ceases business at this time.

● Calculate the amount of cash invested in the business by removing depreciation from asset values.

[13] **References:** Bennett Stewart summarized the Stern Stewart approach as it developed in *The Quest for Value*. New York: HarperBusiness, 1991. Another summary is by Stern Stewart's Al Ehrbar in his book *EVA: The Real Key to Creating Wealth*. New York: John Wiley & Sons, Inc., 1998.

● Calculate the firm's CFROI as the internal rate of return of the above cash flows.

To calculate the CFROI of the firm's planned growth in assets, HOLT and LCRT apply a "time fade model" in which the firm's future growth rate is slowly reduced over a 40-year period to an economy-wide average number. This methodology deals with the problem of supernormal growth, and, according to HOLT and LCRT, more closely matches market values.

CFROIs are compared to the company's cost of capital to determine if the firm is adding value for its investors. Investments with CFROI greater than the cost of capital add value; those with CFROI less than the cost of capital should be abandoned. A company that maximizes its CFROIs will maximize its Total Business Return and this should also maximize its Total Shareholder Return.

HOLT and LCRT recommend the use of TBR and CFROI as a both a valuation model and a measure of corporate financial performance. They have conducted extensive research into their models and have concluded that they are more accurate than competing approaches such as EVA. However, since the calculation of CFROI requires extensive cash flow forecasting and somewhat higher-order mathematics than the EVA methodology, it is more difficult than EVA to communicate. As a result, this approach has found its major success with corporate strategic planners and professional money managers.[14]

Communicating Shareholder Value

Investors in the financial markets cannot evaluate a company unless they know quite a bit about it. An important part of increasing share price, therefore, is to communicate the company's successes to investors fully and promptly. A company's failures should also be disclosed; if the financial markets hear of failures from third parties such as the news media, the company may lose the opportunity to tell the complete story in a believable and favorable manner.

1. Reports of Company Performance

All publicly-held corporations in the U.S. are required to distribute an "Annual Report to Shareholders." This is typically a glossy booklet that describes the company's current condition, tells of the company's products and services, and contains financial statement information. In addition, corporations with stock registered on a national securities exchange, with assets in excess of $10 million, or with 500 or more shareholders are required to file periodic documents with the Securities and Exchange Commission (SEC), the government agency that regulates the stock markets. Among the required SEC filings are Form 10-K, a comprehensive annual report containing audited financial statements; Form 10-Q, a quarterly report containing quarterly financial statements which may be unaudited; and Form 8-K, used to report any material changes to the company's business since the most recent Form 10-Q filing.

---

[14] **References:** A good summary of the HOLT/LCRT approach is by HOLT's Bartley J. Madden in his book *CFROI Vaulation: A Total System Approach to Valuing the Firm*. Woburn, MA: Butterworth Heinemann, 1999.

"This is the part of capitalism I hate."

Beyond formal reports to shareholders and the SEC, most public corporations provide "earnings guidance" to investment analysts. These communications are intended to prevent surprises when the company formally announces its financial results since surprises could cause a sharp change in the company's stock price. Further, when the investment community finds it can trust the firm's earnings guidance, it is more likely to trust other news coming from the company.

Once per year, corporations hold an "annual meeting" of their shareholders. Shareholders vote to select members of the board of directors, to ratify management's choice of external auditors, and to acccept or reject key company initiatives. At the meeting, senior management discusses the company's performance over the past year and responds to shareholder questions.

Companies also typically issue press releases on an ongoing basis to communicate the acquisition of new customers and contracts, to report progress in research and development efforts, to introduce new products and services, and to announce changes in management structure or personnel.

SERVING FINANCE'S CUSTOMERS

Investor Relations at Corning, Incorporated

The investor relations group of Corning, Incorporated conveys both strategic and financial information to financial analysts so they can accurately assess the company's market value. The group works to move the investment community away from a short-term valuation approach by putting events in strategic context and by acting as a teacher, helping analysts perform better analyses. The group considers a good investor relations program as one marked by availability, listening, preparation, and credibility. While they constantly deal with how much they can tell their analyst customers—given the availability of information and legal and ethical boundaries—they want to "leave them all feeling they got the best information available."

2. The Investor Relations Function

NET Present Value
For an example of an investor relations website go to: www.ibm.com/investor

Large corporations typically have a unit within the finance organization devoted to serving the special needs of shareholders and investment analysts. In addition to sending out copies of the Annual Report and SEC filings on request, these units maintain extensive data about the firm on the company's website. They also assist investors with dividends, dividend reinvestment plans, account registration, share transfer, replacement of lost stock certificates, etc.

*B*ill Lin swayed gently to the music he was playing on the grand piano in the corner of his living room. It was time to relax, and playing the piano was Bill's favorite way to unwind.

Yesterday, Bill had completed his flowchart of how his company's actions turned into stock price movements. Between the box containing financial managing activities and the box labeled "stock price" were several new boxes showing how shareholders and financial analysts evaluated the firm and how the company communicated its activities to the financial markets. Bill had found some of the information he was seeking in his finance textbooks. Other insights had come from looking at professional publications aimed at security analysts. Bill also had shared his concerns with several colleagues who had given him useful suggestions that he had incorporated into the flowchart.

Earlier today, Bill had called several financial analysts to discuss how they evaluated his company. One talked about focusing on free cash flow. Another discussed earnings multiples and promised to send Bill a recent research report on his company and industry. Still another mentioned value based management, prompting Bill to print out a series of articles from the websites of several well-known consulting firms.

Since clear communication with the financial markets was important, Bill made a note to study his firm's investor relations function and to locate best-practice firms he could benchmark. He also planned to look at the company's Annual Report and the information for investors on his company's website to see where improvements could be made.

Bill smiled as his hands flew over the keyboard. He remembered an old saying he once had heard about poor communication: "It had the words but not the music." 'No longer' he thought. 'From now on, the financial community will get just the performance it's looking for.'

Summary of Key Points

■ **State the relationship between good financial managing and a company's stock price.** Good financial managing, consistent with the prescriptions of finance theory, should increase a company's stock price. However management does not control the company's stock price directly. Rather, investors evaluate the company's performance and set its stock price equal to the present value of the future cash flows they anticipate receiving.

■ **Identify four key financial managing techniques for adding value to a firm.** Four financial managing activities that add value are (1) investing in positive NPV projects; (2) improving process, both in finance and elsewhere in the firm; (3) raising money at the lowest cost; and (4) reducing the risk borne by the company's investors.

■ **Describe techniques used by the financial community to place a value on common stock.** Since the value of a share of common stock is the present value of the future benefits it will provide, the basis of common stock valuation is the dividend-growth model. This model has been modified over time to account for supernormal-growth companies, variable-growth companies, and non-dividend-paying companies. Today, most analysts use free cash flow instead of dividends in the model. Equity analysts look at economy data, industry data, market position, risk exposure, order backlog, quality of management, and quality of earnings as they forecast a company's future free cash flow and risk. Ratio-based models using multiples of earnings and cash flow are also used.

■■ **Identify the agency barrier to good financial managing, and discuss techniques for minimizing agency costs.** In a corporation with professional management, the interests of the manager-agents are often not the same as those of the shareholder-principals. This "agency problem" leads to agency costs reducing the value of the company to its owners. Agency costs arise from a number of sources including differences in time horizon and risk aversion, management's control of its own compensation, information asymmetry, and attitudes toward risk and retaining earnings. Agency theory frames the firm as a nexus of contracts, a series of implicit and explicit agreements among all those affected by the firm that define relationships and are designed to limit conflicts of interest. Well established methods of minimizing agency costs include the "carrots" of various incentive compensation schemes and the "sticks" of management control systems, corporate governance, and the market for corporate control. However, the use of financial measures for day-to-day managerial guidance, the emphasis on preventing conflict rather than building cooperation, and the focus on relationships delineated by the formal organization chart often prevent companies from achieving high shareholder wealth.

■■ **Identify the finance theory barrier to good financial managing, and describe the nature of "value based managment" systems.** Finance theory tells us that a company adds to its worth when it increases the present value of its free cash flows. However, many managers and analysts persist in using financial accounting data for valuation and decision making, numbers that are not consistent over time, do not equal cash flow, rarely incorporate time value of money, and do not include a cost of capital. Value based management systems attempt to overcone these shortcomings by creating new internal measures to replace traditional financial accounting measures and goals. The Stern Stewart approach, based on net present value and net annual benefit, has managers maximize Economic Value Added so as to maximize Market Value Added. The HOLT/LCRT approach, based on internal rate of return, has managers maximize Cash Flow Return on Investment and Total Business Return so as to maximize Total Shareholder Return.

■■ **Describe how companies communicate value-adding activities to their shareholders and the investment community.** Companies distribute an Annual Report to shareholders and file Forms 10-K, 10-Q, and 8-K as required with the Securities and Exchange Commission. They provide regular earnings guidance to the investment community and issue press releases to inform of customer, product, or management news. The investor relations function is the company unit that serves shareholders and investment analysts.

Questions

1. Why is it that a company's management does not control its stock price?

2. Describe the implication of each of the following theories for common stock valuation:
   a. Technical theory
   b. Fundamental theory
   c. Efficient market theory

3. Identify four financial managing activities that can add value to a company. Why does each add value?

4. In what ways is the dividend-growth present value model a simplification of reality? What techniques do financial analysts use to overcome these limitations?

5. Why is free cash flow better than dividends as an input to stock valuation models?

6. Identify seven inputs used by financial analysts as they estimate the worth of common stock. What is the value of each?

7. What is a multiplier? Identify four accounting figures often used with multipliers.

8. What is normalized earnings? Why do analysts make this calculation.

9. What is the meaning of a company's price/earnings ratio?

10. What is the agency problem?

11. Why does the agency problem not exist in a proprietorship?

12. Identify six sources of the agency problem.

13. Give an example of an agency cost. If you were a shareholder of a company, how would you attempt to minimize it?

14. Why do traditional methods of minimizing agency costs sometimes fail?

15. In what ways do financial accounting data fail to provide financial managers and analysts with signals consistent with finance theory?

16. Define the following value based management terms:

    a. Market Value Added
    b. Economic Value Added
    c. Total Shareholder Return
    d. Total Business Return
    e. Cash Flow Return on Investment

17. What are the commonalities between the EVA and CFROI approaches to value based management? In what ways are these approaches different?

18. Identify three forms that must be filed periodically by most large corporations with the Securities and Exchange Commission.

Problems

1. (**Calculating free cash flow**) A company is expected to generate cash flow from operations (net of debt service) of $6.50 per share in the coming year. How much free cash flow per share will it produce if the per-share amount it will reinvest to finance future growth is:

    a. nothing?   c. $4.00?
    b. $1.50?   d. $7.50?

2. (**Calculating free cash flow**) A company expects to reinvest $5.00 per share this year to finance its future growth. How much free cash flow per share will it produce if it generates cash flow from operations per share (net of debt service) of:

    a. $4.00?   c. $ 7.00?
    b. $5.00?   d. $10.00?

3. (**Using free cash flow**) What is the value of one share of stock of a company expected to grow at 6% per year if investors require a 14% rate of return and forecast free cash flow per share in the coming year of:

    a. $1.50?   c. $ 6.00?
    b. $3.00?   d. $12.00?

4. (**Using free cash flow**) What is the value of one share of stock of a company expected to grow at 4% per year if investors require an 11% rate of return and forecast free cash flow per share in the coming year of:

    a. $15.00?   c. $3.75?
    b. $ 7.50?   d. $2.00?

5. (**Using multipliers**) A company reported the following financial data this year:

EBITDA	3,000,000
EBIT	2,500,000
Net income	2,000,000
Cash flow from operations	3,500,000

If analysts have determined that the total value of the company's stock is $50,000,000, what numbers have they assigned to the following multipliers:

    a. Earnings multiplier?
    b. Cash flow from operations multiplier?
    c. EBIT multiplier?
    d. EBITDA multiplier?

6. (**Using multipliers**) A company most recent income statement is:

Sales	$10,000,000
– Cost of goods sold	6,000,000
Gross profit	4,000,000
– Operating expenses	3,000,000
EBITDA	1,000,000
– Depreciation	200,000
EBIT	800,000
– Interest expense	50,000
– Taxes	100,000
Net income	650,000

In addition, the company had cash flow from operations of $2,000,000. What would a financial analyst who assigned the following multipliers calculate as the total value of the company's stock?

    a. Earnings multiplier: = 25
    b. Cash flow from operations multiplier = 8
    c. EBIT multiplier = 21
    d. EBITDA multiplier = 15

7. (**Normalized earnings**) Normalize the per share earnings of a company with earnings per share of $4.00 if the amount of per share earnings due to non-repeatable events was:

    a. nothing   c. $1.50
    b. $0.25   d. $5.00

8. (**Normalized earnings**) What was the earnings per share of a company if $0.50 of its per share earnings was due to non-repeatable events and normalized earnings per share was:

    a. $5.00?   c. $0.50?
    b. $2.00?   d. zero?

9. (**Price/earnings ratio**) Calculate the price/earnings ratio of a company with earnings per share of $7.50 and a stock price of:

    a. $37.50   c. $112.50
    b. $60.00   d. $187.50

10. (**Price/earnings ratio**) Calculate the price/earnings ratio of a company whose stock price is $90.00 per share if its per share earnings is:

    a. $3.00   c. $ 6.00
    b. $4.50   d. $10.00

PART VI

LOOKING

AHEAD

Part VI consists of only one chapter, one that is somewhat different from the others in this book. We have stepped back from our study of financial managing to summarize where we are: what we know and what we don't know about finance. We know quite a bit, yet in many respects what we don't know is as striking as what we do know. An ongoing part of every finance professional's work is to continue to learn the new as it develops and integrate it with the old.

Chapter 18 looks ahead, but first we look back by summarizing six central concepts of financial managing that have appeared repeatedly throughout the book. Then, we focus our attention toward the future. We identify forces for change in finance theory and discuss innovations in important financial concepts and practices that may be occurring as a result of changes in the global competitive environment and the evolution of financial thought. We distinguish between analytical and operational finance theory and summarize five central concepts in operational finance theory. We identify the benefits and dangers of using a financial perspective in thinking about business decisions and highlight ways to avoid the dangers. Finally we discuss reasons for being humble about what we know about financial managing.

CHAPTER 18

THE FUTURE:

YOURS AND

FINANCE'S

*F*INANCIAL MANAGEMENT THEORY AND PRACTICE: WHAT'S STABLE AND WHAT'S CHANGING?" Carrie Finch wrote in big block letters on the flip-chart. "Okay," she said to the other five members of her group, "here's how I tried to organize my thoughts."

For four days the seminar speakers and participants from Carrie's company had discussed key concepts in financial managing and how they are used. During the week, Carrie found herself particularly interested when seminar members speculated about the future of finance or emphasized what is not known about financial managing. Perhaps those parts especially interested her because a business degree with a finance minor and a half-dozen years in various finance jobs made her reasonably comfortable with the finance concepts that were widely accepted. Or perhaps it was because she knew this question would be discussed at the end of the seminar. Now was the time for each of the groups to bring their thoughts together and to prepare to share their ideas with the seminar leaders and the other teams.

"Four themes keep coming up for me," she said and wrote four words on the flip-chart: THEORY, PRACTICE, CAUSALITY, and SO? "First, theory. What do we think we know about finance, what don't we know, and how is what we don't know likely to change what we think we do know? Second, practice. What's being done the same in finance as it was 5, 10, or 20 years ago, and what's likely to be done differently? I am not convinced that theory and practice are always the same. Third, causality. What is likely to cause these changes we are predicting? I guess I need a theory of change—some sense of causality—so I can have some grounding for talking about what might be stable and what might be changing. And finally, so? as in 'so what?' Why do we care what's changing, and what does it imply for how we do our jobs?

"I'd like to hear what you people think about all of these, but we have only a little time. So which ones do we get to talk about?"

We find ourselves in a situation much like Carrie's. This is the book's last chapter, and we have many remaining thoughts—and questions—about financial managing we'd like to share. And we have only a moderate amount of space for doing so. We also feel we have a "last chapter" opportunity we should not miss—a chance to review and bring together some of the things we discussed in earlier chapters.

Key Points You Should Learn from This Chapter

After reading this chapter, you should be able to:

- Understand why we wrote this chapter the way we did.
- Summarize six central concepts of financial managing.
- Identify three possible forces for change in finance theory and discuss four changes in important financial concepts that may be occurring as a result of changes in the global competitive environment and the evolution of financial thought.
- Distinguish between analytical and operational finance theory and summarize five central concepts in operational finance theory.
- Describe the areas of financial practice that seems to be changing the most as a result of changes in the global competitive environment and the evolution of financial thought.
- Describe the benefits and dangers of using a financial perspective in thinking about business decisions and ways to avoid the dangers.
- Discuss three reasons for being humble about what we know about financial managing.

Introductory Concepts—The Last-Chapter Game Plan

The subject of finance is a bit like the subject of medicine. We have made significant strides in understanding the financial aspects of the organism we call the business organization, in helping it function better, and in curing some of its worst financial diseases. But there is still much we do not know and many ailments that remain uncured. We are in the same position as the doctor who can do so much yet still does not have the answers to many medical questions.

In this last chapter we have taken a step back from our study of financial managing to summarize where we are: what we know and what we don't know about finance. We know quite a bit, yet in many respects what we don't know is as striking as what we do know. Like doctors, an ongoing part of every finance professional's work is to learn the new as it develops and integrate it with the old.

We begin the chapter by reviewing six key concepts in the book. They have been recognized as important for a number of years and are recognized as important right now. We think most professors will agree that Carrie, you, and we will continue finding them useful 10 or 20 years from now. They are so important and enduring that we have devoted about 90% of the book to presenting them.

Then we shift to what is changing, and we simultaneously become much more speculative in our writing. We do so in part because it is easy to make mistakes in recognizing which changes are important and which are not. We continue to consider the six key concepts and speculate about forces that may lead to changes in them and what some of those changes might be. Also, we have introduced a number of topics in this book that are not normally found in finance texts but we believe are important—for example, managing financial processes in Chapter 13 and global sustainability which appears throughout the book; and we have reported some things that are new to finance practice and that only a few companies are currently doing. As textbook authors we see these topics as suggesting possible changes in how finance defines itself as a field and in the ways finance is practiced. Accordingly, in this part of the chapter, we intentionally go well beyond simply reviewing what we have written earlier—we speculate about what may be emerging in the future.

Finally, we close with a review of the value of the finance perspective, some dangers in using it, ideas on how to avoid the dangers, and thoughts about maintaining some humility about what the field of finance knows about financial managing and the world in which financial managing takes place.

Important Concepts in Financial Managing

Much of the content of this book is a report on the established insights of finance theory. In the section that follows, we summarize six of the most important conclusions of finance theory and connect them to their appearance(s) in this text. We anticipate that each of these concepts will continue to be useful to Carrie and her co-workers for many years to come. They have been widely discussed in the finance literature, are widely taught in finance courses, and influence the day-to-day decisions of all financial managers.

1. Importance of Cash Flows

A core concept in finance is that financial value depends upon cash flows. An investor who purchases a share of a company or an entire business exchanges cash today for anticipated cash in the future. This has two major implications.

Cash flows vs. financial accounting   One implication of the recognition that cash flows are the underpinnings of value is that financial accounting numbers—income, asset values, book value, and so on—are the wrong numbers to use in financial valuation analysis. While financial accounting numbers can provide one useful picture of a company, their dependence on accounting rules and conventions means that they are not always consistent with cash flows. In 1987, this understanding led the Financial Accounting Standards Board, the rule-making body for financial accounting, to include a "statement of cash flows" as one of the required outputs of public financial reporting. In Chapter 2 we introduced the concept of cash flows as the basis for financial decision making and illustrated the dangers of using accounting data.

Expectations vs. historical flows   A second implication is that historical cash flows, such as those reported in financial statements and other accounting data do not contribute to financial value. It is future cash flows that matter. Historical information is useful only to the extent that it enables individuals to predict or improve future flows. Expectations of cash flows influence financial decisions. The importance of expectations and the corresponding lesser importance of historical data were discussed throughout the book, but particularly in Chapters 2 (Data), 4 (Money Rates), 5 (Planning), 9 (Value of Securities), 11 (Capital Budgeting), 12 (Permanent Working Capital), and 15 (Managing Risk).

Book value vs. market value   Concerns about financial accounting and historical flows have led finance theorists and practitioners to make the important distinction between book values and market values. Book values, the numbers on a company's accounting books that are made public on its financial statements, are historical in nature and are based on accounting rules. Market values, on the other hand, represent investors' evaluation of future cash flows and are the relevant measures for financial decision making.

2. Time Value as an Evaluation Tool

A corollary to the framework of cash flow analysis is the importance of time to the worth of those cash flows. In Chapter 3 we introduced the concept of time value: that the value of money depends not only on its amount but also on when it is paid or received. Since virtually all business exchanges involve paying (or receiving) cash now in return for receiving (or paying) cash later, it is impossible to evaluate financial opportunities without applying time value.

Chapter 3 presented the calculations for basic and some more-complex time value analyses and introduced the power of the financial calculator and spreadsheet as analytical aids. We then applied these time value concepts to some common financial analyses and decisions. In Chapter 9 we showed that the value of long-term securities can be modeled as the present value of the cash flows anticipated by investors. In Chapter 11 we used time value concepts to perform a cost-benefit analysis of the long-term investments available to a company; we extended the analysis to permanent working capital decisions in Chapter 12.

3. The Risk-Return Relationship

A third core concept of finance is that value depends on a tradeoff between returns and risk. It is not enough to estimate the amount and timing of future cash flows because not all anticipated cash flows are equally likely, hence equally desirable to investors. In Chapter 8 we introduced the concept of risk as the uncertainty of future cash flows. We identified investors as risk averters—requiring higher returns to assume greater risk.

Chapter 8 also contained an introduction to the statistical risk modeling commonly done in finance. For an asset held by itself—for example, a small business owned by an investor-manager without substantial other assets—the total risk model applied and risk could be measured by the standard deviation of returns. However, for an asset held in a well-diversified portfolio, the relevant risk is the systematic risk, the incremental risk from adding that asset to the portfolio. Systematic risk is measured by an asset's beta, the relationship of its returns to those from the overall market. These powerful concepts of portfolio risk are summarized in the capital asset pricing model.

The importance of risk to value appears elsewhere in the book as well. In Chapter 4, we saw from the Fisher model that risk enters the determination of every interest rate. In Chapter 10, we showed how a company's cost of capital—the composite rate it must earn on an investment to justify raising the funds—depends on the risks its investors are asked to take. In later chapters we saw that the financial industry has developed tools for reducing risks by shifting them to individuals and organizations better able to assume them. In particular, Chapter 15 introduced the concept of hedging, of balancing assets and liabilities and also cash inflows and outflows to reduce risk.

4. Perfect Market Learnings and the Importance of Market Imperfections

A particularly fruitful line of finance research has come from the analysis of perfect markets, markets with complete and fully shared information, universal and equal access to borrowing and lending, and no taxes or transactions costs. In such perfect markets, several decisions of financial managers, which seem on the surface to be of critical importance, become irrelevant to the value of the firm. In particular, in Chapters 14 and 16 we highlighted the work of Professors Modigliani and Miller (MM) who showed that if markets were perfect, a company's debt/equity mix and dividend decisions would not change its value.

It is the imperfections in financial markets that create opportunities for adding value. In these realistic markets, some companies have the opportunity to act on better information than their competitors. Others have superior access to resources. Still other companies can structure their activities to reduce tax obligations and other operating costs. Investors in imperfect markets cannot always substitute their own financing activities for those of corporations and, in contrast to MM's perfect-market conclusions, are no longer indifferent to corporate financing activity.

Since it is the imperfections in financial markets that make many financial choices meaningful, financial managers have learned to focus their attention on imperfections rather than those market conditions that approach economic perfection.

5. Insights from Financial Economics

Several financial economic concepts play a vitally important role in finance thought and action. In Chapter 4 we discussed the model of interest rates developed by Professor Irving Fisher. That model demonstrated that interest rates are critically dependent on anticipated inflation and risk; it also provided a valuable framework for many subsequent analyses.

Also, in Chapter 4, we saw that companies that do business in multiple currencies face transaction, translation, and economic exposure to exchange rates. Understanding the relationships among currencies and between spot and foward rates is a useful financial managing skill.

6. Importance of Stakeholder Alignments

Agency theory, as noted in Chapter 17, has provided a powerful way to examine the need for alignments between the organization and its various stakeholders. In corporations where ownership and management are separated, the interests of managers and shareholders are not always the same. Managers have many ways to enrich themselves and other stakeholders at the expense of shareholders, thus violating their implicit responsibility as agents to their shareholder-principals.

Agency theory was framed initially in terms of conflicts of interests between professional managers and shareholders. However, it can be looked at as raising a more encompassing and more important issue—the requirement to create ways of aligning and balancing the needs and interests of all stakeholders of the organization. The legal system origin of agency theory has not encouraged either this larger view nor has it emphasized the positive potential of seeking such alignments. So far, discussions of the "agency problem" have emphasized the abuses arising from manager-shareholder conflicts. Suggested solutions have tended to emphasize either legalistic, contractual ways to restrain self-interested managers from exploiting shareholders, or economic incentives in an attempt to ensure that shareholders benefit from managers' self-interest.

The emergence of global sustainability as a societal goal and the public's increasing awareness of how businesses can both contribute to and damage the world's ecological and social well-being are encouraging many companies to reconsider how their business activities impact all of their stakeholders. Finance theory is likely to continue to address the importance of seeking stakeholder alignments and is likely to broaden the scope and creativity of its analysis and possible solutions.

Changes in Finance Theory

NET Present Value
A good place to keep up to date on developments in finance theory is: www.fma.org, the website of Financial Management Association International

In this section, we look at three sets of forces that lead to the continual evolution of finance theory, identify three sources of change we have emphasized in this book, and then speculate on possible changes in finance theory that might come from these forces.

1. Three Sets of Forces for Change

Finance theory is like all other theory—subject to change and evolution—and it is changing in many ways for many reasons. Some new theory is coming from academic researchers who are using logical and mathematical tools to find relationships that have not been seen before or to disprove relationships previously thought to hold. Other new theory is coming from researchers who study financial practice and synthesize and explain what they observe.

Three sets of forces that have led to changes in finance theory in the past are likely to lead to additional changes in the future. These are: (1) changes in the environment in which finance is practiced, (2) new discoveries within the framework of existing finance theory, and (3) the adoption of insights from other fields into finance theory.

Environmental changes   Changes in the environment in which finance is practiced bring new issues onto the agenda of financial managers and onto the plate of finance theory. As Figure 1.3 summarized, finance theory has regularly added new topics and insights and raised new issues for managers and scholars as the economy and technology have evolved. For example, in Chapter 1 we mentioned that the ongoing shift from physical to human capital is forcing a reevaluation of how firms attract, measure, utilize, and reward resources and that increased awareness of global sustainability is changing how firms determine their goals and activities.

Discoveries in finance   Discoveries within the framework of existing finance theory lead to adjusting, refining, and even overthrowing existing theoretical formulations. For example, the theory of the debt-equity mix, presented in Chapter 14, has changed dramatically over the past 50 years from the traditional theory of Durand, to the perfect market theory of Modigliani and Miller, to the market imperfection theories of today—and yet we still have much to learn. The continual testing of theory against data that is the heart of the scientific process supports some theories and not others, leading to further changes in finance theory.

Borrowing insights   Borrowing from other fields also contributes greatly to finance—just as it does to all fields. Much of finance theory comes from economics, particularly those parts dealing with markets and incremental and optimization decision making. Portfolio theory has its roots in statistics. Many of the concepts of agency theory, including the name itself, derive from the field of law. Psychology and sociology contribute to our understanding of investors' and managers' behavior.

2. Important Sources of Change

In this book we have emphasized the impacts on finance theory and practice arising from several sources including changes brought about by the increasing globalization of business, changes brought about by revolutionary rates of quality improvement and by the adoption of quality-management practices by financial managers, and changes brought about by the awareness of and concerns about global sustainability. We believe that each of these sources of change are real and deserve the most serious attention of business executives.

However, in paying particular attention to these worldwide changes in financial management practices we do not rest on uncontested ground. While quality management has been widely accepted, there remain some who do not see its value. The concept of global sustainability as an imperative for business is also not universally accepted. Some people do not believe that environmental degradation exists or that if it does exist it is the result of human activity. Others recognize the existence of environmental and social problems but do not believe that business has a role in addressing them. For some the jury is still out. Still others believe it is just one more management fad, likely to pass away after a short period of attention.

3. Possible Changes in Well-Established Finance Concepts

As we have indicated throughout this book, these global competitive developments seem to be changing the practice of corporate finance in a number of ways. And, as practice changes, finance theory is also likely to change, although what those changes will be is not clear. Four areas of possible change relate to: (1) the purpose(s) of the firm, (2) agency theory, (3) time value of money, and (4) the theory of perfect and imperfect markets.

The purpose(s) of the firm   As we discussed in Chapter 1, defining the purpose of the firm as the maximizing of share price has been a very attractive simplification for analytical finance theory for many years. However, like every theoretical concept in the social sciences, it is not in any sense an ultimate truth—nor is it an indispensable piece of finance theory. It is a simplification of a complex set of relationships, a value judgment, and a view of the world that carries significant risks with its advantages. The continuing global competitive successes of companies apparently pursuing alternative purposes and the dramatic failures of some companies that practiced shareholder wealth maximization seem to be reducing the advantages of this simplification and calling for new attempts to integrate the valuable insights of this perspective with alternate and often broader views of the purposes of all organizations.

Rethinking agency theory   As we noted in Chapter 17, agency theory is in a very similar situation. It is a powerful and useful framing, containing a major and important kernel of truth that is ripe for greater intellectual development and increased conceptual sophistication. One possible way of achieving a fuller contribution of the insights of agency theory is to shift from a relatively negative and competitive framing to a more positive and collaborative framing. In the coming years, finance theory may offer new insights and guidance to managers working to align the interests of all stakeholders.

Intergenerational implications of the timing of benefits and costs Money today is clearly worth more than the same amount of money tomorrow. However, it is not at all clear that social, environmental, political, or any other benefits are worth more today than tomorrow. Thus, any attempt to put monetary values on noncash items and then discount them to the present is a value judgment that needs to be addressed very explicitly. (Just such an approach has been used often in economic development work where social costs and benefits of alternative projects are translated into monetary terms and then discounted to the present.) If time value of money concepts are applied uncritically to nonmonetary phenomena, they can lead to a selfish exploitation of future generations by our own generation. As the inventor and home of this powerful financial evaluation technique, the field of finance has a special responsibility for learning how to avoid abusing this technique and for teaching others to use it properly.

Limitations of the concept of perfect markets   Financial markets are amazingly efficient in many respects. Like many other markets, they have proven to be very powerful disciplinarians of those who think they are smarter than the markets, those who feel they can fool them forever, or those who think that somehow the realities that drive the forces of supply and demand in those markets do not apply to them. However, the wisdom of financial markets can be exaggerated and may not capture every social value we assume they capture. In particular, we are asking an enormous amount from financial markets if we assume they respond quickly and accurately enough to be a useful guide to managerial decisions in the short run. In the coming years, finance theory may make rich discoveries about when and how financial markets are useful guides to financial and other managerial decisions and when they are not.

◼◼ A Second Focus for Finance Theory

As we consider ways in which increased global competitiveness may be influencing the evolution of finance theory and practice, one observation stands out for us. The things finance theory historically has paid the most attention to seem more objective and analytical than subjective and behavioral. Finance theory seems to deal largely with *what* should be done in managing corporate finance—which decisions to make and the mathematical techniques for doing the analysis. Much less attention seems to be paid to *how* things should be done—how decisions should be made and how they should be carried into action. Let's try to illustrate this distinction.

1. What vs. How

The first area encompasses many topics, including the value today of receiving $100 next year, the exchange rate between dollars and pounds sterling in today's market, and the cost of capital for a particular firm. Some of these topics—like the present value of $100—are *relatively* simple, in the sense that they are factual, definitional, or involve only a few related assumptions or data. Others are more complex, involve more assumptions, and frequently require considerable amounts of data in their construction, like the cost of capital of a large, diversified firm. Whether fairly simple or fairly complex, these topics have a long and respected history in the field of finance. Research and conceptualization on topics such as these give managers a better sense of the workings of the financial environment and a better understanding of financial analytical techniques. It tells them what they *should* do in making decisions about a company's financial resources and what to expect in the financial markets important to those decisions. It has made many contributions to the successful management of organizations.

The second area focuses on how finance actually gets done in organizations. This area includes such topics as the factors that determine which approach to capital budgeting a particular firm chooses to use, how a firm chooses to manage its accounts payable function, how financial managers perceive and execute their role in a particular firm, and which data are collected to make financial decisions. This aspect of finance has received scant attention from teachers and researchers in the field of finance, and it does not even have a widely accepted name to distinguish it from finance theory and decision making.

Although finance theory and research have focused almost exclusively on the first area, there is no reason why theory and research are not appropriate for the second area as well. In fact, the very modest attention paid so far to the second area makes it a particularly promising one for research contributions. For many organizations, major improvements in the practice of financial operations (translating theory and decisions into action) will make great contributions to organizational performance, contributions that may well match or exceed the benefits from increased conceptual understanding of financial frameworks, tools, and techniques.

analytical finance theory—theory about the factual nature of finance and what decisions should be made

operational finance theory—theory about how financial actions are taken in an organization

To call attention to the importance of finance theory for both of these areas of finance, we have chosen to call the first area **analytical finance theory** and the second **operational finance theory.** We are neither enchanted with nor wedded to those labels and expect better ones to emerge in the future. We use them for the present simply because we have not found in the literature widely accepted alternative labels that we could adopt in their place. In understanding and meeting the financial needs of organizations, both areas are important and both are necessary and appropriate fields of research, theory, and conceptualization by finance practitioners, researchers, and teachers.

2. Possible Important Concepts Related to Financial Operations

Although the operational theory of finance is not yet as developed as the analytical theory, at least five central concepts seem to be emerging. Each has influenced the writing of much of this book on financial managing. The concepts relate to: (1) internal and external customers, (2) quality, (3) business processes, (4) continuous improvement, and (5) stakeholders.

Internal and external customers   The concept of finance's customers has appeared throughout this book. The logical application, that finance members can look at their work as "serving finance's customers," has been illustrated in virtually every chapter. This customer focus has been changing the ways in which finance members look at their jobs and how they do their work. It fits well with the changes described by Patrick J. Keating and Stephen F. Jablonsky in a series of studies of the changing roles of financial managers.[1]

Quality   In many places, this book suggests that a broad definition of *financial quality* is emerging in the field of financial management. Although some people still think of financial quality largely in terms of the analytical sophistication of financial decisions or the lack of default risk in financial instruments, broader, more pervasive, and more dynamic definitions are coming into use. They include explicit recognition that finance's customers define quality financial work and that internal as well as external customers need to be served. They include the ideas of anticipating customer needs, exceeding expectations, and even delighting customers—not just meeting needs. They include providing finance's services more quickly—reducing cycle time. And they include "joy in work"—making finance people more fun to work with and finance work more fun for finance people to do.

Business processes   In Chapter 13 we looked at the financial processes that exist in an organization. Because finance is so intimately involved in all parts of the company, much of finance's work is intertwined with the work of other organizational units. Said another way, many finance processes are really cross-func-

---

[1] **References:**   Patrick J. Keating and Stephen F. Jablonsky, *Changing Roles of Financial Management: Getting Close to the Business* (Morristown, N.J.: Financial Executives Research Foundation, 1990) and Stephen F. Jablonsky, Patrick J. Keating, and James B. Heian, *Business Advocate or Corporate Policeman? Assessing Your Role as a Financial Executive* (Morristown, N.J.: Financial Executives Research Foundation, 1993).

tional business processes. One of Chapter 13's key points about financial processes—that they *exist*—comes as a new insight to many finance professionals. Recognizing the existence of financial processes has not always been a part of the perspective of many financial managers. Another of Chapter 13's key points—that it is important that financial processes be understood and well managed—is becoming increasingly apparent to financial managers.

Continuous improvement   In Chapter 13 we examined how financial and other business processes can be improved. The tools of process planning, control, and improvement that have emerged from the global quality revolution apply to financial processes—just as to every other part of the organization. When finance people use these tools, they can add significant value to their companies. In the growing number of places where these tools are being used skillfully and appropriately, revolutionary rates of defect reduction, cycle time reduction, customer satisfaction improvement, and cost reduction are being achieved.[2]

Stakeholders   In many places, this book also suggests that finance is coming to recognize that it has an important role to play in identifying and seeking to exceed the expectations of the organization's many stakeholders. Chapter 1 paid particular attention to this possibility. Many financial managers who once held the view that finance has a special obligation to serve only one stakeholder—the owners of equity shares—are coming to see that serving all stakeholders is often a superior way to serve the company's shareholders.

Changes in Financial Practice

NET Present Value
A good place to keep up to date on developments in finance practice is: www.fei.org, the website of Financial Executives International

To explore ways in which financial practice is changing, we look at two themes that have run throughout this book: quality management and global sustainability. For each we ask four questions: "What's new in finance practice as companies adopt approaches that respond to these major global developments?" "What continues to be done but in new ways?" "What continues to be done in well-established ways?" and "What is no longer done?"

However, one early warning is appropriate: these suggestions must be considered very tentative. In many cases these questions are just starting to be asked, and the field of finance knows very little about the answers. And, as we will argue at the very end of this chapter, there are a variety of reasons why even the few things we might *think* we know may be inaccurate.

1. Changes Driven by Quality Management

What's new?   Adoption of systematic quality-management practices brings with it the use of all of the tools of quality management introduced in Chapter 13. The quantitative and analytical tools are as useful in finance as anywhere else

---

[2] **Reference:** James A.F. Stoner and Frank M. Werner, *Managing Finance for Quality: Bottom-Line Results from Top-Level Commitment* (Milwaukee: Quality Press, and Morristown, NJ: Financial Executives Research Foundation, 1994).

in the organization. And because of the "numerical literacy" of most finance people, these tools are often grasped quickly and enthusiastically.

The behavioral tools are also useful in financial managing as are the techniques of competitive benchmarking. These tools may be more difficult for many finance members to master than the quantitative/analytical ones because of the preference of many finance members for the "hard" side of management versus the "soft" side. However, this greater difficulty of mastering the "soft tools" of quality management is not unique to finance. David Kearns, ex-CEO and chairman of the board of Xerox, has echoed many other quality champions in noting that, for many people, "the hard stuff is easy and the soft stuff is hard."

Competitive benchmarking for financial and other organizational processes also comes naturally to many finance people because of its large analytical component. It is attractive to finance members because of its superiority to a somewhat similar process, the comparing of elements of organizational performance against the average of comparable companies. Competitive benchmarking stimulates strong organizations to new initiatives by revealing how far they lag behind the very best practices; comparisons against averages run the risk of encouraging complacency in organizations that are near or slightly above average.

Developing, collecting, and reporting new measures to capture key success factors that are not captured in existing financial measures are a challenge both to companies and to the field of finance as a whole.

The empowerment and increased training that are part of systematic quality management support and encourage aggressive efforts of finance members to train nonfinancial members in the tools and skills of financial analysis. Together, these efforts to "distribute" financial tools, skills, and capabilities resemble the "distributed data processing" phenomenon that occured with personal computers and other technological changes in information systems and practices.

What's done differently?   Companies are using the tools of quality management to perform well-established financial practices more effectively and more efficiently. For example, planning and budgeting, capital project analysis, and measuring the performance of the total organization are long-established financial processes which, in some leading companies, are being performed at least somewhat differently from the ways they were in the past.

Corning Incorporated's Treasury KRIs (key results indicators) in Chapter 2 is an example of the new steps taken to measure and report finance's performance within the corporation and even to outsiders.

Finance organizations are also beginning to frame and treat the people and organizations with which they work as "customers." In Chapter 1 we noted the framing of all relationships, both inside and outside the organization, as customer/supplier alignments. Doing so improves communication and reduces unnecessary work and rework. It also leads to reductions in operating costs and increases in profitability that are sometimes quite dramatic.

What's done the same?   Not everything in financial practice is changing as a result of developments in global competitiveness. To the contrary, many financial activities do not seem to be changing appreciably. A large number of financial analyses are performed today much as they were 20 or more years ago. Cost of capital calculations, financing mix analyses, and dividend policy seem to be relatively unchanged. It is difficult to predict the future of these activities as finance functions gain in mastery of modern quality-management approaches and as those approaches themselves evolve and change. The quality revolution is still somewhat new in corporate finance, so the future may yield much greater impact on finance than can be seen today. But, at present, changes in these areas are much more difficult to detect than in the others.

What's no longer done?   A major contribution of quality-management approaches involves uncovering nonvalue-added activities that can be eliminated. When finance takes a customer-serving approach to its relationships with internal and external customers and suppliers, an early question is "What do you need from me and why?" The answers frequently reveal that finance toils to produce reports and analyses not really needed in the form provided—or not needed in any form. In a similar way, cycle time and defect-reducing projects often remove multiple steps from financial and cross-functional processes: removing inspections, analyses, reports, rework, and other nonvalue-added work.

The shift in roles of finance members to more collaborative, team-based partnerships with other organizational members has also eliminated many aspects of the police, judge, and inspector roles of finance.

2. Changes Driven by Global Sustainability

What's new?   As companies respond to society's demand for global sustainability, they discover profitable opportunities that they might not have seen before. Among the "low-hanging fruit"—opportunities that are easy to achieve—are reducing energy consumption by installing additional insulation or by using smart light switches, reducing water consumption by installing rainwater collectors and low-flow plumbing fixtures, and finding markets for outputs previously considered to be waste. An example: in the 1990s, in an effort to become "greener," DuPont spent $200 millon on energy upgrades which now save the company more than $300 million annually.[3]

NET Present Value
Wal-Mart discusses its sustainability efforts on its website at:
http://walmartstores.com/sustainability

Some companies are looking internally to discover where more sustainable operations can yield financial benefits. In 2005, Wal-Mart kicked off its "Business Sustainability Strategy" in which the company looked deeply into its supply chain to find how it could be more sustainable. In doing so, the company discovered ways to further cut the cost and ensure a continued supply of the products it sells while at the same time making them more acceptable to many of its customers and other stakeholders. Herman Miller, the upscale furniture manufacturer, found that by making its products easier to disassemble for recycling, it has also made them easier to assemble reducing the cost of manufacturing the furniture in the first place.

---

[3] **Source:**   Marc Karell, President, Climate Change & Environmental Services, LLC.

The Fiesta deck has two swimming pools, two food courts, two casinos . . .

The emergence of carbon markets—such as those established in the European Union under the Kyoto Protocols, the Regional Greenhouse Gas Initiative (RGGI) of ten northeastern U.S. states, and the private Chicago Climate Exchange—has provided a market value for some sustainability activities. This has encouraged companies to seek out tradable carbon credits and to incorporate their value into investment decisions. Weather-related derivatives now give companies new ways to manage the risk of exposure to an increasingly variable climate.

A classic rule of management is that it is difficult if not impossible to manage something that cannot be measured. Many companies are now measuring and reporting their ecological impact—within their traditional financial reports; as a separate environmental report; or to international agencies, such as the Carbon Disclosure Project, which make the data public. These companies can now benchmark their efforts against other reporting companies and set practical and realistic goals to further their sustainability efforts.

Companies are also finding financial value in communicating their sustainability efforts to their stakeholders. The payoffs include increased loyalty and sales from customers; increased loyalty, contributions, and morale from employees; and increased support from their communities.

What's done differently? Companies incorporating sustainability into their operations find that awareness of climate change often leads them to reconsider where they locate, what products and services they sell, and where they source their raw materials. For centuries, people and businesses have located along rivers and coastlines for access to water and shipping routes, however, rising sea levels are threatening the viability of these locations. Rising global temperatures mean that areas of the world that are now hospitable to certain agricultural products and provide excellent grazing areas for animals may not be in the future. Companies are changing their product mix as consumers increasingly demand goods and services that meet minimum standards of sustainability. And, many companies, concerned with the damaging effects of fossil fuels on the environment and the rising price of petroleum, are obtaining an increasing amount of their energy from renewable sources such as solar and wind power.

NET Present Value
You can learn more about the Equator Principles at: http://www.equator-principles.com

As of the date this is written, seventy-two banks, including some of the world's largest, have adopted the Equator Principles which commit the banks to assessing and managing environmental and social risks in project finance, financing in which the use of the proceeds is known. These banks have realized that while a loan may be profitable, their reputations could be at stake if the loan proceeds are used in ways that harm the environment or undermine social justice. Other banks have discovered that they can enhance their reputations by seeking out and lending to companies engaged in environmentally healthy activities, regardless of how the proceeds of any specific loan are used.

NET Present Value
In the United States, the standard for "green" buildings is LEED (Leadership in Energy and Environmental Design) promulgated by the U.S. Green Building Council: http://www.usgbc.org

Real estate developers are constructing buildings to increasingly higher levels of energy efficiency and environmental friendliness. They have discovered that a small additional investment at the time of construction can pay big dividends in reducing operating costs and increased rental and occupancy rates.

Ultimately, the most significant business difference driven by global sustainability may be the emergence of a new goal for the for-profit business firm, one that adds environmental and social objectives to the traditional shareholder wealth management objective to create a goal that better serves society's multiple needs.

What's done the same?   The emergence of global sustainability, like the development of quality management, leaves many financial activities unchanged. Robust economic performance is still necessary for companies to compete and thrive, and the many existing financial tools and activities that contribute to economic success remain important and necessary. However, similar to quality management, it is difficult to predict the future of these activities as finance functions learn ways to manage for global sustainability and as those ways evolve and change.

What's no longer done? Global sustainability encourages companies to look at their activities through a new lens, one that uncovers the firm's impact on the environment and society. In doing so, companies often discover activities that harm the environment and can be eliminated or replaced with cheaper, more environmentally-friendly activities. When McDonald's replaced polystyrene foam packages for their hamburgers with paper wrappers they not only significantly reduced environmental waste, they also saved millions of dollars, and the project led to a corporate Waste Reduction Action Plan that promised additional savings.

NET Present Value
The Cradle-to-Cradle framework is described at the website of the consulting company McDonough and Braungart founded:
http://www.mbdc.com

A new zero-waste business philosophy, championed by architect William McDonough and chemist Michael Braungart under the name "Cradle-to-Cradle," urges manufacturers to stop producing anything that cannot be reused at the end of its lifetime. For McDonough and Braungart, the goal is that "waste=food" with biological waste becoming nutrients for some other organism and technological waste becoming inputs for some other product.

So What? Benefits and Dangers of the Financial Perspective

And now we come to Carrie's last question: "So what?" We take her question considerably further than merely the implications of these changes for financial practice, and we take it in three pieces. First, we look at the benefits of the financial perspective as presented in this book (and essentially all other finance texts). What special contributions will you bring to an organization when you put on your financial manager's hat? Second, we look at the dangers that accompany finance thinking. What unintended consequences might flow from the approaches and analyses used in the name of finance. And third, we suggest ways to capture the benefits of the financial perspective without being ensnared by the dangers. Naturally, we are positive about what finance has to contribute—it is inconceivable to us that a modern company could be run without drawing heavily on the contributions of finance theory. However, we do not feel that the financial perspective, or the perspective of any single discipline or philosophy for that matter, can be embraced without careful regard for possible blind spots it may encourage.

1. Benefits—Finance Thinking as a Useful Mindset

The finance perspective—looking at the money flows through an organization with an eye toward shareholder value—has proven to be a particularly valuable perspective for managers, investors, and analysts of organizational performance. The value of this perspective comes from at least five sources: (1) focus, (2) tools and concepts, (3) a big, integrated picture, (4) wide acceptance, and (5) separation of signal from noise.

Focus   The finance perspective is grounded in a fundamental truth which gives focus to managerial actions: all organizations need to achieve a balance among their money flows in both the longer and the shorter terms. For businesses this need for balance is immediate and obvious, but it also applies to not-for-profit organizations and even to governments. Ongoing surpluses in funds flows are associated with short-term organizational health and long-term survival; ongoing deficits are associated with crisis and termination. An obvious and major contribution of the financial perspective is its call to managers to take explicit account of the impact of business decisions on the financial health of the organization.

Tools and concepts   This first benefit is made real by the second, a set of tools and concepts to analyze the financial implications of organizational actions.

Big, integrated picture   The financial perspective provides a big, integrated picture of the organization that enables us to capture the enormous complexity of its many activities in a small group of numbers. Perhaps the most widely reported is net income, but other accounting numbers such as return on assets and earnings per share, and cash-flow-based numbers such as net cash from operations, free cash flow, and net present value are also recognized as valuable "integrators" of the organization's performance. Analytical finance theory argues that summary numbers such as these are effective in capturing the most important activities of an organization, providing a powerful merging and netting out of a wide range of managerial behavior. Nobel laureate in economics Milton Friedman has made perhaps the most famous argument about the value of one of these measures, net economic profit. He has concluded that corporate profit captures so many of the benefits of an organization's impact on society that it provides a safe and uniquely correct measure of those benefits. In this view, the only social responsibility of managers is to maximize profit.[4]

Widely accepted   The finance perspective is widely accepted. Many people have learned to think very comfortably in terms of budgets, revenues, expenses, and time value of money. The financial perspective provides a language for communicating within and about organizations.

Signal from noise   Like any useful framework or theory, the finance perspective enables us to separate what is important from what is not—to separate the "signal" from the "noise" to use Professor Stewart Myers's terms.[5] In one of its boldest manifestations, analytical finance theory has concluded that data and actions that impact share price are important—the true signals—and those that do not are simply noise.

2. Dangers of Using the Finance Perspective Carelessly

As valuable as the finance perspective is, its use is not without danger. At least three sources of danger exist: (1) expecting too much from analytical finance theory, (2) acting as though the financial perspective is the only important one, (3) acting as though it is always a complete and accurate one.

Expecting too much   It is possible to ask too much from analytical finance theory. The benefits of the focus and tools described above can be carried to extremes, such as suggesting that managers make moment-by-moment managerial decisions to maximize moment-by-moment share price. Thus, omniscient financial markets enable managers to select courses of action that will increase share price the most today. This *reductio ad absurdum* of analytical finance theory is based upon a misconception of the research findings that financial markets are remarkably efficient in the short term. The research has shown that for widely followed stocks public information is impounded into stock prices very quickly. But not all

---

[4] **Reference:**   Milton Friedman, *Capitalism and Freedom* (Chicago: University of Chicago Press, 1963), page 133.

[5] **Reference:**   Stewart Myers, "The Evaluation of an Acquisition Target," in Joel M. Stern and Donald H. Chew Jr., ed., *The Revolution in Corporate Finance* (New York: Basil Blackwell, 1986), page 394.

stocks are widely followed, nor is all information bearing on a company's worth necessarily public—making it incorrect to conclude that a company's stock price accurately captures its value in real time.

This distortion of valuable financial insights is directly contrary to the experience of most managers we have spoken to, who believe they are regularly faced with the choice between decisions with differing shorter- versus longer-run impacts on organizational performance (and share price.) These managers believe they know ways they can make their own and the organization's performance look better for a day or a week or a month or even a year or two before the piper has to be paid. Contrary to the predictions of agency theory, they believe that one of their major challenges is to avoid unwise, self-serving decisions that benefit them in the short run and harm the organization and its stakeholders in the longer run. To the extent that analytical finance theory appears to urge managers to focus on today's share price, it both misses an opportunity to contribute and does a significant disservice to the practice of financial management.

Only important perspective   Because financial losses can eventually lead to the end of any organization, the big financial picture of the company may be mistaken for the only one that matters. Bethany McLean and Peter Elkind's description of the very public fall of Enron Corporation in 2001,[6] then the seventh largest corporation in the U.S., repeatedly calls attention to the company's financially-centered culture where the desire for ever-increasing profits and share price led the company's executives to commit fraud on a massive scale. Using accounting loopholes and offshore accounts, Enron's executives overstated profits and hid billions of dollars of losses. Top management was so entranced by their apparent power and large paychecks that they piled one questionable practice upon another until the fraud eventually became too large to conceal and destroyed the company. Shareholders lost nearly $11 billion, creditors lost tens of billions of dollars, 15,000 employees lost their jobs and pensions, and the company's external auditor, Arthur Andersen—then one of the "Big Five" accounting firms—which had "overlooked" the company's accounting excesses, lost most of its clients and was dissolved with their 85,000 employees also losing their jobs.

Complete and accurate perspective   The financial perspective is never a complete picture of the organization, and it is not even always an accurate one. As David Halberstam reports in *The Reckoning,* his study of the American and Japanese automobile industries, the deep competitive hole the American auto industry made for itself in the 1950s through the 1970s was dug with shovels that seemed to be unearthing endless lodes of gold. Record operating profits and high share prices masked deteriorating product quality, declining customer satisfaction, inefficient management practices, poor industrial relations, and steady market share incursions by Japanese and other competitors. During this period, Ford's financial and analytical "whiz kid," Robert McNamara, first played the role of hero and then the role of villain. His heroic role involved bringing badly needed financial discipline to a company whose finances were in disarray, building sophistication and talent into Ford's finance function, and increasing its influence

---

[6] **Reference:**   Bethany McLean and Peter Elkind, *The Smartest Guys in the Room: The Amazing Rise and Scandalous Fall of Enron* (New York: Penguin Group / Portfolio Hardcover, 2003).

in business decision making. The role of villain arose from too much of a good thing: the finance function's growing dominance over company decisions, even product and manufacturing decisions. As David Halberstam noted, "The coming of McNamara to the Ford Motor Company, his protege Lee Iacocca once said, was one of the best things that ever happened to the company, and his leaving it, Iacocca added, was also one of the best things that ever happened."[7]

3. Capturing the Benefits Without Being Captured by the Dangers

Financial managers are widely recognized as key players in bringing the benefits of the financial perspective to their organizations. They are also well placed to protect their organizations from being captured by the dangers of the financial perspective. Unfortunately, their training may make them slow to see this second opportunity and may cause them to increase the dangers by pushing too aggressively for the use of financial perspectives at the expense of others. Four things they can do to avoid those dangers relate to: (1) multiple perspectives, (2) nonfinancial factors, (3) serving multiple stakeholders, and (4) work styles.

Multiple perspectives   Finance is in a strong position to support other organizational functions and other managers in insisting that a variety of framings or perspectives be used on an on-going basis: that customer satisfaction be emphasized, that investments in the organization's human resources be sustained and increased, that continuous quality improvements be given high priority, that global sustainability be pursued, and that progressively higher ethical standards be sought and achieved. Insisting that increased profits, increased shareholder value, or other financial measures be pursued in concert with these other goals rather than in conflict with them reduces the danger that the financial perspective will become an excuse for what later turn out to be very bad business decisions.

Measuring nonfinancial dimensions   Finance has a well-established role in collecting the numbers and defining and calculating the scorecard by which organizational and unit performance are measured. This traditional role puts it in the ideal position to add new, nontraditional measures to that scorecard and to play a leading role in collecting and reporting those numbers. Finance members are well placed to be key players in doing the conceptual and intellectual work required to figure out how to measure the frequently soft and qualitative dimensions that are not caught in traditional financial measures.

Serving all stakeholders   Finance traditionally has played the role of and been seen as the guardian of shareholder interests—the police officers in the company, making certain that corporate members do not neglect their obligations to the company's owners. From this historical position finance is particularly well placed to insist that the interests of all stakeholders be kept in mind and that all members of the organization are just as responsible as finance for safeguarding organizational assets and the interests of all stakeholders.

---

[7] **Reference:**   David Halberstam, *The Reckoning* (New York: William Morrow, 1986), (page 207 in Avon paperback edition).

Modeling the new organizational style   Finance's traditional roles have not always supported collaborative, team-based working methods. To the extent that finance has perceived the shareholder as its prime or only customer, finance has been tempted to downplay the arguments of other organizational units advocating the needs of other stakeholder groups. When finance members use collaborative, team-based, customer-focused work styles, they set an example that is noticed throughout the organization.

The Appropriateness of Humility—Some Closing Thoughts

Finance provides a very powerful way of looking at organizations, and the tools of financial analysis are key tools for managing those organizations. Financial officers play important roles in making things happen, as well as figuring out afterwards what actually did happen. It is very tempting to be confident and proud of the power of the finance perspective. While that confidence and feeling of power are appropriate, there are also at least three reasons for tempering those feelings with some modesty and intellectual caution—or even a healthy dose of humility.

First, although many current theories of finance have held up well, it is in the very nature of theories to be replaced. It is normal for newer theories to replace older ones. What we know to be true today will very likely no longer be true in the future—either because the situation will have changed or because new insights will have taught us that what we thought we knew to be true never was true. Ewald Nyquist, former chancellor of the Board of Education of the State of New York, expressed this concern eloquently in a commencement address when he told the graduating class, "I'm convinced that half of everything I say to students is false. The problem is that I don't know which half!"

Second, even our best theories are partial in scope and limited in applicability. All theories, and thus all knowledge, are based upon enormous simplifications of reality, so what we "know" is always limited and partial.

However, the third reason is in many ways the most important. During a period of major change of the kind we appear to be undergoing now, it is particularly difficult to know what is really happening and why. A time of major change is a time of replacement of a whole network of theories, an entire reframing of the way we look at the relevant part of the world. During such times, major errors of interpretation and prediction are particularly likely. For example, throughout the 1960s and 1970s most American business leaders and academics completely misinterpreted the early stages of the global quality revolution. Initially they believed the Japanese were not producing high-quality goods but rather that they were producing low-quality goods with cheap labor and selling them below cost overseas to buy market share. Later they accepted that Japan actually was producing high-quality goods but by a unique national and culture-based management system unavailable to the West—"Japanese management." Only in the 1980s did many American observers discover that Japanese companies were adopting a new way of managing more rapidly than companies elsewhere and were reaping the competitive benefits. Those early mistakes may seem almost ridiculous today, but they were not so illogical at the time—and a few still make them.

Ultimately, the major changes in management methods, global sustainability, and competitive patterns that are occurring provide the possibility for great contributions by those who see the newly emerging world more accurately and ahead of others. Leadership involves discovering what we do not yet know and applying it before it becomes conventional wisdom. Great opportunities come from worlds in flux; great contributions come from those who can combine the timeless basics and newly emerging framings, approaches, and tools.

*C*arrie Finch looked around the table and smiled. "These last four days have been an outstanding experience," she said. "It was great to work with the five of you."

Carrie and the other members of her seminar group were at a restaurant two blocks from the hotel where the seminar had been held. They had become close during the past four days and had eagerly agreed to go to dinner together to celebrate the end of their experience.

Carrie continued exuberantly, "This was a special week for me. Of course, you five are a good part of what made it so special. But there was so much more. During this week, I got the chance to review finance theory and practice. It was a good feeling to realize how much I remembered, and it was fascinating to see how much the field has evolved in just the past ten years. Of course, the big eye-opener for me was how finance practice is changing. I never thought of it in terms of analytical and operational finance, but that seems to capture a distinction I was sure existed but never could explain. And while I guess we've made some progress in improving our financial operations around the office, the things the speakers told us about what other companies are doing was just wonderful. Also, now I think I understand a little more about what is causing all these changes, especially how much is coming from the globalization of business, from the new management systems of quality and continuous improvement, and from global sustainability. My goodness! Until this week, I never even connected the words global sustainability to finance work."

Carrie paused, and the others picked up the conversation, sharing their feelings about what they had learned. There was a general consensus that the seminar had been very worthwhile. When it was Carrie's turn to speak again, she was quieter and more thoughtful. "This afternoon, my last question was 'So what? Why do we care about the changes in financial managing?' It wasn't all that clear to me then, but it's a lot clearer now. I think we're really lucky. We're at the right place at the right time. The changes in financial managing we talked about are giving us the knowledge and tools to make a big difference in our careers and for our company."

Carrie picked up her glass and raised it in the air. "I want to make a toast," she said. "To us. There are few things better than being with friends like you and knowing we can make a difference."

Summary of Key Points

■■ **Understand why we wrote this chapter the way we did.** We see this last chapter as an opportunity to share our thoughts about what is known in financial managing and what is less well known. We review key financial managing concepts that we believe will endure and speculate on where financial managing research and practice might be heading.

■■ **Summarize six central concepts of financial managing.** Six central concepts in the analytical theory of corporate finance are: (1) the importance of cash flows, (2) time value of money as an evaluation tool, (3) the significance of risk in determining value, (4) the necessity to study perfect markets to understand the meaning of market imperfections, (5) the market equilibrium insights from financial economics, and (6) the importance of stakeholder alignment which traditionally has been characterized as the problem of principal-agent conflicts.

■■ **Identify three possible forces for change in finance theory and discuss four changes in important financial concepts that may be occurring as a result of changes in the global competitive environment and the evolution of financial thought.** Three forces that have led to changes in finance theory in the past and are likely to lead to additional changes in the future are changes in the environment in which finance is practiced, new discoveries within the framework of existing finance theory, and the adoption of insights from other fields into finance theory. The need to pursue multiple goals, the limitations of agency theory, the intergenerational implications of careless use of time value of money as an evaluation tool, and the dangers of reading too much into the concept of perfect markets all may offer insights and guidance in the future considerably different from those of the past.

■■ **Distinguish between analytical and operational finance theory and summarize five central concepts in operational finance theory.** Analytical finance theory deals with the content of financial decision making, the ways in which markets operate, and the tools of financial analysis. It emphasizes how financial decisions *should* be made. Operational finance theory deals with the ways in which the financial operations of an organization are performed—particularly how finance's own productive processes are designed, executed, and improved—and *how* financial decisions are actually made (the behavioral processes of decision making). Five central concepts in the operational theory of financial practice are internal and external customers, quality, business processes, continuous improvement, and stakeholders.

■■ **Describe the areas of financial practice that seems to be changing the most as a result of changes in the global competitive environment and the evolution of financial thought.** Although each of the five areas of financial practice discussed in this book appears to be changing, the greatest changes may be occurring in the planning, using, and improving of financial processes, and in the recognition of the opportunities deriving from global sustainability. In connection with the increased focus on financial processes, the roles, attitudes, and actions of many financial practitioners are changing significantly. Finance members are becoming more like partners and less like judges and police officers in their day-to-day work. They are spending more time improving their own financial processes and working as team members to improve cross-functional processes. With respect to sustainability, companies are discovering that what they once considered extra costs of doing business are really opportunities to increase profitability while contributing to society's well being.

■■ **Describe the benefits and dangers of using a financial perspective in thinking about business decisions and ways to avoid the dangers.** A financial perspective provides a simple integrated framework for the many complex costs and outcomes of business activities. It uses a language that is widely used and understood inside and outside the organization, and it emphasizes the fundamental importance of financial health for organizational survival. However, the financial picture of the company may be mistaken for the only framework important for managers to use, as a complete framework that captures all aspects of organizational performance, and as one based on full and accurate data. Four things financial managers can do to avoid the dangers are: (1) learning and supporting the use of multiple perspectives to guide organizational decisions, (2) measuring and reporting the organization's key non-financial dimensions, (3) looking for opportunities to serve multiple stakeholders, and (4) modeling modern, collaborative, team-based managerial styles.

■■ **Discuss three reasons for being humble about what we know about financial managing.** Our current theories very likely will be replaced. It is normal for newer theories to replace older ones. All theories, and thus all knowledge, are based upon enormous simplifications of reality, so even what we "know" is limited and partial. During a period of major change—a "shift of paradigms"—it is particularly difficult to know what is truly happening, making errors of interpretation and prediction particularly likely. Yet, even with this humility, it is important to remember that without theory there is no knowledge and that often we must take action—no matter how limited our knowledge.

Questions

1. Identify six concepts that are central to analytical finance. Why is each so important to understand?

2. Why are global competitive developments changing the practice of financial management? Identify four areas where this might be happening.

3. What is the difference between analytical finance theory and operational finance theory?

4. Identify five concepts that are central to operational finance. Why is each so important to understand?

5. Select any task done by financial people in an organization. Which portions of the task are best approached through analytical finance and which through operational finance?

6. What's new in financial practice? Why?

7. What's done differently in financial practice? Why?

8. What's done the same in financial practice? Why?

9. What's no longer done in financial practice? Why?

10. Give five reasons why the finance mindset is valuable. What might happen to someone who attempted to address business issues without this mindset? Why?

11. Why might careless use of financial thinking lead to conclusions and actions that could be detrimental to an organization?

12. How can finance professionals reap the benefits of the finance perspective without falling into the potential traps?

13. Why do we feel the need to caution you about humility in thinking about and applying financial theory?

SUMMARY OF MATHEMATICAL RELATIONSHIPS

Numbers in parentheses refer to the chapter and page on which the definition appears, e.g., (3:60) means Chapter 3, page 60.

Chapter 3—The Time Value of Money

1. Compound interest (3:60)

$$FV = PV(1 + r)^n$$

where:
    FV = future value
    PV = present value
    r = interest rate per period
    n = number of time periods

2. Present value (3:66)

$$PV = \frac{FV}{(1 + r)^n}$$

where:
    PV = present value
    FV = future value
    r = interest rate per period
    n = number of time periods

3. Growing cash stream (3:78)

$$PV = \frac{CF_1}{r - g}$$

where:
    PV = present value
    CF_1 = first cash flow, one period past PV
    r = interest rate per period
    g = growth rate of cash flows

4. Perpetuity (3:79)

$$PV = \frac{PMT}{r}$$

where:
    PV = present value
    PMT = annuity amount
    r = interest rate per period

Chapter 4—Money Rates

1. Fisher model of interest rates (4:88–89)

$$Nominal\ rate = (1 + r_p)(1 + r_i)(1 + r_r) - 1$$

where:
r_p = pure rate of interest
r_i = inflation premium
r_r = risk premium

2. Real rate of interest (4:90)

$$Real\ rate = (1 + r_p)(1 + r_r) - 1$$

where:
r_p = pure rate of interest
r_r = risk premium

3. Risk-free rate of interest (4:91)

$$Risk\text{-}free\ rate = (1 + r_p)(1 + r_i) - 1$$

where:
r_p = pure rate of interest
r_i = inflation premium

4. Forward discount or premium (4:104)

$$Forward\ discount\ or\ premium = \frac{forward - spot}{spot} \times \frac{12}{months\ forward}$$

Chapter 6—Financial Instruments

1. Net credit (6:140)

$$Net\ credit = accounts\ receivable - accounts\ payable$$

Chapter 8—Risk and Its Measurement

1. Expected value (8:198)

$$E(r) = \sum_i p_i \times r_i$$

where:
$E(r)$ = expected rate of return
Σ = summation operator
p_i = probability of ith forecasted rate of return
r_i = i^{th} forecasted rate of return

2. Variance and standard deviation (8:199-200)

$$\sigma^2(r) = \sum_i p_i[r_i - E(r)]^2$$

$$\sigma(r) = \sqrt{\sigma^2(r)}$$

where: $\sigma^2(r)$ = variance of returns
Σ = summation operator
p_i = probability of ith forecasted rate of return
r_i = i^{th} forecasted rate of return
$E(r)$ = expected rate of return
$\sigma(r)$ = standard deviation of returns

3. Capital market line (CML) (8:202)

Required rate of return = r_f + (market price of total risk) × σ

where: r_f = risk-free rate of interest
σ = standard deviation of returns

4. Security market line (SML) (8:212)

Required rate of return = r_f + (market price of portfolio risk) × β

$$= r_f + (r_m - r_f) \times \beta$$

where: r_f = risk-free rate of interest
β = relationship between investment's returns and market returns
r_m = required rate of return on the "market portfolio"

Chapter 9—The Value of Securities

1. Traditional bond value (9:224)

Price of bond = PV of interest annuity + PV of face value

$$= PMT \left(\frac{1 - \frac{1}{(1 + r)^n}}{r} \right) + FV \left(\frac{1}{(1 + r)^n} \right)$$

where: PMT = bond coupon
FV = face value
n = number of interest periods until the bond's maturity date
r = bond investors' required rate of return per interest period

2. Preferred stock value (9:230)

$$Value = PV = \frac{D_p}{r_p}$$

where: $\qquad$ D_p = preferred stock dividend
r_p = preferred stock investors'
required rate of return

3. Preferred stock yield (9:230)

$$Yield = r_p = \frac{D_p}{market\ price}$$

where: $\qquad$ D_p = preferred stock dividend

4. Common stock value (9:232)

$$Value = PV = \frac{D_1}{r_c - g}$$

where:
D_1 = investors' next anticipated dividend
r_c = common stock investors' required rate of return
g = investors' anticipated growth rate of dividends

5. Rate of return on common stock (9:233)

$$Rate\ of\ return = r_c = \frac{D_1}{stock\ price} + g$$

where:
D_1 = investors' next anticipated dividend
g = investors' anticipated growth rate of dividends

Chapter 10—The Cost of Capital

1. Break point (10:255)

$$Total\ new\ financing = \frac{amount\ of\ money\ from\ each\ source}{its\ proportion}$$

Chapter 12—Investing in Permanent Working Capital Assets

1. Definition of working capital (12:288)

$$Working\ capital = current\ assets - current\ liabilities$$

Chapter 14—Selecting the Best Debt-Equity Mix

1. Bottom half of the income statement (14:341)

$$EPS = \frac{(EBIT - interest) \times (1 - tax\ rate)}{number\ of\ shares}$$

where: EPS = earnings per share
            EBIT = earnings before interest and taxes

2. Compromise (market imperfections) approach to the value of a firm with leverage (14:349)

$$V_{levered} = V_{unlevered} + CT - BC - AC$$

where:
   $V_{levered}$ = the value of a firm with leverage
   $V_{unlevered}$ = the value of the same firm if it had no debt financing
   CT = the added value from the corporate tax effect
   BC = the reduction in value from the bankrupty cost effect
   AC = the reduction in value from the agency cost effect

Chapter 16—Dividend Policy

1. Dividend-growth model (16:386)

$$Stock\ Value = PV\ of\ dividend\ stream = \frac{D_1}{r_c - g}$$

where:
   D_1 = investors' next anticipated dividend
   r_c = common stock investors' required rate of return
   g = investors' anticipated growth rate of dividends

Chapter 17—Increasing Share Price

1. Free cash flow (17:411)

   $free\ cash\ flow = cash\ flow\ from\ operations - cash\ flow\ reinvested$

2. Market value added (17:421)

   $Market\ Value\ Added = market\ value - invested\ capital$

3. Economic value added (17:421)

   $Economic\ Value\ Added = NOPAT - k_w\ CAPITAL$

SUMMARY OF FINANCIAL RATIOS

Ratios that Measure Profitability

1. Profitability compared to sales

$$\text{Gross profit margin} = \frac{\text{gross profit}}{\text{sales}}$$

● Measures pricing policy relative to production costs.

$$\text{Operating profit margin} = \frac{\text{EBIT}}{\text{sales}}$$

● Measures economic earnings from delivering products and services to customers.

$$\text{Pretax profit margin} = \frac{\text{earnings before taxes}}{\text{sales}}$$

● Measures profit after satisfying creditors but before taxes and shareholders.

$$\text{Net profit margin} = \frac{\text{earnings after taxes}}{\text{sales}}$$

● Measures profitability as seen by shareholders.

$$\text{Contribution margin} = \frac{\text{contribution}}{\text{sales}}$$

● Measures the change to profit from a $1 change in sales.

2. Profitability compared to assets

$$\text{Basic earning power} = \frac{\text{EBIT}}{\text{average total assets}}$$

● Shows economic earnings in relation to investment in assets.

$$\text{Return on assets (ROA)} = \frac{\text{earnings after taxes}}{\text{average total assets}}$$

● Shows total earnings in relation to investment in assets.

3. Profitability compared to equity

$$\text{Return on equity (ROE)} = \frac{\text{earnings after taxes}}{\text{average total equity}}$$

● Shows total earnings in relation to equity funding.

Ratios that Measure Effective Use of Working Capital

1. Measures of overall liquidity

$$\text{Current ratio} = \frac{\text{current assets}}{\text{current liabilities}}$$

● Measures ability to generate cash to meet upcoming obligations.

$$\text{Quick ratio} = \frac{\text{quick assets}}{\text{current liabilities}}$$

● Measures ability to generate immediate cash to meet existing or emergency obligations.

2. Measures of the effective use of accounts receivable

$$\text{Accounts receivable turnover} = \frac{\text{credit sales}}{\text{average accounts receivable}}$$

● The number of times per year that credit is extended and accounts receivable collected.

$$\text{Collection period} = \frac{\text{average accounts receivable}}{\text{credit sales}} \times 360$$

● The number of days it takes to collect the typical account receivable.

3. Measures of the effective use of inventories

$$\text{Inventory turnover} = \frac{\text{cost of goods sold}}{\text{average inventory}}$$

● The number of times per year that inventories are sold and replenished.

$$\text{Inventory days} = \frac{\text{average inventory}}{\text{cost of goods sold}} \times 360$$

● The number of days the average item remains in inventory.

4. Measures of the effective use of accounts payable

$$Accounts\ payable\ turnover = \frac{purchases}{average\ accounts\ payable}$$

- The number of times per year that purchases are made and accounts payable paid.

$$Payables\ period = \frac{average\ accounts\ payable}{purchases} \times 360$$

- The number of days it takes to pay the typical account payable.

5. The cash conversion cycle

$$Cash\ conversion\ cycle = inventory\ days$$
$$+ collection\ period - payables\ period$$

- The number of days it takes to recover the funds invested in inventories and accounts receivable.

Ratios that Measure the Use of Fixed and Total Assets

1. A measure of the productivity of fixed assets

$$Fixed\ asset\ turnover = \frac{sales}{average\ fixed\ assets}$$

- Measures the effectiveness of fixed assets in generating sales.

2. A measure of the productivity of total assets

$$Total\ asset\ turnover = \frac{sales}{average\ total\ assets}$$

- Summarizes the relationship of all assets to sales.

Ratios that Measure the Choice and Management of Funding

1. Measures of the financing mix

$$The\ debt\ ratio = \frac{total\ liabilities}{total\ assets}$$

- Measures the fraction of assets financed with debt.

$$\text{The funded debt ratio} = \frac{\text{funded debt}}{\text{total assets}}$$

● Measures the fraction of assets financed with interest-bearing debt.

$$\text{The debt/equity ratio} = \frac{\text{total liabilities}}{\text{total equity}}$$

● Measures the amount of debt relative to equity financing.

$$\text{The assets/equity ratio} = \frac{\text{total assets}}{\text{total equity}}$$

● Measures the amount of assets supported by each dollar of equity financing.

2. Measures of the ability to service debt

$$\text{Times interest earned} = \frac{\text{EBIT}}{\text{interest}}$$

● Tests the ability of operating earnings to cover interest obligations.

$$\text{Fixed charge coverage} = \frac{\text{EBIT}}{\text{interest} + \text{principal}\left(\dfrac{1}{1-t}\right)}$$

● Tests the ability of operating earnings to cover interest and principal repayment obligations.

3. Measures of payments against equity

$$\text{Dividend payout ratio} = \frac{\text{dividends}}{\text{earnings after taxes}}$$

● Measures the fraction of earnings paid to shareholders in the form of dividends.

$$\text{Retention ratio} = \frac{\text{earnings retained}}{\text{earnings after taxes}}$$

● Measures the fraction of earnings retained within the firm.

Ratios that Measure the Market's Reaction to the Firm

$$\text{Price/earnings ratio} = \frac{\text{stock price}}{\text{earnings per share}}$$

● Compares stock price to earnings.

$$\text{Market/book ratio} = \frac{\text{stock price}}{\text{book value per share}}$$

● Compares the market value of equity to its accounting value.

In this section we show where to locate the time-value keys on eight popular financial calculators that can handle the full range of time value calculations in this book. Notes with each calculator give additional helpful pointers.

The featured calculators are:

- Hewlett-Packard 10bII, 10bII+, 12c, 12c Platinum, 17bII+, 20b
- Texas Instruments BAII PLUS, BAII PLUS Professional

The following examples translate the notation employed throughout the book to the keystrokes for each of the calculators.

		Using Your Financial Calculator to Solve a Basic Time Value Problem				
Example						

A problem requires you to find the future value of an annuity of $1,000 paid at the beginning of each of the next 15 years, at an interest rate of 9%.

Question: Solve this problem using your financial calculator.

Solution steps:

Step	As illustrated in the text	Using an HP–10bII or HP–10bII+	Using an HP–12c or HP–12c Platinum	Using an HP–17bII+	Using an HP–20b	Using a BAII PLUS or BAII PLUS Professional
Select the correct menu				MAIN (Blue EXIT) FIN then TVM		
Set payments per year to 1	32,003.40	1 P/YR (Orange PMT)		OTHER 1 P/YR EXIT	1 P/YR[1] (Blue PMT)	P/Y (2nd I/Y) 1 ENTER QUIT (2nd CPT)
Clear	Clear TVM	CLEAR ALL (Orange C) C MEM TVM (Blue C 1)	CLEAR FIN (f x≷y)	CLEAR DATA (Blue INPUT)	Reset TVM (Blue Reset INPUT)	CLR TVM (2nd FV)
	Set BEG Enter	BEG/END (Orange MAR) until BEGIN or BEG appears	g 7	OTHER BEG EXIT	Blue PV	BGN (2nd PMT), then SET until BGN appears, then QUIT (2nd CPT)
Enter data	−1,000 as PMT	1000 +/− PMT	1000 CHS PMT	1000 +/− PMT	1000 +/− PMT	1000 +/− PMT
	15 as n	15 N	15 n	15 N	15 N	15 N
	9 as i	9 I/YR	9 i	9 I%YR	9 I/YR	9 I/Y
Calculate the result	Compute FV	FV	FV	FV	FV	CPT FV

Answer: The annuity has a future value of $32,003.40.

[1] **Warning:** On the HP–20b you must clear TVM prior to setting payments per year to 1 since clearing TVM sets P/YR to 12.

Example

Using Your Financial Calculator to Solve a Cash Flow List Problem

A problem requires you to find the present value of an investment which costs $10,000 and returns the following cash flows. The interest rate is 7.5%.

Year	Cash flow	Year	Cash flow	Year	Cash flow
1	$1,000	5	4,000	8	$ 0
2	2,000	6	4,000	9	3,000
3	2,000	7	1,000	10	3,000
4	2,000				

Question: Solve this problem using your financial calculator.

Solution steps:

Step	As illustrated in the text	Using an HP–10bII or HP–10bII+	Using an HP–12c or HP–12c Platinum	Using an HP–17bII+	Using an HP–20b	Using a BAII PLUS or BAII PLUS Professional
Select the correct menu	**4,769.59**			**MAIN (Blue EXIT) FIN** then **CFLO**	**CshFl**	**CF**
Clear	Clear the cash flow list	**CLEAR ALL (Orange C) C MEM CFLO (Blue C 0)**	**CLEAR REG (f CLx)**	**CLEAR DATA (Blue INPUT)** then **YES**	**Reset CshFl (Blue ← ▽▽ INPUT, INPUT, CshFl)**	**CLR Work (2nd CE/C)**
Enter data	Enter the cash flows −10,000 as FLOW 0	**10,000 +/− CFⱼ**	**10000 CHS CF₀ (g PV)**	**10000 +/− INPUT**	**10000 +/− INPUT, INPUT**	**10000 +/− ENTER ↓**
	1,000 as FLOW 1	**1000 CFⱼ**	**1000 CFⱼ (g PMT)**	**1000 INPUT INPUT**	**1000 INPUT INPUT**	**1000 ENTER ↓**
	2,000 as FLOW 2 3 as TIMES	**2000 CFⱼ 3 Nⱼ (Orange CFⱼ)**	**2000 CFⱼ (g PMT) 3 Nⱼ (g FV)**	**2000 INPUT 3 INPUT**	**2000 INPUT 3 INPUT**	**2000 ENTER ↓ 3 ENTER ↓**
	4,000 as FLOW 3 2 as TIMES	**4000 CFⱼ 2 Nⱼ (Orange CFⱼ)**	**4000 CFⱼ (g PMT) 2 Nⱼ (g FV)**	**4000 INPUT 2 INPUT**	**4000 INPUT 2 INPUT**	**4000 ENTER ↓ 2 ENTER ↓**
	1,000 as FLOW 4	**1000 CFⱼ**	**1000 CFⱼ**	**1000 INPUT INPUT**	**1000 INPUT INPUT**	**1000 ENTER ↓ ↓**
	0 as FLOW 5	**0 CFⱼ**	**0 CFⱼ (g PMT)**	**0 INPUT INPUT**	**0 INPUT INPUT**	**0 ENTER ↓ ↓**
	3,000 as FLOW 6 2 as TIMES	**3000 CFⱼ 2 Nⱼ (Orange CFⱼ)**	**3000 CFⱼ (g PMT) 2 Nⱼ (g FV)**	**3000 INPUT 2 INPUT**	**3000 INPUT 2 INPUT**	**3000 ENTER ↓ 2 ENTER ↓**
Switch to the calculation menu				**EXIT CALC**	**NPV**	**NPV**
Enter the interest rate	Enter the interest rate 7.5 as i	**7.5 I/YR**	**7.5 i**	**7.5 I%**	**7.5 INPUT**	**7.5 ENTER ↓**
Calculate the result	Calculate the result NPV	**NPV (Orange PRC)**	**NPV (f PV)**	**NPV**	**▽**	**CPT**

Answer: The investment has a present value of $4,769.59.

▓▓ Hewlett-Packard HP–10bII

Basic time value calculations

(n) Press **N** to enter or calculate a number of time periods

(i) Press **I/YR** to enter or calculate an interest rate

(PV) Press **PV** to enter or calculate a present value

(PMT) Press **PMT** to enter or calculate an annuity payment

(FV) Press **FV** to enter or calculate a future value

(BEG) (END) Press **BEG/END** (the two key sequence **Orange-Shift-Key** then **MAR**) to switch between BEGIN and END

Clearing the financial part of your calculator

(CLEAR) Press **CLEAR ALL** (the two key sequence **Orange-Shift-Key** then **C**)

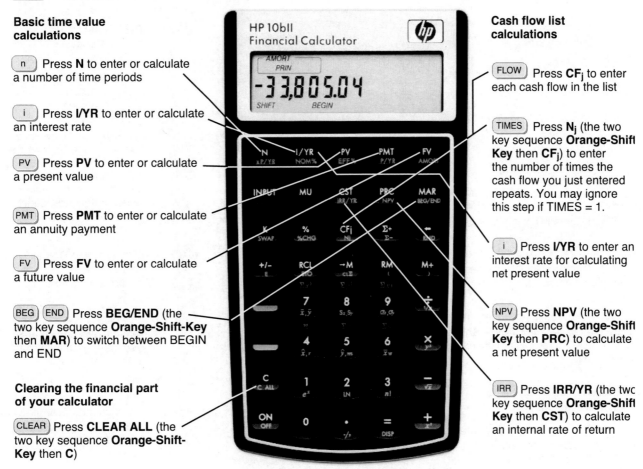

Cash flow list calculations

(FLOW) Press **CF_j** to enter each cash flow in the list

(TIMES) Press **N_j** (the two key sequence **Orange-Shift Key** then **CF_j**) to enter the number of times the cash flow you just entered repeats. You may ignore this step if TIMES = 1.

(i) Press **I/YR** to enter an interest rate for calculating net present value

(NPV) Press **NPV** (the two key sequence **Orange-Shift Key** then **PRC**) to calculate a net present value

(IRR) Press **IRR/YR** (the two key sequence **Orange-Shift Key** then **CST**) to calculate an internal rate of return

Other Helpful Hints about the HP–10bII and HP–10bII+ Calculators

1. To enter data, key in the number and then press the key describing that item. To calculate a result, press the appropriate key without first keying in a number.

2. Be sure to set payments-per-year equal to 1 to avoid unwanted compounding within each period. The keystroke sequence is:
   Key in the number 1 then press **P/YR** (the two key sequence **Orange-Shift-Key** then **PMT**)

3. In the **BEG** mode, "BEGIN" (HP-10bII) or "BEG" (HP-10bII+) appears in the display. If "BEGIN" or "BEG" does not appear, you are in the **END** mode.

4. If you hold down the **CLEAR ALL** key when you clear, the setting for payments-per-year will be displayed. Also, the value of j is displayed as you enter each value of **CF_j** and **N_j** (hold down the **CF_j/N_j** key to see the value of j for a longer time).

5. To set the number of decimal places displayed, press **DISP** (the two key sequence **Orange-Shift-Key** then **=**) followed by the number of decimal places desired (for example, **DISP** then **2** sets the display to show 2 decimal places).

Hewlett-Packard HP–10bII+

Basic time value calculations

[n] Press **N** to enter or calculate a number of time periods

[i] Press **I/YR** to enter or calculate an interest rate

[PV] Press **PV** to enter or calculate a present value

[PMT] Press **PMT** to enter or calculate an annuity payment

[FV] Press **FV** to enter or calculate a future value

[BEG] [END] Press **BEG/END** (the two key sequence **Orange-Shift-Key** then **MAR**) to switch between BEGIN and END

Clearing the financial part of your calculator

[CLEAR] Press **C MEM TVM** (the three key sequence **Blue-Shift-Key** then **C** then **1**) to clear prior to basic time value calculations. Press **C MEM CFLO** (the three key sequence **Blue-Shift-Key** then **C** then **0**) to clear before cash flow list calculations

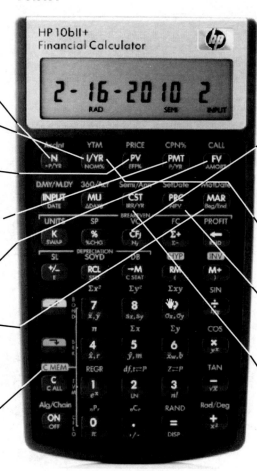

Cash flow list calculations

[FLOW] Press **CFj** to enter each cash flow in the list

[TIMES] Press **Nj** (the two key sequence **Orange-Shift-Key** then **CFj**) to enter the number of times the cash flow you just entered repeats. You may ignore this step if TIMES = 1.

[i] Press **I/YR** to enter an interest rate for calculating net present value

[NPV] Press **NPV** (the two key sequence **Orange-Shift-Key** then **PRC**) to calculate a net present value

[IRR] Press **IRR/YR** (the two key sequence **Orange-Shift-Key** then **CST**) to calculate an internal rate of return

Hewlett-Packard HP–12c

Basic time value calculations

Cash flow list calculations

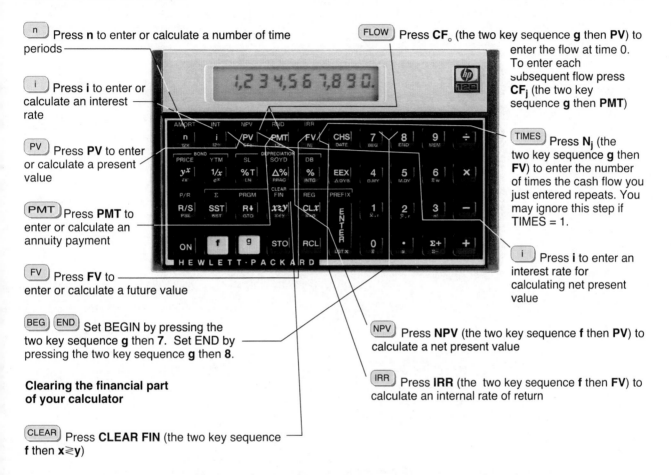

`n` Press **n** to enter or calculate a number of time periods

`i` Press **i** to enter or calculate an interest rate

`PV` Press **PV** to enter or calculate a present value

`PMT` Press **PMT** to enter or calculate an annuity payment

`FV` Press **FV** to enter or calculate a future value

`BEG` `END` Set BEGIN by pressing the two key sequence **g** then **7**. Set END by pressing the two key sequence **g** then **8**.

Clearing the financial part of your calculator

`CLEAR` Press **CLEAR FIN** (the two key sequence **f** then **x≥y**)

`FLOW` Press **CF₀** (the two key sequence **g** then **PV**) to enter the flow at time 0. To enter each subsequent flow press **CFⱼ** (the two key sequence **g** then **PMT**)

`TIMES` Press **Nⱼ** (the two key sequence **g** then **FV**) to enter the number of times the cash flow you just entered repeats. You may ignore this step if TIMES = 1.

`i` Press **i** to enter an interest rate for calculating net present value

`NPV` Press **NPV** (the two key sequence **f** then **PV**) to calculate a net present value

`IRR` Press **IRR** (the two key sequence **f** then **FV**) to calculate an internal rate of return

Other Helpful Hints about the HP–12c Calculator

1. To enter data, key in the number and then press the key describing that item. To calculate a result, press the appropriate key without first entering a number.

2. In the **BEG** mode, "BEGIN" appears in the display. If "BEGIN" does not appear, you are in the **END** mode.

3. When calculating n, the HP–12c rounds the answer up to the nearest integer. If you enter a non-integer value for **n**—for example, n = 1/2 to represent 1/2 year—be sure the calculator is set properly for nominal or compound calculations. Toggle between "nominal mode" and "compound mode" using the two key sequence **STO** then **EEX**. In the compound mode, the letter "C" appears in the display. If "C" does not appear, you are in the nominal mode.

4. To set the number of decimal places displayed, press the two key sequence **f** then the number of decimal places desired (for example, **f** then **2** sets the display to show 2 decimal places).

Hewlett-Packard HP–12c Platinum

Keystrokes are identical to those for the HP-12c.

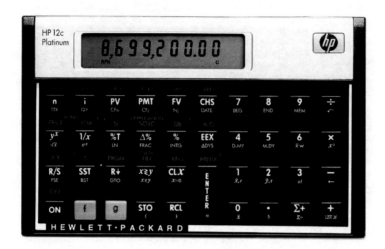

Hewlett-Packard HP–17bII+

You must first display the correct menu for the kind of problem you are doing. For basic time value problems, display the TVM menu (from the main menu press **FIN** then **TVM**). For cash flow list problems, display the cash flow menu (from the main menu press **FIN** then **CFLO**).

Other Helpful Hints about the HP–17bII+ Calculator

1. To enter basic time value data, key in the number and press the key describing that item. To calculate a result, press the appropriate key without first keying in a number.

2. Be sure to set payments-per-year equal to 1 to avoid unwanted compounding within each period. From the TVM menu, the keystroke sequence is:
   Press **OTHER** to bring up the next menu, then key in the number 1 and press **P/YR**, then press **EXIT** to return to the TVM menu

3. The words "BEGIN MODE" or "END MODE" appear in the display when you enter the TVM menu to let you know which mode you are in.

4. To set the number of decimal places displayed, press **DSP** then **FIX** then the number of decimal places desired, then **INPUT** (for example **DSP FIX** 2 **INPUT** sets the display to show 2 decimal places).

Basic time value calculations

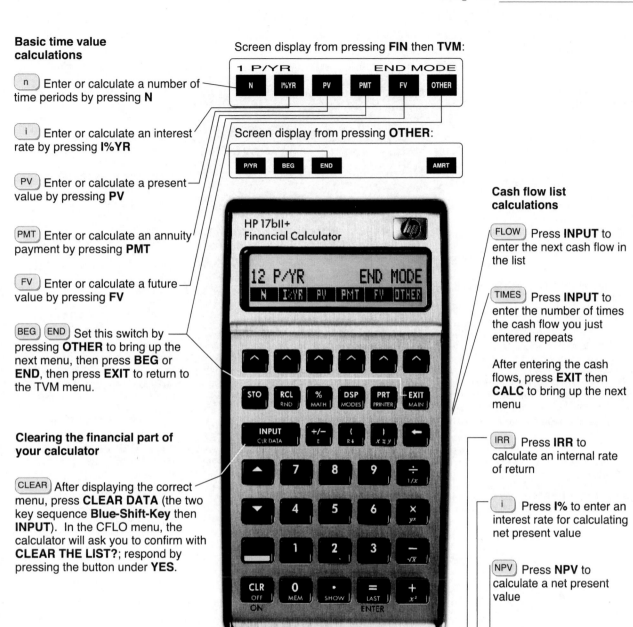

Screen display from pressing **FIN** then **TVM**:

Screen display from pressing **OTHER**:

n Enter or calculate a number of time periods by pressing **N**

i Enter or calculate an interest rate by pressing **I%YR**

PV Enter or calculate a present value by pressing **PV**

PMT Enter or calculate an annuity payment by pressing **PMT**

FV Enter or calculate a future value by pressing **FV**

BEG **END** Set this switch by pressing **OTHER** to bring up the next menu, then press **BEG** or **END**, then press **EXIT** to return to the TVM menu.

Clearing the financial part of your calculator

CLEAR After displaying the correct menu, press **CLEAR DATA** (the two key sequence **Blue-Shift-Key** then **INPUT**). In the CFLO menu, the calculator will ask you to confirm with **CLEAR THE LIST?**; respond by pressing the button under **YES**.

Cash flow list calculations

FLOW Press **INPUT** to enter the next cash flow in the list

TIMES Press **INPUT** to enter the number of times the cash flow you just entered repeats

After entering the cash flows, press **EXIT** then **CALC** to bring up the next menu

IRR Press **IRR** to calculate an internal rate of return

i Press **I%** to enter an interest rate for calculating net present value

NPV Press **NPV** to calculate a net present value

Screen display from pressing **FIN** then **CFLO** then **CALC**

Hewlett-Packard HP-20b

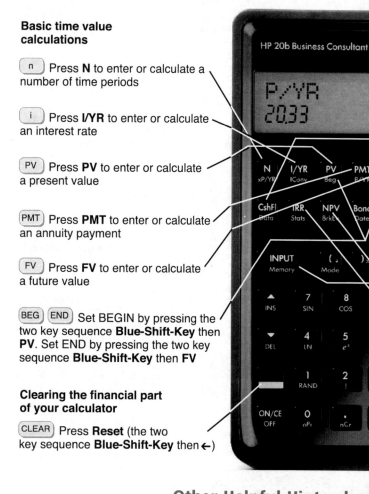

Basic time value calculations

n Press **N** to enter or calculate a number of time periods

i Press **I/YR** to enter or calculate an interest rate

PV Press **PV** to enter or calculate a present value

PMT Press **PMT** to enter or calculate an annuity payment

FV Press **FV** to enter or calculate a future value

BEG **END** Set BEGIN by pressing the two key sequence **Blue-Shift-Key** then **PV**. Set END by pressing the two key sequence **Blue-Shift-Key** then **FV**

Clearing the financial part of your calculator

CLEAR Press **Reset** (the two key sequence **Blue-Shift-Key** then ←)

Cash flow list calculations

Press **CshFl** to enter the worksheet for entering cash flows. Press Reset (the two key sequence **Blue-Shift-Key** then ←) INPUT, INPUT, CshFl to clear the cash flow list

FLOW Press **INPUT** to enter each cash flow in the list. The flows are identified as **CF(0)**, **CF(1)**, etc.

TIMES Press **INPUT** to enter the number of times the cash flow you just entered repeats. **#CF(0)** is the number of repeats for flow **CF(0)**, etc. You may ignore this step if TIMES = 1

i **NPV** Press **NPV** to enter the worksheet for keying in an interest rate and then calculating net present value

IRR Press **IRR** to enter the worksheet for calculating an internal rate of return

Other Helpful Hints about the HP-20b Calculator

1. To enter data, key in the number and then press the key describing that item. To calculate a result, press the appropriate key without first keying in a number.

2. Be sure to set payments-per-year equal to 1 to avoid unwanted compounding within each period. The keystroke sequence is:

    Key in the number 1 then press **P/YR** (the two key sequence **Blue-Shift-Key** then **PMT**)

    Note: clearing the financial part of your calculator sets **P/YR** back to 12.

3. In the **BEG** mode, "BEG" appears in the display. If "BEG" does not appear, you are in the **END** mode.

4. To set the number of decimal places displayed, press **Mode** (the two key sequence **Blue-Shift-Key** then ↓) then the number of decimal places desired then **INPUT** (for example, **Mode 2 INPUT** sets the display to show 2 decimal places). After pressing **Mode** you can also press the = key to cycle through decimal place settings. Press **INPUT** when done.

▓▓ Texas Instruments BAII PLUS

Cash-flow-list calculations, switching between BEGIN and END, setting the display, and many other calculations and settings are done in "prompted worksheets." Once in a worksheet, use the keys on the top row:

- Use ↑ and ↓ to move around within a worksheet.
- Key in a number and press **ENTER** to enter data into a worksheet.
- Press **SET** (the two key sequence **2nd** then **ENTER**) to switch a setting among alternatives within a worksheet.
- Press **QUIT** (the two key sequence **2nd** then **CPT**) to exit a worksheet.

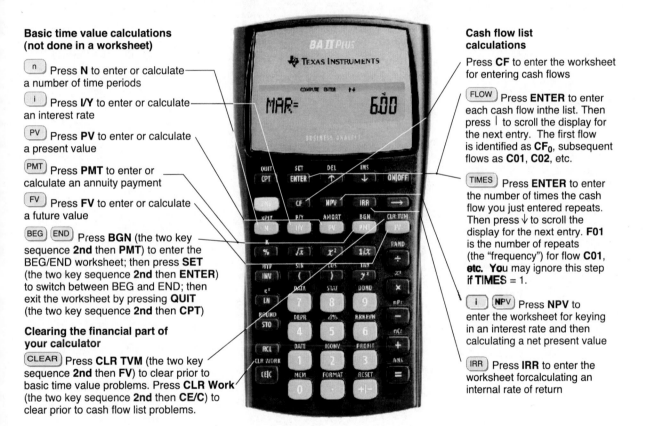

Basic time value calculations (not done in a worksheet)

[n] Press **N** to enter or calculate a number of time periods

[i] Press **I/Y** to enter or calculate an interest rate

[PV] Press **PV** to enter or calculate a present value

[PMT] Press **PMT** to enter or calculate an annuity payment

[FV] Press **FV** to enter or calculate a future value

[BEG] [END] Press **BGN** (the two key sequence **2nd** then **PMT**) to enter the BEG/END worksheet; then press **SET** (the two key sequence **2nd** then **ENTER**) to switch between BEG and END; then exit the worksheet by pressing **QUIT** (the two key sequence **2nd** then **CPT**)

Clearing the financial part of your calculator

[CLEAR] Press **CLR TVM** (the two key sequence **2nd** then **FV**) to clear prior to basic time value problems. Press **CLR Work** (the two key sequence **2nd** then **CE/C**) to clear prior to cash flow list problems.

Cash flow list calculations

Press **CF** to enter the worksheet for entering cash flows

[FLOW] Press **ENTER** to enter each cash flow in the list. Then press ↓ to scroll the display for the next entry. The first flow is identified as CF_0, subsequent flows as **C01, C02**, etc.

[TIMES] Press **ENTER** to enter the number of times the cash flow you just entered repeats. Then press ↓ to scroll the display for the next entry. **F01** is the number of repeats (the "frequency") for flow **C01**, etc. You may ignore this step if **TIMES** = 1.

[i] [NPV] Press **NPV** to enter the worksheet for keying in an interest rate and then calculating a net present value

[IRR] Press **IRR** to enter the worksheet for calculating an internal rate of return

Other Helpful Hints About the TI BAII PLUS Calculator

1. To enter data, key in the number and then press the key describing that item. To calculate a result, press the **CPT** key then press the appropriate key.

2. In the **BEG** mode, the indication "BGN" appears in the display. If "BGN" does not appear, you are in the **END** mode.

3. To set the number of decimal places displayed, press the key sequence **FORMAT** (**2nd** then **.**), then the number of decimal places desired followed by **ENTER**, then **QUIT** (the two key sequence **2nd** then **CPT**). For example, **FORMAT** then **2** then **ENTER** then **QUIT** sets the display to show 2 decimal places.

Texas Instruments BAII PLUS Professional

Keystrokes are identical to those for the BAII PLUS.

SPREADSHEET FUNCTIONS

Calculation	Microsoft Excel Function	Corel Quattro Pro Function
<u>Time Value of Money</u>		
FV (future value)	=FV(rate, nper, pmt, pv, type)	@FVAL(rate, nper, pmt, pv, type)
PV (present value)	=PV(rate, nper, pmt, pv, type)	@PVAL(rate, nper, pmt, pv, type)
N (number of periods)	=NPER (rate, pmt, pv, fv, type)	@NPER (rate, pmt, pv, fv, type)
i (interest rate)	=RATE(nper, pmt, pv, fv, type, guess)	@IRATE(n, pmt, pv, fv, type)
PMT (annuity payment)	=PMT(rate, nper, pv, fv, type)	@PAYMT(rate, nper, pv, fv, type)
<u>Cash Flow List</u>		
NPV (net present value)	=NPV(rate, value1, value2, . . .)	@NPV(rate, block, type)
IRR (internal rate of return)	=IRR (value1, value2, . . ., guess)	@IRR (guess, block)

missing value (N)

TABLE 1 Future Value Factors $= (1 + r)^n$ (FV of \$1 after n periods at interest rate r)

n	1%	2%	3%	4%	5%	6%	7%	8%	9%	10%	11%	12%	13%	14%	15%	20%	25%	30%	35%	40%
1	1.0100	1.0200	1.0300	1.0400	1.0500	1.0600	1.0700	1.0800	1.0900	1.1000	1.1100	1.1200	1.1300	1.1400	1.1500	1.2000	1.2500	1.3000	1.3500	1.4000
2	1.0201	1.0404	1.0609	1.0816	1.1025	1.1236	1.1449	1.1664	1.1881	1.2100	1.2321	1.2544	1.2769	1.2996	1.3225	1.4400	1.5625	1.6900	1.8225	1.9600
3	1.0303	1.0612	1.0927	1.1249	1.1576	1.1910	1.2250	1.2597	1.2950	1.3310	1.3676	1.4049	1.4429	1.4815	1.5209	1.7280	1.9531	2.1970	2.4604	2.7440
4	1.0406	1.0824	1.1255	1.1699	1.2155	1.2625	1.3108	1.3605	1.4116	1.4641	1.5181	1.5735	1.6305	1.6890	1.7490	2.0736	2.4414	2.8561	3.3215	3.8416
5	1.0510	1.1041	1.1593	1.2167	1.2763	1.3382	1.4026	1.4693	1.5386	1.6105	1.6851	1.7623	1.8424	1.9254	2.0114	2.4883	3.0518	3.7129	4.4840	5.3782
6	1.0615	1.1262	1.1941	1.2653	1.3401	1.4185	1.5007	1.5869	1.6771	1.7716	1.8704	1.9738	2.0820	2.1950	2.3131	2.9860	3.8147	4.8268	6.0534	7.5295
7	1.0721	1.1487	1.2299	1.3159	1.4071	1.5036	1.6058	1.7138	1.8280	1.9487	2.0762	2.2107	2.3526	2.5023	2.6600	3.5832	4.7684	6.2749	8.1722	10.541
8	1.0829	1.1717	1.2668	1.3686	1.4775	1.5938	1.7182	1.8509	1.9926	2.1436	2.3045	2.4760	2.6584	2.8526	3.0590	4.2998	5.9605	8.1573	11.032	14.758
9	1.0937	1.1951	1.3048	1.4233	1.5513	1.6895	1.8385	1.9990	2.1719	2.3579	2.5580	2.7731	3.0040	3.2519	3.5179	5.1598	7.4506	10.604	14.894	20.661
10	1.1046	1.2190	1.3439	1.4802	1.6289	1.7908	1.9672	2.1589	2.3674	2.5937	2.8394	3.1058	3.3946	3.7072	4.0456	6.1917	9.3132	13.786	20.107	28.925
11	1.1157	1.2434	1.3842	1.5395	1.7103	1.8983	2.1049	2.3316	2.5804	2.8531	3.1518	3.4785	3.8359	4.2262	4.6524	7.4301	11.642	17.922	27.144	40.496
12	1.1268	1.2682	1.4258	1.6010	1.7959	2.0122	2.2522	2.5182	2.8127	3.1384	3.4985	3.8960	4.3345	4.8179	5.3503	8.9161	14.552	23.298	36.644	56.694
13	1.1381	1.2936	1.4685	1.6651	1.8856	2.1329	2.4098	2.7196	3.0658	3.4523	3.8833	4.3635	4.8980	5.4924	6.1528	10.699	18.190	30.288	49.470	79.371
14	1.1495	1.3195	1.5126	1.7317	1.9799	2.2609	2.5785	2.9372	3.3417	3.7975	4.3104	4.8871	5.5348	6.2613	7.0757	12.839	22.737	39.374	66.784	111.12
15	1.1610	1.3459	1.5580	1.8009	2.0789	2.3966	2.7590	3.1722	3.6425	4.1772	4.7846	5.4736	6.2543	7.1379	8.1371	15.407	28.422	51.186	90.158	155.57
16	1.1726	1.3728	1.6047	1.8730	2.1829	2.5404	2.9522	3.4259	3.9703	4.5950	5.3109	6.1304	7.0673	8.1372	9.3576	18.488	35.527	66.542	121.71	217.80
17	1.1843	1.4002	1.6528	1.9479	2.2920	2.6928	3.1588	3.7000	4.3276	5.0545	5.8951	6.8660	7.9861	9.2765	10.761	22.186	44.409	86.504	164.31	304.91
18	1.1961	1.4282	1.7024	2.0258	2.4066	2.8543	3.3799	3.9960	4.7171	5.5599	6.5436	7.6900	9.0243	10.575	12.375	26.623	55.511	112.46	221.82	426.88
19	1.2081	1.4568	1.7535	2.1068	2.5270	3.0256	3.6165	4.3157	5.1417	6.1159	7.2633	8.6128	10.197	12.056	14.232	31.948	69.389	146.19	299.46	597.63
20	1.2202	1.4859	1.8061	2.1911	2.6533	3.2071	3.8697	4.6610	5.6044	6.7275	8.0623	9.6463	11.523	13.743	16.367	38.338	86.736	190.05	404.27	836.68
21	1.2324	1.5157	1.8603	2.2788	2.7860	3.3996	4.1406	5.0338	6.1088	7.4002	8.9492	10.804	13.021	15.668	18.822	46.005	108.42	247.06	545.77	1171.4
22	1.2447	1.5460	1.9161	2.3699	2.9253	3.6035	4.4304	5.4365	6.6586	8.1403	9.9336	12.100	14.714	17.861	21.645	55.206	135.53	321.18	736.79	1639.9
23	1.2572	1.5769	1.9736	2.4647	3.0715	3.8197	4.7405	5.8715	7.2579	8.9543	11.026	13.552	16.627	20.362	24.891	66.247	169.41	417.54	994.66	2295.9
24	1.2697	1.6084	2.0328	2.5633	3.2251	4.0489	5.0724	6.3412	7.9111	9.8497	12.239	15.179	18.788	23.212	28.625	79.497	211.76	542.80	1342.8	3214.2
25	1.2824	1.6406	2.0938	2.6658	3.3864	4.2919	5.4274	6.8485	8.6231	10.835	13.585	17.000	21.231	26.462	32.919	95.396	264.70	705.64	1812.8	4499.9
26	1.2953	1.6734	2.1566	2.7725	3.5557	4.5494	5.8074	7.3964	9.3992	11.918	15.080	19.040	23.991	30.167	37.857	114.48	330.87	917.33	2447.2	6299.8
27	1.3082	1.7069	2.2213	2.8834	3.7335	4.8223	6.2139	7.9881	10.245	13.110	16.739	21.325	27.109	34.390	43.535	137.37	413.59	1192.5	3303.8	8819.8
28	1.3213	1.7410	2.2879	2.9987	3.9201	5.1117	6.6488	8.6271	11.167	14.421	18.580	23.884	30.633	39.204	50.066	164.84	516.99	1550.3	4460.1	12348
29	1.3345	1.7758	2.3566	3.1187	4.1161	5.4184	7.1143	9.3173	12.172	15.863	20.624	26.750	34.616	44.693	57.575	197.81	646.23	2015.4	6021.1	17287
30	1.3478	1.8114	2.4273	3.2434	4.3219	5.7435	7.6123	10.063	13.268	17.449	22.892	29.960	39.116	50.950	66.212	237.38	807.79	2620.0	8128.5	24201
31	1.3613	1.8476	2.5001	3.3731	4.5380	6.0881	8.1451	10.868	14.462	19.194	25.410	33.555	44.201	58.083	76.144	284.85	1009.7	3406.0	10974	33882
32	1.3749	1.8845	2.5751	3.5081	4.7649	6.4534	8.7153	11.737	15.763	21.114	28.206	37.582	49.947	66.215	87.565	341.82	1262.2	4427.8	14814	47435
33	1.3887	1.9222	2.6523	3.6484	5.0032	6.8406	9.3253	12.676	17.182	23.225	31.308	42.092	56.440	75.485	100.70	410.19	1577.7	5756.1	19999	66409
34	1.4026	1.9607	2.7319	3.7943	5.2533	7.2510	9.9781	13.690	18.728	25.548	34.752	47.143	63.777	86.053	115.80	492.22	1972.2	7483.0	26999	92972
35	1.4166	1.9999	2.8139	3.9461	5.5160	7.6861	10.677	14.785	20.414	28.102	38.575	52.800	72.069	98.100	133.18	590.67	2465.2	9727.9	36449	130161
40	1.4889	2.2080	3.2620	4.8010	7.0400	10.286	14.974	21.725	31.409	45.259	65.001	93.051	132.78	188.88	267.86	1469.8	7523.2	36119	*******	*******
50	1.6446	2.6916	4.3839	7.1067	11.467	18.420	29.457	46.902	74.358	117.39	184.56	289.00	450.74	700.23	1083.7	9100.4	70065	*******	*******	*******
60	1.8167	3.2810	5.8916	10.520	18.679	32.988	57.946	101.26	176.03	304.48	524.06	897.60	1530.1	2595.9	4384.0	56348	*******	*******	*******	*******
70	2.0068	3.9996	7.9178	15.572	30.426	59.076	113.99	218.61	416.73	789.75	1488.0	2787.8	5193.9	9623.6	17736	*******	*******	*******	*******	*******
80	2.2167	4.8754	10.641	23.050	49.561	105.80	224.23	471.95	986.55	2048.4	4225.1	8658.5	17631	35677	71751	*******	*******	*******	*******	*******
360	35.950	1247.6	41822	*******	*******	*******	*******	*******	*******	*******	*******	*******	*******	*******	*******	*******	*******	*******	*******	*******

******* Factor > 99999

TABLE 2 Present Value Factors $= \dfrac{1}{(1+r)^n}$ (PV of \$1 to be received after n periods at interest rate r)

	1%	2%	3%	4%	5%	6%	7%	8%	9%	10%	11%	12%	13%	14%	15%	20%	25%	30%	35%	40%
1	0.9901	0.9804	0.9709	0.9615	0.9524	0.9434	0.9346	0.9259	0.9174	0.9091	0.9009	0.8929	0.8850	0.8772	0.8696	0.8333	0.8000	0.7692	0.7407	0.7143
2	0.9803	0.9612	0.9426	0.9246	0.9070	0.8900	0.8734	0.8573	0.8417	0.8264	0.8116	0.7972	0.7831	0.7695	0.7561	0.6944	0.6400	0.5917	0.5487	0.5102
3	0.9706	0.9423	0.9151	0.8890	0.8638	0.8396	0.8163	0.7938	0.7722	0.7513	0.7312	0.7118	0.6931	0.6750	0.6575	0.5787	0.5120	0.4552	0.4064	0.3644
4	0.9610	0.9238	0.8885	0.8548	0.8227	0.7921	0.7629	0.7350	0.7084	0.6830	0.6587	0.6355	0.6133	0.5921	0.5718	0.4823	0.4096	0.3501	0.3011	0.2603
5	0.9515	0.9057	0.8626	0.8219	0.7835	0.7473	0.7130	0.6806	0.6499	0.6209	0.5935	0.5674	0.5428	0.5194	0.4972	0.4019	0.3277	0.2693	0.2230	0.1859
6	0.9420	0.8880	0.8375	0.7903	0.7462	0.7050	0.6663	0.6302	0.5963	0.5645	0.5346	0.5066	0.4803	0.4556	0.4323	0.3349	0.2621	0.2072	0.1652	0.1328
7	0.9327	0.8706	0.8131	0.7599	0.7107	0.6651	0.6227	0.5835	0.5470	0.5132	0.4817	0.4523	0.4251	0.3996	0.3759	0.2791	0.2097	0.1594	0.1224	0.0949
8	0.9235	0.8535	0.7894	0.7307	0.6768	0.6274	0.5820	0.5403	0.5019	0.4665	0.4339	0.4039	0.3762	0.3506	0.3269	0.2326	0.1678	0.1226	0.0906	0.0678
9	0.9143	0.8368	0.7664	0.7026	0.6446	0.5919	0.5439	0.5002	0.4604	0.4241	0.3909	0.3606	0.3329	0.3075	0.2843	0.1938	0.1342	0.0943	0.0671	0.0484
10	0.9053	0.8203	0.7441	0.6756	0.6139	0.5584	0.5083	0.4632	0.4224	0.3855	0.3522	0.3220	0.2946	0.2697	0.2472	0.1615	0.1074	0.0725	0.0497	0.0346
11	0.8963	0.8043	0.7224	0.6496	0.5847	0.5268	0.4751	0.4289	0.3875	0.3505	0.3173	0.2875	0.2607	0.2366	0.2149	0.1346	0.0859	0.0558	0.0368	0.0247
12	0.8874	0.7885	0.7014	0.6246	0.5568	0.4970	0.4440	0.3971	0.3555	0.3186	0.2858	0.2567	0.2307	0.2076	0.1869	0.1122	0.0687	0.0429	0.0273	0.0176
13	0.8787	0.7730	0.6810	0.6006	0.5303	0.4688	0.4150	0.3677	0.3262	0.2897	0.2575	0.2292	0.2042	0.1821	0.1625	0.0935	0.0550	0.0330	0.0202	0.0126
14	0.8700	0.7579	0.6611	0.5775	0.5051	0.4423	0.3878	0.3405	0.2992	0.2633	0.2320	0.2046	0.1807	0.1597	0.1413	0.0779	0.0440	0.0254	0.0150	0.0090
15	0.8613	0.7430	0.6419	0.5553	0.4810	0.4173	0.3624	0.3152	0.2745	0.2394	0.2090	0.1827	0.1599	0.1401	0.1229	0.0649	0.0352	0.0195	0.0111	0.0064
16	0.8528	0.7284	0.6232	0.5339	0.4581	0.3936	0.3387	0.2919	0.2519	0.2176	0.1883	0.1631	0.1415	0.1229	0.1069	0.0541	0.0281	0.0150	0.0082	0.0046
17	0.8444	0.7142	0.6050	0.5134	0.4363	0.3714	0.3166	0.2703	0.2311	0.1978	0.1696	0.1456	0.1252	0.1078	0.0929	0.0451	0.0225	0.0116	0.0061	0.0033
18	0.8360	0.7002	05874	0.4936	0.4155	0.3503	0.2959	0.2502	0.2120	0.1799	0.1528	0.1300	0.1108	0.0946	0.0808	0.0376	0.0180	0.0089	0.0045	0.0023
19	0.8277	0.6864	0.5703	0.4746	0.3957	0.3305	0.2765	0.2317	0.1945	0.1635	0.1377	0.1161	0.0981	0.0829	0.0703	0.0313	0.0144	0.0068	0.0033	0.0017
20	0.8195	0.6730	0.5537	0.4564	0.3769	0.3118	0.2584	0.2145	0.1784	0.1486	0.1240	0.1037	0.0868	0.0728	0.0611	0.0261	0.0115	0.0053	0.0025	0.0012
21	0.8114	0.6598	0.5375	0.4388	0.3589	0.2942	0.2415	0.1987	0.1637	0.1351	0.1117	0.0926	0.0768	0.0638	0.0531	0.0217	0.0092	0.0040	0.0018	0.0009
22	0.8034	0.6468	0.5219	0.4220	0.3418	0.2775	0.2257	0.1839	0.1502	0.1228	0.1007	0.0826	0.0680	0.0560	0.0462	0.0181	0.0074	0.0031	0.0014	0.0006
23	0.7954	0.6342	0.5067	0.4057	0.3256	0.2618	0.2109	0.1703	0.1378	0.1117	0.0907	0.0738	0.0601	0.0491	0.0402	0.0151	0.0059	0.0024	0.0010	0.0004
24	0.7876	0.6217	0.4919	0.3901	0.3101	0.2470	0.1971	0.1577	0.1264	0.1015	0.0817	0.0659	0.0532	0.0431	0.0349	0.0126	0.0047	0.0018	0.0007	0.0003
25	0.7798	0.6095	0.4776	0.3751	0.2953	0.2330	0.1842	0.1460	0.1160	0.0923	0.0736	0.0588	0.0471	0.0378	0.0304	0.0105	0.0038	0.0014	0.0006	0.0002
26	0.7720	0.5976	0.4637	0.3607	0.2812	0.2198	0.1722	0.1352	0.1064	0.0839	0.0663	0.0525	0.0417	0.0331	0.0264	0.0087	0.0030	0.0011	0.0004	0.0002
27	0.7644	0.5859	0.4502	0.3468	0.2678	0.2074	0.1609	0.1252	0.0976	0.0763	0.0597	0.0469	0.0369	0.0291	0.0230	0.0073	0.0024	0.0008	0.0003	0.0001
28	0.7568	0.5744	0.4371	0.3335	0.2551	0.1956	0.1504	0.1159	0.0895	0.0693	0.0538	0.0419	0.0326	0.0255	0.0200	0.0061	0.0019	0.0006	0.0002	0.0001
29	0.7493	0.5631	0.4243	0.3207	0.2429	0.1846	0.1406	0.1073	0.0822	0.0630	0.0485	0.0374	0.0289	0.0224	0.0174	0.0051	0.0015	0.0005	0.0002	0.0001
30	0.7419	0.5521	0.4120	0.3083	0.2314	0.1741	0.1314	0.0994	0.0754	0.0573	0.0437	0.0334	0.0256	0.0196	0.0151	0.0042	0.0012	0.0004	0.0001	0.0001
31	0.7346	0.5412	0.4000	0.2965	0.2204	0.1643	0.1228	0.0920	0.0691	0.0521	0.0394	0.0298	0.0226	0.0172	0.0131	0.0035	0.0010	0.0003	0.0001	*******
32	0.7273	0.5306	0.3883	0.2851	0.2099	0.1550	0.1147	0.0852	0.0634	0.0474	0.0355	0.0266	0.0200	0.0151	0.0114	0.0029	0.0008	0.0002	0.0001	*******
33	0.7201	0.5202	0.3770	0.2741	0.1999	0.1462	0.1072	0.0789	0.0582	0.0431	0.0319	0.0238	0.0177	0.0132	0.0099	0.0024	0.0006	0.0002	0.0001	*******
34	0.7130	0.5100	0.3660	0.2636	0.1904	0.1379	0.1002	0.0730	0.0534	0.0391	0.0288	0.0212	0.0157	0.0116	0.0086	0.0020	0.0005	0.0002	*******	*******
35	0.7059	0.5000	0.3554	0.2534	0.1813	0.1301	0.0937	0.0676	0.0490	0.0356	0.0259	0.0189	0.0139	0.0102	0.0075	0.0017	0.0004	0.0001	*******	*******
40	0.6717	0.4529	0.3066	0.2083	0.1420	0.0972	0.0668	0.0460	0.0318	0.0221	0.0154	0.0107	0.0075	0.0053	0.0037	0.0007	0.0001	*******	*******	*******
50	0.6080	0.3715	0.2281	0.1407	0.0872	0.0543	0.0339	0.0213	0.0134	0.0085	0.0054	0.0035	0.0022	0.0014	0.0009	0.0001	*******	*******	*******	*******
60	0.5504	0.3048	0.1697	0.0951	0.0535	0.0303	0.0173	0.0099	0.0057	0.0033	0.0019	0.0011	0.0007	0.0004	0.0002	*******	*******	*******	*******	*******
70	0.4983	0.2500	0.1263	0.0642	0.0329	0.0169	0.0088	0.0046	0.0024	0.0013	0.0007	0.0004	0.0002	0.0001	0.0001	*******	*******	*******	*******	*******
80	0.4511	0.2051	0.0940	0.0434	0.0202	0.0095	0.0045	0.0021	0.0010	0.0005	0.0002	0.0001	0.0001	*******	*******	*******	*******	*******	*******	*******
360	0.0278	0.0008	*******	*******	*******	*******	*******	*******	*******	*******	*******	*******	*******	*******	*******	*******	*******	*******	*******	*******

******* Factor < 0.0001

TABLE 3 Future Value Annuity Factors $= \dfrac{(1+r)^n - 1}{r}$ (FV of \$1 per period for n periods at interest rate r)

n	1%	2%	3%	4%	5%	6%	7%	8%	9%	10%	11%	12%	13%	14%	15%	20%	25%	30%	35%	40%
1	1.0000	1.0000	1.0000	1.0000	1.0000	1.0000	1.0000	1.0000	1.0000	1.0000	1.0000	1.0000	1.0000	1.0000	1.0000	1.0000	1.0000	1.0000	1.0000	1.0000
2	2.0100	2.0200	2.0300	2.0400	2.0500	2.0600	2.0700	2.0800	2.0900	2.1000	2.1100	2.1200	2.1300	2.1400	2.1500	2.2000	2.2500	2.3000	2.3500	2.4000
3	3.0301	3.0604	3.0909	3.1216	3.1525	3.1836	3.2149	3.2464	3.2781	3.3100	3.3421	3.3744	3.4069	3.4396	3.4725	3.6400	3.8125	3.9900	4.1725	4.3600
4	4.0604	4.1216	4.1836	4.2465	4.3101	4.3746	4.4399	4.5061	4.5731	4.6410	4.7097	4.7793	4.8498	4.9211	4.9934	5.3680	5.7656	6.1870	6.6329	7.1040
5	5.1010	5.2040	5.3091	5.4163	5.5256	5.6371	5.7507	5.8666	5.9847	6.1051	6.2278	6.3528	6.4803	6.6101	6.7424	7.4416	8.2070	9.0431	9.9544	10.946
6	6.1520	6.3081	6.4684	6.6330	6.8019	6.9753	7.1533	7.3359	7.5233	7.7156	7.9129	8.1152	8.3227	8.5355	8.7537	9.9299	11.259	12.756	14.438	16.324
7	7.2135	7.4343	7.6625	7.8983	8.1420	8.3938	8.6540	8.9228	9.2004	9.4872	9.7833	10.089	10.405	10.730	11.067	12.916	15.073	17.583	20.492	23.853
8	8.2857	8.5830	8.8923	9.2142	9.5491	9.8975	10.260	10.637	11.028	11.436	11.859	12.300	12.757	13.233	13.727	16.499	19.842	23.858	28.664	34.395
9	9.3685	9.7546	10.159	10.583	11.027	11.491	11.978	12.488	13.021	13.579	14.164	14.776	15.416	16.085	16.786	20.799	25.802	32.015	39.696	49.153
10	10.462	10.950	11.464	12.006	12.578	13.181	13.816	14.487	15.193	15.937	16.722	17.549	18.420	19.337	20.304	25.959	33.253	42.619	54.590	69.814
11	11.567	12.169	12.808	13.486	14.207	14.972	15.784	16.645	17.560	18.531	19.561	20.655	21.814	23.045	24.349	32.150	42.566	56.405	74.697	98.739
12	12.683	13.412	14.192	15.026	15.917	16.870	17.888	18.977	20.141	21.384	22.713	24.133	25.650	27.271	29.002	39.581	54.208	74.327	101.84	139.23
13	13.809	14.680	15.618	16.627	17.713	18.882	20.141	21.495	22.953	24.523	26.212	28.029	29.985	32.089	34.352	48.497	68.760	97.625	138.48	195.93
14	14.947	15.974	17.086	18.292	19.599	21.015	22.550	24.215	26.019	27.975	30.095	32.393	34.883	37.581	40.505	59.196	86.949	127.91	187.95	275.30
15	16.097	17.293	18.599	20.024	21.579	23.276	25.129	27.152	29.361	31.772	34.405	37.280	40.417	43.842	47.580	72.035	109.69	167.29	254.74	386.42
16	17.258	18.639	20.157	21.825	23.657	25.673	27.888	30.324	33.003	35.950	39.190	42.753	46.672	50.980	55.717	87.442	138.11	218.47	344.90	541.99
17	18.430	20.012	21.762	23.698	25.840	28.213	30.840	33.750	36.974	40.545	44.501	48.884	53.739	59.118	65.075	105.93	173.64	285.01	466.61	759.78
18	19.615	21.412	23.414	25.645	28.132	30.906	33.999	37.450	41.301	45.599	50.396	55.750	61.725	68.394	75.836	128.12	218.04	371.52	630.92	1064.7
19	20.811	22.841	25.117	27.671	30.539	33.760	37.379	41.446	46.018	51.159	56.939	63.440	70.749	78.969	88.212	154.74	273.56	483.97	852.75	1491.6
20	22.019	24.297	26.870	29.778	33.066	36.786	40.995	45.762	51.160	57.275	64.203	72.052	80.947	91.025	102.44	186.69	342.94	630.17	1152.2	2089.2
21	23.239	25.783	28.676	31.969	35.719	39.993	44.865	50.423	56.765	64.002	72.265	81.699	92.470	104.77	118.81	225.03	429.68	820.22	1556.5	2925.9
22	24.472	27.299	30.537	34.248	38.505	43.392	49.006	55.457	62.873	71.403	81.214	92.503	105.49	120.44	137.63	271.03	538.10	1067.3	2102.3	4097.2
23	25.716	28.845	32.453	36.618	41.430	46.996	53.436	60.893	69.532	79.543	91.148	104.60	120.20	138.30	159.28	326.24	673.63	1388.5	2839.0	5737.1
24	26.973	30.422	34.426	39.083	44.502	50.816	58.177	66.765	76.790	88.497	102.17	118.16	136.83	158.66	184.17	392.48	843.03	1806.0	3833.7	8033.0
25	28.243	32.030	36.459	41.646	47.727	54.865	63.249	73.106	84.701	98.347	114.41	133.33	155.62	181.87	212.79	471.98	1054.8	2348.8	5176.5	11247
26	29.526	33.671	38.553	44.312	51.113	59.156	68.676	79.954	93.324	109.18	128.00	150.33	176.85	208.33	245.71	567.38	1319.5	3054.4	6989.3	15747
27	30.821	35.344	40.710	47.084	54.669	63.706	74.484	87.351	102.72	121.10	143.08	169.37	200.84	238.50	283.57	681.85	1650.4	3971.8	9436.5	22047
28	32.129	37.051	42.931	49.968	58.403	68.528	80.698	95.339	112.97	134.21	159.82	190.70	227.95	272.89	327.10	819.22	2064.0	5164.3	12740	30867
29	33.450	38.792	45.219	52.966	62.323	73.640	87.347	103.97	124.14	148.63	178.40	214.58	258.58	312.09	377.17	984.07	2580.9	6714.6	17200	43214
30	34.785	40.568	47.575	56.085	66.439	79.058	94.461	113.28	136.31	164.49	199.02	241.33	293.20	356.79	434.75	1181.9	3227.2	8730.0	23222	60501
31	36.133	42.379	50.003	59.328	70.761	84.802	102.07	123.35	149.58	181.94	221.94	271.29	332.32	407.74	500.96	1419.3	4035.0	11350	31350	84703
32	37.494	44.227	52.503	62.701	75.299	90.890	110.22	134.21	164.04	201.14	247.32	304.85	376.52	465.82	577.10	1704.1	5044.7	14756	42324	*******
33	38.869	46.112	55.078	66.210	80.064	97.343	118.93	145.95	179.80	222.25	275.53	342.43	426.46	532.04	664.67	2045.6	6306.9	19184	57138	*******
34	40.258	48.034	57.730	69.858	85.067	104.18	128.26	158.63	196.98	245.48	306.84	384.52	482.90	607.52	765.37	2456.1	7884.6	24940	77137	*******
35	41.660	49.994	60.462	73.652	90.320	111.43	138.24	172.32	215.71	271.02	341.59	431.66	546.68	693.57	881.17	2948.3	9856.8	32423	*******	*******
40	48.886	60.402	75.401	95.026	120.80	154.76	199.64	259.06	337.88	442.59	581.83	767.09	1013.7	1342.0	1779.1	7343.9	30089	*********	*******	*******
50	64.463	84.579	112.80	152.67	209.35	290.34	406.53	573.77	815.08	1163.9	1668.8	2400.0	3459.5	4994.5	7217.7	45497	******	*********	*******	*******
60	81.670	114.05	163.05	237.99	353.58	533.13	813.52	1253.2	1944.8	3034.8	4755.1	7471.6	11762	18535	29220	*******	*******	*******	*******	*******
70	100.68	149.98	230.59	364.29	588.53	967.93	1614.1	2720.1	4619.2	7887.5	13518	23223	39945	68733	*******	*******	*******	*******	*******	*******
80	121.67	193.77	321.36	551.24	971.23	1746.6	3189.1	5886.9	10951	20474	38401	72146	*******	*********	*******	*******	*******	*******	*******	*******

Factor > 99999

TABLE 4 Present Value Annuity Factors $= \dfrac{1 - \dfrac{1}{(1+r)^n}}{r}$ (PV of \$1 per period for n periods at interest rate r)

n	1%	2%	3%	4%	5%	6%	7%	8%	9%	10%	11%	12%	13%	14%	15%	20%	25%	30%	35%	40%
1	0.9901	0.9804	0.9709	0.9615	0.9524	0.9434	0.9346	0.9259	0.9174	0.9091	0.9009	0.8929	0.8850	0.8772	0.8696	0.8333	0.8000	0.7692	0.7407	0.7143
2	1.9704	1.9416	1.9135	1.8861	1.8594	1.8334	1.8080	1.7833	1.7591	1.7355	1.7125	1.6901	1.6681	1.6467	1.6257	1.5278	1.4400	1.3609	1.2894	1.2245
3	2.9410	2.8839	2.8286	2.7751	2.7232	2.6730	2.6243	2.5771	2.5313	2.4869	2.4437	2.4018	2.3612	2.3216	2.2832	2.1065	1.9520	1.8161	1.6959	1.5889
4	3.9020	3.8077	3.7171	3.6299	3.5460	3.4651	3.3872	3.3121	3.2397	3.1699	3.1024	3.0373	2.9745	2.9137	2.8550	2.5887	2.3616	2.1662	1.9969	1.8492
5	4.8534	4.7135	4.5797	4.4518	4.3295	4.2124	4.1002	3.9927	3.8897	3.7908	3.6959	3.6048	3.5172	3.4331	3.3522	2.9906	2.6893	2.4356	2.2200	2.0352
6	5.7955	5.6014	5.4172	5.2421	5.0757	4.9173	4.7665	4.6229	4.4859	4.3553	4.2305	4.1114	3.9975	3.8887	3.7845	3.3255	2.9514	2.6427	2.3852	2.1680
7	6.7282	6.4720	6.2303	6.0021	5.7864	5.5824	5.3893	5.2064	5.0330	4.8684	4.7122	4.5638	4.4226	4.2883	4.1604	3.6046	3.1611	2.8021	2.5075	2.2628
8	7.6517	7.3255	7.0197	6.7327	6.4632	6.2098	5.9713	5.7466	5.5348	5.3349	5.1461	4.9676	4.7988	4.6389	4.4873	3.8372	3.3289	2.9247	2.5982	2.3306
9	8.5660	8.1622	7.7861	7.4353	7.1078	6.8017	6.5152	6.2469	5.9952	5.7590	5.5370	5.3282	5.1317	4.9464	4.7716	4.0310	3.4631	3.0190	2.6653	2.3790
10	9.4713	8.9826	8.5302	8.1109	7.7217	7.3601	7.0236	6.7101	6.4177	6.1446	5.8892	5.6502	5.4262	5.2161	5.0188	4.1925	3.5705	3.0915	2.7150	2.4136
11	10.368	9.7868	9.2526	8.7605	8.3064	7.8869	7.4987	7.1390	6.8052	6.4951	6.2065	5.9377	5.6869	5.4527	5.2337	4.3271	3.6564	3.1473	2.7519	2.4383
12	11.255	10.575	9.9540	9.3851	8.8633	8.3838	7.9427	7.5361	7.1607	6.8137	6.4924	6.1944	5.9176	5.6603	5.4206	4.4392	3.7251	3.1903	2.7792	2.4559
13	12.134	11.348	10.635	9.9856	9.3936	8.8527	8.3577	7.9038	7.4869	7.1034	6.7499	6.4235	6.1218	5.8424	5.5831	4.5327	3.7801	3.2233	2.7994	2.4685
14	13.004	12.106	11.296	10.563	9.8986	9.2950	8.7455	8.2442	7.7862	7.3667	6.9819	6.6282	6.3025	6.0021	5.7245	4.6106	3.8241	3.2487	2.8144	2.4775
15	13.865	12.849	11.938	11.118	10.380	9.7122	9.1079	8.5595	8.0607	7.6061	7.1909	6.8109	6.4624	6.1422	5.8474	4.6755	3.8593	3.2682	2.8255	2.4839
16	14.718	13.578	12.561	11.652	10.838	10.106	9.4466	8.8514	8.3126	7.8237	7.3792	6.9740	6.6039	6.2651	5.9542	4.7296	3.8874	3.2832	2.8337	2.4885
17	15.562	14.292	13.166	12.166	11.274	10.477	9.7632	9.1216	8.5436	8.0216	7.5488	7.1196	6.7291	6.3729	6.0472	4.7746	3.9099	3.2948	2.8398	2.4918
18	16.398	14.992	13.754	12.659	11.690	10.828	10.059	9.3719	8.7556	8.2014	7.7016	7.2497	6.8399	6.4674	6.1280	4.8122	3.9279	3.3037	2.8443	2.4941
19	17.226	15.678	14.324	13.134	12.085	11.158	10.336	9.6036	8.9501	8.3649	7.8393	7.3658	6.9380	6.5504	6.1982	4.8435	3.9424	3.3105	2.8476	2.4958
20	18.046	16.351	14.877	13.590	12.462	11.470	10.594	9.8181	9.1285	8.5136	7.9633	7.4694	7.0248	6.6231	6.2593	4.8696	3.9539	3.3158	2.8501	2.4970
21	18.857	17.011	15.415	14.029	12.821	11.764	10.836	10.017	9.2922	8.6487	8.0751	7.5620	7.1016	6.6870	6.3125	4.8913	3.9631	3.3198	2.8519	2.4979
22	19.660	17.658	15.937	14.451	13.163	12.042	11.061	10.201	9.4424	8.7715	8.1757	7.6446	7.1695	6.7429	6.3587	4.9094	3.9705	3.3230	2.8533	2.4985
23	20.456	18.292	16.444	14.857	13.489	12.303	11.272	10.371	9.5802	8.8832	8.2664	7.7184	7.2297	6.7921	6.3988	4.9245	3.9764	3.3254	2.8543	2.4989
24	21.243	18.914	16.936	15.247	13.799	12.550	11.469	10.529	9.7066	8.9847	8.3481	7.7843	7.2829	6.8351	6.4338	4.9371	3.9811	3.3272	2.8550	2.4992
25	22.023	19.523	17.413	15.622	14.094	12.783	11.654	10.675	9.8226	9.0770	8.4217	7.8431	7.3300	6.8729	6.4641	4.9476	3.9849	3.3286	2.8556	2.4994
26	22.795	20.121	17.877	15.983	14.375	13.003	11.826	10.810	9.9290	9.1609	8.4881	7.8957	7.3717	6.9061	6.4906	4.9563	3.9879	3.3297	2.8560	2.4996
27	23.560	20.707	18.327	16.330	14.643	13.211	11.987	10.935	10.027	9.2372	8.5478	7.9426	7.4086	6.9352	6.5135	4.9636	3.9903	3.3305	2.8563	2.4997
28	24.316	21.281	18.764	16.663	14.898	13.406	12.137	11.051	10.116	9.3066	8.6016	7.9844	7.4412	6.9607	6.5335	4.9697	3.9923	3.3312	2.8565	2.4998
29	25.066	21.844	19.188	16.984	15.141	13.591	12.278	11.158	10.198	9.3696	8.6501	8.0218	7.4701	6.9830	6.5509	4.9747	3.9938	3.3317	2.8567	2.4999
30	25.808	22.396	19.600	17.292	15.372	13.765	12.409	11.258	10.274	9.4269	8.6938	8.0552	7.4957	7.0027	6.5660	4.9789	3.9950	3.3321	2.8568	2.4999
31	26.542	22.938	20.000	17.588	15.593	13.929	12.532	11.350	10.343	9.4790	8.7331	8.0850	7.5183	7.0199	6.5791	4.9824	3.9960	3.3324	2.8569	2.4999
32	27.270	23.468	20.389	17.874	15.803	14.084	12.647	11.435	10.406	9.5264	8.7686	8.1116	7.5383	7.0350	6.5905	4.9854	3.9968	3.3326	2.8569	2.4999
33	27.990	23.989	20.766	18.148	16.003	14.230	12.754	11.514	10.464	9.5694	8.8005	8.1354	7.5560	7.0482	6.6005	4.9878	3.9975	3.3328	2.8570	2.4999
34	28.703	24.499	21.132	18.411	16.193	14.368	12.854	11.587	10.518	9.6086	8.8293	8.1566	7.5717	7.0599	6.6091	4.9898	3.9980	3.3329	2.8570	2.5000
35	29.409	24.999	21.487	18.665	16.374	14.498	12.948	11.655	10.567	9.6442	8.8552	8.1755	7.5856	7.0700	6.6166	4.9915	3.9984	3.3330	2.8571	2.5000
40	32.835	27.355	23.115	19.793	17.159	15.046	13.332	11.925	10.757	9.7791	8.9511	8.2438	7.6344	7.1050	6.6418	4.9966	3.9995	3.3332	2.8571	2.5000
50	39.196	31.424	25.730	21.482	18.256	15.762	13.801	12.233	10.962	9.9148	9.0417	8.3045	7.6752	7.1327	6.6605	4.9995	3.9999	3.3333	2.8571	2.5000
60	44.955	34.761	27.676	22.623	18.929	16.161	14.039	12.377	11.048	9.9672	9.0736	8.3240	7.6873	7.1401	6.6651	4.9999	4.0000	3.3333	2.8571	2.5000
70	50.169	37.499	29.123	23.395	19.343	16.385	14.160	12.443	11.084	9.9873	9.0848	8.3303	7.6908	7.1421	6.6663	5.0000	4.0000	3.3333	2.8571	2.5000
80	54.888	39.745	30.201	23.915	19.596	16.509	14.222	12.474	11.100	9.9951	9.0888	8.3324	7.6919	7.1427	6.6666	5.0000	4.0000	3.3333	2.8571	2.5000
360	97.218	49.960	33.333	25.000	20.000	16.667	14.286	12.500	11.111	10.000	9.0909	8.3333	7.6923	7.1429	6.6667	5.0000	4.0000	3.3333	2.8571	2.5000
999	99.995	50.000	33.333	25.000	20.000	16.667	14.286	12.500	11.111	10.000	9.0909	8.3333	7.6923	7.1429	6.6667	5.0000	4.0000	3.3333	2.8571	2.5000

GLOSSARY

Numbers in parentheses refer to the chapter and page on which the definition appears, e.g., (14:350) means Chapter 14, page 350.

acceptable range—the set of debt-equity mixes that produces a weighted-average cost of capital at or near its minimum value (14:350)

accounting profits—the bottom number on an income statement using rules of measurement determined by accounting authorities (1:15)

accrual accounting—a system of recording accounting numbers when economic events have been achieved (2:44)

adding value—making the output of a process worth more for its customers (13:316)

agency cost—the reduction in a principal's wealth when an agent does not act in the principal's best interests (17:417)

agency problem—the possibility that an agent will not act in the best interests of his/her principal (17:416)

agent—a person who acts on behalf of and by the authority of another (17:416)

aggressive security—an investment with a beta greater than 1 (8:209)

alpha—the extra return from an investment above that of the average security of the same risk (18:442)

analytical finance theory—theory about the factual nature of finance and what decisions should be made (18:440)

annuity—a series of cash flows that are equal in amount, direction of flow, and time distance apart (3:72)

annuity due (annuity in advance, BEGIN annuity)—an annuity in which the cash flows occur at the beginning of each time period (3:76)

annuity in advance (annuity due, BEGIN annuity)—an annuity in which the cash flows occur at the beginning of each time period (3:76)

annuity in arrears (ordinary annuity, END annuity)—an annuity in which the cash flows occur at the end of each time period (3:75)

asset-based loan—a loan backed with a pledge of assets (6:142)

assignment—giving a lender the right to collect accounts receivable as collateral for a loan (6:142)

asymmetric information hypothesis—a theory that explores the ramifications of management having better information about a company's prospects than investors (14:354)

average cost—total cost divided by the number of units made (2:45)

balanced-budget unit—an individual or business that spends exactly what it earns (7:169)

balance of payments—the net difference between money inflows and outflows for a country during a period of time (4:99)

banker's acceptance—a promissory note which carries a bank's promise of payment (6:139)

bankruptcy—the condition of being unable to make payments on debt (14:348)

BEGIN annuity (annuity due, annuity in advance)—an annuity in which the cash flows occur at the beginning of each time period (3:76)

benchmark comparison—comparison to a norm which is valid across many companies and/or industries (2:34)

beta—the numerical relationship between the returns from an investment and the returns from the overall market (8:208)

bond—a type of financial instrument that is a long-term loan, giving the holder the right to receive interest payments and repayment of the loan principal (1:6)

bond indenture—the formal agreement between a bond's issuer and buyer (6:151)

break point—a point on the cost of capital schedule where the firm's cost of capital increases (10:255)

bridge loan—a loan to provide temporary financing until future, more permanent financing is arranged (6:147)

broker—an individual or company that locates buyers and sellers and brings them together (7:169)

budget—a time-oriented statement of the financial resources allocated to carry out an organization's activities (5:114)

business risk—the total variability of a firm's operating results (8:196)

business system—the set of integrated and overlapping work processes that constitute an entire business organization (13:312)

buying stock on margin—purchasing stock using borrowed money for part of the purchase price (14:347)

call risk—the risk that a lender will retire a security prior to maturity, taking a good earning opportunity away from an investor (4:96)

capital asset pricing model (CAPM)—the finance model relating asset prices and rates of return to the asset's beta, its impact on the risk of a well-diversified portfolio (8:213)

capital budget—a financial plan showing a firm's intended outlays for long-term assets (11:264)

capital budgeting—the process of discovering, evaluating, and deciding whether to pursue investments in long-term assets (11:264)

capitalist economic system—an economy marked by private ownership of businesses and the resources necessary for producing goods and services (1:14)

capital market line (CML)—a graph of investors' required rate of return as a function of an asset's total risk (8:201)

capital markets—the markets for securities with maturity greater than one year (7:170)

capital structure—the combination of long-term debt and equity financing employed by a firm, often used as a synonym for *the debt-equity mix* (14:335)

cash conversion cycle—the length of time from the outflow of cash to purchase inventory until the inflow of cash from the collection of accounts receivable (2:40)

cash cow—a firm that regularly generates more cash than it needs for operations and growth (5:113)

cash flow—money received or paid by an organization (2:44)

certificate of deposit—a receipt for a bank deposit in which the depositor commits not to withdraw funds from the bank for a specified period of time in return for a better rate of interest (3:74)

characteristic line—the relationship of an investment's rate of return to the overall rate of return available in the market (8:208)

chief financial officer (CFO)—the senior finance professional responsible for all of a company's financial activities (1:6)

clientele—a group of investors with a similar preference for dividends (16:392)

closely held firm—a company in which a small number of shareholders own a significant percentage of the outstanding common stock (14:353)

collateral—property pledged in support of a loan (6:142)

commercial banker—an individual or organization that specializes in taking deposits from investors and in making loans to individuals and organizations (1:6)

commercial paper—short-term, unsecured notes issued by large corporations (6:144)

common causes of variation—factors that cause natural variation in a stable process (13:319)

common stock—ownership shares in a corporation (6:158)

competitive benchmarking—using the best example available, regardless of source, as the firm's target (2:34)

competitive market—a market in which no participant has enough economic power to influence prices (1:15)

compounding—adding compound interest to a present value to produce a future value (3:62)

compound interest—interest paid on both the initial principal and previously paid interest (3:60)

concentration banking—the practice of instructing customers to mail payments to a local bank which then forwards the payment electronically (12:295)

consignment—shipping goods to a buyer but not requiring payment until the goods are resold (6:140)

contract—an agreement between parties specifying each party's role in the relationship (17:418)

correlation coefficient—a measure of the relationship between the returns from two investments (8:204)

cost of a source of funds—the rate a firm must earn from the use of funds to provide the rate of return required by that investor (10:242)

cost of capital—the minimum rate of return a firm must earn on new investments to satisfy its creditors and stockholders (10:240)

cost of capital schedule—a graph showing how a firm's cost of capital will increase with the amount of capital it attempts to raise (10:255)

coupon—the amount of cash interest paid annually by a bond (9:223)

credit analysis—a study to determine the ability of a customer to repay a loan (6:142)

cross rate—the price of one foreign currency in terms of another, calculated via their relationships to a third currency (4:102)

cross-section comparison—comparison of some number to equivalent data from other companies or from the industry over a common period of time (2:34)

customer-supplier alignment—a close working relationship between two parties, one of whom supplies the other, to ensure that the needs of each are being met (1:21)

cycle time—the time from the beginning to the end of any process or process step (2:49)

date of declaration—the date a company's board of directors votes to pay a dividend (16:400)

date of record—the date a company determines who will receive a dividend (16:400)

debenture—a bond with no collateral (6:152)

debt—a loan (6:138)

debt equity mix—the combination of debt and equity financing employed by a firm (14:335)

debt maturity mix—the blend of debt maturities used by a firm (15:368)

deep discount bond—a bond with a price significantly less than its face value (9:227)

default—to breach a loan agreement (6:152)

default risk—the risk that a borrower will delay or not make scheduled payments, or otherwise violate a loan agreement (4:95)

defensive security—an investment with a beta less than 1 (8:209)

deficit-budget unit—an individual or business that spends more than it earns (7:169)

derivative—a contract whose value is defined by a financial market rate or the price of a financial instrument (15:377)

dilute—to reduce the percentage of a firm owned by each common share by increasing the number of shares outstanding (14:353)

direct exchange rate—the number of units of domestic currency required to purchase one unit of a foreign currency (4:100)

direct lease—a lease with only one investor, the lessor, who owns the leased asset (6:148)

discount bond—a bond with a price less than its face value (9:224)

discounting—removing compound interest from a future value to produce a present value (3:66)

discretionary account—a balance sheet account whose value does not change with sales but rather is set by a management decision (5:120)

diversify—to spread your money across several investments, i.e., to purchase a portfolio (8:202)

dividend—a payment made by a corporation directly to its stockholders (16:386)

dividend policy—a company's plan for the level and pattern of its dividend payments (16:385)

dividend yield—the portion of a stock's rate of return coming from dividend payments (9:233)

EBIT-EPS analysis—a graph showing how EPS responds to EBIT for various financing alternatives (14:341)

economic exposure—exposure to a reduction in monetary asset values, an increase in monetary liabilities, or a reduction in cash flow due to adverse exchange rate movements (4:106)

economic profits—the money returns to the investors in a firm (1:15)

efficient allocation of resources—directing the resources of an economy (money, labor, machinery, land, etc.) to those businesses where they can produce goods and services of the greatest value (1:15)

efficient capital market—a financial market in which security prices fully contain the meaning of all known information (1:17)

electronic funds transfer—the computerized exchange of money between bank accounts (12:295)

END annuity (ordinary annuity, annuity in arrears)—an annuity in which the cash flows occur at the end of each time period (3:75)

environmental risk—unexpected changes outside the firm that impact its operations (8:195)

equity—investment in a business (6:138)

Eurobond—a bond denominated in a currency other than that of the country in which it is sold (6:154)

Euronote facility—a contract for the issuance of Euronotes (6:146)

Euronotes—short-term, unsecured, standardized notes issued by large corporations and governments in the Eurodollar market (6:146)

excess cash—the amount of spontaneous financing produced by a firm over and above what it needs to acquire the assets necessary to support its sales forecast (5:126)

(foreign) exchange rate—the value of one currency in terms of another (4:98)

ex-dividend date—the date by which stock must be purchased to receive the next dividend (16:401)

expectations hypothesis—a theory of the term structure focusing on investors' forecasts of future interest rates (4:94)

expected value—the weighted average of the forecasted rates of return from an investment (8:198)

external financing needed—the amount of financing a firm must raise from outside sources to acquire the assets necessary to support its forecasted level of sales (5:126)

factor—a company that purchases accounts receivable (6:143)

factoring—selling accounts receivable (6:143)

finance—the study and practice of how money is raised and used by organizations (1:4)

financial analysis—the use of financial and other data to understand the financial health of an organization (2:30)

financial environment—the business and social forces which impact the financial operations of an organization (1:6)

financial instrument—a document giving the holder a claim to present or future cash flows (1:6)

financial intermediary—an organization that takes funds from surplus-budget units and provides them to deficit-budget units (7:170)

financial lease—a lease providing long-term use of an asset (6:149)

financial leverage—the use of debt to magnify the returns to equity investors (2:41); magnification of changes in earnings per share (EPS) in response to changes in EBIT that is caused by the existence of fixed financing costs (interest obligations) in the firm's cost structure (14:339)

financial manager—a person responsible for analyzing and improving the money flows of an organization (1:6)

financial managing—the art of integrating financial theory and practice with the rest of an organization's management systems to support the delivery of low-cost, high-quality goods and services to customers and to maximize the value of the organization to its stockholders and other stakeholders (1:3)

financial risk—the increased variability in a firm's financial results caused by its financing mix (8:196)

fixed cost—a cost that remains constant when sales changes (2:46)

fixed exchange rate system—a system in which exchange rates are kept constant by government policy (4:98)

floating exchange rate system—a system in which exchange rates are allowed to change freely with market conditions (4:99)

flotation costs—the total amount paid to third parties in order to raise funds (10:242)

foreign bond—a bond issued by a foreign borrower in the currency of the country of issue (6:154)

(foreign) exchange rate—the value of one currency in terms of another (4:98)

foreign exchange risk—the possibility of variation in exchange rates which makes uncertain the value of assets, liabilities, cash flows, and income denominated in a foreign currency (4:98)

forward contract—a contract binding the parties to a future transaction on a specified date and at a specified price or rate (15:376)

forward discount—the condition when forward rates are less than the spot rate, also the amount of the difference (4:104)

forward exchange contract—a contract binding the parties to a future trade of currencies on a specified date and at a specified exchange rate, the forward rate (4:103)

forward (exchange) rate—an exchange rate for a contract to be entered into today (forward exchange contract) but with the trade of currencies to take place on a specified future date (4:103)

forward premium—the condition when forward rates are greater than the spot rate, also the amount of the difference (4:104)

forward rate agreement (FRA)—a contract binding the parties to a future loan on a specified date, for a specified period, and at a specified interest rate (15:377)

free cash flow—the cash flow distributed by a firm to its investors, equal to the firm's cash flow from operations less cash reinvested in the company (17:411)

FRICTO—an acronym (flexibility, risk, income, control, timing, other) summarizing practical considerations in setting the debt-equity mix (14:351)

full-service lease—a lease for an asset and also its operation and maintenance (6:148)

future—an exchange-traded standardized forward contract (15:379)

future value—a single cash flow or value at the end of a time frame (3:62)

goal—the objective of (a business's) actions (1:13)

global sustainability—the long term maintenance and improvement of human well-being through the combination of economic success, a cleaner and healtheir environment, and increased social justice (1:9)

growing cash stream—an infinitely long series of equally spaced cash flows in which each flow is greater than the previous one by a constant rate of growth (3:77)

hedge—to balance liabilities with assets of equal amount and maturity (4:95)

hedging—balancing a risky financial position with an opposite position to cancel out the risk (15:362)

holding-period yield—the rate of return an investor actually earns from an investment (9:228)

homemade dividends—selling shares of stock to augment a company's dividends (16:392)

homemade leverage—borrowing by stock investors to leverage their investment portfolio (14:347)

incremental cost—the additional cost from taking a particular action (2:46)

indifference point—the level of EBIT that produces the same EPS regardless of the debt-equity mix (14:341)

industry-average ratio—a ratio calculated by averaging the ratios of firms within an industry (2:34)

inflation premium—the component of interest rates demanded by investors as compensation for anticipated inflation (4:89)

information asymmetry—the condition in which a firm's manager-agents know more about the firm than its shareholder-principals (17:417)

initial public offering (IPO)—the first public sale of a company's stock (7:172)

interest-rate risk—the risk that interest rates will rise, reducing the value of securities (4:95)

intermediation—moving funds through financial intermediaries (7:170)

internal rate of return—the rate of return from an investment, the discount rate that equates the present value of all benefits from a proposed investment to the present value of all costs (11:278)

international bond—a bond issued outside the borrower's home country (6:154)

intrinsic value—the true economic worth of an asset (7:183)

inverted yield curve—a downward-sloping yield curve in which short-term rates exceed long-term rates (4:94)

investment banker—an individual or organization that specializes in helping firms issue new securities and in trading existing securities (1:6)

junk bond—a speculative grade bond (6:153)

just-in-time inventory system—a system in which inventory is received and produced only as needed keeping the balance of inventory-on-hand as close as possible to zero (2:39)

leveraged lease—a lease with both equity (the lessor) and debt investors (6:148)

life-cycle numbers—numbers which cover the full life-span of some activity and which are not limited to any time period (11:267)

line of credit—a relationship in which a bank offers to lend up to a specified amount for a given time period with no guarantee that funds will be available (6:141)

liquidity—the ability to have access to cash quickly and in full amount (2:38)

liquidity preference hypothesis—a theory of the term structure focusing on investors' loss of liquidity as maturities lengthen (4:95)

listing—arranging for a company's securities to trade on a stock exchange (7:178)

lock box—a post office box to which customers mail their payments (12:295)

London inter-bank offering rate (LIBOR)—a base rate used for dollar-denominated loans made outside the United States (6:142)

macroeconomics—the study of the functioning of economies taken as a whole (1:4)

managed (dirty) float—a system in which government influences a floating exchange rate system through central bank intervention in the currency markets (4:100)

marginal cost—the cost of making one additional unit (2:45)

marginal cost of capital (MCC)—a synonym for "cost of capital" emphasizing its use as a measure of the marginal cost of capital funds (10:254)

marketability risk—the risk that a security will be difficult, hence costly, to sell (4:96)

marketable security—an investment with a ready market that may be sold easily to obtain its value in cash (15:372)

market price of portfolio risk—the additional return demanded by investors to take on one unit of portfolio risk (8:212)

market price of total risk—the additional return demanded by investors to take on one unit of total risk (8:202)

market return—the rate of return from the economy, commonly measured by a major stock market index (8:208)

maturity—the time remaining until the expiration of a security (4:92)

microeconomics—the study of individual units within an economy, specifically consumers and producing firms (1:4)

money markets—the markets for (debt) securities with maturity of one year or less (7:170)

mortgage bond—a bond with collateral (6:151)

multicurrency bond—a bond denominated in more than one currency (6:154)

multiplier—a number used to estimate the value of common stock by multiplying an accounting performance figure (17:413)

mutual fund—a pool of money from many investors that is invested in a portfolio of securities (8:206)

naive diversification—the construction of a portfolio at random (8:207)

natural variation—the random variation inherent in any process (13:319)

net annual benefit (NAB)—the amount by which the annual benefit from an investment exceeds the amount required to cover the firm's cost of capital (12:291)

net lease—a lease for an asset without any supporting services (6:148)

net present value—the present value of all benefits from a proposed investment less the present value of all costs, using the weighted-average cost of capital as the discount rate (11:275)

nexus of contracts—an interconnection of many contracts (17:418)

nominal interest rate (nominal rate of interest)—a quoted rate of interest; in the context of the Fisher model, the rate of interest including the premiums for inflation and risk (4:89)

normalized earnings—earnings that reflect the true earning power of a company (17:414)

normal yield curve—an upward-sloping yield curve in which long-term rates exceed short-term rates (4:94)

off-balance-sheet financing—financing that is not included in balance sheet liabilities (6:149)

offering basis loan—a short-term loan with no prenegotiation (6:141)

operating lease—a lease providing temporary use of an asset (6:149)

operating leverage—magnification of changes in operating earnings (EBIT) in response to changes in sales that is caused by the existence of fixed operating costs in the firm's cost structure (14:337)

operational finance theory—theory about how financial actions are taken in an organization (18:440)

opportunity cost—a benefit forgone by the making of a financial decision (2:46)

ordinary annuity (annuity in arrears, END annuity)—an annuity in which the cash flows occur at the end of each time period (3:75)

par bond—a bond with a price equal to its face value (9:224)

par value—the minimum amount of money per share a shareholder is required to invest (6:161)

payables float—the dollar amount of outgoing checks that have been written but have not yet been covered by bank deposits (12:294)

payment—one of the cash flows in an annuity (3:72)

payment date—the date a dividend is paid (16:400)

pecking-order approach—a pattern of financing in which a company raises funds in the same sequence each year (14:353)

pegged float—a system in which a currency is fixed against another which itself is free to float against other currencies (4:100)

permanent working capital—the level of working capital required at all times (12:288)

perpetuity—an annuity that continues forever; also, a growing cash stream with a zero rate of growth (3:78)

perquisite ("perq")—compensation in a form other than money (17:417)

portfolio—a group of investments held at the same time (8:202)

preferred stock—stock with one or more features better than common stock and without any ownership claim (6:155)

premium bond—a bond with a price greater than its face value (9:224)

present value—a single cash flow or value at the beginning of a time frame (3:66)

primary financial markets—the markets for the initial issue of securities (7:172)

prime rate—a base rate used in the United States, traditionally the rate available to the most credit worthy customers (6:142)

principal—a person who employs another to act in his/her behalf (17:416)

private placement—the sale of a new issue of securities directly to an investor (7:174)

probability distribution—a listing of all possible results of some activity showing the chance of each result taking place (8:196)

process boundary—the line separating a process from other business activities (13:315)

process capability—how well a process functions under normal operating conditions (13:319)

process risk—unnecessary variability caused by systems within the firm that are out of control (8:196)

process stability—the variation in the output of a process (13:319)

professional managers—individuals employed by a firm to direct its activities because of their expertise. They are distinguished from owner-managers, individuals who find themselves managing a firm because they own it (1:16)

profit maximization—the act of managing a firm so as to increase its economic profits to the maximum possible level (1:15)

pro-forma financial statement—a financial statement that projects a firm's condition or operating results into the future (5:117)

prospectus—a booklet of data about a company that must be given to potential investors prior to soliciting any money (7:173)

purchasing power—the value of money measured by the goods and services it can purchase (4:89)

pure rate of interest—the interest rate prior to inclusion of the premiums for inflation and risk (4:89)

random walk—a process in which successive changes are independent of each other (7:185)

real rate of interest—the rate of interest excluding the premium for inflation (4:90)

receivables float—the dollar amount of incoming checks that have been mailed but have not yet been collected (12:294)

reciprocal exchange rate—the number of units of a foreign currency required to purchase one unit of domestic currency (4:100)

reinvestment risk—the risk that interest rates will fall, limiting reinvestment opportunities (4:96)

required rate of return—the minimum acceptable rate of return on an investment which will appropriately compensate the investor for time and risk (9:220)

revolving credit line—a line of credit containing a guarantee that funds will be available for the period of the line (6:141)

rework—an activity performed to correct an error or omission in an earlier stage of a work process (13:316)

risk—the possibility that the result of some activity will not be exactly as (and particularly, will be worse than) forecast (1:15)

risk averter—an individual willing to pay to avoid risk (8:192)

risk-free rate of interest—the rate of interest excluding the premium for risk; it is the rate available on a risk-free investment (4:91)

risk neutral—indifferent to risk (8:192)

risk premium—the component of interest rates demanded by investors as compensation for risk (4:90)

risk seeker—an individual willing to pay to assume additional risk (8:192)

sale and leaseback—a transaction in which a company sells an asset to a lessor and then leases it back (6:148)

seasonal—a firm or market whose activity varies in a pattern throughout the year (2:38)

seasonal dating—invoicing several months' worth of shipments at a strong point in the buyer's seasonal pattern (6:140)

secondary financial markets—the markets for trading existing securities (7:176)

securitization—issuing securities backed by the cash flows of a group of financial assets (1:9)

security—a financial instrument such as a bond or share of stock (1:6)

security market line (SML)—a graph of investors' required rate of return as a function of an asset's portfolio (systematic) risk (8:211)

segmentation or hedging hypothesis—a theory of the term structure focusing on investors' desire for specific maturity instruments to hedge their liabilities (4:95)

serial bond issue—a bond issue composed of bonds of many maturities (6:155)

shareholder wealth—the total value of an investment in the common stock of a company, measured by the price at which the stock could be sold (1:16)

shelf registration—advance SEC approval to make small public security issues (7:175)

signaling—the process of conveying economic information (1:17)

simple interest—interest paid only on the initial principal and not on previously paid interest (3:60)

sinking fund—an account set up to accumulate the cash to retire debt (6:155)

six sigma—a statistical measure of process accuracy, only 3.4 errors per million opportunities (2:49)

special causes of variation—factors that cause excessive variation and make a process unstable (13:319)

specific-item forecasting—a forecasting technique in which each account on a firm's financial statements is projected without reference to the other accounts (5:117)

spontaneous account—a balance sheet account whose value changes with sales without the need for specific management action (5:120)

spot (exchange) rate—an exchange rate available for the immediate trade of currencies (4:103)

stakeholders—persons and organizations affected by the actions of a business firm (1:5)

standard deviation—the square root of the variance (8:200)

stock—a type of financial instrument that gives the holder ownership of a portion of a corporation (1:6)

sunk cost—money previously spent (2:46)

surplus-budget unit—an individual or business that spends less than it earns (7:169)

swap—an exchange of financial obligations (15:379)

synthetic security—an artificial security constructed from real securities and derivatives (15:379)

systematic risk—the variability in an investment's rate of return caused by factors that impact all investments (8:206)

tampering—modifying a system in response to special causes of variation, further destabilizing the system's performance (5:115)

target capital structure—the percentage mix of financing sources management plans to use in the future (10:254)

temporary working capital—increases to working capital due to fluctuations in business activity (12:289)

term loan—a loan with a maturity of more than one year (6:147)

term structure of interest rates—the relationship between a security's yield and maturity (4:92)

time-series comparison—a tracking of some number across time to see if it is changing, and if so, the direction and amount of change (2:34)

time value of money—the concept that the value of money depends on the date of its receipt or payment (3:57)

total cost—the sum of the costs of making each unit (2:45)

traditional bond—a bond that returns a fixed periodic interest payment plus a fixed principal value at maturity (9:223)

transaction exposure—exposure to foreign exchange losses on day-to-day transactions due to adverse exchange rate movements (4:105)

translation exposure—exposure to reduction of accounting income and values due to adverse exchange rate movements (4:105)

trustee—a third party to a bond indenture, responsible for representing the bondholders to the issuing company (6:151)

underwriting—guaranteeing the proceeds of a security issue by purchasing the issue at an agreed-upon price (7:172)

unsystematic risk—the variability in an investment's rate of return caused by factors that only impact that investment (8:206)

value based management—a system of management emphasizing adherence to finance theory (17:421)

variable cost—a cost that changes with changes in sales (2:46)

variance—a measure of the variability of rates of return (8:199)

weighted-average cost of capital (WACC)—a synonym for "cost of capital" emphasizing the method by which it is constructed (10:254)

working capital—a firm's current assets minus its current liabilities (2:37); also, liquid resources available for the day-to-day operations of the firm (12:288)

work process—a series of work activities intended to produce a specific result (13:312)

yield—the rate of return available from a security (4:92)

yield curve—a graph of the term structure, most commonly of U.S. Treasury securities (4:93)

yield-to-maturity—the rate of return an investor would earn from a bond if it were purchased at today's price and held until its maturity date—provided it made all promised payments (9:227)

zero-coupon bond—a bond which makes no cash interest payments (9:227)

INDEX